Studies in Contemporary Economics

Alois Wenig
Klaus F. Zimmermann (Eds.)

Demographic Change and Economic Development

London Paris Tokyo

ISBN 3-540-51140-7 Springer-Verlag Berlin Heidelberg New York
ISBN 0-387-51140-7 Springer-Verlag New York Berlin Heidelberg

Printing and Binding: Weihert-Druck GmbH, Darmstadt.
2142/3140 – 543210

INTRODUCTION

The articles in this volume cover issues related to the interaction
between demographic processes and economic activities. They are revised
and refereed versions of papers presented at a conference on "DEMOGRA-
PHIC CHANGE AND ECONOMIC DEVELOPMENT" held at the FERNUNIVERSITÄT HAGEN
in fall 1986.

Financial support by the DEUTSCHE FORSCHUNGSGEMEINSCHAFT,
the LAND BADEN-WÜRTTEMBERG and the FERNUNIVERSITÄT HAGEN is gratefully
acknowledged.

The role of demographic factors has never been completely overlooked in the analysis of economic development. However, in recent
years population economics has become increasingly popular in both
theory and policy analysis. In fact, for the inquiry into the long
term development of an economy the interaction between demographic
change and economic activity cannot be neglected without omitting major
aspects of the problems. This volume may help to further enhance our
knowledge of population economics.

The book has two parts. The first part deals with theoretical
studies of both macroeconomic and microeconomic nature and with policy
issues. The second part is a collection of applied studies. It contains
three sections: a case study of the demographic history of Hungary,
articles on developing countries, and demographic economic models.

The first article in part I, "MALTHUSIAN CRISES, BOSERUPIAN ESCAPES
AND LONGRUN ECONOMIC PROGRESS", discusses the interaction between demographic change and economic development in the very long term. In this
paper G. STEINMANN presents a model to explain "technical switches,
Malthusian crises and temporary escapes in the history of Western Europe
as well as the final escape from the Malthusian trap in the last century".
Economic history is seen in this context as the result of rational
choices by economic agents rather than the outcome of a random process.
According to STEINMANN the driving forces behind the laws of motion
in economic history are the relative scarcities of exhaustible and
renewable resources and labor. The ratios between population (labor)
and resources determine the decisions about technology which produce
a certain rate of technical progress as well as some direction of technical change. Thus it is mainly the relative population pressure which
controls the pace of economic development in STEINMANN's analysis.
His model can explain both the succession of technical stages in economic
history as well as the empirical observation that technical progress
occurs in jumps rather than in smooth steps.

In the literature concerning endogenous population growth, it
has always been argued that fertility and, consequently, population

fluctuates with the business cycle. At periods of recession or depression
the decline in income reduces the parents' propensity to have more
children. Prosperity, on the other hand, makes people optimistic and
induces them to enlarge their families. The paper "ENDOGENOUS FLUCTUATIONS
IN THE BARRO-BECKER THEORY OF FERTILITY" by J. BENHABIB and K. NISHI-
MURA explains this behavior in terms of the outcome of an individual
optimization procedure in which parents maximize the sum of discounted
future utilities subject to some resource constraint. Inter alia the
optimal solution has the property that fertility and income are positively correlated and that they may fluctuate endogenously.

The contribution "MORTALITY CHANGES AND THEIR ECONOMIC CONSE-
QUENCES, WITH PARTICULAR REFERENCE TO CAUSE OF DEATH" by J. H. POLLARD
develops conceptual instruments to analyze the economic consequences
of changes in key demographic indicators. POLLARD's focus is mainly
the impact of changes in mortality rates on the payment of different
kinds of annuities such as, for example, pensions, hospital insurance
premiums, etc. Though rather technical these calculations are of eminently practical importance if policy makers are to assess the economic
implications of fluctuations in demographic data.

The policy section begins with an article by N. BERTHOLD and M.
PFLÜGER. They are concerned with optimal capital accumulation. In their
paper "MARKET FAILURE POPULATION GROWTH AND GOVERNMENT INTERVENTION
IN A LIFE-CYCLE MODEL", they introduce endogenous population growth
into a DIAMOND-type life-cycle growth model assuming that the growth
rate of the population is an increasing function of per-capita income.
Under this condition "golden rules" of optimal economic growth are
derived and compared to optimal paths of capital accumulation when
population growth is constant. In both cases decentralized economies
may produce "market failure" in the sense that the growth path is dynam-
ically inefficient: everybody could be better off if the process of
allocation was planned by a central agency. Findings similar to those
by BERTHOLD and PFLÜGER have been published previously. However, BERT-
HOLD and PFLÜGER summarize the results of this debate in a very concise
and systematic way.

It is an interesting question whether this kind of market failure
disappears if agents decide on the number of their children rather
than following an exogenous "population law". B. BENTAL addresses this
issue in his contribution "CAPITAL ACCUMULATION AND POPULATION GROWTH
IN TWO SECTOR CLOSED AND OPEN ECONOMIES". While BERTHOLD and PFLÜGER
simply assume a given functional relation between the growth rate of
the population and per capita income BENTAL explains individual be-

havior as the result of rational choices. Within a two-sector overlapping generations model agents decide between physical capital or
children as two alternatives to provide old age security. The return
on investment in children is exogenous. It then depends on the rate
of profit of physical capital which "pension system" (selfish) parents
prefer. For less developed countries in which the rate of return on
children is relatively high BENTAL's model predicts the empirical observation of high interest rates which discourages capital accumulation.
Population, however, grows at a high rate. To overcome this structural
failure, government intervention is required as in the BERTHOLD and
PFLÜGER model.

The paper by H. P. GRAY "POPULATION DRAG AND THE ROLE OF THE IN-
TERNATIONAL SECTOR" discusses alternative policies to reduce the burden
of excess population. The author argues that steps towards an export-
led and labor-intensive industrialization is a well-suited strategy
to enhance the demand for labor by the productive sector. Internationalist (free trade) rather than protectionist measures are required.
In particular, the richer nations' threat of protectionism against
the developing countries is seen as a major obstacle to cushion the
population drag in the Third World which causes so much social and
political tension.

The last two theoretical papers are of microeconomic rather than
macroeconomic nature. A. CIGNO analyzes "THE TIMING OF BIRTH..." in
the framework of a dynamic optimization problem to be solved by the
family. The parents' preferences are given by a utility function with
two arguments: a time sequence of consumption bundles as well as a
quality weighted and dated index of the number of children. CIGNO shows
that the timing of birth is particularly sensitive to the wife's and
the husband's education and earnings. Women married to men with higher
incomes or women who marry late or are endowed with a substantial human
capital at the time of marriage tend, for example, to have their children
early in their married life. This and similar results can be used to
assess the implications of various economic, social, and fiscal policies.

U. BEN-ZION and M. GRADSTEIN ("EQUILIBRIUM AND EFFICIENCY IN IN-
TERGENERATIONAL TRANSFERS") examine the wealth transfers between parents
and their children. They show that the interaction between altruistic
parents and selfish children result in an inefficient allocation within
the family. The imposition of a compulsory social security can restore
efficiency if the parents' pension is financed by a lump-sum tax on
the children.

The second part of the volume is a collection of eight papers on economic change and demographic development. Section one contains two papers on "The Case of Hungary: A Historical Perspective", section two three papers on "Development Issues", and section three presents three "Demographic-Economic Models".

The demographic transition in Europe is well documented. It describes how societies adjust from a period of high fertility and mortality to that of a low fertility and mortality. In comparison to most other European countries, Hungary lagged behind in this development. In his contribution on "ECONOMIC CHANGE AND FAMILY SIZE IN HUNGARIAN HISTORICAL DEMOGRAPHY", R. A. HORVÁTH seeks to explain this phenomenon. He employs a new theory of the demographic transition suggested by K. DAVIS. According to this approach, the changing pattern of the division of labor and the reversal of the sex roles within the family, caused by the Industrial Revolution, was the driving force behind the demographic transition. In a case study, HORVÁTH covers the period of feudalism until its abolishment in 1848, and the capitalistic period until the end of World War II. He shows the perseverance of the feudal agrarian economy even during the capitalist area with a preservation of the traditional family size in the agrarian population. This, as well as a slow and rudimentary industrialization, is identified as the main cause of late demographic transition in Hungary.

From the perspective, it was remarkable that after World War II, Hungary was the first among the advanced societies in which the level of fertility declined below the level of simple replacement. In 1958, the net reproduction rate was already below 1. Within only a few years, a rapid adjustment towards Western European population development patterns took place. Consequently, as early as 1953 and later again in the sixties, pro-natalist population policy measures were undertaken to attain the level of simple replacement. In his paper "DEMOGRAPHIC CHANGE AND ECONOMIC DEVELOPMENT IN HUNGARY SINCE THE SECOND WORLD WAR", R. ANDORKA summarizes this development and the measures undertaken, evaluating the causes and effects. The modernization of the Hungarian economy and society resulted in the acceptance of the two-children family norm by all classes. No spontaneous upswing or oscillations around the replacement level of fertility are to be expected. Cultural values and norms concerning the derived family size have exogenous effects, though they are partly dependent upon economic and social conditions. ANDORKA finds that Hungarian abortion policies had no impact on cohort fertility, whereas financial family support was moderately successful.

The papers by HORVATH and ANDORKA are contained in the section
"The Case of Hungary. A Historical Perspective". It is followed by
three papers on "Development Issues" by TANGRI, FEIGE and BHATTACHARYYA.
S. S. TANGRI makes "A CASE FOR SOME SIMPLE ANALYTICS OF DEMOGRAPHIC
CHANGE AND ECONOMIC DEVELOPMENT". He argues that understanding the
relationships between population growth and economic development is
crucial to policy making in most developing countries. The paper suggests
that simple concepts such as the theory of the firm and the Harrod-
Domar model are useful for analyzing the subject, because the policy
conclusions are unlikely to change in more complex models. For instance,
opening a closed economy to international trade results in a once-and-
for-all shift of the production possibility curve. Unless it can be
shown that an increase of population size improves the terms of trade,
little can be learned from dropping the assumption of a closed economy. TANGRI concludes that for most underdeveloped countries during
the next decade, optimum population growth is negative.

In recent years, the shadow economy has received much interest
in developed countries. In the context of less developed nations, the
informal sector is even more important. In his paper "MONETARY METHODS
OF ESTIMATING INFORMAL ACTIVITIES IN DEVELOPING NATIONS", E. L. FEIGE
presents a small macro monetary model for estimating the size and growth
of the informal sector in developing countries. Successful efforts
to empirically characterize the relationship between demographic change
and economic development crucially depend on the ability to adequately
measure the nature and extent of relevant economic activities. Informal
and unrecorded income growth may itself be related to underlying demographic forces. A population shift from rural to urban areas would
be an example. New urban populations initially locate on the peripheries
of urban centers and engage in economic activities which constitute
an informal sector whose output typically escapes measurement in conventional official statistics. After a discussion of the formal model,
Feige presents empirical estimates for the Peruvian economy examining
a variety of specifications. The outcome of the general currency ratio
model suggests that the informal economy of Peru is sizable and appears
to have grown considerably during the last two decades. Although efforts
have already been made to impute informal income in the official Peruvian statistics, a sizable amount of unrecorded informal income remains.

The contribution by D. BHATTACHARYYA "INTERACTION BETWEEN MACRO-
ECONOMIC ACTIVITIES AND DEMOGRAPHIC CHANGES IN SELECTED DEVELOPING
COUNTRIES" is an attempt to test opposing theories concerning the im-
pact of population change on economic performance, an issue with much

relevance to developing nations. The Malthusian approach suggests that per capita production and per capita consumption have to be reduced with increasing population. Contradicting hypotheses suggest an induced change of agricultural practices and a higher rate of technical progress. Much of the post World War II literature suggests that the introduction of capital-intensive processes by the firms is caused by lack of labor. Consequently, these capital intensive processes have proven to be the major source of technical innovations. These conflicting hypotheses suggest the need for an econometric investigation. In the paper, a dynamic macro-economic model is specified assuming that the Government minimizes a loss function and uses government expenditures and money supply as instruments. Five countries from three continents are selected to obtain empirical results to examine the outlined theories: United Kingdom, India, Pakistan, Ethiopia, and the Central African Republic. The findings show very little support for the Malthusian theory, but also limited evidence for a positive impact of population change on technical progress.

Finally, the volume contains three applied studies on "Demographic-Economic Models" by LUPTÁCIK and SCHMORANZ, ALESSIE and KAPTEYN, and VAN PRAAG and PRADHAN. The contribution by M. LUPTÁCIK and I. SCHMORANZ is "AN EXTENSION OF A STATIC INPUT-OUTPUT MODEL FOR DEMOGRAPHIC-ECONOMIC ANALYSIS". It incorporates demographic-economic linkages in a static Leontief input-output model. Interrelationships between population and the production of goods and services and employment are studied. Changes in size and structure of the population may imply changes in the level and structure of demand for consumption goods. Consequently, changes in production may be induced in particular industrial sectors of the economy, finally inducing changes in the demand for labor as well as in the primary income distribution. The paper keeps demographic patterns as predetermined and seeks to evaluate their impact on economic variables. After the formal presentation of the approach, the model is applied to Austrian data. The authors find a significant structural demographic effect and a relevant impact on the labor market, hence demographic unemployment.

ALESSIE and KAPTEYN study the influence of the demographic composition of a population on the size and composition of private consumption and savings within the life cycle hypthesis framework. In their paper, "CONSUMPTION, SAVINGS AND DEMOGRAPHY", they outline and econometrically estimate an expected multi-period utility maximization model of the joint determination of savings and of expenditures on different goods using panel data. There are two major channels through

which the demographic composition of a population influences consumption and savings. Firstly, age and family composition can act as "taste
shifters". For example, older people may have different tastes than
younger people and large families may have different preferences than
small families. In the second place, age is an important planning variable. For example, the simpler version of the life cycle hypothesis
implies that a consumer will start dissaving when he approaches the
end of his life. The authors give emphasis to an appropriate modelling
of demographic effects and to the estimation of within-period-preferen-
ces that are consistent with intertemporal two-stage budgeting under
uncertainty. The cost function employed is based on the Almost Ideal
Demand System. The econometric findings demonstrate that the exogenously
given demographic factors are important determinants of behavior through
their role as "taste shifters".

Finally, B. M. S. VAN PRAAG and M. P. PRADHAN present "A FLEXIBLE
PROGRAMMING MODEL TO STUDY PROBLEMS OF POPULATION ECONOMICS". In their
opinion, population issues treated in the theory of economic growth
yield elegant results, but are too stylized to be of much value for
the investigation of real world problems. Stylized facts like the marked
fall of the birth rate in Western European countries, prove that the
use of an exponentially growing population is unrealistic. Therefore,
they suggest to use simulation models with no specific exponential
law, but maintain the assumption of exogenous population changes. They
employ a dynamic programming model where optimal solutions are found
by numerical methods. A normative model to calculate optimum growth
patterns for economies with arbitrary population developments, arbitrary utility functions, production functions and social security systems
is built and explored. They find the general wage level to be the easiest
instrument to manipulate for a central planner or government. The contribution by VAN PRAAG and PRADHAN completes the volume.

The interesting issues raised and the results presented in this
volume should clearly pay handsome dividends in better understanding
the interdependence between economic development and demographic processes. The editors have to thank the authors and numerous referees
for their contributions and, in particular, for their help and patience
in improving the first drafts of the papers. Finally, we are indebted
to Ms. K. ALFSMANN for carefully typing all manuscripts and to
J. DE NEW for editorial assistence.

Hagen and Mannheim, December 1988

A. WENIG   K. F. ZIMMERMANN

Contents

Part I

Theoretical Studies on Economic Change and Demographic Development

I,1
Macroeconomic Models

MALTHUSIAN CRISES, BOSERUPIAN ESCAPES AND LONGRUN ECONOMIC PROGRESS

Gunter Steinmann
University of Paderborn

Paderborn / West Germany

ABSTRACT: The model presented in this paper features the characteristics of long-run growth cycles in West European economic history. Population is considered as the key factor for the dynamic process. Population growth leads to capital dilution in the short run but increases the rate of technical progress in the long run. Population density also determines the optimum technology and, therefore, the technique to be adopted.
     The model takes into account all three functions of population. By implementing a production function for new technical knowledge and the possibility of technical choices into a neoclassical growth model, we were able to explain and simulate the historical experience of recurrent and persistent economic crises, technical revolutions, temporary escapes from crises and, finally, unlimited and steady economic progress.

I.   Introduction

The history of mankind is marked by dynamic changes in all areas: demographic growth and catastrophes, recurrent famines, economic crises and recoveries, epochs of slow technical progress and stagnation and periods of abrupt technical revolutions, rise and fall of nations, societies and institutions. Historians, anthropologists and archeologists provide us with the data and give us some explanations of why and how the specific circumstances at a time led to the events of that period. They tend most often, however, to prefer ecclectic explanations, attaching much weight to random elements like diseases, strong or weak leadership, accidental inventions and discoveries.

     There can be no doubt that such attributes and random events have had major impacts on the historical process. If, however, we focus totally on the unpredictable randomness and uniqueness of each epoch we risk the ability to trace any regularities or "laws" in history. Therefore, the ecclectic approach is to be supplemented - not to be substituted - by a general approach or "theory of history" to find out regularities in history and to develop a vision of the historical process in the very long run.

     The task before us is to build a theory of history on the principles of economic theory. We hope and believe that this theoretical model is a step in this direction. The aim of our model is to demonstrate that

---

*
  This project was supported by a grant from the Volkswagen Foundation
  and a travel grant from the Fulbright Commission.

Studies in Contemporary Economics
A. Wenig, K. F. Zimmermann (Eds.)
Demographic Change and Economic Development
© Springer-Verlag Berlin Heidelberg 1989

the technical revolutions starting from the age of hunting and gathering to the ages of ranching and farming until the age of industrialization, the recurrences of Malthusian crises and famines in human history and the final escape from them in recent times are by no means stochastic historical events but are to be understood as inevitable results of the reactions of men to changes in the available amounts of exhaustable and renewable resources and labor.

The model contains three crucial assumptions. First, we hypothesize that men have known several technological alternatives ever since the beginning of history and, consequently, have always been able to make technological choices (assumption of technical choice). Second, we assume that people have chosen that technique that gave them the highest output (assumption of economic optimization). They have switched to a different technique when increasing or decreasing shortages of labor, capital, land and other resources made the existing technology inferior to the new one. Third, we explain the rate of technical progress endogenously by a technical progress function (assumption of endogenous technical progress). We argue that new technical knowledge has been created more easily when people were more numerous and better educated and when preexisting knowledge was relatively high. Furthermore, we can also expect an increase of the labor productivity when people become better acquainted with a new technique and learn how to use the technique more effectively (hypothesis of learning-by-doing).

Notice the twofold role of population for technology in this model. Population density (= ratio between population, land and capital) determines the choice of optimal technology while population size and growth determine the rate of technical progress (= rate of growth of the scale factor in the production function). The first relationship can be classified as Boserupian technological change. It explains the new adoption of previously known technical knowledge and shows the technological response to shortages and price changes of labor, land (incl. resources) and capital. The second relationship describes the creation of new technical knowledge. The technical progress function reflects the assumption that technical progress is "produced" by inputs like any other commodity.

The model differs from other models of economic growth not only by the assumption of technical choice but also by the length of the time-scale. While in most other growth models the time validity is limited by the assumption of given technology and institutions, this model measures time in centuries and millenia rather than in decades. The longrun perspective is due to our goal to develop a theory capable to model the long growth-cycles in economic-technological history.

In a recent article STEINMANN and KOMLOS formulated a model similar to this model. They adopted the assumption of technical choice and showed how an output-maximizing society responds in form of switching technologies to changes in factor-endowments. Their model remained incomplete. It did not explain how, if at all, the growth of technical knowledge is achieved. That explanation is necessary to overcome the Malthusian trap.

The present model fills this gap by adding a technical progress function that offers the last missing element of an economic model of history. It explains technical switches, Malthusian crises and temporary escapes in the history of Western Europe as well as the final escape from the Malthusian trap in the last century. The model offers a new view of history. We can interpret the history of longrun economic and technological change as definite outcome of rational decision-making and do not need to refer to ad hoc hypotheses or random factors. The impact of randomness in economic history should not be overstated and is likely to be of minor importance compared to the forces of economic and technological needs.

II. Structure of the Model

We assume that, at any moment in time, the society has in infinite number of technologies available from which to choose and that all possibilities of input-output-relationships can be characterized by COBB-DOUGLAS-Functions with three inputs: land (R), capital (K) and labor (L).

The alternative techniques i = 1, 2, ... differ in the output elasticities (α, β, γ) and scale levels (A).

(1) $Q_t = A(i)_t * R_t^{\alpha(i)} * K_t^{\beta(i)} * L_t^{\gamma(i)}$

We restrict the range of possible values of the output elasticities by stipulating maximum and minimum values for the output elasticities of all three factors and assuming constant returns of scale for all techniques.

$$a_1 \ >= \ \alpha(i) \ \ >= \ a_0$$

(2a) $$b_1 \ >= \ \beta(i) \ \ >= \ b_0$$

$$g_1 \ >= \ \gamma(i) \ \ >= \ g_0$$

(2b) $$\alpha(i) + \beta(i) + \gamma(i) = 1 \qquad i = 1, 2, \ldots$$

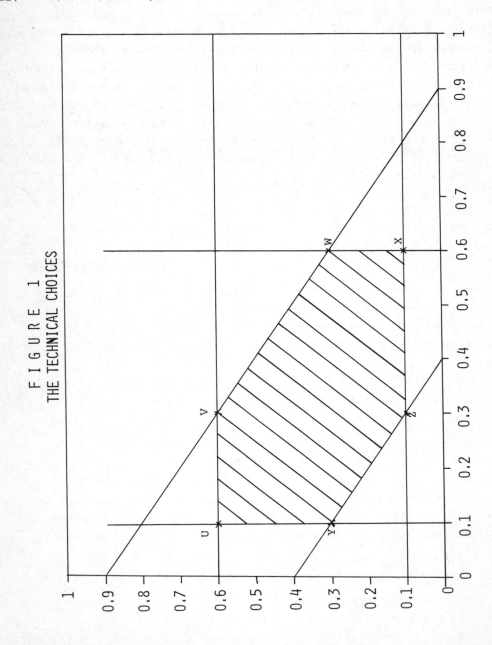

F I G U R E   1
THE TECHNICAL CHOICES

The technical choices are illustrated by the polygon Y-U-V-W-X-Z in figure 1. People can choose any combinations of output elasticities which are on the curve Y-U-V-W-X-Z or in the area included. Neglect for a moment any differences in the scale factor and assume that the scale levels are the same for all techniques [A(i) = A for i = 1, 2,...]. The ISO-output-curve (in Logs) is then[1]:

$$\gamma = F * Log(Q) + G * \beta - H$$

with $F = \dfrac{1}{Log(L)-Log(R)}$ $\qquad G = \dfrac{Log(R)-Log(K)}{Log(L)-Log(R)}$ $\qquad H = \dfrac{Log(A)+Log(R)}{Log(R)-Log(L)}$

The optimum solution depends on the position and the slope of the ISO-Output Curves, i. e. on the ratios between land, capital and labor. Only the corner solutions represent optimal solutions. The relative abundance of land, labor and capital determines, which of these six techniques leads to the highest production. Notice that the relative abundancy or scarcity of an input can only be defined for specific periods and can alternate in other periods. The people choose in each period the technique with the highest possible output elasticity for the currently most abundant factor and the lowest possible output elasticity for the currently most scarce factor[2]. Figure 2 shows the choice of the optimum technique in relation to the input-ratios between land, capital and labor. Technical revolutions (switches of technology) occur when different growth rates of the input factors lead to a change in the order of relative scarcity between land, capital and labor. Although the model does not explicitly refer to prices, it is, of course, the price response to shortages of inputs which determines the technological decisions and induces the people to switch from one technology to another.

_____

[1] Substituting (2b) in (1) and taking the logs.

[2] We suppose R_t = R = constant, i. e. we assume that all re sources are nonexhaustable. Then the technique that gives the largest output and, consequently, the largest investment in period t, provides the society with a larger stock of capital in the next period (t+1) than other techniques do while it has the same labor size and the same stock of resources. The technique with the largest output is therefore the optimal technique in period t regardless of the time preference of society.

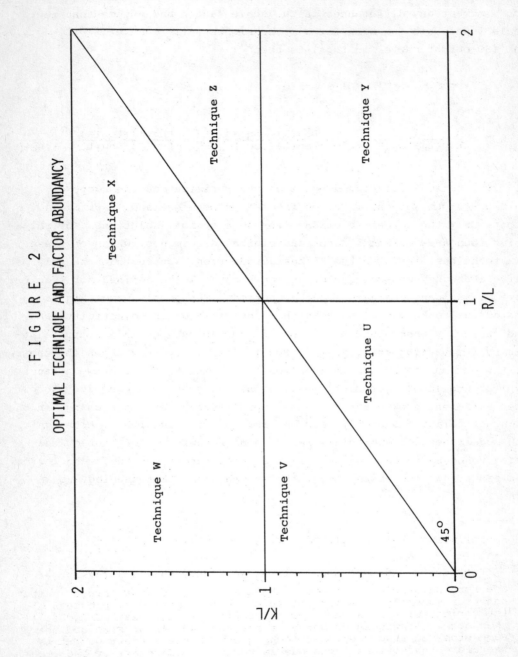

F I G U R E   2

OPTIMAL TECHNIQUE AND FACTOR ABUNDANCY

Next, we have to drop the assumption of given and identical scale factors. We hypothesize that the scale level of a technique depends both on the experiences made with that specific technique in the past $[B(i)_t]$ and on the current standard of the general technological knowledge $[M_t]$.

(3) $A(i)_t = B(i)_t * M_t$

The differences in the scale levels of the various techniques are due to learning-by-doing-effects. "Old" techniques (techniques that have been used previously) can be expected to have higher scale factors than "new" techniques (techniques that have not yet been used) because the people have learned by their adoption and can use them more effectively. The hypothesis of learning-by-doing can be stated as follows[3],[4]:

$$B(i)_t = B_0 + \frac{B_1 - B_0}{1 + \psi/(t - lag - t_i)} \quad (t_j \geq t \geq (t_i + lag), j \neq i)$$

(4)

$$B(i)_t = B_0 \qquad\qquad \text{if } t < (t_i + lag)$$

with t_i : Year of first adoption of technique i

   lag : Time lag in the process of learning

   B_0 : B-level if technique has not yet been adopted ($t < t_i$)

   B_1 : B-level if technique has been adopted for so long time that the full effect from learning by doing has been reached [$(t - t_i) \to$ infinite]

   ψ : measure for the speed of the learning-by-doing-process

The process of learning-by-doing retards the technological switches because it increases only the scale level of the technique that is in use and leaves the scale levels of the other techniques unaffected.

---

[3] According to the learning-by-doing hypothesis, the rate of technical progress depends on the cumulative production of the past and not on time. Formula (4) is therefore not a correct description of the learning-by-doing hypothesis but is an approximation to simplify the analysis.

[4] Eq. (4) is applicable as long as technique i is used [$t_j \geq t \geq (t_i + lag), j \neq i$]

Furthermore, learning-by-doing will have a relative strong impact on the productivity of labor if the technique is relatively new in use. On the other side, if the technique has been adopted for a long time, most benefits from learning-by-doing will already have been exploited and further increases of the productivity of labor will be relatively modest. We can therefore expect that learning-by-doing will improve the output per capita in periods following technical revolutions. The gains may be lost again in later periods when the effects of learning-by-doing are too weak to overcome or neutralize the pressure from decreasing returns of scale.

Learning-by-doing is not the only source of the growth of technological knowledge. New technical knowledge is also produced by men. We suppose that this type of technical knowledge [M] affects the scale levels of all techniques and that the creation of new technical knowledge depends (1) on the amount of existing knowledge [M], (2) on the number of people [L] and (3) on the education of people. We use the capital-labor-ratio [K/L] as proxy variable for the level of education and assume the technical progress function

$$M_t - M_{t-1} = m * M_{t-1} * F[\frac{K_{t-1}}{L_{t-1}} , L_{t-1}]$$

with $0 \leq F[...] \leq 1$

and   m : a technological multiplier (and also the highest possible
          rate of technical progress effective when F[...] = 1)

We specify the technical progress function by two alternative functions[5]:

(5a) $$\hat{M}_t = \frac{M_t - M_{t-1}}{M_{t-1}} = m * \tanh \left[c * [\frac{K_{t-1}}{L_{t-1}}]^{\epsilon} * L_{t-1}^{\mu} \right]$$

and

(5b) $$\hat{M}_t = \frac{M_t - M_{t-1}}{M_{t-1}} = m * \tanh \left[c_1 * [\frac{K_{t-1}}{L_{t-1}}]^{\epsilon} \right] * \tanh \left[c_2 * L_{t-1}^{\mu} \right]$$

_____

[5] $\tanh[x] = (e^x - e^{-x})/(e^x + e^{-x})$, $\tanh[x->\infty]=1$, $\tanh[x=0]=0$.

with tanh[x]: hyperbolic tangent function (logistic function)

ε, μ, c, c_1, c_2 : constant parameters

Equation (5a) states that the quantity (L) and the quality (K/L) are substitutes in the production of new knowledge (case of unlimited substitutability). Equation (5b) sets minimum requirements on the number and quality of researchers which must be met to acquire new knowledge. This reduces the substitutability (case of limited substitutability)[6].

Land, including resources, is assumed to be given. This does not mean that the resources are "natural". For it is the available stock of labor and capital, the standard of technological knowledge [the scale level A(i)] and the selected technique, that determines the output received from given quantities of "natural" resources and other inputs.

(6) $R_t = R = $ constant

Capital increases through accumulation. The rate of saving out of production is s. We assume that savings equals (net) investment.

(7) $K_t - K_{t-1} = s * Q_t$

The growth of the population is assumed exponential for simplicity. We also neglect the age distribution of population and do not distinguish between population and labor.

(8) $L_t = L_{t-1} * (1 + g_L)$

---

[6] We assume $\varepsilon > \mu$ in the case of unlimited substitutability [eq. (5a)], i. e. the quality of researchers affects the production of new knowledge more than their quantity. We do not set any restrictions on ε and μ in the case of limited substitutionability [eq. (5b)]. We exclude the assumption $\varepsilon < \mu$ in the first case, because it implies the result that population growth stimulates technical progress under all circumstances and never has any adverse effect on the creation of new knowledge.

III. Steady State Solution

The steady state is carried out in continuous form rather than discrete time periods. The equations (1), (6), (7) and (8) form the foundation of the basic neoclassical growth model and lead to the well known steady state solution (9) for a given technique i and a constant rate of technical progress ($g_{A(i)}$).

$$(9) \qquad g_Q = g_K = \frac{g_{A(i)}}{1-\beta(i)} + \frac{\gamma(i)}{1-\beta(i)} * g_L$$

$$(10) \qquad g_q = g_Q - g_L = \frac{g_{A(i)}}{1-\beta(i)} + \frac{\beta(i) + \gamma(i)-1}{1-\beta(i)} * g_L$$

with g_Q, g_q, g_K, g_L: equilibrium growth rates of production, per-capita-production, capital and population

Whether production per capita increases, stagnates or decreases in equilibrium depends on the rate of technical progress and the output elasticity of land.

$$(10a) \qquad g_q \gtreqless 0 \quad \text{if} \quad g_{A(i)} \gtreqless \alpha(i) * g_L$$

Notice that each technology yields a different steady state solution provided that the rate of technical progress is the same. We showed above, that only the six corner solutions Y, U, V, W, X, Z represent optimal technologies. Consequently, we also get six steady state equilibria, each of which corresponds to another technique. A change in the order of the input ratios between land, capital and labor makes the existing technology obsolete and replaces the one steady state equilibrium by the other. The existence of an equilibrium depends on the assumption that the rate of technical progress is given. But the rate of technical progress is an endogenous variable in our model. Therefore we have to examine whether the assumption of a constant rate of technical progress is consistent with equations (4) and (5).

First, consider the case of unlimited substitutionability between quantity and quality of researchers (technical progress function (5a). The logistic function tanh [...] approaches either its maximum tanh [x→∞] = 1 or its minimum tanh [x=0] = 0. Therefore we can derive two alternative steady state rates of M:

$$g_M = m \quad \text{if} \quad g_K > \frac{\varepsilon - \mu}{\varepsilon} * g_L$$

(11a)

$$g_M = 0 \quad \text{if} \quad g_K < \frac{\varepsilon - \mu}{\varepsilon} * g_L$$

Technical knowledge either grows with its maximum rate or stagnates. The outcome depends on the equilibrium rate of capital growth and on the population growth rate. Faster population growth increases the required equilibrium rate of capital growth that is necessary to ensure technical progress although the difference in the required rates is less than the difference in the rates of population growth.

We can neglect learning-by-doing in the steady-state analysis because it affects the rate of technical progress only temporarily during the adjustment. Therefore we replace (4) by

(4a) $B(i) = B_1$

and get by transforming and substituting (3), (4a) and (9) in (10a)

(12a) $g_M = g_{A(i)} = m > 0$ if $m > \frac{\bar{I}}{\underline{I}}\, \alpha(i) - \frac{\mu}{\varepsilon} * [1-\beta(i)]\, \frac{\bar{I}}{\underline{I}} * g_L$

(12a)' $g_M = g_{A(i)} = 0$ if $m < \frac{\bar{I}}{\underline{I}}\, \alpha(i) - \frac{\mu}{\varepsilon} * [1-\beta(i)]\, \frac{\bar{I}}{\underline{I}} * g_L$

and [(12a), (12a)' in (11a)]

(13a) $g_q > 0$ if $g_M > [\alpha(i) * g_L]$

(13a)' $g_q < 0$ if $g_M < [\alpha(i) * g_L]$

Conditions (12a) and (13a) are unlikely to be met for technique Y when α is at its maximum and β at its minimum. Technique Z has the same α and needs the same g_M for a positive growth of production per capita as technique Y. But technique Z has a larger β than technique Y and this lowers the m that is necessary to get technical progress in equilibrium (condition 12a). The two conditions (12a) and (13a) are easier to satisfy for techniques U and X when α is lower. This is even more true for techniques V and W when α is at its minimum. We can therefore conclude that techniques V and W offer better chances for longrun positive growth of technical knowledge and production per capita and bear lower risks of Malthusian crises than all other techniques.

Next, assume the case of limited substitutability between quantity and quality of researchers in the technical progress function (eq. (5b)). Again we get two alternative steady state rates:

$$g_M = m \qquad \text{if } g_K > g_L > 0$$

(11b)

$$g_M = 0 \qquad \text{if } g_K < g_L$$

and from (3), (4a), (9) and (11b):

(12b) $\quad g_M = g_{A(i)} = m > 0 \quad \text{if } m > [\alpha(i) * g_L]$

(12b)' $\quad g_M = g_{A(i)} = 0 \qquad \text{if } m < [\alpha(i) * g_L]$

The condition for a positive steady state rate of per capita production remains unchanged:

(13b) $\quad g_q > 0 \qquad\qquad \text{if } g_M > [\alpha(i) * g_L]$

(13b)' $\quad g_q < 0 \qquad\qquad \text{if } g_M < [\alpha(i) * g_L]$

Conditions (12b) and (13b) coincide. A positive steady state rate of technical progress exists in this case, only for those techniques that generate a positive steady state rate of per capita production. Furthermore, techniques V ad W are more likely to fulfill this condition than any other techniques. Growing production per head is a necessary precondition for growing technical knowledge. That is the main difference compared to the case of unlimited substitutability between quantity and quality of researchers, in which technical progress can merely be achieved by having enough poeople, even if the standard of education (capital-labor-ratio) is low.

IV. Dynamics of Adjustment

We simplify our analysis in this paragraph by assuming that all further adjustments to the capital-labor-land-ratio alterations, to changes in technology or to variations of the rate of technical progress occur after the end of the period and are completed before the beginning of the next period. There is then an equilibrium within each period, allowing us to equate the growth rate of production with the growth rate of capital and to transform equations (1), (6), (7) and (8) into[7]

$$(14) \qquad \hat{Q}_t = \hat{K}_t = \frac{\hat{A}_t(i)}{1-\beta(i)} + \frac{\gamma(i)}{1-\beta(i)} * g_L$$

In addition to this, we also neglect the effects of learning-by-doing.

$$(15) \qquad \hat{A}_t(i) = \hat{M}_t$$

Both restrictions will be dropped in the next paragraph when we simulate the process of adjustment by numerical examples.

We consider first the case of unlimited substitutability and assume that the rate of technical progress reacts to changes of (K/L) and L with a one period lag.

$$(5a)' \qquad \hat{M}_t = \frac{M_t - M_{t-1}}{M_{t-1}} = m * \tanh \left[c * \left[\frac{K_{t-1}}{L_{t-1}}\right]^\varepsilon * L_{t-1}^\mu \right]$$

$$\hat{M}_t \gtreqless \hat{M}_{t-1} \quad \text{if} \quad \hat{K}_{t-1} \gtreqless \frac{\varepsilon-\mu}{\varepsilon} * g_L$$

or using (14) and (15):

(16a) $\hat{M}_t \gtreqless \hat{M}_{t-1}$ if $\hat{M}_{t-1} \gtreqless \begin{matrix} \overline{I} \\ I \\ \underline{I} \end{matrix} \alpha(i) - \frac{\mu}{\varepsilon} * (1-\beta(i)) \begin{matrix} \overline{I} \\ I \\ \underline{I} \end{matrix} * g_L$

We can also determine the condition for growing, constant or de-clining production per capita

(17a) $\hat{q}_t = \hat{Q}_t - g_L \gtreqless 0$ if $\hat{M}_{t-1} \gtreqless [\alpha(i) * g_L]$

We can define the combinations of quantities and qualities of people that yield the same rate of technical progress as ISO-RATE-OF-TECHNICAL-PROGRESS-CURVES (ISO-RTP-CURVES) and can graph them in a diagram with (K/L) and (R/L) scaled on the axis [notice that R is con-stant so that (R/L) changes inversely with L]. Figure 3a shows ISO-RTP-Curves for three different rates of technical progress:

(1) $\hat{M}_t = [\alpha(Y) * g_L]$,

(2) $\hat{M}_t = [\alpha(U) * g_L]$ and

(3) $\hat{M}_t = [\alpha(V) * g_L] = [\alpha(W) * g_L]$

The curves are named CSL-curves (Constant Standard of Living), because the rates of technical progress lead to constant per capita production for technology Y, U and V and W. The curves set for each technology the boundary between the area of increasing and decreasing per capita production.

We can also identify CTP-curves (Constant Rate of Technical Progress) that have the rates of technical progress

$\hat{M}_t = [\alpha(i) - (\mu/\varepsilon) * (1-\beta(i))] * g_L$ [i = Y, U, V, W, X, Z]

and therefore keep the rate of technical progress unchanged (see figure 3b). The rate of technical progress increases in the area above and decreases in the area below CTP.[8]

---

[8] Within the range $m \geq \hat{M}_t \geq 0$

FIGURE 3A

CSL-CURVES

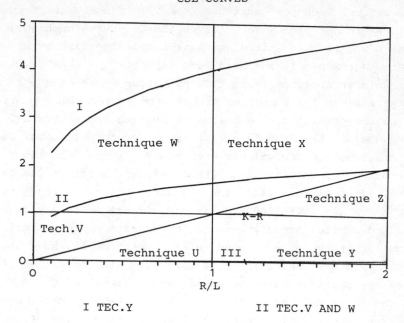

I TEC.Y   II TEC.V AND W

FIGURE 3B

CTP-CURVES

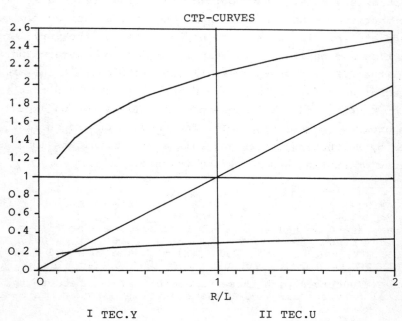

I TEC.Y   II TEC.U

The positions of the CTP- and CSL-curves depend on the technical progress function and on the output elasticities α and β, i. e. on the adopted technique. Technical switches from Y to U and V shift the curves southeast. The change from V to W leaves the CSL-curve unchanged.

Let us start from an initial situation characterized by plenty of land, only a few people and even less capital $[1 > (L/R) > (K/R)]$. The technique most appropriate to this situation is technique Y that provides the maximum for α and the minimum for β. Technique Y can be described as the prehistoric technique of hunting and gathering. Land is affluent and has the most important impact on output. Labor size has less influence and capital has even minor effects than labor due to the low output elasticity of capital. Per capita output can only grow, first, if conditions (12a) and (13a) for positive steady state rates of Q and M are fulfilled and, second, if the initial size of population and capital are high enough to generate the necessary rate of technical progress, i. e. if the initial position is above the CTP-curve. Both are highly unlikely to be fulfilled. The magnitude of m that is required for positive rates of steady state growth of Q and M is very high due to technique's Y maximum α and minimum β. For the same reason are the CLS- and CTP-curves unfavorable. Large population and capital are needed for an escape from the Malthusian trap if the chance of an escape exists at all. But, on the other side, technique Y is only an appropriate technique when labor and capital are scarce relative to land and this is unlikely to be the case for the very large population size and capital stock that is needed to generate the escape [i. e. the STP- and CLS-curves will not intersect in the area in which technique Y is adopted. We can therefore conclude that the technique of hunting and gathering (technique Y) cannot be expected to nourish growing numbers of people. The population growth will be accompanied by Malthusian crises and famine will result as long as the technique of hunting and gathering is used.

Footnote to Figure 3:

* The diagrams are computed from the following parameter values:
  $m = 0.01$, $c = 0.005$, $\varepsilon = 0.8$, $\mu = 0.2$, $\alpha(Y) = 0.6$, $\beta(Y) = 0.1$,
  $\alpha(Y) = 0.6$, $\beta(Y) = 0.1$, $\alpha(U) = 0.3$, $\beta(Y) = 0.1$, $\alpha(V) = 0.1$, $\beta(Y) = 0.3$,
  $\alpha(W) = 0.1$, $\beta(W) = 0.6$, $R = 100\ 000$, $g_L = 0.25$ %. Techniques V and W
  do not have CTP-curves with these parameter values, because the rate of technical progress always increases until it reaches its maximum.

The continuing growth of population and capital leads to increasing shortage of land and eventually makes land more scarce than labor [(L/R > 1 > (K/R)]. The new situation affects the choice of techniques. Technique U with maximum output elasticity of labor and minimum output elasticity of capital becomes the optimal technique and replaces old technique Y. The technological switch from Y to U can be interpreted as corresponding to the neolithic agricultural revolution in history. The technique of hunting and gathering is superseded by the agricultural technique (farming, domestication of wild animals, construction of irrigation systems and use of fertilization methods).

The shift of the technique from Y to U is associated with a downward shift of the CTP- and CLS-curves. This facilitates potential escapes from Malthusian crises. While in the case of technique Y, population size and capital may not have been large enough to produce the high rate of technical progress that is necessary for long-run growth of knowledge and production, they may now generate the escape due to the higher output elasticity of augmentable labor. The stability (and existence) of a steady state equilibrium with positive growth rates of technical knowledge and per capita production is still highly questionable. It is more likely that the agricultural age is similar to the age of hunting and gathering and that people still suffer periodically from famines. These, of course, are the historical experiences.

The age of agriculture comes to an end when the returns to capital surpass that of land [(L/R) > (K/R) > 1] and, consequently, technique V replaces technique U. This is the beginning of the industrialization era. It leads to further shifts of the RTP- and CLS-curves. For this reason, and because population size and capital stock are large after having grown for so long, we get the final escape from famine. The escape is accomplished because a) the then existing size of population represents an enormous ingenious capacity and stimulates new technical progress more than in all ages before, b) the high population density and urbanization favor the creation of new knowledge additionally by establishing a dense network system of communication and transportation and finally c) the high output elasticities of the augmentable inputs labor and capital offer better opportunities for overcoming the Malthusian crises than ever before and allow permanent improvements of the standard of living even with relatively low rates of technical progress.

The series of technical switches does not end with the switch from technique U to V. The age of industrialization is followed by another technical age, which begins when faster capital growth makes the returns to capital greater than that of labor [(K/R) > (L/R) > 1].

It is characterized by technique W with maximum β and minimum α. The adoption of technique W leads to still higher growth rates of capital and per capita income than the adoption of technique V did. Furthermore with capital growing faster than labor and the latter faster than land (= const.), the order of the input ratios will not change any more. This excludes further technical switches, making technique W the technology which finally succeeds.

The case of limited substitutability between quantity and quality of researchers in the technical progress function shows similar results. The positions of the CTP- and CLS-curves are less favorable in this case because the capital-labor-ratio must not fall short of a certain minimum to get technical progress. This makes more questionable both the existence and the stability of a steady state equilibrium with positive growth rates of knowledge and production per capita and worsens the chances of escaping from Malthusian crises.

V.   Simulation Results

The purpose of the simulations is to get a better understanding of the dynamics of longrun technical change and economic growth. Although we made several simulation runs with both alternative technical progress functions, we will only review the results of the case of limited substitutability between quantity and quality of people. We used the technical progress function:

$$(5b)' \quad M_t - M_{t-1} = m*M_{t-1}*\tanh\left[c_1*\left[\frac{K_{t-1}}{L_{t-1}}\right]^{\varepsilon}\right]*\tanh\left[\frac{c_2}{L_0}*(L_{t-1}-L_0)^{\mu}\right]$$

with m: the maximum rate of technical progress

   L_0:   minimum size of population for creating new knowledge

   c_1, c_2, ε, μ: parameters that determine the slope of the technical progress function

The simulations differ in the rate of population growth and in the values assigned to ε and μ. All other parameter values are held constant.[9] The numerical values of g_L, ε and μ are listed in table 1.

Table 1: Alternative Numerical Values
For Population Growth And Technical Progress Function

	ε=0.25 μ=0.75	ε=0.50 μ=0.50	ε=0.75 μ=0.25
g_L = 0.25%	simulation I	simulation II	simulation III
g_L = 0.10%	simulation IV	simulation V	simulation VI
g_L = 0.00%	simulation VII	simulation VIII	simulation IX

The time pattern of output per capita is plotted in figure 4 (Notice the logarithmic scale of the ordinate). While, at early stages of history, fast growing population (0.25 %) leads to a slightly lower output per capita than slow growing (0.1 %) or stagnating population, it overcomes the adverse effects of capital dilution in all cases in the long run, regardless of the chosen parameter values of ε and μ. The positive result is due to two reasons:

(1) Rapid population growth shortens the process of technological switches. The early adoption of the industrial techniques V and W allows fast expansion of output, capital and knowledge at a time when the slow growing population is still trapped by techniques less benign to economic

---

[9] savings rate: s = 0.05
output elasticities: the maximum (minimum) values of $\alpha(i)$, $\beta(i)$ and $\gamma(i)$ are 0.6 (0.1)
technical progress function: m = 0.01, c_1 = 1/2, c_2 = 1/8, L_0 = 30000

learning-by-doing function: ψ = 100 (i. e. one third of the potential gain from learning-by-doing occurs within the first 50 years) B_1 = 1.5*B_0 (i. e. the scale factor can be increased by 50 %)
lag = 50 (lag of 50 periods)
initial conditions: R = 100000, L = 30000, K = 20000, M = 1.25, A(i) = 0.007

and technical growth. Zero population growth is even worse because it
prevents the introduction of the industrial techniques V and W. [10)]

(2) Rapid population promotes the creation of new knowledge and
increases the rate of technical progress, especially in the case
$\varepsilon = 0.25$, $\mu = 0.75$ (see figure 4a). A larger population eventually enjoys a higher output per capita than a smaller population even in the
case $\varepsilon = 0.75$, $\mu = 0.25$ (see figures 4c and 4d) although it needs much
longer to overcome the dismal effect of capital dilution than in the
more favorable cases $\varepsilon = 0.25$, $\mu = 0.75$ and $\varepsilon = 0.5$, $\mu = 0.5$. A high
education standard (capital-labor-ratio) alone cannot produce rapid
technical progress, if there are not enough people to invent new ideas
and to form a dense network of communication.

Figure 5 shows the time pattern of the growth rate of production.
The diagrams demonstrate the disruption of existing economic-technological equilibria and the beginning of new economic-technological
eras when population and/or capital have grown so much that the size
of population and capital allows and enforces the adoption of a new
technology. The graphs also reveal the effects of technical changes.
They lead to:

(1) temporary escapes from Malthusian crises in the periods
following technical revolutions. The improvements of the productivity
of labor are due to increasing experience in using the new technologies
(effect of learning-by-doing). The growth rates of output decrease
again in later periods when the gains from learning-by-doing-cause
become smaller.

(2) the permanent escape from Malthusian trap when technical
progress becomes stronger and when techniques are adopted that are
more benign to economic growth (techniques with high output elasticities
of the augmentable inputs labor and capital). Both the higher rates of
technical progress and the adoption of the new favorable techniques
are ultimately caused by population growth and are absent in the case
of zero population growth. It is true that capital accumulation also
leads to a technical revolution in the case of zero population (from
technique Y to Z, see figure 5). However, the process of technical
changes ends in this case with technique Z instead with the more favorable techniques V and W.

[10)] Unless the stabilization of population size takes place late in
the industrial age when population size is sufficient high to get
the maximum rate of technical progress.

23

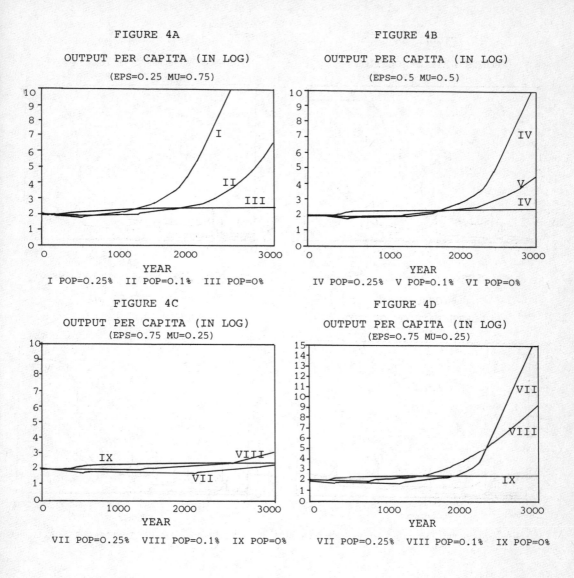

FIGURE 4A

OUTPUT PER CAPITA (IN LOG)

(EPS=O.25 MU=0.75)

YEAR

I POP=O.25%   II POP=O.1%   III POP=O%

FIGURE 4B

OUTPUT PER CAPITA (IN LOG)

(EPS=O.5 MU=0.5)

YEAR

IV POP=O.25%   V POP=O.1%   VI POP=O%

FIGURE 4C

OUTPUT PER CAPITA (IN LOG)

(EPS=O.75 MU=0.25)

YEAR

VII POP=O.25%   VIII POP=O.1%   IX POP=O%

FIGURE 4D

OUTPUT PER CAPITA (IN LOG)

(EPS=O.75 MU=0.25)

YEAR

VII POP=O.25%   VIII POP=O.1%   IX POP=O%

24

FIGURE 5A

GROWTH RATE OF OUTPUT
(EPS=0.25 MU=0.75)

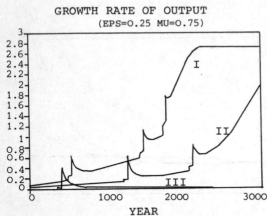

I POP=0.25%   II POP=0.1%   III POP=0%

FIGURE 5B

GROWTH RATE OF OUTPUT
(EPS=0.5 MU=0.5)

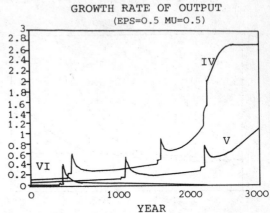

IV POP=0.25%   V POP=0.1%   VI POP=0%

FIGURE 5C

GROWTH RATE OF OUTPUT
(EPS=0.75 MU=0.25)

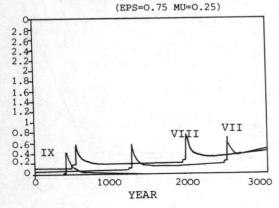

VII POP=0.25%   VIII POP=0.1%   IX POP=0%

FIGURE 5D

GROWTH RATE OF OUTPUT
(EPS=0.75 MU=0.25)

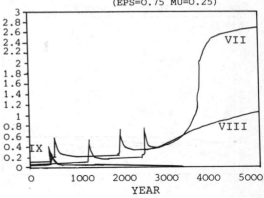

VII POP=0.25%   VIII POP=0.1%   IX POP=0%

VI. Extensions

1. Lengthening of working time. Ester BOSERUP emphasizes that (1) most
new agricultural techniques in history have had higher labor requirements than the preceding techniques and (2) therefore led to longer
working time of laborers. Our model contains only the first argument
and links optimum technology to population size. The second argument
can easily be incorporated into the model, too. Both growing population
and growing working time per laborer increase the labor input and eventually lead to technical change. An extension of working time can make
a new technique optimal that, otherwise, would not have become optimal
before population had been grown enough. This accelerates the process
of technical revolutions and leads to an earlier escape from Malthusian
crises than in the cases with constant working time.

2. Endogenous growth of population. Demographic adjustments to economic
conditions have been an important element in the dynamics of history.
This suggests adding a population function to our model. There is no
doubt that a population function would fit in the model and complete
it. We may, for instance, include feedbacks of Malthusian crises to
fertility and mortality and other positive or preventive checks (fertility controls, random shocks like epidemic catastrophes or wars).
We did not introduce a population function because we wanted to concentrate on the essential forces in action, demonstrating that population growth, though it may have been adverse to the standard of
living in the very short run and aggregated the economic problems of
some of our ancestors, eventually has caused the economic and technical revolutions and the unprecedented economic progress that we enjoy today.

3. Scale effects. The assumption of constant returns to scale,

$$\alpha(i) + \beta(i) + \gamma(i) = 1 \quad (i = 1, 2, \ldots)$$

might be too restrictive, because land is explicitly included in the
production function. Positive scale effects are likely to exist, if
all inputs (incl. land) are increased. Neoclassical growth models usually assume that the output elasticities of labor and capital add to 1.
Suppose, for instance, that

$$\alpha(i) + \beta(i) + \gamma(i) = 1.2 \quad i = 1, 2, \ldots$$

Then we do not even need technical progress to finally escape the Malthusian trap. With the same maximum and minimum values of the output elasticities as hypothesized in the simulations

$$[a_0 = b_0 = g_0 = 0.1, \quad a_1 = b_1 = g_1 = 0.6]$$

α decreases from 0.6 in technique Y, to 0.5 in technique U and to 0.1 in techniques V and W. As consequence, the sum of β and γ increase from 0.6 (technique Y) to 0.7 (technique U) to finally 1.1 (techniques V and W). It is still true, that the growth of capital and labor does not allow a long-run growth of per-capita-output for techniques Y and U. However, with techniques V and W, the high output elasticities of the two augmentable inputs make a long-run increase of per-capita-output achievable even in the absence of any technical progress.

VII. Conclusion

Our aim was to emphasize the key role of population growth for longrun economic and technological development. We implemented a production function for technical knowledge and the potential of technical choices into the standard growth model of neoclassical theory. A change in population pressure influences the creation of new knowledge and induces technological adjustments.

We were able to theorize and simulate the historical experience of technical revolutions: Malthusian crises, Boserupian overcomings and final escape. We offered an explanation of the reasons economic and technological progress in history proceeded in abrupt technical and economic revolutions rather than in small and smooth changes. Growing population size and population density are the central dynamic forces in history.

Since MALTHUS, mainstream thinking in growth and development economies has focused on the capital dilution effect of population growth, and has overseen the impact of population on creation and adoption of new technology. The traditional view is not only onesided and misleading but also contrary to historical experience. The greatest technical, economic and cultural achievements of west European history occured in the 11th, 12th and 13th and in the 18th, 19th and 20th centuries when West European population grew most rapidly. The immense economic and technological benefits that we enjoy today have been attained due to, rather than in spite of, the enormous increase in population.

References

BOSERUP, Ester, 1983, "The Impact of Scarcity and Plenty on Development". Journal of Interdisciplinary History, 14: 383-407.

BOSERUP, Ester, 1981, "Population and Technological Change: A Study of Long-Term Trends". Chicago, University of Chicago Press.

CIGNO, Alessandro, 1984, "Consumption vs. Procreation in Economic Growth". In Gunter STEINMANN (ed.), "Studies in Contemporary Economics. Economic Consequences of Population Change in Industrial Countries". Proceedings of a Conference on Population Economics held at the University of Paderborn June 1 - June 3, 1983. Berlin (Germany), Springer, pp. 2-28.

JONES, E. L., 1981, "The European Miracle. Environment, Economies, and Geopolitics in The History of Europe and Asia". Cambridge, The Cambridge University Press.

KOMLOS, John and ARTZROUNI, Marc, 1985, "A Simulation Model of Malthusian Population Dynamics in a Two-Sector Economy with Capital Accumulation Between the First and Second Economic Revolution". Unpublished manuscript, Carolina Population Center, University of North Carolina at Chapel Hill.

KUZNETS, Simon, 1960, "Population Change and Aggregate Output". In Universities - National Bureau of Economic Research, Demographics and Economic Change in Developed Countries. Princeton, N. J., Princeton University Press.

LEE, Ronald Demos, 1984, "Malthus and Boserup: A Dynamic Synthesis". Working Paper no. 15. Berkeley, Program in Population Research, University of California.

NORTH, Douglas, 1981, "Structure and Change in Economic History". New York, Norton.

SIMON, Julian L., 1986, "Theory of Population and Economic Growth". Oxford, Basil Blackwell.

SIMON, Julian L., 1978, "An Integration of the Invention-Pull and Population-Push Theories of Economic-Demographic History". In: Julian L. SIMON (ed.), "Research in Population Economics", Vol. I. Greenwich, JAI Press.

SIMON, Julian L. and STEINMANN, Gunter, 1984, "The Economic Implications of Learning-by-Doing for Population Size and Growth". European Economic Review, 26: 167-85.

SIMON, Julian L. and STEINMANN, Gunter, 1986, "Population Growth and the Longrun Standard of Living". Mimeo.

STEINMANN, Gunter, 1986, "Bevölkerungsentwicklung und Technischer Fortschritt". In Bernhard FELDERER (ed.), "Beiträge zur Bevölkerungsökonomie". Berlin (Germany), Duncker & Humblot, pp. 85-115.

STEINMANN, Gunter, 1984, "A Model of the History of Demographic-Economic Growth". In Gunter STEINMANN (ed.) "Studies in Contemporary Economics. Economic Consequences of Population Change in Industrial Countries". Proceedings of a Conference on Population Economics

held at the University of Paderborn June 1 - June 3, 1983.
Berlin (Germany), Springer, pp. 29 - 49.

STEINMANN, Gunter and KOMLOS, John, 1986, "Population Growth and Econ-
    omic Development in the Very Long Run: A Simulation Model of Three
    Revolutions". Forthcoming. Mathematical Social Sciences.

STEINMANN, Gunter and SIMON, Julian L., 1980, "Phelps' Technical Progress
    Model Generalized". Economic Letters, 5: 177-182.

ENDOGENOUS FLUCTUATIONS IN THE
BARRO-BECKER THEORY OF FERTILITY

Jess Benhabib[*], New York University
and
Kazuo Nishimura[*], Kyoto Institute of Economic Research

New York/USA and Kyoto/JAPAN

ABSTRACT: One of the recent interesting hypotheses of population growth is due to EASTERLIN (1973) (see also BECKER (1981) chapter 7) who suggests the possibility of self-generating fluctuations in population growth. A large population will face stiffer economic competition, lower incomes, congestions and crowding if other means of production as well as the social infrastructure do not expand simultaneously. The result may be a decline in fertility as parents try to maintain an adequate standard of living for themselves. But why should capital and other means of production or the social infrastructure not expand with population size at a uniform rate? Are fluctuations a necessary or even possible outcome of this analysis? Using the BARRO-BECKER framework (1985) and relaxing some of their assumptions, we will answer this question. Our results show that under a broad class of preferences, fertility and per capita incomes not only move together but endogenously oscillate.

I.   The Model and Theorems

BARRO and BECKER consider a model where parents derive utility from their own consumption as well as from the utility of their children. Starting with a given stock of capital k_o, they maximize their utility, assuming that their children will do the same:

(1)
$$V(k_o) = \max_{c_o, n_0, k_1} [U(c_o) + \sum_{t=1}^{\infty} \prod_{w=1}^{t} \alpha(n_w) n_w U(c_t)]$$

S.T.

$$(1-g)k_0 + F(k_0) = c_0 + n_0(k_1 + B_0)$$

where c_t is the consumption of generation t, n_t is one plus the endogenous population growth rate, B is the cost of raising children and is constant over time, k_t is the per capita stock, $F(k)$ is the production function, $U(c_0)$ is the utility derived from consumption and g is the depreciation rate. $\alpha(n)$ can be taken as a parameter of altruism towards children[1][2]. BARRO and BECKER assume $\alpha(n) \cdot n$ to be concave. In dynamic

---

[1] We will assume that $\alpha(n) \cdot n$ is small enough, possibly bounded by 1 so that the sum converges.

[2] In a competitive market and under constant returns, wages plus profit income will be a function of the given capital stock per worker and will equal $f(k)$. To save space we simply specify income to be equal to output.

[*] We thank Sadao Kanaya for calling our attention to Barro and Becker's work on the fertility choice problem. We are grateful to Gary Becker for valuable comments and corrections.

Studies in Contemporary Economics
A. Wenig, K. F. Zimmermann (Eds.)
Demographic Change and Economic Development
© Springer-Verlag Berlin Heidelberg 1989

programming form we can write the problem as

(2) $V(k_0) = \underset{c_0,n_0,k}{\text{Max}} \; [U(c_0) + a(n_0)V(k_1)]$

S.T.

$f(k_0) = c_0 + n_0(k_1 + b_0)$

where $\alpha(n_0) \cdot n_0 = a(n_0)$ and $f(k) = F(K) + (1-g)k$. Here $a(n_0)$ is increasing and concave, which reflects that the utility of the parents is increasing at a diminishing rate with the number of children, for a given level of well-being $V(k_1)$ per child. We assume that there is a maximum sustainable level of capital stock $\bar{k}$ such that $f(k) < k$ for all $k > \bar{k}$. Substituting the budget constraint into the problem, we obtain[3]

(3) $V(k_0) = \underset{k_1,n_0}{\text{Max}} \; [U(f(k_0) - n_0(k_1+B)) + a(n_0)V(k_1)]$

The above problem, after choosing n_0 optimally as a function of (k_0,k_1) can also be written as

(4) $V(k_0) = \underset{k_1}{\text{Max}} \; W(k_0,k_1,n(k_0,k_1))$

Define $\bar{W}(k_0,k_1) = W(k_0,k_1,n(k_0,k_1))$ and $\bar{W} = \partial\bar{W}/\partial k_0$. Let k^* be a steady state satisfying $V(k^*) = \bar{W}(k^*,k^*) = \underset{k_1}{\text{max}}\,\bar{W}(k^*,k_1)$. Let E be the set of steady states. We will use the following lemma to prove our main result.

Lemma 1:   (i) If $\bar{W}_1(k_0,k_1)$ is strictly increasing in k_1, then an optimal path $\{\hat{k}_t\}$ from any $k_0 > 0$, $k_0 \notin E$, is strictly monotone, i. e. $(\hat{k}_{t-1}-\hat{k}_t)(\hat{k}_t-\hat{k}_{t+1}) > 0$.

(ii) If $\bar{W}_1(k_0,k_1)$ is independent of k_1, then the capital stock jumps to its steady state value in one period, i.e. $\hat{k}_2 = \hat{k}^*$.

(iii) If $\bar{W}_1(k_0,k_1)$ is strictly decreasing in k_1, then an optimal path from any $k_0 > 0$, $k_0 \notin E$, fluctuates, i. e., $(\hat{k}_{t-1}-\hat{k}_t)(\hat{k}_t-\hat{k}_{t+1}) < 0$.

---

[3] BARRO and BECKER limit $a(n_0)$ to be of the constant relative risk aversion class. We will allow a broader class of functions $a(n)$.

Note that at a steady state in Lemma 1 above we may have $k^* > 0$ or $k^* = 0$. Note also that we do not need to use the differentiability of the value function $V(k)$ to prove this lemma. This lemma may be rigorously proved in the manner given in BENHABIB, MAJUMDAR and NISHIMURA (1985). A short proof using the differentiability of $V(k_1)$ is given in the Appendix of the present paper. In the rest of the paper, we shall give the interpretation of the conditions imposed on $\overline{W}_1(k_0, k_1)$. To do so, we assume the differentiability of $V(k_1)$.

We can now apply the above Lemma 1 to our problem given by (1). Let e be the elasticity of (a/a') with respect to n; that is,

(5) $\qquad e = (na'/a) \cdot d(a/a')/dn$, where $a' = da(n)/dn$

Theorem 1: If $e < 1$ (>1), the capital stock oscillates (is monotonic). If $e = 1$ (the BARRO-BECKER case), the capital stock jumps to its steady state value in the first period.

Proof: The theorem follows from Lemma 1 if we can establish that the sign of $\overline{W}_{12}$ is the same as that of e-1. We set

(6) $\qquad W(k_0, k_1, n_0) = U(f(k_0) - n(k_1 + B)) + a(n_0)V(k_1)$.

Maximizing $W(k_0, k_1, n_0)$ with respect to n and k_1 yields

(7) $\qquad W_n = -(k_1 + B)U'(c_0) + a'(n_0)V(k_1) = 0$

and

(8) $\qquad W_{k_1} = -nU'((c_0) + a(n_0)V'(k_1) = 0$.

Using (7), we can obtain the optimal value of n_0 as $n(k_0, k_1)$ with the derivatives

(9) $\qquad \dfrac{dn}{dk_0} = \dfrac{(k_1 + B)U''(c_0)f'(k_0)}{a''(n_0)V(k_1) + (k_1 + B)^2 U''(c_0)} > 0$

(10) $\qquad \dfrac{dn}{dk_1} = \dfrac{-U'(c_0) - a'(n_0)V'(k_1) - (k_1 + B)n_0 U''(c_0)}{a''(n_0)V(k_1) + (k_1 + B)^2 U''(c_0)}$

Using (6) and (7), we can evaluate $\overline{W}_{12}$ as follows:

$$(11) \quad \overline{W}_{12} = W_{k_0 k_1} + W_{k_0 n_0}(\frac{\partial n_0}{\partial k_1}) + W_{n_0 k_1}(\frac{\partial n_0}{\partial k_1}) + W_{n_0 n_0}(\frac{\partial n_0}{\partial k_1}) \cdot (\frac{\partial n_0}{\partial k_0})$$

where $W_{k_0 k_1} = -n_0 f'(k_0)U''(c_0)$, $W_{k_0 n_0} = -(k_1+B)^2 U''(c_0)[f'(k_0)+1]$,

$W_{n_0 n_0} = (k_1+B)''U''(c_0) + a''(n_0)V(k_1)$, $W_{k_1 k_0} = -U'(c_0) + n_0(k_1+B)U''(c_0)$

$\quad\quad + a'(n_0)V'(k_1)$.

Substituting into (11) and cancelling, we obtain

$$\overline{W}_{12} = \frac{f'(k_0)U''(c_0)}{a''(n_0)V(k_1)+(k_1+B)^2 U''(c_0)}[(k_1+B)(a'(n_0)V'(k_1)$$

$$- U'(c_0)) - n_0 a''(n_0)V(k_1)]$$

Solving for $V(k_1)$ and $V'(k_1)$ from (7) and (8) and substituting, we obtain

$$\overline{W}_{12} = [\frac{f'(k_0)U''(c_0)}{a''(n_0)V(k_1)+(k_1+B)^2 V''(c_0)}][(k_1+B)(\frac{n_0 a'(n)U'(c)}{a(n_0)}$$

$$- U'(c)) - \frac{n_0 a''(n_0)(k_1+B)U'(c)}{a'(n)}]$$

$$(12) = [\frac{f'(k_0)U''(c_0)(k_1+B)U'}{a''(n_0)V(k_1)+(k_1+B)^2 V''(c_0)}][\frac{n_0 a'(n_0)}{a(n_0)} - 1 - \frac{n_0 a''(n_0)}{a'}]$$

The first square bracket on the right is positive by concavity. The second can be further simplified so that it equals

$$(13) \quad [(\frac{n_0 a'}{a})\frac{(a'(n_0))^2 - a(n_0)a''(n_0)}{(a'(n_0))^2} - 1] = (\frac{n_0 a'}{a})\frac{d(a/a')}{dn} - 1 = e-1$$

Therefore the sign of $\overline{W}_{12}$ is the same as that of e-1, as was to be proved.   Q.E.D.

Theorem 1 gives conditions under which the capital stock is oscillatory or monotonic. We now turn to the analysis of how the fertility rate n changes with the capital stock. Theorem 2 below gives a result for the oscillatory case:

Theorem 2: If $e = (\frac{n_0 a'}{a})\frac{d(a/a')}{dn_0} < 1$, the fertility rate n oscillates in phase with the per capita stock k.

Proof: We have $dn_0(dk_0 = \partial n_0/\partial k_0 + (\partial n_0/\partial k_1)dk_1/dk_0$. From the proof of Lemma 1, we know that e < 1 implies $dk_1/dk_0 < 0$. Also from (9) in the proof of Theorem 1 we have $\partial n_0/\partial k_0 > 0$. From (8) and (10) in the proof of Theorem 1 we can compute how the optimal value of n_0 changes with k_1:

$$(14) \qquad \frac{\partial n_0}{\partial k_1} = \frac{U'(c_0)(1-\frac{n_0 a'}{a}) - (k_1+B)n_0 U''(c_0)}{a''(n_0)V(k_1) + (k_1+B)^2 U''(c_0)}$$

However, we also have

$$(15) \qquad 1 - \frac{n_0 a'}{a} \geq 1 - \frac{n_0[(a')^2 - aa'']}{aa'}$$

$$= 1 - e > 0.$$

Thus, under our concavity assumptions $\partial n_0/\partial k_1 < 0$ and $dn_0/dk_0 > 0$. Since under e < 1 the capital stock oscillates, so does n.   Q.E.D.

Theorem 2 therefore lends support to the hypothesis that under some reasonable conditions on preferences, the fertility rate n_0 will tend to be high (low) when the per capita stock k_0 and per capita income $f(k_0)$ are high (low).

Remark 1: It should be noted that in the oscillatory case the optimal trajectory can converge to the steady state or to a period-two cycle. These possibilities may be studied by the formal methods presented in BENHABIB and NISHIMURA (1985). If e-1 changes sign, the dynamic behavior of trajectories can become more complicated and even chaotic.

II. Examples

In this section we give several examples which illustrate the monotonic and oscillatory cases discussed above. We also show that the special case considered by BARRO and BECKER, who use a constant relative risk aversion function for a(n), corresponds to a parameter configuration on the borderline of the monotonic and oscillatory behavior in the class of Hyperbolic Absolute Risk Aversion (HARA) functions.

The general example which contains the monotonic, oscillatory as well as the BARRO-BECKER case is illustrated by a HARA function for (a(n) given by $\delta(n+Z)^A$. In this case, e = n/(n+Z). Therefore if Z > 0 (e < 1), the capital stock oscillates (Theorem 1) and n and k move in phase with each other (Theorem 2). Since k is bounded by $\bar{k}$ and $f(\bar{k}) \le c + n(\bar{k}+B)$, we have $n \le f(\bar{k})/(B+\bar{k}) = \bar{n}$. Since $a = \delta(n+Z)^A$, we can choose δ (for any given A and Z) such that $a = \delta(\bar{n}+Z)^A < 1$. Therefore the utility sums in (1) will converge.

Note that the case Z = 0 corresponds exactly to the BARRO-BECKER case with e = 1. The monotonic case with e > 1 will correspond to Z ≤ 0, with Z ≥ -n along the optimal path.

Figure 1 below illustrates the relation between the initial stock $\hat{k}_0$ and the optimal choice $\hat{k}_1$, where $\hat{k}_1 = h(\hat{k}_0)$ and h(k) is the policy function for the monotonic case. Intersections of $h(\hat{k}_0)$ with the 45° line are steady states. Note that we may have multiple steady states, with stable ones alternating with unstable ones. Figure 2 illustrates the BARRO-BECKER case and Figure 3 the oscillating case which converges to the steady state. If the steady state becomes unstable, the trajectories may converge to a periodic cycle and can also become chaotic.

Remark 2: Differentiating (2) along an optimal path, we have $V'(k_t) = V'(c_t)f'(k_t)$. Using (7), we obtain

$$n_t = \frac{a(n_t)V'(c_{t+1})}{V'(c_t)} f'(k_{t+1})$$

At a steady state, this becomes

$$a(n^{\#}) = \frac{U^*}{f'(k^*)}$$

Thus if the steady state is efficient in the usual sense, that is, if
$f'(k^*) > n^*$, then there is positive discounting of the future. On the
other hand, at the steady state $V = U/(1-a)$, so that $U/U' = (k+B)(1-a)/a'$.
If U/U' is increasing in c and $(1-a) > 0$, then an increase in costs of
child rearing will increase consumption provided we ignore the effect
of B on the steady state values of n^*, k^* and $F'(k^*)$. This is discussed
by BARRO and BECKER (1985). Also, changing the steady state interest
rate via a perturbation of the production function will affect U/U'
as well as the steady state consumption levels only via its impact
on steady state values k^* and n^*.

The steady state value of n can be either bigger or smaller
than one and will, among other things, depend on B, the cost of raising
children. The following numerical example demonstrates this point. Let
$U = 20^{.5}$, $f(k) = k^{.333} + 0.75 k$ and $a = 0.5(n+1)^{.667}$. For $B = 0.3385$,
steady state values are $n^* = 0.9995$, $k^* = 0.5291$, a = 0.7936. For
$B = 0.3383$, we have $n^* = 1.0003$, $k^* = 0.5280$, a = 0.7938. The effects
of increasing δ on steady state values are ambiguous, since a higher
marginal valuation of the future may lead to a higher steady state
k (see equation (9)) and since $n = a \cdot f'(k)$, n may either increase or
decrease.

APPENDIX

(i) If $\bar{W}_{12} > 0$, then an optimal path is strictly monotone.

Proof: Consider optimal paths $(\hat{k}_t)$, $(\hat{k}_t')$ from $\hat{k}_0$, $\hat{k}_0'$ respectively, where $\hat{k}_0' > \hat{k}_0$. Then

$$(16) \qquad \bar{W}(\hat{k}_0, \hat{k}_1) \geq \bar{W}(\hat{k}_0, \hat{k}_1')$$

$$(17) \qquad \bar{W}(\hat{k}_0', \hat{k}_1') \geq \bar{W}(\hat{k}_0', \hat{k}_1)$$

Hence

$$(18) \qquad \bar{W}(\hat{k}_0', \hat{k}_1') - \bar{W}(\hat{k}_0, \hat{k}_1') + \bar{W}(\hat{k}_0, \hat{k}_1) - \bar{W}(\hat{k}_0', \hat{k}_1) \geq 0$$

$$\int_{\hat{k}_0}^{\hat{k}_0'} [\bar{W}_1(s, \hat{k}_1') - \bar{W}_1(s, \hat{k}_1)] ds \geq 0$$

$$(19) \qquad \int_{\hat{k}_1}^{\hat{k}_2'} \int_{\hat{k}_0}^{\hat{k}_0'} \bar{W}_{12}(s, t) ds \, dt \geq 0$$

Since $\bar{W}_{12} > 0$ and $\hat{k}_0' > \hat{k}_0$, $\hat{k}_1' \geq \hat{k}_1$ must hold. We note that along the optimal paths,

$$(20) \qquad \bar{W}_1(\hat{k}_0, \hat{k}_1) = W_{k_1} + W_n(\partial n/\partial k_0) = 0.$$

$\bar{W}_{12} > 0$ implies

$$(21) \qquad 0 = \bar{W}_1(\hat{k}_0, \hat{k}_1) > \bar{W}_1(\hat{k}_0', \hat{k}_1)$$

for $\hat{k}_0' > \hat{k}_0$. Hence $(\hat{k}_0', \hat{k}_1, \ldots)$ cannot be an optimal path: $\hat{k}_1'$ must differ from $\hat{k}_1$. We have shown that $\hat{k}_0' > \hat{k}_0$ implies $\hat{k}_1' > \hat{k}_1$. This also means that $\hat{k}_0 \underset{(<)}{>} \hat{k}_1$ implies $\hat{k}_t \underset{(<)}{>} \hat{k}_{t+1}$.   Q.E.D.

(ii) If $\overline{w}_{12} = 0$, every optimal path from any $\hat{k}_0 > 0$ jumps to a steady state in one step.

<u>Proof:</u> Let k^* be a steady state. It satisfies

(22) $\overline{w}_2(k^*,k^*) = 0$.

Since $\overline{w}_{12} = 0$, $\overline{w}_2$ is independent of the value of $\hat{k}_0$. Hence $(\hat{k}_0,k^*)$ for any $\hat{k}_0 > 0$ satisfies

(23) $\overline{w}_2(\hat{k}_0,k^*) = 0$.

Therefore $(\hat{k}_0,k^*,k^*, \ldots)$ is an optimal path from any $\hat{k}_0 > 0$.   Q.E.D.

(iii) Over the domain where $\overline{w}_{12}(k_0,k_1) < 0$ holds, optimal paths oscillate.

<u>Proof:</u> The inequality (19) and $\overline{w}_{12}$ are used to get $\hat{k}_0' > \hat{k}_0 \rightarrow \hat{k}_1' \leq \hat{k}_1$. $\hat{k}_1' = \hat{k}_1$ is excluded by the same argument as in the proof of (i). Q.E.D.

References

BARRO, R., and BECKER, G., "Fertility Choice in a Model of Economic Growth", Working paper from University of Rochester, October, 1984.

BECKER, G., A Treatise on the Family Harvard University Press, 1981.

BENHABIB, J., and NISHIMURA, K., "Competitive Equilibrium Cycles", Journal of Economic Theory 35 (1985), 284-307.

BENHABIB, J., MAJUMDAR, M., and NISHIMURA, K., "Global Equilibrium Dynamics with Stationary Recursive Preferences", presented at the Workshop on the Advances in the Analysis of Economic Dynamic Systems, Venice, January 1986.

EASTERLIN, R., "Relative Economic Status and the American Fertility Swing", in E. B. SHELDON, ed., Family Economic Behavior: Problems and Prospects Philadelphia: Lippincott, 1973.

KEMP, M., and KONDO, H. "Overlapping Generations, Competitive Efficiency and Optimal Population", Working paper from University of New South Wales, 1985.

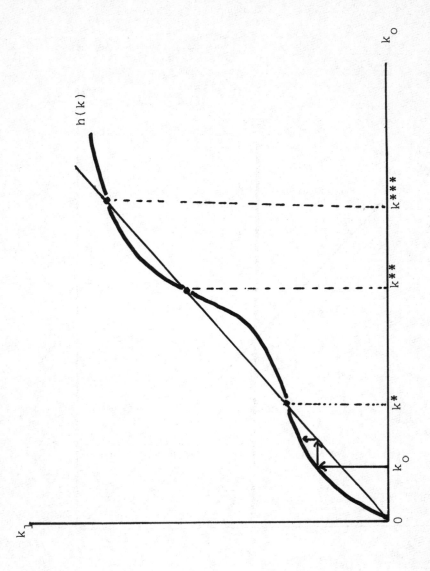

Figure 1

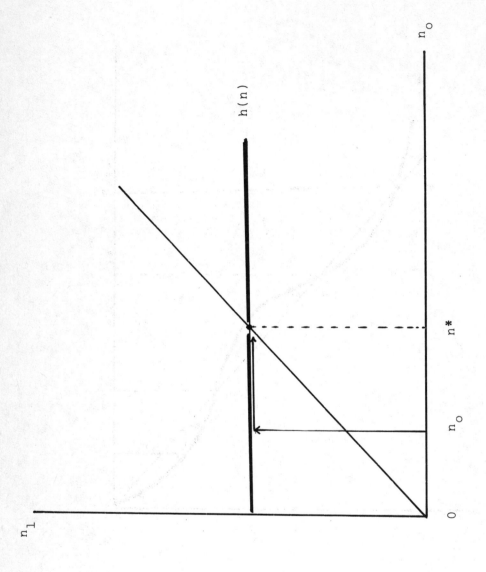

Figure 2

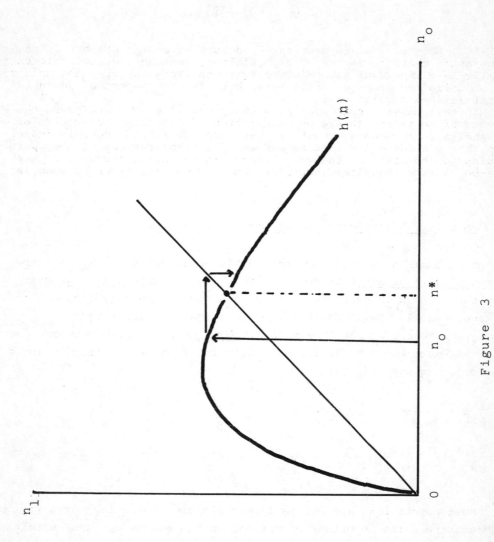

Figure 3

MORTALITY CHANGES AND THEIR ECONOMIC CONSEQUENCES,

WITH PARTICULAR REFERENCE TO CAUSE OF DEATH

J. H. Pollard
Macquarie University

Sydney / Australia

ABSTRACT: Economic development can lead to substantial changes in the demographic characteristics of a population, and these demographic changes usually have important economic implications. This is true, not only for the so-called developing populations, but also in respect of advanced industrialised populations.

In this paper, techniques previously developed for analysing the effects of mortality change on expectation of life are extended to allow the analysis of changes in certain key demographic and economic indicators. The methods allow concise and ready interpretations of the factors leading to the observed changes. Changes in the net reproduction rate of a population, hospital insurance and pensions are given as examples.

1. Mortality and Expectation of Life

In the standard actuarial and demographic notation, the complete expectation of life at age x is denoted by $\overset{o}{e}_x$ and the probability of surviving from exact age x to exact age x+t by ${}_tp_x$. The probability that a life now aged exactly x will die between exact ages x+t and x+t+dt is ${}_tp_x\,\mu_{x+t}dt$, where μ_{x+t} is the force of mortality (or instantaneous death rate) at exact age x+t. These life table functions are connected in the following ways [10][11]

$$ {}_tp_x = \exp\left\{- \int_o^t \mu_{x+u}du\right\} \; ; \tag{1} $$

$$ \overset{o}{e}_x = \int_o^\infty {}_tp_x \, dt \; . \tag{2} $$

Most populations are currently experiencing improving mortality rates, although there are important exceptions in Eastern Europe and certain Third-World countries. To account for these secular changes in mortality, we shall introduce a superscript 1 to indicate a life table function evaluated in terms of the mortality prevailing at time 1 and a superscript 2 to indicate a life table function evaluated in terms of the mortality prevailing at time 2. Thus, for example, $\overset{o}{e}{}_o^1$ will denote the complete expectation of life at birth at time 1 and ${}_tp_x^2$ will denote the probability of survival from exact age x to exact age x+t in terms of the mortality prevailing at time 2. There should be no confusion

Studies in Contemporary Economics
A. Wenig, K. F. Zimmermann (Eds.)
Demographic Change and Economic Development
© Springer-Verlag Berlin Heidelberg 1989

between these superscripts and powers.

From relations (1) and (2), we see that the change in expectation of life at birth between time 1 and time 2, given by

$$\overset{o}{e}{}^2_o - \overset{o}{e}{}^1_o = \int_o^\infty (_tp_o^2 - {}_tp_o^1)dt$$

$$= \int_o^\infty (_tp_o^2/{}_tp_o^1 - 1)_tp_o^1 \, dt$$

$$= \int_o^\infty [\exp\{\int_o^t (\mu_u^1-\mu_u^2)du\} - 1]_tp_o^1 \, dt. \qquad (3)$$

But, according to (2),

$$_tp_o^1 \, \overset{o}{e}{}^1_t = {}_tp_o^1 \int_o^\infty {}_rp_t^1 \, dt = \int_t^\infty {}_up_o^1 \, du \ , \qquad (4)$$

so that $-_tp_o^1$ is the derivative of (4) with respect to t, and (3) may be written

$$\overset{o}{e}{}^2_o - \overset{o}{e}{}^1_o = \int_o^\infty [\exp\{\int_o^t (\mu_u^1-\mu_u^2)du\} - 1] \, \frac{d}{dt} \, (-_tp_o^1 \, \overset{o}{e}{}^1_t)dt. \qquad (5)$$

The derivative of the term in square brackets in (5) is

$$(\mu_t^1-\mu_t^2) \, \exp\{\int_o^t (\mu_u^1-\mu_u^2)du\} = (\mu_t^1-\mu_t^2)_tp_o^2/{}_tp_o^1 \ . \qquad (6)$$

Integrating (5) by parts therefore, we obtain

$$\overset{o}{e}{}^2_o - \overset{o}{e}{}^1_o = \int_o^\infty (\mu_t^1-\mu_t^2) \, {}_tp_o^2 \, \overset{o}{e}{}^1_t \, dt \ . \qquad (7)$$

This formula for the change in expectation of life at birth represents a weighted average of the changes in the force of mortality at the individual ages.

An alternative exact formula can be obtained by interchanging the superscripts 1 and 2 in (7) and reversing the differences on both sides:

$$\overset{o}{e}{}^2_o - \overset{o}{e}{}^1_o = \int_o^\infty (\mu_t^1-\mu_t^2) \, {}_tp_o^1 \, \overset{o}{e}{}^2_t \, dt \ . \qquad (8)$$

Both (7) and (8) are exact formulae but the weights differ slightly. To ensure a unique symmetrical partition of the change in expectation of life at birth in terms of the age-specific mortality rates, the following formula has therefore been adopted in previous analyses [1] [12][13]:

$$\overset{\circ}{e}{}^2_0 - \overset{\circ}{e}{}^1_0 = \int_0^\infty (\mu^1_t - \mu^2_t) w_t \, dt \, , \tag{9}$$

where

$$w_t = \frac{1}{2} [\,_t p^1_0 \, \overset{\circ}{e}{}^2_t + \,_t p^2_0 \, \overset{\circ}{e}{}^1_t] \, . \tag{10}$$

Formula (9) combines the various interactions between the mortality improvements at the various ages with the main effects. This is justified on two grounds. First, the interaction terms are relatively small, even in extreme cases [12]. Second, the interaction terms are difficult to interpret in practice.

Table 1 shows, in hundredths of a year of life, the contributions of mortality improvements in the various age groups to the improvements in expectation of life at birth of Australian males and females over the 50-year period 1921-1971 and the subsequent decade 1971-1981. From this table we see inter alia that in the decade 1971-1981 a mortality 'revolution' took place. Whereas in earlier decades, the larger proportion of the improvement in life expectancy was due to mortality improvements in infancy and early childhood, the major contributions are now coming from ages over 50.

Table 2 summarises a similar analysis in respect of Kuwait over the period 1970-1980, during which male expectation of life rose 4.64 years to 66.39 and female expectation of life 4.88 years to 71.99. The author, A.A.K. ABAZA, remarks that his analysis does not only show a substantial increase in expectation of life at birth due to reduced infant mortality, but also at the adult and older ages, indicating that the "Kuwaiti population takes good care not only of its youngsters but also of its elders". This writer does not really concur with the strength of this statement.

The methods used to derive formula (9) can also be used to prove a more general result in respect of the expected number of years of life to be lived between ages x+m and x+m+n by a life now aged x. We first note that if T_t is used to denote the expected number of years of life to be lived after age t by a life now aged 0,

$$T_t = \int_t^\infty {}_u p_o \, du, \tag{11}$$

and the weight w_t in (10) may be written

$$w_t = \frac{1}{2} \left[({}_t p_o^1 / {}_t p_o^2) T_t^2 + ({}_t p_o^2 / {}_t p_o^1) T_t^1 \right]. \tag{12}$$

The change in the expected number of years of life to be lived between ages x+m and x+m+n by a life now aged x can be expressed in terms of the mortality changes between ages x and x+m+n as follows:

$$\int_o^{m+n} (\mu_{x+t}^1 - \mu_{x+t}^2) w_t' \, dt, \tag{13}$$

where, for $0 \leq t \leq m+n$,

$$w_t' = \frac{1}{2} \left[({}_t p_o^1 / {}_t p_o^2)(T_{x+\alpha}^2 - T_{x+m+n}^2) \right.$$

$$\left. + ({}_t p_o^2 / {}_t p_o^1)(T_{x+\alpha}^1 - T_{x+m+n}^1) \right] , \tag{14}$$

with $\alpha = \max(t,m)$. \tag{15}

These formulae can also be deduced from the later formulae (33) and (35).

2. Cause of Death

According to the usual model of mortality by cause, the force of mortality at age x is the sum of the forces of mortality for the various individual causes. In other words

$$\mu_x = \sum_i \mu_x^{(i)} , \tag{16}$$

where $\mu_x^{(i)}$ is the force of mortality by cause i. Substituted in (9), formula (16) allows the partition of $\overset{o}{e}_o^2 - \overset{o}{e}_o^1$ by cause of death as well as age. We obtain

$$\overset{o}{e}_o^2 - \overset{o}{e}_o^1 = \sum_i \int_o^\infty (\mu_t^{(i)1} - \mu_t^{(i)2}) \, w_t \, dt , \tag{17}$$

where w_t is as previously defined.

The central mortality rate between ages x and x+n for cause i, $_nm_x^{(i)}$ will usually provide an accurate estimate of

$$\frac{1}{n} \int_o^n \mu_{x+t}^{(i)} \, dt$$

provided n is not too great, and for numerical purposes, the following weighted-sum formula can be used.

$$\overset{o2}{e}_o - \overset{o1}{e}_o = \underset{i}{\Sigma}[_1m_o^{(i)1} - {}_1m_o^{(i)2}]w_o$$

$$+ 4 \underset{i}{\Sigma}[_4m_1^{(i)1} - {}_4m_1^{(i)2}]w_2$$

$$+ 5 \underset{i}{\Sigma}[_5m_5^{(i)1} - {}_5m_5^{(i)2}]w_{7.5}$$

$$+ 5 \underset{i}{\Sigma}[_5m_{10}^{(i)1} - {}_5m_{10}^{(i)2}]w_{12.5}$$

$$+ \ldots \quad . \tag{18}$$

Formula (18) has been used to analyse the change in expectation of life at birth of a number of populations [13]. The results of two of these analyses are repeated here, in tables 3 and 4.

Table 3 shows that Australian males and females both enjoyed substantial improvements in life expectancy over the decade 1971-1981. These were remarkable after the previous decade of mortality stagnation. For both sexes, the major contributing cause to the improvement was ischaemic heart disease (IHD), and for males, reduced IHD mortality in the age range 50-69 alone made the single most important contribution (0.70 years) to the sizable improvement in life expectancy. Reduced mortality from all diseases of the circulatory system in fact contributed 54 % of the male and 58 % of the female increase in expectation of life at birth.

Mortality from neoplasms had a slight negative effect on the trend in male life expectancy and a small positive effect in respect of females. Disturbing in relation to the females are the negative trends in respect of mortality from both neoplasms of the respiratory systems and from bronchitis, emphysema and asthma.

Although developed in terms of a single population at two distinct points of time, the methods we have described also allow the analysis of differentials between two populations, and have been used in the third section of Table 3 to analyse the Australian sex differential in 1981.

Among modern developed populations, Hungary is unusual in that it is one of the few experiencing deteriorating mortality for most major causes of death, and, for males, a reduction in expectation of life at birth. Table 4 summarises the Hungarian experience over the decade 1970-1980.

In the case of males, improvements in mortality from infective and parasitic diseases, respiratory disease (excluding bronchitis, emphysema and asthma) and neonatal causes and congenital anomalies added 1.16 years of life. Neoplasms of the respiratory system, bronchitis, emphysema and asthma on the other hand reduced the expectation of life by 0.55 years, and diseases of the circulatory system led to a decline of 0.76 years. Increases in mortality from cirrhosis of the liver and suicide reduced the expectation of life at birth by 0.47 years.

Hungarian male mortality improved generally at ages under 30, and led to an increase in life expectancy of 1.09 years. At the older ages however, mortality deteriorated considerably, reducing life expectancy by 1.95 years.

Hungarian females enjoyed a modest increase in expectation of life at birth of 0.62 years between 1970 and 1980. We see that the following causes made important contributions to this improvement: infective and parasitic diseases, diseases of the circulatory system (excluding cerebrovascular disease), respiratory disease (excluding bronchitis, emphysema and asthma), and neonatal causes and congenital anomalies. Deteriorating mortality from cerebrovascular disease, bronchitis, emphysema and asthma and cirrhosis of the liver however considerably reduced the overall improvement.

As with the males, mortality at ages under 30 generally improved, producing an increase in life expectancy of 0.90 years. There was also an improvement in overall mortality at ages over 70. Deteriorating mortality at middle ages reduced the overall improvement in life expectancy by 0.43 years.

Analyses of trends in life expectancies of other populations and comparisons among populations may be found in [13].

3. Present Values and Annuities

The present value at rate of interest i per annum of a sum of 1 payable in t years' time is

$$(1+i)^{-t} \text{ or } e^{-t\delta} , \tag{19}$$

where the force of interest δ is given by

$$\delta = \ln(1+i) . \tag{20}$$

In the standard actuarial notation, the present value of an annuity of 1 per annum payable continuously while a life now aged exactly x remains alive is $\bar{a}_x$. This present value may be written

$$\bar{a}_x = \int_o^\infty {}_tp_x \, e^{-t\delta} \, dt . \tag{21}$$

From (1), we see that

$${}_tp_x \, e^{-t\delta} = \exp \{ -\int_o^t (\mu_{x+u} + \delta) du \} .$$

It follows that formulae for the present values of annuities and changes in these present values can be deduced from the earlier formulae simply by replacing μ_t by $(\mu_t + \delta)$, ${}_tp_x$ by ${}_tp_x$ by ${}_tp_x \, e^{-t\delta}$, and $\overset{o}{e}_x$ by $\bar{a}_x$. In particular, we note that

$$\bar{a}_o^2 - \bar{a}_o^1 = \int_o^\infty (\mu_t^1 - \mu_t^2) w_t^* \, dt , \tag{23}$$

where

$$w_t^* = \frac{1}{2} e^{-t\delta} [{}_tp_o^1 \, \bar{a}_t^2 + {}_tp_o^2 \, \bar{a}_t^1] , \tag{24}$$

and more generally, at age x,

$$\bar{a}_x^2 - \bar{a}_x^1 = \int_o^\infty (\mu_{x+t}^1 - \mu_{x+t}^2) w_{x+t}^{*\prime} \, dt , \tag{25}$$

with

$$w_{x+t}^{*\prime} = \frac{1}{2} e^{-t\delta} [{}_tp_x^1 \bar{a}_{x+t}^2 + {}_tp_x^2 \bar{a}_{x+t}^1] . \tag{26}$$

Table 5 shows the effects of mortality changes between 1971 and 1981 by age and cause on the value of an annuity to an Australian male aged 50, for interest rates of 3 % and 5 % per annum.

4.   Variable Annuities

The formulae derived in section 3 above assume a constant rate of payment throughout life. In many situations, this assumption is not realistic. Consider the average expenditure rate on hospitalisation of an
individual aged t as an example. At the younger ages, the frequency
of hospitalisation will usually be low and the average duration in
hospital low. The converse will be true at the older ages. As a result,
the average expenditure rate on hospitalisation will be a function
of age and can be expected to rise with age, at least over the adult
ages.

Let us denote the rate of payment (or rate of expenditure) at
age t by $\lambda(t)$, and the expected total undiscounted payment throughout
life for a life now aged x by $\overset{o}{\varepsilon}_x$. Then

$$\overset{o}{\varepsilon}_x \;=\; \int_o^\infty {}_tp_x \; \lambda(x+t)dt \; , \tag{27}$$

with (2) a special case when $\lambda(t) \;=\; 1$ for all t.

As we have seen above, age-specific mortality rates change over
time. Age-specific expenditure rates (e.g. on hospitalisation) may
also vary. Superscripts 1 and 2 will therefore be used again to denote
functions evaluated at times 1 and 2 respectively.

From (27), we see that the change in the total expected payment
throughout life is given by

$$\overset{o2}{\varepsilon_o} - \overset{o1}{\varepsilon_o} \;=\; \int_o^\infty [{}_tp_o^2 \; \lambda^2(t) - {}_tp_o^1 \; \lambda^1(t)] \; dt \tag{28}$$

which may be written

$$\overset{o2}{\varepsilon_o} - \overset{o1}{\varepsilon_o} \;=\; \int_o^\infty [\lambda^2(t) - \lambda^1(t)] \; {}_tp_o^1 \; dt$$

$$+ \int_o^\infty \lambda^2(t) \; {}_tp_o^2 \; [1 - \exp\{\int_o^t (\mu_u^2 - \mu_u^1)du\}]dt \; , \tag{29}$$

(the second term in the second integral cancelling the first term in
the first integral).

But, according to (27),

$$_tp_o^2 \; \overset{o2}{\varepsilon_t} \;=\; {}_tp_o^2 \int_o^\infty {}_rp_t^2 \; \lambda^2(t+r)dr \;=\; \int_t^\infty {}_up_o^2 \; \lambda^2(u)du \; , \tag{30}$$

so that $-\,{}_up_0^2\,\lambda^2(u)$ is the derivative of (30) with respect to t, and we may integrate the second integral in (29) by parts to obtain (on simplification)

$$\overset{\circ}{e}{}_0^2 - \overset{\circ}{e}{}_0^1 = \int_0^\infty [\lambda^2(t) - \lambda^1(t)]\, {}_tp_0^1\, dt$$

$$+ \int_0^\infty (\mu_t^1 - \mu_t^2)\, {}_tp_0^1\, \overset{\circ}{e}{}_t^2\, dt. \tag{31}$$

This exact formula partitions the change in total expected expenditure throughout life in terms of the changes to the age-specific payment rates and the changes in the age-specific forces of mortality.

An alternative exact formula can be obtained by interchanging the superscripts 1 and 2 in (31) and reversing the difference on both sides:

$$\overset{\circ}{e}{}_0^2 - \overset{\circ}{e}{}_0^1 = \int_0^\infty [\lambda^2(t) - \lambda^1(t)]\, {}_tp_0^2\, dt + \int_0^\infty (\mu_t^1 - \mu_t^2)\, {}_tp_0^2\, \overset{\circ}{e}{}_t^1\, dt. \tag{32}$$

Both (31) and (32) are exact formulae, but the weights differ slightly. We shall adopt the following symmetric partition formula which is the arithmetic mean of (31) and (32):

$$\overset{\circ}{e}{}_0^2 - \overset{\circ}{e}{}_0^1 = \int_0^\infty [\lambda^2(t) - \lambda^1(t)]\, w_t^\lambda\, dt + \int_0^\infty (\mu_t^1 - \mu_t^2)\, w_t^\mu\, dt, \tag{33}$$

where

$$w_t^\lambda = \tfrac{1}{2}({}_tp_0^1 + {}_tp_0^2), \tag{34}$$

and

$$w_t^\mu = \tfrac{1}{2}({}_tp_0^2\, \overset{\circ}{e}{}_t^1 + {}_tp_0^1\, \overset{\circ}{e}{}_t^2). \tag{35}$$

As in section 1, interactions between mortality changes at the various ages and rate of payment changes at the various ages are combined with the main effects. Formulae (9) and (10) are clearly special cases when $\lambda^1(t) = \lambda^2(t) = 1$ for all t. Formulae (13), (14) and (15) can also be deduced as special cases by setting $\lambda^1(t) = \lambda^2(t) = 1$ for $x+m < t < x+m+n$ and $\lambda^1(t) = \lambda^2(t) = 0$ elsewhere.

Using the same argument as that following (22), the change in the discounted values of these variable annuities payable throughout life from age 0 is

$$\bar{\alpha}_o^2 - \bar{\alpha}_o^1 = \int_o^m \lfloor \lambda^2(t) - \lambda^1(t) \rfloor w_t^{\lambda *} \, dt + \int_o^m (\mu_t^1 - \mu_t^2) w_t^{\mu *} \, dt \tag{36}$$

where

$$w_t^{\lambda *} = \frac{1}{2} e^{-t\delta} (_t p_o^1 + _t p_o^2) , \tag{37}$$

$$w_t^{\mu *} = \frac{1}{2} e^{-t\delta} (_t p_o^2 \, \bar{\alpha}_t^1 + _t p_o^1 \, \bar{\alpha}_t^2) , \tag{38}$$

and $\quad \bar{\alpha}_t = \int_o^\infty {}_r p_t \, \lambda(t+r) \, e^{-r\delta} \, dr .$ \tag{39}

5.   Variable Annuities - Applications

In this section we demonstrate a few applications of the formulae of
the preceding sections.

The net reproduction rate

The net reproduction rate of a population R_o is defined as the expected
number of daughters a newly-born female will bear during her lifetime
[9] [11]. Thus,

$$R_o = \int_o^\infty {}_t p_o \, \lambda(t) \, dt , \tag{40}$$

where $_t p_o$ is the proportion of newly-born females in the population
surviving to age t, and $\lambda(t)$ is the age-specific rate of bearing daughters. It is clear that R_o has the form of (27) with x = 0.

Development generally affects both mortality and fertility, and
it is clear from (40) above that the net reproduction rate R_o is affected by both these demographic factors. Formula (33) can be used to
determine the contribution of each factor by age to the change in the
net reproduction rate.

The net reproduction rate of Australian females in 1921 was 1.317,
which increased to 1.397 in 1971. Table 6 sets out the respective contributions of the mortality and fertility changes in the various age
groups. We see, for example, that the overall effect of fertility changes
over the half century was to reduce the net reproduction rate by 0.061,
but mortality decline meant that a greater number of females survived
to produce daughters, resulting in an increase in the net reproduction
rate of 0.140, and a net increase of 0.079. The effect of fertility

change in the various age groups on the net reproduction rate is summarised in column (3), from which the tendency for reproduction to become more concentrated in recent years between ages 15 and 30 is evident.

Values of the age specific fertility rates $\lambda^1(t)$ and $\lambda^2(t)$ were provided by the Australian Bureau of Statistics in quinquennial age ranges (3), and the two integrals in (33) were evaluated numerically in five-year sections, apart from infancy where a single year period was adopted because of the rapid change in mortality with age and the following early childhood range where a four-year interval was adopted.

Over the age range (n, n+5), the following numerical formula was adopted to evaluate the relevant section of the second integral in (33):

$$\ln({}_5p_n^1 / {}_5p_n^2) \ w_{n+2.5}^{\mu} \tag{41}$$

Similar formulae were used elsewhere in the calculations.

Formula (33) may be modified in a simple manner to take account of cause of death. We see from section 2 of the paper that all that is required is for indices (i) to be attached to the forces of mortality in the second integral and for the integral (which now depends on the cause i) to be summed over all causes i. This procedure has been adopted in Table 7, in which the contributions of changes in age-specific mortality by selected causes to the increase in net reproduction rate of Australian females between 1921 and 1971 are analysed. We see for example that almost one-third of the positive contribution to the change in net reproduction rate due to improved mortality could be attributed to a decline in mortality from infectious diseases. Deteriorating external cause mortality made a negative contribution.

For fertility analysis, use of cohort rather than period data may be preferable. The methods demonstrated remain unchanged. We have adopted the period approach purely because of the readily-available data.

Pensions

The manner in which pensions are determined and paid varies from country to country. In this example, we restrict ourselves to a particularly simple case. A flat-rate pension of 50 % of a published index of average weekly earnings is paid to all persons over 65 years of age and contributions are made by or on behalf of all members of the population aged between 25 and 65. The cost of pensions in any year is spread equally across all those currently aged 25-65.

For a stable population with intrinsic growth rate r, the number of persons in the age-range m to n (n>m) per new-born individual is [9][11]

$$\int_m^n e^{-rt} \, {}_tp_o \; dt \; . \tag{42}$$

Once again, this is an example of (27), with x=0 and $\lambda(t) = e^{-rt}$. The methods of section 4 can therefore be used to analyse the contributions of mortality change and intrinsic growth rate change on the numbers of pensioners and active persons per new-born child under stability.

Table 8 shows the numbers of persons in the various age-groups per new-born child under stability according to the fertility and mortality rates prevailing in 1961 and 1981 in a certain population. The mortality rates are in fact those of Australian males in 1961 and 1981 respectively, and the intrinsic growth rates are 0.017 for 1961 and 0.007 in 1981. The changes in the numbers in the various age-groups per new-born child are substantial. We see, for example, that if the 1961 rates were to have continued, lives beween 25 and 65 would have had to contribute approximately 7.14 % of average weekly earnings in the long term. With the reduction in both mortality and intrinsic growth rate, the long-term contribution rate (at 1981 levels of mortality and fertility) has risen to 11.37 %.

Table 9 sets out the contributions to the change in numbers of active lives and pensioners per new-born child of mortality changes in the various age groups and the change in intrinsic growth rate. The latter is the major contributor (which we would expect as the decline in intrinsic growth rate is very large), although the mortality effect is by no means insignificant (nearly 22 % of the over-65 change). The largest contributions to the mortality component of the change in the number of age pensioners result from mortality improvements between ages 55 and 75, which is in line with the figures in Table 1. For the 'active population', infant mortality improvement made the most significant contribution.

The proportion of the increase in contribution rate ascribable to mortality improvement is difficult to determine uniquely. From the figures presented in Table 9, however, it would seem that at least 29 % of the increase in contribution rate from 7.14 % of average weekly earnings to 11.37 % of average weekly earnings is due to mortality improvements.

The figures in Tables 8 and 9 were calculated on the basis of stability. There is no reason why the method should be restricted to stable populations. In the case of a population which is not in a stable condition, the exponential term in (42) is replaced by B(t), where B(t) is the ratio of the birth rate t years ago to the current birth rate.

The effects of changes in the mortality rates for the various causes of death on the numbers of active lives and age pensioners can also be readily determined. The relevant formula is obtained by adding a superscript (i) to the force of mortality i and summing for all causes i, in the manner of section 2. This approach was adopted in Table 10 to partition the mortality contributions of Table 9 into those due to ischaemic heart disease and those due to all other causes. From the policy-maker's point of view, this type of analysis allows an appreciation of the likely future cost in terms of pensions resulting from further improvement in ischaemic heart disease mortality if further resources are allocated to this end.

Hospital insurance premiums

An insurer offers private hospital insurance to cover the cost of a hospital bed. The premium for this benefit is fixed for life at the time the policy is written, apart from being indexed according to an official government index of daily hospital bed cost.

If the insurer assumes that the force of interest he will earn on his investments exceeds the force of increase in the index of bed cost by an amount δ, the annual premium for a new individual aged x, as a proportion of the daily hospital bed cost (before loadings for expenses and profits) is

$$ P = \left\{ \frac{\int_x^\infty {}_uP_o \lambda(u)\, e^{-u\delta}\, du}{\int_x^\infty {}_uP_o\, e^{-u\delta}\, du} \right\} , \tag{43} $$

where $\lambda(u)$ is the expected number of days hospitalised at age u.

The effects of changes over time in hospitalisation rates and mortality rates on the numerator integral N in (43) and the denominator integral D can be analysed exactly using the methods of section 4 above. Then, provided the changes in the denominator are relatively small (which will usually be the case, since they are caused by mortality changes alone), the change in the premium is given by

$$P \doteq \frac{1}{D} \sum_i \{\Delta(\lambda_i)N + \Delta(\mu_i)N\}$$

$$- \frac{N}{D^2} \sum_i \Delta(\mu_i)D \ , \tag{44}$$

where $\Delta(\lambda_i)N$ is the change in the numerator caused by a change in the hospitalisation rate in age group i, and $\Delta(\mu_i)N$ and $\Delta(\mu_i)D$ are the changes in the numerator and denominator respectively, caused by mortality changes in age group i.

Some hospitalisation and life table data are given in Table 11. From these data, the premium for a new policyholder aged exactly 25 is found to be equivalent to the cost of 2.930 bed days in 1971 and 2.426 bed days in 1981, a reduction equivalent to the cost of 0.504 bed days.

The contributions of the changes in the hospitalisation rates and mortality rates to this reduction were calculated independently using (44) and the formulae of section 4, and are set out in Table 12. We see from this table, for example, that beyond age 75, decreased hospitalisation had the effect of reducing the premium, but that this favourable effect was largely counteracted by decreased mortality beyond 75 which allowed lives to live longer.

6.   Concluding Remarks

Techniques recently developed, which enable concise and readily inter-pretable summaries of changes in expectation of life in terms of age-specific mortality change by cause, have been generalised in this paper to allow the analysis of variable annuities. The generalisation incorporates both change in mortality and change in the rate of payment of the annuity.

The variable annuity formulae find application in a number of areas of interest to demographers and economists concerned with the consequences of socio-economic change associated with development. Changes in the net reproduction rate, dependent population for pensions, and hospital insurance premiums were given as examples.

From the policy maker's point of view, the availability of a con-cise and readily interpretable summary of changes in key indicators as a result of changes in more basic variables is almost essential, if decisions on the allocation of resources are to be made in a rational manner. The consequences of devoting substantial sums of money to the prevention and treatment of heart disease, for example, will have a considerably different effect on the contribution rate for pensions than the same sums spent on accident prevention. The methods of this paper allow such analyses.

References

[1]   ABAZA, A.A.K. (1986) The improvement in expectation of life for the Kuwaiti population between 1970-1980. Arab Journal of Social Science (in press).

[2]   Australian Bureau of Statistics (undated) Commonwealth Demography 1921. Bulletin Number 39.

[3]   Australian Bureau of Statistics (1974) Demography, 1971. Bulletin Number 87. Reference No. 4.9.

[4]   Australian Bureau of Statistics (1980) Hospital and Nursing Home In-patients - New South Wales 1978. Australian Bureau of Statistics Catalogue No. 4306.1.

[5]   Australian Bureau of Statistics (1985) Hospital and Nursing Home In-patients - New South Wales 1983. Australian Bureau of Statistics Catalogue No. 4306.1.

[6]   Australian Government Actuary (1976) Australian Life Tables 1970-72, Australian Government Publishing Service, Canberra.

[7]   Australian Government Actuary (1981) Australian Life Tables 1980-82. Australian Government Publishing Service, Canberra.

[8]   Commonwealth Statistician and Actuary (1925) Census of the Commonwealth of Australia 1921. Part XXVII - Life Tables.

[9]   KEYFITZ, N. (1968) Introduction to the Mathematics of Population. Reading, Mass.: Addison-Wesley.

[10]   NEILL, A. (1977) Life Contingencies. Heinemann, London.

[11]   POLLARD, J.H. (1973) Mathematical Models for the Growth of Human Populations. Cambridge University Press.

[12]   POLLARD, J.H. (1982) The expectation of life and its relationship to mortality. Journal of the Institute of Actuaries, 109, 225-240.

[13]   POLLARD, J.H. (1986) Cause of death and expectation of life: some international comparisons. Seminar on Comparative Studies of Mortality and Morbidity. Siena, Italy, 7-12 July, 1986.

Table 1

Australian males and females. Improvements in expectation of life at
birth 1921 - 1971 and 1971 - 1981. The figures shown indicate (in
hundredths of a year of life) the contributions of mortality improvements in the various age groups.

Age group	Period 1921-1971		Period 1971-1981	
	Males	Females	Males	Females
0	342	288	63	60
1-4	147	141	10	10
5-14	73	73	7	6
15-29	87	147	22	17
30-49	169	204	47	50
50-69	42	149	121	102
70+	13	126	74	149
All ages	875	1,129	342	394

Sources: [12], [13].

Table 2

Kuwaiti males and females. Improvements in expectation of life at birth
1970-1980. The figures shown indicate (in hundredths of a year of life)
the contributions of mortality improvements in the various age groups.

Age Group	Males	Females
0	187	171
1-4	53	86
5-14	62	57
15-29	75	58
39-49	41	50
50-69	40	26
70+	26	15
All ages	464	488

Source: [1]

Table 3

AUSTRALIA. Expectation of life at birth. Contributions of the various causes of death to the change in expectation of life between 1971 and 1981 and to the 1981 sex differential. The figures shown are hundredths of a year of life.

Code	Cause	Males 1971/1981 Age group								Females 1971/1981 Age group								Males/Females 1981 Age group							
		0	1-4	5-14	15-29	30-49	50-69	70+	All ages	0	1-4	5-14	15-29	30-49	50-69	70+	All ages	0	1-4	5-14	15-29	30-49	50-69	70+	All ages
1	Infective, parasitic	7	3	0	0	1	0	0	12	5	2	1	0	0	0	0	9	-1	0	0	0	0	0	0	1
2	Neoplasm excl. 3,4,5	0	0	1	1	0	-2	-4	-3	0	1	1	2	2	4	-3	8	0	1	1	3	4	18	30	55
3	Neoplasms digestive	0	0	0	0	0	0	2	1	0	0	0	0	0	4	4	9	0	1	0	0	2	20	15	37
4	Neoplasm respiratory	0	0	0	0	0	0	-4	-5	0	0	0	0	0	-4	-2	-6	0	0	0	0	5	43	30	77
5	Neoplasms of breast	0	0	0	0	0	0	0	0	0	0	0	0	0	1	0	3	0	0	0	0	-11	-21	-9	-42
6	Endocrine disease	1	0	0	0	1	2	1	7	1	1	0	0	1	4	5	12	1	-1	0	0	0	3	2	4
7	Blood,mental,sense	0	1	0	-2	2	3	0	3	0	-1	0	0	4	2	-1	5	1	0	0	4	1	4	4	13
8	Circulat'y excl. 9,10	0	0	0	0	4	6	13	22	0	0	0	1	5	10	31	46	0	0	0	0	4	19	16	40
9	Ischaemic heart dis.	0	0	0	0	19	70	33	122	0	0	0	0	6	41	55	101	0	0	0	0	25	133	86	244
10	Cerebrovascular dis.	0	0	0	0	3	17	21	40	0	0	0	0	8	24	47	80	0	0	0	0	1	12	6	18
11	Respiratory disease	16	2	1	0	3	5	5	32	13	2	0	1	2	4	7	30	0	0	0	0	0	4	8	14
12	Bronch,emphys,asthma	0	0	0	0	0	7	3	11	0	0	0	0	1	-4	-3	-5	0	0	0	0	1	17	38	54
13	Digestive excl. 14	1	0	0	0	0	1	-1	2	1	0	0	0	2	1	-2	2	0	0	0	0	2	4	3	10
14	Cirrhosis of liver	0	0	0	0	0	-3	0	-5	0	0	0	0	0	-1	0	-1	0	0	0	0	5	10	1	16
15	Genito-urinary syst.	0	0	0	0	1	3	2	8	0	0	0	0	5	6	0	13	0	0	0	0	-1	-1	3	2
16	Pregnancy,childbirth	0	0	0	0	0	0	0	0	0	0	0	0	2	0	0	2	0	0	0	-1	0	0	0	-1
17	Skin,tissue disease	0	0	0	0	0	0	0	1	0	0	0	0	0	0	0	3	0	0	0	0	0	0	0	-1
18	Congenital anomalies	48	2	0	0	0	0	0	51	46	1	1	0	0	0	0	50	12	0	0	0	0	0	0	13
19	Ill-defined condit's	-13	-1	0	0	0	0	0	-10	-9	0	0	0	0	0	2	-5	5	0	0	0	0	0	0	8
20	External excl.21.22	3	2	2	3	5	3	1	22	3	2	0	2	0	2	5	15	1	3	2	14	14	6	2	42
21	Motor veh. accidents	0	1	2	14	6	4	1	29	0	1	1	3	1	3	0	10	0	0	3	36	13	4	3	60
22	Suicide,self inflict	0	0	0	0	2	1	0	3	0	0	2	0	5	2	0	11	0	0	0	12	10	5	1	29
	Total all causes	63	10	7	22	47	121	74	342	60	10	6	17	50	102	149	394	20	3	8	70	76	276	240	693

Source: [13].

Table 4

HUNGARY. Expectation of life at birth. Contributions of the various causes of death to the change in expectation of life between 1970 and 1980 and to the 1980 sex differential. The figures shown are hundredths of a year of life.

Code	Cause	Males 1970/1980								Females 1970/1980								Males/Females 1980							
		0	1-4	5-14	15-29	30-49	50-69	70+	All ages	0	1-4	5-14	15-29	30-49	50-69	70+	All ages	0	1-4	5-14	15-29	30-49	50-69	70+	All ages
1	Infective, parasitic	12	1	0	1	4	7	3	27	10	2	0	0	1	3	2	18	0	0	0	0	2	8	2	13
2	Neoplasm excl. 3,4,5	0	0	-1	-4	-8	-3	-3	-17	0	1	0	1	2	-2	-1	0	0	1	3	-2	10	14	14	29
3	Neoplasms digestive	0	0	0	-3	-3	-3	0	-4	0	0	0	-1	-1	1	3	4	0	0	1	6	6	27	11	43
4	Neoplasm respiratory	0	0	0	-7	-12	-5	0	-22	0	0	0	-1	-1	-3	0	-4	0	0	0	1	11	38	16	66
5	Neoplasms of breast	0	0	0	0	0	0	0	0	0	0	0	0	-3	-4	-1	-7	0	0	0	-12	-12	-16	-4	-32
6	Endocrine disease	0	0	0	0	-1	-3	-1	-6	-1	0	0	0	0	-4	-4	-10	0	0	0	-3	-3	-3	-4	-5
7	Blood, mental, sense	3	1	1	-1	-1	0	0	5	3	2	0	1	0	1	0	8	3	1	1	3	4	4	0	14
8	Circulat'y excl. 9,10	0	1	0	-1	-3	1	2	3	0	1	1	3	3	4	8	16	0	0	0	3	8	25	14	50
9	Ischaemic heart dis.	0	0	0	-2	-22	-26	9	-41	0	0	0	-3	-3	4	18	10	0	0	0	3	45	93	28	167
10	Cerebrovascular dis.	0	0	0	-8	-22	-8	3	-38	0	0	0	-5	-5	-9	-4	-18	0	0	0	0	8	32	13	53
11	Respiratory disease	16	3	0	0	-1	2	3	22	14	3	0	0	0	1	4	16	5	-1	0	4	4	6	2	19
12	Bronch, emphys, asthma	0	0	0	-3	-3	-14	-16	-33	0	0	0	0	-2	-5	-10	-16	0	0	0	4	6	21	21	45
13	Digestive excl. 14	0	1	-1	-1	-2	-2	-1	-6	0	0	0	0	0	0	0	-6	1	0	0	6	6	7	2	17
14	Cirrhosis of liver	0	0	0	-1	-11	-12	-1	-27	0	0	0	-6	-6	-4	0	-11	0	0	2	9	9	18	3	32
15	Genito-urinary syst.	0	0	0	0	0	0	2	4	0	0	1	0	7	1	0	8	0	0	0	0	1	1	5	7
16	Pregnancy, childbirth	0	0	0	0	0	0	0	0	0	0	0	1	2	0	0	2	0	0	0	-2	0	0	0	-2
17	Skin, tissue disease	1	0	0	0	0	0	0	2	0	0	0	0	0	0	0	2	0	0	0	0	-1	0	0	-1
18	Congenital anomalies	67	1	0	-1	0	0	0	67	53	0	-1	0	0	0	0	51	31	0	1	0	0	0	0	32
19	Ill-defined condit's	-1	0	0	0	0	0	0	0	-1	0	0	0	0	2	0	1	0	0	0	0	0	0	0	0
20	External excl. 21,22	-2	3	1	-5	-6	-6	-1	-6	-2	3	1	-2	1	0	0	-3	0	2	4	15	23	16	2	61
21	Motor veh. accidents	0	0	1	1	1	1	0	4	0	0	1	0	1	0	0	0	0	0	2	15	11	6	1	38
22	Suicide, self inflict	0	0	-1	-3	-11	-3	-2	-20	0	0	0	-6	-6	-2	0	-9	0	0	1	19	34	15	3	75
	Total all causes	94	12	2	-1	-75	-100	-19	-87	76	12	3	-1	-16	-27	15	63	38	5	9	62	163	309	136	721

Source: [13].

Table 5

Australian males aged 50. Contributions of changes in mortality at the various ages, by cause, to the change in annuity values* between 1971 and 1981 at 3 % per annum and 5 % per annum. The figures shown are hundredths of a unit.

	3% per annum interest					5% per annum interest				
	50-59	60-69	70-79	80+	Total	50-59	60-69	70-79	80+	Total
Neoplasms	-2	1	-3	-5	-5	-2	0	-1	0	-3
Ischaemic heart disease	22	22	10	4	58	16	15	6	1	38
Cerebrovascular disease	4	6	6	3	19	2	4	4	2	12
Other circulatory system	1	3	3	3	10	1	2	2	1	6
Bronchitis, emphysema, asthma	2	3	1	0	6	1	2	1	0	4
Other respiratory disease	1	2	2	1	6	1	2	0	0	3
Cirrhosis of liver	-2	-1	0	0	-3	-1	-1	0	0	-2
External causes	5	2	0	0	7	4	1	0	0	5
All other causes	4	4	3	0	11	3	3	1	0	7
Total	35	42	22	10	109	25	28	13	4	70

* Annuity values were as follows: 15.81 (1971, 3%)
12.88 (1971, 5%)
16.91 (1981, 3%)
13.60 (1981, 5%)

Table 6

Australian females. Contributions of age-specific mortality and fertility changes to the change in net reproduction rate (NRR) between 1921 and 1971.

| Age group | Contribution to change in NRR of | | Total |
	age-specific mortality rate	age-specific fertility rate	
0	.057	.000	.057
1-4	.029	.000	.029
5-14	.017	-.009	.008
15-19	.008	.062	.070
20-24	.012	.086	.098
25-29	.010	.065	.075
30-39	.007	-.194	-.187
40-49	.000	-.071	-.071
Total	.140	-.061	.079

Table 7

Australian females. Contribution of changes in age specific mortality
by selected causes to the increase in the net reproduction rate (NRR)
between 1921 and 1971*.

Age group	Contribution to increase in NRR of change in age-specific mortality due to				Total
	infectious diseases	complications of pregnancy	external causes	all other causes	
0	0.0036	0.0000	-0.0001	0.0536	0.0571
1-4	0.0076	0.0000	0.0016	0.0197	0.0289
5-14	0.0048	0.0000	0.0010	0.0109	0.0167
15-19	0.0042	0.0004	-0.0014	0.0049	0.0081
20-24	0.0056	0.0025	-0.0011	0.0049	0.0119
25-29	0.0037	0.0021	-0.0003	0.0041	0.0096
30-39	0.0024	0.0016	-0.0003	0.0038	0.0075
40-49	0.0001	0.0000	0.0000	0.0002	0.0003
Total	0.0320	0.0066	-0.0006	0.1021	0.1401

* Note that the International Classification of Diseases changed
several times over this period and to this extent the results
shown in this table must be treated with some caution.

Table 8

Stable numbers of active lives and age pensioners per new-born child, 1961 and 1981 intrinsic growth rates and mortalities.

Age range	Active lives			Pensioners	
	1961 rates	1981 rates		1961 rates	1981 rates
25-34	5.6883	7.7983		–	–
35-44	4.7044	7.1662		–	–
45-54	3.7815	6.4406		–	–
55-64	2.7931	5.4163		–	–
65-69	–	–		0.9779	2.1554
70-74	–	–		0.6946	1.6875
75-79	–	–		0.4307	1.1691
80-84	–	–		0.2178	0.6765
85-89	–	–		0.0797	0.3004
90-94	–	–		0.0186	0.0912
95+	–	–		0.0025	0.0172
	16.9673	26.8214		2.4218	6.0973

Table 9

Changes in stable numbers of active lives and age pensioners per new-born child: effect of mortality changes in the various age groups and the change in intrinsic growth rate.

Age group	Contribution of mortality change in age-group to change in	
	number of active lives	number of age pensioners
0	0.2430	0.0473
1-4	0.0413	0.0080
5-14	0.0386	0.0075
15-24	0.0050	0.0010
25-34	0.0476	0.0109
35-44	0.0999	0.0348
45-54	0.1156	0.0736
55-64	0.1030	0.2123
65-74	-	0.2487
75-84	-	0.1157
85+	-	0.0311
Total mortality change effect	0.6940	0.7909
Growth rate change effect	9.1601	2.8846
Level at 1961 rates	16.9673	2.4218
Level at 1981 rates	26.8214	6.0973

Table 10

Changes in stable numbers of active lives and age pensioners per
new-born child: effect of changes in mortality from ischaemic heart
disease (IHD) and other causes in the various age-groups.

| Age group | Contribution of mortality change in age-group to change in | | | |
| | number of active lives | | number of age pensioners | |
	IHD	Other causes	IHD	Other causes
0	0.0000	0.2430	0.0000	0.0473
1-4	0.0000	0.0413	0.0000	0.0080
5-14	0.0000	0.0386	0.0000	0.0075
15-24	0.0000	0.0050	0.0000	0.0010
25-34	0.0033	0.0443	0.0008	0.0101
35-44	0.0354	0.0645	0.0123	0.0225
45-54	0.0698	0.0458	0.0444	0.0292
55-64	0.0636	0.0394	0.1311	0.0812
65-74	-	-	0.1227	0.1260
75-84	-	-	0.0543	0.0614
85+	-	-	0.0130	0.0181
Total	0.1721	0.5219	0.3786	0.4123

Table 11

Hospitalisation rates (bed days per annum) and life table data for a certain population in 1971 and 1981

Age group	Hospitalisation rate		Integral[a] of μ_t over age group		Mid-age t	Survival probability ${}_tp_o$	
	1971	1981	1971	1981		1971	1981
0	4.5	5.1	.01968	.01154	0	1.00000	1.00000
1-4	0.8	0.9	.00332	.00268	2	.97904	.98761
5-14	0.9	0.7	.00444	.00328	10	.97437	.98425
15-24	1.5	1.0	.01716	.01426	20	.96473	.97661
25-34	1.5	1.1	.01463	.01327	30	.94916	.96207
35-44	2.0	1.2	.02871	.02165	40	.93150	.94818
45-54	2.7	2.4	.08109	.06265	50	.88798	.91396
55-64	3.9	3.2	.22099	.16632	60	.77574	.82433
65-74	6.7	5.4	.54948	.42988	70	.54616	.63063
75+	12.8	11.2	.27166	1.04437	80	.23399	.32025

[a]Note $\int_x^{x+n} \mu_t \, dt = -\ln {}_np_x$.

Table 12

Effect of changed hospitalisation rates and changed mortality rates
on the premium for hospital bed insurance in respect of a 25 year old.

Age group	Change in premium level due to			
	changed hospitali- sation rate	changed mortality affecting claims	changed mortality affecting pre- mium payments	Total
25-34	-0.124	0.003	-0.003	-0.124
35-44	-0.201	0.015	-0.012	-0.198
45-54	-0.059	0.031	-0.019	-0.047
55-64	-0.101	0.064	-0.031	-0.068
65-74	-0.113	0.081	-0.025	-0.057
75+	-0.054	0.047	-0.008	-0.015
Total	-0.651	0.242	-0.098	-0.507

I,2
Policy Issues

MARKET FAILURE, POPULATION GROWTH AND
GOVERNMENT INTERVENTION IN A LIFE-CYCLE GROWTH MODEL

Norbert Berthold
University of Hamburg

Michael Pflüger
Cambridge University

ABSTRACT: This paper firstly gives a detailed, modified analytical and graphical description of the allocation process in the one-good Diamond life-cycle growth model. The independence of the optimal growth path and the optimal division of output - making up the Two-Part-Golden rule - is stressed.
   Market failure resulting from the additional Modigliani-Diamond capital market conditions is discussed.
   Using an endogenous population growth rate, a more comprehensive "modified" Two-Part Golden rule (encompassing Phelps', Davis' and Diamonds Golden rule respectively) is derived.

I.   Introduction

In 1965, P. A. DIAMOND suggested a growth model incorporating the neo-classical one-sector Solow-growth model and the overlapping generations model due to SAMUELSON (DIAMOND, 1965, 1126-1150; SAMUELSON, 1958, 477-482; SOLOW, 1956, 65-94). Several writers have commented on this paper and have made the neoclassical growth model a useful tool for the analysis of problems in public finance as well as in social security and optimal population (SAMUELSON, 1965; 1967; 1968; 1975a; 1975b; 1976; ASIMAKOPULOS, 1967; BIERWAG/GROVE/KANG, 1969; STEIN, 1969; DIAMOND, 1970; IHORI, 1978; ATKINSON/STIGLITZ, 1980).

   The present paper gives a detailed and modified description of the analytical and graphical exposure of the allocation process in the DIAMOND model first set down by IHORI (IHORI, 1978, 389-396). The independence of the optimal growth path (i. e. the Golden Rule) and the optimal division of output (i. e. the Biological Interest Rate), making up the Two-Part-Golden rule is especially stressed. Market failure resulting from the additional Modigliani-Diamond-capital market condition is also discussed.

   Exogenous population growth is an unsatisfying factor in the neo-classical life-cycle growth model. Following DAVIS' (DAVIS, 1969, 177-181) analysis, the authors derive a more comprehensive "modified" Two-Part-Golden Rule. The paper then concludes by (1) comparing the results with those formerly derived, (2) outlining the role of population growth, (3) criticizing the inherant feature of market failure in the Diamond-

Studies in Contemporary Economics
A. Wenig, K. F. Zimmermann (Eds.)
Demographic Change and Economic Development
© Springer-Verlag Berlin Heidelberg 1989

model and (4) by giving a surprising interpretation of optimal social security as forwarded by SAMUELSON (SAMUELSON, 1975).

II. The Life-Cycle Framework

1. The Centrally Planned Economy

The neoclassical life-cycle economy, as introduced by P. A. DIAMOND, con- sists of a goods market and the factor markets for capital and labor (DIAMOND, 1965; IHORI, 1978), and by assumption, has an infinitive future.

The supply of goods can be represented by a "well behaved" linear-homogeneous production function,

$$(1) \quad Y_t \ = \ F(K_t, \ L_t) = L_t \cdot F(K_t/L_t, \ 1) = L_t \cdot f(k_t)$$

$$dF/dK \ > \ 0; \quad dF/dL \ > \ 0$$
$$d^2F/dK^2 \ < \ 0; \quad d^2F/dL^2 \ < \ 0$$

where Y_t is output, K_t denotes durable capital, L_t is labor (which is assumed to be identical to population; a labor participation rate of 100 % is thus assumed) and k_t represents the capital-labor ratio. Technology is unchanging and no depreciation takes place.

Real output can either be consumed or invested. Consumption can be divided, according to SAMUELSON, into that consumed by the young gen-eration, and that by the old,

$$(2) \quad Y_t \ = \ C_t + I_t$$

$$= \ c_t^1 \cdot L_t + c_t^2 \cdot L_{t-1} + K_{t+1} - K_t,$$

where C_t expresses life-cycle consumption (c_t^1 and c_t^2 being per capita consumption in t of the young and the old, respectively).

The supply of labor is assumed to grow exogenously at constant rate n,

$$(3) \quad L_t \ = \ (1+n)^t.$$

Equilibrium in the labor market is obtained at the point in which the wage rate (w_t) equals the marginal product of labor (dY/dL), i. e.,

$$(4) \quad w_t \;=\; dY/dL = f(k_t) - f'(k_t) \cdot k_t$$

Capital supply amounts to

$$(5a) \quad S_t \;=\; L_t \cdot s_t = K_{t+1},$$

where (S_t) stands for total savings and per capita savings (s_t) are derived from

$$(5b) \quad s_t \;=\; w_t - c_t^1,$$

while the wage rate constrains the individual's life cycle consumption,

$$(5c) \quad w_t \;=\; c_t^1 + c_{t+1}^2/(1+r_{t+1})$$

Equations (5a), (5b), (5c) of course give us the supply of savings in a centrally planned economy, whereas the supply of savings in a competitive economy is derived by individuals' maximizing behaviour, as will be shown below. Equilibrium in the capital market is again neoclassically determined by equating the interest rate with the marginal product of capital, such that,

$$(6) \quad r_t \;=\; dY/dK = f'(k_t).$$

Equations (1) to (6) are not mutually independent, so that equilibrium in two markets imply that the third is also.

Assuming that the economy is at a steady state, or analogously, that the central authorities decide to preserve a constant capital-labor-ratio,

$$(7a) \quad ..k_{t-1} = k_t = k_{t+1} = ... = k,$$

capital stock will grow at the same rate as labor,

$$(7b) \quad (L_{t+1} - L_t)/L_t = n = (K_{t+1} - K_t)/K_t.$$

Using this assumption, we can derive from equations (1), (2) and (3)

a relation between a centrally planned economy's first and second period
steady state consumption levels, which we will denote as a "consumption
possibility curve" in a centrally planned economy,

$$(8) \quad c^1 = f(k) - nk - c^2/(1+n)$$

According to SAMUELSON (SAMUELSON, 1958), all persons are assumed to
have identical preferences, so that utility of society can be expressed
by a Million representative man's quasi-concave utility function,

$$(9) \quad u = u(c^1, c^2).$$

This utility function can be transformed into steady state utility
of society by replacing c^1 in (9) through the consumption constraint
(8), so that:

$$(10) \quad u = u(c^1, c^2) = u(f(k) - nk - c^2/(1+n), c^2).$$

2. The Two-Part Golden Rule

The problem of selecting the optimal golden age path, i. e. the golden
age path on which each individual's utility is maximized subject to
the constraint given by the consumption possibility curve, thus becomes
(SAMUELSON, 1975a, 534),

$$(11a) \quad \underset{k,c^2}{\text{Max}} \quad u(f(k) - nk - c^2/(1+n), c^2).$$

This formulation treats the allocation of consumption in a single year
between the young and the old in a similar fashion to the allocation
of consumption over the lifetime of an individual. DIAMOND reminds
us that this maximization process decomposes into the separate problems
of selecting the optimal capital-labor ratio and the utility maximizing
consumption allocation (DIAMOND, 1965). First order conditions[1] are
obtained by differentiating (11a) with respect to (k) and (c^2),

___

[1] Second order conditions for a maximum require that
$-(u_{22}+(1/(1+n)^2) \cdot u_{11}) > 0$ and that $(u_{11} \cdot f'')/(1+n)-u_{22}(u_{11} \cdot (f'+n)^2$
$- f'')) < 0$.

(11b) $du/dk = u_1(f'(k) - n) = 0$

(11c) $du/dc^2 = -u_1(1/(1+n)) + u_2 = 0$

Rearranging terms gives the Two Part Golden Rule (SAMUELSON, 1968),

(12a) $f'(k) = n$

(12b) $u_1/u_2 = (1+n)$

Equation (12a) is the wellknown PHELPS production Golden Rule requiring the marginal product of capital (i. e. the interest rate) to equal population growth. The identification of the optimal k therefore gives the maximum steady state consumption, $f(k) - n \cdot k$.

The optimal intergenerational consumption allocation is specified by (12b) and is known as the SAMUELSON Biological Interest Rate (SAMUELSON, 1958). Steady state consumption will be socially optimally distributed among all individuals and all generations, when the ratio of marginal utilities in period one and two equals the growth factor. The central planning agency will strive to fulfill this technological double condition in order to obtain the optimal vector (c_g^1, c_g^2, k_g), and thus $r = n$. [2]

Substituting the optimal capital-labor ratio (kg) into (8) and rearranging terms, a graphical exposition of this technocratic welfare optimum can be obtained:

(13) $c^2 = -(1+n)c^1 + (1+n)(f(kg) - nk_g)$.

This linear relationship, denoted "feasibility line", is shown in Figure 1.

Note that the slope of the feasibility line is independent of (k_g), while the maximum levels of consumption in period one and two are dependent on the optimal k-level.

---

[2] Questions of stability and initial conditions are excluded from this analysis.

78

An explanation of the Two Part Golden Rule, as suggested by the authors, would be the following: The feasibility line represents maximum consumption possibilities in a centrally planned economy. Any further increase of (k) would lead to dynamical inefficiency; a situation in which $(k < k_g)$ (a parallel to the left of the feasibility line) would be suboptimal, as an increase in (k) would result in higher consumption levels in both periods. The relevant part of the feasibility line is point G, as only G fulfills the additional condition as required by the Biological Interest Rate, such that $G = G(c_g^1, c_g^2, k_g)$.

Figure 1: The feasibility line and the two part golden rule (G).

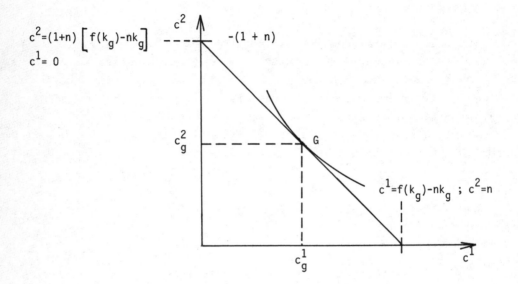

III. The Competitive Economy

The Two Part Golden Rule, amounting to the technocratic determination of (k), (c^1) and (c^2), was derived in II. In a competitive economy one must pay attention to, not only the constraint given by the goods markets equilibrium, i. e. the identity of production and aggregate demand, but also the factor markets. The capital market gives the individuals freedom to supply savings; thus the capital market will be a decentralized arrangement where the individuals supply as much savings as is derived from utility maximization of their preferences subject to their budget constraints (DIAMOND, 1965, 1130 ff.).

In order to give a graphical exposition of the competitive solution, we will first ask what consumption alternatives a competitive economy in steady state has. The six equations (3), (4), (5a), (5b), (5c) and (6), i. e. capital and labor market conditions, contain all the constraints of the market process in the neoclassical life cycle growth model. Again using the steady state assumption (7a) we can transform these into a pair of equations expressing the golden age/consumption levels,

(14a) $c^1 = f(k) - (f'(k) + 1 + n) \cdot k$

(14b) $c^2 = (1 + n)(1 + f'(k)) \cdot k.$

Note that these equations contain the restrictions for steady state consumption levels, being solely dependent on (k). Each value of the capital-labor ratio will thus be associated with a pair of golden age/consumption levels.

Assuming that (c^1) reaches a single maximum in the range where (c^2) is increasing with respect to (k) and that equation (14b) has at best a single maximum (IHORI, 1978, 390; also ATKINSON/STIGLITZ, 1980, 243), we can construct the consumption possibility curve in the market process.

The movement from the origin in the (c^2-c^1)-diagram to the right and then again to the left along the market consumption possibilities is associated with an increasing level of the capital-labor ratio. The maximizing behavior of an individual in a competitive economy will result in the selection of an equilibrium value of (k) on this curve.

As already noted, the capital market is a further restriction to be considered in a competitive economy. The supply of savings will be governed by decentralized decisions; not by authoritarian regulation. Individuals will maximize their life-time utility subject to their budget equation in order to determine the amount of savings they are willing to supply to the capital market,

(15a) Max $u(c_t^1, c_{t+1}^2)$

s.t. $c_t^1 + c_{t+1}^2/(1+r_{t+1}) = w_t,$

which is solved by,

(15b) $s_t = s(w_t, r_{t+1})$.

(Equations (15a) and (15b) replace (5b) and (5c) of the central planning framework).

Figure 2: Consumption possibilities in the market process[3]

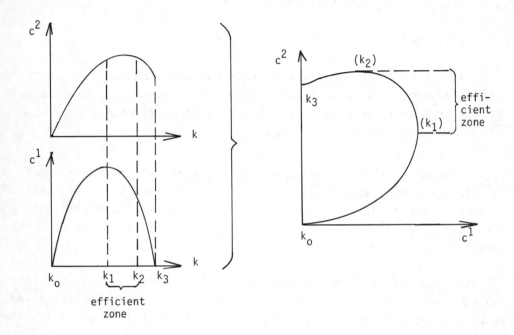

The market process leads to the vector (c_m^1, c_m^2, k_m) as is shown graphically in figure 3:

[3] Only the interval between (k_1) and (k_2) will be efficient (IHORI, 1978, 390).

Figure 3: Market allocation (CE)

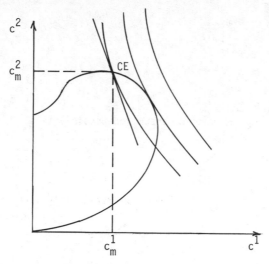

Individual maximizing behavior leads to a unique selection of one point along the market consumption possibility curve.

Using (15b), equilibrium in the capital market can be reformulated as

$$(15c) \quad s \;=\; c^2/(1+r) = (1+n) \cdot k$$

in steady state. This condition will be denoted as the "MODIGLIANI-DIAMOND"-condition or the life cycle savings-investment-condition (SAMUELSON, 1975a, 535.

IV. Market Failure

Using the results of the discussion above, we can carry through with a comparison of the allocation process in a centrally planned economy, to that of a competitive one.

Let us first note, that the consumption possibilites in the market process are except for one point (i. e. the Golden Rule) more restricted than those of a centrally planned economy. This can be graphically demonstrated by the tangency of the feasibility line with the market consumption possibilities (IHORI, 1978, 390 ff.).

Figure 4: The feasibility line and market consumption possibilities

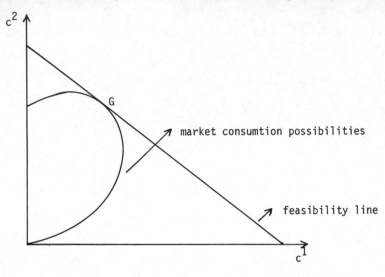

Analytically this result is obtained by comparing the slope of the consumption possibility curve in the market process,

(16) $(dc^2/dc^1)_m = -(1+n)(1+f'+kf'')/(1+n+kf'')$,

with the slope of the feasibility line,

(17) $(dc^2/dc^1) = -(1+n)$

Only when $f'(k) = n$, i. e. where the Golden Rule condition is satisfied, will these slopes be equal.

A comparison of the allocation solutions as shown below will in general produce the result that the market allocation will not coincide with the Two Part Golden Rule (DIAMOND, 1965; STEIN, 1969; SAMUELSON, 1975a; 1975b; IHORI, 1978; ATKINSON/STIGLITZ, 1980).

This non-coincidence, as proved by DIAMOND for an economy with COBB-DOUGLAS preferences and technology (DIAMOND, 1965, 1134-1135), points out that the decentralized arrangement of the market will not lead to the socially optimal allocation. In other words, the selfish behavior of individuals will, in general, result in an allocation in which everybody is worse off than in a centrally planned economy. Only when the Two Part Golden Rule is satisfied and this allocation is sus-

tained by the additional capital market MODIGLIANI-DIAMOND condition,
will market equilibrium will be optimal.

Figure 5: Market failure

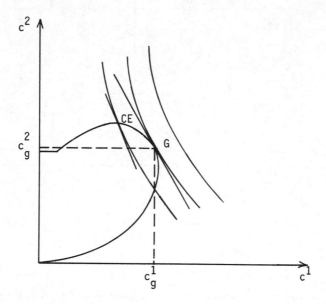

The literature already published concerning the problem of this
market failure has either tried to cure such failure through the introduction of government intervention and through the determination of
an optimal population growth rate, or has accepted the fact, that the
market allocation will always be inferior to the Two Part Golden Rule
and has therefore suggested second best solutions or analyses of incidence of government policy instruments.

84

Figure 6: Market failure and government intervention

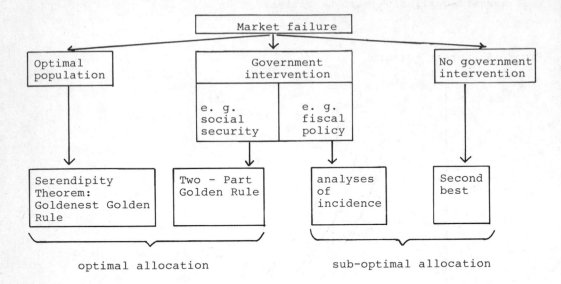

V. Population Growth

The assumption of exogenous population growth is unsatisfying in long
run growth models, as are the models proposed by SOLOW (SOLOW, 1956)
and the one in question. The invariable growth rate also plays an important role in the neoclassical life cycle growth model:

(1) In a life cycle economy caracterized by COBB-DOUGLAS technology
     and preferences, the competitive economy would only realize the
     optimal Two Part Golden rule state, if the exogenous population
     growth rate amounted to a certain value as determined by the para-
     meters of the preference and production functions. This is the
     DIAMOND result (DIAMOND, 1965).

(2) SAMUELSON's analysis of optimal population and optimal social
     security argues that at a very high (low) population growth rate,
     given an interest rate (r = n), life cycle savings might not suffice
     (might be excessive) to supply exactly the amount of saving, that
     would be needed to maintain the optimal capital-labor ratio
     (SAMUELSON, 1975a, 535-536; see also DEARDORFF, 1976). SAMUELSON
     also advanced his serendipity theorem demonstrating that at a
     certain "goldenest golden rule" level of population, growth savings
     would just match the needed capital growth in order to maintain
     (k_g) and thus the state of social optimality.

(3) Classical and neoclassical theory, as well newer approaches on
     the theory of fertility, make population growth dependent on econ-
     omic factors, e. g. the level of per capita income, per capita
     output or the wage rate.

     In this chapter we will follow E. DAVIS' analysis and assume that
population growth is dependent on per capita income (DAVIS, 1969).
We will then ask how the results, as obtained above, i. e. the allocation
of durable capital in a centrally planned and a competitive economy,
change.

     Refering to the demographic work by J. BUTTRICK, DAVIS interprets
population growth as being the result of birth and death rates[4]; while
death rates vary inversely with per capita income, the economic effect
on birth rates is such that the relationship between population growth
and per capita income is positive and monotonic overall. Figure 7 illustrates this theory.

Figure 7: Population growth

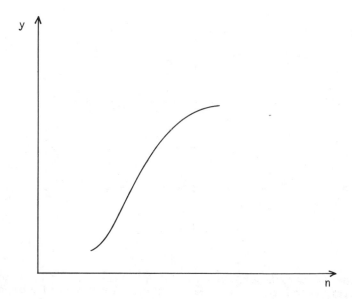

---

[4] Migration is excluded from the argument, but this would only strength-
    en the results (DAVIS, 1969, 178).

Analytically, this can be stated as

(18a) $n = n(y)$; $dn/dy > 0$

Applying the relationship as given by the neoclassical production function, (18a) changes to[5] (18b)

(18b) $n = n(f(k))$,

and thus the supply of labor (still assuming a labor participation rate of 100 %[6] to

(3') $L_t = (1+n(y))^t = (1+n(f(k))^t$.

---

[5] The dependence of n on the capital-labor ratio can be illustrated graphically by using the production function and the functional relation n(y):

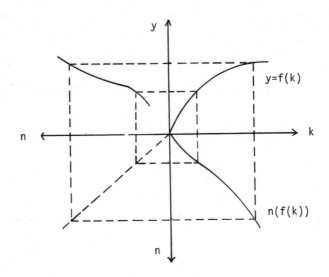

[6] L. SAMUELSON (L. SAMUELSON, 1980, 752 ff.) suggests an endogenous labor participation rate; such a rate could also be incorporated in the DIAMOND-model.

VI. A Modified Two Part Golden Rule

The modified model consists of the eight equations (1), (2), (3'), (4), (5a), (5b), (5c) and (6). Following through with the same analysis as in II and III, and assuming that the economy is on a steady state, a modified consumption possibility curve in a centrally planned economy can be identified:

$$(8') \quad c^1 = f(k) - n(f(k)) \cdot k - c^2/(1+n(f(k))).$$

The maximization problem for the representative individual thus becomes

$$(11a') \quad \underset{k,c^2}{\text{Max}} \; u(f(k) - n(f(k)) - c^2/(1+n(f(k))), \; c^2).$$

The Modified Two Part Golden Rule giving the optimal allocation and distribution in a centrally planned economy, is obtained by setting the total differentials of (u) with respect to (k) and (c^2) equal to zero[1].

---

[1] Second order conditions for a maximum require

$$\begin{vmatrix} u_{11} & 0 & 1 \\ 0 & u_{22} & 1/1+n \\ 1 & 1/1+n & 0 \end{vmatrix} > 0 \text{ resp. } -(u_{22} + 1/(1+n)^2 u_{11}) > 0 \quad \text{and}$$

$$\begin{vmatrix} u_{11} & 0 & 0 & 1 \\ 0 & u_{22} & -\lambda n'f'/(1+n)^2 & 1/1+n \\ 0 & -\lambda n'f'/(1+n)^2 & L_{33} & \lambda\{\frac{-f'+n+(k-c^2)n'f'}{(1+n)^2}\} \\ 1 & 1/1+n & \lambda\{\frac{-f'+n+(k-c^2)n'f'}{(1+n)^2}\} & 0 \end{vmatrix} < 0$$

where

$$L_{33} = \lambda[c^2(\frac{-2}{(1+n)^4}(n'f')^2 - \frac{n''f'+f''n'}{(1+n)^2}) - f''+n'f'+[n''f'+nf'']k]$$

(11b') $du/dk = \delta u/\delta c^1 \cdot dc^1/dk + \delta u/\delta c^2 \cdot dc^2/dk = 0$

(11c') $du/dc^2 = \delta u/\delta c^1 \cdot dc^1/dc^2 + \delta u/\delta c^2 = 0$

Rearranging terms gives

(12a') $n = f'(1-kn' - c^2 \cdot n'/(1+n)^2)$

(12b') $u_1/u_2 = 1+n.$

In order to get a socially optimal allocation, the central planning agency would use equations (8'), (12a') and (12b'), and thus obtain (c_g^1, c_g^2, k_g).[7]

The capital market in a competitive economy is dependent on individuals maximizing saving behavior. The modified MODIGLIANI-DIAMOND condition, which is derived from (5a), (6) and (3'),

(15c') $c^2/(1+f'(k)) = k(1+n(f(k)))$ where $f = f'(k)$,

is the additional constraint that has to be satisfied. The competitive solution is socially optimal only when it produces (c_g^1, c_g^2, k_g) consistent with (15c'). Otherwise the decentralized solution will result in suboptimal (c_m^1, c_m^2, k_m).

---

[7] Existence of the modified two part golden rule is assumed. Specification of the relevant function will need two non-linear equation systems, which can only be solved numerically. Thanks go to an anonymous referee for pointing out to us, that further restrictions on the population function might be necessary in order to allow for its existence.

VII. Interpretation and Comparison

A Modified Two Part Golden Rule was deduced, using the assumption of an endogenous population growth rate. This comprehensive formulation of the optimality condition in the life cycle growth model again describes distributional, as well as, allocational optimality. Equation (12b') gives the Biological Interest Rate with a slight modification of the DIAMOND case. The ratio of marginal utilities in period one and two must now allow for population growth and will thus be associated with optimal (k). The PHELPS production Golden Rule now requires a population growth rate less than the marginal product of capital (and therefore less than the interest rate). An economy on the optimal growth path will grow with an even smaller rate than DAVIS' economy (DAVIS, 1969, 179 ff.). Economies with relatively low population growth rate compared to the return on capital might thus be on the optimal balanced growth path, contrarily to the original SAMUELSON and PHELPS results (SAMUELSON, 1958; PHELPS, 1961).

The Modified Two Part Golden Rule of course allows for the DIAMOND case, where n = const. and thus n' = 0 and for the DAVIS formulation of the golden rule, when ordinary (not life cycle) consumption is considered. Figure 8 summarizes these conclusions.

Although endogenous population growth rate is important for the resulting optimality in a life cycle economy, it will not affect the conclusion that a competitive economy will in general produce a suboptimal allocation, or, as J. L. STEIN puts it, that in the neoclassical life cycle economy, there will be no "invisible hand" (STEIN, 1969, 139 ff.). Only by chance will the optimal solution be sustained by the decentralized capital market.

Figure 8: Golden rules in comparison

	Exogenous population growth (n)	Endogenous population growth (n=n(y))
Neoclassical-Solow-growth-model	Phelps Golden Rule	Davis' Golden Rule
$c = f(k) - n*k$	$f' = n$	$f'(1-kn') = n$
Diamond-neoclassical life-cycle growth model	Diamond Two Part Golden Rule	Modified Two Part Golden Rule
	$f' = n$	$f'(1-kn' - c^2n') = n$
$c^1 + c^2(1+n)$		
$= f(k)-n*k$	$u^1/u^2 = 1+n$	$u_1/u_2 = 1+n$

A surprising result of our analysis was gained by chance. Having identified the problem of market failure in the neoclassical life cycle growth
model with the analytical fact that the decentralized solution is over-
determined if optimality is required, i. e. the four equations (8),
(12a), (12b) and (15c) in the conventional model and (8'), (12a'),
(12b') and (15c') in the modified model are to determine the values
of (c^1, c^2, k), it can now be seen, why SAMUELSON's optimal social
security lifts the competitive economy on the Two Part Golden Rule
level (SAMUELSON, 1975b, 539 ff.). By introducing two policy parameters,
per capita taxes and a social capital stock, into the model and thus
into the MODIGLIANI-DIAMOND condition, there remain four equations
to determine five variables. Therefore it is no surprise, that an infinite number of combinations of the two policy parameters will fulfill
this task.

VIII.   Conclusions

The present paper sheds light on the allocation process in the neoclassical life cycle model. Though a more comprehensive formulation of
the Two Part Golden Rule, containing the SAMUELSON, PHELPS, and DAVIS

golden rule was given, some questions still remain.

No definitive answer could be given to the problem of market failure in a model that is free from the usual sources of inefficiency encountered in price theory, that explicitly assumes perfect competition, perfect foresight and no external economies or diseconomies. The "over-determination hypothesis" makes this problem formally plausible, but does not state any economic reason for this problem willingly or unwillingly incorporated in this model. Further research should be invested in this problem.

The presented model still requires further specification changes. We suggest to direct further study in a COBB-DOUGLAS economy where the population function is specified. Some remaining questions can only be solved by examplary analysis.

References

ASIMAKOPULOS, A. (1967), The Biological Interest Rate and the Social
    Utility Functions, in: American Economic Review, Vol. 57 (1967),
    pp. 185-189

ATKINSON, A. B. and STIGLITZ, J. E. (1980), Lectures on Public Economics.
    London a. o. 1980

BIERWAG, G. O., GROVE, M. A. and KHANG, Ch. (1969), National Debt in a
    Neoclassical Growth Model: Comment, in: American Economic Review,
    Vol. 59 (1969), pp. 205-210

DAVIS, E. (1969), A Modified Golden Rule: The Case with Endogenous
    Labor Supply, in: American Economic Review, Vol. 59 (1969),
    pp. 177-181

DEARDORFF, A. V. (1976), The Optimum Growth Rate for Population: Comment,
    in: International Economic Review, Vol. 17 (1976), pp. 510-515

DIAMOND, P. A. (1965), National Debt in a Neoclassical Growth Model,
    in: American Economic Review, Vol. 55 (1965), pp. 1126-1150

DIAMOND, P. A. (1970), Incidence of an Interest Income Tax, in: Journal
    of Economic Theory, Vol. 2 (1970), pp. 211-214

IHORI, T. (1978), The Golden Rule and the Role of Government in a Life
    Cycle Growth Model, in: American Economic Review, Vol. 68 (1978),
    pp. 389-396

PHELPS, E. S. (1961), The Golden Rule of Accumulation: A Fable for
    Growthmen, in: American Economic Review, Vol. 51 (1961),
    pp. 638-643

SAMUELSON, L. (1980), The Golden Rule with Endogenous Labor Participa-
    tion Rate, in: American Economic Review, Vol. 70 (1980),
    pp. 752-755

SAMUELSON, P. A. (1958), An Exact Consumption-Loan Model of Interest
    with or without the Social Contrivance of Money, in: Journal of
    Political Economy, Vol. 66 (1958), pp. 467-482

SAMUELSON, P. A. (1965), A Catenary Turnpike Theorem Involving Consump-
    tion and the Golden Rule, in: American Economic Review, Vol. 55
    (1965), pp. 486-496

SAMUELSON, P. A. (1967), A Turnpike Refutation of the Golden Rule in
    a Welfare Maximizing Many-Year Model, in: K. SHELL (ed.), Essays
    in the Theory of Optimal Economic Growth, 1967, pp. 269-280

SAMUELSON, P. A. (1968), The Two-Part Golden Rule Deduced as the Asymp-
    totic Turnpike of Catenary Motions, in: Western Economic Journal,
    Vol. 6 (1968), pp. 85-89

SAMUELSON, P. A. (1975a), The Optimum Growth Rate for Population, in:
    International Economic Review, Vol. 16 (1975), pp. 531-538

SAMUELSON, P. A. (1975b), Optimum Social Security in a Life-Cycle Growth
    Model, in: International Economic Review, Vol. 16 (1975),
    pp. 539-544

SAMUELSON, P. A. (1976), The Optimum Growth Rate for Population. Agree
    ment and Evaluations, in: International Economic Review, Vol. 17
    (1976), pp. 516-525

SOLOW, R. M. (1956), A Contribution to the Theory of Economic Growth,
    in: Quarterly Journal of Economics, Vol. 70 (1956), pp. 65-94

STEIN, J. L. (1969), A Minimal Role of Government in Achieving Optimal
    Growth, in: Economica, May 1969, pp. 139-150

CAPITAL ACCUMULATION AND POPULATION GROWTH
IN TWO SECTOR CLOSED AND OPEN ECONOMIES

Benjamin Bental
Faculty of Industrial Engineering and Management
Technion - Israel Institute of Technology

Haifa 32000 / Israel

ABSTRACT: An overlapping generations model with endogenous capital accumulation and population growth is explored. The rate of return on children is set exogenously, and dictates the required rate of return on capital. If that return is believed to be low, no capital is accumulated. In an international trade context it is shown that a fast population growth economy will have a high interest rate but may accumulate no capital. The policy conclusion is that high population growth countries may be justified in supporting capital accumulation in order to direct domestic investment away from children.

I.   Introduction

The stylized facts are all too well known: poor countries have a high population growth rate while the population of the rich countries hardly grows at all. Some economists, who attempted to explain these facts, claimed that the motives for having children in LDC's and in developed countries are different. Children in LDC's provide for their parents in old age (the "Old Age Security Hypothesis"), and therefore their number depends on the rate of return on "investment" in children. NEHER (1971) and WILLIS (1980) represent this idea. On the other hand, in developed countries children are presumed to be a "consumption good", and their number is determined by the marginal utility derived from an additional child as compared to other forms of consumption. Recent contributions taking up this approach include ECKSTEIN and WOLPIN (1985) and NERLOVE, RAZIN and SADKA (1986). Thus, whether an economy is an LDC or developed, is predetermined by the modeller.

The approach taken below favors the old age security motive for having children. However, it is very explicit about alternatives to children in providing that security. In particular, physical capital may be used to provide this service (as in DIAMOND, 1965).[1]

---

[1] The theoretical importance of the existence of an alternative asset in the context of the old age security hypothesis is discussed in WILLIS (1980) and NERLOVE et al. (1986), but is not analysed in full in these papers.

Studies in Contemporary Economics
A. Wenig, K. F. Zimmermann (Eds.)
Demographic Change and Economic Development
© Springer-Verlag Berlin Heidelberg 1989

Clearly, if the return on investment in children is high, there is little incentive to invest in the alternative asset. On the other hand, as education costs increase and family ties weaken, we should expect to find more investment in capital and less in children. Capital labor ratios should increase and interest rates should decrease. It is well known that capital labor ratios in LDC's are much lower than in the rich countries. Although hard to document, we maintain the hypothesis that the economic return on children is indeed lower in the developed countries than in LDC's.

Finally, the issue of trade between developed and less-developed countries is constantly discussed. LDC's participation rates in international trade are very low. Furthermore, LDC's are known to control heavily capital flows, while encouraging domestic capital formation explicitly or implicitly.

The model developed below lends itself to an analysis of the interrelationship between population growth rate, capital accumulation and international trade. In particular it turns out that LDC's may be justified in their attempt to encourage capital formation. Specifically, because of the high return on children in the LDC's, no capital is accumulated if the return on capital is perceived to be low. Under these circumstances, government intervention may be needed.

Formally the analysis is carried out using an overlapping generations structure in conjunction with a standard two sector growth model. The specific technology is described in section II, while section III discusses the agents who populate the economy and their saving strategies. In section IV, steady states characterized by positive capital labor ratios are discussed. In section V some relevant comparative static exercises are carried out, ascertaining the effect of the rate of return on children on the population growth rate, capital accumulation and the capital labor ratio. Section VI discusses the steady state in which no capital is accumulated, and section VII compares the population growth rates in the two steady states. Trade issues are the subject of section VIII. Section IX concludes the paper.

II.   Technology

Let technology be described by a standard two sector model (in which the results obtained by RYBCZYNSKI, STOLPER and SAMUELSON hold). That is, there are two factors of production, labor and capital, producing two goods: a consumption good (C, in sector 1) and capital (K, in sector 2). Both production processes are assumed to exhibit constant returns to scale. Specifically, output per worker in sector i is given by

$$y_i = f_i(k_i) \tag{1}$$

where $k_i \equiv \dfrac{K_i}{L_i}$ is sector i's capital labor ratio. The production functions satisfy

$$f_i'(\cdot) > 0, \quad f_i''(\cdot) < 0, \quad \lim_{k \to 0} f_i'(k) = \infty, \quad \lim_{k \to 0} k\, f_i'(k) = 0, \quad \lim_{k \to \infty} f_i'(k) = 0.$$

Further, we assume that capital depreciates at a rate of 100 %. Finally we assume that capital is essential only for the production of the capital good, whereas the consumption good may be produced with labor alone, so that $f_1(0) > 0$, $f_2(0) = 0$.

Given a positive capital labor ratio k we can define the production possibilities frontier of the economy. In particular, if all markets are competitive, given a relative price of the capital good in terms of the consumption good p, the amount of each good produced can be found as a tangency point between the production possibilities frontier and the price (see figure 1). Moreover, there exist two functions $\underline{p}(k)$ and $\overline{p}(k)$ such that the economy produces both goods only if $\underline{p}(k) < p < \overline{p}(k)$. Specifically, the amount of capital produced is given by

$$S(p,k) = \begin{cases} 0 & p < \underline{p}(k) \\ a(p)k + b(p) & \underline{p}(k) \le p \le \overline{p}(k) \\ f_2(k) & \overline{p}(k) < p \end{cases} \tag{2}$$

We also know that given k the wage function is given by

$$\tilde{w}(p,k) = \begin{cases} f_1(k) - k f_1'(k) & p < \underline{p}(k) \\ w(p) & \underline{p}(k) \le p \le \overline{p}(k) \\ p(f_2(k) - k f_2'(k)), & \overline{p}(k) < p \end{cases} \tag{3}$$

and the rental function is given by

$$\tilde{r}(p,k) = \begin{cases} f_1'(k) & p < \underline{p}(k) \\ r(p) & \underline{p}(k) \le p \le \overline{p}(k) \\ p f_2'(k) & \overline{p}(k) < p \end{cases} \tag{4}$$

Furthermore, we have $a(p) = r'(p)$ and $b(p) = w'(p)$.

The assumption that sector 1 can produce with no capital but sector 2 cannot do so implies that for sufficiently low economy-wide capital labor ratio and for p that satisfies $\underline{p}(k) < p < \overline{p}(k)$, $k_1 < k_2$. If we assume that in a capital-rich economy sector 1 is more capital intensive than sector 2, by continuity there must exist a critical capital-labor ratio $\hat{k}$ such that $k_1 = k_2 = \hat{k}$. At that capital-labor ratio the economy's PPF is linear, and $\underline{p}(\hat{k}) = \overline{p}(\hat{k}) = \hat{p} = \dfrac{f_1(\hat{k})}{f_2(\hat{k})}$. Figures 2 and 3 show the wage and rental correspondences for the case in which capital intensity reverses.

III. Agents

Consider a discrete-time, deterministic overlapping generations econ-omy with the aforementioned technology. Agents live three periods and care only for consumption in all periods of their lives. In the first period they make no decisions, and consume an amount which is allo-cated to them by their "parents". In the second period agents are en-dowed with 1 unit of non-storable labor. The labor endowment can be sold, and the proceeds may be consumed, spent on a capital good or on transfers to a new generation. A certain fixed amount is transferred to the "parents". Consumption in the third period is financed through dissaving and by transfers from "children".

Formally, let the utility function satisfy all smoothness con-ditions. In addition assume that second period and third period consump-tion are normal goods and gross substitutes. The problem faced by an age 2 agent is

$$\underset{\substack{c_t(t),c_t(t+1)\\s(t+1),n(t+1)}}{\text{Max}} \quad \{u(c_t(t), c_t(t + 1))\} \tag{5}$$

s.t.

$$c_t(t) + p(t)s(t+1) + en(t+1) + d \le w(t) \tag{6}$$

$$c_t(t+1) \le r(t+1)s(t+1) + dn(t+1) \tag{7}$$

where

$c_t(t+i)$ - time t+i consumption of an agent who works at t, i = 0, 1

n(t+1) - number of children of an agent who works at t

p(t) - time t price of capital in terms of the time t consumption good

w(t) - time t wage rate in terms of the time t consumption good

r(t) - time t gross rental in terms of the time t consumption good

e   - transfers per "child", in terms of the consumption good

d   - transfers to "parent", in terms of the consumption good.

We regard n(t) as a continuous variable with $n(t) \geq 0$. Further, we treat d and e as fixed positive parameters.[2]

An agent faced with problem (5) and constraints (6) and (7) has the following decision rule

$$p(t)s(t + 1) + en(t + 1) = F(w(t) - d, R(t + 1))) \tag{8}$$

where R(1 + 1) is the return earned on saving given by

$Max\{\dfrac{r(t + 1)}{p(t)} , \dfrac{d}{e}\}$. The normalcy and gross-substitution assumptions imply $F_1 > 0$, $F_2 > 0$. Furthermore, we get

$$s(t + 1) = 0 \text{ if } \frac{d}{e} > \frac{r(t + 1)}{p(t)} \tag{9}$$

and

$$n(t + 1) = 0 \text{ if } \frac{r(t + 1)}{p(t)} > \frac{d}{e} \tag{10}$$

An <u>equilibrium</u> is a path of

$\{c_t(t), c_{t-1}(t), n(t + 1), s(t + 1), p(t)\}_{t=1}^{\infty}$ such that for a given k(o)

---

[2] In this respect this paper follows the tradition set in the "old age security hypothesis" literature. Given the fact that no theory concerning the determinants of the intergenerational transfers is provided here, analytical convenience dictated the formulation of the model.

i)   agents optimize

ii)   labor and capital markets clear at competitive prices, and

iii) perfect foresight prevails.

It is clear that n(t) = 0 for any t ≥ 1 cannot be an equilibrium since $f_i(\infty) \to 0$, and condition (9) is violated. On the other hand, s(t) = 0 for some t cannot be ruled out. However, we start with the case where s(t) > 0 for all t ≥ 1.

IV. Equilibria With Capital Accumulation

Formally, an equilibrium is a solution to the following system of equations

$$p(t)s(t+1) + en(t+1) = F(w(p(t)) - d, \frac{r(p(t+1))}{p(t)}) \tag{11}$$

$$\frac{r(p(t+1))}{p(t)} = \frac{d}{e} \tag{12}$$

and

$$s(t+1) = S(p(t), \frac{s(t)}{n(t)}) \tag{13}$$

We first analyze the properties of a steady state of the system (11) - (13), assuming it exists. The dynamic properties are briefly discussed later on.

Proposition 1: For any steady state p^* which solves (12), there exist unique steady state values of n and s which solve (11) and (13).

Proof: At steady state we get

$$s = a(p^*) \frac{es}{F(w(p^*) - d, \frac{d}{e}) - p^* s} + b(p^*) \tag{14}$$

Omitting the stars, the solution of (14) is given by

$$s = \frac{-(ae - F - pb) \overset{+}{-} \sqrt{(ae - F - pb)^2 - 4pbF}}{2p} \tag{15}$$

If sector 1 is more capital intensive we get a < 0, b > 0; so that s > 0 taking both roots. However we also require

$$en = F - ps > 0. \tag{16}$$

To satisfy (16) we need

$$\pm \sqrt{(ae - F - pb)^2 - 4pbF} < (ae - F - pb) + 2F \tag{17}$$

If the RHS of (17) is negative, obviously the bigger root of (15) is ruled out. If the RHS of (17) is positive and the LHS is taken to be positive as well, then

$$-4pbF < 4F(ae - F - pb) + 4F^2 \tag{18}$$

or

$$0 < ae \tag{19}$$

which contradicts a < 0. Therefore this case too admits only the smaller root of (15).

If sector 2 is more capital intensive, then a > 0 and b < 0. As a result only the bigger root in (15) is positive. Furthermore, (17) holds because the RHS is positive and a > 0.   Q.E.D.

Remark 1: If sector 1 is more capital intensive, there exists a unique steady state.

The result stated above is due to the fact that r'(p) < 0, so that equation (12) has a unique steady state solution. As a corollary we note that if capital intensities reverse, (12) may not have a unique solution, and accordingly the steady state need not be unique.

A dynamic analysis of the system (10) - (13) reveals that steady states may be unstable. Furthermore, this model (like many other decen-tralized growth models) may have multiple perfect foresight paths. It is also possible for the system to oscillate around the steady state. In particular, under the "usual" capital intensity conditions whereby sector 1 is more capital intensive population growth rates may vary over time, and capital accumulation patterns may be quite complicated.

V. Comparative Statics

In this section we investigate how steady states depend on the exogenous variables d and e. The validity of this analysis in a dynamic sense depends on the stability results of the previous section. If the system is stable then at steady state the following relationships hold

$$
\begin{bmatrix}
p & s' - F_1 w' - F_2\left[\dfrac{r'p - r}{p^2}\right] & e \\[3ex]
0 & \dfrac{r'p - r}{p^2} & 0 \\[3ex]
1 - \dfrac{S_2}{n} & -S_1 & \dfrac{s}{n^2}S_2
\end{bmatrix}
\begin{bmatrix}
ds \\[3ex] dp \\[3ex] dn
\end{bmatrix}
=
\begin{bmatrix}
-F_1 dd - nde \\[3ex]
\dfrac{1}{e}\,dd - \dfrac{d}{e^2}de \\[3ex]
0
\end{bmatrix}
\quad (20)
$$

The determinant of the LHS of (20) is given by

$$
D \equiv \frac{r'p - r}{p^2}\left[p\,\frac{s}{n^2}\,S_2 - e\left(1 - \frac{S_2}{n}\right)\right] \quad (21)
$$

The stability of the dynamic system requires $D > 0$. Note that $D > 0$ when sector 1 is more capital intensive. If $k_1 > k_2$ and if

$$
\left(s - F_1 w' - F_2\,\frac{r'p - r}{p^2}\right) > 0, \text{ (that is, } F_1 \text{ small) we get}
$$

$$
\frac{\partial n}{\partial e} < 0. \quad (22)
$$

If we assume further that $\left(s - F_1 w' - F_2\left(\dfrac{r'p - r}{p^2}\right)\right)\dfrac{s}{n^2}S_2 + eS_1 < 0$, (that is, e small) we get also

$$
\frac{\partial s}{\partial e} < 0. \quad (23)
$$

The signs of $\dfrac{\partial n}{\partial d}$ and $\dfrac{\partial s}{\partial d}$ are ambiguous, and depend on the value of F_1. However, if F_1 is sufficiently small, we get

$$
\frac{\partial n}{\partial d} > 0 \quad (24)
$$

and

$$\frac{\partial s}{\partial d} > 0. \tag{25}$$

These results imply that under certain conditions if the return on children increases in a given economy, both steady-state capital accumulation and population growth rates increase.[3] The changes in the steady-state relative price of capital are given by

$$\frac{\partial p}{\partial e} = - \frac{d}{e^2} \frac{p^2}{(r'p - r)} \tag{26}$$

$$\frac{\partial p}{\partial d} = \frac{1}{e} \frac{p^2}{(r'p - r)} \tag{27}$$

As returns on children increase the relative price of capital must increase because the rate of return on capital has to increase as well.

The sign of the change in the capital labor ratio, as e changes, is given by the sign of $\frac{1}{s}\frac{\partial s}{\partial e} - \frac{1}{n}\frac{\partial n}{\partial e}$. The latter expression is

$$\frac{n}{s}\frac{\partial}{\partial e}\left[\frac{s}{n}\right] = \frac{1}{D}\left[-\frac{r'p - r}{p^2} - \frac{d}{e^2}\left[(\frac{e}{s} + \frac{p}{n})S_1 + (s - F_1 w' - F_2 \frac{r'p - r}{p^2})\frac{1}{n}\right]\right] \tag{28}$$

The first element in (28) is positive if sector 1 is more capital intensive. The second is negative. However, for sufficiently small $\frac{d}{e}$ the first element dominates, so that $\frac{s}{n}$ increases as e increases: higher costs of raising children (i. e., lower return on saving) will reduce investment in children by more than investment in capital.

---

[3] The assumptions needed to get these results demonstrate that the "Old Age Security Hypothesis" cannot be rejected by a naive correlation of population growth against rates of return. In particular, it is not just tastes that determine the response to changes in rates of return (as represented by the magnitude of F_1 in this model) but also technology and the capital intensity conditions. See also WILLIS (1980) on this point.

If the dynamic stability conditions for the system are not satis
fied the sign of D (equation (21)) may be negative. However, if the
saddle-point property holds the results obtained above remain valid,
subject only to a possible sign reversal of D. Clearly, if the system
is unstable, comparative statics exercises are meaningless.

VI.   Steady States Without Capital Accumulation

A path without capital accumulation is an equilibrium. The relative
price path is indeterminate in such an equilibrium. The following proposition states this result.

Proposition 2: Any sequence $\{p(t)\}_{t=1}^{\infty}$ such that $\frac{r(p(t + 1))}{p(t)} < \frac{d}{e}$
for all t is an equilibrium.

Proof: It is obvious that conditions (i) and (ii) of the definition
of an equilibrium are fulfilled: agents optimize and markets clear
since both supply and demand for capital are zero for all t. This price
sequence satisfies the perfect foresight requirement in the sense that
there is no actual price sequence which contradicts it.   Q.E.D.

The equilibrium path in this case is unique and steady and is
given by

$$en = F(f_1(0) - d, \frac{d}{e}).$$ (29)

Denote the solution to (29) by $\hat{n}$. Obviously $\hat{n}$ exists only if

$$f_1(0) - d > 0.$$

VII.   A Comparison of the Steady States

Denote the steady state population growth with capital accumulation
by n^*. In general, nothing can be said about the relationship between
$\hat{n}$ and n^*. However, it can be shown (from (16)) that en^* is small if
a (which is $r'(p)$) is small in absolute value. Since

$$r'(p) = \frac{f_2(k_2)}{k_2 - k_1} \tag{30}$$

en* will be small if the capital labor ratios in the two sector diverge from each other. Accordingly, an economy that displays large discrepancies between the capital labor ratios in the two sectors is likely to have a steady state population growth rate that is lower than the population growth rate it would have if it did not accumulate any capital.

Along the equilibrium path, the wage rate in an economy with capital must be higher than $f_1(0)$, as w(p) is monotone decreasing when sector 1 is less capital intensive and increasing otherwise (see figure 2). The rate of return on saving is the same in both cases, $\frac{d}{e}$. Accordingly, total saving in an economy with capital must be higher (since both c_1 and c_2 are normal). Furthermore, the utility level achieved by a representative agent in an economy with capital must be higher (see figure 4) at any date. The equilibrium with capital accumulation clearly PARETO dominates the path in which no capital is accumulated.

VIII.   Trading Economies

Consider a world which consists of two economies with identical technologies (described in section II) and identical utility functions. The economies may differ from each other by d and e, and in particular by $\frac{d}{e}$. Let $\frac{d^1}{e^1} \geq \frac{d^2}{e^2}$, where the superscript denotes the economy.

Let both economies be open to trade, and assume there are no taxes, tariffs, transportation costs, etc., so that both economies face the same price. We can now define a trading equilibrium as follows:

A <u>trading equilibrium</u> consists of sequences

$$\{c_t^i(t), \; c_{t-1}^i(t), \; n^i(t + 1), \; s^i(t + 1), \; p(t)\}_{t=1}^\infty, \; i = 1, \; 2$$

with $s^i(t) > 0$ for i = 1, 2 and all t

such that

$$e^i n^i(t + 1) + p(t)s^i(t + 1) = F(w^i(t) - d^i, \frac{d^i}{e^i}), \; i = 1, \; 2 \tag{31}$$

$$\frac{r^i(p(t+1))}{p(t)} = \frac{d^i}{e^i} \tag{32}$$

and

$$\sum_{i=1}^{2} N^i(t)s^i(t+1) = \sum_{i=1}^{2} N^i(t)S(p(t), \frac{s^i(t)}{n^i(t)}) \tag{33}$$

where $N^i(t)$ is the size of country i's new generation born at t. We require further that perfect foresight prevails.

Trading equilibria are characterized by the following results.

Proposition 3: If $\frac{d^1}{e^1} > \frac{d^2}{e^2}$ then generically for any p(t) at least one economy specializes for all $t \geq 2$.

Proof: Suppose both economies diversify at t = 2. If the same industry in both economies is the capital intensive one, then r(p(t + 1)) is the same; a contradiction results.

If the two industries have opposite capital intensities in the two economies, then conditions (31) and (33) (3 equations) must determine $n^i(t+1)$ and $s^i(t+1)$, i = 1, 2, so that the equilibrium is indeterminate. However, this is a measure zero case, since there exists (at most) one pair (p(t), p(t + 1)) which satisfies both equations (32).   Q.E.D.

Proposition 3 leads us into the analysis of the steady states of the trading economies.

Proposition 4: In steady state generically one economy diversifies.

Proof: Generically $n^1 \neq n^2$. Clearly the economy with the larger n has to be self sufficient in both goods, while the low population growth economy specializes according to the internal price of the large n economy. [4]   Q.E.D.

According to proposition 4 the steady state may take only a limited number of forms. First we state the following proposition.

---

4) KEMP (1969) discusses this result in a context of a model with an exogenous population growth rate.

<u>Proposition 5:</u> In steady states, $\dfrac{s^1}{n^1} < \dfrac{s^2}{n^2}$.

<u>Proof:</u> Given p, the rental function is globally a strictly decreasing function of $\dfrac{s}{n}$ (see figure 5). Therefore, the economy with the higher $\dfrac{d}{e}$ has a lower $\dfrac{s}{n}$.   Q.E.D.

<u>Remark 2:</u> There need not exist a steady state trading equilibrium.

<u>Proof:</u> Suppose that $n^i > n^j$ and economy i diversifies in steady state. Then p is determined by

$$\frac{r(p)}{p} = \frac{d^i}{e^i} .$$ (34)

The specialized economy's capital labor ratio is determined by

$$\frac{\tilde{r}(p, \frac{s^j}{n^j})}{p} = \frac{d^j}{e^j}$$ (35)

where $\tilde{r}(\cdot)$ is defined in (4).

Suppose now that economy 1 is the large one, and $p = p^1$. Clearly, economy 2's wage rate (w_1^2) is higher (see figure 6). Therefore, if d^1 is sufficiently large relative to economy 1's wage rate (w_1^1) while d^2 is sufficiently small relative to w_1^2 it is possible that $n^2 > n^1$, which contradicts the presumption that economy 1 is dominating. If, on the other hand, economy 2 dominates and the price is p^2, its wage rate may decrease to w_2^2, while economy 1's wage rate may increase to w_2^1. Accordingly we may get $n^1 > n^2$, which is another contradiction.[5]   Q.E.D.

Remark 2 opens the question whether equilibria and steady states in which no trade may exist. Such a situation emerges when at least one of the two economies accumulates no capital. First, we rule out the following possibilities.

---

[5] An example of this nature can be easily constructed for a COBB-DOUGLAS technology and a log utility function. However, this example does not satisfy $f_1(0) > 0$.

Proposition 6: If $n^i > n^j$ and $s^i > 0$ at steady state, then $s^j > 0$ for i, j = 1, 2 and i ≠ j.

Proof: The slower growing economy (j) is clearly a price taker in this situation. Since there exists a specific, positive price that economy j faces, there exists a unique positive s^j such that $\frac{r^j(p)}{p} = \frac{d^j}{e^j}$.

Q.E.D.

As a corollary to proposition 6, we obtain that if economy i has the faster growing population and it does not accumulate capital, then the smaller economy j may or may not accumulate capital. This inconclusive result is due to the fact that economy j which is a price taker has no price to take. On the other hand, even if the price of capital in economy j is positive, it cannot serve as an indication for economy i's population, because this price would change if economy i accumulated capital. This conclusion may be sharpened somewhat if we assume that income effects dominate substitution effects and that $d^2 < d^1$ while $e^2 = e^1$ so that $\hat{n}^2 > \hat{n}^1$ (see equation (29)). In this case $n^1 = \hat{n}^1$, so that $n^1 > n^2$ and $s^1 = 0$ imply $s^2 > 0$. The economy with the high interest rate also has a high population growth rate and accumulates no capital. Furthermore, it does not participate in international trade. However, the economy with the lower interest rate has the lower population growth rate and necessarily has a positive capital labor ratio.

IX. Conclusion

The model presented in this paper argues that if children may be viewed as a store of value that competes with capital and if capital (unlike labor) is not essential for production, then economies may be characterized by high population growth rates and no capital accumulation. Furthermore, the model shows that populous high interest rate economies may fail to accumulate capital and to participate in international trade. This result mimics quite nicely the North-South split of the world today. The North consists of low population growth countries with low interest rates and high capital labor ratios. The South consists of countries with the opposite characteristics. Within the North there is a very substantial trade activity while the South is almost excluded from this activity.

The model clearly admits other equilibria as well. As a matter
of fact, the equilibria in which capital accumulation in zero are, in
some sense, "sun-spot" equilibria. They are purely a result of agents'
subjective views about relative rates of return, views that can never
be tested because they are self-justifying. Accordingly, if the model
captures reality, any policy which tries to solve the problem must
address the expectations issue. In particular, it must convince agents
that investment in capital may be as good as investment in the alternative asset (children). To do so, subsidies to encourage capital formation may be considered. In fact, the most direct approach is for the
government to guarantee a high rate of return on capital. Notice that
as the target group of such a policy is the local population, it is
reasonable to place capital controls as long as the government intervention is needed. There is no reason to subsidize foreign investors.

Alternative policies aim at reducing the rate of return on investment in children by taxing large families. These policies may indeed
reduce population growth rates (see China), but may fail to encourage
capital formation because the rate of return on capital may be still
perceived to be low.

References

DIAMOND, Peter: "National Debt in a Neoclassical Growth Model"., <u>AER</u> 55, No. 5, 1965.

ECKSTEIN, Zvi and Kenneth I. WOLPIN: "Endogenous Fertility and Optimal Population Size," <u>Journal of Public Economics</u>, 27, No. 1, 1985.

KEMP, Murray C.: <u>The Pure Theory of International Trade and Investment</u>, Prentice-Hall, Inc., 1969.

NEHER, Philip A.: "Peasants, Procreation and Pensions," <u>AER</u> 61, No. 3, 1969.

NERLOVE, Marc, Assar RAZIN and Efraim SADKA: "Some Welfare Theoretic Implications of Endogenous Fertility," <u>IER</u> 27, No. 1, 1986.

WILLIS, Robert J.: "The Old Age Security Hypothesis and Population Growth" in Thomas K. BURCH (ed.): <u>Demographic Behavior - Interdisciplinary Perspectives on Decision Making</u>. Westview Press, 1980.

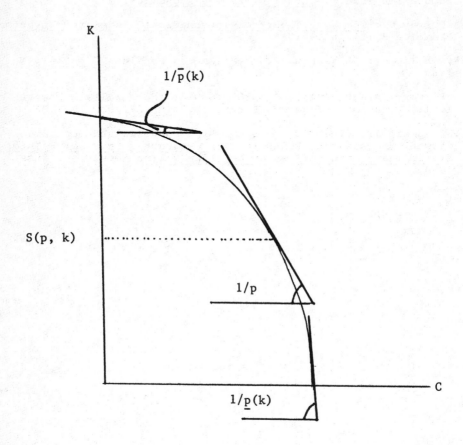

Figure 1: Production Possibilities Frontier

111

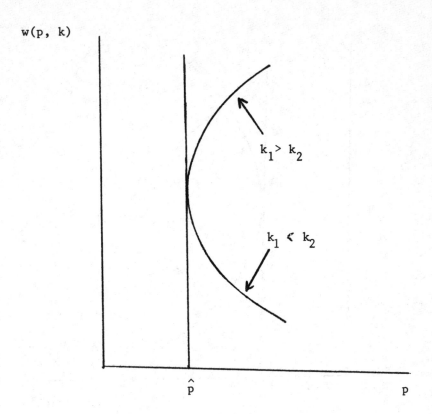

Figure 2: The Wage Correspondence

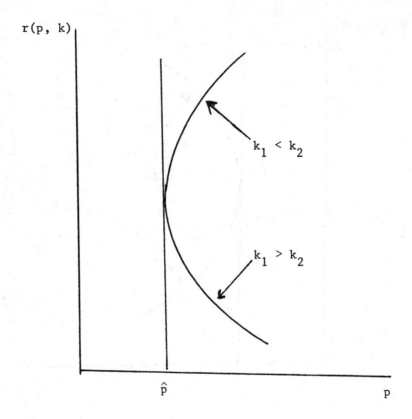

Figure 3: The Rental Correspondence

113

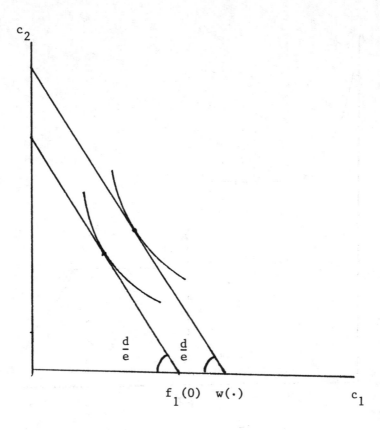

Figure 4: Saving With and Without Capital

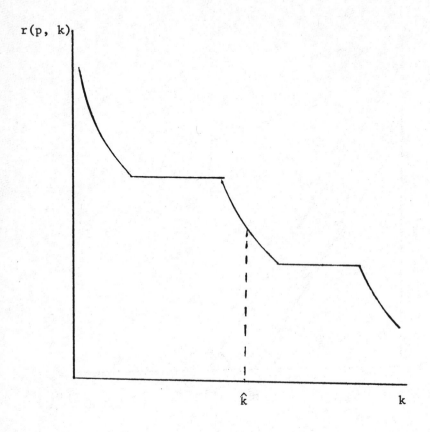

Figure 5: Rental As Function of the Capital
Labor Ratio

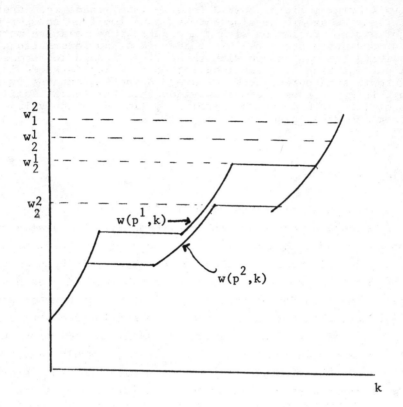

Figure 6:   Wages As a Function of the Capital
            Labor Ratio, and $p^1 > p^2$.

"POPULATION DRAG" AND THE ROLE OF THE INTERNATIONAL SECTOR

H. Peter Gray[*]
School of Business - Rutgers University

New Brunswick, N.J. / USA

ABSTRACT: Differing policies toward international trade and investment in the course of economic development may have implications for the pressure of excess population within a country. The relative merits insofar as population pressures are concerned of an internationalist set of policies are contrasted with those of an inward-looking strategy of import substitution. Internationalist policies as featured in export-led growth strategies, seem to have distinct advantages over a strategy of import substitution provided that the industrialized countries of the world do not set arbitrary limits to the volume of imports from the developing world.

I. Population Drag

Any assessment of the role of demographic factors on the rate of economic growth or development must distinguish explicitly between static conditions and changes through time[1]. As normally defined, both actual and optimum population are static concepts. Changes in both measures over time are simply changes in stocks although such changes have obvious implications for future population size. The concept of population drag is developed here in a comparative static framework since the issue is the effect of alternative international policies on the amount of excess population. Steady state analysis would be unsuitable because there can be no supposition that the effect of the international sector on the quantity of labor demanded will evolve steadily through time under either policy option.

The fact that optimum population is usually defined in static terms and the difficulties of definition and measurement are so great, has led to the suggestion that the concept is sterile for policy purposes. This assertion relies on a more precise concept of economic

---

[1] This paper does not follow the usual practice of distinguishing between growth and development by having the latter necessarily involve structural change. One feature of this analysis is to examine the role of the alternative policies on the acquisition of human capital: if the human capital of the population increases over time, social and structural change will occur inevitably.

[*] I am indebted to Shanti S. Tangri for long and insightful discussions on the interactions between population pressures and economic development as well as for comments on an earlier draft of this paper.

Studies in Contemporary Economics
A. Wenig, K. F. Zimmermann (Eds.)
Demographic Change and Economic Development
© Springer-Verlag Berlin Heidelberg 1989

modeling and policy formulation than is possible or practical in reality. Provided that the difference between actual and optimum population (however defined) is substantial, economic policy need only be
aware of the necessary direction of change and an exact knowledge
about the ultimate magnitude of change (the gap between actual and
optimum) is not necessary. This point is at the basis of TANGRI's
(1986) concept of the "optimum rate of population growth" which measures
the rate and direction or sign of the change in actual population
needed to approach optimum. This focus on the direction of change (and
the lack of need for precise knowledge of magnitudes) is also a feature
of traditional macroeconomic policy in industrialized countries. When
actual and target rates of capacity utilization are quite different,
the diagnosis of the appropriate policy measures is straightforward
in terms of the need for expansion or restraint: since the reaction of
target variables to instrument variables is not instantaneous, macro-
economic policy proceeds by increments. The precision embodied in
TINBERGEN's "The Theory of Economic Policy" (1970) is not required until
the actual rate of capacity utilization approaches the target rate quite
closely. Then, if further improvement is to result from manipulation of
instrument variables, the analytic model must portray all inter-sectoral
relationships and feedback mechanisms with precision in addition to
being furnished with accurate and speedily-provided data. In this paper,
it is assumed that actual population exceeds the optimum by a substantial amount, so that any reduction in the gap between optimum and actual
will reduce population drag and enhance the rate of economic development.
Thus, if the adoption of one of a pair of mutually-exclusive policies
(or some exogenous change) will reduce the rate of population growth
and enhance the amount of population needed by the productive sector,
it will reduce population drag: an internationalist stance will have
positive externalities if it generates a larger optimum population
than that which would have been generated by inward-looking policies[2].

Optimum population can be defined as that which can be fully uti-
lized by the existing stock of capital, the embodied technology and
other available resources so that the marginal product of labor is at
least equal to subsistence income (however defined)[3]. Thus, optimum

---

[2]   The comparison must assume that each set of policies has been in
place long enough for its effect on optimum population to have
taken hold.

[3]   This assumption is tacit in Keynesian models of full employment in
industrialized economies and implies a labor-skill profile which may
not always exist - particularly in times of rapid technological
change.

population is defined in terms of the demand for labor with a given endowment of (physical) capital. The endowment of capital must also assume the existence of a given stock of human capital (skills and education) so that the embodied technology can be used. The definition of optimum population can be further constrained (implying a higher marginal product of labor) by the requirement that the rate of saving be adequate to allow capital formation at a rate which will not impair the marginal product of labor given the national fertility rate. Yet another constraint is that the technology embodied in the physical capital not sacrifice the precision or quality of output simply to accommodate the supply of labor: the suitable technolgy is, at a minimum, that which permits the economy to penetrate foreign markets for quality products so that all needed non-competitive imports can be paid for by export earnings[4]. In practical terms, the comparison between the two international strategies can be considered in terms of their alternative effects on population drag and these, in turn, can be considered in terms of

> the rate of saving;
> the mix of goods produced;
> the stock of human capital;
> the fertility rate.

That international policy that most reduces population drag, other things equal, will be the one which increases the rate of national saving and the skills of the population; which enhances the need for labor through changes in the product mix and which reduces the fertility rate. This multi-dimensional comparison of the outcomes of two different policies will provide an unequivocal answer only if the effect of one policy outranks the other in all four dimensions (so-called vector dominance). If the comparison were to yield mixed results, the benefits of the internationalist stance would depend upon the relative importance of the individual variables and the magnitude of the difference in the effects. Given the complexity of the interrelationships and the lack of precision in available data, a common-sense interpretation might allow some inferences to be drawn without permitting a clearcut answer.

---

[4]   For a definition of non-competitive goods, see GRAY (1976, pp. 46-9). GRAY (1986) argues that manufactured exports will necessarily have quite high ratios of human capital to pure labor.

The four aspects of population drag can be briefly considered. The role of the rate of saving is straightforward: higher saving permits higher rates of capital formation. The mix of goods produced can contribute to the demand for labor both quantitatively and qualitatively. Any quantitative additions to the demand for labor will reduce population drag. If a policy increases the quantity of exports of manufactured goods using labor-intensive technology, an outward looking policy will also have the external benefit that it eases the foreign-exchange constraint and allows the nation to derive its gains from international trade less constrained by bureaucratic controls. Contributions to the stock of human capital may evolve through raising the level of general education throughout the country and by increasing the directness of education so that the skills acquired are specific to the task required in the productive sector. The provision of general education (human capital) is extremely capital intensive and, frequently, is so generally directed that the cost per unit of directly-applicable knowledge is very high. The capital intensity derives from three factors: the time-lag between the first and final inputs into education (and this delay greatly exceeds that in physical capital); the high rate of wastage of human capital as it is depreciated by disuse; and because the "upstream activity" of educating the educators is itself very capital-intensive. This general education is prerequisite to much product-specific training. But a higher level of human capital implies a more educated population and this, in turn, is likely to reduce the fertility rate (ADELMAN, 1963) (GRAY, 1971). As the general level of human capital in the country is raised, the ability of the workforce to use physical capital with more advanced technology and to broaden the range of potential export goods is enhanced.

If production units need workers with certain skills, they may be prepared to train new entrants to the manufacturing workforce to the level of skill required and they may be able to do so at lower social cost than the public sector which lacks the knowledge of the end use of the human capital[5]. Feedback mechanisms may be important here. Any increase in the directness of the educational process provided by firms rather than by the local "ministry of education" will have externalities in terms of the general education acquired by the workers trained. Possibly more important is the inter-generational saving in the costs

---

[5]   BIRDSALL (1984, pp. 63-5) provides data on the importance of human capital in export industries.

of education provided as intra-familial communication better prepares
children for the formal education process and both increases the quality
of the education and reduces the costs of provision.

Whichever of the two policies makes the greater contribution to
raising the rate of saving, increasing the demand for labor, raising
the quantity and quality of human capital (and by so doing reduces fertility), will prove the more effective policy in reducing population
drag. In addition to the externalities of the two policies with reference to population pressures, the policies will generate their own
Myrdalian spread effects whose strengths must also be considered in deciding between the two development policies.

II. The Role of the International Sector

This section addresses the ways in which a high level of international
economic involvement will reduce population drag by increasing the optimum population. The section intentionally omits considerations of
any gains in allocative efficiency which derive from the elimination
of the overvalued currency, high tariffs and non-tariff barriers as
well as what KEOHANE and OOMS (1975) refer to as "image" - the need
for a country to feel and see itself independent of foreign nations.
"Image" can be a very important phenomenon for ex-colonies, particularly in their formative years, and, to the extent that image is fostered
by a non-internationalist policy set, there may be benefits which are
not considered in this paper.

The first consideration is the effects generated by current transactions. Export-led growth involves a conscious decision to rationalize
the economy (with particular attention paid to the degree of overvalu-
ation of the currency, controls over foreign transactions and other
barriers to international trade) so that sectors with export potential
are encouraged to seek out foreign markets[6]. Export-led growth places
heavy reliance on the accuracy and use of price signals from the global
market and involves a conscious decision to make foreign exchange avail-

---

[6] The contrast between export-led growth and Prebisch policy is ex-
     treme. There exists a whole intermediate range (YANNOPOULOS, 1986)
     but the effects on population drag can be expected to be monotonic-
     ally related along the continuum of policies.

able for investments in exporting sectors (KRUEGER, 1983)[7]. Following
the examples of the four Asian newly-industrializing countries, an internationalist policies will increase the demand for labor by increasing
the volume of exports of manufactured goods and, in this way, increase
the number of workers employed in labor-intensive production in the
modern sector. The effect on human capital acquisition will be relatively
small in quite backward countries where firms are unlikely to put much
emphasis on training beyond what is directly applicable to the task at
hand.

The expected benefits from the internationalist stance are likely
to be much greater when foreign direct investment by multinational corporations is encouraged and when the multinational corporations (MNCs)
are allowed to establish themselves in the developing country and are
required to meet certain standards of social performance. In straightforward analysis, MNCs can be expected to add substantially to GDP and
GDP per capita, to increase the stock of capital, to ease any foreign
exchange constraint, at least temporarily, and to introduce new technologies. The key feature of an MNC is its ability to transfer a compa-
tible collection of factors of production which are simply unavailable
in the host (developing) nation. Technology and trained personnel are
the key. MNCs, if oriented towards export markets, will enhance foreign
exchange earnings.

Such "best practice" examples of the effects of inward direct investment on the host economy do not always work out in practice. The
difficulty is to ensure that the MNC will locate in the economy and,
at the same time that the policies of the MNC are socially beneficial.
The biggest concern is with the possible lack of congruence between the
goals of the MNC and those of the host government (WALTER, 1975). One
of the most common problems in goal incongruence is the "appropriateness"
of the technology introduced by the MNC to the level of development of
the host economy. The host economy with a heavy awareness of its excess
population will seek very labor-intensive technologies while the MNC
will be more interested in using a proven method of production even if
that does not maximize current employment. Such an incongruence does
not necessary imply an indifference to the host's goals on the part of

---

[7] As noted, this does not imply a free-trade policy in its pure form.
Import controls and similar measures may co-exist with export-led
growth but their severity is likely to be reduced.

the MNC but merely indicates risk-aversion on the part of the MNC. To
juxtapose this well-known problem with the problem of population drag
sheds new light on the question: the less-demanding and the more labor-
intensive the technology used by the MNC, the smaller is the probable
contribution of the MNC to the host's stock of human capital.

There already exists a well-established preference for policies
of "indigenization" on the part of host governments. These policies
require MNCs rapidly to train up local people to replace foreign experts who have been used to establish the subsidiary venture: on occasion the emphasis is so great as to eliminate foreign experts too quickly[8]. Clearly, the more advanced the technology introduced into the
host economy (relative to the general level of technology in use there),
the greater is the need for training local people. This training will
ordinarily be performed at the expense of the MNC and the MNC can, with
appropriate urging by the host government, develop quite general as well
as direct or specific training programs. This potential benefit will
be facilitated by the acceptance by many large corporations of the advantages of in-house general educational programs.

The disaster in Bhopal in December, 1984, provides an excellent
example of the need for MNCs to invest heavily in the education/training
of local personnel when it introduces a technology which exceeds that
accepted as standard by the local population. With the Bhopal example
serving as an enduring goad, MNCs are likely to be more amenable to
host government pressures for educational upgrading of employees working
with advanced technologies[9].

In addition to training local workers in the host country, MNCs
have a practice of sending executives abroad for further training.

Another benefit which can derive from the presence of an outward-
oriented MNC is the development of experience on the part of host-country

---

[8] DUNHAM (1984) terms this practice "localization" and considers it
     as a part of a large range of problems which include joint owner-
     ship, nationalization and other aspects of establishing host-country
     control over the MNC. He labels the larger set as "indigenization".

[9] This problem of very disparate technological levels may also set
     limits to the degree to which indigenization is feasible or,
     at least, to the rate of indigenization.

nationals in dealing with foreign markets. This experience is necessary
if nationals are to sell sophisticated products in foreign markets.
This type of MNC will raise the level of education of both management
and workers and add substantially to the educational upgrading contributed by the MNC.

None of this suggests that there do not exist actual and potential
costs which derive from being host to an MNC but the argument does
suggest that the more internationalist development policy is, the less
serious will population drag on development. It is important that the
internationalist stance exceed a simple reliance on exporting by locally-
owned firms operating with local technology. The benefits from an internationalist stance will be smaller the more skilled the country in
acquiring foreign technology through licensing and the more efficient
its own educational system.

III. The Question of the Duration of Benefits from an Internationalist Approach

Tacitly underlying the argument of the two preceding sections is the
presumption that developed countries will be content to accept ever
larger amounts of imports from the developing world[10]. This presumption also underlies much of the endorsement of export-led growth as a
development strategy. This presumption hinges on a continuation on the
part of the industrialized North of a liberal policy towards international trade and particularly towards imports from the Third World. The
presumption also tacitly assumes that the existence of cheap labor in
labor-surplus countries will continue to provide the developing world
with a comparative-cost advantage in labor-intensive standardized products. Neither of these conditions can be relied on indefinitely.

General equilibrium analysis in which the argument for liberal
trade policies is couched, pays little attention, if any, to the social
costs of moving from one equilibrium to another. MEADE (1955, p. 52)
whose treatment of the benefits of free trade is the modern classic,
explicitly assumes "that there are no real costs of movements of fac-

---

[10] YANNOPOULOS (1986) argues that since exports from the Third World
continue to increase, the presumption is valid. There may be a considerable lag between the creation of political opposition and it
finally becoming effective in the industrialized world.

tors when they turn from one industry to another." Arguments for protection are seen as selfish demands by pressure groups who fear some
slight loss of income in response to a new set of international trading
conditions. The smallness of the loss to be experienced by workers
threatened with displacement derives from the assumption of large
elasticities of factor substitution in all production functions. In
the real world in which international trade and economic development
take place, life is less simple. Workers have industry-specific or
product-specific skills and capitalists have product-specific equipment. Inroads by foreign goods from export-oriented developing countries
will displace workers more quickly than product-specific capital can
be depreciated. This is particularly true for human capital which
may have a very long potential life. The facile assumption of zero costs
of adjustment or relocation simply does not hold. Workers threatened
with displacement by developing countries' exports are likely to foresee
substantial economic costs and protracted unemployment[11].

The degree of resistence to imports of manufactured goods from developing countries pursuing internationalist policies has grown in recent years and can be expected to continue to grow steadily. The historical growth of imports from Third World nations will have increasing
social costs: at first, displaced workers would have been those with
the greatest ease of relocation or those for whom unemployment holds the
fewest evils. These will be people with few industry-specific skills
(i. e. little seniority within the industry) and those who are close
to normal retirement. As imports and displacements grow, those workers
who are displaced are less and less adaptable to alternative employment
and/or are likely to find early retirement more and more costly. Thus,
greater protectionist political pressure will emerge unless the government in the importing industrialized country can cushion the process
of adjustment by programs which give protracted economic support and
provide training for re-employment in expanding industries. Only under
these conditions can displaced workers be expected passively to bear
the costs imposed on them by the change in international trading conditions.

---

[11] PFALLER (1986) points out that when the impetus for change is growth
in the industrialized economies, the problem conforms to the free
trade argument and adjustment costs are small: when the problem
is the reallocation of a given volume of global output among
countries, the social costs of displacement can be high.

If the motivation to resist displacement by imports made from "cheap foreign labor" is positively related to the perceived loss of income, then political pressures are likely to grow over time as more and more people are displaced and as the marginal displaced workers perceive increasing costs of displacement with the less buoyant local labor markets. The legislative response to this kind of political pressure is also likely to involve an important time dimension. The protectionist pressures will have to overcome an inclination towards maintaining a liberal trade policy but when the cumulative pressures become sufficient, the resulting legislation may be both severe and longlasting. Government, when finally moved to action, will probably overreact[12].

The pressures for protectionism in the industrialized world will be greater because imports of manufactured goods made abroad with large amounts of low-wage labor will interact with the effects of the modern technologies of the microchip and the robot. Both the new technologies and the increased integration of global production of manufactures will tend to displace workers employed in more routine jobs in the industrialized countries. While it is possible that time will steadily extend the range of displaced workers up the skill ladder, the main emphasis of the new conditions will be felt by lower-skilled workers in the industrialized countries. There can be little expectation that job displacement caused by technological advances can be stopped but the existence of that displacement will accentuate the pressure against imports: workers displaced by the new technologies will have the same or similar characteristics as those displaced by international competition making alternative employment increasingly difficult to find.

The internationalist policies of outward-looking developing economies coupled with the transfer of technology to those countries under the aegis of MNCs, threatens to integrate the global labor market. This integration can be slowed by the erection of barriers to international trade between the North and the South although the political repercussions for the free enterprise democracies may be negative. From the point of view of workers in industrialized countries, the threat of imports from the Third World may be overwhelming. Industrialized econ-

---

12) By, for example, imposing measures that actual reduce the volume of imports from the Third World rather than by arranging for a period of very gradual growth.

omies have generated high rates of pay and relatively safe working
conditions by virtue of their stock of capital, their infrastructure,
their technology and by the relative scarcity of workers. If the economies of low population growth rates are to be integrated with those
with high rates of population growth, the effect could be disasterous
for workers in industrialized countries. Their working conditions
will be forced down to near those existing in developing countries -
even to the point of reductions of safety measures and similar legislation designed to prevent outright exploitation. The workers in the
industrialized countries will be asked to share the excess burdens
of the excess population in the world and of the excess rate of population growth. None of this can occur without violent social strain
in the industrialized nations and without extreme political pressures
for import limitation. (CULBERTSON, 1984).

It is quite possible that the technological gains of recent years
will thwart the success of internationalist policies as effectively as
protectionism. The displacement of low-skilled workers which is likely
to follow from the widespread introduction of the robot and the microchip, will rob the labor-surplus countries of their competitive advantage in the production of standardized manufactured goods. As technology progresses and substitutes automating machinery for human workers
at higher and higher levels of skill and to ever greater degrees,
the best location for production may well switch back to the countries
in which goods are to be sold - to the industrialized North.

If workers are destined to become surplus everywhere, the problems
will be most serious (and most socially-upsetting) in those countries
with large endowments of labor and high rates of population growth.
If the new technologies can automate out of existence all of those
jobs which have historically allowed workers with low skill attainments
to exist at an acceptable economic level and with some self-respect in
an achievement-reward environment, the world faces serious problems
of political stability. This state of affairs lies further in the
future than the threat of protectionism against Third World exports
but it has similar origins.

IV. Conclusion

This inquiry into the effects of an internationalist (export-led)
strategy for economic development on population pressures in the Third
World (and accompanying population drag) has developed three arguments.

1. Optimum population must be seen in terms of both its number and its
human capital content. In a country with surplus labor, the ability
to use population productively derives from the stock of capital and
the embodied technology and the human capital available must be compa-
tible with the capital stock.

2. An internationalist strategy of economic development does seem
to offer quite considerable benefits in terms not only of economic
growth and the release or diminution of foreign-exchange constraints,
but it will also have positive externalities on population pressures.
This argument will apply particularly to the benefits to be realized
by inward foreign direct investment provided that the MNCs can be required to devote considerable resources to the training of local personnel in general as well as job-related skills. This requirement
is unlikely to confront great reluctance from the MNCs because they
are accustomed to this practice "at home" and because the danger of
inadequate training of local personnel has been made evident by Bhopal.

3. Unfortunately, the current trend of economic evolution is likely
to make this window of opportunity short-lived on two counts. The mu-
tually-reinforcing quality of new technologies and imports from labor-
surplus countries will intensify worker resistance to unlimited imports
from the developing nations (whether under straightforward, arm's-
length trade or through MNC-linkages). This resistance which has been
gathering strength for the last decade will continue to gain momentum
and the wave of protectionism will not have peaked as yet.

The message of this paper is not one of optimism. The apparent
ability of the newly-industrializing countries in Asia to eliminate
surplus labor from their economies is not likely to prove an option
available to succeeding generations of NICs. The South cannot look to
the industrialized world as a repository for its surplus population
(either through trade or emigration) and population pressures must be
solved at home. Lower rates of population growth are mandatory. Indeed,
the possible spread of modern technology to labor-surplus countries

suggests that the optimum rate of population growth is becoming increasingly negative. This state of affairs adumbrates significant strains in North-South relations as well as within blocs.

References

ADELMAN, Irma, "An Econometric Analysis of Population Growth", <u>AER</u> 53, (June, 1963), pp. 314-339.

BIRDSALL, Nancy, et al., "Population Change and Economic Development", (New York: Oxford University Press, 1984.)

BURNELL, Peter J., "Economic Nationalism in the Third World, (Boulder: Westview Press, 1986), pp. x and 294.

CULBERTSON, John M., "International Trade and the Future of the West", (Madison, Wisconsin: Twenty-First Century Press, 1984).

GRAY, H. Peter, "Education and Fertility", The Indian Journal of Economics, LII, (October, 1971) pp. 187-190.

GRAY, H. Peter, "A Generalized Theory of International Trade" (London: Macmillan Press, 1976).

GRAY, H. Peter, "Domestic Efficiency, International Efficiency, and Gains from Trade", Weltwirtschaftliches Archiv 121, (Fall 1985), pp. 460-470.

GRAY, H. Peter "North-South Technology Transfer: Two Neglected Problems", Journal of Economic Development 11, (July, 1986) pp. 27-46.

KEOHANE, Robert O. and van DOORM, Ooms "The Multinational Firm and International Regulation", in C. Fred BERGSTEN and Lawrence B. KRAUSE, "World Politics and International Economics (Washington, D.C.: The Broolings Institution, 1975), pp. 169-209.

KRUEGER, Anne O., "The Effects of Trade Strategies on Growth", Finance and Development (June, 1983), pp. 6-8, reprinted in Robert E. BALDWIN and J. David RICHARDSON, International Trade and Finance: Readings, (Third edition) (Boston: Little Brown, 1986) pp. 216-221.

MEADE, J. E., "Trade and Welfare" (Oxford: Oxford University Press, 1955).

PFALLER, Alfred, "The Changing North-South Division of Labor", Kyklos (1986), pp. 85-108.

TANGRI, Shanti S., "Towards a Theory of Optimum Population Growth", paper presented at the Hagen Conference, September 1986.

TINBERGEN, Jan, "On the Theory of Economic Policy" (Amsterdam: North-Holland, 1970).

WALTER, Ingo, "A Guide to Social Responsibility of Multinational Enterprise", in Jules BACKMAN (ed.), Social Responsibility and Accounting (New York: New York University Press, 1975).

YANNOPOULOS, George N. "Trade Policy Options in the Design of Development Strategies", University of Reading Discussion Paper Series A, No. 181, November, 1986.

I,3
Microeconomic Models

THE TIMING OF BIRTHS: A THEORY OF FERTILITY, FAMILY EXPENDITURES AND LABOUR MARKET PARTICIPATION OVER TIME

Alessandro Cigno
University of Hull

Hull / Great Britain

ABSTRACT: An intertemporal microeconomic model of family decisions emphasising the effects of the mother's age on the "quality" of the child and the financial implications of interrupting the mother's career to care for a child is developed to analyse the effects of personal characteristics and of several economic variables on the time-profiles of childbearing and of income raising and spending activities of married couples. The model's predictions are then used to interpret the decline of completed fertility and the reversal of an earlier tendency towards younger motherhood that has characterised Western Europe over recent years.

I. Introduction

According to recent demographic studies, the level of completed fertility in Western Europe is now so low, that fluctuations in the "period" birth rate are overwhelmingly associated with changes in the timing of births.[1] Any attempt at explaining these, often very marked, fluctuations and the way in which they might be controlled by government policy must thus begin with a dynamic theory of parental decisions.

However, truly dynamic analyses have been late coming. Earlier studies have tried to capture aspects of the timing decision within an essentially static model: RAZIN (1980) postulates that parents-to-be simultaneously choose the number and the average interval between births, under the assumption that the quality of the average child is an increasing function of the length of that interval; SCHULTZ (1976) and LEE (1980) use a stock-adjustment model in which the speed of adjustment to the desired number of children is not derived from intertemporal optimisation. More recent attempts at dynamic analysis have been based on drastic simplifications of the decision framework. CIGNO (1983) assumes that the quality of children and, therefore, their utility to parents are independent of the time distribution of births, so that timing decisions are taken entirely on the basis of financial considerations. HAPPEL, HILL and LOW (1984) restrict their attention to the timing of the first birth, taking the time profile of subsequent births as given. Others concentrate almost solely on the stochastic aspects of the problem.

---

[1] See HÖPFLINGER (1984) and MUÑOZ-PEREZ (1986).

Studies in Contemporary Economics
A. Wenig, K. F. Zimmermann (Eds.)
Demographic Change and Economic Development
© Springer-Verlag Berlin Heidelberg 1989

While not attempting to model uncertainty, the present paper analyses a richer set of dynamic interrelations than any of its predecessors. In particular, it allows for the quality of a child or, more generally, the utility that parents derive from a birth to depend on both the age of the mother and the amount of resources expended on the child. Furthermore, it takes account of the interrelations between the time patterns of child bearing and maternal earnings, and explicitly recognises the simultaneous nature of the parents' life time consumption, employment and reproduction plans.

Before plunging into the theory, it will be useful to summarise some of the known facts. The econometric evidence regarding the effects of economic parameters on total fertility is fairly firm and consistent with the predictions of the (static) economic theory of the family. BUTZ and WARD (1979), ERMISCH (1979) and WINEGARDEN (1984) all agree that the overall birthrate is positively correlated with male earnings and negatively correlated with female wage rates. The econometric analysis of birth timing, on the other hand, is still in its infancy, but a recent study of U. K. data by DeCOOMAN, ERMISCH and JOSHI (1985) comes to the conclusion that labour market conditions favourable to the employment of women tend to delay childbearing, while labour market conditions favourable to male employment have the opposite effect. What would a dynamic economic theory of the family have to say on the matter?

In trying to answer the last question, the analysis that follows takes the date of (legal or de facto) marriage as exogenous. A reason for so doing is that births to women who have not yet formed a stable relationship are likely to include a large proportion of unplanned pregnancies, which can be scarcely explained by a deterministic decision model. Another is that we do not have an economic theory of the timing of marriage. The model will thus be concerned with the fertility, labour force participation and consumption/saving decisions of married couples. The way in which these decisions are affected by exogenous changes in the date of marriage, initial assets, male earnings and female career prospects will also be examined, along with the consequences of possible correlations between the exogenous variables.

II. The Framework of Parental Choice

According to the economic model of the family, parents choose the number of children so as to maximise a utility function,

$$U = U(C,B), \tag{1}$$

where C denotes parental consumption of market goods and B a quality weighted index of the number of children.[2] The quality of a child is, in general, a function of the quantities of parental time and financial resources expended on the child and may be interpreted as the parental perception of the child's lifetime utility. The function U( ) is thus a kind of family welfare function.

With the exception of the CIGNO (1983) and HAPPEL et al. (1984) versions, this model takes no account of the distribution of births and expenditures over the parents' lifetime. That is not a serious omission where income expenditure is concerned because, with perfect capital markets, we can always interpret the sum allocated to, say, adult consumption or the welfare of a particular child, as the present value of an optimally timed stream of payments. Not so, however, where childbearing is concerned, because in that case the quality or utility of a child may depend on the date when the child is born (e.g. because of the effect of the mother's age) and, also, because the present value of parental earnings may depend on the time profile of births.

A natural way of introducing timing considerations into family welfare is to define the adult consumption index as

$$C = \sum_{t=a}^{T} u_t(C_t), \tag{2}$$

where C_t is parental consumption at date t, a is the date of marriage and T is the date of death (assumed to be the same for both parents). The functions $u_t(\ )$, assumed to be increasing and concave, and dated to allow for possible time preference, may be interpreted as "instantaneous" utility functions. Similarly,

$$B = \sum_{t=a}^{T} v_t(I_t)B_t, \tag{3}$$

where B_t denotes the rate of birth at t, while I_t is the present value at t of the (optimally timed) stream of voluntary parental expenditures, including any bequests, on a child born at date t. The functions $v_t(\ )$, also increasing, concave and dated to reflect the physiological and psychological effects of parental ageing as well as possible time preference, may be interpreted as parental perceptions of their children's (indirect) utility functions. Thus, $v_t(I_t)$ may be interpreted as the parents' assessment of the lifetime utility of a child born at t, given that the child has been allocated a lump sum (or equivalent payment stream) I_t.

---

[2] See, for example, WILLIS (1973). More general formulations, e.g. BECKER (1981) or CIGNO (1986), have quality and number of children as separate variables.

The omission of parental time from the arguments of $v_t($ $)$ requires some explanation. In general, the welfare of a child may be thought to be affected by the amount of maternal attention enjoyed at various stages of its life. But, maternal time becomes increasingly substitutable with paternal time, with the services of hired hands and with other goods as the child grows older. To allow for all these potential substitutions would make an already complex model virtually unmanageable. A simplifying assumption will thus be made that a certain minimum amount of maternal time is absolutely required over the first period of a child's life (suitably extended to include an appropriate portion of the pregnancy period), but that income expenditure is a perfect substitute for maternal time in all subsequent periods. The length of this crucial first period will be taken as the unit of time of the analysis and conventionally referred to as the year.

This assumption simplifies also the specification of the parental labour supplies. Taking leisure as given, as is common practice in the fertility literature, the father's labour supply will then be simply equal to his work capacity, while the mother's will be given by

$$L_t = m - B_t, \tag{4}$$

where m is her annual work capacity, expressed as a multiple of the minimum amount of time required for each child.

The woman's wage rate in year t is given by

$$W_t = K_t w \tag{5}$$

where K_t is her stock of human capital at t, and w is the (real) market rate of return to human capital. Human capital is supposed to accumulate with work experience, so that

$$K_t = K_a + \beta \sum_{r=a}^{t-1} L_r \tag{6}$$

where β is a positive constant. K_a will depend on the woman's natural talent, education and pre-marital work experience. The husband's wage rate will be determined by a similar mechanism, the only difference being that his work experience is independent of the number and time distribution of births, while hers depends crucially on both.

Keeping in mind that any bequests made to a child born at t are included in I_t, we can then write the parents' lifetime budget constraint as

$$\sum_{t=a}^{T} \{B_t(q+I_t) + C_t\}(1+r)^{a-t} = A_a + \sum_{t=a}^{T} L_t W_t (1+r)^{a-t} \tag{7}$$

where r is the real rate of return to financial assets, and q is the fixed cost of a child, which includes all unavoidable expenditures associated with childbirth, plus the minimum cost of supporting the child. A_a is the couple's stock of wealth at marriage defined as their endowment of financial assets, plus the present value at marriage of the husband's lifetime earnings.

Additional restrictions on the choices of individual families are that $\{B_t, C_t, I_t, L_t\}$ must be nonnegative and, furthermore, that each B_t must be an integer. Our aim, however, is to predict the aggregate or average behaviour of a group of families with similar characteristics. Under the common assumption that aggregate behaviour is determined as if it were the outcome of a single optimising decision by the group as a whole, we shall then side-step the integer problem by interpreting our variables as averages over large numbers of similar families. By the same argument, we shall also assume that the boundary constraints are not binding for realistic values of the parameters, and can thus be ignored.

III. Efficient Paths

Parents are thus assumed to choose a sequence of birth and expenditure rates $\{B_t, C_t, I_t\}$ which maximises (1) subject to (7). The first order conditions are that, for each t,

$$U_c u_t(C_t) = \lambda(1+r)^{a-t}, \tag{8}$$

$$U_B v_t(I_t) = \lambda(1+r)^{a-t} \tag{9}$$

and

$$U_B v_t(I_t) = \lambda P_t (1+r)^{a-t}, \tag{10}$$

where

$$P_t = q + I_t + W_t + \beta w \sum_{r=t+1}^{T} L_r (1+r)^{t-r} \tag{11}$$

and λ is the Lagrange multiplier, equal to the marginal utility of wealth.

Being the sum of the three costs associated with the birth of a child in year t,

(i)   an actual disbursment, $(q + I_t)$,

(ii)   a loss of earnings, as the mother becomes temporarily unavailable for employment, W_t,

(iii)   a loss of future earning potential (evaluated at date t), as the mother has to forego an increment in her stock of human capital,

$$\beta w \sum_{r=t+1}^{T'} L_r (1+r)^{t-r}$$

the endogenously determined variable P_t represents the "price" that parents must pay in order to have a baby at t. Alternatively, since B_t is equal to the amount of time expended on child raising activities in year t, we can also interpret P_t as the price of keeping mother at home for a unit of time in year t.

3.1 Some General Rules

From (8) we derive the familiar Ramsey-Keynes Rule that the marginal utility of consumption must decline at the rate of interest:

$$\{u'_t - u'_{t+1}\} / u'_{t+1} = r. \tag{12}$$

Similarly, from (9) we find that the marginal utility of the wealth invested in children must decline at the rate of interest,

$$\{v'_t - v'_{t+1}\} / v'_{t+1} = r, \tag{13}$$

while the price of a birth of unit quality must grow at the same rate

$$\{[P_{t+1}/v_{t+1}] - [P_t/v_t]\} / [P_t/v_t] = r. \tag{14}$$

Condition (13) is another instance of the Ramsey-Keynes Rule, while (14) is the Hotelling Rule that the rate of extraction of a natural resource must be such, that its price will grow at the rate of interest. The resource being "extracted", in the present case, is the mother's time supplied to the labour market and, therefore, diverted from child raising activities, where it would attract the price P_t.

It should be noted that the rules in question do not hinge on a particular form of the utility function. Rather, they are efficiency criteria flowing from the assumption of perfect capital markets implicit in (7). Subject to that assumption, some such set of rules will apply to any couple, irrespectively of tastes and personal circumstances. If, on the other hand, parents had no access to borrowing and lending as assumed in HAPPEL et al. (1984), (7) would break into a sequence of annual budget constraints, and the nature of the solution could be quite different.

The dynamic system (12)-(13)-(14) determines the efficient paths of B_t, C_t and I_t up to arbitrary initial conditions. The profiles of C_t and I_t can be readily inferred from (12) and (13) without solving the system explicitly, but the same cannot be said of B_t, because the value of P_t at any t depends on the entire birth profile before and after t. Let us then specify

$$u_t(C_t) = C_t^{\gamma}(1+\delta)^{a-t}, \quad 0 < \gamma < 1, \tag{15}$$

and

$$v_t(I_t) = I_t^{\alpha}(1+\phi)^{-t}, \quad 0 < \alpha < 1, \tag{16}$$

where t is now measured from the beginning of the woman's reproductive span (assumed to be not later than the date of marriage). While the parameter δ reflects mere time preference, the parameter ϕ shows the effects of the mother's age on the quality of the child. Therefore, δ can have any sign, but ϕ must be positive and sufficiently large for $v_t(I_t)$ to become virtually zero (i.e. for no children to be born) at the end of the reproductive span whatever the value of I_t. Given a span of at most 40 years, this means that ϕ must be well in excess of 10 %.

3.2. Efficient Expenditure Profiles

Given (15), the solution of (12) is

$$C_t = C_a\{(1+r)/(1+\delta)\}^{\frac{t-a}{1-\gamma}}, \tag{17}$$

indicating that parental consumption will grow or decline over married life according to whether the real interest rate exceeds or falls short of the rate of time preference. Only if r happens to equal δ will consumption remain constant.

Similarly, for (16), the solution of (13) is

$$I_t = I_a(1+\pi)^{t-a} \tag{18}$$

where

$$\pi = \{(1+r)/(1+\phi)\}^{\frac{1}{1-\alpha}} - 1. \tag{19}$$

Therefore, the amount spent on each child depends, in general, on birth order. If r is less than ϕ, it is optimal to spend most on the first born, less on the second and so on; vice versa if r is greater than ϕ. If we allowed ϕ to vary over the woman's lifetime, assuming perhaps more realistically that ϕ is small over most of the reproductive span but rising very rapidly towards the end of it, then the parents would spend increasing amounts of money on successive children up to a point and rapidly decreasing amounts thereafter (if it is optimal to have children so late in life, which is generally not the case).

Whether ϕ is constant, as assumed here, or variable, it is only if r happens to equal ϕ at all dates that children will be equally treated. This is hardly surprising since B is, in effect, a Benthamite welfare function: a more general formulation would be needed to allow for the possibility that parents might wish to treat all their children equally, come what may, or to sustain the folklore that the middle child comes off worst.

3.3 Efficient Birth Profiles

Since

$$I_t = \alpha P_t \tag{20}$$

for (9), (10) and (16), we can also write, for (11),

$$\alpha P_{t+1} = \alpha\{q+I_{t+1}+K_a w+\beta w[m(t+1-a)-N_{t+1}+ \sum_{\tau=t+2}^{T} L_\tau (1+r)^{t-\tau}]\}$$

$$= I_a(1+\pi)^{t+1-a} \tag{21}$$

and

$$\alpha(1+r)P_t = \alpha(1+r)\{q+I_t+K_a w+\beta w[m(t-a)-N_t+ \sum_{\tau=t+1}^{T} L_\tau (1+r)^{t-\tau}]\}$$

$$= I_a(1+r)(1+\pi)^{t-a}, \tag{22}$$

where

$$N_t = \sum_{\tau=a}^{t-1} B_\tau \tag{23}$$

is the total number of children at t.

By subtracting (22) from (21) and using (4) we then find

$$I_{t+1} - (1+r)I_t = (I_a/\alpha)(\pi-r)(1+\pi)^{t-a}$$

$$+ rw\{K_a + \beta m(t-a)\} + rq$$

$$- \beta w\{N_{t+2} + 2N_{t+1} - (1+r)N_t\}. \tag{24}$$

On the other hand, for (18),

$$I_{t+1} - (1+r)I_t = I_a(\pi-r)(1+\pi)^{t-a}. \tag{25}$$

Therefore,

$$N_{t+2} - 2N_{t+1} + (1+r)N_t =$$

$$= \frac{1-\alpha}{\alpha} \frac{I_a}{\beta w} (\pi-r)(1+\pi)^{t-a} + r\{\frac{K_a w+q}{\beta w} + m(t-a)\}. \tag{26}$$

This is the fundamental equation governing the movement of the number of children through time.

The general solution of (26) is given by

$$N_t = \xi(\sqrt{1+r})^t \cos(tx+\rho)+\frac{K_a w+q}{\beta w} + m(t-a)+\frac{n}{\pi}I_a(1+\pi)^{t-a}, \tag{27}$$

where x is an angle with cosine equal to $(1+r)^{-\frac{1}{2}}$, ξ and ρ are arbitrary constants, and

$$n \equiv \frac{1-\alpha}{\alpha\beta w} \; \frac{\pi(\pi-r)}{r+\pi^2} \tag{28}$$

The desired birth profile is thus

$$B_t \equiv N_{t+1} - N_t$$

$$= m + nI_a(1+\pi)^{t-a} + \xi \sin \rho \sin tx(1-\sqrt{r})(\sqrt{1+r})^t . \tag{29}$$

Assuming that the number of children is zero at the date of marriage,

$$N_a = \xi(\sqrt{1+r})^a \cos(ax + \rho) + \frac{K_a w+a}{\beta w} + \frac{n}{\pi} I_a = 0 , \tag{30}$$

the value of ξ is given by

$$\xi = - \frac{\beta n I_a + \pi K_a + (\pi/w)q}{\beta\pi \cos(ax+\rho)} (\sqrt{1+r})^{-a} . \tag{31}$$

Thus,

$$B_t = m + nI_a(1+\pi)^{t-a} - \frac{\beta n I_a + \pi K_a + (\pi/w)q}{\beta\pi} \frac{\sin \rho \sin tx}{\cos(ax+\rho)}(1-\sqrt{r})(\sqrt{1+r})^{t-a} \tag{32}$$

On the other hand,

$$B_a = m + nI_a - \frac{\beta n I_a + \pi K_a + (\pi/w)q}{\beta\pi} \frac{\sin \rho \sin ax}{\cos(ax + \rho)}(1-\sqrt{r}) . \tag{33}$$

Hence, finally,

$$B_t = m + nI_a(1+\pi)^{t-a} - (m+nI_a-B_a)(\sqrt{1+r})^{t-a} \frac{\sin tx}{\sin ax} . \tag{34}$$

It is clear, from (28) and (34), that the properties of efficient birth profiles depend crucially on the values of ϕ and r. The former, as we have already established, must be greater than 10 %. The latter, on the other hand, is highly unlikely to be either negative or as high as 10 % for any extended period. Hence, in view of (19),

$$0 < 1+\pi < 1 . \tag{35}$$

If the real interest rate were zero, the efficient birth rate would then follow a path of exponential decline

$$B_t^* = B_a^* - nI_a^* \{1-(1+\pi)^{t-a}\}.\qquad(36)$$

If the real interest rate is positive, however, the efficient birth rate will fluctuate around (B_t^*). In other words, so long as borrowing is costly, births will tend to come in clusters.

It is also clear, from (36), that an increase in B_a would raise the whole birth profile. By contrast, an increase in nI_a would lower B_t^* at each t, but more at later ones. Therefore, the total number of children (completed fertility) is an increasing function of B_a and a decreasing one of nI_a, while the proportion born in the earlier years of marriage (the tempo of fertility) is increasing in nI_a. We are thus interested in how the choice of B_a and I_a is affected by differences in personal characteristics or changes in the exogenous variables.

IV. Comparative Dynamics

Having determined the efficient paths of B_t, C_t and I_t up to initial conditions (B_a, C_a, I_a), the optimisation problem reduces to choosing these initial conditions so as to maximise (1), where now

$$C = cC_a^\gamma \qquad (37)$$

and

$$B = \frac{I_a^\alpha}{(1+\phi)^a} \{b_2 B_a - \frac{b_1}{\beta w} I_a - b_0\}\ ,\qquad(38)$$

subject to the lifetime budget constraint, which can now be written as

$$A = E + F\ ,\qquad(39)$$

with

$$A = A_a + a_o K_a w + a_1 \beta w\ ,\qquad(40)$$

$$E = eC_a \qquad(41)$$

and

$$F = (q + I_a + K_a w)(f_2 B_a - \frac{f_1}{\beta w} I_a - f_0)\ .\qquad(42)$$

The constants a_i, b_i, c, e and f_i are defined in the Appendix.

By standard methods we then find that, at an optimum,

$$\frac{\partial B_a}{\partial A_a} = \frac{\partial A}{\partial A_a} \, i_B \, , \tag{43}$$

$$\frac{\partial B_a}{\partial K_a} = \frac{\partial^2 F}{\partial I_a \partial K_a} \, s_{BI} + \frac{\partial^2 F}{\partial B_a \partial K_a} \, s_{BB}$$

$$+ \left\{ \frac{\partial A}{\partial K_a} - \frac{\partial F}{\partial K_a} \right\} i_B \, , \tag{44}$$

$$\frac{\partial B_a}{\partial q} = \frac{\partial^2 F}{\partial I_a \partial q} \, s_{BI} + \frac{\partial^2 F}{\partial B_a \partial q} \, s_{BB} - \frac{\partial F}{\partial q} \, i_B \, , \tag{45}$$

$$\frac{\partial B_a}{\partial \beta} = - \frac{U_{CB}}{U_C} \frac{\partial E}{\partial C_a} \frac{\partial B}{\partial \beta} \, s_{BC}$$

$$- \left\{ \frac{U_B}{\lambda} \frac{\partial^2 B}{\partial I_a \partial \beta} + \frac{U_{BB}}{U_B} \frac{\partial F}{\partial I_a} \frac{\partial B}{\partial \beta} - \frac{\partial^2 F}{\partial I_a \partial \beta} \right\} s_{BI}$$

$$- \left\{ \frac{U_B}{\lambda} \frac{\partial^2 B}{\partial B_a \partial \beta} + \frac{U_{BB}}{U_B} \frac{\partial F}{\partial B_a} \frac{\partial B}{\partial \beta} - \frac{\partial^2 F}{\partial B_a \partial \beta} \right\} s_{BB}$$

$$+ \left\{ \frac{\partial A}{\partial \beta} - \frac{\partial F}{\partial \beta} \right\} i_B \, , \tag{46}$$

$$\frac{\partial B_a}{\partial w} = - \frac{U_{CB}}{U_C} \frac{\partial E}{\partial C_a} \frac{\partial B}{\partial w} \, s_{BC}$$

$$- \left\{ \frac{U_B}{\lambda} \frac{\partial^2 B}{\partial I_a \partial w} + \frac{U_{BB}}{U_B} \frac{\partial F}{\partial I_a} \frac{\partial B}{\partial w} - \frac{\partial^2 F}{\partial I_a \partial w} \right\} s_{BI}$$

$$- \left\{ \frac{U_B}{\lambda} \frac{\partial^2 B}{\partial B_a \partial w} + \frac{U_{BB}}{U_B} \frac{\partial F}{\partial B_a} \frac{\partial B}{\partial w} - \frac{\partial^2 F}{\partial B_a \partial w} \right\} s_{BB}$$

$$+ \left\{ \frac{\partial A}{\partial w} - \frac{\partial F}{\partial w} \right\} i_B \tag{47}$$

and [3)]

$$\frac{\partial B_a}{\partial a} = - \frac{U_{CB}}{U_C} \frac{\partial E}{\partial C_a} \frac{\partial B}{\partial a} s_{BC}$$

$$- \{ \frac{U_B}{\lambda} \frac{\partial^2 b}{\partial I_a \partial a} + \frac{U_{BB}}{U_B} \frac{\partial F}{\partial I_a} \frac{\partial B}{\partial a} \} s_{BI}$$

$$- \{ \frac{U_B}{\lambda} \frac{\partial^2 B}{\partial B_a \partial a} + \frac{U_{BB}}{U_B} \frac{\partial F}{\partial B_a} \frac{\partial B}{\partial a} \} s_{BB} , \qquad (48)$$

where i_B denotes the effect on B_a of an increase in A, and s_{BJ} the compensated effect on B_a of an increase in the marginal cost of J $(J = B_a, C_a, I_a)$. [4)]

Similarly,

$$\frac{\partial I_a}{\partial A_a} = \frac{\partial A}{\partial A_a} i_I , \qquad (49)$$

$$\frac{\partial I_a}{\partial K_a} = \frac{\partial^2 F}{\partial I_a \partial K_a} s_{II} + \frac{\partial^2 F}{\partial B_a \partial K_a} s_{IB}$$

$$+ \{ \frac{\partial A}{\partial K_a} - \frac{\partial F}{\partial K_a} \} i_I , \qquad (50)$$

$$\frac{\partial I_a}{\partial q} = \frac{\partial^2 F}{\partial I_a \partial q} s_{II} + \frac{\partial^2 F}{\partial B_a \partial q} s_{IB}$$

$$- \frac{\partial F}{\partial q} i_I , \qquad (51)$$

[3)] Strictly speaking we should not differentiate with respect to the date of marriage, because time is a discrete variable, but as usual we shall seek to approximate the effects of finite changes in the exogenous variables by those of infinitesimal changes.

[4)] The presence of substitution and cross-substitution effects side by side in the same expression - characteristic of fertility models - is due to the fact that a rise in child quality increases the marginal cost of giving birth, while a rise in the birth rate increases the marginal cost of quality.

$$\frac{\partial I_a}{\partial \beta} = -\frac{U_{CB}}{U_C} \frac{\partial E}{\partial C_a} \frac{\partial B}{\partial \beta} s_{IC}$$

$$-\{\frac{U_B}{\lambda} \frac{\partial^2 B}{\partial I_a \partial \beta} + \frac{U_{BB}}{U_B} \frac{\partial F}{\partial I_a} \frac{\partial B}{\partial \beta} - \frac{\partial^2 F}{\partial I_a \partial \beta}\} s_{II}$$

$$-\{\frac{U_B}{\lambda} \frac{\partial^2 B}{\partial B_a \partial \beta} + \frac{U_{BB}}{U_B} \frac{\partial F}{\partial B_a} \frac{\partial B}{\partial \beta} - \frac{\partial^2 F}{\partial B_a \partial \beta}\} s_{IB}$$

$$+\{\frac{\partial A}{\partial \beta} - \frac{\partial F}{\partial \beta}\} i_I , \tag{52}$$

$$\frac{\partial I_a}{\partial w} = -\frac{U_{CB}}{U_C} \frac{\partial E}{\partial C_a} \frac{\partial B}{\partial w} s_{IC}$$

$$-\{\frac{U_B}{\lambda} \frac{\partial^2 B}{\partial I_a \partial w} + \frac{U_{BB}}{U_B} \frac{\partial F}{\partial I_a} \frac{\partial B}{\partial w} - \frac{\partial^2 F}{\partial I_a \partial w}\} s_{II}$$

$$-\{\frac{U_B}{\lambda} \frac{\partial^2 B}{\partial B_a \partial w} + \frac{U_{BB}}{U_B} \frac{\partial F}{\partial B_a} \frac{\partial B}{\partial w} - \frac{\partial^2 F}{\partial B_a \partial w}\} s_{IB}$$

$$+\{\frac{\partial A}{\partial w} - \frac{\partial F}{\partial w}\} i_I \tag{53}$$

and

$$\frac{\partial I_a}{\partial a} = -\frac{U_{CB}}{U_C} \frac{\partial E}{\partial C_a} \frac{\partial B}{\partial a} s_{IC}$$

$$-\{\frac{U_B}{\lambda} \frac{\partial^2 B}{\partial I_a \partial a} + \frac{U_{BB}}{U_B} \frac{\partial F}{\partial I_a} \frac{\partial B}{\partial a}\} s_{II}$$

$$-\{\frac{U_B}{\lambda} \frac{\partial^2 B}{\partial B_a \partial a} + \frac{U_{BB}}{U_B} \frac{\partial F}{\partial B_a} \frac{\partial B}{\partial a}\} s_{IB} , \tag{54}$$

where i_I is the effect on I_a of an increase in A.

The expressions describing the overall effects of a, A_a, K_a and q may be signed by assuming that income effects are positive but small (relative to substitution and cross-substitution effects), and that the marginal utility of B does not fall too quickly as B increases (U_{BB} small in size relative to U_B). Under these assumptions, we find that B_a is increasing in A_a, but decreasing in a, K_a and q, while I_a is increasing in all four exogenous variables. Consequently, the tempo of fertility increases with all these exogenous variables, while completed fertility decreases with a, K_a and q, and may increase or decrease, as A_a increases, depending on the relative size of the income effects on B_a and I_a.

By contrast, the responses of B_a and I_a to changes in β or w cannot be signed under any plausible set of assumptions. It may be surmised, therefore, that these responses are generally inelastic. Since, on the other hand, n is inversely proportional to β and w, we can then conclude that nI_a and, therefore, the tempo of fertility decreases as β or w increase.

V.   Discussion and Conclusion

The predictions of the model under the special assumptions stated are summarised in Table 1, where completed fertility is represented by N (equal to N_T) and the tempo of fertility by ν (an increasing function of nI_a).

Table 1
Effects of exogenous variables

	B_a	I_a	N	ν
a	−	+	−	+
A_a	+	+	?	+
K_a	−	+	−	+
q	−	+	−	+
β	?	?	?	−
w	?	?	?	−

N = completed fertility   ν = tempo of fertility

Other things being equal, women with greater financial assets at
marriage, or married to men with higher incomes, may thus be expected
to have a larger proportion of their children earlier in married life -
but not necessarily to have more children, because they will also spend
more on each child. The same is predicted for women who marry late or
are endowed with more human capital (greater earning ability) at the
time of marriage, except that these women will definitely have fewer
children. On the other hand, women in occupations characterised by
steeper earning profiles will tend to have their children later. Therefore, if women with greater initial human capital, or women who marry
late, tend to be in professions where the wage rate rises sharply with
seniority of service, that could offset the tendency to earlier motherhood.

Paradoxically, a rise in q would raise the amount that parents
spend voluntarily for each child in addition to q, and increase the
proportion of early births, but it would reduce the total number of
births. A general rise in married men's wages (higher A_a) would also
raise expenditure per child and the tempo of fertility, but it is not
clear what would happen to completed fertility: possibly little. By
contrast, a general rise in married women's wage rates (higher w) would
lower the tempo of fertility.

These predictions could help us to interpret the post-war experience
of Western Europe. As reported in HÖPFLINGER (1984) and MUÑOZ PEREZ
(1986), completed fertility has been falling over successive cohorts
of women born since 1940. Such a decline was initially offset, in the
1950s and 1960s, by a tendency to have children at younger ages, but
not any more since the 1970s, when the tempo of fertility went into reverse. Even though there are now signs that completed fertility is
levelling out, period fertility is nonetheless declining and, in many
countries, it has already fallen below replacement level.

The fall of completed fertility and the tendency to younger motherhood observed in the two earlier decades could be explained, in the
light of our model, by the contemporaneous rise in female education and
labour force participation before marriage, both of which would lead
to rising K_a and, therefore, falling N and rising ν. As the proportion
of educated and working women increased, however, the rate of increase
in that proportion will have fallen. At the same time and for the same
reason, an increasing proportion of women is likely to have entered
occupations characterised by steep career structures (high β), thus
helping to explain why the earlier trends in the quantum and tempo
of fertility have tended to flatten out, and why the tempo has eventu-

ally moved into reverse. Rises in w relative to A_a due to lessening
sex discrimination over pay and, in some countries, to increases in
male relative to female unemployment - might have further strengthened
the advantages of delaying motherhood.

The model's predictions have also implications for the demographic
consequences of various economic policies. Higher taxes on married
women's earnings - equivalent to a fall in w - would raise the tempo of
childbearing, probably without any noticeable consequence for the quality and number of children. By contrast, higher taxes on married men's
earnings - equivalent to a fall in A_a - would delay childbirth and lower
the quality of children, possibly without much change in number. And
finally, a rise in child benefits - equivalent to a fall in q - or
a policy resulting in lower ages of marriage would increase completed
fertility, but the tempo of fertility and the amount spent on each
child would fall.

If a government were content with the existing trend of completed
fertility and were simply concerned to counter the current tendency
to late motherhood, a less favourable tax treatment of married women's
earnings would probably do the job with a minimum of side effects. In
most West European countries, however, that would entail a negative
rate of population growth in the long run, because the completed fertility of recent cohorts of women is expected to be less than 2.

Confronted with the prospect of long term demographic decline,
the typical response of a society is to call for incentives to natility -
usually in the form of higher subsidies to families with children - and
of measures, particularly in the housing field, designed to facilitate
early marriage. But, while raising period fertility in the long run,
such policies lower the tempo of childbearing and, therefore, reduce
period fertility in the short run; they also reduce the amount spent
on each child. To counter these negative side effects, taxes on married
men's earnings must then be cut at the same time. Higher taxes on married
women's earnings are a useful adjoint to the policy package in that
they help ensure that its net effect on the tempo of fertility is indeed positive and, not least, help raise finance for the other policies.

Appendix

The constants figuring in equations (38) to (43) are defined as follows:

$$a_o \equiv m \sum_{t=a}^{T} (1+r)^{a-t} \tag{A.1}$$

$$a_1 \equiv m^2 \sum_{t=a}^{T} (t-a)(1+r)^{a-t} , \tag{A.2}$$

$$b_o \equiv - m \sum_{t-a}^{T} \left\{ 1 - \frac{\sin tx}{\sin ax} (1+r)^{\frac{t-a}{2}} \right\} \left\{ \frac{(1+\pi)^\alpha}{1+\phi} \right\}^{t-a} , \tag{A.3}$$

$$b_1 \equiv - \frac{1-\alpha}{\alpha} \frac{\pi(\pi-r)}{r+\pi^2} \sum_{t-a}^{T} \left\{ 1 - \frac{\sin tx}{\sin ax} [\frac{\sqrt{1+r}}{1+\pi}]^{t-a} \right\} \left\{ \frac{(1+\pi)^{1+\alpha}}{1+\phi} \right\}^{t-a} , \tag{A.4}$$

$$b_2 \equiv \sum_{t=a}^{T} \frac{\sin tx}{\sin ax} \left\{ \frac{(1+\pi)^\alpha (1+r)^{\frac{1}{2}}}{1+\phi} \right\}^{t-a} , \tag{A.5}$$

$$c \equiv \sum_{t=a}^{T} \left\{ \frac{(1+0)^\gamma}{1+\delta} \right\}^{t-a} , \tag{A.6}$$

$$c \equiv \sum_{t=a}^{T} \left\{ \frac{1+0}{1+r} \right\}^{t-a} , \tag{A.7}$$

$$f_o \equiv - m \sum_{t=a}^{T} \left\{ 1 - \frac{\sin tx}{\sin ax} (1+r)^{\frac{t-a}{2}} \right\} [\frac{1+\pi}{1+r}]^{t-a} , \tag{A.8}$$

$$f_1 \equiv - \frac{1-\alpha}{\alpha} \frac{\pi(\pi-r)}{r+\pi^2} \sum_{t=a}^{T} \left\{ 1 - \frac{\sin tx}{\sin ax} [\frac{\sqrt{1+r}}{1+\pi}]^{t-a} \right\} \left\{ \frac{(1+\pi)^2}{1+r} \right\}^{t-a} \tag{A.9}$$

and

$$f_2 \equiv \sum_{t=a}^{T} \frac{\sin tx}{\sin ax} [\frac{1+\pi}{\sqrt{1+r}}]^{t-a} \tag{A.10}$$

References

BECKER, G., A Treatise on the Family. Harvard University Press, 1981

BUTZ, W. P. and M. P. WARD, The emergence of countercyclical US fertility. American Economic Review, 1979.

CIGNO, A., Human capital and the time profile of human fertility. Economics Letters, 1983.

CIGNO, A., Fertility and the tax benefit system: a reconsideration of the theory of family taxation. Economic Journal, 1986.

DE COOMAN, E., J. ERMISCH and H. JOSHI, The next birth and the labour market; a dynamic model of births in England and Wales. Discussion Paper No. 37, Centre for Economic Policy Research, 1985.

ERMISCH, J., The relevance of the Easterlin hypothesis and the 'New Home Economics' to fertility movements in Great Britain. Population Studies, 1979.

HAPPEL, S. K., J. K. HILL and S. A. LOW, An economic analysis of the timing of childbirth. Population Studies, 1984.

HÖPFLINGER, F., Cohort fertility in Western Europe: comparing fertility trends in recent birth cohorts. Gonus, 1984.

LEE, R. D., Aiming at a moving target: period fertility and changing reproductive goals. Population Studies, 1980.

MUÑOZ-PEREZ, P., Changements recents de la fecondite en Europe occidentale et nouveaus traits de la formation des familles. Population, 1986.

RAZIN, A., Number, spacing and quality of children, in J. L. Simon and J. Da Vanzo (eds.). Research in Population Economics, Vol. 2, JAI Press, 1980.

SCHULTZ, T. P., An economic interpretation of the decline in fertility in a rapidly developing country, in R. Easterlin (ed.) Population and Economic Change in Developing Countries. University of Chicago Press, 1976.

WILLIS, R. J., A new approach to the economic theory of fertility behaviour. Journal of Political Economy, 1973.

WINEGARDEN, C. R., Women's fertility, market work and marital status: a test of the 'New Household Economics' with international data', Economica, 1984.

EQUILIBRIUM AND EFFICIENCY IN INTERGENERATIONAL TRANSFERS

Uri Ben-Zion and Mark Gradstein
Faculty of Industrial Engineering and Management
Technion - Israel Institute of Technology

Haifa 32000 / Israel

ABSTRACT: The focus of our study concerns a family consisting of two altruistic agents, the parent and the child. The model is cast within a two period framework where, in the first period, the parent decides on the allocation of his resources between consumption and investment in the human capital of his child, and, in the second period, the child has to decide how much of his (acquired through the parent's transfer) wealth to give away for the support of his parent. Our first result establishes that the outcome of the game of transfer is inefficient; then we proceed by investigating possible means of attaining efficiency; finally, we analyze the impact of uncertainty regarding child's preferences on the game equilibrium.

I.   Introduction

In two well known papers, BECKER has analyzed a model of intrafamily transfers (BECKER, 1974, 1976). His model presumes a family consisting of two agents - an altruistic parent and a selfish child. The child chooses an action which affects the family's income; subsequent to this choice the parent makes a transfer to the child which determines his own and his child's consumption. If child's consumption is a normal good, the larger the total income is the bigger is the parent's transfer and, consequently, the child's final consumption level. Therefore, the child, in his attempt to maximize his own welfare, will choose an action which maximizes the family's income. In other words (this is the content of BECKER's "rotten kid theorem"), altruistic parents transfers to selfish children provide the latter with optimal incentives.

In our model, as in BECKER's, there are two agents - a parent and a child. However, in contrast to BECKER, both of them are altruists. The sequence of moves is as follows. First, the parent (who initially holds all the wealth) decides on the allocation of his resources between consumption and investment in the human capital of his child; in the second stage, the child has to decide how much of his (acquired through the parent's transfer) wealth to give away for the support of his parent. Thus, we make use of HIRSHLEIFER's insightful remark that the sequence of moves between parents and children might be important and that it

We are grateful to Alois Wenig for the opportunity to present this paper at the Conference on Demographic Change and Economic Development, Hagen (West Germany), 29-30 September, 1986, and to an anonymous referee for his helpful remarks.

is tenable to assume the children as having the last word (HIRSHLEIFER,
1977). Our main result establishes that externalities between the parent
and his child, due to their mutual utility interdependence, result in
inefficient equilibrium transfers.[1] That is, there is a system of
transfers such that the position of at least one of the agents is better
off while the position of the other is not worse off than in equilibrium.
Thus, laissez-faire fails, and the government should intervene to ensure
efficiency in intrafamily transfers. It turns out that one possible means
of attaining efficiency consists of providing the parent with social
security. Specifically, there exists a level of social security for the
parent (financed by a lump-sum tax on the child), such that the resulting
equilibrium is efficient. In this equilibrium, although the child makes
no transfer to the parent, the latter attains his maximal utility. Another possibility is to subsidize the child by means of a lump sum tax
on the parent's first period wealth. We prove that if the tax level is
sufficiently high, the resulting equilibrium is efficient. Then we proceed by considering the case in which the parent can transfer part of
his wealth into the second period by means of saving. It turns out that,
generally, this possibility does not solve the inefficiency problem but
may restore efficiency, in particular cases (for example, when the
parent and the child are sufficiently egoistic). Finally, we investigate
the impact of incomplete information about child's preferences on the
equilibrium.

Section II describes the basic model; Section III compares laissez-
faire and centralized solutions; Section IV deals with government intervention in form of social security; Section V introduces the possibility of saving; Section VI analyzes the case of uncertainty regarding
child's preferences. Section VII summarizes the findings.

II. Formulation

Consider a family consisting of two persons - P (a parent) and C (a
child) - both of whom are altruistic towards each other. The meaning of
the latter assumption is that each of them derive utility not only
from their own consumption, but also from that of the other family
member. The respective preferences of P and C over different consumption bundles are represented by utility functions $u^P(x,y)$ and $u^C(x,y)$
which are assumed to increase in both arguments and satisfy the standard
concavity conditions. In addition we assume that $\lim_{x \to 0} u_1^i(x,y) = \infty$,
$\lim_{y \to 0} u_2^i(x,y) = \infty$ for $i = P, C$. Initially the whole family wealth - W -
belongs to P who has to decide on its allocation between his own con-

sumption and the transfer to C. The total amount made over by P to C in the first period is denoted x_{PC}. We assume that it is made in form of investment in the human capital of C: thus, x_{PC} represents not only direct money transfers from the parent to the child but also includes expenses for education, health care, etc. The return on this investment is $g(x_{PC})$ where $g(\cdot)$ is an increasing, concave function. In fact, $g(x_{PC})$ is the amount of C's wealth. In the first period P derives utility from his own consumption and from C's wealth: $u^P[W-x_{PC}, g(x_{PC})].$[2] C is assumed to possess no utility in the first period.[3]

In the second period C has to decide which part of his wealth to consume and which part to transfer to P. The amount of C's transfer to P, denoted x_{CP}, represents the only source of P's consumption in the second period; thus, P's subsistence depends on C's transfer. C's utility in the second period (in fact, his total utility) is $u^C[x_{CP}, g(x_{PC}) - x_{CP}]$. P's second period utility is $u^P[x_{CP}, g(x_{PC}) - x_{CP}]$ hence, his total utility equals $u^P[W-x_{CP}, g(x_{PC})] + \beta u^P[x_{CP}, g(x_{PC}) - x_{CP}]$ where $0 < \beta < 1$ is the discount rate. (Note that we assume additive utility; for a similar approach see also RAZIN and BEN-ZION (1975).)

The described situation can be represented by a leader-follower game. In the first stage of the game P makes his move, and then it is C's turn to respond. The players' strategies are (x_{PC}, x_{CP}) where $0 \leq x_{CP} \leq g(x_{PC})$, and their respective payoffs are as follows:

$$u^P[W-x_{PC}, g(x_{PC})] + \beta u^P[x_{CP}, g(x_{PC}) - x_{CP}] \qquad (1)$$

$$u^C[x_{CP}, g(x_{PC}) - x_{CP}] \qquad (2)$$

It can be easily established that under our assumptions the game has an equilibrium. The next section contains equilibrium and efficiency analysis.

III. Equilibrium and Pareto Optimality

To characterize the equilibrium in our game, we proceed by backward reasoning. In the second stage the child C maximizes his utility for every possible amount of transfer x_{PC} made by the parent in the first period. Thus, he has to solve the following problem:

$$\max_{0 \leq x_{CP} \leq g(x_{PC})} u^C[x_{CP}, g(x_{PC}) - x_{CP}] \qquad (3)$$

Under our assumptions, (3) always has a unique solution. Denote

$$x_{CP}^{*}(x_{PC}) = \underset{0 \le x_{CP} \le g(x_{PC})}{argmax} \; u^{C}[x_{CP}, y(x_{PC}) - x_{CP}] \qquad (4)$$

($x_{CP}^{*}(x_{PC})$ is the child's best response function.) Given $x_{CP}^{*}(x_{PC})$, P maximizes his total utility by choosing the optimal bequest x_{PC}. Substituting from (4) into (1), the parent's problem is given as follows:

$$\underset{0 \le x_{PC} \le W}{max} \; u^{P}[W - x_{PC}, g(x_{PC})] + \beta u^{P}[x_{CP}^{*}(x_{PC}), g(x_{PC}) - x_{CP}^{*}(x_{PC})] \qquad (5)$$

Differentiating (5) with respect to x_{PC} and assuming an internal solution we obtain:

$$-u_{1}^{P} + u_{2}^{P}g' + \beta[u_{1}^{P}\frac{dx_{CP}^{*}}{dx_{PC}} + u_{2}^{P}g' - u_{2}^{P}\frac{dx_{CP}^{*}}{dx_{PC}}] = 0 \qquad (6)$$

where x_{CP}^{*} satisfies

$$u_{1}^{C} - u_{2}^{C} = 0 \qquad (7)$$

(as usual, functions with subscript i denote partial derivatives with respect to the ith argument). By total differentiation of (7) with respect to x_{CP}^{*} and x_{PC}, we obtain

$$\frac{dx_{CP}^{*}}{dx_{PC}} = \frac{u_{22}^{C} - u_{12}^{C}}{u_{11}^{C} - 2u_{12}^{C} + u_{22}^{C}} \; g' \qquad (8)$$

which after substituting into (6) finally yields:

$$-u_{1}^{P} + u_{2}^{P}g' + \beta u_{2}^{P}g' + \beta(u_{1}^{P} - u_{2}^{P})\frac{(u_{22}^{C} - u_{12}^{C})g'}{u_{11}^{C} - 2u_{12}^{C} + u_{22}^{C}} = 0 \qquad (9)$$

The equilibrium system of transfers satisfies simultaneously (7) and (9).

The system of Pareto optimal transfers is defined as a pair (x_{PC}, x_{CP}) such that no other pair exists which betters off the position of at least one of the agents without worsening the position of the other. To find the efficient system of transfers we have to maximize parent's utility while keeping child's utility on a fixed level. That is, we have to solve

$$\max_{0 \leq x_{PC} \leq W} \quad u^P[W-x_{PC}, g(x_{PC})] + \beta u^P[x_{CP}, g(x_{PC})-x_{CP}]$$

$$0 \leq x_{CP} \leq g(x_{PC})$$

$$\text{(10)}$$

$$\text{s.t.} \quad u^C[x_{CP}, g(x_{PC}) - x_{CP}] = \bar{u}^C$$

Again assuming an internal solution, we obtain after solving (10)

$$-u_1^P + u_2^P g' + \beta u_2^P g' + \beta (u_1^P - u_2^P) \frac{u_2^C g'}{u_2^C - u_1^C} = 0 \tag{11}$$

It can be seen that generally the solution of (7) and (9) differs from that of (11), which implies that the equilibrium is inefficient.

IV.   Government Intervention to Ensure Efficiency

In the preceding section we have seen that in the game of intrafamily transfers equilibrium is inefficient, and the question arises how the government can secure efficiency. We will explore two possible means of attaining efficiency. One such means is to provide the parent with social security in the second period, such that his subsistence would not depend solely on his child's transfers. It turns out that if the level of social security is high enough, then in equilibrium C does not make any transfer to P; P's second period wealth (and consumption) consists of the social security provided by the government, and the equilibrium is efficient. The second possibility is to make a lump sum transfer from the parent to the child in the first period (consider, for example, taxes on the parent used to finance the education of the child). Again, if the level of the lump sum transfer is high enough, then effi-ciency is attained: in the equilibrium the parent will make no volun-tarily transfer to the child (the corner solution).

(i)   Social Security

Let I denote the amount of social security alloted to P in the second period and assumed to be financed by a lump-sum tax on C's second period wealth. Under this assumption the respective payoffs of P and C are as follows

$$u^P[W-x_{PC},g(x_{PC})] + \beta u^P[x_{CP}+I,g(x_{PC})-x_{CP}-I] \qquad (12)$$

and

$$u^C[x_{CP}+I,g(x_{PC})-x_{CP}-I] \qquad (13)$$

From (12) it is evident that for each x_{PC} there is a level of I --
$I^*(x_{PC}) \leq g(x_{PC})$, such that P's maximal utility is attained at $x_{CP} = 0$.
Similarly, from (13) it follows that there is $I^{**}(x_{PC}) \leq g(x_{PC})$ such
that C's maximal utility is attained at $x_{CP} = 0$. Denote

$$\bar{I} = \max_{0 \leq x_{PC} \leq W} [I^*(x_{PC}), I^{**}(x_{PC})].$$

Thus, $\bar{I}$ is the level of social security under which both P and C prefer
C's transfer to P to be equal to zero, regardless of the amount of P's
bequest. We assert that $\bar{I}$ is the required level of social security.

Indeed, let

$$\bar{x}_{PC} = \underset{0 \leq x_{PC} \leq W}{\operatorname{argmax}} \; u^P[W-x_{PC},g(x_{PC})] + \beta u^P[\bar{I},g(x_{PC})-\bar{I}].$$

Then $(\bar{x}_{PC},0)$ is clearly equilibrium (both agents prefer not to deviate
from the equilibrium strategy). Moreover, this equilibrium is efficient
since P arrives in $(\bar{x}_{PC},0)$ at his maximal utility.

(ii) Lump Sum Transfer from the Parent to the Child

Let T denote the amount of lump sum taxes on the parent's first period
wealth transferred as a subsidy to the child. The respective utility
functions of the parent and the child are as follows:

$$u^P[w-T-x_{PC},g(x_{PC}+T)] + \beta u^P[x_{CP},g(x_{PC}+T) - x_{CP}]$$

$$u^C[x_{CP},g(x_{PC}+T)-x_{CP}].$$

Using our assumptions it can be easily shown that there exists a sufficiently high level of T --T^*, $T^* \leq W$ -- such that in the equilibrium the amount of the parent's voluntarily transfer to the child is zero. Let $x_{CP}^* = \underset{x_{CP}}{\mathrm{argmax}}\ u^C[x_{CP}, g(T^*)-x_{CP}]$. Clearly $(0, x_{CP}^*)$ is the equilibrium. Moreover, since the parent attains his maximal utility, this equilibrium is efficient.

V.   Saving as a Means of Attaining Efficiency

The model developed in the previous sections did not allow for the possibility of saving: the only means for the parent to secure his subsistence in the second period was by a transfer to his child. In the present section we allow for the possibility of saving and examine its impact on intergenerational transfers. As we shall see, in some cases provision for saving may lead to efficiency.

Let s denote the amount of P's saving. The respective utility functions of P and C are now formulated as follows:

$$u^P[w - x_{PC} - s, g(x_{PC})] + \beta u^P[s(1+r)+x_{CP}, -x_{CP}] \qquad (14)$$

$$u^C[s(1+r) + x_{CP}, g(x_{PC}) - x_{CP}] \qquad (15)$$

(here r denotes the interest rate). The parent now chooses the vector (x_{PC}, s), while the child controls x_{CP}. When equilibrium is internal, it is given by differentiating (14) with respect to x_{PC} and s, and (15) with respect to x_{CP} and equating the resulting expressions to zero. As can be verified directly by comparing these equilibrium conditions to the conditions for Pareto optimality, this equilibrium is not efficient. However, when the equilibrium is not internal, it can be efficient as the following argument shows.

Denote U^P the class of P's utility functions for which the maximum of P's utility is attained when $x_{CP} = 0$. That is,

$$U^P = \{u^P : \Omega^P \text{ is not empty}\}$$

where

$$\Omega^P = \{(s, x_{PC}, x_{CP}): (s, x_{PC}, 0) = \mathrm{argmax}\ u^P\}.$$

Clearly, U^P is not empty (consider for example the case when the child is egoist). Similarly, let $U^C = \{u^C:\Omega^C$ is not empty$\}$ where

$$\Omega^C = \{(s,x_{PC},x_{CP}) \; : \; (s,x_{PC},0) = \text{argmax } u^C\}.$$

Now choose $u^P \varepsilon U^P$ and $u^C \varepsilon U^C$ in such a way that $\Omega^P \cap \Omega^C \neq \phi$.[4] The elements of $\Omega^P \cap \Omega^C$ are of the form $(s,x_{PC},0)$, they constitute equilibrium and satisfy the efficiency condition, since the parent attains his maximal utility. This completes the argument.

VI.   Uncertainty Regarding Child's Preferences

In this section we deal with the case in which the information on the child's preferences is incomplete. We shall assume for simplicity that the child's utility is of the Cobb-Douglas type, and that the parameter measuring the elasticity of demand under this specification is the source of the incomplete information. In other words,

$$u^C[x_{CP},g(x_{CP}) - x_{CP}] = x_{CP}^{\tilde{\alpha}}[g(x_{PC}) - x_{CP}]^{1-\tilde{\alpha}}$$

where $\tilde{\alpha}$ is a random variable, such that $\Pr(0 < \tilde{\alpha} \leq 1) = 1$. In this case equilibrium is represented by a pair $(x_{PC}^*, \tilde{x}_{CP}^*)$ where $\tilde{x}_{CP}^*$ is a random variable (being a function of $\tilde{\alpha}$).

Since C's best response function is given by $x_{CP} = \tilde{\alpha}g(x_{PC})$, P's problem is to maximize his expected total utility, which is written as follows:

$$E\{u^P[W-x_{PC},g(x_{PC})] + \beta u^P[\tilde{\alpha}g(x_{PC}),(1-\tilde{\alpha})g(x_{PC})]\} \tag{16}$$

The certainty case analogue of (16) is obtained by substituting instead of the random variable $\tilde{\alpha}$ its expected value $-\bar{\alpha}$:

$$u^P[W - x_{PC},g(x_{PC})] + \beta u^P[\bar{\alpha}g(x_{PC}), (1-\bar{\alpha})g(x_{PC})] \tag{17}$$

In this section our major concern is to compare the equilibrium transfers in the case of certainty with that of uncertainty. Denote the maximizing value of (16) x_{PC}^*, and that of (17) will be denoted x_{PC}^{**}. (Note that, given our assumptions on the parent's preferences, both values are unique.) Our aim is to prove that $x_{PC}^* < x_{PC}^{**}$, that is the amount of P's transfer is less in the certainty case. To pursue this aim we first need the fact that the function

$$E\{u^P(\tilde{\alpha}g(x_{PC}), (1-\tilde{\alpha})g(x_{PC})) - u^P(\bar{\alpha}g(x_{PC}),(1-\bar{\alpha})g(x_{PC}))]$$

decreases in x_{PC}. The proof of this fact, being rather cumbersome, is relegated to the Appendix.

Suppose that $x_{PC}^* \geq x_{PC}^{**}$. Since x_{PC}^{**} maximizes (17), it turns out that

$$u^P[W - x_{PC}^{**}, g(x_{PC}^{**})] + \beta u^P[\bar{\alpha}g(x_{PC}^{**}), (1-\bar{\alpha})g(x_{PC}^{**})] >$$

$$u^P[W - x_{PC}^*, g(x_{PC}^*)] + \beta u^P[\bar{\alpha}g(x_{PC}^*), (1-\bar{\alpha})g(x_{PC}^*)] \qquad (18)$$

while from the result in the Appendix it follows that

$$\beta E[u^P(\tilde{\alpha}g(x_{PC}^{**}), (1-\tilde{\alpha})g(x_{PC}^{**})) - u^P(\bar{\alpha}g(x_{PC}^{**}), (1-\bar{\alpha})g(x_{PC}^{**}))] \geq$$

$$\beta E[u^P(\tilde{\alpha}g(x_{PC}^*),(1-\tilde{\alpha})g(x_{PC}^*)) - u^P(\bar{\alpha}g(x_{PC}^*),(1-\bar{\alpha})g(x_{PC}^*))] \qquad (19)$$

Adding (18) and (19), we have

$$u^P[W-x_{PC}^{**},g(x_{PC}^{**})] + \beta E[u^P(\tilde{\alpha}g(x_{PC}^{**}),(1-\tilde{\alpha})g(x_{PC}^{**}))] >$$

$$u^P[W-x_{PC}^*,g(x_{PC}^*)] + \beta E[u^P(\tilde{\alpha}g(x_{PC}^*),(1-\tilde{\alpha})g(x_{PC}^*))] \qquad (20)$$

But (20) contradicts the assumption that x_{PC}^* is the maximizer of (16). Therefore, $x_{PC}^* < x_{PC}^{**}$. The expected value of the child's transfer in the second period is likewise clearly less than in the certainty case.

It is interesting to note that in the case of uncertainty both parent and child are at a disadvantage; the expected utility of both of them is less than in the certainty case. Thus, it would be better for both that the child's behavior be certain.

VII. Concluding Remarks

In this paper we concentrated on the equilibrium and efficiency analysis of intrafamily transfers. Assuming a family which consists of two altruistic agents - a parent and a child - we first proved that the cecentralized system of transfers - from the parent to the child and from the child to the parent - is inefficient. This result is obtained due to the utility interdependence between the two agents. Then we

proceed by showing that the government can ensure efficiency by providing the parent with a social security which makes him independent
of his child's transfer. Another means of attaining efficiency is by
a subsidy to the child financed by a lump sum tax on the parent's wealth.
In some cases efficiency also can be attained in a model allowing for
the possibility of parent's saving. An intuitive explanation for this
is that the possibility of saving decreases parent's dependence on the
provision made by his child. In the last section of the paper we investigate the impact of uncertainty about the child's preferences on
the equilibrium. It turns out that in the uncertainty case, the amount
of transfers, both from the parent to the child and from the child
to the parent, is less than in the certainty case analogue.

Recently there have been made some attempts in the literature
of modelling intrafamily transfers - see, for example, BECKER (1976),
BERNHEIM et al. (1985), NERLOVE et al. (1985). Invariably, in these
papers, some externalities (via utility interdependence of the family
members) were introduced and their impact on the efficiency of transfers were scrutinized. Our paper can be viewed as an additional attempt
in this direction. We arrived at the conclusion that in the absence of
saving opportunities, intrafamily transfers result in inefficiency
and we indicated how the government can overcome this problem by different
means.

Appendix

<u>Claim</u>. The function $E[u^P(\tilde{\alpha}g(x_{PC}), (1-\bar{\alpha})g(x_{PC})) - u^P(\bar{\alpha}g(x_{PC}), (1-\bar{\alpha})g(x_{PC}))]$ decreases in x_{PC}.

<u>Proof</u>. We have to prove that

$$E[\tilde{\alpha}g'u_1^P(\tilde{\alpha}g(x_{PC}), (1-\tilde{\alpha})g(x_{PC})) + (1-\tilde{\alpha})g'u_2^P(\tilde{\alpha}g(x_{PC}), (1-\tilde{\alpha})g(x_{PC})) -$$
$$- \bar{\alpha}g'u_1^P(\bar{\alpha}g(x_{PC}),(1-\bar{\alpha})g(x_{PC})) - (1-\bar{\alpha})g'u_2^P(\bar{\alpha}g(x_{PC}),(1-\bar{\alpha})g(x_{PC}))] \quad (21)$$

is less than 0.

Add to and subtract from (21) the expression

$$E[\tilde{\alpha}g'u_1^P(\bar{\alpha}g(x_{PC}),(1-\bar{\alpha})g(x_{PC})) - (1-\tilde{\alpha})g'u_2^P(\bar{\alpha}g(x_{PC}),(1-\bar{\alpha})g(x_{PC}))].$$

Then (21) can be rewritten as

$$g'E[\tilde{\alpha}u_1^P(\tilde{\alpha}g(x_{PC}),(1-\tilde{\alpha})g(x_{PC}) + (1-\tilde{\alpha})u_2^P(\tilde{\alpha}g(x_{PC}),(1-\tilde{\alpha})g(x_{PC}))$$
$$- \tilde{\alpha}u_1^P(\bar{\alpha}g(x_{PC}),(1-\bar{\alpha})g(x_{PC})) - (1-\bar{\alpha})u_2^P(\bar{\alpha}g(x_{PC}),(1-\bar{\alpha})g(x_{PC}))]$$
$$+ g'E[(\tilde{\alpha}-\bar{\alpha})u_1^P(\bar{\alpha}g(x_{PC}),(1-\bar{\alpha})g(x_{PC}))+u_2^P(\bar{\alpha}g(x_{PC}),(1-\bar{\alpha})g(x_{PC}))$$
$$- u_1^P(\bar{\alpha}g(x_{PC}),(1-\bar{\alpha})g(x_{PC}))-u_2^P(\bar{\alpha}g(x_{PC}),(1-\bar{\alpha})g(x_{PC}))] =$$
$$g'E[\tilde{\alpha}u_1^P(\tilde{\alpha}g(x_{PC}),(1-\tilde{\alpha})g(x_{PC})) + (1-\tilde{\alpha})u_2^P(\tilde{\alpha}g(x_{PC}),(1-\tilde{\alpha})g(x_{PC}))$$
$$- \tilde{\alpha}u_1^P(\bar{\alpha}g(x_{PC}),(1-\bar{\alpha})g(x_{PC})) - (1-\tilde{\alpha})u_2^P(\bar{\alpha}g(x_{PC}),(1-\bar{\alpha})g(x_{PC}))]$$

which (applying TAYLOR expansion) yields in turn

$$g'E\{(\tilde{\alpha}-\bar{\alpha})[\tilde{\alpha}(u_{11}^P(\bar{\alpha}g(x_{PC}),(1-\bar{\alpha})g(x_{PC}))+u_{12}^P(\bar{\alpha}g(x_{PC}),(1-\bar{\alpha})g(x_{PC})))$$
$$+ (1-\tilde{\alpha})(u_{12}^P(\bar{\alpha}g(x_{PC}),(1-\bar{\alpha})g(x_{PC})) + u_{22}^P(\bar{\alpha}g(x_{PC}),(1-\bar{\alpha})g(x_{PC})))]\}.$$

The expression in brackets decreases in $\tilde{\alpha}$ because of the quasiconcavity of u^P. Denoting this expression $\Delta(\tilde{\alpha})$, we obtain

$$\tilde{\alpha} > \bar{\alpha} \implies \Delta\,(\tilde{\alpha}) < \Delta\,(\bar{\alpha}) \quad \text{and}$$

$$\tilde{\alpha} < \bar{\alpha} \implies \Delta\,(\tilde{\alpha}) > \Delta\,(\bar{\alpha}).$$

Therefore,

$$g'E[\,(\tilde{\alpha}-\bar{\alpha})\Delta\,\tilde{\alpha})\,] \;<\; g'E[\,(\tilde{\alpha}-\bar{\alpha})\Delta\,(\bar{\alpha})\,] \;=\; g'\Delta\,(\bar{\alpha})E(\tilde{\alpha}-\bar{\alpha}) \;=\; 0.$$

Footnotes

1. This conclusion seems to provide a support for the view maintained
   in NERLOVE et al., 1985 (see also NERLOVE et al., 1986) that intrafamily externalities may result in allocative inefficiency. Note,
   however, that our model differs from that of NERLOVE et al. (1985)
   in several important aspects.

2. A more consistent assumption is that P can decide how much of his
   transfer C is to spend on his first period consumption and how much
   he is to save. Under this specification P can derive utility from
   C's first period consumption. However, since the results of this
   case are identical to those presented in the paper, we preferred
   the simplified formulation.

3. More exactly, C's first period utility is disregarded. This assumption
   is justified, since in the first period C is not a decision maker in
   his own right.

4. That this is feasible can be seen by considering the (trivial) case
   of the egoistic child.

References

BECKER, G.S., "A Theory of Social Interaction", JPE, 82(1974),
    1063-1093.

BECKER, G.S., "Altruism, Egoism and Genetic Fitness: Economics and
    Sociobiology", Journal of Econ. Lit., 14 (1976), 817-826.

BERNHEIM, D.R., SHLEIFER, A., and SUMMERS, L.M., "The Strategic Be-
    quest Motive", JPE, 93(1985), 1045-1076.

HIRSHLEIFER, J., "Shakespeare vs. Becker on Altruism: the Importance
    of Having the Last Word," Journal of Econ. Lit., 15(1977),
    500-502.

NERLOVE, M., RAZIN, A. and SADKA, E. "Bequests and the Size of Popu-
    lation when Population is Endogenous", JPE, 92(1985), 527-531.

NERLOVE, M., RAZIN, A. and SADKA, E. "Some Welfare Theoretic Appli-
    cations of Endogenous Fertility", IER, 27(1986), 3-32.

RAZIN, A. and BEN-ZION, U., "An Intergenerational Model of Population
    Growth", AER, 65(1975), 923-933.

Part II
Applied Studies on Economic Change and Demographic Development

II,1
The Case of Hungary: A Historical Perspective

ECONOMIC CHANGE AND FAMILY SIZE IN HUNGARIAN HISTORICAL DEMOGRAPHY

Robert A. Horváth
Institut International de Statistique

Budapest / Hungary

ABSTRACT: The present paper is a verification of the new theory of demographic transition forwarded by Kingsley Davis in 1984 based on the
changing pattern of the division of labor and the reversal of the sex
roles within the family or the household as a consequence of the Industrial Revolution. As a test case the end of the era of feudalism
and the capitalist era till to World War II in Hungary was chosen because of its predominantly agrarian economic structure and was relatively well documented by historical demographic and economic statistics
for the above periods. The results of the author show a relatively long
survival of the feudal agrarian economy, and this also during the capitalist era, with preservation of the traditional family size in the
agrarian population, but with a marked differentiation within the peasantry itself. This specific development, united with a slow and rudimentary industrialisation parallel to it, is identified as the main cause
of the late demographic transition in Hungary, resulting in a rapid
collapse of the old demographic growth pattern and in a rapid approximation to Western European population development patterns.

I.   Introduction

To explain the interrelation between demographic changes and economic
development the majority of scholars is inclined to study the underlying economic changes, which transform not only the economic system,
but also the whole social framework, resulting in a fundamental demographic change. Among these scholars it was Kingsley DAVIS who recently, with the publication of a remarkable paper[1] reversed his earlier
approach and elaborated on a model for the explanation of the interrelation
in question via demographic changes, i. e. by the demographic transition
theory developed in a special form for the purposes of population economic analysis instead of following the usual line of argument of population economics.

Notably, this new theory of demographic transition is based on
the changing pattern of the division of labor and the reversal of sex
roles within the family, or within the household as an economic unit,
as a consequence of the Industrial Revolution. According to this theory,
demographic change and economic development arose from the abandonment
of the so-called "agricultural household economy system" universally

---

[1]   Kingsley DAVIS, Wives and Work: The Sex Role Revolution and Its Consequences, Population and Development Review, Vol. 10 No. 3,
Sept. 1984, pp. 397 ff.

Studies in Contemporary Economics
A. Wenig, K. F. Zimmermann (Eds.)
Demographic Change and Economic Development
© Springer-Verlag Berlin Heidelberg 1989

maintained before the Industrial Revolution, built on the family type
of a unique gainfully employed head of family. However, in reality,
it was based on the collective work of all family members working together to be able to secure an acceptable general level of life for
the family as an entity. This family pattern was transformed after the
first preindustrial phase of economic development by the rise of the
Industrial Revolution, and in a second phase parallel with the formation
of a new family pattern, called by DAVIS "the breadwinner system", pene-
trating all sectors of the economic system.

This new pattern transformed the gainfully employed heads of family
into workers and employees and reduced the housewives either to a full-
time child-raising occupation or to full-time workers, in principle
on an egalitarian basis. But the consequences in the latter case resulted
in decreased natality and fertility, because in a family with a non-
working wife the quality of life drastically fell, and gave no possibility of raising several children on the former standard of living. If
the wife were also gainfully employed, the difficulties of child-raising
led to the same demographic results.

Within his exposition of these ideas, DAVIS has given a comprehensive analysis of the established controls - economic, social and demographic - of phase one, i. e. those of the agricultural household economy system, which were collapsing with it. The most outstanding consequence
of this process from the demographic point of view, according to DAVIS,
may be represented by the fact that in Western countries ahead in the
process of the Industrial Revolution the family size were at their zenith
around 1890 and began to fall rapidly after this traditional period.[2]
For scholars of the demographic transition, it is a common fact that
there were significant differences among countries according to the
rise, the duration and the extent of the Industrial Revolution and of
the demographic transition. The correspondence and parallellism varied
considerably from country to country, especially in the eastern and
southern directions on the European continent. It is my country's case,
belonging to the south-eastern part of Europe, where the Industrial
Revolution and especially the demographic transition, were lagging behind Western European development.[3]

The problem dealt with in my present paper is the verification of
the applicability of the recent DAVIS-model to the Hungarian case: to
raise the question whether it is suitable to confirm findings of scholars

---

[2] Ibidem, pp. 404 ff.

[3] ACSÁDY, György and KLINGER, András, The Population of Hungary between
the Two Wars. Budapest, 1965. (Hungarian text)

of economic and demographic development with some new insights into
the underlying trends and peculiarities of these processes of the Hungarian development, or whether a full application as a working hypothesis seems to be unworkable, because of the built-in weaknesses of
the model to cover more general facts or more peripheral developments.

As the Hungarian historical demography covers the period including
feudalism until its abolishment in 1848 and the capitalistic period
until the end of World War II, my paper tries to raise two basic questions connected with the ideas of DAVIS. First, I wish to demonstrate
the necessity of analysing the agricultural household economy system
more thoroughly according to the main population strata in this era,
especially the peasantry, and second, to show the coexistence of the
two systems as identified by DAVIS, i. e. that the breadwinner system
was not replacing the agricultural household economy system. On the
contrary, this latter system was existing simultaneously with the former
in Hungary and gave a very peculiar character to the whole period of
capitalist development there. This trend is characterised by calling
this period "half feudal - half capitalistic".

It would be an alluring task to demonstrate also that remnants
of this agricultural household economy system survived even after World
War II, not only in the radical agrarian reform immediately after the
war, but also in new and very sophisticated forms in the recent period of
the "new economic mechanism", giving a unique feature to Hungarian socialism. However, as there is another Hungarian paper dealing with this
period of socialism,[4] I do not delve into the problems of this third
period.

II. The Era of Feudalism

The era of feudalism began in Hungary practically in the second milleni-
um, after the conquest at the end of 9th century, when Hungarians slowly
went over to agricultural ways of life, abandoning nomadism. For modern
historical demography, however, it has not been possible to study only the
end of this era (i. e. from the end of 18th century till to its abolishment in 1848), because of the lack of comprehensive, i. e. synthetic

---

[4] ANDORKA, Rudolf, Interrelations of Demographic and Economic Changes
     during the Demographic Transition in Hungary, this volume.

statistical data. The same statement may be valid for economic history proper and consequently also for population economics in the historical perspective. If we realize that the process of abolishing feudalism was initiated by the absolutist Habsburg-rule after the loss of the Hun- garian war of independence in 1848-1849, continuing until the 1860's. One may say that Hungarian historical demography is able to cover, even if with rather conjectural data, nearly a century of development at the end of Hungarian feudalism.

The statistical sources of this period are very mixed; one may find first attempts of official statistical activities, contemporary descriptive or analytical statistical ventures written by individual scholars, and an abundant, up-to-date corpus of historical demographic and economic historical literature produced in the last decades of our time, partly reinterpreting and partly complementing the older sources.

The best starting point for our analysis is with the 1784-85 first census in Hungary, the so-called Josephine or military census, ordered by Joseph II and carried out by the civilian administration with the help of the military in order to cover only the privileged population of nobility. The results of this census[5], covering the totality of the historic territory of Hungary existing till 1920, show an overwhelmingly agrarian economy with a population around 9 million. In the 70 large towns, varying between 5 and 30 thousand inhabitants, only 5 % of the population was conglomerated and industrialisation was making its first steps. It was furthered mainly by the economic policy of enlightened absolutism and rather sporadically by private initiatives.

Even if we are willing to consider the population of the some 650 smaller towns and market-places as "urban", and these latter sometimes were really "peasant-towns" around the 20-30 thousand inhabitant-limit, the proportion of the "urban" or "quasi-urban" population amounts to no more than 10 %. The share of nobility and clergy in the adult male population amounted to some 8 %, and that of the clerks and free occupations was nearly the same. The urban industrial and commercial population represented not more than 4 %, with the army representing 1 % in the total male adult population. So the bulk of the population, nearly 80 %, was the peasantry among the gainfully employed, and the family-size (cal-

---

[5] HORVÁTH, Robert A., The First Hungarian Census in the Era of Joseph II. Statisztikai Szemle, 1986. Nr. 6., pp. 624 ff. - A French version from the same author was given as a lecture in the Hungarian Cultural Institute in Paris in 1984 under the title: "La Hongrie à la Lumière de Deux Recensements - 1784 - 1980", - available in manuscript.

culated on average for the whole country with five family-members) -
has to correspond roughly for the whole peasantry.

Its average must be even slightly over this value if one admits that
in the non-peasant or non-rural population the number of children was
most probably less than 3 - 4.

My research has demonstrated[6] that even in the peasantry, strong
signs of stratification were already present at the end of the 18th
century with the beginning of the agricultural-technical revolution,
involving an early family planning which was necessary to maintain a
better standard of living, to provide against the division of serf-
tenures, or even to multiply it by marriages between single children.
The contemporary authors I studied, FEJES (1803), TESSEDIK and BERZEVICZY
(1804-1806), who all signalled this process, strongly emphasised the
accelerated pauperisation ensuing from the exhausted agricultural territory and its diminution by the enclosures of the nobility's estates,
which were switching to capitalist farming, and by the impoverishment
of the growing peasant population with its outmoded production methods
and lack of capital. As the efforts of the Habsburg-rulers, Maria The-
resia and Joseph II, were not able to modernize the Hungarian serfdom
with legal measures, serfdom's outmoded production techniques, combined with the population growth corresponding to the traditional demographic regime, induced this rapid pauperisation-process, denominated
by historiographers as the "era of the second serfdom" in Hungary.

---

[6] From the same author, Les Débuts de la Démographie en Hongrie - János
FEJES, Population, 1965, No. 1, pp. 109 ff., - with reference to
FEJES, János: De Vicissitudinibus Populationis in Senioratu Evangelico
Kis-Hontensi, Anno 1803 - Interventis, in De Populatione in Genere
et in Hungaria in Specie, Pestini, 1812, - from the s. a.: Tessedik
als Sozialwissenschaftler. Acta Universitatis Szegediensis, Juridica
et Politica, Tomus XVI. Fasciculus 6., Szeged, 1969. - with reference
to TESSEDIK, Samuel: Memorabilia Szarvasiensa, oder ökonomische Chro-
nik des Marktfleckens Szarvas, Szarvas, 1805, first published by
NÁDOR, Jenö, Budapest, 1938, in Hungarian translation, - from the
s. a.:Problems of Statistical Method and Theory in the Works of Gergely Berzeviczy, Budapest, 1972 (Monography in Hung. with English
summary). A French summary published under the title: L'Interdépen-
dance des Facteurs Economiques et Démographiques dans la Pensée de
Grégoire Berzeviczy, Population, 1970. No. 5, pp. 975 ff., - both
of them with reference to BERZEVICZY, Gergely: De Conditione et In-
dole Rusticorum in Hungaria, anonymous edition, no place, no date,
most probably from 1804 - 1806.

I am insisting on the stability of this traditional demographic regime,
with its 40 - 45 % birth rate and 30 - 35 % mortality rate, producing
on average, a population growth of 10 %o or 1 %. Therefore without any
"population explosion" as in Western Europe, it added in half a century
some 50 % more people to the existing population, coexisting with a
nearly stagnant agrarian economy and a very slow industrialisation process. BERZEVICZY, by analysing the production of a full serf-tenure
at the beginning of the 19th century of some 16 - 20 cadastral yoke
arable land and some 6 - 10 c. y. pastures, came to the conclusion that
its productivity was near to or under the subsistence level;[7] and more
so for tenures of 1/2, 1/4, or 1/8 size having to nourish even more
people, compared to the chosen "unique sample tenure" by BERZEVICZY.
Notably, this unique sample was chosen by BERZEVICZY himself, a pro-
prietor of big family-estates, a practising agrarian, and a scholar
of political economy, to represent the full-size tenure all over the
country. We therefore may consider it also as representative for the
family and household-size of the people living on it, i. e. two parents
with one single child and two servants as helping hands. From BERZE-
VICZY's line of argument, however, it is absolutely clear that the full-
size tenure does not correspond to the most frequent or modal size of
the serf tenures at the beginning of the 19th century in Hungary. This
problem was dealt with for the first time by LE PLAY himself, when he
came in 1846 to Hungary to find out the representative Hungarian household or family for his monograph on European working classes.[8]

LE PLAY, with the help of Hungarian scholars, found that this family in Hungary was not industrial but agrarian and was living on a half-
tenure on the Great Hungarian Plain, near the imaginary weight center
of the Hungarian population. The family usually nourished two parents,
two children, with two other ones already having died at younger ages, and
two adult bachelor members of the family, an uncle and an aunt, i. e.
six persons in all. If we contrast LE PLAY's results with those of the

[7] From the same author, Berzeviczy-monography, as cited under 6),
chapter III, pp. 43 ff.

[8] From the same author, Tentatives de Quantification de la Consommation
par Tête en Hongrie dans la Période Proto-Statistique - 1804 - 1887,
Papers of the "Famine in History" Symposium, Vevey, 1981. - With
reference to LE PLAY, Frédéric: Les Ouvriers Européens, 2nd Ed.,
in 6 Vol.s, Tours-Paris, 1877 - 1879, Vol. 2: Paysans (à corvées)
des Plaines de Theiss (Hongrie), pp. 272 ff.

recent Hungarian historiography, they seem to exceed the real value of this frequency. According to recent findings[9] the modal value of serf tenures around the turn of the 18th and 19th century was rather the 2/5 tenure, i. e. not 50 %, but only 40 % of size of the full tenure. However calculated on basis of the next 1828 census it fell back to 1/3 the tenure, i. e. to 33 % of the size of the full tenure as a consequence of the above-mentioned "second serfdom process". By comparing the data of the 1828 census and those of the 1848 abolishment period, rapid deterioration and acceleration of the pauperisation may be best documented by statistically differentiating between serf family-heads, in Latin "jobbagiones", in Hungarian "jobbágy", with tenures, and landless agrarian family heads, "inquilini" or "zsellér" respectively:[10]

Table 1

Category	1828	1846	Increase
	in absolute number		in %
Family-heads with tenure	546,643	619,527	+ 9.6
Landless family-heads	687,288	911,754	+ 32.6

These data refer to the territory of historic Hungary excluding Transylvania, which was ruled administratively separately under Habsburg-rule in this period. According to data for 1848, the landed property's distribution was the following:[11]

---

[9] The History of Hungary, University Textbook, Vol. III: 1790 – 1849, A collective work, Budapest, 1975. – The development of market economy, pp. 62 ff.

[10] Ibid, pp. 93 ff.

[11] Ibid pp. 150 ff.

Table 2

Category	abs. number	%
A) Family-heads with		
Full tenure	40,380	2.6
2/3 "	6,458	0.4
1/2 "	281,264	18.3
1/4 "	254,160	16.5
1/8 "	41,872	2.7
Total	624,134	40.5
B) Landless family-heads with		
some land and house	32,120	2.1
only with house	773,528	50.3
without house	108,314	7.1
Total	913,963	59.3
A) + B) Peasantry together	1,538,096	100.0

From the above two tables, it is evident that different Hungarian historiographers calculated slightly differently the number of peasants with
tenure between 1846 and 1848 - 619,527 and 624,134, respectively - but
the difference is only 0.1 % i. e. negligible. The second table's data
confirm the fact that the majority of tenures was between the 1/2 and
1/4 size as the two categories amount to 86 % of all tenures, with the
average of them being around the 1/3 tenure size with a dispersion of
7.4 % above and 6.6 % under the modal values. As for the standard of
living, or rather of misery of families under the global mode, and that
of the landless families, it is hard to imagine, because of a lack of
data in a more detailed structure. Among the families above the general
level, there was a farmer-type stratum, in which such a farmer, by imita-
ting the capitalist agrarian technology of the big estates, by practising
usury and commerce and especially family planning, came to augment his
estate by two or more tenure-sizes, and was even able to buy his freedom and abandon the serf-status. An individual example near the town
Kecskemét on the Great Hungarian Plain, is in the 1820's a family-head
with some 400 c. y. land, a livestock of 60 horses and some 1000 sheep,
leaving open the question of his family's size; unfortunately from our
point of view.

    The major conclusion for this whole period at the end of the feudal
era characterized by the "second serfdom" is the marked differentiation
of the peasantry in Hungary, not only from the economic point of view,
but also according to demographic behavior. Namely, some wealthier strata
were far ahead of the so-called "demographic transition", while the

bulk lagged far behind. As a consequence of this latter phenomenon, they were maintaining the traditional demographic pattern country-wide, by securing a 1 % population growth annually. To be able to do that, their family size ought to have been above the country average and the same seems to be very probable for the strata with 1/2 and 1/4 tenures, for whom helping hands within the family were absolutely necessary to fulfill their duties to the landlords and to secure a subsistence level of the family. To a greater or lesser extent this also may be true concerning the landless families of the "zsellér" with only a house, for whom the prospect of acquiring some tenure represented the only outlook to raising the quality of life, if migration possibilities into towns were minimal, as in fact they were in Hungary in that period. According to another assessment of economic historians,[12] the number of industrial family heads rose between 1828 and 1846 from 95 to 243 thousand heads and that of commercial families from 1 to 22 thousand. That is, the growth rates were 148 and 137 %, respectively, as compared to the total of the peasantry's corresponding rate (26 %). But in absolute numbers even this accerlerated rate was not able to provide satisfactory migration possibilities into towns. The percentage of real urban population, according to my own calculations, may be estimated around 1800 as no more than 6 % and around 1850 as 12 %.

For this analysis one may conceive of a research programme for rian historical demography, specifically to elucidate by comprehensive calculations and estimations the demographic development of the different strata of population, or at least that of the bulk of peasantry, which was maintaining and reinforcing the traditional demographic pattern of feudalism as the propelling force of subsistence agriculture.

III. The Era of Capitalism

Paradoxically, the process of the demographic transition according to social strata in the era of capitalism is practically no better known than in the era of feudalism. Despite the take-off of official statistics, these were far better developed in the demographic than in the economic statistical field. This does not mean that the process of capitalist development in Hungarian agriculture is not one of the statistically best-documented in Europe from the economic aspect. It is only the elucidation of its interdependence with the demographic process, which

---

[12] Ibid.

is missing from the picture to be able to demonstrate the parallel survival of out-moded, small-size subsistence agriculture and its role
in the prolongation of the "traditional" demographic order.

Regarding the economic side of the Hungarian development in capitalism, we know that in 1848 the abolition of feudalism freed some
255 thousand "jobbágy"-tenures, representing some 20 % of the whole
cultivation area and some 37 % of the arable land and pastures from
the whole territory of the country (calculated again without Transylvania)[13]. The so-called "Urbarial patent" of the absolute Habsburg-
rule in 1853 ordered the abolishment process to continue and finish
under less favourable conditions - the introduction of a down-payment
for the redemption - and completed this process by the end of the
1860's. The resulting situation was statistically first wholly eluci-
dated by the big 1895 agricultural census official statistics, the
summary of which may be given in the following synthetic table, with
the remark that here the territory of historic Hungary is given together with Transylvania, but without the old Croatian-Slavonian territory, which became autonomous in the Hungarian constitutional era after
1867. With the inclusion of the latter territories as "Croatia", the
denomination applied was "Hungarian empire", but it may be omitted in
the present paper as the distribution of landed property in its percentage shares was hardly different[14].

Table 3

Category of landed properties in cad. yoke	in abs. Nr.	Percentage share from all landed properties (%)
Under 1 c. y.	562,946	33.56 (H. e. 32.08)
1 - 5 "	716,769	30.01 (30.15)
5 - 10 "	458,535	19.20 (20.37)
10 - 50 "	590,562	24.73 (25.13)
50 - 100 "	36,032	1.51 (1.39)
100 - 500 "	16,723	0.70 (0.62)
500 - 1000 "	3,144	0.13 (0.12)
over 1000 -	3,768	0.16 (0.14)
Total	2.388,482	100.00 (100.00)

[13] Ibid.

[14] Agricultural Statistics of the Countries of the Hungarian Crown,
Part I: Main Results, Hungarian Statistical Publications, New Series.
Vol. XV., Budapest, 1897, pp. 204x ff. - and Part IV: The Distribution of Landed Properties by Character and Size, Budapest, 1900,
pp. 3x ff.

For a comprehensive interpretation of these data, it is necessary to know that the so-called "dwarf" farms' share (under 5 c. y.) of the total number of farms was over half of them with 53.57 %, but that from the agrarian territory only 5.84 %. As for the so-called "small" farms, (between 5 and 100 c. y.), the corresponding values were 45.44 and 46.50 %, respectively. As for the "medium" size estates, from 100 to 1000 c. y., their share in the total number was only 0.83 %, but from the total territory 15.37 %, and the same values for the "big" estates - over 1000 c. y. - were 0.16 and 32.29 %, respectively.

To sum up, the "dwarf" and "small" farms became overwhelming in number, nearly 99 % of the total, but their territory hardly surpassed the half of agrarian territory with its 52.34 % share. In the long run one may say that the situation since BERZEVICZY's estimation - from the beginning of the 19th century till 1848 changed more slowly as the peasantry's territory augmented from about 20 % to about 30 % than in the capitalist era. During another half century, capitalist small-holders augmented their share to nearly half of the territory, while some 20 thousand medium-size farms owned more than 1/3 of the remaining half, and less than 4000 big estates the remaining 2/3, demonstrating "ad oculos" the survival of the subsistence agriculture under the harder conditions of home and international competition.

It is no wonder the international emigration to the United States and Canada began already with the 1870's and continued until World War I, with some 2 million people leaving historic Hungary. However, some 900 thousand - after successfully saving enough capital to buy land in the old country - came back and according to may estimations, the majority settled on the territory of the later postwar Hungary. So the net loss fell to the peripheral parts of historic Hungary, the poorer population of which stayed overseas.[15]

The fall of the Austrian-Hungarian Dual-Monarchy after World War I created a radically worse situation for the new Hungary, not only by the loss of territory and population - from 323 thousand square km to 93, and from 21 million inhabitants to 8 - but by destroying the econ-

---

[15] HORVÁTH, Robert A., Die Gestaltung der Bevölkerungszahl Ungarns und die ungarische bevölkerungsstatistische Wissenschaft, Történeti Statisztikai Közlemények, 1959. No. 1 - 2 pp. 118 ff.

omically well-balanced unit[16] and creating an artificial new one. This
new unit was overwhelmingly agrarian and practically without industrial
raw materials. The emigration era closed with the end of the war just
as American, Canadian and Soviet grain exports were slowly being dumped,
but successfully ruining Hungarian agriculture. This was manifest in
the world agrarian crisis and later with the overall economic crisis
of the early 1930's. The second big agrarian census of 1935 gave a statistically correct assessment of this desperate situation, summed up
in this paper on a comparative basis with the 1895 census:[17]:

Table 4

Category of landed properties in cad. yoke	Number of landed properties in abs. Nr.	Percentage share from all landed properties (%)
Under 1 c. y.	628,431	38.5
1 - 5 c. y.	556,352	34.2
5 - 10 "	204,471	12.5
10 - 50 "	217,849	13.2
50 - 100 "	15,240	1.0
100 - 500 "	9,632	0.5
500 - 1000 "	1,362	0.1
over 1000 -	1,070	0.0
Total	1,634,407	100.0

The character of subsistence agriculture is clearly shown by these
data, as the number of "dwarf" farms is overwhelming: 72.7 % of the
total while the share of their territory is hardly 10 %. The "small"
farms became fewer in number, only some 26.7 %, but the territory's
share much less so with 41.8 %. The corresponding values for the "medium" size and "big" estates changed, with 0.6 % medium estates occupy-
ing 18.2 % of the whole agrarian territory, and less than 0.1 "big"
ones some 29.8 %.

---

[16] John Maynard KEYNES, The Economic Consequences of the Peace, London,
1920. - where the destroying of the European economic order by the
peace-treaties, and especially that of Germany was dealt with, even
if the Hungarian situation was not mentioned.

[17] Agrarian property conditions of Hungary in the year 1935, Part I,
Hung. Stat. Publications, New Ser., Vol. 99, Budapest, 1936, pp.
12[x] ff., - and Part II: Landed Properties by size, Vol. 102, Budapest, 1937, pp. 10[x] and ff.

This structure could be maintained only by a very moderate "land reform" in 1920, which redistributed only 1/16 of the agrarian territory among some 114 thousand dwarf- and smallholders, 187 thousand landless agrarian workers and 41 thousand small craftsmen or industrial workers - diminishing the territory of the landed properties over 100 c. y. from 53.5 % to 48.0 %[18]. According to the population census of 1910, people living of agriculture were some 68.5 % and on the post-war territory at the same time some 58.3 %. For this smaller unit the recalculated data for 1910 show[19] a population living from industry and mining of 21.3 % and the latter portion was not more than 24.4 % according to the 1941 census. In other words, the industrialization process during the interwar years was minimal, some-textile- and chemical industry was added to the inherited industrial framework, but only in the 1930's.

The misery of the agricultural day-workers, agricultural workers, and the "dwarf holders" was great and steadily growing in the interwar years. Hungary was characterized by a contemporary author in 1928[20] as the "country of 3 million beggars", corresponding to 1.3 million family-heads with 1.7 million family-members, representing 67 % of the Hungarian peasantry and 34 % of the total Hungarian population. It is no wonder their family size - calculated globally - was no more than 2.3 members. According to up-to-date calculations[21], their yearly per head average income at the end of the 1920's was only 36 - 46 % of the global per-head income (some 500,- Pengö.), and so among the day and agricultural workers the share of the childless families was 18 %, those of 1 or 2 children 40 %, and those of 3 or more some 30 %. The same values for the dwarfholders were 15, 60 and 25 %, respectively.

---

[18] KERÉK, Mihály: The Hungarian Agrarian Problem, Budapest, 1939. (Hung. text)

[19] Hungarian Statistical Pocket-Book, Vol. XV. Budapest, 1948, p. 54. (Hung. text)

[20] OLÁH, György: Three Million Beggars, Budapest, 1928.

[21] GUNST, PÉTER: The Income Situation of the Peasantry in the years 1920 - 1930, Századok, 1985. Nr. 3, pp. 677 ff. (Hung. text)

These recent calculations demonstrate the reality of my line of thought. Notably that the so-called delayed demographic transition in Hungary was not a result of the industrialisation process, but rather of the long survival of subsistence agriculture in Hungary until the inter-war years, and especially of its relatively late breakdown in this period. This latter was the consequence of the Hungarian peace treaty and the failure of the old regime to reorganize the economic and social structure under the new conditions - despite the utmost scarcity of capital - towards a somewhat more effective economy and a more tolerable social framework. Such a policy, one has no illusions surely, would not have prevented the beginning of the demographic transition in the inter-war years, but with a retarding effect, it could have been able to avoid the transition's rapid acceleration in the years following World War II.

DEMOGRAPHIC CHANGE AND ECONOMIC DEVELOPMENT IN HUNGARY
SINCE THE SECOND WORLD WAR

Rudolf Andorka
University of Economics

Budapest / Hungary

ABSTRACT: The modernization of the Hungarian economy and society resulted in the acceptance of the two-children family norm by all classes
of society. As a consequence, the level of fertility is lower than
that necessary for simple replacement. From the population policy measures
introduced in the last decades, the restriction of induced abortions
had no effect on cohort fertility, but the financial assistance given
to families with children had a moderate impact, at least stopping
the decline of fertility and also slightly increasing the desired and
planned number of children of young couples.

I.   Introduction

Hungary was the first among the advanced societies after World War II
in which the level of fertility declined below the level of simple
replacement; the gross reproduction rate declined to 1.005 in 1959 and
0.975 in 1960 (the net reproduction rate was already below 1.0 in 1958)
and has remained below 1.0 since that time except for the period 1974 –
1978. Relatively early, first in 1953, and starting up again during
the mid-1960's, population policy measures with pro-natalist aims were
introduced in order to attain the level of simple replacement. It might
be of interest for societies which experienced a decline of fertility
more recently and which are still contemplating the introduction of a
pro-natalist population policy, to have some information about the
possible causal mechanisms of the decline of fertility and about the
impact of different population policy measures in Hungary.

The main theses of this paper are:

1. the modernization of the economy and of society produces conditions which tend to result in the post-transition period with a fertility level lower than required for the replacement of the population;
therefore no spontaneous upswing or oscillations around the replacement
level of fertility might be expected;

2. the economic and social conditions exert their influence through
the cultural values and norms concerning the desirable number of children,
with these values and norms being influenced, but not completely determined by the economic and social conditions, so that culture can have
an independent depressing or enhancing impact of fertility;

Studies in Contemporary Economics
A. Wenig, K. F. Zimmermann (Eds.)
Demographic Change and Economic Development
© Springer-Verlag Berlin Heidelberg 1989

3. adequate pro-natalist measures have a moderate impact on the level of fertility which in the present conditions of Hungary would be sufficient to increase it to the level of simple replacement.

II. The Development of Fertility in Hungary during the Demographic Transition

Historical demographic research proved, that already before the beginning of the demographic transition, there were some regions in Hungary where the level of marital fertility was remarkably low (DEMENY, 1960; ANDORKA, 1978; ANDORKA, BALAZS-KOVACS, 1986). This can be explained only by the widespread knowledge and practice of birth control in marriage by peasant population groups long before the onset of industrialization.

Although mortality began to decline slightly in the 1850's, the great cholera epidemic of the 1870's increased the level or mortality again to the pre-transition level, so that the continuous improvement of mortality dates to the second half of the 1870's. It was relatively soon followed by the onset of the sustained decline of fertility around 1890. The period of rapid growth therefore was relatively short. Already before the Second World War the net reproduction rate declined below 1.0.

The postwar recuperation period of fertility was relatively short, with the birth rate beginning to fall already in 1951. In 1953 a vigorous pro-natalist policy was iniciated, consisting essentially of severely applying the existing penal law measures against illegal abortions. The birth rate increased for one year in 1954, then began to decline and parallelly with the gradual liberalization of induced abortions, continued on that trend until 1962, when the gross reproduction rate attained 0.868. Beginning from the mid-1960's a completely different population policy was accepted: while the induced abortions remained free (performed on demand by women in all cases), family allowances were increased and the so-called child-care allowance was introduced. This allowance provided the possibility for mothers who were employed to remain at home until the third birthday of the child, establishing the right to return to the working place, and provided an allowance which was more or less equivalent to the minimal wage. In the following years the level of fertility increased (the gross reproduction rate attained 0.997 in 1968), but failed to reach the level of replacement. For this reason, the conception of the population policy was changed again in 1973: while the family allowances and the child care allowance were increased, the system of free abortions was somewhat restricted, permitting induced abortions for married women living with their hus- band and having less than 3 children only in specified exceptional cases. The specified exceptions were, however, rather broadly defined (most of all for women having already 2 children), so that the demand for an induced abortion was refused in the subsequent years only in very few cases (some thousands per year). In the following 5 years, the gross reproduction rate was above 1.0, but began to decline again in 1970 and since 1979 has been again permanently below 1.0 (in 1985 0.892). The level, however, seems to be stabilized in the mid-1980's. In 1984 family allowances were again increased and the child care allowance was transformed so that until the 2nd birthday of the child, it amounts to about 75 percent of the previous wage of the mother (i. e. it is proportional to the wage of the women).

III. <u>The Influence of Economic and Social Modernization on Fertility</u>

Recently, the concept of economic and social modernization is often used in the Hungarian social sciences to describe the changes that happened since 1945. Modernization means industrialization, urbanisation, the disappearance of feudal habits and traditional values, the dominance of rational decision making etc. According to the modernisation inter- pretation of the past century of Hungarian history, the take-off period of economic development in the second half of the 19th century achieved some progress toward a modern economy and society. In the interwar period, however, the process of modernization was blocked and the rapid transfortmations of the post-1945 decades might be seen as an attempt to catch up with the more advanced economies and societies.

It is a truism that the economic and social modernization causes a decline of fertility. The development of the social differences of fertility in Hungary might, however, explain the causative mechanism, the reason of the early and rapid decline in Hungary in the 1950's and the unlikeliness of an automatic important increase of it in the near future.

During the decades of the demographic transition, very high fer- tility differences by social strata developed (see Table 1). In the 1960's and 1970's, however, these differences diminished. According to the Hungarian part of the World Fertility Survey in 1977 the average number of children born by married women below 40 and economically active,

Table 1: Number of births per 1000 women aged 15-49
by social strata in Hungary

Social stratum	1900 to 1901	1910 to 1911	1920 to 1921	1930 to 1931	1940 to 1949	1959
Agricultural worker and cooperative peasant	195	212	178	199	233	69
Self-employed peasant	157	137	106	57	56	43
Industrial and construction worker	212	171	153	97	–	76
Transport worker	220	189	141	105	84	100
Service worker	87	77	50	42	–	47
Self-employed artisan, merchant	154	125	97	75	67	49
Non-manual	104	82	56	37	55	46
Total	156	144	118	80	76	61

Source: Klinger, 1964.

was the following (KLINGER et al, 1982):

agricultural manual	1.93
non-agricultural manual	1.40
non-manual	1.29
total active	1.43

The differences with respect to location of residence were even lower.
The average number of children born by married women below 40 was the
following:

villages	1.75
smaller towns	1.54
Budapest	1.30
total	1.60

The family plans of the different social strata were even more similar,
most of all among the younger couples. According to longitudinal sample
surveys of the couples married in 1966 and in 1974, the number of children
desired at marriage was almost identical in all social strata and in
all residential groups, although after 6, respectively 14 years of
marriage the desired (achieved plus still desired) number of children
became somewhat more differentiated (KLINGER et al, 1983, 1986)

Table 2: Desired number of children at marriage and in 1980
by social and residential strata of the marriage cohorts
of 1966 and 1974

Social stratum	marriage cohort 1966		marriage cohort 1971	
	in 1966	in 1980	in 1974	in 1980
agricultural manual	1.91	2.33	2.15	2.21
nonagricultural manual	1.89	2.06	2.14	1.89
non-manual	1.89	1.78	2.18	1.89
dependant	1.94	2.48	2.30	2.16
Villages	1.93	2.17	2.17	2.02
smaller towns	1.90	1.94	2.16	1.96
Budapest	1.82	1.74	2.19	1.89

It might be concluded that the two-children family ideal was accepted
in all social strata in Hungary. Nevertheless some fertility differences by social strata still exist. The agricultural manual families
and the families residing in villages have an average number of children
sufficient for the simple replacement. An average of two children per
family in the other strata is obviously somewhat less than the number
necessary for the simple reproduction of the population, as about 5
percent of the women do not marry (in 1984 8.8 percent of the children
were born by unmarried women), about 5 percent of married women fail
to have children because of biological reasons, and part of the women
cannot have a second, due to death, divorce, or sterility.

The path of development of fertility in the particular social
strata can be explained in terms of their economic and social conditions. The non-manuals were the forerunners in reducing their fertility, similarily to other European societies. This process was additionally stimulated by the hardships of this stratum in the interwar
years, when the inflow of Hungarian non-manuals from the neighbouring
areas belonging to Hungary in the pre-1914 period caused widespread
unemployment among them. Therefore their fertility already in the 1930's
was not sufficient for simple reproduction. In the post-1945 period
the number of non-manuals increased strongly the new non-manual families
adopted rapidly the low fertility norms of the traditional non-manual
stratum. Nevertheless it seems that the average number of children
did not decline in the non-manual families in the postwar decades.

The most interesting aspect of the demographic transition of the
Hungarian society is the early decline and the low level of fertility
of self-employed peasants. In order to understand it, some characteristics of this peasant stratum should be mentioned. They were not
farmers in the American sense, producing for the market, using rational calculation and having a relatively high level of living. Most
Hungarian self-employed peasants were smallholders, whose land was
barely enough to provide work and sustenance for a family. Therefore
they were in no need of additional family manpower and, in the case
of several inheritors, had to divide their small land among them, leading
to their pauperization. Since the country was industrialized only slowly, their sons could not escape from agriculture through social mobility
into other branches of the economy. The peasant stratum was affected
especially severly by the economic crisis of the 1890's and by the
world crisis after 1929, as the price or the agricultural products
declined more than the price of industrial products. The reaction of
the peasant families among others was the widespread adoption of birth

control, which - by limiting the number of their children to one in-
heritor (a two-child family with one son and one daughter) - promised
the avoidance of pauperization.

The social position of agricultural workers was quite different.
They amounted at the end of the 19th century to about 40 percent of the
agricultural population and about 1/3 of the total society. Most of
them worked on the large estates partly on the basis of year-long contracts, and also by engaging in shorter employment periods. They had
no land; those who worked at the large states on year-long contracts
had no house of their own. Therefore they had nothing to loose but had
no hope to achieve upward mobility. On the other hand a larger family
assured some advantages, as male children began to work very early
along with their father. The cost of educating the children was also
very low, as they went to school for very few years. These circumstances explain why agricultural workers usually did not practice birth
control. Their situation, however, completely changed after the Second
World War. First, they received some land through land reform. After
becoming smallhoders, they usually adopted the norms and values of
the traditional smallhoders, including their fertility controlling
behavior.

When the agricultural sector was collectivized around 1960, both
self-employed peasants and former agricultural workers became either
cooperative members of workers on state farms. Their working conditions
and social situation today are similar to those of the industrial workers, i. e. they receive fixed wages, work fixed hours, and have the
right to the same social security such as pension and sickness pay.
Therefore their fertility became very similar to the fertility of urban
workers. By this process, the social stratum, which until the Second
World War had compensated the low fertility of the other strata by
its high fertility, disappeared from the Hungarian society. Today there
is no social stratum which would follow the traditional norms of high
fertility. It probably would be unrealistic to expect a fundamental
change in the future, such as producing a baby-boom, as the economic
and social condition of no social stratum could change in such a way
that the families belonging to it would be interested to have more
than 2 children.

The other most important factor contributing to the rapid decline
of fertility might have been that the high and growing employment of
women. In 1980 only 7 percent of the women aged 15-54 were dependents
and not going to school.

The almost complete employment of women can be explained by the fact that single-earner families are very disadvantaged in terms of family income. In order to achieve the minimal living level considered to be adequate in Hungary, two earnings are necessary for a family with children. The decision to engage in employment outside the home, however, obviously meant that the couple had to limit the number of their children. Although the child-care allowance was established in order to alleviate the difficulties of employed mothers having very young children, it is still a rather hard task to reconcile the requirements of child care and education and those of an occupational career.

All the other corrolaries of the very rapid economic and social transformations of the postwar period, such as mass social mobility, resulted in the disappearance of the remaining traditional high-fertility groups. Although the fertility differences by social strata diminished strongly, some differences still exist. The main direction of social mobility went from the strata having somewhat higher fertility to those having lower fertility (from the agricultural population into the industrial working strata, from the unskilled strata to the skilled manual strata, from the manual strata into the non-manual strata). In addition, social mobility was usually accomplished at the cost of many hardships and strong problems of adaptation into the new social environment. These hardships induced the families to limit their offspring, as it became very difficult with a larger number of children to achieve upward social mobility, to provide adequate higher education for the children and adequate housing.

The above mentioned explanation of the decline of fertility in Hungary could be expressed in terms of EASTERLIN's (1969,1976) theory of fertility. According to this theoretical framework, the number of children planned and desired by couples is governed by the relationship between their aspirations concerning the level of living and of the resources (income etc.) at their disposition. In Hungary the aspirations increased rapidly paralleling the economic and social transformations, partly as a result of the diffusion of the socialist ideal of equality, while the level of income, although increasing, lagged behind the aspirations. Under these conditions it was a rational strategy for young couples to adopt lower fertility norms.

On the basis of his more general theoretical framework, EASTERLIN (1966, 1980) formulated a more middle-range theory for the explanation of the swings of fertility in the United States. According to this explanation the aspirations of young couples were governed by the standard of living experienced in their parental families, while their

actual relative income level at the beginning of the career was influenced by the size of their cohort. When the ratio of young adults to
older active adults was low, their relative income level was advanta-
geous, as compared to the conditions they experienced in their parental
family, and vice versa. On the basis of this causal mechanism he hypothesized the existence of approximately 40-years long demo-economic
cycles of fertility in the postwar United States and in other advanced
societies.

It might be fascinating to assume similar cycles in Hungary, as
an upswing in fertility could be expected sooner or later, bringin
fertility back to the replacement level. However, the ratio of the
population aged 15-34 to those aged 35-64, which is used by EASTERLIN
to represent the relative size of the young adult cohort, does not
exhibit any positive correlation with fertility in Hungary (Table 3).
Therefore no automatic upswing in fertility could be expected in the
near future.

This statement obviously does not exclude the possibility that
an important improvement in the standard of living would lead to a
moderate increase in fertility, making it possible for young couples
to attain more fully and with less efforts their aspirations. At present,
no such improvement of the economic conditions can be foreseen on the
horizon.

IV. The Influence of Cultural Factors on Fertility

Economic and social conditions and their changes influence the level
of fertility mainly through the values and norms of the social milieu
concerning the ideal or desirable number of children in the families.
Faced with specific economic and social conditions, each society or
special stratum or social community develops an answer in the form
of values and norms. However, these cultural elements are not completely
determined by external conditions as there are usually several alternate
responses to the given situation.

Peasant populations, for example, might respond to an emerging
shortage of land by postponing marriage and increasing celibacy, or
by practising birth control in marriage, or by emigrating. In Western
Europe, as J. HAJNAL (1965) discovered, late marriage and high celibacy
was a widespread response at least since the 18th century, long before
the acceptance of birth control in marriage. In some regions of Hungary,

Table 3:   The age ratio and the gross reproduction rate
in Hungary

Year	Population 35-64/population 15-34	Gross reproduction rate
1921	0.84	1.828
1930-31	0.84	1.385
1940-41	1.04	1.194
1949	1.21	1.223
1950	.	1.259
1951	.	1.234
1952	.	1.198
1953	.	1.328
1954	.	1.428
1955	1.12	1.360
1956	1.14	1.250
1957	1.20	1.102
1958	1.22	1.048
1959	1.24	1.006
1960	1.25	0.975
1961	1.27	0.937
1962	1.29	0.868
1963	1.29	0.880
1964	1.30	0.872
1965	1.30	0.875
1966	1.29	0.907
1967	1.29	0.970
1968	1.28	0.997
1969	1.26	0.984
1970	1.24	0.953
1971	1.22	0.931
1972	1.20	0.931
1973	1.19	0.943
1974	1.18	1.117
1975	1.18	1.157
1976	1.19	1.096
1977	1.19	1.056
1978	1.19	1.010
1979	1.22	0.985
1980	1.22	0.937
1981	1.23	0.919
1982	1.25	0.865
1983	1.28	0.859
1984	1.32	0.849
1985	1.33	0.892

when the land area available for the serf peasants became scarce, these peasants responded with rapidly spreading use of birth control in marriage beginning from the last decade of the 18th century (ANDORKA, 1978). The motivation for practicing birth control was to avoid the fragmentation of the farm area, similar to the case of postponing marriages in Western Europe. Thus the map of Europe, produced by the Princeton European Fertility Project (COALE, WATKINS, 1986) shows two areas of early declining marital fertility: 1. most of France and 2. parts of Southern Hungary. To fully understand the adoption of different cultural responses, we will have to wait for the development of research into the history of mentalities. It might, however, be hypothesized that this long tradition of birth control acceptance in marriage, in at least parts of the peasant population, has played a role in the very early decline of fertility of the total landholding peasant class in Hungary (but not among agricultural workers till 1945) and in the almost universal acceptance of the small family ideal in the Hungarian population since 1945.

According to the longitudinal surveys of selected marriage cohort, an increasing portion of newly married couples desire two children at the time of marriage: 70.1 per cent of the couples in the marriage cohort of 1966, 73.1 percent of the marriage cohort of 1974, and 74.4 percent of marriage cohort of 1982/83 (KLINGER, 1984; KAMARAS, 1984; KLINGER et al, 1986). Although the desired number of children changes somewhat in the later years of marriage, there is a clear tendency of convergence toward the two-children family. Three-children families are considered to be "big" families; e. g. the Association of Large Families, founded in 1987, admits couples to its membership having 3 or more children. Thus the ideal of two children is deeply embedded in the culture of present-day Hungarian society.

However, an average of two children per marriage is insufficient to allow for the replacement of the population. KLINGER, 1984, calculated a hypothetical distribution of married couples by the number of children, necessary for attaining the simple replacement level (Table 4). The reason for the calculation is that the proportion of childless couples cannot be reduced below 5 percent, due to biological sterility and as well, some couples will have only one child because of divorce etc., so that a shift from the couples desiring two children to the families desiring more than two would be necessary. This, however, necessitates a profound change of the values and norms concerning fertility. The problem is whether this can be achieved by pro-natalist population policies, considering the strong pressures originating from the economic

Table 4: Distributions of couples by the desired number
of children in the marriage cohort of 1974 and a
hypothetical distribution sufficient for simple
replacement

Number of children	Desired number at marriage of the 1974 marriage	Born and desired in 1980 after 6 years of marriage	Necessary for simple replacement
0	0.2	1.3	5.0
1	5.7	16.8	10.0
2	73.1	67.1	45.0
3	19.1	13.0	35.0
4 and more	1.9	1.8	5.0
Total	100.0	100.0	100.0
Average	2.17	2.01	2.30

and social conditions, which cause important disadvantages in terms
of per capita income and time constraints for the families having more
children, i. e. the difficulty of being employed and spending a sufficient amount of time caring for and educating the children.

V.   The Influence of Pro-Natalist Population Policies

All over the advanced societies and also in Hungary, a widespread skepticism prevails concerning the efficiency of pro-natalist population
policies. In the case of Hungary, the skepticism is based on the experience of the postwar period. In both cases, when the yearly fertility
rate increased as a consequence of new population policies, in 1954
and again in 1974-1975, the higher level was not sustained and fertility
soon declined below the level of replacement. In clear contradiction
to this skeptical evaluation, I would like to demonstrate that appropriate measures could influence the level of fertility in the desired
direction and that they had such an impact in Hungary in the last decades.

However, it is first necessary to state that coercive population policies, i. e. the strict prohibition of induced abortions in 1953 and the mild restriction in 1973 had most probably no impact on cohort fertility, as the short increase in the yearly rates was completely a consequence of the change of timing of parities. Thus, faced with the restrictions, the couples simply had the number of children they wanted to have during their lifetime earlier than they otherwise would have. The fertility data of the census of 1970 clearly show that the number of children ever born of the birth cohorts of married women monotonously declined - with the exception of the cohort born in 1919 - , although they were affected by the measures introduced in 1953 (being 24-30 years old at that time) (Table 5).

Table 5: Number of children ever born per 100 married women by the birth cohorts which might have been affected by the prohibition of induced abortions in 1953

Year of birth of the married women	Children ever born per 100 married women at the age of	
	40	50
1915	243	242
1916	241	243
1917	242	242
1910	239	238
1919	243	243
1920	236	.
1921	235	.
1922	230	.
1923	228	.
1924	223	.
1925	223	.
1926	220	.
1927	217	.
1920	217	.
1929	212	.
1931-1935	203	.
1936-1940	193	.
1941-1945	190	.

The evaluation of the impact of the population policy introduced since the mid-1960's is more difficult, as the influence of the monetary social benefits and that of the mild restriction of induced abortions in 1973 is difficult to separate. On the other hand, as already mentioned, the yearly fertility measures increased moderately in the second half of the 1960's and strongly after 1973, but after some years fell back in the 1980's to the level of the first half of the 1960's. Since the surplus in 1974-1978, as compared to the previous and subsequent years, consisted almost entirely of first and second parities, it is usually considered that the restriction of the availability of legal induced abortion for women having less than two children (married women having two children could obtain the permission on the basis of social indications) resulted in the earlier birth of children desired and planned anyway.

Meanwhile, some important changes occured in the cohort fertility measures that can be inferred from the census fertility data (see a more detailed analysis in ANDORKA and VUKOVICH, 1985). The distribution of married women by number of children born shows two opposite tendencies:

1. In all age groups the secular decline of the percentage of women having 4 or more children continued.

2. In the younger age groups the secular growth of the one-child family was reversed in favor of the two-children family and also a very slight increase of the three-children family seems to have appeared.

The two opposite tendencies more or less offset each other. If we assume, that the reversal of the growth of the one-child family was due to the increase of family allowances and to the introduction of the child care allowance (which obviously had an impact only on the younger cohorts, who were in the usual age groups of childbearing in Hungary), then in the absence of these population policy measures, the level of fertility would have declined further. The two tendencies are illustrated here with the distribution of married women by number of children born of two birth and marriage cohorts at the censuses from 1949 to 1980 (Table 6).

The two opposite tendencies might also be illustrated from another viewpoint, namely the relationship between fertility and women's educational level (Table 7). On the one hand the tendency of declining fertility was reversed at all educational levels except the lowest after 1970, but educational attainment of women continued to shift toward the higher educational categories having lower fertility.

Table 6: Distribution of married women by number of children born in two age and marriage duration groups.

Age	Marriage duration	Year	Number of children born in percent						
			0	1	2	3	4-5	6 and more	Total
25-29	5-9	1930	10.8	21.3	29.1	21.6	15.7	1.5	100.0
		1949	10.6	30.2	34.5	16.1	8.0	0.6	100.0
		1960	6.7	35.5	40.3	12.3	4.7	0.5	100.0
		1970	8.0	43.0	39.9	6.7	2.1	0.3	100.0
		1980	6.7	20.2	54.5	8.7	1.7	0.2	100.0
45-49	20-29	1949	10.3	14.0	20.3	16.2	19.9	10.5	100.0
		1960	7.9	18.2	26.4	17.9	17.4	12.2	100.0
		1970	7.4	20.4	34.3	19.2	13.0	4.9	100.0
		1980	6.0	27.0	43.6	14.5	6.6	2.3	100.0

Note: The age group of 25-29 in 1980 was influenced by the pro-natalist population policy measures introduced since the second half of the 1960's, while the age group 45-49 was obviously not influenced by them.

Table 7: Children born per 100 married women by education and the distribution of married women by education

Education of married women	1960	1970	1980
Primary school, less than 6 grades	326	311	296
6-7 grades	239	236	226
8 grades	141	152	172
Secondary school diploma	129	118	140
Tertiary school diploma	128	123	137
Total	232	205	189
Primary school, less than 6 grades	24.0	16.0	9.2
6-7 grades	40.5	37.6	24.6
8 grades	22.3	34.4	43.2
Secondary school diploma	4.2	9.7	18.1
Tertiary school diploma	1.0	2.3	4.9
Total	100.0	100.0	100.0

198

It is once again proposed, that in the absence of population policy
measures, this shift toward higher education would have resulted in
a much lower level of fertility.

It might thus be concluded that the pro-natalist measures, providing social benefits to families having children, had a certain impact
on the level of fertility. This impact would probably have been greater,
if the amount of benefits had been higher. Another important problem
is that these benefits are not indexed, so that their real value declines until the next government decision to increase them.

It should be noted that these benefits probably influenced fertility both directly and indirectly, through the slight changes of
values and norms. The direct influence consisted of a moderate reduction of the financial burdens of the couples deciding to have an additional child and of the alleviation of the time constraints by the child-
care allowance in the first years after the birth. The indirect influence consisted of a social atmosphere more, favourable to families
with children, i. e. through the values and norms concerning fertility
and thus through the changes in the desired number of children.

The desired number of children clearly reflects the changes of
population policy. Its average for all 15-49 years old married women
was 2.33 in 1958, with the planned number being 2.14 for married women
in the same age group. Couples married in that year, however, planned
even fewer children. Since that year we have data on the changes in
number of children desired for the same women from longitudinal surveys (Table 8). These data show that the desired number of children
already began to increase in the second half of the 1960's, reaching
the highest value around 1974, then slightly declining, but not as
low as the level of the early 1960's.

Table 8: The desired number of children of married women
by marriage cohorts

| Year | Women married in | | |
	1966	1974	1982/83
1966	1.89	.	.
1972	1.97	.	.
1974	.	2.17	.
1980	2.05	2.01	.
1982/83	.	.	2.06

Source: KAMARAS, 1984.

VI. Economic and Social Problems Caused by the Continuous low Level
     of Fertility and Conclusions for a Population Policy

The analysis of the consequences of the continuous low fertility level
would need a separate paper, perhaps even a book, whereas only some
problems can be mentioned here.

The immediate consequence is that the size of the population has
been declining since 1981. According to the population forecasts prepared in 1980 (HABLICSEK, MONIGL, VUKOVICH, 1985) the population will
diminish by 225 thousand up to the year 2000, if the fertility and
mortality levels of 1980 remain unchanged (from 10.7 million in 1980
to 10.5 million in 2000). All other variants of the projection assumed
somewhat more disadvantageous tendencies and a higher decline of the
population ranging between 600 and 360 thousand people.

The economic and social problems caused by an intensive aging
of the population, well documented recently by SAUVY (1979), are probably even more serious. They are already indicated, among others, by
the fact that although 10.5 percent of the national income is spent
on pensions, the real value of each individual pension, which is reg-
ularily increased by the government in order to avoid the pauperization
of the persons with the lowest pensions), is declining from year to
year, because the automatic 2 percent increase per year is insufficient
to compensate for the increasing costs of living. Since the pensions
are paid from the state budget and not on the basis of an insurance
principle, the indexation of pensions would cause a great burden for
the state budget in the coming years, when the number of the active
population is in decline. (For comparison it might be mentioned that
the total sum of family allowances and child care allowances amounted
to 2.8 percent of the national income, i. e. for much less).

Therefore there is a general agreement in Hungary among politicians,
scientists and the public, that it would be desirable to attain "zero
population growth", thus increasing fertility to the level necessary
for simple replacement. The argument in this paper suggests that this
cannot be expected to happen automatically, but might be achieved by
a conscious and generous population policy providing social benefits
(higher than at present) to families having children.

References

ANDORKA, R., 1978: Determinants of Fertility in Advanced Societies.
London. Methuen, p. 431.

ANDORKA, R., BALAZS-KOVACS, S., 1986: The social demography of Hungarian
Villages in the Eighteenth and Nineteenth Centuries (with special
attention to Sárpilis, 1792-1804). Journal of Family History,
Vol. 11, No. 2, pp. 169-192.

ANDORKA, R., VUKOVICH, Gy., 1985: The Impact of Population Policy on
Fertility in Hungary, 1960-1980. International Population Conference, Florence 1985, Vol. 3. Liege. IUSSP. pp. 403-412.

COALE, A. J., WATKINS, S. C., (eds.), 1986: The Decline of Fertility
in Europe. The revised proceedings of a conference on the Princeton European Fertility Project. Princeton. Princeton University
Press, p. 484.

DEMENY, P., 1968: Early Fertility Decline in Austria-Hungary: A Lesson
in Demographic Transition. Daedalus. Spring. pp. 502-522.

EASTERLIN, R. A., 1966: Economic-Demographic Interactions and Long
Swings in Economic Growth. American Economic Review, Vol. 56,
No. 5. pp. 1063-1104.

EASTERLIN, R. A., 1969: Toward a Socio-Economic Theory of Fertility.
Behrman, S.J., Corsa, L., Jr., Freedman, R., eds.: Fertility and
Family Planning: A World View. Ann Arbor. University or Michigan
Press. pp. 127-156.

EASTERLIN, R. A., 1976: The Conflict Between Aspirations and Resources.
Population and Development Review. Vol. 2, No. 3-4, pp. 417-425.

EASTERLIN, R. A., 1980: Birth and Fortune. The impact of numbers on
a personal welfare. London. Grant McIntyre, p. 205.

HABLICSEK, L., MONIGL, I., VUKOVICH, G.: A Magyar Népességfejlódés
Nénány Hosszu Távu Jellemzoje 1880-2001 Kozott. Demográfia.
Vol. 28, No. 4, pp. 403-457.

HAJNAL, J., 1965: European Marriage Patterns in Persepctive. Glass,
D. V., Eversley, D. E. C., eds.,: Population in History. London,
Edward Arnold, pp. 101-143.

KAMARAS, F., 1984: Longitudinalis Vizsgáľatok Szerepe a Népesedési Foly-
amatok Elemzésében. A gazdasági intenziv fejlodése és a statisz-
tika c. Konferencia eloadásai. Budapest. Kozponti Statisztikai
Hivatal, pp. 97-104.

KLINGER, A., 1964: Differenciális termékenység. Szabady, E., ed.,
Bevezetés a Demográfiába. Budapest. Kozgazdasági és Jogi Kömyv-
kiado, pp. 280-293.

KLINGER, A., JOZAN, P., BARANY, L., MESZAROS, A., 1982: Világ Termé-
kenységi vizsgálat: Magyarország adatai. Budapest. Kozponti
Statisztikai Hivatal, p. 281.

KLINGER, A., JOZAN, P., KAMARAS, F., OROSZI, Zs., 1983: Házasság és
család az 1970-es években. Budapest. Kozponti Statisztikai Hivatal,
p. 93.

KLINGER, A., 1984: The Impact of Policy Measures, Other Family Planning
    Programmes on Fertility. Budapest. Research Reports of the Demo-
    graphic Research Institute, No. 10, p. 14.

KLINGER, A., JOZAN, P., KAMARAS, F., OROSZI, Zs., 1986: A házasság
    elsó tiz esztendeje 1974-1984. Budapest, Központi Statsztikai
    Hivatal, p. 62.

SAUVY, A., 1979: Les Conséquences du Vieillissement de la Population.
    Chaunu, P., Dumont, G. F., Legrand, J., Sauvy, A.: La France ridée.
    Paris. Livre de Poche. pp. 61-118.

II,2
Issues of Developing Countries

A CASE FOR SOME SIMPLE ANALYTICS OF DEMOGRAPHIC CHANGE

AND ECONOMIC DEVELOPMENT

Shanti S. Tangri[*]
Rutgers University

New Brunswick / USA

ABSTRACT: Understanding inter-relationships between population growth
and economic development is critical to policy making in most countries.
For some, survival may depend on their ability to provide satisfactory
employment and incomes to their populations. Economists, until recently, gave little attention to the subject partly because of the complex-
ities involved. This paper argues that (1) simple concepts such as
the theory of the firm and the Harrod-Domar model can be useful for
discussing the subject (2) the assumptions of the models warrant their
use in Less Developed Countries (LDCS) and (3) more complex models
are unlikely to change the policy implications of the simple models.

I. Population, Environment and Welfare

Issues of demographic change and economic development concern policy

makers in most developed and less developed countries. Yet the space

devoted to the subject in economic text books often does not reflect

the intensity of this concern. The reasons may lie in the complexity

of the subject, the lack of agreement among scholars on the nature of

relationships between demographic and economic variables and on the

nature of the appropriate welfare function that is to be maximized

if optimum population growth has to have a clear meaning. At a philo-

sophical level the problem may indeed be insolvable as CANNAN[1] argued

nine decades ago or DASGUPTA[2] and others have argued recently. As

NERLOVE, RAZIN and SADKA ask "What does it mean to compare the allo-

cations in which some individuals are never born with those in which

they are?" Many share their answer that "The criterion of Pareto opti-

---

[1] Edwin CANNAN, "Elementary Political Economy", London 1888, Part I,
Section 7.

[2] P. DASGUPTA, (a) "On the Concept of Optimum Population", Review of
Economic Studies, 1969. (b) "Lives and Welfare", London School of
Economics, 1983.

[*] I am thankful to my colleagues, H. Peter Gray, Gary Gigliotti and
Ira Gang for comments on an earlier and longer paper from which
this is derived.

Studies in Contemporary Economics
A. Wenig, K. F. Zimmermann (Eds.)
Demographic Change and Economic Development
© Springer-Verlag Berlin Heidelberg 1989

mality is minimal only from the standpoint of the present generation
and has no meaning in an intertemporal context when population is variable."[3]

On the other hand it does not seem unreasonable to assume that
the finite bio-mass of earth cannot support an infinitely large population even at some subsistence level, much less could it do so at
an increasing standard of living. In the long run, then, only non-positive population growth rates would be feasible and optimal. If one
assumes that the world's population is already enough or more than
enough, non-positive rates become optimal even in the short run. The
same arguments can be extended to all countries in the long run and
to most in the short run.

Pragmatic policy makers tend to focus on the need to maximize
per capita output or consumption, or their growth rates, or some other
measure of total or average welfare now or at some time in the near
future. This stance seems to imply that the welfare of the living is
more important than the welfare of those not yet born or those who
may never be born.

Most of modern economic theory has been produced by modern industrialized societies which, by and large and until recently, did not experience acute absolute or dynamic pressures of population growth on
their abundant natural resources and relatively abundant capital resources. This may account for the relatively low priority attached
to conservation of natural resources in many such economies.

The increasing pollution of air and water, the mounting destruction of irreplaceable natural resources and the growing disturbance
of ecological systems in the industrialized nations are causing concern.
These problems may all be exaggerated manyfold as the poor majority
of the world struggles to attain levels of living of the affluent mi-
nority. Technology may solve many, but not all, of these problems. Hence,
even the older and static notions of optimum population (in relation to
size or density) may yet turn out to be relevant from the ecological
point of view for even developed economies. Since an economic system
is part of a larger ecological system, economic growth which progressively destroys the environment in which it functions, is self- defeating,
and hence, non-optimal in the long run. In LDCs, development is likely
to improve the environment in some dimensions and worsen it in others
with perhaps a positive net effect in the short run.

---

[3] Marc NERLOVE, Assaf RAZIN and Efraim SADKA, "Socially Optimal Population Size and Individual Choices", paper for the Conference on Optimum Population; drawn from Household and Economy: Welfare Economics
of Endogenous Fertility, Academic Press, New York, 1987.

In the long run their environmental problems may be at least as bad as those of the developed countries. This paper, however is concerned with the narrower economic questions of the relatively short run, for LDCs.

II. A Static Approach to Optimum Population

NURKSE has argued that in "Asia over the last hundred years ... while population has doubled, other things such as techniques, capital supplies and cultivable land have remained too much the same." The changes in other variables vis-a-vis population, in other words, have been small enough to warrant static assumptions. "The economic problem of the East has been largely a consequence of dynamic population growth in an otherwise relatively static environment."[4]

This population growth is attributed to the fall in death rates. If falling death rates are due to new medical technology, international relief, and other factors independent of the level of per capita income, savings and investment, as many demographers believe, NURSKE's argument is applicable to many economies.

In countries like India where population densities are high: land is scarce or very expensive to reclaim: resources for investment are meager, and the marginal product is below the average product, a good case can be made for reducing the absolute size of population, if at all possible (through emigration for example); the case for preventing population size from increasing (i. e., for a zero growth rate of population) is stronger, while the case for reducing the growth rate of population is stronger still.

Reducing the absolute size of population is unlikely to be feasible in any country. More realistically, it needs to minimize its population growth and to raise its volume of savings and investment. It could invest in population control or in physical capital and in other productivity raising programs (such as health, education, and training of the labor force).

The relative effectiveness of investment in raising per capita output by either increasing output or reducing population growth could yield the optimal growth rate of population and of output in a given context.

---

[4] Ragnar NURKSE, "Excess Population and Capital Construction", Malaya Economic Review, Oct. 1957.

Some empirical results[5], as well as theoretical consideration[6], suggest that the returns of investment in population control are much higher than in physical capital. If so, underdeveloped countries could accelerate their pace of development considerably by stepping up investment in birth control programs.

III. A Simple Dynamic Approach

The Harrod-Domar model, despite its simplicity and rigidity of assumptions, has proved to be a rather useful tool in development planning, even though its original purposes were unrelated to this field.

Given the need to attain some growth rate of the economy, it can be used to arrive at needed savings and investment rates consistent with the capital-output ratio for an economy. In the model, in the absence of technical change, equilibrium requires that capital stock, output and labor force grow at the same rate - the rate given by the ratio of the propensity to save (σ) and the capital-output ratio (β).

Since output is a function only of one input, capital, it is assumed that whatever labor force is required for equilibrium growth is always available. If one assumes that population is optimal initially, employment and population will continue to be so over time; both growing at the same rate as output as well as the stock of capital; i. e.,

$$\frac{\sigma}{\beta} = \frac{\Delta L}{L} = \frac{\Delta P}{P} = \frac{\Delta K}{K} = \frac{\Delta Y}{Y}$$

Since this version does not permit per capita output to rise, it is of little interest for development. Introducing technical change makes the model more interesting and relevant. To the extent technical change raises the productivity of the existing labor force, additional labor is not needed to meet the requirements of the production process. The needed growth rate of population G_0 then equals the difference between the growth rate of output (or capital) and the growth rate of productivity (T), i. e.,

$$G_0 = \frac{\sigma}{\beta} - T$$

---

[5] See, for example, Robert Repetto, "India: a Case Study of the Madras Vasectomy Program", Studies in Family Planning, No. 31, May 1968, pp. 8-16.

[6] Stephen ENKE, "The Economic Aspects of Slowing Population Growth", The Economic Journal, No. 301, March 1966, pp. 44-56.

The capital-output ratio remains stable as before (one of the properties of the Harrod-Domar models), but both capital and output now increase faster than population; hence, the capital as well as the output per worker rise. In general, the smaller the savings rate, the larger the capital output ratio, and the faster the gains of productivity due to technical change, the smaller the growth rate of optimum population. As expenditures on research and development continue to increase in amounts and as proportions of national incomes, and as technical knowledge is shared increasingly between nations, the trend of T may be upwards, thereby reducing G_0. But such countries usually start with large pools of unemployed labor force and hence, during their initial and transitional phase, G_0 maybe zero if not negative.

Net savings rates in most economies fall between 20 and 2 percent, with most countries falling between 15 and 5 percent. Incremental capital output ratios range between 5 and 1, with most clustering around 3. The highest and the lowest growth rates of output (20 and 0.4 percent per year) are then given by the unlikely events in which the highest σ is found with the lowest β and vice versa. If one assumes that both β and T are higher in economies with higher rates of investment, and that from country to country and over time, β and T vary less than σ, we can compute some hypothetical and likely values for G_0.

In many poor economies, σ is below 6 percent and β above 3. A 2 percent rise in productivity due to technical change would make population growth undesirable as long as these conditions persist.

Introducing assumptions about the nature of technical change (whether it is neutral, labor-biased, capital-biased, whether it is embodied only in new equipment or newly trained labor, or it raises the productivity of all capital assets and workers) would yield different optimum population paths over time. But even if technical change is labor using, it needs resources that have to be saved from current consumption, which is a major bottleneck in development. Making the model dynamic in this way, thus, does not really make population growth more beneficial.

Obviously this simple modified Harrod-Domar model assumes away difficult and complex questions such as age composition, dependency ratios, labor participation rates, skills, values, institutions, attitudes and possibilities of international trade.

IV. Conclusions

More complex models are needed and are being produced. There has been
a resurgence of intellectual output on the subject since SAMUELSON's
path breaking article in 1958.[7] It is suggested here that sophisticated
demographic-economic models have not eliminated the usefulness of a
simple model any more than the complex models of growth theory have
diminished the usefulness of the original Harrod-Domar models.

Opening a closed economy to international trade results in a once-
and-for-all shift of the production possibility curve. Unless it can
be demonstrated that a country's participation in international trade
improves its terms of trade with increasing population size, little
is gained by dropping the assumptions of a closed economy. Neither
of these propositions have much weight, logically or empirically.

Producing labor intensive goods for domestic and foreign markets
has been one way for LDCs to raise their employment, output and standards
of living. But the thrust of technical change in developed as well
as less developed economies is increasingly creating a class of permanently unemployed or underemployed, low skilled population everywhere.
There may even be increased protectionism in the DCs as a result of
chronic and structural unemployment in DCs. As these pressures increase,
LDs will find that their problems are harder to solve. The need for
curbing population growth will then be stronger.

Considering the limited availability of resources from abroad,
the difficulty of emigration to open spaces, the expensive nature of re-
claiming and settling jungles or deserts, the paucity of internal sources
of savings and investment, the low nutritional and educational levels
(and hence productivity) of the population, the high dependency ratios,
the exhausted nature of most soils, and the stagnant markets for their
traditional exports, the capital-using nature of available technology,
the optimum populations for most underdeveloped countries during the
next decade are likely to be less than what they now have implying
optimal population growth to be negative. More sophisticated models,
based on realistic assumptions, are unlikely to change that conclusion.

[7] P. A. SAMUELSON, (a) "An Exact Consumption Loan Model of Interest
with or without the Social Contrivance of Money", The Journal of Political Economy, 1958, pp. 467-482. (b) "Optimal Social Security in
a Life Cycle Growth Model", International Economic Review, 1975,
pp. 539-544. (c) "The Optimum Growth Rate for Population", International Economic Review, 1975, pp. 531-538. (d) "The Optimum Growth
Rate for Population: Agreements and Evaluations", International
Economic Review, 1976, pp. 516-525.

MONETARY METHODS OF ESTIMATING INFORMAL ACTIVITIES
IN DEVELOPING NATIONS

Edgar L. Feige
University of Wisconsin

Madison, Wisc. / USA

ABSTRACT: This paper presents a simple monetary model for estimating
the size and growth of the informal sector in developing nations. The
model is empirically estimated for the Peruvian economy under a variety
of specifications. Studies of the relationship between demographic
change and economic activity are enhanced by knowledge of both the
secular and cyclical patterns of growth of the informal economy.

I.   Introduction

The quality of macroeconomic analysis and public policy ultimately depends upon the reliability and comprehensiveness of the system of economic accounts used to describe both the structure and intertemporal
changes in economic activity. A prerequisite for efforts to empirically
characterize the relationship between demographic change and economic
development is the ability to adequately measure the nature and extent
of relevant economic activities. The measurement of economic activity
in developing nations poses particular challenges. Resources required
for the construction of National Income and Product Accounts (NIPA)
are often limited and necessary data sources are often unavailable or
of dubious quality. NIPA data sources typically include: 1) government
administrative statistics; 2) economic censuses; 3) household surveys;
4) trade and private source data. The coverage of these data sources
is often limited to those economic units that are well integrated into
the economic and financial structure. Such units would typically include
governmental agencies, larger business and middle and upper income households. To the extent that NIPA data sources also include detailed estimates of agricultural output based on estimates of land in cultivation
and crop yields, reasonably reliable estimates of the agricultural sector
may also be available. These units make up what will be referred to as
the **official** sector of economic activity. The **recorded** sector of economic activity reflects the sum of the measured official sector plus
any imputations made in the NIPA for unofficial or informal economic
activity.

Studies in Contemporary Economics
A. Wenig, K. F. Zimmermann (Eds.)
Demographic Change and Economic Development
© Springer-Verlag Berlin Heidelberg 1989

During the past decade, there has been a growing recognition that
NIPA accounts often understate overall economic activity. The largest
component of omitted income is that produced in the household sector.
The omission of this income is due to accounting conventions that exclude imputations for household production largely on the grounds that
such income is too difficult to measure. In addition to convention based
exclusions, NIPA accounts also tend to understate economic activities
that should in principle be included according to accepted national
accounting conventions. Even developed nations with sophisticated national accounting structures understate economic activity because underlying data sources are systematically biased downward. A particular example is the understatement of income from tax source data. The recent
comprehensive revision of U. S. NIPA [BEA, 1985] reveals that for the
year 1984, personal income in the U. S. required an upward adjustment
of almost $ 100 billion in order to reflect newly discovered [IRS, 1983]
amounts of unreported income in tax source data. This type of problem
is likely to be of even greater significance for developing nations,
whose NIPA accounts are likely to understate the amounts of income generated by economic activites undertaken in the informal sector. We refer
to this omitted income as unrecorded income, namely, the amount of income that should be recorded in NIPA but is not recorded.

Informal and unrecorded income growth may itself be related to underlying demographic forces. An example is a population shift from rural
to urban areas. New urban populations initially locate on the peripheries of urban centers and engage in economic activities which constitute
an informal sector whose output typically escapes measurement in conventional official statistics. Developed economies have witnessed anomalous
increases in aggregate unemployment rates which are often attributed
to changes in the demographic composition of the labor force.[1] An alternative hypothesis which also explains the data is that observed unemployment rates have been artificially inflated as a result of a growing unrecorded sector of economic activity. Individuals actually employed in
the unrecorded sector may be counted in labor market surveys as part of
the unemployed labor force. Efforts to discriminate between these competing hypotheses require some independent estimates of unrecorded activities. Similar problems arise with studies of productivity.[2] Official

---

[1] GRACIA-DIEZ, 1986.

[2] WOLFF, E., 1986

estimates of productivity growth may be downward biased as a result of growth of unrecorded output.[3] As a consequence, empirical studies of the relationship between documented demographic shifts and official estimates of economic growth may produce biased results. This problem arises because the full economic impact of demographic changes may not be registered in conventional measures of economic growth.

The purpose of this paper is to describe a model of economic activity that is capable of providing rough estimates of the magnitude of unrecorded income in developing nations which are most likely to suffer from data inadequacies that lead to underestimates of economic activity. The model of economic activity is a simple monetary model. Its usefulness derives from the fact that the highest quality statistics in most developing nations are typically monetary statistics. Central banks in developing nations generate and collect administrative data on the stocks of currency and demand deposits. Currency data are reliable because Central banks must maintain accurate records of the issuance and redemption of currency notes. Demand deposit data are likely to be reliable because Central bank regulatory functions require commercial banks to provide timely and precise deposit statistics.

The basic hypothesis that motivates the methodology employed in this analysis is that the informal or unrecorded sector of economic activity in developing nations predominantly uses currency as a medium of exchange in the conduct of its economic affairs. Currency is a superior medium of exchange for this sector for several reasons. Its use does not require any formal affiliation with the commercial banking sector, and its use leaves no "paper trail" that can be used by government agencies as a basis for establishing tax liabilities or regulatory compliance. Both factors reduce the implicit transactions costs associated with the process of exchange in the informal sector.

The paper specifies some simple models which can be used to obtain indirect estimates of informal sector activity in most developing nations. Given these provisional estimates, researchers interested in studying the linkages between demographic changes and economic activity can examine the robustness of their hypotheses when economic development is confined to official estimates of income and when the concept is broadened to include the growth of the informal sector.

---

[3] FEIGE (1980) showed that estimates of unrecorded income are significantly related to the unexplained residual component of the productivity decline in the U. S.

Section I specifies a general currency ratio model (GCR) that can be employed to obtain estimates of informal or unrecorded economic activity. Section II presents alternative specifications of the model representing special cases defined by alternative key assumptions. In order to illustrate the use of the model under alternative specifications, empirical estimates of unrecorded income are undertaken for Peru. These results indicate the sensitivity of the estimates to alternative specifying assumptions. They serve to illustrate the application of the model to a situation typical for a developing nation.

II. Theoretical Specifications

i) A General Currency Ratio Model

In order to provide a general conceptual framework for the estimation of the informal sector based on currency ratio methods, it is useful to develop a general currency ratio model (GCR) from which it is possible to derive a number of special cases which represent alternative procedures that have been employed to obtain aggregative inter-temporal estimates of the informal sector.

Let,

C = Actual stock

D = Actual stock of demand deposits

Y_o = Official Income

Y_r = Record Income

i = subscript to denote the "informal" sector

o = subscript to denote the "official" sector

k_o = the ratio of currency to demand deposits in the "official" sector

k_i = the ratio of currency to demand deposits in the "informal" sector

v_i = "informal" sector income velocity

v_o = "official" sector income velocity

The general currency ratio model contains the following specifications:

(1) $C = C_1 + C_o$

(2) $D = D_1 + D_o$

$$(3) \quad k_o = \frac{C_o}{D_o}$$

$$(4) \quad k_i = \frac{C_i}{D_i}$$

$$(5) \quad v_o = \frac{Y_o}{C_o + D_o}$$

$$(6) \quad v_i = \frac{Y_i}{C_i + D_i}$$

$$(7) \quad \beta = \frac{v_i}{v_o}$$

$$(8) \quad Y_o = \gamma \cdot Y_r$$

Equations (1) and (2) decompose the actual stocks of currency and demand deposits[4] into their "informal" and "official" components. Equations (3) and (4) are definitions of the terms k_o and k_i which can be viewed either as functions or constants. Similarly, equations (5) and (6) define income velocity in the two sectors. Equation (7) defines the parameter β as the ratio of the income velocities in the two sectors and equation (8) specifies the relationship between official sector income and the total income actually recorded in the National Income and Product Accounts [$\gamma \leq 1$].

The model can be solved for Y_i in terms of the observable variables, namely C, D and Y_r. Repeated substitution and rearrangement of terms yields the general solution for Y_i as:

---

[4] The appropriate definition of the assets that constitute the money supply must be limited to those assets that function as a final medium of exchange. In practice, currency and demand deposits comprise the final exchange media in most developing nations. Many nations are known to have considerable stocks of U. S. currency that circulate in the economy. These stocks should in principle be included in the analysis as part of the currency supply. To the extent that such U. S. dollar holdings are large and have been growing over time, they would tend to increase the estimates of the informal economy. Travelers checks and credit cards are sometimes considered to be media of exchange, however, since the purchase of travelers checks or the settlement of credit card accounts requires the use of currency or checkable deposits, to include these assets would amount to double counting. The currency ratio method should therefore be applied with (D) defined as demand deposits. This convention is maintained in all following estimates of the informal economy.

$$(8) \quad Y_i = \beta \cdot \gamma \cdot Y_r \cdot \frac{(k_i + 1) \cdot (C - k_o D)}{(k_o + 1) \cdot (k_i D - C)}$$

Equation (8) expresses the informal economy as a function of the observable variables Y_r, C and D and four parameters or functions: β, γ, k_i and k_o.

ii) Special Cases of the General Model

Although equation (8) provides a general solution for the evaluation of the informal sector's income Y_i, empirical estimation requires additional assumptions concerning the appropriate values of the parameters β, γ, k_i and k_o. The particular manner in which these parameters are specified, define the special cases of the general model. The procedure to be followed is to consider alternate possible specifications of these parameters and to empirically evaluate the general solution for Y_i under alternative parametric specifications ranging from the most restrictive to the least restrictive. By providing alternate specifications, experts familiar with the particular institutional arrangements of any developing nation can select the particular set of restrictions that appear most appropriate for the nation's institutional setting. Consideration of alternative specifications also permits a sensitivity analysis of the results to alternative specifying assumptions.

III. Empirical Estimates of Informal Income

In order to provide an illustration of the use of the GCR model, various specifications are applied to data for Peru for the period 1953-1983.[5]

i) The Simple Currency Ratio Method

The most restrictive case of the general model reflects the assumptions used by CAGAN (1956) and GUTMANN (1976). The assumptions are as follows:

[5] The data employed in these calculations are from the IMF International Financial Statistics.

1) That currency is the exclusive medium of exchange in "informal" transactions.
2) That the ratio of currency to demand deposits in the official economy
   remains constant.
3) That the amount of "informal" income produced by a dollar of currency
   is the same as the amount of income produced by a dollar of currency
   in the official economy.
4) That in some benchmark period t_b, informal sector income is negligible.
5) That recorded income is comprised entirely of "official" income.

Assumption 1) implies that informal transactions are never paid by check,
therefore: $k_i \to \infty$.

Assumption 2) asserts that k_o is constant over time.

Assumption 3) implies that $\beta = 1$.

Assumption 4) implies that in the benchmark year t_b, $Y_i/Y_o = 0$, therefore:

$$k_{ot_b} = \frac{C_{t_b}}{D_{t_b}}$$

Assumption 5) implies the $\gamma = 1$.

Under these restrictive assumptions, equation (8) reduces to:

$$(9) \quad Y_i = Y_r \cdot \left\{ \frac{(C - k_o D)}{(k_o + 1)\, D} \right\}$$

and k_o can be approximated by its benchmark value at t_b.[6]

Table (1) presents estimates of the informal sector based on the
foregoing assumptions, and Figure (1) depicts the ratio of the informal
income to recorded income. As depicted in Figure (1), and Table (1)
[Col. 3 and 4], the informal sector appears to have grown secularly,
both in real and nominal terms, except for a decline during the late
1950's and early 1960's. The informal sector, is estimated to have grown
to a maximum of 37.57 % of recorded income by 1982. Figure 2 presents
estimates of total real income in Peru and depicts the real contribution
of both the informal and formal sectors.

---

[6] In the base year $Y_i = 0$. Therefore $k_{otb} = C/D$.

218

Figure 1

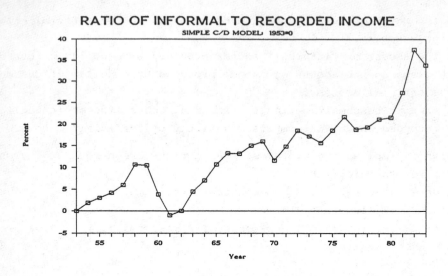

Figure 2

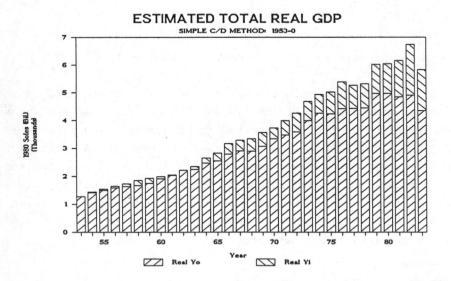

Table 1

Estimates of Informal Income: Assuming $\beta = 1$; $k_i \rightarrow \infty$; $Y_i = 0$ (1953)

YEAR	(1) Nominal GDP	(2) Real GDP	(3) Estimated Nominal Informal Income	(4) Estimated Real Informal Income	(5) Percent Informal
53	22.90	1276.48	.00	.00	.00
54	26.70	1416.45	0.49	26.22	1.85
55	29.60	1497.98	0.89	45.22	3.02
56	33.00	1586.54	1.38	66.36	4.18
57	36.10	1640.91	2.15	97.79	5.96
58	40.30	1679.17	4.32	179.85	10.71
59	47.40	1755.56	4.99	184.67	10.52
60	55.60	1917.24	2.13	73.47	3.83
61	63.90	2061.29	-0.61	-19.77	-0.96
62	73.40	2224.24	0.04	1.11	0.05
63	78.70	2248.57	3.53	100.98	4.49
64	96.70	2479.49	6.83	175.20	7.07
65	114.90	2553.33	12.35	274.46	10.75
66	136.80	2791.84	18.22	371.90	13.32
67	156.90	2905.56	20.68	383.04	13.18
68	185.80	2903.13	27.93	436.41	15.03
69	209.00	3073.53	33.44	491.82	16.00
70	240.70	3343.06	28.02	389.13	11.64
71	264.40	3478.95	39.23	516.24	14.84
72	294.70	3593.90	54.60	665.84	18.53
73	359.20	3991.11	61.99	688.74	17.26
74	447.50	4261.90	70.17	668.26	15.68
75	550.20	4232.31	102.37	787.49	18.61
76	764.50	4419.08	166.32	961.41	21.76
77	1057.90	4426.36	199.36	834.16	18.85
78	1677.50	4449.60	324.48	860.68	19.34
79	3119.30	4967.04	660.30	1051.44	21.17
80	4968.60	4968.60	1074.09	1074.09	21.62
81	8489.70	4840.19	2324.05	1325.00	27.37
82	14134.00	4900.83	5310.49	1841.36	37.57
83	26499.10	4351.25	8964.52	1472.01	33.83

220

Figure 3

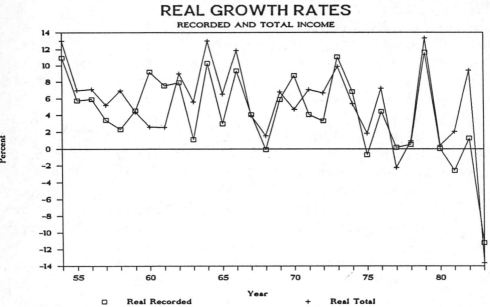

Figure 3 displays the real growth rates of recorded income and
total income, namely the sum of recorded and informal income. Figure 3
suggests that growth rates in recorded income can both overstate and
understate the overall growth in economic activity. In some periods,
declines in recorded growth rates were offset by shifts to the informal
sector, suggesting that apparent recessions were not as severe as suggested by recorded GDP. On the other hand, there are also some periods
during which the growth rate of total real income was actually lower
than the observed growth rate. For example, the severity of the decline
in recorded income in 1983 was sufficiently strong to induce an even
greater decline in the informal economy, making the decline in the growth
of total income greater than the decline suggested by the recorded GDP
figures.

ii) Effect of Changing Benchmark Assumptions

In order to examine the sensitivity of the estimates of the informal
sector to alternative parametric specifications, we first consider the
implications of a relaxation of the benchmark assumption, namely that
in the early part of the period, the informal economy was non existent.
If we modify assumption (4) of the preceding section to permit an informal sector amounting to 10 % of recorded income in the beginning of
the period under study, but retain the remaining restrictive assumptions
of the simple C/D method, it is possible to solve Equation (8) for the
value of k_o that would have prevailed in the benchmark period (k_{otb}).
Since this benchmark value of k_o is assumed to have remained constant
during the remainder of the period, it is then possible to obtain estimates of the informal sector for all other years by applying equation
(9). The results of this change in benchmark specification are displayed
in Figures (4) and (5). The change in the benchmark period assumption,
raises the estimated ratio of informal to recorded income for all years,
and suggests that the informal sector amounted to almost 50 % of recorded income in 1982-1983. A comparison between Figure (1) and Figure
(4) shows that the benchmark assumption affects only the estimated size
of the informal sector, but does not affect its inter-temporal growth
path.

It should be recalled, that the foregoing estimates all assume
that recorded income consists exclusively of income produced in the
formal sector ie. ($\gamma = 1$). The implication of this assumption is that

all informal sector income is unrecorded in the National Income and
Product Accounts of Peru. However, recent analysis undertaken by the
Instituto Libertad y Democracia (ILD) reveals that recorded GDP already
includes some imputations for the income produced in the informal sector.

Figure 4

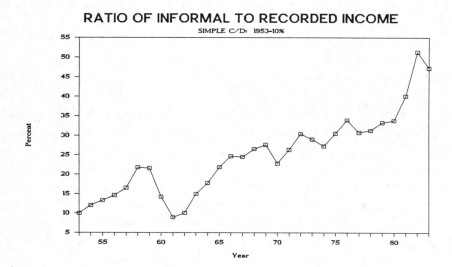

223

Figure 5

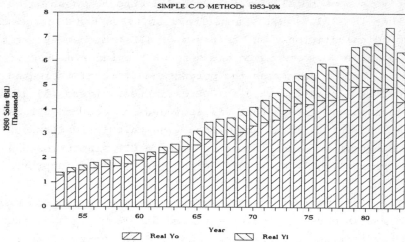

Figure 6

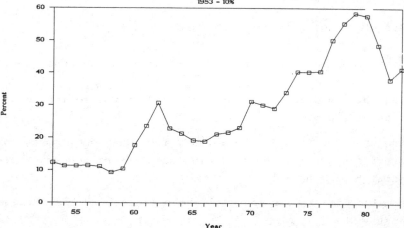

The ILD undertook a detailed evaluation of GDP by sectors for the year 1979 and concluded that recorded GDP in that year already included imputations for the informal sector. These imputations amounted to approximately 14 % of total official recorded output. These calculations suggest that in 1979, γ .86, rather than unity as had been assumed in the forgoing calculations. On the basis of ILD time series estimates of γ, it is possible to reestimate the size of the informal sector from equation (8) and to determine the percentage of total estimated informal income that is already imputed in GDP estimates. Figure (6) displays the percent of informal income that was included in recorded GDP as a result of imputations for informal activities. The calculations suggest that the percentage of informal income imputed in GDP statistics has increased over time from slightly over 10 % during the 1950's to approximately 50 % by 1980.

In the sections that follow, several further simulation experiments are performed in order to indicate the methodology for a further relaxation of the restrictive assumptions embodied in the simplest formulation of the currency ratio approach. The sensitivity simulations concerning the benchmark assumption indicate that the estimates of the size of the informal sector are quite sensitive to the particular specifying assumption employed. On the other hand, the time path of the informal sector is essentially invariant under different assumptions concerning the size of the informal sector in the benchmark year.

iii) Effect of Changing Assumptions Concerning β and k_i

The forgoing simulations have already illustrated the consequences of:

a) Assuming that an irregular sector existed at the beginning of the period under study.

b) Assuming that recorded income already includes some imputations for the irregular economy. The foregoing simulations however, retained the restrictions that:

c) Income velocities in the informal and official sectors being equal ie that $\beta = 1$.

d) Currency being the exclusive medium of exchange in the informal sector, ie. that $k_i \to \infty$.

e) The ratio of currency to demand deposits in the official economy (ko) remaining constant over the period of observation.

As can be seen from equation 9, the estimated size of the informal sector will depend directly on the assumed ratio of the income velocities in the two sectors. Since the informal sector of the economy is likely to be more service intensive than that of the formal sector, it may be more reasonable to assume that $\beta > 1$. Service intensive sectors typically require fewer intermediate transactions than manufacturing intensive sectors so a given amount of the medium of exchange can support a higher amount of final output. If the income velocity of the informal sector is assumed to be 10 % higher than in the official sector, $\beta = 1.10$ and all the earlier reported estimates would be increased by 10 %.

It is also desirable to modify the assumption that currency is the exclusive medium of exchange used in the informal sector. Survey studies undertaken in several developed nations indicate that although check transactions leave an "audit trail", checks are nevertheless used as a medium of exchange in informal activities. In the U. S. for example, survey results indicate that between 30 % and 50 % of some particular informal market transactions are in fact paid for by check rather than currency (SMITH, 1985). In developing nations, banking institutions are neither as extensive nor as accessible as is the case in developed nations. Nevertheless, it is likely that at least some fraction of informal activities employ checks as a medium of exchange. To appreciate the impact of a relaxation of the restriction that $k_i \to \infty$, assume instead that 90 % of informal market transactions use currency as the medium of exchange, whereas 10 % of payments are made by check. This assumption implies that $k_i = 9$.

Table 2 reports the estimates of the informal sector that correspond to the joint hypotheses that:

$\beta \quad = 1.10$

$\gamma \quad = 1$

$k_i \quad = 9.$

226

Table 2

Estimates of Informal Income: Assuming $\beta=1.10$; $ki=9$; $Y_i=0$ and $Y_i=10\%(1953)$

Year	Percent Informal 1953-0	Estimated Nominal Informal Income	Estimated Real Informal Income	Percent Informal 1953=10%	Estimated Nominal Informal Income	Estimated Real Informal Income
53	.00	.00	.00	10.00	2.29	127.65
54	2.50	0.67	35.44	12.73	3.40	180.31
55	4.09	1.21	61.27	14.46	4.28	216.64
56	5.68	1.88	90.16	16.20	5.35	257.01
57	8.13	2.93	133.39	18.87	6.81	309.61
58	14.77	5.95	247.99	26.11	10.52	438.45
59	14.50	6.87	254.53	25.82	12.24	453.22
60	5.20	2.89	99.74	15.68	8.72	300.53
61	-1.29	-0.82	-26.55	8.60	5.49	177.17
62	0.07	0.05	1.50	10.07	7.39	224.06
63	6.11	4.80	137.28	16.66	13.11	374.62
64	9.66	9.34	239.58	20.54	19.86	509.31
65	14.82	17.03	378.50	26.17	30.07	668.24
66	18.48	25.28	515.90	30.16	41.26	841.98
67	18.28	28.68	531.18	29.94	46.98	870.03
68	20.94	38.90	607.79	32.84	61.02	953.36
69	22.34	46.68	686.50	34.37	71.83	1056.26
70	16.08	38.72	537.72	27.55	66.31	920.91
71	20.66	54.62	718.65	32.54	86.02	1131.88
72	26.01	76.66	934.88	38.38	113.10	1379.26
73	24.16	86.78	964.17	36.35	130.58	1450.93
74	21.87	97.87	932.08	33.86	151.52	1443.01
75	26.13	143.76	1105.88	38.50	211.85	1629.65
76	30.78	235.30	1360.12	43.58	333.14	1925.67
77	26.48	280.12	1172.07	38.89	411.38	1721.26
78	27.21	456.45	1210.74	39.68	665.70	1765.77
79	29.91	932.85	1485.42	42.62	1329.58	2117.17
80	30.57	1519.03	1519.03	43.35	2153.98	2153.98
81	39.25	3331.84	1899.56	52.81	4483.70	2556.27
82	55.21	7802.78	2705.54	70.22	9925.52	3441.58
83	49.26	13052.46	2143.26	63.73	16888.96	2773.23

Two sets of simulations are presented. The first assumes that the informal sector was zero in 1953, the second assumed that the informal
sector accounted for 10 % of recorded income in 1953.

Figure 7

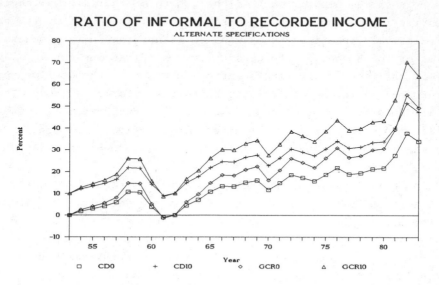

Figure 7 displays the results of these simulations for the general
currency ratio model (GCR) under the foregoing set of specifications
and repeats the results of the most restrictive versions of the model
[labeled CD 0 and CD 10] for comparative purposes. Figure 7 therefore
indicates the sensitivity of the empirical results to alternative specifying assumptions. For the year 1983, the most restrictive forms of the
model [CD 0 and CD 10] produce estimates of the informal economy that
range between 34 % and 47 % of recorded income. The earlier calculations
suggest that less than half of this informal income is already imputed
in recorded GDP. The less restrictive estimates of the GCR model [GCR 0
and GCR 10] produce estimates that suggest that the informal sector accounts for between 49 % and 64 % of recorded activity. The consequence
of relaxing the restrictions on β and k_i is therefore to raise the esti-

mated size of the informal economy. Figure (7) suggests that the final estimates are sensitive to both the choice of an appropriate benchmark and to the appropriate specifications for the parameters β and k_i. Although the estimates of the size of the informal sector depend quite critically on the specifying assumptions, all estimates suggest that the informal economy has grown secularly in relation to recorded GNP. Moreover, since the temporal path of the growth of the informal sector depends primarily on the ratio of currency to demand deposits, its growth path is relatively invariant to changes in either the initial benchmark assumption or to changes in the parametric specifications for β and k_i.

One of the most interesting questions concerning the development of the informal sector is its relationship to the formal economy. In particular, does the informal sector act as a counter cyclical buffer to stabilize fluctuations in recorded economic activity, or does the informal sector also have a business cycle that conforms to that of recorded income?

In the former case, the business cycle in recorded GDP tends to overstate actual fluctuations in overall economic activity. Declines in recorded GDP are buffered by shifts into informal activities and conversely, strong growth in the official sector provides employment opportunities for individuals previously engaged in informal activities. When formal and informal activities are cyclical substitutes, overall economic activity will fluctuate less than recorded economic activity with the informal economy functioning as an automatic stabilizer for overall economic activity.

On the other hand, it is possible that declines in aggregate demand in the official sector spill over to the informal sector. In this case, both sectors will experience similar business cycles, and fluctuations in recorded income will in fact understate fluctuations in overall economic activity.

Figure (8) displays the cycles in real recorded GDP and in the real informal sector as estimated by the less restrictive GCR model for the period 1967 - 1983. With the exceptions of the synchronous movements observed during 78 - 80 and 82 - 83, the results suggest that for the Peruvian case, the informal sector has largely served as a counter cyclical buffer for fluctuations in recorded economic activity. This latter finding has both economic and political implications.

If fluctuations in the official sector are buffered by shifts into the informal sector it suggests that governments should take great care not to over react to observed fluctuations in recorded income with large swings in discretionary monetary and fiscal policy which may tend to

Figure 8

BUSINESS CYCLES
REAL RECORDED GDP AND REAL INFORMAL

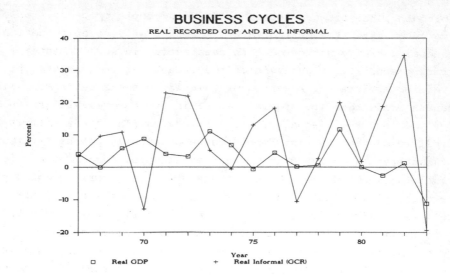

□   Real GDP   +   Real Informal (GCR)

destabilize the economy rather than stabilize it.[7] Conversely, a pro-
cyclical informal sector will require stronger counter cyclical policy
measures than would be called for on the basis of information generated
by fluctuations in observed economic activity.

If developing nations are observed to have differently functioning
informal sectors, these differences may be used to predict the potential
for political instability. If the informal sector serves as a substitute
for official sector activity, any economic decline in the official sector
is less likely to foster widespread political discontent since the economic impact of the decline is cushioned by offsetting shifts into the
informal sector. Nations whose informal sectors are institutionally
structured as complements to the official sector will suffer even greater
economic hardship with the depression of the official sector, becoming
more vulnerable to political instability.

---

[7] [FEIGE and McGEE, 1982] have developed a two sector macroeconomic
model which shows that both automatic and discretionary counter cyclical policies can destabilize economic activity when unobserved
shifts to the informal sector distort the information system.

IV. Summary and Conclusions

The foregoing analysis provides a relatively simple procedure for obtaining rough estimates of the informal sector of developing nations. The general currency ratio model is constructed in such a manner as to permit a sensitivity analysis of the impacts of various assumptions required for estimation. A series of calculations was performed using the general model and its special cases, in order to examine the robustness of the results under alternate assumptions. The study reveals that the final results do in fact depend quite critically on the particular set of assumptions employed in the estimation procedure. Country specific institutional knowledge is therefore essential in determing which particular set of assumptions is most appropriate. Where there is doubt as to the likely value of some of the key parameters, it will only be possible to use the model to obtain a range of plausible estimates.

Overall, the illustrative findings suggest that the informal economy of Peru is sizable and appears to have grown considerably during the last two decades. The results also suggest that although efforts have already been made to impute informal income in the official Peruvian NIPA, there remains a sizable amount of informal income that is unrecorded. Knowledge of the size and growth of this unrecorded component can be of great importance, since any demographic study that relies exclusively an official statistics is likely to be flawed by overlooking the important growth that has taken place in unrecorded components of income.

A further relaxation of the assumptions of the GCR model would permit several of the key parameters of the model to be specified as functions rather than constants. The foregoing simulations have all assumed that the ratio of currency to demand deposits in the official sector remains constant during the period of study. A more plausible assumption would be to consider the ratio a stable function of other economic variables. This latter modification requires that the currency ratio be specified as an additive function of the variables affecting k_o and those affecting the ratio C_u/D.[8] While such a specification would relax the remaining restrictions imposed on the model, it is questionable whether the available data base for most developing nations is sufficiently rich and accurate to improve the reliability of the final estimates.

---

[8] This procedure is discussed in [FEIGE, 1986] which presents the results of an econometric specification of the GCR model for the U. S.

On the basis of the foregoing simulations for Peru, it appears
that the size of the informal sector is considerable, but that the range
of variation in estimates of its size are still uncomfortably large,
as the resulting estimates appear to be quite sensitive to the particular
set of specifying assumptions employed. The temporal patterns of growth
in the informal sector are however less dependent on the particular
assumptions regarding parameter values. The evidence suggests that in
the Peruvian case, the informal sector acts largely as a counter cyclical buffer for the official sector. Thus, observed fluctuations in
recorded activity tend to overstate the true fluctuations in overall
economic activity.

One possible explanation of the observed relationship between the
recorded and unrecorded sectors of the Peruvian economy is that demographic changes have influenced the pattern of the informal sector's
development. For example, the secular trend in the growth of the informal sector may be related to secular trends in urbanization. Similarly,
economic cycles in agricultural areas may provide incentives that produce cyclical patterns of demographic migrations to urban centers. Declines in measured economic growth in agriculture may not be offset
by measured increases in recorded incomes in urban sectors if much of
the urban growth takes place in the informal economy. These asymmetries
in measurement would result in "omitted variables" biases which would
mislead investigators who exclusively investigate the relationships
between demographic changes and measured changes in economic growth.
Assessment of the true relationship between demographic changes and
overall economic development would require indirect estimates of the
omitted variable, namely the growth of unrecorded income. The foregoing procedures for obtaining rough estimates of the magnitude of informal activities facilitate unbiased tests of the linkages between
demographic change and economic development. Although we are far from
obtaining precise estimates of these informal activities, the foregoing
methods can be viewed as a preliminary effort to gain greater insights
into the development of this elusive sector.

232

References

FEIGE, Edgar L.: The Observed and Unobserved Economy: A New Perspective on Macroeconomic Phenomena. American Economics Association Meetings. Denver, Colorado, 1980.

FEIGE, Edgar L. and McGEE, R.: Policy Illusion, Macroeconomic Instability and the Unobserved Economy. Presented at the International Conference on the Unobserved Economy, Wassenaar, 1982.

FEIGE, Edgar L.: A Re-examination of the "Underground Economy in the United States". International Monetary Fund Staff Papers, December, 1986.

GRACIA-DIEZ, Mercedes: Compositional Changes of the Labor Force and the Increase of the Unemployment Rate: An Estimate for the U. S. Paper presented at the International Conference on Demographic Change and Economic Development in Hagen/West-Germany, September 1986.

INSTITUTO LIBERTAD Y DEMOCRACIA: Magnitude of the Informal Economic Activity in Peru. Estudios Economicos, March, 1986.

WOLFF, Edward: Demographic Changes and Long-Term Productivity Trends in Seven OECD Countries, 1870 - 1979. Paper presented at the International Conference on Demographic Change and Economic Development in Hagen/West-Germany, September 1986.

INTERACTION BETWEEN MACRO-ECONOMIC ACTIVITIES
AND DEMOGRAPHIC CHANGES IN SELECTED DEVELOPING COUNTRIES

Dilip Bhattacharyya[*]
University of Leicester

Leicester / Great Britain

Abstract: A dynamic macro-economic model is specified assuming that
the Government minimises a loss function and uses government expenditures and money supply as instruments for control. Through this model
we examine the Malthusian theory as well as Simon and Steinmann's theory
of population growth and technical progress.

I.   Introduction

Demographic changes have important consequences to an economy. In the
case of increasing population, the country generally faces a large number
of young people who need societal support or, more precisely, the support
of the currently working population. Generally, this support is given
with the expectation that these young people will join the labour force
and the economy will adjust to utilise the larger size of the labour
force and in turn will produce more goods and services in the future.
However, this scenario has different implications for different economies.
For a less developed country (LDC) one could utilise BOSERUP's explanation
and suggest that population growth will induce people to change their
agricultural practices.[1] Alternatively, one could take a Malthusian
stand and suggest that the per capita production and the consumption
level will be reduced due to increased population. A casual observation
of the recorded history of the world would suggest that the MALTHUS's
(1798) theory has not found any observational support until now. Particularly, if we examine the history of the more developed countries
(MDC's) we find that the economies are growing fast and there is virtually no evidence to support Malthusian predictions.[2] SIMON (1986)
and STEINMANN (1986) extended BOSERUP's conjecture and argue that population growth induces technical progress using the experience of the

---

[1] Boserup's argument can be seen as an extension of the idea put forward
in Sen (1959).

[2] Simon has put forward this argument since 1977 in many of his writings.

---

[*] I am grateful to the Nuffield Foundation and the University of
Leicester Research Board for research grants. I have benefited from
the comments of Klaus F. Zimmermann and an anonymous referee on an
earlier draft. All errors are mine.

Studies in Contemporary Economics
A. Wenig, K. F. Zimmermann (Eds.)
Demographic Change and Economic Development
© Springer-Verlag Berlin Heidelberg 1989

OECD countries to support their theory. But, it is well known that
the OECD countries are richly endowed with resources and technical
know-how and therefore SIMON's and STEINMANN's study cannot be taken
as a conclusive evidence that population growth is the only or even
the main cause of technical progress. In fact, much of the post World
War II literature suggests that the introduction of capital-intensive
processes by the firms is caused by the lack of a sufficiently large
labour force (see FELLNER (1961)). It is also argued by many authors
that introduction of capital-intensive processes is the major cause
of technical innovations. Hence, it is possible to argue that SIMON
and STEINMANN's findings are spurious and the actual cause of technical
progress is in fact due to the lack of population growth. To resolve
this controversy, it is necessary to perform causality tests with suitable conditioning. Alternatively, one could suggest a plausible econometric model in which technical progress is the outcome of population
growth and other factors. The estimated parameters of the econometric
model and the associated statistical tests will be able to identify
the major causes of technical progress.[3] However, it is well known
that the measurement of technical progress is a very controversial
issue and therefore can cause further ambiguity to the econometric
results. It is also necessary that the econometric specification be
in a position to refute both Malthusian theory as well as SIMON-STEIN-
MANN's type theory.

The data which could refute the theories of MALTHUS or SIMON-STEIN-
MANN are necessarily aggregate in nature and observed only over time.
As these predictions are basically about a very long-run outcome it
may not be possible to verify these theories from a short series. What is
necessary in this situation is several short series of data over a
long period. For example, simple regression analysis of population
growth and per-capita income growth have shown insignificant correlation
in many studies such as KUZNETS, CHESNAIS and SANVEY (for further details see SIMON (1977) chapter 3). As the simple regression does not
take into account any structural changes that has happened over the
long periods under study, it is likely to produce misleading results.
Therefore, the approach we have taken in this paper is distinctly different. We specified a stylised macro model (to be elaborated in the
next section) and estimated that with a short time-series data set. We
then looked at the long-run behaviour of that model for a few selected
countries.

---

[3] The problem of testing through misspecified models is ignored here,
although such a possibility cannot be ruled out.

We focussed our interest on four major variables, (a) Consumption expenditure; (b) Investment expenditure; (c) National income and (d) Population. Consumption expenditure is considered to be a more meaningful variable to study MALTHUSIAN theory than the national income as the later is quite strongly affected by government expenditures and other government activities. To study SIMON-STEINMANN's theory we consider both investment expenditures and the national income as the suitable variables, since technical progress would directly cause an increase in national income and in that process will increase investment expenditure as that is a necessary condition for innovations (and to some extent for inventions). Thus, we need an inter-related structure between the four variables mentioned above along with some other variables which are either exogenous or predetermined to the system.

In this paper, we selected five countries from three continents to obtain some empirical results necessary to examine the theories mentioned above. Our control country is the United Kingdom which is one of the OECD countries and had an average population growth per annum of only 0.2 % during the period 1964-80. The four other countries chosen consist of India, Pakistan, Ethiopia and the Central African Republic; all of whom experienced high average population growth i. e. between 2.2 % to 3.2 % per annum. Thus our comparison of less developed countries and a developed economy will provide further insight into this global problem.

In the next section we present our model followed by sections with empirical results and conclusions.

II. The Analytical Framework

Let X_1, X_2, X_3 and X_4 be the four aggregate variables of interest as mentioned in the last section, namely (i) Consumption expenditure; (ii) Investment expenditure; (iii) National income and (iv) Level of Population. We assume households basically decide about the level of consumer expenditure, the structure of the family and the level of income by choosing the work effort. Thus the ith household makes 'optimum' (or desired) choice X_{1t}^i, X_{3t}^i and X_{4t}^i at time t. Similarly, the jth entrepreneur decides on the 'optimum' (or desired) level of X_{2t}^j and X_{3t}^j at time t. In addition, it is possible that the entrepreneur also takes into account the growth in population to predict the size of the market which in turn is reflected in the level of output decision. We also assume that the Government uses the fiscal and monetary instruments to control the economy. In particular, we assume that the government chooses the level of activities to minimise the expected loss measured as deviations from the desired level. This can be former-ly stated as: The Government wants to minimise,

$$E[\sum_{s=0}^{\infty} (X_{t+s} - X_{t+s}^{*})'W(X_{t+s} - X_{t+s}^{*}) | \Omega_{t+s}] \tag{1}$$

where

$$X_{t+s} = \begin{pmatrix} X_{1t+s} \\ X_{2t+s} \\ X_{3t+s} \\ X_{4t+s} \end{pmatrix}$$

and X_{t+s}^{*} is the vector of aggregate desired level of activities obtained by aggregating individual's desired levels. W is a constant matrix of weights whose magnitude are decided by the Government's preference structure. Ω_{t+s} denotes the information set which in the present study contains government expenditures G_{t+s} money supply M_{t+s} and other exo-genous and pre-determined variables in the system. In addition, it is assumed that the government would like to minimise the cost of adjust-ment to the current level from the previous level of activities. This is measured as

$$(X_{t+s} - X_{t+s-1})'C(X_{t+s} - X_{t+s-1}) \tag{2}$$

where C is the matrix of constants measuring the adjustment cost struc-ture. Thus the government's overall objective is to minimise,

$$I = E[\sum_{s=0}^{\infty} (X_{t+s} - X_{t+s}^{*})'W(X_{t+s} - X_{t+s}^{*}) | \Omega_{t+s}] +$$

$$+ (X_{t+s} - X_{t+s-1})'C(X_{t+s} - X_{t+s-1}) \tag{3}$$

Assuming that the principle of 'Certainty Equivalence' is applicable 'I' can be minimised for each chosen level of G_{t+s} and M_{t+s}. Thus, there could be an infinite number of optimal solutions for infinite possible choices of G_{t+s} and M_{t+s}. We assume that the Government uses other extranous criteria to decide the level of G_{t+s} and M_{t+s} to choose among the many possible alternatives available to them. In particular, it can be argued that among the alternative choices of G_{t+s} and M_{t+s} the government chooses that combination which is politically most agreeable.[4] The optimal solution of 'I' will produce a system of the form.[5]

$$(A_1 - A_2 L + A_3 L^2) \; X_{t+s+1} = D_2 Z_{t+s} \qquad (4)$$

where A_1, A_2, A_3 and D_2 are matrix of constants. L is the lag operator, i. e. $L^r(X_t) = X_{t-r}$ and Z_{t+s} is the vector of all the exogenous and predetermined variables that describe Ω_{t+s}. Hence Z_{t+s} includes G_{t+s} and M_{t+s}. In the empirical analysis we use an approximate equivalent representation of equation (4) which is

$$X_{t+s+1} = H_1 X_{t+s} + H_2 Z_{t+s-1} + H_3 Z_{t+s} + U_{t+s+1} \qquad (5)$$

where U_{t+s+1} is treated as the disturbance term. In the final estimation the parameters in H_3's are 'concentrated out' by a set of auxiliary regressions (see VEALL and ZIMMERMANN (1986) for details). It is important to note that the equation (5) is an approximation derived from the expansion of an expression of the form $(1-\beta L)^{-1}$. Thus, it is possible that variables with lag 2 or lag 3 should not be ignored. To examine the importance of lag structure we use Akaikie Information Criterion (AIC), where AIC $= -\frac{2}{T} \log(L) + \frac{2K}{T}$; where L stands for the liklihood function of the equation under consideration. T is the sample size and K is the number of free parameters in the equation. We choose the equation for which the AIC is lower. The long-run behaviour of the model is extrapolated from the estimated model as specified in equation (5). As

$$E(X_{t+s+1}) = H_1 X_{t+s} + H_2 Z_{t+s-1} + H_3 Z_{t+s} \; ;$$

the stability of the system depends on the eigenvalues of H_1. In our empirical study we examined the stability property from estimated $\hat{H}_1$.

---

[4] It is possible to suggest alternative 'optimising' procedures of choosing G and M. We avoided that because these alternative arguments will not affect our specification or analysis.

[5] For detailed derivation readers can consult NICKELL (1985) or BHATTACHARYYA (1978).

III. Empirical Results

The empirical study is based on data from India, Pakistan, Ethiopia, Central African Republic and the United Kingdom as mentioned earlier. The data period is 1964-1980. Although, for some of the countries (U.K. and India particularly) a longer series of data is available we used the period 1964-80 for all countries so that the comparisons are meaning-ful. The consumer expenditures, investment expenditures, the national income, government expenditures and money supplies were measured in real terms. Lagged G.N.P. price deflators were used as proxies for all exogenous and predetermined variables. The values of AIC based on one-period lag price and two-period lag price are presented below, equation by equation, for each country under study. AIC with one-period lag price is called AIC_1 and similarly with two-periods lag AIC_2, and the results are presented in Table 1. The experiments were extended for three and four periods lag price, but only the results of the first two lags are presented here as the problem reduced to choice between lag-one period and lag-two period specification on numerical grounds.

Table 1

Countries	Equation 1		Equation 2		Equation 3		Equation 4	
	AIC_1	AIC_2	AIC_1	AIC_2	AIC_1	AIC_2	AIC_1	AIC_2
Central African Republic	-2.9310	-2.8592	-5.3591	-5.3451	-2.2656	-2.1918	11.7703	11.8108
Ethiopia	2.5489	1.5850	2.0231	1.5559	3.3576	2.2423	12.0198	12.0158
India	11.9506	12.0768	12.1108	12.2745	13.8450	13.2864	14.5634	14.6547
Pakistan	10.2959	10.3899	8.3005	7.8582	10.7712	10.8954	12.9472	13.0048
U. K.	10.4736	10.5672	6.4897	6.1700	11.3640	11.4460	9.5121	9.6450

Equation 1: Consumer expenditures as the dependent variable.
Equation 2: Investment expenditures as the dependent variable.
Equation 3: National Income as the dependent variable.
Equation 4: Population as the dependent variable.

It can be seen from the results in Table 1 that for Ethiopia, AIC_1 is always higher than the corresponding AIC_2. But for other countries AIC_1 is generally lower than AIC_2 except in two cases. Thus our choice of lag one for the price variable is justified for countries other than Ethiopia. However, our primary aim is to study the long-run behaviour of the model assuming that the economy continued with the present structure. It can be seen from the table 4 that although AIC_2 values have been lower than AIC_1 for Ethiopia, the eigen-values from the estimated $\hat{H}_1$ matrices are not much different in a qualitative sense under the two alternative specifications. Thus with two period lag-prices we have the same qualitative results as with lagged one prices. To keep the comparison between countries meaningful we present the results for Ethiopia also with one period lagged price variables.

The specification of the model in equation (5) is similar to reduced-form equations, but they are estimated using the method suggested by ZELLNER for 'Seemingly Unrelated Regressions' (SUR) as the correlation between the least squares residuals for all four equations are more than 0.3. Thus, our estimates are more efficient than ordinary least squares estimates (see MEHTA ans SWAMY (1976)). The estimated regression coefficients and their 't' values are presented in tables 2 to 6. A goodness-of-fit statistic Q is also presented for each esti-

mated equation where $Q = 1 - \dfrac{S_u^2}{S^2}$; where S_u^2 is the estimated error variance and S^2 is the estimated variance of the dependent variable. According to Q statistics except one equation for Ethiopia all other equations explained more than 80 % of the variations in the dependent variables.

The first major observation that follows from these results is that only for the U. K., the majority of the estimated coefficients are significantly different from zeros according to 't' statistics whereas for Ethiopia only 5 coefficients are significantly different from zero at 5 - 7 % significant levels. This might suggest that in countries like Ethiopia, either Government does not try to control the economy in the way we portray in this paper or alternatively the government activities have very little impact on the movements of the economy. Hence, in our subsequent discussion, we assumed that our 'maintained hypothesis' is the correct description of the governmental objectives with varying degrees of success. First we examined the long-run property of the estimated system. To examine the stability property of the system of equations we calculated the eigen-values of the (4 x 4) $\hat{H}_1$ matrix produced by the coefficients of CP-1, IP-1, YP-1, and PP-1 from the four estimated equations for each country. Our results suggest that

only for Ethiopia and Central African Republic the system is stable,
i. e. the eigen-values are less than @1@ (for technical details of
these analyses see GANDOLFO (1980)). However, for India, Pakistan and
the United Kingdom, the system is unstable and explosive. Although an
unstable dynamic structure does not necessarily mean an undesirable
outcome but it does create additional problems for the Government of
the country.[6] It is clear that in terms of long-run analysis, government can change its priorities which will cause the structure to change
and may avoid this explosive path. We examine the problem of unstable
systems by perturbing the structure to accomodate more significantly
SIMON's and STEINMANN's (S & S) theory. We have explained before that
if the (S & S) theory is correct, then the lagged population should
affect current investment expenditures and current national income
positively. Therefore, we perturbed the system in a way such that the
effect of PP-1 on IP and YP is increased by 25 % above the estimated
coefficients. Then, restricting those two parameters at these new imposed levels, we re-estimated the other parameters of the system by
the restricted SUR method. When carrying out this exercise, the system
achieved a long-run stable structure only for India. Hence we believe
that the technical growth caused by the population growth may not be
the only solution to cure unstable structures. In fact, the most disturbing factor is that by the same perturbation, we find that the Ethiopian
and the Central African Republic's structures become unstable. The
coefficients of PP-1 in IP and YP equations are positive only for the
U. K. and the Central African Republic. Hence, this indirect test suggests that the 'S & S' theory is only partially supported by the experiments conducted here. We have used only part of the empirical results to analyse our theories. It is possible that the results used
in this analysis are all spurious. To check this argument, we examined
the overall results which are not used in our analysis but which corobo-
rates with other studies. For example, for the U. K. we find that the
real lagged government expenditures have negative partial effect on
CP, YP and PP. This fits with the 'crowding out' theory in the following way: Any increase in GP-1 will reduce IP in the product market
but will not compensate fully in the service sector. This will in turn
cause YP to decrease, causing CP to decrease. The negative relation
between PP and GP is the effect of long term decrease in population

---

[6] Whether the unstable structure is desirable or undesirable will
be examined later in this section.

growth (see table 7). On the other hand, for India the effect of increased GP is positive in all the variables under study. An increase
in GP will increase CP as well as YP with a time lag is an established
fact in India due to unutilised resources in the country. Also it is
generally observed in India that any increase in Government expenditure
is always matched by the private investors. Hence, we observe a positive
relation between IP and GP-1. Finally, the demographers have established
that the increased levels of consumption and income has a positive
contribution to population growth in less developing countries. Thus,
all estimated coefficients to some extent 'encompass' the findings
of other studies.[7]

  Finally, we look at the long-run behaviour of the estimated models
along with the growth rates presented in table 7. First, we notice
that the growth rates for the five variables (CP, IP, YP, MP and GP)
have fluctuated quite vigorously throughout the period. For example,
concerning the U. K., the mean rate of population growth is only 0.17 %
and except for GP, no other variables have fluctuated enough to justify
the long-run unstable structure of the economy. Hence, it is not possible
to argue that the explosive long-run structure of the economy is more
desirable than a stable structure. If we look at the growth rates for
India and Pakistan, who have unstable structures in terms of estimated
parameters, we find that the population growth rates are very steady
with very small fluctuations, whereas all other variables exhibit a
fluctuating growth. In terms of a mean growth rates, both countries
with unstable structure may exhibit a fast inprovement in terms of per
capita consumption and income. However, it is not clear whether the
unstable structures are totally related to the mean growth levels. If
the unstable structures are strongly influenced by the growth rates
observed during the periods when the minimum growth rates or near-about
values were observed, then the unstable structures are cause for concern.
In fact, the fluctuating nature of growh rates for the MP and GP variables for all the countries suggest that the governments of these countries do act to minimise loss (or to stabilise the variables) and this
may be in terms of the objective function mentioned in section II. The
growth rates figures for Ethiopia and Central African Republic suggest
that the mean growth rates have dominated the estimated structures.
Thus, we find that a Malthusian crisis is very unlikely to appear for
these countries. On the other hand, we observed that there is only
partial evidence to support SIMON and STEINMANN's theory.

[7] Readers can go through tables 2 - 6 and notice that our claim is
generally correct.

IV. Conclusions

We presented a framework for analysing the long-run behaviour of macro-
economic variables and population where government is assumed to minimise a loss function. The specification derived is very similar to
'error-correcting' models. A similar analysis to the data was possible,
using the recent approach of ENGLE and GRANGER (1987) for co-integrated
variables, where 'error-correcting' models are a particular form of
co-integrated variables. Our empirical results have very little support
for Malthusian theory and only partial support for the SIMON-STEINMANN
theory. However, our empirical analysis is limited in nature on two
grounds. Firstly, we have studied only five countries, although the
population on those countries constitute one-fifth of the world population. Secondly, to examine Malthusian theory it is necessary to examine the time pattern of structural changes over a long period. We
interpret that the Malthusian theory is based on 'invariant' structure.
Hence by studying the pattern of structural changes, we will be in a
position to examine SIMON-STEINMANN's theory more carefully.

We use an unorthodox approach to study the interrelationship between macro-economic variables and population, but we believe that
we have produced some insight into the problem. We hope our study will
encourage other researchers to study and develop the methodology to
examine the long-run behaviour of other countries.

Glossary for the tables 2 to 7

All data were collected from several issues of the Monthly Bulletin of Statistics, published by the United Nations, New York. The table numbers quoted below are all related to the table numbers in 1973 issues.

CP = A real measure of consumption expenditure where consumption expenditure at current prices (from Table 63) divided by wholesale price index.

IP = A real investment expenditure, measured as Gross Fixed Capital Formation divided by price index (Table 62).

YP = National income at constant prices calculated by dividing the national income at market prices by the price index (Table 63).

PP = Estimates of mid-year population (Table 1).

GP = Real government final consumption expenditure calculated from government final consumption expenditure at current prices (Table 62) divided by the price index.

MP = Real money supply calculated from nominal money supply (Table 67) deflated by price index.

P = Index number of wholesale prices (Table 58).
     All one-period lagged variables are denoted with -1.
     Figures in the brackets are the t-statistics.

Q = A measure of goodness of fits as defined in the text.

Perturbation 1 = The coefficients of PP-1 are increased by + 25 % in both IP and YP equations.

Table 2: SUR Estimates for India

Dependent Variable	CP-1	IP-1	YP-1	PP-1	MP-1	GP-1	P-1	Const.	Q
CP	-1.05837 (-1.441)	-1.92093 (-2.053)	1.35477 (1.713)	-0.00465 (-0.673)	0.12065 (0.280)	1.33460 (1.396)	15.5885 (1.721)	4161.056 (1.884)	0.9596
IP	-0.17381 (-0.408)	-0.71928 (-1.326)	0.52093 (1.136)	-0.01392 (-3.479)	0.57187 (2.285)	1.26571 (2.283)	25.0684 (4.774)	4116.150 (3.215)	0.9746
YP	-1.34066 (-1.041)	-2.64975 (-1.615)	1.92321 (1.387)	-0.01388 (-1.146)	1.02769 (1.358	2.22278 (1.326)	35.24819 (2.219)	6679.49 (1.725)	0.9665
PP	-0.84813 (-0.527)	-2.89637 (-1.411)	3.03423 (1.749)	0.94010 (62.076)	-1.68977 (-1.785)	2.99801 (1.429)	87.55747 (4.406)	26861.97 (5.545)	0.9999

The Eigen-values of $\hat{H}_1$ matrix

Real	Imaginary
0.600617	0
-1.00710	+ 0.320767
-1.00710	- 0.320787
0.924157	0

The Eigen-values of $\hat{H}_1$ matrix after Perturbation 1

Real	Imaginary
0.048978	+ 0.473825
0.048978	- 0.473825
0.018788	0
0.970102	0

Table 4: SUR Estimates for Ethiopia

Dependent Variable	CP-1	IP-1	YP-1	PP-1	MP-1	GP-1	P-1	Const.	Q
CP	0.028904 (0.147)	-0.71739 (-2.016)	0.27157 (1.283)	0.001273 (2.208)	-0.75149 (-3.528)	0.11363 (0.348)	0.15594 (4.667)	-14.4277 (-1.890=)	0.9939
IP	0.19432 (1.327)	0.32250 (1.213)	0.08007 (0.507)	-0.000812 (-1.885)	-0.00969 (-0.0609)	-0.07142 (-0.293)	0.03374 (1.352)	10.9945 (1.929)	0.5979
YP	0.61182 (2.093)	0.04081 (0.077)	0.17639 (0.559)	0.000911 (1.060)	-0.42451 (-1.337)	0.31573 (0.649)	0.02500 (0.502)	-7.24324 (-0.637)	0.9903
PP	-53.9493 (-2.401)	84.9998 (2.084)	82.7786 (3.413)	0.87527 (13.249)	-26.9436 (-1.1039)	-22.2396 (-0.595)	12.46799 (3.256)	488.3813 (0.558)	0.9996

The Eigen-values of $\hat{H}_l$ matrix

Real	Imaginary
-0.094848	0
0.989208	0
0.453752	+0.051404
0.453752	-0.051404

The Eigen-values of $\hat{H}_l$ matrix after Perturbation 1

Real	Imaginary
0.400353	+0.412047
0.400353	-0.412047
-0.224366	0
0.975092	0

The Eigen-values of $\hat{H}_l$ matrix when two-period lagged price used

Real	Imaginary
0.991050	0
-0.737813	0
-0.132975	+0.438207
0.132975	-0.438207

Table 5: SUR Estimates for Central African Republic

Dependent Variable	CP-1	IP-1	YP-1	PP-1	MP-1	GP-1	P-1	Const.	Q
CP	-0.59538 (-1.269)	-1.34880 (-1.256)	1.41545 (3.508)	0.0000322 (0.338)	-3.59755 (-2.278)	-0.68031 (-0.557)	0.005260 (2.267)	0.16491 (0.786)	0.9674
IP	0.18293 (1.343)	-0.40233 (-1.291)	-0.15932 (-1.361)	0.0000841 (3.046)	0.362403 (0.791)	-0.464686 (-1.824)	-0.002119 (-3.148)	0.26320 (4.325)	0.8084
YP	0.025624 (0.405)	-0.65973 (-0.462)	0.66661 (1.242)	0.000213 (1.686)	-1.99536 (-0.949)	-3.50867 (-2.158)	-0.0000106 (-0.003)	0.59141 (2.119)	0.9223
PP	557.2213 (0.834)	-2048.308 (-1.339)	-1.66023 (-0.003)	1.00011 (7.380)	-1.986.594 (-0.833)	2510.171 (1.442)	-2.38972 (-0.723)	52.54182 (0.176)	0.9729

The Eigen-values of $\hat{H}_1$ matrix

Real	Imaginary
-0.104405	+0.667621
-0.104405	-0.667621
0.812149	0
-0.872933	0

The Eigen-values of $\hat{H}_1$ matrix after Perturbation 1

Real	Imaginary
-6.535203	0
-0.931393	0
1.070146	0
0.529988	0

Table 6: SUR Estimates for the United Kingdom

Dependent Variable	CP-1	IP-1	YP-1	PP-1	MP-1	GP-1	P-1	Const.	Q
CP	-2.61714 (-1.976)	-4.47835 (-4.577)	2.67670 (3.694)	0.16502 (2.900)	1.57680 (1.437)	-4.43190 (-3.593)	-0.87147 (-2.178)	-8020.004 (-2.660)	0.8184
IP	-0.79882 (-3.666)	-0.97185 (-6.037)	0.62881 (5.275)	0.040849 (4.3637)	0.69694 (3.862)	-0.44079 (-2.172)	-0.38145 (-5.795)	-2015.588 (-4.064)	0.9572
YP	-4.02576 (-1.934)	-7.80008 (-5.071)	4.47487 (3.929)	0.27640 (3.090)	1.75000 (1.015)	-7.23567 (-3.731)	-1.36497 (-2.170)	-13493.97 (2.847)	0.8066
PP	3.00862 (3.576)	0.29439 (0.474)	-0.82644 (-1.796)	0.91350 (25.273)	-1.84405 (-2.646)	-2.81777 (-3.596)	0.42489 (1.672)	4626.859 (2.416)	0.9982

The Eigen-values of $\hat{H}_1$ matrix

Real	Imaginary
-2.646190	0
1.095658	0
0.382933	0
-0.911239	0

The Eigen-values of $\hat{H}_1$ matrix after Perturbation 1

Real	Imaginary
1.845596	0
-0.725709	0
-1.897254	0
-0.104798	0

Table 7: Mean Percentage Growth Rates and their Dispersions

Country	Variable	Mean	Standard Deviation	Minimum	Maximum
India	CP	2.4	3.5	- 5.8	9.7
	IP	5.4	9.5	-12.1	26.8
	YP	3.1	4.1	- 5.5	8.3
	PP	2.2	0.1	2.1	2.4
	MP	2.5	9.1	-12.1	22.8
	GP	3.7	8.0	-10.8	20.8
Pakistan	CP	6.1	5.3	- 5.0	17.8
	IP	4.4	12.4	-17.2	24.4
	YP	5.9	4.6	- 2.0	14.1
	PP	3.0	0.2	2.9	3.9
	MP	4.6	12.0	-20.4	22.4
	GP	5.1	9.4	-13.3	27.0
Ethiopia	CP	3.5	2.8	- 1.5	7.0
	IP	2.1	11.3	-15.6	23.5
	YP	3.3	2.1	- 0.7	6.8
	PP	2.2	0.5	1.5	3.0
	MP	7.5	10.4	- 5.7	26.0
	GP	6.2	8.2	- 7.2	25.7
Central African Republic	CP	5.3	7.3	- 7.2	17.4
	IP	-1.3	14.9	-31.9	26.8
	YP	3.3	8.3	- 6.1	28.8
	PP	3.3	4.1	2.0	18.5
	MP	6.2	11.9	-13.2	35.6
	GP	-0.3	9.7	-20.5	22.6
United Kingdom	CP	0.29	7.53	-17.82	8.31
	IP	0.02	7.99	-17.94	9.93
	YP	0.91	7.43	-19.17	9.29
	PP	0.17	0.14	- 0.06	0.32
	MP	-1.37	9.60	-20.69	10.18
	GP	2.80	8.73	-13.37	20.14

References

BHATTACHARYYA, D. K. (1978), Demand for Financial Assets: An Econometric Study of the U. K. Personal Sector. Saxon House, England.

BHATTACHARYYA, Dilip and Gerd WEINRICH (1985), Food-Feed Controversies Reconsidered: A Formal Analysis. Paper presented at the Fifth World Congress of the Econometric Society. MIT, U.S.A.

DENTON, F. T. and B. G. SPENCER (1984) The time Path of the Economy as the Population Moves towards a Stationary State. In Gunter STEINMANN (ed.) Economic Consequences of Population Change in Industrialized Countries: Proceedings, Paderborn, West Germany, June 1983. Springer-Verlag, Verlin.

FELLNER, W. (1961), Two Propositions in the Theory of Induced Innovations. Economic Journal pp. 305-308.

GANDOLFO, G. (1980), Economic Dynamics: Methods and Models'. North Holland, Amsterdam.

GRANGER, C. W. J. and R. F. ENGLE (1987), Dynamic Model Specification with Equilibrium Constraints: Co-integration and Error-Correction. Econometrica, Vol. 55, no. 2, pp. 251-276.

HENDRY, D. F. (1986), Econometric Modelling with Co-integrated Variables: An Overview. Oxford Bulletin of Economics and Statistics. Vol. 48, pp. 201-212.

JORGENSON, D. W. (1967), The Theory of Investment Behaviour. In FERBER, Robert (ed.) Determinants of Investment Behaviour. NBER, Columbia University Press, New York.

LOTKA, A. J. (1907), Mode of Growth of Material Aggregates. American Journal of Science. Vol. 24, pp. 199-216.

MALTHUS, T. R. (1798), An Essay on the Principle of Population. Printed for J. JOHNSON in St. Paul's Churchyard, London.

MEHTA; J. S. and P. A. V. B. SWAMY (1976), Further Evidence on the Relative Efficiencies of Zellners Seemingly Unrelated Regressions Estimators. Journal of the American Staistical Association, vol. 71, pp. 634-639.

NICKELL, Stephen (1985), Error Correction, Partial Adjustment and All That: An Expository Note. Oxford Bulletin of Economics and Statistics, vol. 47, pp. 119-129.

SAMUELSON, P. A. (1975), The Optimum Growth Rate for Population. International Economic Review, vol. 16, pp. 531-538.

SEN, Amartya (1959), The choice of Agricultural Techniques in Underdeveloped countries. Economic Development and Cultural Change, vol. 7, pp. 279-285.

SIMON, Julian L. (1977), The Economics of Population Growth. Princeton University Press, Princeton, New Jersey.

SIMON, Julian L. (1986), Theory of Population and Economic Growth. Basil Blackwell, Oxford.

STEINMANN, Gunter (1984), A Model of the History of Demographic-Economic Growth. In STEINMANN, Gunter (ed.) Economic Consequences of Population Change in Industrialized Countries: Proceedings, Paderborn, West Germany, June 1983. Springer-Verlag, Berlin.

STEINMANN, Gunter (1986.), Malthusian Crisis, Boserupian Escapes and Longrun Economic Progress. Paper presented at the International Conference on Demographic Change and Economic Development at Hagen, West Germany, 1986.

THEIL, H. (1968). Optimal Decision Rules for Government and Industry. North-Holland, Chicago.

TINBERGEN, J. (1956), Economic Policy: Principles and Design. North-Holland, Amsterdam.

VEALL, Michael R. and Klaus F. ZIMMERMANN (1986), A Monthly Dynamic Consumer Expenditure System for Germany with Different Kinds of Households. The Review of Economics and Statistics, pp. 256-264.

II,3
Demographic Economic Models

AN EXTENSION OF A STATIC INPUT-OUTPUT MODEL FOR
DEMOGRAPHIC-ECONOMIC ANALYSIS

M. Luptácik and I. Schmoranz
Institut für Ökonometrie und Operations Research
Technische Universität Wien

Wien / Austria

ABSTRACT: This paper is concerned with the modelling of demographic-economic linkages within a static Leontief input-output model. The emphasis of the paper is the quantitative analysis of economic conse-quences (production of goods and services, employment and the financial equilibr. m of the public retirement system) of a change in the exogene-ously giv demographic variables. Using activity-commodity framework, useful in. ation about demographic and economic multiplier relation-ships is o ained. The application of the model is demonstrated with reference to data for Austria. The computations show a significant structural effect and a not negligible impact for the labour market.

I.   Introduction

The recent demographic development in industrialized countries with low fertility and aging population has stimulated the interest in the econ-omic consequences of these demographic changes and has initiated research in the modelling of demographic-economic linkages. According to the sub-ject of analysis, different approaches can be adopted to assess the im-pact of demographic changes on the economy. Some authors, for example, have favoured an econometric approach based upon the modelling of aggre-gate demographic and economic relationships within a system of simul-taneous regression equations (e. g. LEDENT, 1982, and TAYLOR, 1982). Others have pointed to the advantages of simulation techniques, capable of handling linkages in a high degree of detail (e. g. ORCUTT et al. 1976; GOLLADAY - HAVEMAN, 1977; DENTON - SPENCER, 1984; FELDERER, 1984; BUHR, 1984). A third approach takes as its starting point the input-output model first developed by LEONTIEF (1951) as a tool in inter-industry analysis. This model can be extended and generalized to take account of the wider socio-economic context in which industrial activity takes place (SCHINNAR, 1976; STONE, 1981; BATEY-MADDEN, 1981; BATEY, 1985).

The primary aim of our paper is the development of the demo-economic accounting linkage between population development and the production of goods and services and, in turn, employment in the context of a compar-ative static analysis. Changes in size and structure of the population may imply changes in the level and structure of demand for consumption goods. These shifts in turn may give rise to changes in production in particular industrial sectors of the economy, resulting in changes in

Studies in Contemporary Economics
A. Wenig, K. F. Zimmermann (Eds.)
Demographic Change and Economic Development
© Springer-Verlag Berlin Heidelberg 1989

the demand for labour as well as changes in primary income distribution. Labour supply is made up of the economically active members of population. The change in size and structure of the labour force affects the primary income distribution, which determines expenditure patterns and thus the level and structure of private consumption. These shifts in consumption as one result of changes in demographic size and structure are coupled with changes in a demographically related part of public consumption.

Furthermore, we recognise the importance of modelling the public retirement system and the effects of a changing population on the financial equilibrium of this system.

For this purpose we use the static Leontief input-output model which can be extended to include demographic-economic relationships. This approach allows us to describe also the indirect (or structural) effects of population changes and represents a closed-loop system in which household income and consumption are treated as endogenous. In this system, "production leads to income determination, which leads to expenditure patterns, which leads to production requirements needed both to supply the goods and to create the income flows" (CLARK, 1975, p. 142).

The term "demographic-economic analysis" in the title of this paper underlines the intention of our contribution. In the presented model, the demographic patterns are exogenously given and we try to assess their impact on economic variables. We do not address the question of how demographic development can be influenced by economic variables or how individual demographic and economic models can be linked together in a recursive framework (see e. g. COAL (1976), SCHULTZ (1974), ZIMMER-MANN (1985), MADDEN and BATEY (1984) and for the input-output type models SCHINNAR (1976), (1977) with his so-called "eco-demographic multiplier").

In the next section, we present the mathematical formulation of the model and in the section 3 the data and the application of the model for Austria.

In section 4 we draw some conclusions about the results presented and try an evaluation of our model.

II. Demographic-Economic Relationships in Input-Output Model

The starting point for our model is an open Leontief input-output system:

$$A\underline{x} + \underline{y} = \underline{x} + \underline{m} \tag{1}$$

or

$$\underline{x} = (I-A)^{-1}(\underline{y}-\underline{m}) \qquad (2)$$

where $A = \{a_{ij}\}$ is an n x n matrix of technical coefficients, I is an n x n identity matrix, $(I-A)^{-1}$ is the Leontief inverse, $\underline{x}$ is an n-dimensional vector of gross production, $\underline{y}$ is an n-dimensional vector of final demand and $\underline{m}$ is an n-dimensional vector of imports.

Final demand is divided into three components:

$$\underline{y} = \underline{c} + \underline{y}^{D} + \underline{y}^{ND} \qquad (3)$$

where $\underline{c}$ denotes private consumption, $\underline{y}^{D}$ is that part of public consumption which depends on size and structure of the population (schools, hospitals, etc.) and $\underline{y}^{ND}$ that fraction of final demand which is not directly affected by the demographic patterns and is classified as an exogenous variable for the model to be discussed.

According to the modern theory of the consumer we consider the household, rather than the individual or family, as a consumption unit. A household can be defined as a socioeconomic unit, consisting of individuals who live together. We classify households according to the number of adults, children (persons up to 15 years old), and income receivers. The number of the households of type k (k = 1, 2, ..., h) is described by a vector $\underline{d} = (d_1, d_2, ..., d_h)$, which is exogenously given by demographic development.

The structure of consumption expenditure in the different households can vary considerable. It has also been observed that consumer behaviour of large households may be more economical [with respect to specific items, as well as all items of consumption taken together], because of the existence of economies of scale. The smaller the household, the higher the per-capita expenditure required to provide a given standard of living.

The consumption patterns for each household in relation to the m commodities is described by matrix C^{H}. The coefficients of this matrix, c_{rk}, indicate the proportion of consumption expenditure on commodity group r (r = 1, ..., m) in the total consumption expenditure of the household k (k = 1, 2, ..., h). We postulate that these percentage distributions remain stable regardless of a change in the number of households.

The household income is determined first by the number of wage earners:

$$\underline{w} = Q \, \hat{W}_o \hat{L} \underline{x} \qquad\qquad (4)$$

where $\underline{w}$ is an h-dimensional vector of wage income by household type, Q is an h x n matrix showing the proportion of people from the various household making up the workforce for each industry, $\hat{W}_o$ is an n x n diagonal matrix of labour income per employee and $\hat{L}$ is an n x n diagonal matrix of labour coefficients (number of employees per unit of gross production). Obviously the following condition holds:

$$\sum_{k=1}^{h} q_{kj} = 1 \qquad (j = 1, 2, \ldots, n)$$

It would be possible to include also income from profits in our model by modifying matrix $\hat{W}_o \hat{L}$. The elements of the matrix $Q \, \hat{W}_o \hat{L}$ represent the share of value generated in sector j that is received by household k (see also GROOTAERT, 1983, matrix V on page 10).

The other source of household income are old age pensions and children's allowances, which are determined by demographic development. The total income of the households is then given by following equation:

$$\underline{i} = Q \, \hat{W}_o \hat{L} \underline{x} + \underline{t} \qquad\qquad (5)$$

where $\underline{i}$ is an h-dimensional vector of total income by household type and $\underline{t}$ is an h-dimensional vector of transfer payments. This income is translated into household consumption by the following expression:

$$\underline{c}^P = C^H (I - \hat{S}) \, \{ (I - \hat{b}_s - \hat{\delta}) Q \, \hat{W}_o \hat{L} \underline{x} + (I - \hat{\delta}) \underline{t} \} \qquad\qquad (6)$$

where $\underline{c}^P$ is an m-dimensional vector giving the total consumption of each of m commodities and $\hat{S}$ is an h x h diagonal matrix of savings ratios, $\hat{b}_s$ is an h x h diagonal matrix of the rate of old-age security contribution paid by employees and $\hat{\delta}$ is an h x h diagonal matrix of (average) tax rates of the households.

The model distinguishes the primary income distribution, described by equation (4), from the secondary income distribution which is given after government intervention via taxes and transfers.

However the consumption vector $\underline{c}^P$ relates to commodities rather than to the industrial scheme. Using an n x m conversion matrix T we get the vector of private consumption $\underline{c}$ by industrial sectors:

$$\underline{c} = T \underline{c}^P . \qquad\qquad (7)$$

The coefficients t_{jr} ($j = 1, 2, \ldots, n$; $r = 1, 2, \ldots, m$) of matrix T indicate the proportion of consumption of commodity r, produced by sector j. Obviously

$$\sum_{j=1}^{n} t_{jr} = 1 \qquad (r = 1, 2, \ldots, m).$$

Substitution of equation (6) into equation (7) yields:

$$\underline{c} = T C^H (I-\hat{S}) \{I-\hat{b}_s-\hat{\delta}) Q \hat{W}_o \hat{L} \underline{x} + (I-\hat{\delta})\underline{t}\}. \tag{8}$$

Setting

$$U = T C^H (I-\hat{S})(I-\hat{b}_s-\hat{\delta}) Q \hat{W}_o \hat{L} \tag{9}$$

$$V = T C^H (I-\hat{S})(I-\hat{\delta}) \tag{10}$$

we get

$$\underline{c} = U\underline{x} + V\underline{t}. \tag{11}$$

The first term on the right side of equation (11) describes the private consumption of a household generated by wages and salaries of working population, the second term part of private consumption generated by transfer payments. The elements of the matrix U are the labour-input coefficients expressed in terms of goods consumed by the employees (including the members of their household) per unit of sectoral gross output. We are now able to analyse the influence of different instruments of government policy (for example, an increase in children's allowance or a reduction of taxed for households with more children) for consumer demand.

For lack of data and for simplicity, we postulate that the part of final demand $\underline{y}^D$ is a linear function of the number of the households:

$$\underline{y}^D = Y_d^D \underline{d} \tag{12}$$

where y_d^D is an $n \times h$ matrix of consumption coefficients for public consumption.

We are now in a position to establish the effect of demographic change upon gross output of the particular sectors. In our previous work (LUPTACIK - SCHMORANZ, 1980, p. 58-59) we derived so-called demo-economic multiplier (an $n \times h$ matrix) whose coefficients describe the total (direct and indirect) deliveries of sector j for one unit of

demographic group k. Under the assumption of the Leontief production
function permits our model - for given labour and capital coefficients
of the sectors - an assessment of the demographic impact for the labour
and capital demand in the particular sector of the economy:

$$\hat{L}\underline{x} = \underline{l} \tag{13}$$

$$\hat{K}\underline{x} = \underline{k} \tag{14}$$

where $\hat{L}$ is a diagonal n x n matrix of labour coefficients, $\hat{K}$ is a diagonal matrix of capital coefficients, $\underline{l}$ is an n-dimensional vector of
employment and $\underline{k}$ is an n-dimensional vector of capital stock.

In this way the model allows the evaluation of demographic unemployment through change of labour demand because of demographic effects on
the composition of commodity demand (WAGNER, 1984, p. 300). If the
changes in the size and structure of population shift the commodity
demand from sectors with high labour intensity to sectors with high
capital intensity - all other factors being constant - demographic
unemployment is possible. An indication of this dependence and its
possible evaluation as a structural version of the so-called Guenther
paradox[1]) in the context of LUPTACIK - SCHMORANZ (1980) model is given
by WAGNER (1980b, p. 128-129).

Now let us turn to the part of model concerning the relationship
between the demographic development of a country and the development
of its public old-age security system. In our model, not only direct
demographic impact (i. e., size and (age-) structure of the population)
is considered, but possible economic consequences of a changing population are also taken into account (e. g., declining real growth rates
and reduced employment rates).

The retirement system in Austria is primaly based on the public
retirement system financed on a pay-as-you-go principle. That means,
old age pensions in one year are to be financed by the contributions
of employees (of working population) of the same year. Therefore, the
financial equilibrium condition of this system implies that the total
sum of contributions (EIN) equals to the total sum of retirement payments (AUS) in each period. In this context, we shall consider the
(direct and indirect) effects of a changing population on the financial
equilibrium of the system.

---

[1]) The presumed connexion of declining birth rates and rising unemployment respectively of rising birth rates and declining unemployment
in a transition period of about 15 to 20 years is called Guenther
paradox (GUENTHER, 1931 and WAGNER, 1980a).

The total sum of revenues can be calculated as follows:

$$EIN = \underline{b}\,\hat{W}_o\underline{l} \tag{15}$$

where $\underline{b} = (b, ..., b)$ is an n-dimensional vector of the full rate of contribution (in Austria, old-age security contributions are financed in equal parts by the insured and by their employers) and $\underline{l} = \hat{L}\underline{x}$ expresses the level of employment in the particular sector of the economy.

On the other hand, the retirement payments are given by:

$$AUS = r\,P \tag{16}$$

where r denotes the average retirement income and P is the number of pension recipients.

For the purpose of our analysis we decompose the vector of transfer payments $\underline{t}$ into two components:

$$\underline{t} = \underline{t}_1 + \underline{t}_2 \tag{17}$$

where $\underline{t}_1$ is an h-dimensional vector of retirement payments and $\underline{t}_2$ is an h-dimensional vector of children's allowances. The retirement payments $\underline{t}_1$ are now described by the form:

$$\underline{t}_1 = r\,P = r\hat{\alpha}\underline{d} \tag{18}$$

where $\hat{\alpha}$ is an h x h diagonal matrix showing an average number of pension recipients in the household type.

For the children's allowances we write:

$$\underline{t}_2 = \rho\hat{\beta}\underline{d} \tag{19}$$

where ρ denotes the level of children's allowance and $\hat{\beta}$ is an h x h diagonal matrix expressing the (average) number of children in the household type.

According to the financial equilibrium condition we now obtain the following relationship:

$$\underline{b}\,\hat{W}_o\underline{l} - r\hat{\alpha}\underline{d} + \xi = 0 \tag{20}$$

where ξ is the difference between the (total) sum of contributions and the (total) sum of retirement payments. $\xi > 0$ indicates the financial

deficit in the pay-as-you-go retirement system. (To simplify the any-
lysis, we have disregarded from state subsidies.)

At this point it may be helpful to draw together the main elements
of our mathematical model by setting the block equation structure of
the model within an activity-commodity framework. Expressing the model
in this form enables us to see more clearly how the conventional input-
output model has been extended and we shall see that the framework
provides a convenient means of studying relationships between demograhic
and economic change.

We consider the model as seven blocks of equations:

$$(I-A)\underline{x} - T\underline{c}^P - Y_d^D\underline{d} = \underline{y}^{ND} - \underline{m} \tag{21}$$

which can be obtained from equation (1) using the relationships expressed
in equations (3), (7) and (12).

$$(I-\hat{b}_s-\hat{\delta})Q\,\hat{W}_o\underline{1} = \underline{w}_N \tag{22}$$

corresponding to equation (4), where $\underline{w}_N$ denotes an h-dimensional vector
of net labour income by household type.

$$C^H(I-\hat{S})\underline{w}_N + C^H(I-\hat{S})(r\hat{\alpha}+\rho\hat{\beta})\underline{d} = \underline{c}^P \tag{23}$$

which we get from equation (6) and (17) - (19).

The remaining four blocks are given by equations (13), (14), (20)
and

$$I\underline{d} = \underline{d} \tag{24}$$

which represents exogeneous inputs. Assembling these equations as an
activity-commodity framework, we obtain:

$$\begin{bmatrix} I-A & 0 & 0 & 0 & -T & 0 & -Y^D \\ -\hat{L} & I & 0 & 0 & 0 & 0 & 0 \\ -\hat{K} & 0 & I & 0 & 0 & 0 & 0 \\ 0 & -(I-\hat{b}_s-\hat{\delta})Q\hat{W}_o & 0 & I & 0 & 0 & 0 \\ 0 & 0 & 0 & -C^H(I-\hat{S}) & I & 0 & -C^H(I-\hat{S})(r\hat{\alpha}+\rho\hat{\beta}) \\ 0 & b\hat{W}_o & 0 & 0 & 0 & 1 & -r\hat{\alpha} \\ 0 & 0 & 0 & 0 & 0 & 0 & I \end{bmatrix} \begin{bmatrix} \underline{x} \\ \underline{1} \\ \underline{k} \\ \underline{w}_N \\ \underline{c}^P \\ \xi \\ \underline{d} \end{bmatrix} = \begin{bmatrix} \underline{y}^{ND}-\underline{m} \\ 0 \\ 0 \\ 0 \\ 0 \\ 0 \\ \underline{d} \end{bmatrix}$$

The framework has three main components: a square matrix of coefficients (partitioned to show how the basic input-output model has been extended), a vector of activity levels (unknows), and a vector of constraints (inputs).

Inverting the matrix of coefficients and expressing the inverse in compart-mentalised form we obtain:

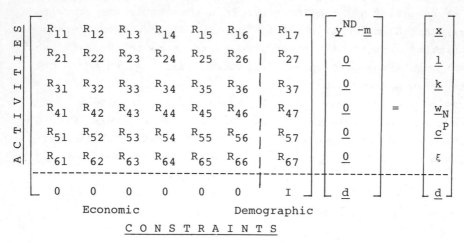

$$
\begin{array}{c}
\text{A C T I V I T I E S}
\end{array}
\left[\begin{array}{cccccc|c}
R_{11} & R_{12} & R_{13} & R_{14} & R_{15} & R_{16} & R_{17} \\
R_{21} & R_{22} & R_{23} & R_{24} & R_{25} & R_{26} & R_{27} \\
R_{31} & R_{32} & R_{33} & R_{34} & R_{35} & R_{36} & R_{37} \\
R_{41} & R_{42} & R_{43} & R_{44} & R_{45} & R_{46} & R_{47} \\
R_{51} & R_{52} & R_{53} & R_{54} & R_{55} & R_{56} & R_{57} \\
R_{61} & R_{62} & R_{63} & R_{64} & R_{65} & R_{66} & R_{67} \\
\hline
0 & 0 & 0 & 0 & 0 & 0 & I
\end{array}\right]
\left[\begin{array}{c}
\underline{y}^{ND}-\underline{m} \\
\underline{0} \\
\underline{0} \\
\underline{0} \\
\underline{0} \\
\underline{0} \\
\underline{d}
\end{array}\right]
=
\left[\begin{array}{c}
\underline{x} \\
\underline{l} \\
\underline{k} \\
\underline{w}_N^P \\
\underline{c} \\
\xi \\
\underline{d}
\end{array}\right]
$$

Economic   Demographic

C O N S T R A I N T S

A major distinction is made between economic activities and commodities and demographic activities and commodities. Within these four compartments are a number of sub-matrices, identified by R_{ij} ($i = 1, \ldots, 6$; $j = 1, \ldots, 7$). Each sub-matrix contains coefficients which describe the effects upon activity levels of unit change in constraints (or, in case where the constraint is zero in the framework, in commodity levels). In such a way yields this inverse matrix a wealth of information about demographic and economic multiplier relationships. We shall give the interpretation of the particular submatrices in the Appendix.

Null sub-matrices mean that population is an exogeneous variable and cannot be influenced in our model by changes in any of the economic constraints/commodity levels. An identity matrix reflects the fact that change in one demographic group cannot influence any other demographic group.

Because of his static character, the model described here is more appropriate as tool for impact analysis than for medium - and long - term forecasting.

For illustration of the possibilities of the presented model, some results of its application for Austria are given in the next section.

III. Application of the Model for Austria

We use the data of population projections for Austria for the period
1981-2051 provided to us by "Arbeitskreis für ökonomische und soziologische Studien" (Working group for economic and sociological studies).
From the different variants of population development we consider the
following two projections: the first one is a stagnation variant with
considerable decreasing mortality rate (variant I), the second projection is shrinking variant with moderate decreasing mortality rate (variant II). The population development in Austria according to the above
projections is described in table 1.

The projections of working population is given in table 2.

The last part of population projections of "Arbeitskreis für ökonomische und soziologische Studien" contains the development of households, which are the consumption units in our model (table 3 and 4).

	variant I	variant II
1986	7.592.000	7.551.000
1991	7.601.000	7.522.000
1996	7.777.000	7.462.000
2001	7.854.000	7.364.000

Table 1: Population development in Austria 1986-2001 (source: Arbeitskreis für ökonomische und soziologische Studien).

	variant I	variant II
1986	3.438.000	3.459.000
1991	3.455.000	3.499.000
1996	3.431.000	3.495.000
2001	3.397.000	3.460.000

Table 2: Working population in Austria 1986-2001 (source: Arbeitskreis
für ökonomische und soziologische Studien).

number of persons per household

year	total	1	2	3	4	5+	average
1986	2.842	752	804	555	413	317	2,67
1991	2.938	753	905	586	407	287	2,61
1996	3.020	752	989	612	403	264	2,57
2001	3.083	759	1.043	629	402	250	2,55

Table 3: Projections of households (in 1000) for Austria 1986-2001, variant I.

number of persons per household

year	total	1	2	3	4	5+	average
1986	2.836	750	810	555	410	311	2,66
1991	2.920	747	935	585	391	262	2,58
1996	2.987	741	1.048	611	373	215	2,50
2001	3.029	741	1.133	627	354	174	2,43

Table 4: Projections of households (in 1000) for Austria 1986-2001, variant II.

The model comprises nineteen production sectors, based on the input-output table for 1976 (see RICHTER, 1981) and the following six commodity groups:

1. Food, beverages, tobacco, clothing, and footwear
2. Heating and lighting
3. Household operation, rents, furniture
4. Transport and communication
5. Medical care and health expenses
6. Entertainment, education, and miscellaneous goods.

The consumption data, the matrix C^H, is given by "Konsumerhebung 1984" (collection of consumption data for 1984) of "Österreichischen Statistischen Zentralamtes" (Austrian statistical office).

The following computations are of a comparative static character. Taking two different demographic developments (variant I and variant II of population projections described above), we want to analyse the economic effect of this change in the demographic pattern. For this

264

Production sectors	Decline in gross production (in billions of Austrian shillings, i.e. 10^9)	Labour input coefficients (per billion of production)	Decline in employment
1 Agriculture, etc.	0,655	4.950	3.242
2 Mining, etc.	0,073	1.613	118
3 Manufacture of food, etc.	1,101	900	991
4 Textiles, etc.	0,648	2.470	1.601
5 Manufacture of wood, etc.	0,217	2.080	451
6 Manufacture of paper, etc.	0,238	1.580	376
7 Manufacture of chemicals	0,465	850	395
8 Crude petroleum	0,673	220	148
9 Manufacture of non-metallic mineral products	0,088	1.410	124
10 Basic metal industries	0,202	1.250	253
11 Manufacture of fabricated metal products	0,863	1.700	1.467
12 Electricity, gas, water	0,250	560	140
13 Construction	0,260	2.450	637
14 Trade	1,096	710	778
15 Restaurant and hotels	0,153	3.400	520
16 Transport, etc.	0,486	2.200	1.069
17 Financing, etc.	1,028	1.600	1.645
18 Social and personal services	0,496	2.612	1.296
19 Public administration and defence	1,054	3.200	3.373
total			18.624

Table 5: Decline in the gross production and in the employment in year 1996 induced by shrinking population.

purpose we hold constant the other parameters of the model (e. g. income
per employee, input output coefficients, the matrix C^H). Under this
assumption we solve our model for the year 1996 with demographic data
corresponding to the two above mentioned variants. The values for the
stagnation variant minus the values for the shrinking variant indicate
the impact of changing population size and structure for selected economic variables.

Table 5 shows the results of our computations for gross output
and employment in the nineteen production sectors.

A comparison of gross production values between stagnation and
shrinking variant shows that only in sectors manufacture of food, trade,
financing, and public administration is the decline greater than one
billion Austrian shillings. It is interesting to note, that the labour
input coefficients in these sectors (excluding the sector public administration) are relatively small. Nevertheless the level of employment
would decrease because of demographic effects on commodity demand approximately by 19.000 employees. According to the data in table 2 the working population of the shrinking variant is in 1996 by 64.000 higher
than in the stagnation variant. Therefore the demographic impact for
labour market or demographic unemployment can be estimated approximately
by 83.000, which is for the Austrian economy a not negligible number.

IV.   Conclusions

In this paper, we have presented one way in which a static Leontief
input-output model can be extended to include demographic-economic
relationships. The merits of this type of model lie in the possibility
of assessment of the direct and indirect (structural) effects of
changing population size and structure. Second, the activity-commodity
framework yields more insight on the nature of demographic-economic
interaction. The inverse of the activity-commodity model contains -
partly novel - multiplier relationships.

The application of the model for Austria illustrates the working
of this model and gives some information about the magnitude of changes
in economic variables due to demographic changes. The numerical results
for Austria show some interesting shifts in the structure of production
and a not negligible demographic impact for the labour market. For
further results, especially regarding the sensitivity analysis, see
LUPTACIK-SCHMORANZ (1980), (1986).

Certainly, our model has all merits and shortcoming of the static Leontief input-output model (such as assumption of linearity, errors in the input-output coefficients) which have been discussed extensively in the literature on input-output models. Due to the structural simplicity, the type of model presented in the paper provides a powerful tool for the analysis of demographic-economic linkages and delivers new insights into real demo-economic processes.

Acknowledgements: The authors wish to thank K. F. Zimmermann and two anonymous referees for helpful comments on an earlier draft of the paper.

References

BATEY, P. W. J. and MADDEN, M., 1981: "Demographic-economic forecasting within an activity-commodity framework: Some theoretical considerations and empirical results", Environment and Planning A, vol. 13, 1067-1083.

BATEY, P. W. J., 1985: "Input-output models for regional demographic-economic analysis: some structural comparisons", Environment and Planning A, vol. 17, 73-99.

BUHR, W., 1984: "A model of regional economic growth. Simulation results for the case of population decline" in: STEINMANN, G. (Ed.) 1984, 147-166.

CLARK, P., 1975: "Intersectoral consistency and macro-economic planning" in "Economy-wide Models and Development Planning" Eds. C. BLITZER, P. CLARK, L. TAYLOR, Oxford University Press, New York, pp. 129-154.

COAL, A. J. (Ed.): "Economic Factors in Population Growth", Proceedings of a Conference held by the International Economic Association at Valescure, 1976.

DENTON, F. T. and SPENCER, B. G., 1984: "The time path of the economy as the population moves towards a stationary state" in: STEINMANN, G. (Ed.) 1984, 109-131.

GOLLADAY, F. L. and HAVEMAN, R. H., 1977: "The Economic Impacts of Tax-transfer Policy: Regional and Distributional Effects", Academic Press, New York.

GROOTAERT, Ch., 1983: "The Relation Between Final Demand and Income Distribution: With Application to Japan", Springer, Berlin.

GUENTHER, E., 1931:"Der Geburtenrückgang als Ursache der Arbeitslosigkeit? Untersuchung einiger Zusammenhänge zwischen Wirtschaft und Bevölkerungsbewegung" in: Jahrbücher für Nationalökonomie und Statistik, 134, Bd. III, Folge 79, Bd., Jg. 1931/I, 921-973.

FELDERER, B., 1984: "Population and per-capita income in simulation models" in STEINMANN, G. (Ed.) 1984, 132-146.

LEDENT, J., 1982: "Long-range regional population forecasting: specification of a minimal demo-economic model", with a test for Tucson, Arizona. Papers of the Regional Science Association 49, 37-67.

LEONTIEF, W., 1951: "The Structure of the American Economy", Oxford University Press, New York.

LUPTACIK, M. and SCHMORANZ, J., 1980: "Demographic changes and economic consequences: demo-economic multiplier for Austria", Empirical Economics, vol. 5, 55-67.

LUPTACIK, M. and SCHMORANZ, J., 1986: "Economic consequences of a change in demographic patterns: An integrated approach" in 'Integrated Analysis of Regional Systems' edited by P. W. J. BATEY and M. MADDEN, London Papers in Regional Science 15, Pion Publication, 107-121.

MADDEN, M. and BATEY, P. W. J., 1984: "A demographic-economic model of a metropolis" in: Developments in Spatial Demography. Eds. R. WOODS, P. H. REES (George Allen and Unwin, Hemel Hempstead, Herts.).

MIYAZAWA, K., 1976: "Input-Output Analysis and the Structure of Income Distribution", Springer, Berlin.

ORCUTT, G., CALDWELL, S. and WERTHEIMER, R., 1976: "Policy Exploration Through Micro-analytic Simulation", The Urban Institute, Washington, D.C.

RICHTER, J., 1981: "Strukturen und Interdependenzen der Österreichischen Wirtschaft", Schriftenreihe der Bundeskammer der gewerblichen Wirtschaft 41, Wien.

SCHINNAR, A. P., 1976: "A multi-dimensional accounting model for demographic and economic planning interactions", Environment and Planning A 8, 455-475.

SCHINNAR, A. P., 1977: "An eco-demographic accounting-type multiplier analysis of Hungary", Environment and Planning A 9, 373-384.

SCHULTZ, T. W. (Ed.): "Economics of the Family. Marriage, Children, and Human Capital". A Conference Report of the National Bureau of Economic Research. Chicago 1974.

STEINMANN, G. (Ed.), 1984: "Economic Consequences of Population Change in Industrialized Countries", Springer, Berlin.

STONE, R., 1981: "The relationship of demographic accounts to national income and product accounts" in Social Accounting Systems: Essays on the State of the Art (Edited by F. T. JUSTER and K. L. LAND), Academic Press, New York, 307-376.

TAYLOR, C. A., 1982: "Demographic disaggregation in the construction of regional econometric models: a statistical evaluation", International Regional Science Review 7, 25-51.

WAGNER, A., 1980a: "Der Geburtenrückgang als Ursache von Arbeitslosigkeit? Einige Bemerkungen zum Günther-Paradoxon" in: Jahrbücher für Nationalökonomie und Statistik, Bd. 195/3, Jg. 1980, 261-269.

WAGNER, A., 1980b: "Verursacht der Geburtenrückgang Arbeitslosigkeit?" in: Wechselwirkungen zwischen Wirtschafts- und Bevölkerungsentwicklung (zusammengestellt und bearbeitet von O. HATZOLD), Ifo-Institut für Wirtschaftsforschung e. V. München, 124-129.

WAGNER, A., 1984: "Aspects of demographic unemployment" in: STEINMANN, G. (Ed.) 1984, 295-302.

ZIMMERMANN, K. F., 1985: "Familienökonomie". Theoretische und empirische Untersuchungen zur Frauenerwerbstätigkeit und Geburtenentwicklung. Springer-Verlag Berlin, Heidelberg, New York, Tokyo.

Appendix

The particular sub-matrices of the inverse in the activity-commodity
model yield the following information about economic and demo-economic
multiplier relationships:

R_{11}: a typical element r_{ij}^{11} describes the effect of a unit change of
final demand in sector j upon gross production in sector i.

R_{14}: a typical element r_{ik}^{14} describes the effect of a unit change of
net labour income in household k upon gross output in sector i.

R_{15}: a typical element r_{is}^{15} describes the effect of a unit change of
consumption of product s upon gross output in sector i.

R_{21}: a typical element r_{ij}^{21} describes the effect of a unit change of
exogeneously given final demand in sector j upon employment in
sector i.

R_{24}: a typical element r_{ik}^{24} describes the effect of a unit change of
net labour income in household k upon employment in sector i.

R_{25}: a typical element r_{is}^{25} describes the effect of a unit change of
consumption of product s upon employment in sector i.

R_{31}: a typical element r_{ij}^{31} describes the effect of a unit change of
exogeneously given final demand in sector j upon capital demand
in sector i.

R_{41}: a typical element r_{kj}^{41} describes the effect of a unit change of
final demand in sector j upon net labour income in household k.

R_{44}: a typical element r_{lk}^{44} describes the effect of a unit change of
net labour income in household k upon net labour income in household l. It is interesting to note that this sub-matrix corresponds
very closely to the inter-relational income multiplier, K, put
forward by MIYAZAWA (1976). However, Miyazawa's formulation ignores
the effect of taxation and savings and so he is able to interpret
the coefficients in K as the effect of income changes in one demo-

graphic group upon consumption in another demographic group, since household income is assumed to equal household consumption, for any demographic group.

R_{45}: a typical element r_{ks}^{45} describes the effect of a unit change in consumption of product s upon net labour income in household k.

R_{54}: a typical element r_{sk}^{54} describes the effect of a unit change of net labour income in household k upon consumption of product s.

R_{61}: a typical element r_{j}^{61} describes the effect of a unit change of exogeneously given final demand in sector j upon balance condition of the public retirement system.

R_{62}: a typical element r_{j}^{62} describes the effect of a unit change of employment in sector j upon balance condition of the public retirement system.

R_{64}: a typical element r_{k}^{64} describes the effect of a unit change of net labour income in household k upon balance condition of the public retirement system.

Of special interest are the demographic-economic multipliers $R._{7}$, expressing the economic effects of changes in the size and structure of population.

R_{17}: a typical element r_{ik}^{17} describes the effect of a unit change of population in demographic group k upon gross production in sector i. This sub-matrix corresponds to demo-economic multiplier Z developed in our previous paper (LUPTACIK - SCHMORANZ, 1980) and which is the subject of further discussion and empirical analysis in LUPTACIK - SCHMORANZ (1986).

R_{27}: a typical element r_{ik}^{27} describes the effect of a unit change of population in demographic group k upon employment in sector i.

R_{37}: a typical element r_{ik}^{37} describes the effect of a unit change of population in demographic group k upon capital demand in sector i.

R_{47}: a typical element r_{lk}^{47} describes the effect of a unit change of population in demographic group (household) k upon net labour income of household l.

R_{57}: a typical element r_{sk}^{57} describes the effect of a unit change of population in household k upon consumption of product s.

R_{67}: a typical element r_{k}^{67} describes the effect of a unit change of population in household k upon balance condition of the public retirement system.

CONSUMPTION, SAVINGS AND DEMOGRAPHY

Rob J. M. Alessie

Arie Kapteyn

Tilburg University, Tilburg / Netherlands

ABSTRACT: This paper estimates and tests an expected (multiperiod) utility maximization model of the joint determination of savings and of expenditure on different goods using panel data. The emphasis is on appropriate modelling of demographic effects (as taste shifters) and on the estimation of within period preferences that are consitent with intertemporal two stage budgeting under uncertainty. The parameters of the intratemporal utility function depend on demographic factors in a flexible way.

Certain implications of the rational expectations-life cycle hypothesis are tested along the lines of HALL(1978). The empirical results indicate rejection of the hypothesis and suggest the existence of liquidity constraints. However, for some forms of liquidity constraints the functional form of the within period demand functions is not affected. Therefore we have estimated a within period demand system, based on the Almost Ideal Demand System (A. I. D. S.) cost function. Both the allocation of consumption across the life cycle and the allocation of expenditures within a given period depend heavily on demographics.

I.   Introduction

Only since the pioneer work of MODIGLIANI and BRUMBERG (1955), have many economists paid much attention to the Life Cycle Hypothesis (LCH). Today it is hardly conceivable that one would attempt an economic analysis of consumption and savings over a consumer's life cycle without using some version of the LCH as a starting point. In this paper, we model the influence of the demographic composition of a population on the size and composition of private consumption and savings within the LCH-framework.

There are two major channels through which the demographic composition of a population influences consumption and savings. In the first place, age and family composition can act as taste shifters. For example, older people may have different tastes than younger people and large families may have different preferences than small families. In the second place, age is an important planning variable. For example, the simpler version of the LCH imply that a consumer will start dissaving when the end of his life draws nearer.

Financial support by the Netherlands Organization for the Advancement of Pure Research (ZWO) and by the NMB bank is gratefully acknowledged. We thank an anonymous referee, Raymond Gradus and Arie de Graaf for their research assistance and Yannis Ioannides, Bertrand Melenberg, Robert Moffitt, John Muellbauer and Theo Nijman for their valuable comments.

Studies in Contemporary Economics
A. Wenig, K. F. Zimmermann (Eds.)
Demographic Change and Economic Development
© Springer-Verlag Berlin Heidelberg 1989

Although our emphasis is on the role of demographic characteristics, a fair amount of space is devoted to a discussion of assumptions and proper estimation strategies for LCH-models. Recently, various new approaches have been suggested to the estimation of LCH-models, like the constant λ variety of HECKMAN (1978), HECKMAN and MaCURDY (1980), MaCURDY (1981) and BROWNING, DEATON and IRISH (1985). As discussed in Section 2, these approaches are based on rather restrictive assumptions of consumer preferences. Another area of the literature conditions on within-period total expenditures (or "full expenditures" if labor supply is modelled jointly with consumption). See, e. g., BLUNDELL and WALKER (1986) and ALTONJI (1986). In the latter case, preference assumptions are less stringent, but since in the applications by BLUNDELL and WALKER and ALTONJI only cross-section data are used, no real test of the LCH can be performed. It is not possible, for instance, to check whether consumers are liquidity constrained.

In Section 2 we present the LCH-model in rather general terms and we discuss some of the estimation strategies proposed in the literature. Also, we outline our own estimation method which is closely related to the approach by MaCURDY (1983). Section 3 gives details on functional specifications. For the explanation of consumption expenditures on various goods within periods, a flexible specification (AIDS) is chosen with cubic splines of ages of family members to represent demographic effects. These demographic effects are allowed to influence both the intercept and the slope of the ENGEL curves within periods.

For the modelling of the distribution of total expenditures (and hence of savings) across periods, a more restrictive, yet convenient functional form is chosen. Once again, the influence of age is modelled by means of cubic splines. Next, Sections 4, 5, and 6 discuss the data and present estimation results. One of the most striking empirical outcomes is that age is a strong taste shifter for total expenditures, in the sense that older people tend to consume substantially less, saving more than young people. This taste effect dominates the planning effect (i. e. that at the end of the life cycle one could deplete physical wealth), and as a result, older people save more than younger people. Further, in an aging population, one may expect private savings to go up rather than down, as simpler versions of the LCH would suggest. However, tests of the first stage part of the model (the explanation of the allocation of consumption across the life cycle) indicate rejection, so that this implication has to be viewed with some reservation. The rejection of the first stage part does not invalidate the second stage of the model (the allocation of expenditures within each period). The second stage model appears to be consistent with the data Section 7 concludes.

II. The Life Cycle Hypothesis and Two-Stage Budgeting

Consider a single consumer (or household), who has to plan consumption from the present period t up to a terminal period T in an uncertain environment. We assume that the consumer maximizes the following inter-temporally additive utility function:

$$U(t) = E_t \sum_{\tau=t}^{T} \left(\frac{1}{1+\rho}\right)^{\tau-t} u(z(\tau),q(\tau)), \tag{2.1}$$

with

E_t: = mathematical expectation conditional on all information available at the beginning of period t (expectations are rational)

$q(\tau)$: = vector of consumption goods in period τ, $\tau = t,\ldots,T$

$z(\tau)$: = vector of taste shifters at age τ

$u(z(\tau),q(\tau))$: = subutility function for period τ, strictly concave

ρ: = rate of subjective time preference.

This utility function is maximized subject to the following constraints:

$$A(\tau) = (1+r) A(\tau-1) + y(\tau) - p(\tau)' q(\tau), \quad \tau = t,\ldots,T, \tag{2.2a}$$
$$A(t-1) \text{ given}, \tag{2.2b}$$
$$A(T) = 0 \text{ ("no bequest motive")}, \tag{2.2c}$$

where

$A(\tau)$: = value of assets at the end of period τ

r: = interest rate

$p(\tau)$: = vector of prices in period τ

$y(\tau)$: = labor income in period τ, plus income transfers received in period t, next of taxes.

In this specification, credit markets are assumed to be perfect (no liquidity constraints and equal borrowing and lending rates). We have also assumed a constant interest rate over time. Relaxation of this assumption has little impact on the empirical model. In our model $p(\tau)$, $z(\tau)$ and $y(\tau)$ are exogenous variables.

The vectors $v(\tau)$: = $(p(\tau), z(\tau), y(\tau))'$, $\tau > t$, contain all the variables that are uncertain prior to period t. The random vector $\nu(\tau)$ is realized at the beginning of period τ. With respect to the probability distribution of the $\nu(\tau)$, we only assume the existence of certain moments. The distribution of $\nu(\tau)$ represents the consumer's subjective judgements about future variables.

Optimization of (2.1) subject to the budget constraints (2.2) implies the following first order conditions for period t[1] (see MaCURDY (1983)):

$$\frac{\partial\, u(z(t),q(t))}{\partial\, q(t)} = \lambda(t)\, p(t) \tag{2.3}$$

$$\lambda(t) = E_t \frac{(1+r)}{(1+\rho)} \lambda(t+1), \tag{2.4}$$

where $\lambda(\tau)$, $\tau = t,\ t + 1$, is the Lagrange multiplier associated with the budget constraint of period τ. The quantity $\lambda(\tau)$ is the marginal utility of after tax wealth in period τ. From equations (2.3) and (2.4) it follows that intertemporal additivity allows for two-stage budgeting. In the first stage, the household derives total consumption x(t) at time t by equalizing the marginal utility of suitably discounted after tax wealth in all periods of the life cycle (see the Euler equation (2.4)). As a result, also the optimal savings-decision is determined in this stage. In the second stage the amount of total expenditures x(t) in period t is allocated to consumption goods according to condition (2.3).

There is another important implication of the life cycle-rational expectations hypothesis. One can rewrite the Euler equation (2.4), for example, in the following two ways

$$\lambda(t+1) = \frac{(1+\rho)}{(1+r)} \lambda(t) + \varepsilon(t+1),\quad E_t\varepsilon(t+1) = 0 \tag{2.4a}$$

and

$$\lambda(t+1) = \frac{(1+\rho)}{(1+t)} \lambda(t)\, (1+\varepsilon(t+1)),\quad E_t\varepsilon(t+1) = 0 \tag{2.4b}$$

The condition $E_t\varepsilon(t+1) = 0$, in both formulations, implies that $\varepsilon(t+1)$ will be uncorrelated with all lagged variables in the consumer's information set. This econometric implication of rational expectations has been exploited in a number of estimation methods, which have been proposed in the literature and which will be discussed below. In this dis-

---

[1] For the moment, only interior solutions are assumed.

cussion, the cardinal period specific utility function associated with
period t is parameterized as

$$u(z(t),q(t)) = F(u^*(z(t),q(t)),z(t)),\qquad (2.5)$$

where $F(.)$ is a monotonically increasing function in $u^*(.)$, and $u^*(.)$
possesses all the conventional properties of a utility function[2].
The choice of the monotonic transformation is irrelevant in static
analysis. However, this is not the case in a multiperiod setting.

BROWNING, DEATON and IRISH (1985) use the first order conditions
(2.3) and (2.4) to construct the so-called λ-constant (or FRISCH) functions, which take the following form

$$q(t) = f(p(t),\ z(t),\ \lambda(t))\qquad (2.6)$$

The general properties of the demand equations (2.6) are described
in detail in BROWNING, DEATON and IRISH (henceforth referred to as
B. D. I.) and the use of these functions provides a useful interpretation of life-cycle behavior. Since the marginal utility of wealth
$\lambda(t)$ changes only when new information becomes available and all information about future variables is summarized in this sufficient statistic,
one can compute equation anticipated (intertemporal) price elasticities
from this.

B. D. I. want to estimate (2.6) by using panel data and treating
$\ln \lambda(t)$ as a fixed effect. Fixed effects can most easily be dealt with
by differencing, provided that they appear additively in the demand
equations, i. e. it is required the FRISCH demand of good i is of the
form

$$\zeta_i(q_i(t)) = \mu_i\ n\ell\lambda(t) + \eta_i(p(t),\ z(t)),\qquad (2.7)$$

where $\eta_i(.)$ and $\zeta_i(.)$ are suitable functions. In an environment of un-

---

[2] Of course, if $u^*(.)$ represents the intratemporal preferences with
respect to $q(t)$, then so does $F(u^*(.),\ z(t))$. It is a matter of
notational convenience to pick an arbitrary representation $u^*(.)$
and then to highlight the cardinal nature of the intertemporal utility function by showing the uniqueness of the transformation F,
given $u^*(.)$.

certainty, one can apply the estimation procedure of B. D. I. if the random variable ℓn λ(t+1) - ℓn λ(t) is a sum of an observable variable and a random variable ω(t+1), which satisfies $E_t\omega$(t+1) = 0. This property does not follow directly from the EULER equations (2.4a) or (2.4b). One needs some extra distributional assumptions about the forecast error appearing in (2.4a) or (2.4b) in order to justify the estimation procedure of B. D. I..

The major disadvantage associated with the use of the B. D. I. approach is, as they point out, the requirement that ln λ(t) enters additively in (2.7), thereby imposing severe restrictions on within period preferences. (see B. D. I. and BLUNDELL, FRY and MEGHIR (1985)).

An alternative estimation method proposed in the literature (see e.g. BLUNDELL and WALKER (1986)) is to condition on within period total (or "full") expenditures rather than marginal utility of wealth. In other words, this approach only requires the estimation of a complete static demand system. By using this approach one does not have to impose a priori restrictions on within period preferences and one can deal easily with corner solutions (see BLUNDELL and WALKER (1986) and MaCURDY (1983)). Obviously, with this procedure one can only estimate the parameters of the ordinal utility function u^*(.) in (2.5) and not the parameters of the monotonic transformation F(.). BLUNDELL and WALKER (1986) have retrieved intertemporal (constant-λ) price elasticities through the addition of some arbitrarily chosen identifying assumptions on the monotonic transformation F(.).

To obtain a feeling for the advantages and disadvantages of the approach we explore first the properties of the solution for q(t) derived from the optimization of (2.1) subject to (2.2) and a liquidity constraint of the form

$$A(\tau) \geqq M(\tau) \qquad\qquad , \tau = t,\ldots,T \qquad\qquad (2.9)$$

where M(τ) may be a function of current income.

$$M(\tau) = \Psi_0 + \Psi_1 y(\tau) \qquad \Psi_1 < 0 \qquad\qquad (2.10)$$

This formulation of the liquidity constraints is the same as that of, inter alia, MUELLBAUER (1983), ZELDES (1985), IOANNIDES (1986) and MARIGER (1987).

Optimization of (2.1) subject to (2.2) and (2.9) gives the following first order conditions.

$$\frac{\partial\ u(q(t),z(t))}{\partial\ q(t)} = \lambda(t)\ p(t) \qquad\qquad (2.11)$$

$$\lambda(t) - \mu(t) = E_t \frac{(1+r)}{(1+\rho)} \lambda(t+1) \qquad (2.12)$$

$$\mu(t) [A(t) - M(t)] = 0 \qquad (2.13)$$

If $\mu(t)$ is equal to zero, the liquidity constraint is not binding. As before, the optimal plan then follows from the first order conditions (2.3) and (2.4). However, if $\mu(t)$ is greater than zero, then it follows from (2.13) that total expenditures $x(t)$ are completely determined by the liquidity constraint (2.9). Thus, consumption is not entirely determined by the FRISCH demand functions. The optimal allocation of total expenditures over the different goods follows from (2.11) and can be described by a complete demand system. From the first order conditions (2.3) and (2.11), it is clear, that the functional form of the demand systems, which are derived from the two optimization problems mentioned above, are the same.

Since the two optimization problems yield the same demand system for $q(t)$, the strategy of BLUNDELL and WALKER yields estimates of the parameters appearing in $u^*(.)$ that are more robust with respect to the possible presence of liquidity constraints than the constant λ approach, used by B. D. I. and MaCURDY. However, in this way one cannot identify the parameters appearing in the function $F(.)$ introduced in (2.5), because the within-period demands are invariant with respect to choices of F. This implies, that BLUNDELL and WALKER have to assume that the life cycle hypothesis is true, before they can derive intertemporal elasticities.

The discussion so far motivates the choice of estimation method adopted in this paper. In order to explain our procedure we rewrite the EULER equation (2.4). Combining this equation with (2.3) and (2.5), one obtains the equation

$$F'(t)\frac{\partial \Psi^*(x(t), p(t), z(t))}{\partial x(t)} = E_t \frac{(1+r)}{(1+\rho)} F'(t+1)\frac{\partial \Psi^*(x(t+1), p(t+1), z(t+1))}{\partial x(t+1)}$$

$$(2.14)$$

where $F'(t)$ is the derivative of $F(.)$ with respect to $u^*(t)$, $x(t)$ denotes total expenditures, and $\Psi^*(.)$ is the indirect utility function corresponding to $u^*(t)$. This equation implies the relation

$$F'(t+1) \frac{\partial \Psi^*(x(t+1),p(t+1),z(t+1))}{\partial x(t+1)} =$$

$$\frac{(1+\rho)}{(1+r)} F'(t) \frac{\partial \Psi^* (x(t), p(t), z(t))}{\partial x(t)}[1+\varepsilon(t+1)] \qquad (2.15)$$

where $\epsilon(t+1)$ is a forecast error with $E_t \epsilon(t+1) = 0$ and consequently uncorrelated with variables observed by period t. Taking natural logs of (2.15) yields

$$\ln \left[F'(t+1) \frac{\partial \Psi^*(x(t+1), p(t+1), z(t+1))}{\partial x(t+1)} \right] = \gamma(t+1) +$$

$$\ln[F'(t) \partial \Psi^*(x(t), p(t), z(t))/\partial x(t)] + \xi(t+1), \qquad (2.16)$$

where $\quad \gamma(t+1) = \ln \frac{(1+\rho)}{(1+r)} + E_t \ln(1+\epsilon(t+1))$

$$\xi(t+1) = \ln(1+\epsilon(t+1)) - E_t \ln(1+\epsilon(t+1))$$

In our approach we obtain the parameters of the function $F(.)$ and $\Psi^*(.)$ by simultaneously estimating a demand system with total expenditures as the conditional variable and equation (2.16). Since the innovation $\xi(t+1)$ will, in general, be correlated with variables dated t+1, an instrumental variable estimator is required to estimate (2.16).

Although we allow $E_t \ln(1+\epsilon(t+1))$ to correlate with other variables on the right hand side of (2.16) dated t, we will assume that $E_t \ln(1+\epsilon(t+1))$ is constant across households.[3] This means among other things that we do not allow for heteroskedasticity of the forecast error. We will also assume that ρ and r are constant across households so that $\gamma(t+1)$ may be treated as a constant.

Our estimation method is very similar to the estimation procedure which MaCURDY (1983) has used in his empirical analysis. However, he rewrites the EULER equation (2.4) in a different manner. He uses the following equation

$$\lambda(t) = [\partial u(q_i(t), z(t))/\partial q_i(t)]/P_i(t) \qquad (2.17)$$

and imposes restrictions on the within period preferences $u^*(.)$, such as additivity. Furthermore, he estimates the parameters of the within

---

[3] The approach that seems preferable to imposing this expectational assumption, is to estimate the EULER equation (2.15) directly by using the method of generalized instrumental variables estimation of nonlinear rational expectional models proposed by HANSEN and SINGLETON (1982). This procedure does not require specific assumptions about the forecast errors. However, given our specification of $F(.)$ and $u^*(.)$, which will be presented in section 3, our estimation method is much simpler to carry out than the alternative method. In various other papers (for instance B.D.I. (1985), MaCURDY (1983), the estimation problem has been reduced considerably in the same manner as we do namely by transforming the EULER equation (2.4a) and (2.15) and consequently by making some distributional assumptions about the forecast error.

period utility function $u^*(.)$ by estimating marginal utilities instead
of using a demand system.

Notice, finally, that by our procedure (as well as by MaCURDY's)
one can estimate both the parameters of $u^*(.)$ and $F(.)$. Moreover, we
can choose a flexible functional form for the within-period preferences
and we are able to test some theoretical implications of the life cycle
hypothesis along the lines set out by HALL (1978). A consequence of
the life cycle hypothesis is that, apart from consumption prices and
taste shifters, none of the lagged variables should have explanatory
power with respect to current consumption (see equation (2.15)). We
test this implication in the empirical part of the paper by adding
lagged income to equation (2.16). It is clear from the equations (2.10),
(2.11), (2.12) and (2.13), that lagged income, $y(t)$, has a significant
effect on consumption in period t+1 if the household is liquidity constrained in period t.

III. Specification of the Model

In order to analyse the life cycle model empirically, we adopt explicit
functional forms for the within period indirect utility function
$F(u^*(t), z(t)) = F(\Psi^*(x(t), p(t), z(t)), z(t))$. Suppose $\Psi^*(.)$ can be
described by the Almost Ideal Demand System (AIDS) utility function
of DEATON and MUELLBAUER (1980)

$$\Psi^*(x(t), p(t), z(t)) = \frac{(\ln x(t) - \ln a(z(t), p(t)))}{b(z(t), p(t))} \qquad (3.1)$$

where
$$\ln a(z(t), p(t)) := \alpha_0(z(t)) + \sum_{i=1}^{I} \alpha_i(z(t)) \ln p_i(t) +$$

$$\sum_{i=1}^{I} \sum_{j=1}^{I} \gamma_{ij} \ln p_i(t) \ln p_j(t), \qquad (3.2)$$

$$b(z(t), p(t)) := \prod_{i=1}^{I} (p_i(t))^{\beta_i(z(t))},$$

with I the number of goods, $z(t)$ the vector of taste shifters and

$$\sum_{i=1}^{I} \alpha_i(z(t)) = 1; \quad \sum_{i=1}^{I} \beta_i(z(t)) = \sum_{i=1}^{I} \gamma_{ij} =$$

$$\sum_{j=1}^{I} \gamma_{ij} = 0; \quad \gamma_{ij} = \gamma_{ji}. \qquad (3.3)$$

The functional form of the monotonic transformation $F(u^*(t))$ is given by

$$F(u^*(t), z(t)) = \beta_0(z(t)) \, u^*(t) \tag{3.4}$$

This leaves the following function to be maximized subject to (2.2)

$$E_t \sum_{\tau=t}^{T} \left(\frac{1}{1+\rho}\right)^{\tau-t} F(u^*(\tau), z(t)) \tag{3.5}$$

The estimation model becomes

$$\frac{\beta_0(z(t))}{b(z(t),p(t))x(t)} = E_t \frac{\beta_0(z(t+1))}{b(z(t+1),p(t+1))x(t+1)} \frac{(1+r)}{(1+\rho)} \tag{3.6}$$

$$w_i(t) = \alpha_i(z(t)) + \sum_{j=1}^{I} \gamma_{ij} \ln p_j(t) +$$

$$\beta_i(z(t)) \, [\ln x(t) - \ln a(z(t), p(t))], \qquad i = 1,\ldots I \tag{3.7}$$

where $w_i(t)$ is the budget share of good i in period t.

The linear form chosen for $F(.)$ greatly simplifies estimation. However, it is also restrictive. It turns out, for example, that the intertemporal (constant-λ) price elasticity

$$\frac{\partial \ln q_i(t)}{\partial \ln p_j(t)} = -\delta_{ij} - \beta_j + \frac{(\gamma_{ij} - \beta_i \beta_j - \beta_i (\alpha_j + \sum_{k=1} \gamma_{jk} \ln p_k(t)))}{w_i(t)}$$

can be recovered from knowledge of $u^*(.)$ alone and is therefore completely determined by the estimated cross-section demand system. These remarks also apply to the elasticities $\partial \ln q(t) / \partial \ln \lambda(t)$, and $\partial \ln x(t) / \partial \ln p_i(t)$. The elasticity $\partial \ln x(t) / \partial \ln \lambda(t)$ is equal to -1. Only the constant λ elasticities $\partial \ln q_i(t) / \partial \ln z(t)$ $i=1,\ldots I$ depend on parameters of the function $F(.)$. For these reasons, in future work richer specifications for $F(.)$ will be considered.

To incorporate demographic effects into the second stage model (3.7) we parameterize $\alpha_0(z(t))$, $\alpha_i(z(t))$ and $\beta_i(z(t))$, as follows:

$$\alpha_0(z(t)) = \alpha_0 + \rho \ln fs(t) \tag{3.8}$$

$$\alpha_i(z(t)) := \alpha_i + \sum_{j=1}^{fs(t)} \delta_j \, f^i(a_j(t)) + \theta_i^1 Q_1(t) + \theta_i^2 Q_2(t) \tag{3.9}$$

$$\beta_i(z(t)) := \beta_i + \eta_i \ln fs(t), \tag{3.10}$$

where

$fs(t) :=$ family size (i.e. number of household members) in period t

$a_1(t) :=$ age of head of household in period t

$a_2(t) :=$ age of partner of head of household in period t (if present)

$a_3(t), \ldots, a_{fs}(t) :=$ ages of the remaining household members, arranged in order of declining age (if present)

$f^i(.) :=$ a cubic spline function with knots at the ages 0, 6, 18, 65 and 79.

$\delta_j := 1$ if $j = 1$

$\quad := \ln(j/(j-1))$ if $j > 2$

$Q_1(t) := 1$ if head of household has a paid job

$\quad := 0$ otherwise

$Q_2(t) := 1$ if both the head of the household and his or her partner have a paid job

$\quad := 0$ otherwise

Thus $\alpha_i(z(t))$ depends on family composition and the labor force participation of both the head of the household and his or her partner, whereas $\alpha_0(z(t))$ and $\beta_i(z(t))$ only depend on family size. The definition of δ_j implies a weighting of household members which increases logarithmically with their rank number. The cubic spline $f^i(.)$ is defined on the interval $[0,79]$ and if the age of the j-th member of the household exceeds 79 it is set equal to 79. For this study we restrict the form of the cubic spline $f^i(a_j(t))$ at the end points 0 and 79. In particular we restrict the second order derivatives at 0 and 79 in the following way: $f^{i''}(0) = \frac{1}{2} f^{i''}(6)$ and $f^{i''}(79) = \frac{1}{2} f^{i''}(65)$.

Without these restrictions the data matrix would be extremely ill-conditioned (see BLUNDELL (1980)). Moreover these restrictions permit us to write the cubic spline as follows (see POIRIER (1976))

$$f^i(a) = \sum_{j=1}^{5} SPL_j(a)\xi_{ij} \qquad \begin{array}{l} i = 1,\ldots,I \\ a = 0,\ldots,79 \end{array}$$

with $\sum_{j=1}^{5} SPL_j(a) = 1$ for all a.

In this equation, the 80 x 5 values of $SPL_j(a)$ are known and the ξ_{ij} are ordinates of the spline function corresponding to the abscissa values 0, 6, 18, 65, 79. Details can be found in POIRIER (1976, ch. 3). Given estimates of ξ_{ij} we can derive estimates of $f^i(a)$. The functional form of $\sum_{j=1}^{fs(t)} \delta_j f^i(a_j(t))$ is given by

$$\sum_{j=1}^{fs(t)} \delta_j f^i(a_j(t)) = \sum_{k=1}^{5} [\sum_{j=1}^{fs(t)} \delta_j SPL_k(a_j(t))]\xi_{ik} =$$

$$\equiv \sum_{k=1}^{5} WSPL_k \xi_{ik} \tag{3.11}$$

Note that

$$\sum_{k=1}^{5} WSPL_k(t) = 1 + \ln fs(t)$$

By choosing these functional forms for $\alpha_o(z(t))$, $\alpha_i(z(t))$ and $\beta_i(z(t))$, we have adopted an approach similar to RAY's (1983), who has introduced the use of a price and/or utility dependent 'Engel scale'. The Engel scale $m(u^*(t), p(t), fs(t), a_1(t),..., a_{fs}(t))$ corresponding to our functional specification is given by

$$\ln m(u^*(t), p(t), fs(t), a_1(t),..,a_{fs}(t)) = \rho \ln fs(t)$$

$$+ \sum_{i=1}^{I} (\sum_{j=1}^{fs(t)} \delta_j f^i(a_j(t)) + \theta_i^1 Q_1(t) + \theta_i^2 Q_2(t)) \ln p_i(t)$$

$$+ u^*(t) \prod_{i=1}^{I} p_i^{\beta_i}[\prod_{i=1}^{I} p_i^{\eta_i} \ln fs(t)_{-1}] \tag{3.12}$$

Since we only consider expenditures within one period, we set all prices equal to one, without loss of generality. Inserting (3.8)-(3.11) into (3.7) yields

$$w_i(t) = (\alpha_i - \beta_i \alpha_o) + \sum_{k=1}^{5} WSPL_k(t) \xi_{ki} + \theta_i^1 Q_1(t) + \theta_i^2 Q_2(t) +$$

$$+ \beta_i \ln x(t) + \eta_i \ln x(t) \ln fs(t) - (\beta_i \rho + \eta_i \alpha_o) \ln fs(t) -$$

$$- \eta_i \rho \ln^2 fs(t) \tag{3.13}$$

Since $\sum_{k=1}^{5} WSPL_k(t) = 1 + \ln fs(t)$, model (3.13) can be rewritten as

$$w_i(t) = (\alpha_i^* + \beta_i \rho) + \sum_{k=1}^{5} WSPL_k(\xi_{ki}^* - \beta_i \rho) +$$

$$\theta_i^1 Q_1(t) + \theta_i^2 Q_2(t) + \beta_i \ln x(t) + \eta_i \ln x(t) \ln fs(t) -$$

$$- \eta_i \rho \ln^2 fs(t), \qquad (3.13')$$

with $\alpha_i^* = \alpha_i - \beta_i \alpha_0 + \eta_i \alpha_0$

$\xi_{ki}^* = \xi_{ki} - \eta_i \alpha_0$

Comparison of these functions to the Working-Leser Engel functions that follow from the standard AIDS-model without demographic effects,

$$w_i(t) = (\alpha_i - \beta_i \alpha_0) + \beta_i \ln x(t), \qquad (3.14)$$

reveals that family composition is allowed to influence both the slope and the intercept of the Engel functions. In addition, total expenditures are scaled by fs^ρ. Finally, we have allowed, in a somewhat ad hoc manner, for effects of non-separability of consumption and leisure by the incorporation of 2 dummies in (3.12), that indicate whether a family has zero, one, or two or more earners.

The Euler equation (3.6), which describes the first stage model, can be replaced by

$$\frac{(1+r)}{(1+\rho)} \frac{\beta_0(z(t+1))}{b(z(t+1),p(t+1))\, x(t+1)} = \frac{\beta_0(z(t))}{b(z(t),p(t))\, x(t)} (1+\epsilon(t+1)),$$

$$(3.15)$$

where $\epsilon(t+1)$ is a forecast error uncorrelated with variables observed by period t ($E_t \epsilon_{t+1}=0$). We have specified the parameter of the monotonic transformation $\beta_0(z(t))$ as follows

$$\ln \beta_0(z(t)) = \xi_0 + \xi_1 Q_1(t) + \xi_2 Q_2(t) +$$

$$\sum_{j=1}^{fs(t)} \delta_j h(\bar{a}_j(t)) \qquad (3.16)$$

where

h(.):= cubic spline function with knots at ages 0, 6, 18, 65 and 79 years.

The variables $a_j(t)$ and δ_j were defined before. Given this specification of $\beta_0(z(t))$ and given $p_i(t) = 1$ for all $i = 1,\ldots,I$, we may rewrite (3.15) in the following manner

$$\ln x(t+1) = \gamma_0(t+1) + \ln x(t) + \zeta_1 \, \Delta Q_1(t+1) + \zeta_2 \, \Delta Q_2(t+1) +$$

$$\Delta \sum_{j=1}^{fs(t+1)} \delta_j \, h(a_j(t+1)) - [\sum_{i=1}^{I} \eta_i \ln p_i(t+1)] \ln fs(t+1) + \tilde{\xi}(t+1)$$

$$(3.17)$$

where

$$\gamma_0(t+1) := \ln \frac{(1+\rho)}{(1+r)} + E_t \ln(1+\varepsilon(t+1)) - \sum_{i=1}^{I} \beta_i \ln p_i(t+1)$$

$$\tilde{\xi}(t+1) := \ln(1+\varepsilon(t+1)) - E_t \ln(1+\varepsilon(t+1)),$$

and Δ is a first difference operator. Since we assume that all consumers face the same prices, we may treat the terms $\sum_{i=1}^{I} \beta_i \ln p_i(t+1)$ and $\sum_{i=1}^{I} \eta_i \ln p_i(t+1)$ as constants in a cross-section. Along the same lines as in (3.11) the function $\Delta \sum_{j=1}^{fs(t+1)} \delta_j h(a_j(t+1))$ can be replaced by

$$\Delta \sum_{j=1}^{fs(t+1)} \delta_j h(a_j(t+1)) = \sum_{k=1}^{5} \Delta WSPL_k(t+1) \, \zeta_{k+2} \qquad (3.18)$$

As a result equation (3.17) becomes

$$\ln x(t+1) = \gamma_0(t+1) + \ln x(t) + \zeta_1 \Delta Q_1(t+1) + \zeta_2 \Delta Q_2(t+1)$$

$$+ \sum_{k=1}^{5} \Delta WSPL_k(t+1) \, \zeta_{k+2} - \gamma_1(t+1) \ln fs(t+1) + \tilde{\xi}(t+1),$$

$$(3.19)$$

where $\gamma_1(t+1) = \sum_{i=1}^{I} \eta_i \ln p_i(t+1)$

Thus the relative change in total expenditures in period $t+1$, $\Delta \ln x(t+1)$, can be expressed as a function of changes in the labor force participation of both the head of the household and his or her partner, and family composition. Once again, the incorporation of the labor force participation dummies can be seen as a rather crude way to allow for a possible non-separation between consumption and leisure.

IV.   Data, Identification and Estimation

The data used to estimate the model developed above comes from the
1980-1981 Consumer Expenditure Survey of the Netherlands Central Bureau
of Statistics. We have used 1579 observations of households whose expenditures, income, family composition, occupational status, etc.,
are known for both 1980 and 1981. Expenditures are classified according
to the following seven categories

1. Food (including outdoor meals)
2. Housing (including rent, maintenance, appliances, tools, heating,
   electricity)
3. Clothing and footwear
4. Personal care and medical expenditures (including payments for domestic services)
5. Education and recreation (including holidays, smoking, stationary
   and subscriptions)
6. Transportation (including public transportation, bicycles, mopeds,
   motor cycles, cars)
7. Other expenditures.

Table 1 gives some sample information on the budget shares of these
categories and some general household characteristics.
    The complete model consists of (3.13') and (3.19), with error
terms added to (3.13'). We estimate model (3.13') for period t+1. The
complete model can be summarized as follows:

Table 1: Sample means and standard deviations of some variables

	1980 Mean	1980 Standard deviation	1981 Mean	1981 Standard deviation
Budget Shares				
1. Food, w_1	0.218	0.072	0.215	0.070
2. Housing, w_2	0.313	0.106	0.331	0.107
3. Clothing/Footwear, w_3	0.083	0.044	0.079	0.043
4. Personal care and medical expenditure, w_4	0.130	0.044	0.132	0.044
5. Education and recreation, w_5	0.140	0.075	0.130	0.074
6. Transportation, w_6	0.105	0.089	0.102	0.086
7. Other expenditures, w_7	0.012	0.018	0.011	0.017
General Characteristics of the households				
1. Total expenditures, x (Dfl x 1,000)	33,019	13,970	33,248	14,070
2. After tax income, y (Dfl x 1,000)	35,590	15,004	37,035	15,955
3. Family size, fs	2.985	1.394	3.003	1.394

$$\ln x(t+1) = \gamma_0(t+1) + \ln x(t) + \sum_{k=1}^{5} \Delta WSPL_k(t+1) \ \zeta_{k+2}$$

$$\zeta_1 \ \Delta Q_1(t+1) + \zeta_2 \ \Delta \ Q_2(t+1) + \gamma_1(t+1) \ \ln \ fs \ (t+1) + \tilde{\xi}(t+1) \quad (4.1)$$

$$w_i(t+1) = (\alpha_i^* + \beta_i \rho) + \sum_{k=1}^{5} WSPL_k(t)(\xi_{ki}^* - \beta_i \rho) + \theta_i^1 Q_1(t+1) + \theta_i^2 Q_2(t+1)$$

$$+ \ \beta_i \ln x(t+1) + n_i \ln x(t+1) \ \ln \ fs(t+1) - n_i \rho \ \ln^2 fs(t+1) +$$

$$+ \ \omega_i(t+1) \quad\quad\quad (4.2)$$

$i \in \{1, \ldots, I\}$ (I = number of goods)

$$\gamma_0(t+1) = \ln \frac{(1+r)}{(1+\rho)} - E_t \ \ln(1+\epsilon(t+1)) - \sum_{i=1}^{I} \beta_i \ \ln \ p_i(t+1)$$

$$\gamma_1(t+1) = - \sum_{i=1}^{I} n_i \ \ln \ p_i(t+1)$$

$$\alpha_i^* = \alpha_i - \beta_i \alpha_0 + n_i \alpha_0$$

$$\xi_{ki}^* = \xi_{ki} - n_i \alpha_0$$

$$\sum_{i=1}^{I} \alpha_i = 1; \quad \sum_{i=1}^{I} \xi_{ki} = 0; \quad \sum_{i=1}^{I} n_i = 0; \quad \sum_{i=1}^{I} \beta_i = 0$$

$$\sum_{i=1}^{I} \theta_i^1 = 0; \quad \sum_{i=1}^{I} \theta_i^2 = 0.$$

Since the budget shares add to unity, any one equation in (4.2) can be dropped from the estimation. We have chosen to drop the last one. With respect to the stochastic specification of the model we make some simplifying assumptions. First we assume that the distribution of $\tilde{\xi}(t+1)$ in (4.1) is the same across consumers. Consequently, $\gamma_0(t+1)$ is a period specific parameter, which has the same value for all consumers. Furthermore, we assume $\omega(t+1) := (\tilde{\xi}(t+1), \ \omega_1(t+1), \ldots, \omega_6(t+1))' \equiv (\tilde{\xi}(t+1), \ \omega^*(t+1))'$ to be (normally) independently and identically distributed across observations with mean zero and variance covariance matrix V, given by

$$V = \begin{pmatrix} \sigma^2_{\tilde{\xi}} & V'_{\omega^*,\tilde{\xi}} \\ V_{\omega^*,\tilde{\xi}} & V_{\omega^*,\omega^*} \end{pmatrix} \qquad (4.3)$$

with V symmetric positive definite but otherwise unrestricted. We have
estimated (4.1) and (4.2) separately by using (non-linear) two stage
least squares methods for both equations and by ignoring the restric-
tion $\gamma_1(t+1) = -\sum_{i=1}^{I} n_i \ln p_i(t+1)$. We need an instrumental variable estimator in (4.1), because the taste shifters dated t+1 may be correlated
with $\tilde{\xi}(t+1)$. We use a number of household characteristics like $Q_1(t)$,
$Q_2(t)$, region, family size etc.. Since our panel consists of 2 waves
we have only levels and not first differences of these instruments,
such as $\Delta Q_1(t)$, at our disposal. Therefore, the correlation between
the instruments and the endogenous variables on the right hand side
tends to be small. Some instruments deserve further comment: given
the size and age composition of the family in 1980, we have computed
the following variables

$$WSPLI_k(t): = \sum_{j=1}^{fs(t)} \delta_j SPL_k(a_j(t)+1)$$

Good instruments for $\Delta WSPL_k(t+1)$ may be

$$\Delta WSPLI_k(t) = WSPLI_k(t) - WSPL_k(t) \quad k = 1,\ldots 5 \qquad (4.4)$$

Since $\sum_{k=1}^{5} WSPL_k(t) = \sum_{k=1}^{5} WSPLI_k(t) = 1 + \log fs(t)$, we have added only

four of the five variables in (4.4) to the set of instruments.

We have to estimate model (4.2) by means of nonlinear two stage
least squares, because $\ln x(t+1)$ and $\ln x(t+1) \ln fs(t+1)$ are endogenous
variables, due to assumption (4.3). We have used the following instruments $\ln x(t)$ and $\ln x(t) \ln fs(t+1)$. (We assume that we may treat
taste shifters in period t+1, such as $\ln fs(t+1)$, as exogenous variables
in the second stage model.)

As a result our estimation procedure will yield consistent, but
not fully efficient estimates of the parameters in (4.1) and (4.2).

Finally, we pay some attention to the identification of the structural parameters in model (4.2). Under the statistical assumptions made,
all reduced parameters can be estimated consistently. However, the re-

duced form parameters do not contain enough information to identify all structural form parameters. This can be seen as follows: β_i, η_i, θ_i^1, θ_i^2 are reduced form parameters and hence identified. Next use the reduced form parameter corresponding to $\ln^2 fs(t)$ to determine ρ. Then, it is easy to see that the parameters ξ_{ki}^* and α_i^* are also identified. However, knowing ξ_{ki}^* and α_i^* still leaves us one piece of information short to be able to solve for the structural parameters α_i, α_0 and ξ_{ki}.

291

H(age)

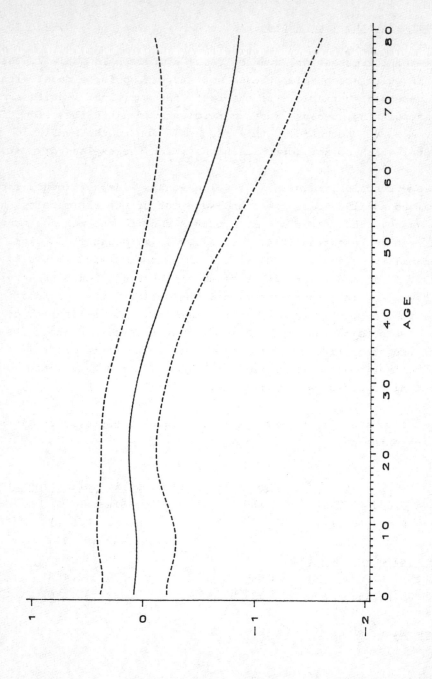

FIG. 5.1: Estimated age function (cubic spline), H(age), plus the corresponding confidence interval.

V.   Results for the First Stage

The parameter estimates for equation (4.1) are given in Table 2. The R^2-value is quite acceptable, though not surprising for a model with a lagged dependent variable. For the rest, the empirical results are a bit disappointing, because most coefficients do not differ significantly from zero. Undoubtedly, this is partly due to the available instruments, which do not correlate highly with the explanatory variables.

The age function drawn in Fig. 5.1 also has wide confidence intervals (defined as 1.96 times the standard error of the estimate of the function value), and a test of the hypothesis of a constant age function does not lead to rejection (F(4,1570) = 1.83), although it is close (the probability of an F(4,1570)-statistic exceeding 1.83 equals 0.12.). From (2.5), (3.4) and (3.16) it is clear that the age function serves to weight utility in different periods. The shape of the age function suggests, that beyond the age of twenty one, there is a tendency to give lower weights to consumption at older ages (over and above the effect of the subjective discount rate). Since the taste shift is foreseen (i. e. "rational"), the _ceteris paribus_ effect of age on consumption is a monotonic decrease after the age of twenty.

Table 2: Estimation results for the first stage (asymptotic t-values in parentheses)

Equation 4.1

Ordinates of the cubic spline function

$\gamma_0(1981) = 0.030$ (1.786)

$\gamma_1(1981) = 0.002$ (0.112)

age	ordinates
0	0.080 (0.527)
6	0.053 (0.297)
18	0.128 (1.002)
65	-0.679 (-2.446)
79	-0.833 (-2.156)

Labor participation dummies

$\zeta_1 = -0.025$ (-0.309)

$\zeta_2 = 0.010$ (0.116)

total expenditures

$\gamma_2 = 1$

$\text{var}(\eta(1981)) = 0.059$ $R^2 = 0.710$

We have also estimated an equation of the following form by means of 2SLS.

$$\ln x(t+1) = \alpha_0(t+1) + \alpha_1 \ln x(t) + \alpha_2 Q_1(t+1) + \alpha_3 Q_2(t+1)$$

$$\alpha_4 Q_1(t) + \alpha_5 Q_2(t) + \sum_{j=1}^{5} \alpha_{j+5} WSPL_j(t+1)$$

$$+ \sum_{j=1}^{5} \alpha_{j+10} WSPL_j(t) + \xi(t+1) \qquad\qquad (5.1)$$

Note that equation (4.1) is nested in (5.1).[4] We can thus use an asymptotic F-test to investigate whether the restrictions implied by (4.1) are valid. The test rejects the restriction decisively $F(7,1563) = 27.82$. A possible explanation is, that the functional form of the monotonic transformation F is not correct.

Finally, we have added lagged income to equation (5.1). The corresponding coefficient differs significantly from zero ($t(1562) = 5.107$).

One can interpret this result as a contradiction of the life cycle-rational expectations hypothesis, which says that of the lagged variables, only lagged consumption and taste shifters (in our case demographic factors and labor participation dummies) should have a nonzero coefficient in such a regression (see HALL (1978)). A possible cause for the departure of the life cycle-rational expectation hypothesis is the presence of liquidity constraints and the possibility of consumer expectations not being rational.

The significance of the lagged income coefficient may also be due to a violation of some other assumptions we made. We assumed, for example:

1. The within period preferences are weakly separable between consumption and leisure.

2. The consumer is not subject to rational habit formation.

3. The coefficient $\gamma_0(t+1)$ is the same across individuals. This means that we neither allow for a varying rate of time preference ρ nor for heteroskedasticity of the forecast error. One can somewhat relax this assumption by treating $\gamma_0(t+1)$ as a random effect, provided that it does not correlate with variables dated t.

---

[4]
Note that $\sum_{j=1}^{fs(\tau)} WSPL_j(\tau) = 1 + \log fs(\tau)$, $\tau = t, t+1$.

If assumptions 1 or 2 are violated, the within period demand system will be misspecified. The violation of the third assumption, or non-rational expectations, or liquidity constraints, need not induce mis-specification of the second stage model. Maintaining assumptions 1 and 2 we present estimation results for the within period demand system in the next section.

VI. Results for the Second Stage

Parameter estimates for model (4.2) are given in Table 4. Once more, the results for the spline functions are given in graphs, see Figures 6.1 through 6.6. The R^2-s are rather low, which suggests that it might be useful to add more explanatory variables to the model. Lagged budget shares (as an indication of (myopic) habit formation) may be especially important determinants of current budget shares. One should note, however, that although the explanation of variation in budget shares across households leaves something to be desired, the explanation of expenditures is much better. Rewriting (4.2) in terms of expenditures reveals that more than 50 % of the variance of expenditures across households is explained by the model.

In our model the expenditure elasticity of good i is equal to

$$1 + \frac{\beta_i + \eta_i \ln fs(t)}{w_i}$$

The resulting expenditure elasticities for different family sizes are displayed in Table 3.

Table 3: Expenditure elasticities for different family sizes (evaluated at the 1981 sample means of $w_1, \ldots, w_6, w_7$)

good \ fs	1	2	3	4
1. food	0.740	0.691	0.663	0.643
2. housing	0.964	0.960	0.957	0.955
3. clothing	1.063	1.125	1.161	1.186
4. personal care	1.061	0.856	0.736	0.651
5. education	1.092	1.215	1.287	1.338
6. transportation	1.490	1.633	1.716	1.776
7. other	0.364	0.679	0.863	0.994

We observe that food and housing are necessities irrespective of the size of the family. Personal care and medical expenditures are also necessities, if the family size is at least equal to two.

The other consumption categories are mostly luxuries. The estimate of $\rho (=0.24)$ implies substantial economies of scale: An increase of family size by 10 % increases the cost of maintaining a certain utility level by only 2.4 % (cf. (3.12) with all prices equal to one). The estimates of the θ-s show that one and two-earner families have a lower budget share for food and a higher budget share for personal care, medical expenditures and transportation than households with zero earners. For the remaining, the differences are slight.

Table 4: Second stage estimates (t-values in parentheses)

$\rho = 0.236$

$\alpha_1^{**} = 0.248\ (\ 4.78)$	$\beta_1 = -0.056\ (-5.65)$	$\eta_1 = -0.015\ (-1.59)$
$\alpha_2^{**} = 0.433\ (\ 5.07)$	$\beta_2 = -0.012\ (-0.75)$	$\eta_2 = -0.002\ (-0.15)$
$\alpha_3^{**} = 0.068\ (\ 1.91)$	$\beta_3 = 0.005\ (\ 0.78)$	$\eta_3 = 0.007\ (\ 1.04)$
$\alpha_4^{**} = -0.047\ (-1.31)$	$\beta_4 = 0.008\ (\ 1.18)$	$\eta_4 = -0.039\ (-5.69)$
$\alpha_5^{**} = 0.220\ (\ 3.66)$	$\beta_5 = 0.012\ (\ 1.09)$	$\eta_5 = 0.023\ (\ 2.13)$
$\alpha_6^{**} = 0.040\ (\ 0.60)$	$\beta_6 = 0.050\ (\ 3.96)$	$\eta_6 = 0.021\ (\ 1.80)$
$\alpha_7^{**} = 0.038$	$\beta_7 = -0.007$	$\eta_7 = -0.005$
$\theta_1^1 = -0.013\ (-2.43)$	$\theta_1^2 = -0.024\ (-3.36)$	$R_1^2 = 0.2152$
$\theta_2^1 = 0.004\ (\ 0.42)$	$\theta_2^2 = -0.000\ (-0.01)$	$R_2^2 = 0.1044$

$\theta_3^1 = -0.003 \ (-0.78)$ $\theta_3^2 = -0.005 \ (-0.91)$ $R_3^2 = 0.0388$

$\theta_4^1 = 0.005 \ (1.39)$ $\theta_4^2 = 0.016 \ (3.22)$ $R_4^2 = 0.1019$

$\theta_5^1 = -0.001 \ (-0.13)$ $\theta_5^2 = 0.008 \ (0.10)$ $R_5^2 = 0.0764$

$\theta_6^1 = 0.008 \ (1.17)$ $\theta_6^2 = 0.011 \ (1.19)$ $R_6^2 = 0.1639$

$\theta_7^1 = 0.000$ $\theta_7^2 = -0.007$

Our attempt to make the specification of demographic effects as general as possible, makes it difficult to attach a direct interpretation to the parameter estimates. This is slightly different for the age functions incorporated in (3.13) since these represent an additive effect on the budget share of a good. The age functions are presented in Figures 6.1 through 6.6. The small seventh expenditure category has been omitted. Fig. 6.1 suggests that food consumption goes up until one reaches adulthood and afterwards remains constant. For housing, it would seem that in particular, the young and the elderly need a lot of space. It should be noted, of course, that people in the 30-50 range frequently will have children in the younger age-range. And it is only the sum of the age effects, logarithmically weighted, which appears in (3.13).

Fig. 6.3 suggests that the need for clothing only starts declining after the retirement age. The demand for personal and medical care (Fig. 6.4) shows a dip at the healthy ages between 3 and 25. Old people do not consume more medical care than younger people since in The Netherlands health insurance premiums are in principle constant across age groups. Not surprisingly, Fig. 6.5 shows that education and recreation are least consumed by the very young and the very old. Finally, Fig. 6.6 suggests that the budget share of transportation are more or less constant across the life cycle, with a slight dip around the age of ten.

VII. Concluding Remarks

The life-cycle hypothesis provides a convenient and powerful approach to the modelling of consumption and savings decisions. Even though the first stage model is rejected by the data, the additive separability of the intertemporal utility function allows for a flexible specification of the second stage expenditure allocation decision, which is not rejected by the data. For both the first and second stage model,

F1(age)

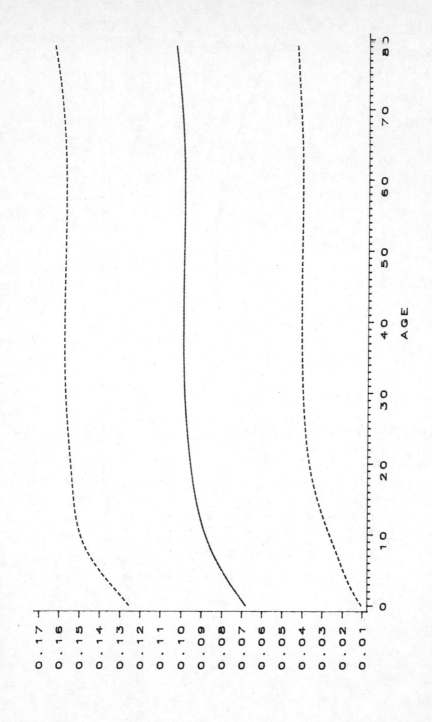

FIG. 6.1: Estimated age function (cubic spline), F1(age), of food plus the corresponding confidence interval.

298

F2(age)

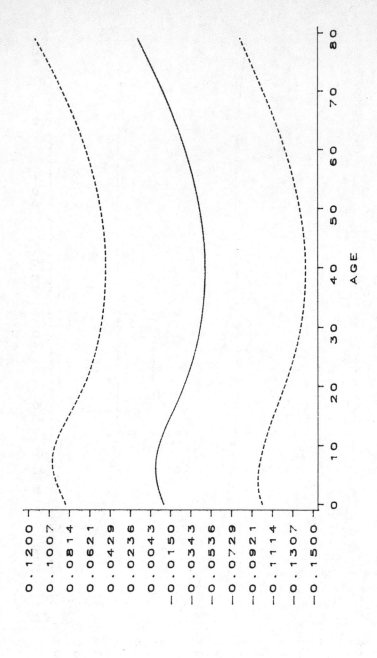

FIG. 6.2: Estimated age function (cubic spline), F2(age), of housing plus the corresponding confidence interval.

F3(age)

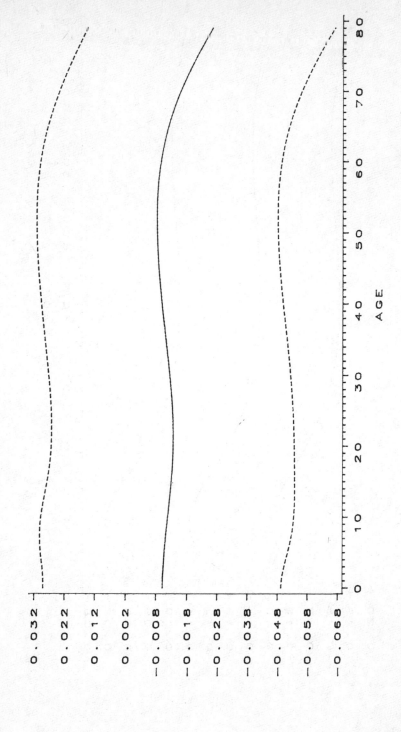

FIG. 6.3: Estimated age function (cubic spline), F3(age), of clothes, footwear plus the corresponding confidence interval.

300

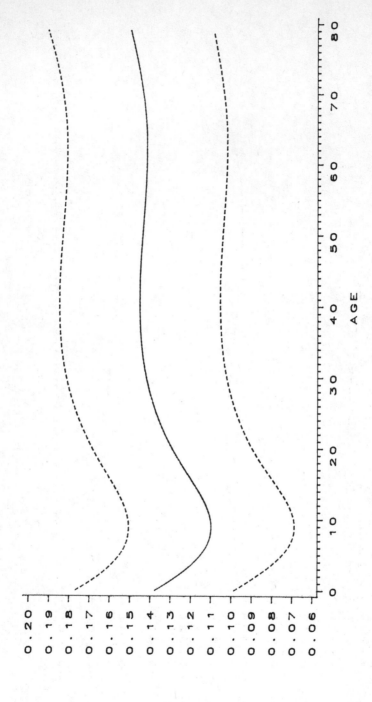

F⁴(age)

FIG. 6.4: Estimated age function (cubic spline), F4(age), of personal and medical care plus the corresponding confidence interval.

301

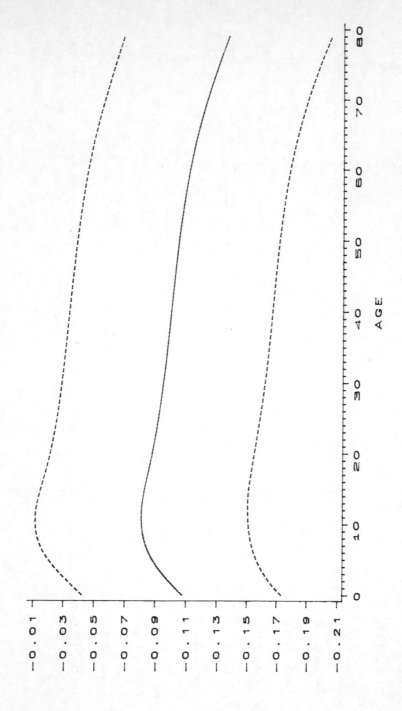

F5(age)

FIG. 6.5: Estimated age function (cubic spline), F5(age), of education and recreation plus the corresponding confidence interval.

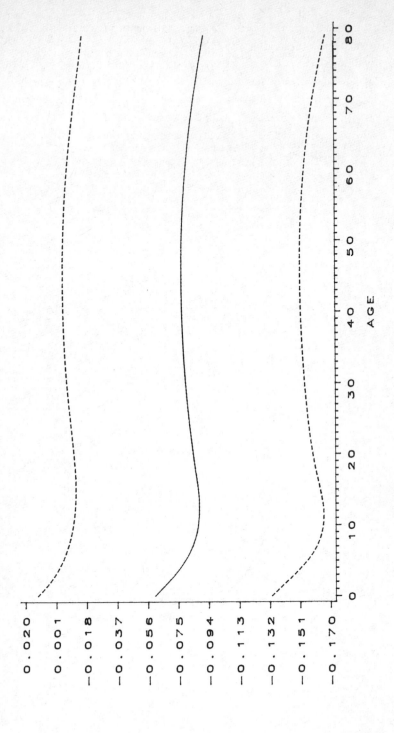

F6(age)

FIG. 6.6: Estimated age function (cubic spline), F6(age), of transportation plus the corresponding confidence interval.

demographic factors appear to be important determinants of behavior, through their role as taste shifters

The rejection of the first stage model suggests the need to relax the stringent assumption of perfect capital markets. The low R^2 s for the second stage model indicate the need to pay more attention to the influence of taste shifters. In ALESSIE and KAPTEYN (1985) we have therefore incorporated habit formation and preference interdependence into the second stage model.

304

References

ALESSIE, R. and KAPTEYN, A. (1985), Habit formation and interdependent preferences in the almost ideal demand system. Mimeo, Tilburg University.

ALTONJI, J. G. (1986), Intertemporal substitution in labor supply: Evidence from micro data. Journal of Political Economy, 94, pp. 5176-5215.

BLUNDELL, R. (1980), Estimating continuous consumer equivalence scales in an expenditure model with labour supply. European Economic Review, 14, pp. 145-157.

BLUNDELL, R., FRY, V. and MEGHIR, C. (1985), A constant and alternative empirical models of life cycle behaviour under uncertainty. Mimeo, University College London.

BLUNDELL, R. and WALKER, I. (1986), A life cycle consistent empirical model of family labour supply using cross-section data. Review of Economic Studies, 53, pp. 539-558.

BROWNING, M. J., DEATON, A. and IRISH, M. (1985), A profitable approach to labor supply and commodity demands over the life cycle. Econometrica, 53, pp. 503-542.

DEATON, A. and MUELLBAUER, J. (1980), Economics and consumer behaviour. Cambridge University Press.

FRIEDMAN, M. (1957), A theory of the consumption function. Princeton University Press.

HALL, R. E. (1978), Stochastic implications of the life cycle-permanent income hypothesis: theory and evidence. Journal of Political Economy, 86, pp. 971-987.

HANSEN, L. P. and SINGLETON, K. P. (1982), Generalized instrumental variables estimation of nonlinear rational expectations models. Econometrica, 50, pp. 1269-1286.

HECKMAN, J. J. (1978), A partial survey of recent research on the labor supply of women. American Economic Review, 68, pp. 200-207.

HECKMAN, J. J. and MaCURDY, T. E. (1980), A life cycle model of female labour supply. Review of Economic Studies, 47, pp. 47-74.

IOANNIDES, Y. M. (1986), An empirical investigation of intertemporal decisions and liquidity constraints. Mimeo. The Athens School of Economics and Business Sciences.

MaCURDY, T. E. (1981), An empirical model of labor supply in a life cycle setting. Journal of Political Economy, 89, pp. 1059-1085.

MaCURDY, T. E. (1983), A simple scheme for estimating an intertemporal model of labor supply and consumption in the presence of taxes and uncertainty. International Economic Review, 24, pp. 265-289.

MARIGER, R. P. (1987), A life cycle consumption model with liquidity constraints: theory and empirical results. Econometrica, 55, no. 3, pp. 533-557.

MUELLBAUER, J. (1983), Surprises in the consumption function. Economic
    Journal, Supplement (Conference Papers), pp. 34-49.

PALM, F. C. and WINDER, C. C. A. (1986), The stochastic life cycle
    consumption model: theoretical results and empirical evidence.
    Mimeo. Free University Amsterdam.

POIRIER, D. (1976), The econometrics of structural change. North
    Holland, Amsterdam.

RAY, R. (1983), Measuring the costs of children: an alternative
    approach. Journal of Public Economics, 22, pp. 89-112.

ZELDES, S. (1985), Consumption and liquidity constraints: an empirical
    investigation. Mimeo 24-85. The Wharton School, University of
    Pennsylvania.

A FLEXIBLE PROGRAMMING MODEL TO STUDY PROBLEMS
OF POPULATION ECONOMICS

Bernard M. S. van Praag[*/**] and Menno P. Pradhan[*]
Econometric Institute
Erasmus University Rotterdam / Netherlands

ABSTRACT: In this paper, a normative model is constructed in order
to calculate optimal growth patterns for economics with arbitrary
population development, arbitrary social welfare functions, production
functions and social security systems. It turns out that in almost
all cases an optimal growth pattern is not synonymous with full employment, except in the classical case of exponential population growth.

I.   Introduction

In the sixties and seventies, population was not much of an issue
in economics. It first appeared in the theory of economic growth.
Invariably it was assumed that population increases at an exponential
rate with the main problem being the determination of optimal savings
behavior such that some social welfare function is maximized. The
solution was found by using differential calculus. It appears feasible
to find a growth path in which capital and population grow proportionally
and the total labor force is employed all the time, such as found in
the now classic textbook by BURMEISTER and DOBELL (1970). In recent
years it has been realized that those approaches yield elegant results
but are too stylized to be of much value in the investigation of real
problems.

The major point, which should be accounted for, is that population
does not grow exponentially. This is due to the fact that age-specific
birth rates are not constant, but subject to rather strong fluctuations
that seem to occur in reality. A specific example is the marked fall
of the birth rate in many Western European countries, even below that
of the reproduction rate. Given that observation, the use of an exponentially growing population is unrealistic. It follows that all convenient instruments of calculus loose their value, forcing us to use
simulation models instead. Optimization techniques become discrete
and tend to be of the dynamic programming type (see also RITZEN and
van PRAAG (1985) and BUHL (1984)).

---

[*]   Erasmus University Rotterdam
[*/**] Member of the Scientific Council for Government Policy (WRR),
        The Hague, The Netherlands

Studies in Contemporary Economics
A. Wenig, K. F. Zimmermann (Eds.)
Demographic Change and Economic Development
© Springer-Verlag Berlin Heidelberg 1989

The main purpose of this paper is to construct a rather pedestrian programming model which can be used to study the impact of various policy instruments and assumptions on an economy, in which the development of the population is not governed by a specific exponential law. We shall maintain the assumption that population changes are exogenously determined. The model will not be used to derive results in the form of theorems, as we are only interested in one result, viz., that the program works. Along the line, we shall work out some examples. Our main policy instrument will be the general wage level. We assume that the relative income structure is fixed, but that the general wage level may be manipulated by the policy maker. As we have sacrificed our preoccupation with elegant results for flexibility, the model should be able to deal simultaneously with various elements considered important in demo-economic problems. We mention:

1. it must deal with any population pattern
2. investment in physical capital (savings problem)
3. investment in schooling (human capital)
4. unemployment
5. social security
6. age-differentiated need and wage patterns
7. population policy

A short discussion of these points follows. The first requirement arises because there is no real-world evidence for an exponential or other tractable specification of population as a function of time. A functional specification is only helpful in rather theoretical stylized situations, whereas it is actually a nuisance when the situation becomes somewhat more complicated to fit reality (see also RITZEN and van PRAAG (1985)). The oldest problem relevant in the population context is that of savings, as was first posed by RAMSEY (1928): Which part of the present product should be laid aside for investment to build up the physical capital for future periods? As HARROD (1960) and DOMAR (1957) have shown, the optimal savings behavior depends critically on the population growth rate, especially if population evolves according to a given law.

Recently, notably by BECKER (1981) it has been stressed that schooling, apart from its consumption aspect, has the investment aspect of making the labor force more productive. So, the problems of saving in physical or human capital are roughly isomorphic. If population fluctuates, we may get mismatches in the labor market, except if we assume that wages are completely flexible so that demand and supply

are always adjusted. In this paper, we assume that relative wages
are fixed but that the absolute wage is flexible.

A major issue in the modern welfare state is <u>social security</u>
(see also van PRAAG, POETH (1975)). Sizeable transfers are made from
the workers to the elderly, children and unemployed. As most of those
transfers are affected by population changes, it is impossible to
study social security without its demographic aspects. It is well-known
that people's needs vary with age, family size and other characteristics.
Many of them are demographically determined. The same holds for <u>wages</u>
which are strongly correlated with age. It follows that the levels
of the wage bill and of the distribution of consumption should be
evaluated in light of the demographical composition of the population.

Finally, in contrast to earlier work it is now understood that
the evolution of the population is not exogenously determined, but
that the population growth itself is partly determined by socio-economic factors like income, unemployment and the level of social security (see e. g. NERLOVE, RAZIN, SADKA (1987)) Although our model seems
able to cope with an endogenous population, we shall not elaborate
that feature in this paper.

II. <u>Population, Schooling and Ability, Consumption, Welfare</u>

Time t is running discretely from t=0 to t=T. Each period will be
called a year. Population P_t at time t will be subdivided according
to age i in I age brackets P_{it}. Part of the population will be employed
and part will be unemployed at time t. We denote the <u>working</u> population
by $P_{it}^{(1)}$ and the <u>jobless</u> by $P_{it}^{(2)}$. We have

$$P_{it} = P_{it}^{(1)} + P_{it}^{(2)}$$

$$P_t^{(1)} = \sum_{i=1}^{I} P_{it}^{(1)}$$

$$P_t^{(2)} = \sum_{i=1}^{I} P_{it}^{(2)}$$

and $\quad P_t = P_t^{(1)} + P_t^{(2)}$

It might be possible to make multi-dimensional subdivisions on the basis of (age, sex) or (age, region) etc., but we shall not do so in this paper.

Individuals have different labor endowments. At time t a person of age i will have a labor endowment of λ_{it} labor efficiency units (l. e. u.). The volume of l. e. u. at time t in age bracket i will be denoted by $L_{it} = \lambda_{it} P_{it}$. Moreover the total volume available will be $L_t = \sum_i L_{it}$; labor supply may be decomposed as $L_{it} = L_{it}^{(1)} + L_{it}^{(2)}$

Their consumption will be denoted by $C_{it} = c_{it}^{(1)} + c_{it}^{(2)}$. The wage of workers is denoted by w_{it}, while non-workers get a social security benefit b. Physical capital in period t will be K_t. Let $c_{it}^{(1)}$, $c_{it}^{(2)}$ stand for per capita consumption of the employed and unemployed, then individual welfare per period will be measured by a utility function $u_{it}(c)$ yielding an α-discounted utility flow

$$U = \sum_{t=0}^{T-1} \sum_{i=1}^{I} \alpha_t [P_{it}^{(1)} u_{it}^{(1)} (c_{it}^{(1)}) + P_{it}^{(2)} u_{it}^{(2)} (c_{it}^{(2)})]$$

Notice that this specification is extremely flexible. We leave room for utility functions that may vary per age group, over time and between employed and unemployed. The discount vector $(\alpha_0, \ldots, \alpha_{T-1})$ is not necessarily exponential. The traditional specification $\sum \alpha^t U(c_t)$ is a special case; if each person has the same utility function, there is equal per capita consumption and population grows exponentially.

III. Optimal Investment Policy

The consumption flow $\{c_{i\tau}\}$ over the period [t,T] with t = 0, ..., T-1 depends on capital $\{K_\tau\}_{\tau=t}^{T}$ which in turn depends on investment $\{I_\tau\}_{\tau=t}^{T}$ and initial capital K_t. If investment is low, consumption will be low and hence the resulting utility flow will be low. But if investment is high, consumption will also be low. The problem is to find the optimum investment policy. $\{K_t\}_{t=0}^{T}$ will be our vector of control variables. We shall assume K_0 and K_T to be given.

In the traditional exponential growth context, the problem may be solved by control theory, yielding some convenient differential equations. In our model, where we do not assume a specific population growth pattern, such methods cannot be used. Therefore, we have to find optimal solutions by numerical methods, in which we employ dynamic programming (BELLMAN (1957)).

Let us assume that there is a planning authority deciding on investment. National capital in year $(\tau + 1)$ equals

$$(3.1) \qquad K_{\tau+1} = (1 - \delta)K_\tau + I_\tau$$

where δ stands for a constant depreciation rate.

National product is

$$(3.2) \qquad Y_\tau = f(L_\tau^{(1)}, K_\tau)$$

where f stands for the national production function and Y_τ is produced jointly by employed labor $L_\tau^{(1)}$ and capital K_τ.

National product is decomposed into

$$(3.3) \qquad Y_\tau = C_\tau + I_\tau.$$

A national savings rate is defined by $s_\tau = I_\tau/Y_\tau$. As population does not grow exponentially, it is not helpful to cast our analysis in per capital units.

First, let us derive some natural boundaries on the control sequence. When we consider a finite period $[0,T]$ and start with an initial capital K_0, it is clear that K_1 is bounded from below and from above by

$$(3.4) \qquad (1 - \delta)K_0 \le K_1 \le (1 - \delta)K_0 + f(L_0, K_0) = (1 - \delta)K_0 + Y_0.$$

We denote the interval (3.4) by $\kappa_1(K_0)$. In words $\kappa_1(K_0)$ is the set of capital values that is reachable at t=1 from a capital K_0 at t=0. Similarly if K_1 is fixed, K_0 has to satisfy

$$(3.5) \qquad g(K_1) \le K_0 \le K_1(1 - \delta)^{-1}$$

where $g^{-1}(K) = (1 - \delta)K + Y_0(K)$. The interval (3.5) is denoted by $\kappa_{-1}(K_1)$.

Similarly by assuming that for two periods nothing is invested or all is invested we find that $K_1 \epsilon \kappa_1(K_0)$, $K_2 \, \epsilon \, \kappa_2(K_0)$ and also $K_1 \, \epsilon \kappa_{-1}(K_2)$, $K_0 \, \epsilon \kappa_{-2}(K_2)$. If K_0 and K_2 are fixed, it implies for K_1 that $K_1 \, \epsilon (\kappa_1(K_0) \cap \kappa_{-1}(K_2))$. Similarly we may construct feasible capital development paths over longer periods $[t,T]$, where $(T-t) \ge 2$. Given K_t and K_T, $K_\tau \, \epsilon (\kappa_{\tau-t}(K_t) \cap \kappa_{T-\tau}(K_t))$ for $\tau = t, \ldots, T$.

Second, we have to outline the way in which age-specific employment is determined. When we assume that labor endowments λ_{it} vary over subgroups, say age cohorts, then it implies that there are people with zero or very low marginal labor productivity. We notably think of children and the old-aged. A modern society will not indulge in a reward system which rewards people according to their labor productivity if that would be zero. This implies that wages will not be proportional to marginal productivity and that there will be unemployment. Further, given the wage system w_{it} per person or $w_{it}/\lambda_{it} = \hat{w}_{it}$ per labor efficiency unit, unemployment in a period t is determined by capital K_t in that period, since marginal labor productivity depends on capital K_t. But then employment $P_{it}^{(1)}$ in a specific subgroup i in period t is a function of capital K_t, i. e.

$$(3.6) \qquad P_{it}^{(1)} = \min\{P_{it}, \hat{P}_{it}^{(1)}(K_t)\} = P_{it}^{(1)}(K_t)$$

where $\hat{P}_{it}$ stands for labor demand of type i by industry with capital K_t. The same holds for $P_{it}^{(2)} = P_{it}^{(2)}(K_t) = P_{it} - P_{it}^{(1)}(K_t)$ and similarly $L_{it}^{(1)} = P_{it}^{(1)}(K_t)$, $L_{it}^{(2)} = L_{it}^{(2)}(K_t)$. The details of the hiring-and-firing process will be outlined in the next section.

At this point we observe that period-utility U_t may written as a function of K_t, for

$$(3.7) \qquad U_t = \alpha_t \sum_{i=1}^{I} [P_{it}^{(1)}(K_t)u_{it}^{(1)}(c_{it}^{(1)}) * P_{it}^{(2)}(K_t)u_{it}^{(2)}(c_{it}^{(2)})]$$

$$= U_t(K_t)$$

where $c_{it}^{(1)}$ and $c_{it}^{(2)}$ are defined in a way to be discussed in the next section; they satisfy the constraint $\sum_i P_{it}^{(1)}c_{it}^{(1)} + \sum_i P_{it}^{(2)}c_{it}^{(2)} = C_t$. It follows that the utility flow is still separable over time and may be written as

$$(3.8) \qquad U = \sum_{\tau=0}^{T-1} U_\tau(K_\tau).$$

The optimal investment path and resulting capital development, given final and initial capital K_T and K_0 can now be found by dynamic programming as follows. Consider the problem for the two-year period $[T-2,T]$.

(3.9) $U_{T-2,T-1}(K_{t-2};K_T) = U_{T-2}(K_{T-2}) * U_{T-1}(K_{T-1})$

where $K_{T-2} \varepsilon (\kappa_{T-2}(K_0) \cap \kappa_{-2}(K_T))$.

We maximize (3.9) with respect to $K_{T-1} \varepsilon (\kappa_1(K_{T-2}) \cap \kappa_{-1}(K_T))$ subject to (3.1), (3.2) and (3.3). The optimal capital is $\hat{K}_{T-1} = \hat{K}_{T-1}(K_{T-2};K_T)$. The optimal value of (3.9) is

(3.10) $\hat{U}_{T-2,T-1}(K_{T-2};K_T) = \max_{K_{T-1}} U_{T-2,T-1}(K_{T-2};K_T)$.

Consequently we define

(3.11) $U_{T-3,T-1}(K_{T-3};K_T) = U_{T-3}(K_{T-3}) + \hat{U}_{T-2,T-1}(K_{T-2};K_T)$

with $K_{T-3} \varepsilon (\kappa_{T-3}(K_0)) \cap \kappa_{-3}(K_T))$ and maximize (3.11) with respect to $K_{T-2} \varepsilon (K_1(K_{T-3}) \cap K_{-2}(K_T))$ subject to (3.1), (3.2), (3.3). This procedure is repeated until we reach $U_0(K_0;K_T)$ with corresponding optimal investment policy $\{\hat{K}_t\}_{t=1}^{T-1}$. Finally if K_T is not known, which in practice will be the case, we solve

(3.12) $\max_{K_T} \hat{U}_{0,T-1}(K_0;K_T)$

where $K_T \varepsilon \kappa_T(K_0)$.

IV. __Wages, Unemployment and Social Security__

Before we can operationalize the model we have to fill out a number of details. Let nominal wage of type i in period t be w_{it} and __real__ labor cost $\hat{w}_{it} = w_{it}/\lambda_{it}$. Our assumption will be that nominal wage w_{it} will reflect λ_{it} but not proportionally. More specifically we assume

(4.1) $w_{it} = w_{\cdot t} \lambda_{it}^{1-\gamma}$

where $w_{\cdot t}$ is the general wage level. If $\gamma = 0$, $w_{it}/\lambda_{it} = w_{\cdot t}$; it implies that every labor efficiency unit is equally paid, irrespective of the fact that some people get very low wages. If $\gamma = 1$, every employed

person gets the same wage regardless of his labor efficiency unit
input. In reality γ will be somewhere in between.

Employers will hire the cheapest workers first. That is, the
labor force is ordered according to required real wage $\hat{w}_{it}$. Let the
cheapest workers be in group i_0 with labor-force endowment $L_{i_0,t}$.

Its marginal productivity is $\frac{\partial}{\partial L} f(L_{i_0,t}, K_t)$. If

$$(4.2) \qquad \frac{\partial}{\partial L} f(L_{i_0,t}, K_t) \geq \hat{w}_{it_0}$$

the group i_0 is employed. If (4.2) does not hold, not all of type
i_0 are employed but only a fraction $0 \leq \xi < 1$ such that

$$(4.3) \qquad \frac{\partial}{\partial L} f(\xi L_{i_0,t}, K_t) = \hat{w}_{it_0}.$$

If the type i_0 is competely employed we go to the next-cheapest labor
type i_1 and repeat the test (4.2).

In this way the employed and unemployed are determined. Notice
that children and old-age will belong to the unemployed as their labor
endowment is small or zero. There are two loose ends: the social assistance to the unemployed, and the value of $w_{.t}$.

We assume that social assistance is given by taxing wages proportionally with premium rate θ_t, with the contributions being distributed
among the unemployed such that they get as a social benefit a fraction
ε of net wage $(1 - \theta_t)w_{.t}$. Hence the sum of premiums is

$$(4.4) \qquad \theta_t w_{.t} \sum_{i=1}^{I} \lambda_{it}^{1-\gamma} P_{it}^{(1)}.$$

The sum of benefits equals

$$(4.5) \qquad \varepsilon w_{.\tau}(1 - \theta_\tau) . P_\tau^{(2)}.$$

Given ε, equalization of (4.4) and (4.5) yields the social security
premium θ_τ.

It follows from the equation

$$\frac{\theta_\tau}{1-\theta_\tau} = \varepsilon \frac{\Sigma P_{i\tau}^{(2)}}{\Sigma P_{i\tau}^{(1)} \lambda_{i\tau}^{1-\gamma}}$$

As $P_{i\tau}^{(1)}$ and $P_{i\tau}^{(2)}$ depend on $w_{.\tau}$ and K_τ we have $\theta_\tau = \theta(w_{.\tau}, K_\tau)$. If we assume that wage is totally spent on consumption and on premiums to a pay-as-you-go fund from which social benefits are given to the unemployed, who also do not save, the gross-wage sum (demand for consumption goods) equals consumption C_τ

$$(4.6) \qquad \sum_{i=1}^{I} w_{i\tau} P_{i\tau}^{(1)} = w_{.\tau} \sum \lambda_{i\tau}^{1-\gamma} P_{i\tau}^{(1)} = C_\tau.$$

Given a specific $w_{.t}$, $P_{it}^{(1)}(K_t)$ may be calculated and values for $c_{it}^{(1)}$, $c_{it}^{(2)}$ and Y_t, I_t and K_{t+1} may be calculated for arbitrary $w_{.t}$, K_t; those values will not maximize the utility flow $U_t + \hat{U}_{t+1,T}$. By trial and error, $w_{.t}$ and consequently K_{t+1} are determined such that an optimum is found. We use the backwards solution version of dynamic programming.

The idea behind this procedure is that the relative wage structure is fixed but that the absolute wage level, that is w_τ is used as our policy instrument. In the next section we shall study the model by numerical examples.

V.   The Model at Work

In this section we try to study the system's behavior on the basis of some simulations. First, let us try to specify the basic and less basic components of the model.

1.   The Real Structure

a. The _production function._ We assume the production function to be constant over time. For convenience we take a Cobb-Douglas function

$$y = 6 \cdot K^{1/4} L^{3/4}$$

b. The _depreciation_ structure is assumed to be constant and exponential.

c. The individual _utility_ function $u(c)$ is assumed to be logarithmic, $u(c) = \ln c$, with all individuals having the same utility function.

d. The _time-discount_-rate α

e. The _population development._ In this experiment we assume the population to consist of 12 age brackets, in which everybody dies after finishing the twelfth year. The birth process is described by

$$(5.1) \qquad P_{1t} = (\beta_3 P_{3t-1} + \beta_4 P_{4t-1}) \; [\tfrac{1}{4} \sin(\tfrac{t\pi}{8}) + 1].$$

2. Parameters

a. The time discount rate α.

b. The labor endowment profile λ_{it}, a vector of length 12. We set it equal to (0, 0, .8, 2, 2.8, 4, 4, 3.6, 3, 2.2, 2.6, 0). Individuals are non-productive as a child and when they are old, and most productive in midlife.

c. The wage profile parameter γ is set at 0.3.

d. The social security parameter ε.

Some of the non-specified parameter values will be varied.

3. Initial and Final Conditions

We shall take 20 periods. The initial and final conditions do not have much importance, provided that one can reach the final situation from the initial and vice versa. What really counts is the behavior in the middle period. The initial population composition is defined to be

$$P = [8, 8, 9, 8, 8, 9, 8, 8, 9, 8, 8, 9].$$

Initial capital is K_0 and final capital K_f is defined by $K_f/P_f = K_0/P_0 = \eta$. If $\eta = 1$ capital per head at the start is equal to final capital per head.

As a human life in this model takes only 12 "years" a "model year" is about 6 calendar years. It follows that all parameters defined per time unit cannot directly be compared with real life parameters. More specifically, a <u>depreciation</u> rate per <u>calendar</u> year of $(1-\delta_c)$ is roughly equivalent to $(1-\delta_c^6) = (1-\delta)$ in model years. We take $1-\delta = (1-\delta_c^6) = (0.9)^6 = 0.53$. Similarly we have to interpret the time discount parameters and the savings rate.

The outcome parameters.

Most interesting for the evaluation of results are the behavior over time of

a. average instantaneous utility $\bar{u}$
b. average dependency ratio $P^{(1)}/P$
c. average employment ratio $L^{(1)}/L$
d. average capital per employed labor efficiency unit $K/L^{(1)}$
e. the utilization ratio of the production apparatus $f(L^{(1)},K)/f(L,K)$
f. the wage level parameter $w_{.t}$
g. average gross savings ratio (in calendar years)
h. the social security premium.

First let us consider a case more in detail. We call it the <u>central</u> problem. See Table 1.a and 1.b. In Table 1.a we present the typical employment and consumption pattern. Most classes are 100 % employed; some 0 % and some partially.

In Table 1.b population moves slowly according to (5.1). The dependency ratio varies considerably about the mean of 66.8 %. The same holds for the unemployment ratio that varies about the mean of 6.05 %. Capital is more than doubled from 400 to about 900. The final condition on capital leads to a forced capital reduction in the last several years. Except in the last two years, slack capacity is small; being about 4 %. The wage level stays rather constant and the same holds for the savings ratio of about 5 % per calendar year. Social security is rather stable at 23 %, while average utility remains rather stable at 1.69 over the whole period. The most interesting conclusion is that even under an optimal control, a fluctuating but not structurally growing population development (0.7 + 0.3 = 1) will yield an unemployment ratio in terms of labor efficiency units of about 10 %. Let us now look at other cases.

In table 2 some parameter values of the first case are changed. First we vary the <u>time discount</u> factor $\alpha = 1.0$, $\alpha = .9$, $\alpha = .7$, $\alpha = .53$.

Second, the population structure is varied $\beta_3 = .8$, $\beta_3 = .6$, $\beta_3 = .9$, $\beta_3 = .7$ and $\beta_4 = .3$. In the third line we also introduce a mortality of 5 % per age bracket. In the fourth line we return to the constant population but we increase the sinusoidal fluctuation compared to (5.1) by setting

$$P_{it} = (0.7\ P_{3t-1} + 0.3P_{4t-1})(\tfrac{1}{2} \sin \tfrac{2\pi t}{8} + 1).$$

Third, we vary the social security parameter $\varepsilon = .8$, .9, 1.0, 1.1. Fourth, we change the final capital constraint $\eta = 1$, 1.25, 1.5 and 1.25 with

K_0 = 1000. The main lesson to be drawn from Table 2 is that the impact of various parameter changes is apparently not very strong, except for the capital-labor ratio under various population developments. However, we have to keep in mind, that also in the real world, tiny fractions of percentages, such as in unemployment, may be the subject of fierce political discussion. The major fixed factor is the utility function, that is assumed to be logarithmic. A change in the specification of the utility function may have a much stronger impact.

VI.   Discussion and Conclusion

In this paper, we built a normative model to calculate optimal growth patterns for economies with arbitrary population developments, arbitrary utility functions, production functions and social security systems. The basic trick seems to be the endogenization of employment. It is obvious that we have dropped the ambition of building convenient theories. However, we have got an instrument, a flexible program, which makes it possible to evaluate and even to formulate optimal policies for large varieties of problems as listed in the introduction. Although several variables may be chosen as policy instruments, we opted for the general wage level $w_{.t}$ as the easiest instrument to manipulate for central government. It is our intention to generalize this setting by making population an endogenous variable as well.

TABLE 1a. Employment and consumption profile per age bracket in the central solution

- EMPLOYMENT PER AGE BRACKET

periods / years	1	2	3	4	5	6	7	8	9	10	11	12
0	0.0	0.0	100.0	100.0	100.0	100.0	100.0	100.0	100.0	100.0	100.0	0.0
1	0.0	0.0	85.4	100.0	100.0	100.0	100.0	100.0	100.0	100.0	100.0	0.0
2	0.0	0.0	0.0	100.0	100.0	100.0	100.0	100.0	100.0	100.0	100.0	0.0
3	0.0	0.0	0.0	100.0	100.0	100.0	100.0	100.0	100.0	100.0	100.0	0.0
4	0.0	0.0	92.5	100.0	100.0	100.0	100.0	100.0	100.0	100.0	100.0	0.0
5	0.0	0.0	97.5	100.0	100.0	100.0	100.0	100.0	100.0	100.0	100.0	0.0
6	0.0	0.0	97.7	100.0	100.0	100.0	100.0	100.0	100.0	100.0	100.0	0.0
7	0.0	0.0	95.8	100.0	100.0	100.0	100.0	100.0	100.0	100.0	100.0	0.0
8	0.0	0.0	95.0	100.0	100.0	100.0	100.0	100.0	100.0	100.0	96.8	0.0
9	0.0	0.0	0.0	100.0	100.0	100.0	100.0	100.0	100.0	100.0	100.0	0.0
10	0.0	0.0	0.0	100.0	100.0	100.0	100.0	100.0	100.0	100.0	97.2	0.0
11	0.0	0.0	0.0	100.0	100.0	100.0	100.0	100.0	100.0	100.0	97.5	0.0
12	0.0	0.0	0.0	100.0	100.0	100.0	100.0	100.0	100.0	100.0	97.9	0.0
13	0.0	0.0	0.0	100.0	100.0	100.0	100.0	100.0	100.0	100.0	98.5	0.0
14	0.0	0.0	0.0	100.0	100.0	100.0	100.0	100.0	100.0	100.0	98.4	0.0
15	0.0	0.0	0.0	100.0	100.0	100.0	100.0	100.0	100.0	100.0	97.7	0.0
16	0.0	0.0	0.0	100.0	100.0	100.0	100.0	100.0	100.0	100.0	97.3	0.0
17	0.0	0.0	0.0	100.0	100.0	100.0	100.0	100.0	100.0	100.0	97.5	0.0
18	0.0	0.0	0.0	100.0	100.0	100.0	100.0	100.0	100.0	100.0	0.0	0.0
19	0.0	0.0	0.0	0.0	99.5	100.0	100.0	100.0	100.0	0.0	0.0	0.0
20	0.0	0.0	0.0	0.0	100.0	100.0	100.0	100.0	100.0	0.0	0.0	0.0

CONSUMPTION PER AGE BRACKET

periods	1	2	3	4	5	6	7	8	9	10	11	12
0	3.9584	3.9584	3.9584	4.3982	5.5663	6.6369	6.6369	6.1117	5.5663	4.3982	3.7622	3.9584
1	4.2176	4.2176	4.2176	4.6862	5.9307	7.0715	7.0715	6.5118	5.9307	4.6862	4.0085	4.2176
2	4.3754	4.3754	4.3754	4.8615	6.1526	7.3361	7.3361	6.7555	6.1526	4.8615	4.1585	4.3754
3	4.0678	4.0678	4.0678	4.5198	5.7202	6.8204	6.8204	6.2807	5.7202	4.5198	3.8662	4.0678
4	4.4215	4.4215	4.4215	4.9128	6.2175	7.4134	7.4134	6.8267	6.2175	4.9128	4.2023	4.4215
5	4.4363	4.4363	4.4363	4.9293	6.2384	7.4383	7.4383	6.8496	6.2384	4.9293	4.2164	4.4363
6	4.4447	4.4447	4.4447	4.9386	6.2501	7.4523	7.4523	6.8625	6.2501	4.9386	4.2244	4.4447
7	4.5121	4.5121	4.5121	5.0134	6.3449	7.5653	7.5653	6.9666	6.3449	5.0134	4.2884	4.5121
8	4.5434	4.5434	4.5434	5.0482	6.3889	7.6178	7.6178	7.0149	6.3889	5.0482	4.3182	4.5434
9	4.6235	4.6235	4.6235	5.1372	6.5015	7.7520	7.7520	7.1385	6.5015	5.1372	4.6235	4.6235
10	4.5479	4.5479	4.5479	5.0533	6.3953	7.6254	7.6254	7.0219	6.3953	5.0533	4.3225	4.5479
11	4.8093	4.8093	4.8093	5.3436	6.7628	8.0636	8.0636	7.4254	6.7628	5.3436	4.8093	4.8093
12	4.8388	4.8388	4.8388	5.3765	6.8044	8.1131	8.1131	7.4710	6.8044	5.3765	4.8388	4.8388
13	4.9092	4.9092	4.9092	5.4546	6.9033	8.2311	8.2311	7.5796	6.9033	5.4546	4.9092	4.9092

14	4.9657	4.9657	5.5174	6.9827	7.6669	8.3258	8.3258	6.9827	5.5174	4.9657	4.9657
15	4.9335	4.9335	5.4817	6.9375	7.6173	8.2719	8.2719	6.9375	5.4817	4.9335	4.9335
16	4.8860	4.8860	5.4289	6.8707	7.5439	8.1922	8.1922	6.8707	5.4289	4.8860	4.8860
17	4.8313	4.8313	5.3681	6.7938	7.4595	8.1005	8.1005	6.7938	5.3681	4.8313	4.8313
18	4.7116	4.7116	5.2351	6.6254	7.2746	7.8998	7.8998	6.6254	5.2351	4.7116	4.7116
19	4.0473	4.0473	4.0473	5.6913	6.2489	6.7860	6.7860	5.6913	4.0473	4.0473	4.0473
20	3.6962	3.6962	3.6962	5.1976	5.7068	6.1973	6.1973	5.1976	3.6962	3.6962	3.6962

$(1 - \delta) = 0.53$
$\quad \dfrac{K_f/P_f}{K_0/P_0} = 1.25$
$\quad K_0 = 400$
$\quad \beta_3 = .7$
$\quad \beta_4 = .3$
$\quad \epsilon = .9$

TABLE 1b. The main indices over the years in the central problem

t	population	dependency rate	unempl %	labour av	capital	cap/lab	actual product	maximum product	used capacity f(L(1))/f(L)
0	100.0000	0.7500	0.0000	95.0000	400.0000	4.2105	816.5052	816.5023	1.0000
1	100.5319	0.7344	0.0156	95.0000	545.0420	5.7800	882.1683	877.2734	0.9945
2	102.2986	0.6549	0.1067	95.0000	647.5231	7.1787	920.9961	885.8700	0.9619
3	104.1459	0.6337	0.1262	95.3192	676.6315	7.5517	933.5218	891.1900	0.9547
4	106.4863	0.7191	0.0094	96.5919	727.9499	7.5707	960.2455	956.9799	0.9966
5	110.4231	0.7145	0.0031	98.6198	774.6800	7.8669	990.6147	989.5123	0.9989
6	113.9847	0.7126	0.0032	101.6824	811.5946	7.9940	1025.4638	1024.2722	0.9988
7	116.9228	0.7263	0.0058	106.4262	845.7607	7.9693	1072.1349	1069.8767	0.9979
8	120.6853	0.7325	0.0065	111.7066	882.3910	7.9240	1123.6358	1120.9990	0.9977
9	123.2475	0.6469	0.1326	116.9452	923.8777	8.4312	1176.3642	1120.3404	0.9524
10	123.9864	0.6769	0.1229	122.4418	900.7213	7.8063	1209.8905	1157.2010	0.9565
11	125.0751	0.6989	0.1102	126.4334	926.2577	7.7263	1248.0458	1199.2313	0.9609
12	125.2668	0.7062	0.1014	127.8086	930.6330	7.6428	1259.6965	1214.7629	0.9643
13	123.4119	0.7170	0.0950	127.0686	939.3897	7.7346	1257.1625	1215.2613	0.9667
14	121.2833	0.7236	0.0870	124.1190	943.6663	7.9255	1236.6150	1198.6710	0.9693
15	119.0815	0.7103	0.0851	118.7084	937.4850	8.2274	1193.9976	1157.8921	0.9698
16	115.5662	0.6945	0.0896	112.1723	917.8311	8.5476	1138.2987	1101.6158	0.9678
17	112.2051	0.6810	0.0945	105.7602	885.5707	8.7751	1079.4403	1042.1642	0.9655
18	109.4330	0.6580	0.1013	99.7461	844.8698	8.9106	1020.9881	982.9054	0.9627
19	107.0583	0.3755	0.4761	95.1409	801.0891	12.5075	972.4042	722.6916	0.7432
20	105.5588	0.3692	0.4815	92.8664	626.5476	10.0703	898.0155	665.0016	0.7405
21					529.1969				
mean	113.6406	0.6684	0.1073	107.8360	804.2625	8.0167	1067.4383	1019.5340	0.9533
abs dev	7.4729	0.0640	0.0767	11.1314	117.5844	0.8907	119.3772	132.1790	0.0404

t	wage w.t	savings	annual savings rate	util P1	util P2	average utility	social security premium θ
0	5.5302	0.4079	0.0587	1.6034	1.3758	1.5465	0.2047
1	5.9860	0.4088	0.0588	1.6760	1.4393	1.6132	0.2171
2	6.7481	0.3764	0.0547	1.7626	1.4760	1.6637	0.2796
3	6.4325	0.4144	0.0595	1.6961	1.4031	1.5888	0.2973
4	6.4039	0.4063	0.0585	1.7083	1.4865	1.6460	0.2328
5	6.4656	0.4053	0.0583	1.7071	1.4898	1.6451	0.2376
6	6.4916	0.4058	0.0584	1.7086	1.4917	1.6462	0.2392
7	6.4865	0.4058	0.0584	1.7232	1.5068	1.6640	0.2271
8	6.4773	0.4070	0.0586	1.7370	1.5137	1.6773	0.2206

9	7.1715	0.3669	0.0535	1.8344	1.5311	1.7273	0.2837
10	6.8033	0.3879	0.0562	1.8177	1.5147	1.7198	0.2572
11	7.0167	0.3667	0.0534	1.8713	1.5705	1.7808	0.2384
12	6.9977	0.3673	0.0535	1.8804	1.5767	1.7912	0.2317
13	7.0186	0.3668	0.0535	1.8925	1.5911	1.8072	0.2228
14	7.0615	0.3849	0.0532	1.8946	1.6025	1.8139	0.2187
15	7.1278	0.3636	0.0530	1.8828	1.5961	1.7997	0.2309
16	7.1962	0.3623	0.0529	1.8681	1.5864	1.7820	0.2456
17	7.2436	0.3603	0.0526	1.8482	1.5751	1.7611	0.2589
18	7.2714	0.3595	0.0525	1.8195	1.5500	1.7274	0.2800
19	9.3615	0.2795	0.0419	1.8250	1.3980	1.5584	0.5196
20	8.6641	0.2964	0.0442	1.7356	1.3073	1.4654	0.5260
mean	6.9503	0.3752	0.0545	1.7854	1.5039	1.6869	0.2700
abs dev	0.5407	0.0260	0.0033	0.0758	0.0636	0.0801	0.0539

TABLE 2. The effect of paramter variations

Time discount factor

	utility	dependency rate	L1/L	cap/lab	F(L(1))/F(L)	savings rate	social security premium θ
α = 1.0	1.6667 (0.1010)	0.6649 (0.0971)	0.9253 (0.0958)	8.3815 (1.1831)	0.9408 (0.07772)	0.3756 (0.0333)	0.2758 (0.0850)
α = .9	1.6869 (0.0801)	0.6684 (0.0640)	0.9395 (0.0513)	8.0167 (0.8907)	0.9533 (0.0404)	0.3752 (0.0260)	0.2700 (0.0539)
α = .7	1.6477 (0.0983)	0.6212 (0.0765)	0.8961 (0.0824)	8.1396 (1.9794)	0.9177 (0.0687)	0.3565 (0.0150)	0.3105 (0.0707)
α = .53	1.6752 (0.0789)	0.6390 (0.0540)	0.9180 (0.0479)	7.6784 (1.3167)	0.9365 (0.0390)	0.3592 (0.0094)	0.2937 (0.0486)

Population structure

	utility	dependency rate	L1/L	cap/lab	F(L(1))/F(L)	savings rate	social security premium θ
β3 = .8	1.6610 (0.0728)	0.6742 (0.0506)	0.9541 (0.0400)	7.6674 (0.6458)	0.9648 (0.0309)	0.3842 (0.0242)	0.2665 (0.0424)
β3 = .6	1.6958 (0.0959)	0.6480 (0.0741)	0.9127 (0.0723)	8.4988 (1.5092)	0.9319 (0.0583)	0.3651 (0.0194)	0.2865 (0.0656)
β3 = .9	1.5519 (0.0759)	0.6127 (0.0625)	0.9682 (0.0435)	9.1554 (1.0827)	0.9758 (0.0331)	0.3890 (0.0187)	0.3298 (0.0567)
β3 = .7	1.6491 (0.1526)	0.6019 (0.0747)	0.9225 (0.0688)	10.2901 (1.8017)	0.9402 (0.0535)	0.3660 (0.0295)	0.3313 (0.0679)

Social security

	utility	dependency rate	L1/L	cap/lab	F(L(1))/F(L)	savings rate	social security premium θ
ε = .8	1.6520 (0.1022)	0.6553 (0.0958)	0.9187 (0.0955)	8.4145 (1.3725)	0.9356 (0.0773)	0.3745 (0.0290)	0.2619 (0.0820)
ε = .9	1.6869 (0.0801)	0.6684 (0.0640)	0.9395 (0.0513)	8.0167 (0.8907)	0.9533 (0.0404)	0.3752 (0.0260)	0.2700 (0.0539)
ε = 1	1.6625 (0.1051)	0.6454 (0.0919)	0.9123 (0.0934)	8.3209 (1.4078)	0.9308 (0.0757)	0.3715 (0.0262)	0.3116 (0.0826)
ε = 1.1	1.6657 (0.1048)	0.6454 (0.0919)	0.9123 (0.0934)	8.3209 (1.4078)	0.9308 (0.0757)	0.3715 (0.0262)	0.3309 (0.0833)

Capital $\frac{K_f/P_f}{K_0/P_0}$	utility	dependency rate	L1/L	cap/lab	F(L(1))/F(L)	savings rate	social security premium θ
= 1	1.6571 (0.1054)	0.6477 (0.0940)	0.9138 (0.0939)	8.3683 (1.3855)	0.9319 (0.0761)	0.3731 (0.0274)	0.2893 (0.0828)
= 1.25	1.6869 (0.0801)	0.6684 (0.0640)	0.9395 (0.0513)	8.0167 (0.8907)	0.9533 (0.0404)	0.3752 (0.0260)	0.2700 (0.0539)
= 1.5	1.6973 (0.0702)	0.6813 (0.0460)	0.9541 (0.0301)	7.8673 (0.7243)	0.9651 (0.0230)	0.3793 (0.0224)	0.2587 (0.0379)
= 1.25, K_0 = 1000	1.6774 (0.1084)	0.7066 (0.0295)	0.9743 (0.0255)	8.8097 (0.8984)	0.9806 (0.0192)	0.4140 (0.0452)	0.2386 (0.0224)

References

BECKER, G. B. (1981): A Treatise on the Family. Harvard University Press, Cambridge.

BELLMANN, R. (1957): Dynamic Programming. Princeton University Press, Princeton.

BUHL, H. V. (1984): A discrete Model of Optimal Economic Growth. Journal of Macro-Economics, vol. 6, no. 4, pp. 447-456.

BURMEISTER, E. and DOBELL, A.R. (1970): Mathematical Theories of Economic Growth. MacMillan, London.

DOMAR, E. D. (1957): Essays in the Theory of Economic Growth. Oxford University Press, Oxford.

HARROD, R. F. (1960): A Second Essay in Dynamic Theory. Economic Journal, vol. 70.

NERLOVE, M., RAZIN, A., SADKA, E. (1987): Household and Economy, Welfare Economics of Endogenous Fertility.Academic Press, Boston.

RAMSEY, F. P. (1928): A Mathematical Theory of Saving. Economic Journal, vol. 39, 1928, pp. 543-549.

RITZEN, J. M. M., and van PRAAG, B. M. S. (1985): Golden rules and Non-Stationary Population. Working Paper. Econometric Institute, Rotterdam.

van PRAAG, B. M. S. and POETH, G. G. J. M. (1975): The introduction of an Old Age Pension in a Growing Economy. Journal of Public Economics 4, pp. 87-100.

List of Contributors

Rob J.M. Alessie	*Tilburg University*, Tilburg, Netherlands
Rudolf Andorka	*University of Economics*, Budapest, Hungary
Dilip Bhattacharyya	*University of Leicester*, Leicester, Great Britain
Jess Benhabib	*New York University*, New York, USA
Benjamin Bental	*Israel Institute of Technology*, Haifa, Israel
Uri Ben-Zion	*Israel Institute of Technology*, Haifa, Israel
Norbert Berthold	*University of Hamburg*, Hamburg, West Germany
Alessandro Cigno	*University of Hull*, Hull, Great Britain, and *University of Pisa*, Pisa, Italy
Edgar L. Feige	*University of Wisconsin*, Madison, USA
Mark Gradstein	*Israel Institute of Technology*, Haifa, Israel
H. Peter Gray	*Rutgers University*, New Brunswick, USA
Robert A. Horváth	*Institut International de Statistique*, Budapest, Hungary
Arie Kapteyn	*Tilburg University*, Tilburg, Netherlands
M. Luptácik	*Technische Universität Wien*, Wien, Austria
Kazuo Nishimura	*Kyoto Institute of Economic Research*, Kyoto, Japan
Michael Pflüger	*Cambridge University*, Cambridge, Great Britain
J.H. Pollard	*Macquarie University*, Sydney, Australia
Bernard M.S. van Praag	*Erasmus University Rotterdam*, Rotterdam Netherlands
Menno P. Pradhan	*Erasmus University Rotterdam*, Rotterdam Netherlands
I. Schmoranz	*Technische Universität Wien*, Wien, Austria
Gunter Steinmann	*University of Paderborn*, Paderborn, West-Germany
Shanti S. Tangri	*Rutgers University*, New Brunswick, USA

writing clear essays

ROBERT B. DONALD   **BETTY RICHMOND MORROW**

LILLIAN GRIFFITH WARGETZ   **KATHLEEN WERNER**

Community College of Beaver County

Illustrations by RAYMOND E. DUNLEVY

PRENTICE–HALL, INC., Englewood Cliffs, New Jersey   *07632*

Library of Congress Cataloging in Publication Data
Main entry under title:

Writing clear essays.

Includes index.
1. English language—Rhetoric. I. *Donald Robert B.*
PE1408.W772 1983   808´.042   82-16131
ISBN 0-13-970145-1

TEXT CREDITS

Page 8   Henry David Thoreau, *The Heart of Thoreau's Journals,* Odell Shepard, ed. © 1961 by Dover Publications, Inc. Reprinted by permission of Dover Publications, Inc.

Page 147   From *The Reporter,* 11 September 1956. Copyright 1956 by Malcolm Cowley. Reprinted by permission of the author.

Page 156   From *Ovid, Metamorphoses,* trans. Rolfe Humphries, copyright 1955 by Indiana University Press.

Page 167   Adapted from Robert M. Gorrell and Charlton Laird, *Modern English Handbook,* 5th ed., 1972, p. 93. Used by permission of the publisher, Prentice-Hall, Inc.

Pages 177–78   Mark Twain, "Puddnhead Wilson's Calendar," Harper & Row Publishers, Inc.

Page 207   From *The American Language,* 4th Edition, by H. L. Mencken. Copyright 1936 by Alfred A. Knopf, Inc., and renewed 1964 by August Mencken and Mercantile-Safe Deposit and Trust Co. Reprinted by permission of the publisher.

Pages 216–17   Barbara Tuchman, "The Decline of Quality," 2 October 1980. © 1980 by The New York Times Company. Reprinted by permission.

Pages 218–19   Excerpts from "Politics and the English Language" in *The Collected Essays, Journalism and Letters of George Orwell,* Volume 4, copyright © 1968 by Sonia Brownell Orwell. Reprinted by permission of Harcourt Brace Jovanovich, Inc.

Page 231   "It Ain't Necessarily So" by George Gershwin and Ira Gershwin © 1935 by Gershwin Publishing Corporation. Copyright renewed, assigned Chappelle & Co., Inc. International copyright secured. ALL RIGHTS RESERVED. Used by permission.

Page 251   Lawrence J. Hudson, *The Tribune-Democrat,* Johnstown, Pennsylvania. Reprinted by permission of the author.

Page 264   From "I Have a Dream" by Martin Luther King, Jr. Reprinted by permission of Joan Daves. Copyright ©1963 by Martin Luther King, Jr.

Page 267   Phyllis McGinley, "A Choice of Weapons" in *Times Three.* Copyright 1954 by Phyllis McGinley. Copyright renewed 1982 by Phyllis Hayden Blake. Originally published in *The New Yorker.* Reprinted by permission Viking-Penguin Inc.

Page 268   S. I. Hayakawa and William Dresser, *Dimensions of Meaning,* Indianapolis, Indiana: The Bobbs-Merrill Company, Inc., 1970.

Pages 277–79   Copyright © 1947 by Ray Bradbury, copyright renewed 1975. Reprinted by permission of the Harold Matson Co., Inc.

Pages 286–87   Copyright 1943, 1971 by Lionel Trilling. Reprinted from his volume *Of This Time, Of That Place and Other Stories* by permission of Harcourt Brace Jovanovich, Inc.

Pages 297–98   From *Story and Structure,* Second Edition, by Laurence Perrine, © 1959, 1966 by Harcourt Brace Jovanovich, Inc., and reprinted with their permission.

Page 300   "To Satch," by permission of the author, Samuel Allen.

Page 301   "The Death of a Toad" by Richard Wilbur. From *Ceremony and Other Poems,* copyright 1950, 1978 by Richard Wilbur. Reprinted by permission of Harcourt Brace Jovanovich, Inc.

Printed in the United States of America

10   9   8   7   6

ISBN 0-13-970145-1

Prentice-Hall International, Inc., *London*
Prentice-Hall of Australia Pty. Limited, *Sydney*
Editora Prentice-Hall do Brasil, Ltda., *Rio de Janeiro*
Prentice-Hall Canada Inc., *Toronto*
Prentice-Hall of India Private Limited, *New Delhi*
Prentice-Hall of Japan, Inc., *Tokyo*
Prentice-Hall of Southeast Asia Pte. Ltd., *Singapore*
Whitehall Books Limited, *Wellington, New Zealand*

contents

CHAPTER II
narrating 43

CHAPTER III
describing 72

CHAPTER IV
explaining with examples 98

CHAPTER IX
persuading **240**

CHAPTER X
writing about literature **270**

CHAPTER XI
the essay test **305**

preface

To most teachers of writing, the question "Why write?" is comparable to "Why breathe?" Students, however, usually do not see these questions as obvious parallels.

A supposedly true story, that came out of World War II, gives one answer to the question "why write." A group of rookie soldiers were waiting for their first assignments.

The officer of the day snapped out, "I need a cook."

A rookie put up his hand. "I'm a cook," he said.

"I need a machinist."

"I'm a machinist."

"I need an accountant."

"I'm an accountant."

So it went, until all the soldiers but one had been assigned. The officer looked skeptically at him. "I need someone who can write."

"I can write," said the last man.

When the day finally came for the men to be mustered out of the army, they all came back to the original group. The cook, the machinist, and the ac-

vii

countant had all been working hard at their jobs. But the man who knew how to write had been to the Pentagon, to London, to Paris, to Germany, to the Nuremburg Trials.

The point can be made to even the most reluctant writer that jobs worth having depend upon the ability to communicate clearly. Industrial engineers have long pointed out that all jobs, even the most technical, are more than 60 per cent communication. The National Association of Accountants, in a recent bulletin, states that "written communications, through need analysis, appear now as the most highly required skill among rank-and-file executives and managers in most companies." According to the same bulletin, business experts estimate that American companies spend approximately $70 billion annually in written communications. Such figures provide the practical answer to "why write." And writing is a learnable skill.

Writing Clear Essays is designed to meet the specific needs of students in freshman composition. The text will provide them with a clear structural framework for orderly progression from the writing of a single paragraph to the writing of essays. Based upon the premise that effective expository and persuasive writing is a skill that ordinary students can learn, the text is carefully designed to provide the step-by-step guidance that most freshmen urgently need but few composition texts provide.

Through years of experience in teaching composition, we have found that freshman composition texts frequently intimidate students by offering them examples drawn from the work of professional writers which are far beyond students' levels of skill. This type of formal approach might work well with self-motivated students who are confident of their writing abilities, but large numbers of today's students do not fit into this category. In fact, most students enroll in composition courses because they have to, not because they want to, and it is no secret that required courses often generate immediate resistance. Students can't understand why they have to learn how to write in the first place, and their negative feelings are often compounded by other apprehensions: they expect English to be boring, and they are afraid that they will never be able to master the art of writing anyway, so why try? When these students are presented with a dull, forbidding text, it only confirms their fears about writing. That is why we feel that a light, informal tone is important in motivating such students. An English composition text should be both interesting and easy to read. We have therefore provided essays written by our own students on topics that sparked the interest of their classmates. We have also included numerous illustrations, both humorous and explanatory, to keep the reader interested and to clarify important points. Additional features which enhance the readability of our text include: (1) a reading level that the majority of students can handle (approximately 10.5 grade level), (2) a clear three-part structure (the same organizational pattern that we followed in our book *Writing Clear Paragraphs*), and (3) an effective layout of the printed page.

Written in clear, direct, and informal style, the text emphasizes the development of ideas as clearly and economically as possible. Starting with the single paragraph as a thought unit having one controlling idea, the students will expand the basic structure of Beginning, Middle, and End and apply it to the writing of short essays. The Prologue and Chapter I provide the connecting link between the single paragraph and the essay of five- or six-hundred words. Each of the following chapters, II through IX, deals with one specific method of development: narrating, describing, explaining with examples, comparing and contrasting, dividing and classifying, defining, cause and effect, and persuading. Chapter X discusses writing about literature, and Chapter XI, the concluding chapter, deals with answering essay questions. Through practical writing assignments following the "Organization" section of each chapter, students will immediately put the principles and methods into practice.

Although *Writing Clear Essays* is an autonomous text, as is *Writing Clear Paragraphs,* it is designed to take up where *Writing Clear Paragraphs* leaves off. Both follow the same three-part organization. Each chapter deals with (1) organization, (2) techniques of clear writing, and (3) word power. Thus each chapter begins with a method of organization, gets the students writing, and then takes up various writing techniques and mechanical details as they progress. In addition to considering the persuasive principles as it involves the use of logic, emotion, and language, Chapters VIII and IX examine the relationship between evidence and conclusion and set forth the basic rules of logic. Chapter X, on Writing About Literature, shows how the principles and strategies covered in previous chapters can be applied to writing about character, action, point of view, setting, or ideas embodied in a literary work. Chapter XI, although based upon the principles of good organization presented in the first ten chapters, can be taught at almost any time during the course.

IMPORTANT FEATURES

1. Many clear, relevant examples (for example, ten types of introductions are presented in Chapter II)
2. Interesting and well-written student essays
3. Thorough analysis of essay structure
4. A clear three-part structure
5. Numerous exercises in each section to reinforce learning
6. A light, informal tone
7. An accessible reading level
8. Cartoons to illustrate important grammatical and rhetorical points
9. Essay test practice
19. Fifty suggested topics for each assignment

ACKNOWLEDGMENTS

We appreciate the widespread support we received in writing this book. First, we are grateful to Dr. Terry L. Dicianna, president of our college, who helped us with every request and came up with ideas of his own to encourage us. Thanks also for the support of Dr. William Bauer, our academic dean.

Our colleagues in Community College of Beaver County, too, deserve our thanks, especially Linda Ciana and Dr. John Shaver. We also thank our secretaries, Alice Watson and Mary Williams, and particularly Carol Kunzmann for her tireless and cheerful assistance.

From outside our own college, we received perceptive and painstaking criticism from our reviewers: Terence Burke, *Cuyahoga Community College;* Rosanna Grassi, *Syracuse University;* Joseph C. Harrison, *Jackson State Community College;* Stanley J. Kozikowski, *Bryant College;* James A. Pierce, *Del Mar College;* Cynthia Ricketson, *Central Piedmont Community College.*

We also appreciate the artwork of Dawn Russell, the generous support of Joan Wilson, our Prentice-Hall representative, and the encouragement of Joyce Perkins.

Finally, we thank most warmly our students for contributing their own paragraphs and essays to exemplify our principles: Ron Alberti, Tony Bondi, Mark Custer, Erin Duffy, Janet Gailey, Dorothy Gaydos, Greg Hendry, Nancy Kammerdiener, Tim Kasunic, Jackie Kunzmann, Sharon Schavroni, Vicki Schmidt, Bonnie Shamrock, Pat Tonkovich, and Cathy Windom.

going from paragraph to essay

In an old play, a character called Jourdain is surprised and pleased to find that he has been speaking prose all his life. He had supposed that it was very difficult to do. Like Jourdain, you may be pleased and surprised to find that you know more than you thought you did about writing an essay. An essay is simply a piece of writing built from the paragraph.

The paragraph has a three-part form. First, it has a *topic sentence,* which includes a subject and an attitude toward that subject. The attitude is what you think or feel about the subject. For example, in the sentence, "Despite the appeal of mistletoe and Santa Claus, Thanksgiving has some definite advantages over the more popularly acclaimed Christmas." *Thanksgiving* is the subject and *some definite advantages* is the attitude.

The second part of the paragraph is the *development* (also called the *body*). In the development, you pull together enough supporting detail to convince your reader that you are right to have that attitude toward that subject. For example, to support your idea about Thanksgiving, you might say such things as:

1. Thanksgiving is the first of several big holidays all happily huddled together at the end of the year, so you not only have Thanksgiving itself to enjoy but others to look forward to.

2. Since there are other holidays soon to come, you are not too upset if some little thing goes wrong. You can be relaxed about Thanksgiving.

3. This relaxation extends to getting ready for Thanksgiving. You don't feel as if you have to have the whole house scrubbed and polished. So what if you don't get the upstairs windows washed. There's plenty of time to do them before Christmas.

4. The Thanksgiving cooking is as much work as the Christmas cooking, but you don't have to worry about trimming the tree, wrapping the presents, decorating the whole house. You can just plunk Aunt Miranda's beautiful china turkey in the middle of the table and enjoy making those pumpkin pies and your own special stuffing.

5. On Thanksgiving you have all the joy of gathering with your family, but you don't have to worry about whether to give Uncle John a good sweater or just a case of beer.

6. On Thanksgiving you have a feast day and you love seeing all your family, but you're not broke for the next two months.

These six points make an adequate development. They show why you like Thanksgiving better than Christmas. (They don't have to persuade your reader to like it better. They just have to show why you do.)

The third part of the paragraph form is the *concluding sentence.* This sums up your development and states again your topic idea. It must not, of course, bring in new ideas because it is an ending, not a beginning.

A possible concluding sentence for the paragraph about Thanksgiving might be:

Thanksgiving is an even better holiday than Christmas—feast and family without pressures and with more fun to come.

What Is an Essay?

An essay is a written interpretation of experience. What an essay communicates is not facts or information but an interpretation of such facts or information. There are many ways it can interpret, but the important thing is that it does interpret, not simply report.

As you study this book, you will learn that a good essay requires a good *thesis statement,* a statement of the controlling idea of the essay as a whole. Having written your thesis statement, you then explain it, analyze it, define it, dramatize it in a story, argue for or against it, or try to persuade someone else to see it as you do in the body of your essay.

Since it is *your* interpretation, an essay is highly personal. As the writer, you are extremely important. The information on which you base your interpreta-

3

*going from
paragraph to
essay*

tion may be important or trivial, but the personal expression of your reaction to it is always important.

This emphasis on the personal point of view and the personality of the writer goes back to the so-called father of the essay, the French philosopher Montaigne, who in 1580 published a volume called *Essais*. This means "attempts," efforts to communicate his thoughts and ideas in the light of his own personality. Montaigne said, "It is myself that I portray," and writers since his time have attempted to convey their responses to the world and ideas surrounding them through essays that also portray themselves.

**ESSAYS AND
YOU**

If your experience is like that of many other Freshman Composition students, sometime during the first week of class your instructor will ask you to write a short essay, probably on a subject of your own choosing, perhaps a personal experience. He may refer to it as a "writing sample." This may leave you confused. What does he want? What does he expect you to say? You pick up a pencil or roll a sheet of paper into your typewriter, but the paper remains stubbornly blank.

This confusion comes about because writing for a class is an artificial situation. In a class you write because you must to pass the course; your instructor reads because it's a large part of his job. But the natural arrangement between writer and reader is different: the writer writes because she has something she wants to say; the reader reads because he wants to be entertained or he wants to learn something. If you adopt this natural association between writer and reader, some of your problems will vanish. Change your first question from "What does the instructor want?" to "What do I want to say?" Change your second question from "What does he expect me to say?" to "How can I best say it?"

Every time you think about your writing assignments, you will have to consider two key terms—*narrow* and *choose*. To begin with, among the various forms of writing, your concern will be narrowed to expository writing. *Expository writing* is nonfiction prose which aims at communicating facts, ideas, or opinions. *Exposition,* which means "explanation," does most of the everyday work of communication. It is the writing in textbooks, in business and industry, in politics, in religion, in journalism. Exposition is also the writing of much self-expression. In personal letters, in diaries, in autobiographies, writers say who they are, what they think, what they feel.

Within the wide reaches of expository writing, you will narrow your choice again by the type of expository writing you are doing. Eight chapters in this book are discussions narrowed to one type. Depending on what you want to say, you choose definition, narration, comparison/contrast, persuasion, or whatever type best suits your purpose.

It is true, of course, that usually writers do not stick to just one type of writing. Their essays generally combine several types, each one of which is chosen to make its point effectively and to supplement the other types. After the individual modes, or types, have been discussed and practiced, you will go on in Chapters VII through XI to practice the essay that uses more than one mode.

Finding a Subject

As a writer, your first job is to find a subject. Even if one has been assigned, you still have to decide what you want to say about that subject. Despite a panicky sense of "I don't have a subject," you do. You have all your personal experience to draw on—school, jobs, friendships, hobbies, games, family life, disappointments and pain, successes and joys. You also have all you have learned: Are you interested in solar energy, science fiction, rock music, the Civil War, the novels of Kurt Vonnegut? You can search yourself to find something you have experienced or learned, something that interests you. If it interests you, you can probably make it interesting to others.

You may decide that although it may sound simple, searching yourself is not easy. There are some specialized techniques to help you come up with ideas.

BRAIN-STORMING

Brainstorming is one effective technique for generating ideas. It is usually thought of as a group process, but you don't always need a group of people to brainstorm for ideas. You can plop down in your favorite spot with a pepperoni pizza and come up with dozens of ideas before you reach for your second piece. Either in a group or alone, you can produce a surprising number of ideas in a short period of time.

Brainstorming Within a Group

Brainstorming within a group works on the principle that two heads are often better than one. The size of the group is not important. You can brainstorm with two friends or with your entire English class. The process itself is rather simple: one person throws out an idea and others respond with ideas generated by the first one. Those ideas then generate different responses, and so on. In other words, you bounce ideas off each other until you get as many as you need. The quality of your ideas is not important at this point. Say anything that comes into your head no matter how crazy it sounds. The purpose of brainstorming is to stimulate creative thinking, and you can't be creative if you have to worry about your ideas being criticized. Everyone in the group should follow the same rule: as soon as you think of something, say it.

Suppose that you have been assigned to write a paper in which you compare or contrast two things. After talking to some of your classmates at lunch, you realize that you all have the same problem with the assignment. You all understand *how* to compare and contrast, but none of you can think of a good topic. Three of you therefore decide to have a ten-minute brainstorming session before your next class. You decide to brainstorm the term *junk food*. The jotted-down results might look like this:

TEN-MINUTE BRAINSTORMING SESSION
—junk food
—chemical additives
—can't eat anything anymore without getting cancer
—my brother's a vegetarian
—you are what you eat

4

—a good diet is so important
—my dad's crash diet—avoided restaurants for months
—the funny waiter at Houlihan's
—what a lousy job—on your feet all day
—putting up with crabby customers
—sounds like the job I had last summer
—people can be so insensitive
—too busy trying to make a buck
—parents' generation took more pride in their work
—the good old days
—when you could pull into a gas station and say, "Fill it up," without emptying
    your wallet
—those damn oil companies
—buy a horse
—the urban cowboy
—some good movies showing at Cinema III
—I saw a good documentary in history class on American Indians
—the unfair way that Indians are portrayed in TV westerns
—their respect for the land
—what we can learn from other cultures
—makes me think of the exchange student from Germany that I dated
—some of the characters I dated in high school

Now, with over twenty-five ideas down on paper, you at least have a beginning. What you have to do now is evaluate these ideas. When you look over your list, you will notice that many ideas must be rejected because, for one reason or another, they do not fit the assignment. If, for example, the assignment calls for a personal experience paper, you could not use a topic that required research. You must always consider the requirements for the specific assignment. If, as suggested earlier, the assignment is a comparison-contrast paper, you would examine your list to see if any of your ideas readily suggest a comparison or contrast. For example, these ideas

too busy trying to make a buck
parents' generation took more pride in their work

might lead you to these topics:

the difference in attitudes toward work—past and present

>   *OR*
the difference in the quality of goods produced in this country—past and
present

From these topics, you could then arrive at specific thesis statements:

One of the biggest differences between my parent's generation and mine is our differing attitudes toward work.

OR
The high-quality goods that were once produced in this country contrast sharply with the shoddy workmanship seen so frequently today.

Another idea from your list

some of the characters I dated in high school

might lead you to this topic:

the surprising similarities between two of my high school heartthrobs

From this topic, you could then form a thesis statement:

Although everyone assumed that my two high school heartthrobs were total opposites, I soon discovered that Kazz, the class clown, and Edgar, the walking dictionary, were actually quite similar.

Other ideas that readily suggest a contrast are

I saw a good documentary in history class on American Indians
the unfair way that Indians are portrayed in TV westerns

From these ideas, you might arrive at this topic:

the difference between Indians in real life and Indians on TV westerns

Upon closer examination of your list, you might find more possibilities for a comparison or contrast. For example:

two types of waitresses
two types of diets
two types of restaurants
two jobs . . . and so on

Brainstorming by Yourself
Individual brainstorming consists essentially of thinking aloud. Instead of bouncing ideas off others, you generate your own ideas by letting your mind wander from one thought to another. One idea leads to another, the second idea leads to a third, and so on. Again, it is important that you hold nothing back. As soon as you think of an idea, write it down. As your list grows, it will stimulate other ideas. Suppose that again, you begin your brainstorming session with the term *junk food:*

junk food   [This reminds you of the time you were rushed to the hospital with food poisoning.]
food poisoning

hospitals   [This conjures up grim memories of the emergency room.]
emergency room
the terror-stricken little boy
his hysterical father
the impatient nurse yelling at the little boy
the kind nurse who took care of me
all of the noise and confusion
the doctor who looked just like my Uncle Phil
too bad he didn't act more like my Uncle Phil
no bedside manner
nothing at all like my family doctor
funny to think that he used to date my mother   [This makes you think about your mother.]
poor Mom—how upset she was when I got sick   [This makes you think about your dad.]
how different she is from Dad
his theory that sympathy makes you weak and spineless
how did they ever get together?   [This makes you think about marriage.]
but they have a good marriage
so rare these days

From this list, you can immediately spot several possible topics for a comparison or contrast:

two types of nurses
two types of doctors
two philosophies of raising children
different attitudes toward marriage

Studying the list more closely might yield more topics, but even if you get just one good idea from a few minutes of brainstorming, then it was well worth the effort.

Another way that you can brainstorm by yourself is to concentrate on one subject at a time. Suppose, for example, that you are asked to write an essay on crime. You might start by jotting down every crime-related idea that occurs to you. In just a few minutes you might have a list like this:

stick-up	burglary	white-collar crime	Capone
handguns	forgery	payoff	gangsters
machine guns	arson	bagman	prohibition
drug pushers	rape	loan shark	execution
drug busts	mugging	enforcer	kidnapping
drug smugglers	FBI	the Mob	street crime
rip-offs	shoplifting	swindle	con games

You already have subjects for more than a dozen essays. Now check each item on your list and try to decide which one you are best prepared to write on. Suppose that "arson" triggers your memory of a television program about arson for profit. If you remember some of the main points brought out in the program, you will at least have a start. Of course, you will have to dig up additional information; but in selecting "Arson for Profit," you have narrowed your subject and simplified your search for the information necessary to develop your essay.

KEEPING A JOURNAL

If you make a habit of keeping a journal, it can be of immense help to you in all your future writing. You can begin quite simply by jotting down, each day, the things you experience: little observations about people and events, snatches of conversation, things that people say to you and about you, and, most of all, your thoughts upon any and every subject. One thing that every writer needs is raw material, and everything in life ought to provide grist for your private mill.

In his journal, which eventually grew to some two million words, Thoreau sought to capture the essence of the moment—"to improve the nick of time." The entries in his journal later provided the basis for all his published work, including *Walden*, the book that made him famous.

Perhaps this is the main value of a habit of writing, of keeping a journal —that so we remember our best hours and stimulate ourselves. My thoughts are my company. They have a certain individuality and separate existence, aye, personality. Having by chance recorded a few disconnected thoughts and then brought them into juxtaposition, they suggest a whole new field in which it was possible to labor and to think. Thought begat thought. *Henry David Thoreau*

Carry a notebook with you and jot down in brief notes the fleeting thoughts, immediate impressions, and things that catch your interest throughout the day. Then set aside a specific time each day to record whatever you have in your mental hopper. Don't strain for fancy phrases so as to make the whole thing a chore, but write what you want—what has meaning for you. Just don't waste space on such trivia as "Went to the shopping plaza to look at shoes but couldn't find my size." What did you think as you went about your fruitless errand? Didn't you see at least one unusual person? Didn't at least one peculiar thought strike you? Don't wait for the earth-shattering event; some minor incident or casual bit of conversation may take on significance at a later date, provided that you write it down. If you should get an instructor who insists that you keep a journal, so much the better, but don't wait until it is demanded of you. Do it for yourself.

Sometimes little scenes stand out from the daily routine so that they become detached and seem to take on a life of their own. The following notes are drawn from a humdrum Saturday round of errands:

supermarket jam-up over can of pineapple

the wildman in the tire shop

Working from your journal entries, you might develop something like this:

The checkout blonde at the supermarket sat on the edge of the counter and yelled, "How much is the can of generic crushed pineapple?" The line stopped while first the stock boy and then the assistant to the assistant and then the assistant all checked and inquired, "How much is the generic crushed pineapple?" Two ancient ladies with square chins—two sisters they appeared to be—waited, tight-lipped, until the word came down from on high: "Fifty-nine cents."

The guy who changed the tire had a gleaming beard, black and fierce as that of any Siberian wolf hunter. Every second word he said was profanity, and he moved with a kind of expert furiousness. His blue workshirt hung like a smock from shoulders as broad as a door . . . powerful wrists whipped the snow tire and wheel onto the balance stand as if it were a breakfast cruller. His whole body seemed to signal violence barely held in check. The manager, a slight young man with a neat little moustache, once said, without any authority, "Watch your language." The beard just redoubled his profanity in gleeful defiance. When the job was done—while the manager wrote up the slip—the bearded one ceaselessly paced the concrete floor . . . the stream of profanity slowed to a mocking trickle. Maybe he should have been—would rather be—in some Siberia hunting wolves and bears.

Some of the best subjects for essays are those that emerge from everyday existence. Your journal can prove to be an invaluable source for writing on almost any subject. If you are taking a course on marriage and the family, for instance, and you are asked to write about sibling rivalry or financial planning, ideas drawn from your journal might provide convincing examples to illustrate some of your main points.

In addition, whether you intend to be a city detective or a marine biologist, the habit of keeping a journal can serve you well. You will often find that some of your best ideas come to you at odd moments when you are engaged in activities unrelated to your job. You may suddenly find the answer to a perplexing problem or get a new idea for improving the flow of work. If you take the time to write down your ideas, you will have something specific to discuss the next time you talk with your supervisor. Even facts and ideas on what appear to be totally unrelated subjects can often help you in solving the problems you will face in your occupation. You do need to write those ideas down, however, or they may escape before you get a chance to put them to use.

FREE WRITING Another method that some people find very helpful in getting ideas is *free writing*. You simply write—anything—for ten minutes. You never stop to think of the right word or to correct spelling or grammar. Keep the pencil moving constantly across the page; your aim is to get words, any words, on paper. As in brainstorming, the most important rule is to avoid criticism and discussion. The following is an example of free writing:

that poor old lady that I saw on TV last week - so lonely in her dilapidated one-room apartment - so sad - she had no family and all of her friends were dead - but how she loved her little television set - it was everything to her - how she looked forward to her game shows and soap operas every day - that TV was her only friend - her only company all day long except for the Meals on Wheels driver - the boob tube - everybody always complaining about what's on television today - sex - violence - dumb situation comedies - that phony canned laughter - and how I hate those stupid, insulting commercials - they really make my blood boil – but there are good programs too – like "60 Minutes" – I really look forward to Sunday nights because I can sit down and relax and watch "60 Minutes" – and all the good programs for kids on the educational station – "Sesame Street" and "Mr. Rogers" – how many times I've heard parents say that those programs are such great baby-sitters – they can't wait for them to come on so that they can get an hour of peace while their kids sit glued to the TV – sometimes you even find the parents listening to Kermit the Frog's news report or laughing at Big Bird – you don't hear them complaining about the "boob tube" then

Depending on what your assignment is, this sample of free writing could provide you with several topics. For instance, suppose you had to write an essay supported with examples. You could write about any of the following topics:

ridiculous commercials
insulting commercials
how television is used as a baby-sitter
the adult humor of "Sesame Street"

If you had to write an essay in which you define an abstract term, you could also find several topics:

the meaning of loneliness
the definition of a friend

If you had to write an analysis, you could find several topics that would lend themselves to division and classification. For instance, you could analyze:

the various uses of television
different types of humor

If you had to write a persuasive essay, you might consider one of these topics:

using television as a baby-sitter
restrictions on the amount of violence shown on TV
tighter control of the content of TV commercials

Most free writings contain a number of unrelated ideas, but sometimes they focus primarily on one idea. Both types can produce good topics for writing. Look at the following student free-writing samples to see if they contain any ideas that you could use for an essay:

FREE WRITING THAT FOCUSES ON ONE IDEA
I wish I didn't come to my classes today – when I got out of bed I could hardly bring myself to comb my hair – all I can think about is what John thinks about me after last night – I was so upset – I even went to bed at 9:00 – I took a long bath – it must have lasted an hour – I know I'm not ready for the quiz I'm going to have in Fundamentals tonight but I will probably still go to class because I

feel funny not going when I'm not even sick – that's why I came to my morning classes – I don't see why I seem to have so many problems at once – I wish I could just be left alone for about two weeks and start all over again – then maybe I would do things differently and I wouldn't have so many problems and feel so down all of the time – I don't know what I'll be doing this weekend – it's the first time in a long time that I've had to think about it – what if I have to stay home – I suppose it won't be so bad – I really never did anything that great on the weekends before so why should I worry about what I'm going to miss –

Nancy Kammerdiener

FREE WRITING THAT GOES FROM ONE IDEA TO ANOTHER

This could be tough, primarily because I'm not playing chess, cycling, or walking – at those times I get struck by lightning – I like trucks, farm tractors, and trees – my kids are in the daycare – somehow Scott will be maturing and helping Josh to grow – great Scott – Josh was named after the biblical character who carried on after Moses – know ye that the Lord cares for you – I restrung my classic guitar yesterday – think I will purchase a book on guitar construction – not the one I ordered on classic but rather the one on folk – which means I will need a router to reinforce the neck to withstand steel string tension – Dan wants an old-fashioned mandolin – I wonder if I'm able to build a beetle-back for him – how does a mandolin volume compare with that of a violin – violin was perfected about 300 years ago – technology today can't match that – guitars are nearing perfection now – Colonial Williamsburg has much to teach about ancient technique –

Bob Hilpert

INTERVIEWING YOURSELF

One of the worst mistakes you can make is to assume that you have nothing interesting to write about. Comments such as "Nothing ever happens to me" or "I can't think of anything to write about" can be heard frequently in English classes (especially after the instructor assigns a narrative essay), but nothing could be further from the truth. Never sell yourself short. Your life is unique, and if you think about it for a while, you will realize that you have experienced life in a way unlike any other person in the world because no one else is **exactly** like you. No one else possesses an exact combination of your fears, your talents, your dreams, your hobbies, your opportunities, your problems, your family, your friends, your sweethearts, your jobs, your bosses, your habits, your secrets, or your mistakes. One way to learn more about yourself and get a good topic at the same time is to ask yourself a series of questions. For example:

What makes me laugh?
What makes me cry?
What makes me angry?
What makes me nervous?
What was the most embarrassing experience I've ever had?
What was the most terrifying? The most valuable? The most disappointing?
Have I had any experiences that changed me?
   —made me a vegetarian
   —made me an advocate of gun control
   —made me realize how lucky I am

What do I remember most about my childhood?
Who are the most important people in my life?
From whom have I learned the most? A teacher? My parents? A friend?
Could I be happy living alone or do I need people?
Why do I like (or hate) my job?
What are my pet peeves?
What do I like most about my husband? My wife? My boyfriend? My girlfriend?
What sort of places make me feel uncomfortable?
What's the best thing about having children? What's the worst?
What is more important to me—my time or my money?

**USING THE
LIBRARY**

Sometimes just seeing an interesting book title or newspaper headline is enough to stimulate your thought processes. Libraries are full of interesting ideas which can generate other ideas, and those ideas can lead to still more ideas. After a few minutes of browsing, you might come up with several ideas from book titles such as the following:

BOOKS
1. *What Every Child Would Like His Parents to Know About Divorce*
2. *Eating May Be Hazardous to Your Health*
3. *The Pet Profiteers*
4. *Birth Without Violence*
5. *How to Talk Back to Your Television Set*
6. *Battered Wives*
7. *Indian Medicine*
8. *Single Parents Are People Too*
9. *The Permissible Lie*
10. *The Dictionary of Diseased English*
11. *Death and the Mines*
12. *Changing Careers After Thirty-five*
13. *Concentration Camps: USA*
14. *The Mafia Is Not an Equal Opportunity Employer*
15. *The World's Greatest Rip-offs*

Newspaper headlines and titles of magazine articles can also provide food for thought. For example:

MAGAZINE ARTICLES
1. "How to Stop Fighting Over Housework"
2. "Tested Tips for Taking Tests"
3. "Why Do Critics Love Trashy Films?"
4. "How Teachers Can Help Victims of Child Abuse"
5. "Secretaries are Professional Too"
6. "Injuries at Work Are Fewer Among Older Employees"
7. "The Preservation of Old Buildings"
8. "Origins of the VW Beetle"

NEWSPAPER HEADLINES

1. "Athletes Deserve Human Frailty Like the Rest of Us"
2. " 'Tough Cop' Approach Abandoned"
3. "Easing Auto Rules Could Save Billions"
4. "Fear of Success Makes Losers"
5. "Keeping Jeans Honest"
6. "College Board Is Persuaded to Show and Tell"
7. "Illegal Rent Rates Held Widespread"
8. "Divorce Law and Women"

Narrowing to a Specific Subject and Attitude

Suppose the subject you have found and decided to write about is your family. Your family is, after all, what you know best and feel most strongly about. What's more, all of your readers have family feelings, too, so they are willing to be interested. Therefore, family is a good subject, what is known as a "universal" subject because it has universal appeal. Since you are writing only a short essay, however, you quickly realize that your family is too broad a subject. You must decide on a narrower, a more specific subject.

For example, at the family reunion picnic last summer, twenty-seven relatives showed up. Obviously, you must narrow "family" to a smaller unit—perhaps just one person. Which person? This is a rather hard decision, since you like almost all of them—even some that you didn't like when you were a kid.

Cousin Chris is a good example. When you were both kids, she was a real pain. Your mother used to say she was the type who "got into things." You didn't mind so much that **she** got into things. The real problem was that she got **you** into things, all of them trouble. She always wanted to have adventures; she always wanted to know **why** anything happened. She once persuaded you to "explore" an empty house, where **your** foot went through a rotten board so you had a sprained ankle. She persuaded you to climb into an empty freight car to see how hobos traveled. When the train pulled out, you were both afraid to jump and you ended up thirty-one miles from home. **Your** father had to come for you, and he had tickets for that day's ball game. She was a pain then, but now she's fun.

She's a magazine reporter who has traveled all over Europe. She's met a lot of famous people and quite a few oddballs. She's really enthusiastic about what she's doing, and she can persuade other people that things are as exciting as she sees them.

When you come to think of it, Cousin Chris as a kid had most of these characteristics. She just controls them better now. Maybe, you think, that's what's meant by growing up—channeling your interests and energy to get something good, not just trouble. So, you have found yourself a specific topic, the growing up of Cousin Chris.

Thinking of Cousin Chris reminds you, through the process your psych instructors call "free association," of Cousin Lucy. She was another pain when you were kids. First of all, her looks annoyed you. Her hair, cut very short, curled all over her head. You would have loved a haircut like that, but your ears stuck out.

What was worse, she always managed to stay clean. Even her knees were clean, but yours were always grimy and scabby. Somehow, her hems never came out, looping down in untidy scallops like yours. Worst of all, she always wanted to play with dolls when you wanted to play some good game like kick-the-can. Even in the tree house your grandfather had made, she wanted to have tea parties instead of playing pirates. She certainly was a pain.

But last summer at the reunion you realized that she was a pretty, pleasant, hard-working woman. Although she had a large, rollicking, loving family, she also was a teacher in elementary school. Her childhood characteristics, too, determined the kind of woman she turned out to be, as Chris's had.

As you think about this, you become aware of a third possibility for a subject. You know now that neither of them was a pain; they were just individuals. Perhaps your changed attitude toward your cousins was not so much their growing up as your growing up. As you recognize that, you know you have thought your way to a good subject: growing up means liking people for their own merits, not just for their effect on you.

You could have chosen either Cousin Chris or Cousin Lucy as your narrowed subject; however, by thinking further about these people and your reactions to them, you have come up with a far better subject.

Developing a Thesis Statement

Once you have decided on a subject, the next step is to decide what you want to say about that subject; you have to develop an attitude. This process takes some time and some hard, logical thinking, but it is well worth the effort. It is impossible to write a coherent, focused essay on a broad, vague topic. A narrowed topic does not make your task simple, but it does make it possible.

Suppose you have decided to write about sports:

TOPIC: Sports

You now must decide what you want to say about these sports—your attitude:

TOPIC: Sports
ATTITUDE: taught me a lot

Now you begin the process of narrowing. After deciding on your attitude, you realize your subject is not just sports but:

Sports that I have participated in taught me a lot.

This is narrower, but if you participated in a lot of sports, you still have a broad topic; perhaps it should be narrowed further:

Two sports that I participated in . . . .

And perhaps you want to narrow it by time:

Two sports that I participated in during high school . . . .

And perhaps you can narrow it further by being more specific:

Playing football and tennis in high school . . . .

Once you have a narrowed subject, you should go through the same process with your attitude:

taught me a lot
Playing football and tennis in high school taught me a lot.

This attitude is still broad. Do you want to discuss "a lot" of things that you learned? You would have a better essay if you concentrated on one or two important things these sports taught you rather than merely listing "a lot" of items:

taught me several important things

This is acceptable as an attitude, but perhaps you want to narrow it further, to be more specific:

taught me several important things about myself as a person and as a competitor

Now you put your narrowed subject and narrowed attitude together in a thesis sentence:

THESIS: Playing football and tennis in high school taught me several things about myself as a competitor and as a person.

EXERCISE A
Narrow the following topics to one suitable for a 500-word essay. Add an attitude and write a clearly worded thesis sentence for each.

1. Topic: Pets

   Narrowed subject: _____

   Narrowed attitude: _____

   Thesis sentence: _____

2. Topic: Automobiles

   Narrowed subject: _____

   Narrowed attitude: _____

   Thesis sentence: _____

3. Topic: Classmates

Narrowed subject: _____

Narrowed attitude: _____

Thesis sentence: _____

4. Topic: Disciplinarians

Narrowed subject: _____

Narrowed attitude: _____

Thesis sentence: _____

5. Topic: Cartoon Characters

Narrowed subject: _____

Narrowed attitude: _____

Thesis sentence: _____

Outlining

One way to avoid ending up with a rambling, incoherent essay is to make an outline before you begin to write your first draft. Through the process of making an outline, you can eliminate serious problems that might otherwise appear in the first draft of your essay. For example, you might discover that some of your material is irrelevant or that your essay is not logically organized or that you don't have enough details to prove your point. In other words, a good outline can help to en-sure that your essay will be unified, coherent, and adequately developed.

Having decided that you want to write an essay about your mother, you try brainstorming. You begin by jotting down all the details that stand out in your memory. You might end up with a list like this:

doing housework all day long and then working again at night
living with an alcoholic
having a baby at age 44
trying to keep peace in the family
the steelworkers' strike of 1959—losing the house
cooking extra meals just for my father
moving to West Virginia and raising seven kids alone
making the decision to leave my father
how I thought about my mother when I had my first child
    comparing her to other women in the labor room
    thinking about her after I got home from the hospital
lying to my father in order to protect us
working in an apple orchard
living in a house without running water
learning to drive when she was 59
starting life all over again in her late forties
finally getting a better job in Winchester, Virginia

dealing with the problems of older children
   her sons going to Vietnam
   two of her kids getting divorced

Now that you have your thoughts down on paper, you can begin to narrow your topics; you see that the details reflect primarily your mother's courageous spirit, her determination to face any problem that confronted her. This idea is your thesis. Now you must decide how to arrange the details about your mother's strength in some sort of rough chronological order. Your list might look like this:

living with an alcoholic
cooking extra meals just for him
trying to keep peace in the family
lying to him in order to protect us
doing housework all day long and then working again at night
the way she faced pregnancy at age 44
how I thought about her when I had my first child
   comparing the other women in the labor room to her
   thinking about her when I got home from the hospital
the steelworkers' strike in 1959—losing the house
finally making the decision to leave my father
moving to West Virginia and raising seven kids alone
starting life all over again in her late forties
working in an apple orchard
living in a house without running water
finally getting a better job in Winchester, Virginia
dealing with the problems of older children
   her sons going to Vietnam
   two of her kids getting divorced
learning to drive when she was 59

After you examine this list, you see that most of your details are examples of your mother's courage in facing two situations: living with an alcoholic, and making a new life for herself. You could then arrange all of your details under these two headings:

living with an alcoholic
   cooking extra meals just for him
   trying to keep peace in the family
   lying to him in order to protect us
   doing housework all day long and then taking over my father's chores in the
      evening
   the way she faced pregnancy at age 44
   how I thought about her when I had my first child
   comparing the other women in the labor room to her
   thinking about her after I got home from the hospital
starting life all over again in her late forties
   finally making the decision to leave my father
   moving to West Virginia and raising seven kids alone

the steelworkers' strike in 1959—losing the house
working in an apple orchard in West Virginia
living in a house without running water
finally getting a better job in Winchester, Virginia
dealing with the problems of older children
her sons going to Vietnam
two of her children getting divorced
learning to drive when she was 59 years old

These two ideas should then become the major headings in the body of your outline, and the sum of the two ideas, the two halves of your essay's total idea, will be its thesis, the key ingredient in your essay's introduction.

THESIS STATEMENT: One phase of my mother's personality is consistent: her determination to do whatever needs to be done.

OUTLINE

Introduction   One phase of my mother's personality is consistent: her determination to do whatever needs to be done.

Body   A.   Coping with my father's alcoholism
B.   Facing life alone

Conclusion   Concluding paragraph

You now have a basic outline. Next you decide how you are going to develop each of the paragraphs in the body of your essay. You examine the details you have listed to see how they can be divided further and put under more specific headings. Concentrating first on *A*, "Coping with my father's alcoholism," you find that your mother's actions were basically to protect the children and to set an example of perserverance.

I.   Coping with my father's alcoholism
   A.   Protecting her children
   B.   Setting an example of perserverance

Now you ask yourself, "How did she protect her children?" You look back at your list and see that you have already pointed out several ways in which your mother protected her children. These points would then become supporting details for subtopic A.

I.   Coping with my father's alcoholism
   A.   Protecting her children
      1.   Shielding them from emotional pain
      2.   Shielding them from physical pain

Continuing that way, you might end with a final outline that looks like this:

Introduction   One phase of my mother's personality is consistent: her determination to do whatever needs to be done.

Body   I.   Coping with my father's alcoholism
                  A.   Protecting her children
                       1.   Shielding them from emotional pain
                       2.   Shielding them from physical pain
                  B.   Setting an example of strength and perserverance
                       1.   Overworking herself
                       2.   Enduring pregnancy at the age of 44
            II. Facing life alone
                  A.   Adjusting to financial and emotional traumas
                       1.   Losing her home
                       2.   Leaving her husband
                  B.   Moving to West Virginia
                       1.   Working in an apple orchard
                       2.   Living in a house without running water
                  C.   Moving again, to Winchester, Virginia
                       1.   Improving the family's living conditions
                       2.   Dealing with the problems of her older children
                       3.   Learning and changing at the age of 59

Conclusion   Final paragraph

After reading the outline above, you can see some basic patterns emerging:

1.   An outline has a specific structure. Major ideas are indicated by Roman numerals, subtopics of major ideas are indicated with capital letters, and so forth. In general, as you move from left to right in an outline, your ideas become more and more specific. The basic pattern looks like this:

> I
>
>   A
>   B
>   1
>   2
>   a
>   b

2.   All the major headings—those indicated by Roman numerals—must be expressed in parallel form, and all headings of **equal** rank under the same major heading must be in parallel form. Notice that each detail in the outline above begins with an -*ing* verb (*coping, shielding,* etc.). An outline such as the one above, which uses phrase or incomplete sentence headings, is called a *topic outline*. If each idea in the outline were stated in complete thoughts, it would be called a *sentence outline*. For example:

I.   She coped with my father's alcoholism
    A.   She protected her children
    B.   She set an example of strength and perserverance

Note that even if you are not using a sentence outline, each outline item is capitalized.

19

3. Each heading that has subheadings should have at least two subheadings. In other words, you can't have an A without a B or a 1 without a 2, and so on. The logic behind this concept is clear: you can't divide anything into fewer than two parts.

4. Usually, your final outline will not include everything that you thought of when you were writing your first list of details. For example, you would eliminate the details about the birth of your first child because they have nothing to do with your thesis—your mother's strength of character.

Once you have a good outline, you can begin to write your paper. Your final draft might look like this:

A Tribute to Mom

Today the words "I can't" seem to be a part of everyone's vocabulary. But when my seven brothers and sisters and I were growing up, these were words that we never heard. We were taught, by our mother, that we could do whatever we needed or wanted to do. Anything was possible if the need or desire was strong enough. Mom was and is a perfect example of the truth in these words. There are so many facets in her personality that she reminds me of a chameleon. In the space of a moment, she can change from a gentle, tender mother to a tough, demanding drill sergeant to a lighthearted, laughing gypsy; but **one phase of her personality is consistent—her determination to do whatever needs to be done.**

**Thesis
Statement**

The first example of her courage and determination that I saw as a child was her reaction to my father's alcoholism. Somehow, she shielded us from most of the hurt and ugliness that surrounds an alcoholic. She was our strength; she taught us perserverance, not anger. When Dad came home drunk and obnoxious, she did whatever was necessary to soothe him. Many times, hours after we had eaten our dinner, she would go back into the kitchen to cook another meal for him because he had stayed out and missed his supper. Although she hated lying, sometimes she lied to him to protect us from his anger. Still, when he wasn't drunk, she worked by his side to provide for us. After a full day of washing, ironing, and constant cooking, she would go out and help him plow the garden, and after it was planted, she took complete care of it, protesting offers of help from the older children. At another time, I can remember seeing her on the roof of our house, helping my father put new shingles on it, even though she was always afraid of high places. She stood beside him, drunk or sober, for many years. Her life had to be a living hell, yet she never became the bitter, angry woman she had a right to become. At age forty-four, when other women worry about where to have their hair done, my mother had her last child. I was with her when this child was born, and even during the pain of childbirth, she was a perfect example of strength and courage.

**I. Coping with
my father's
alcoholism**

It was in 1959 that the combination of my father's drinking and a four-month strike by the steelworkers caused them to lose the house that she loved and had worked so hard to care for. Still her courage did not falter. I was married by this time, and so I escaped much of the sadness surrounding this event, but my brothers and sisters were not as fortunate. As time passed, my father's drinking became worse, and it was no longer possible for her to shield the children from his violence. Leaving him, she took her family to West Virginia to live. She still had seven children with her, the oldest being sixteen, the youngest one-and-a-half. Now the courageous example she set sustained all of us. With determination, bred of necessity, she set about raising her children alone. She took a job working in an apple orchard and raised my brothers and sisters in a house without running water. As a result, she soon became thin and haggard-looking. When I visited her, I saw a frightened look in her eyes which tore at

**II. Facing
life alone**

my heart. I could not help her financially, but part of the time I was able to bring the baby home with me in the wintertime, and in the summertime, when the other children were not in school, they were able to visit me too. I hoped that this would ease her plight at least a little. My father contributed nothing, nor did his family, except to offer to split up the children among themselves, which, of course, my mother would not even listen to. She supported the children financially, took care of their physical needs, kept their spirits up, and planted seeds of their dreams. In her early fifties, with five children still in her care, she moved again—this time to Winchester, Virginia. There she took a job in a sewing factory. She rented an apartment, and at last their living conditions improved. She began to regain her health, and the frightened look in her eyes faded. During these next years she watched two of her sons leave for Vietnam, saw two of her daughters married, and another daughter and a son divorced. By this time, Mom should have been too tired to keep on learning and changing, but she continued to do whatever was necessary for the family and herself. For instance, when she was fifty-nine years old, she bought a car and learned to drive it. She's retired now, and the family is scattered over several states, but we never know when we will look up and see her coming down the road in her little car.

To some people it might seem that we were disadvantaged or deprived children, but her desire to raise us well knit the ties of love among us tighter and stronger than most people ever know. **It is the memory of her strength and determination which gives each of her children the will to win against adversity.**

Conclusion

Dorothy Gaydos

Relating to Your Audience

Before you begin to write, you must decide how you are going to address your audience. Your audience will almost always determine the way you say what you have to say. Certainly, you consider your audience when you write a love letter or an application for a job. You don't speak to your boss as you do to your best friend or to your grandmother. Likewise, when you write a theme, you think about your audience even though it is not an individual.

Much writing is presented to a general audience: adult, intelligent, reasonably well-educated people. Yet even if you are writing to a general audience, there are different subclassifications who have special interests. The audience for *Field and Stream,* for example, is a general audience with a special interest in outdoor sports, particularly hunting and fishing. The audience for *Psychology Today* is also a general audience (that is, the magazine is not directed exclusively to practicing psychologists), but one that is especially interested in learning more about psychology. The audience for *Seventeen* is somewhat restricted, as its name suggests; writers writing for *Seventeen* limit their subjects to concerns of high schoolers, particularly girls. You probably would not write a technical article on nuclear fission for *Good Housekeeping* or describe the ten most swinging discotheques in New York for *The Farm Journal.*

Granted, any subject can be made appealing to various audiences. The subject, however, must be tailored to fit the interests of each audience. Your own audience, your instructor and classmates, is essentially a general audience. Your concern as a writer is to handle your writing so you appeal to an interest of theirs.

21

CHAPTER I

from paragraph to essay

ORGANIZATION

Moving from the paragraph to the essay is not a difficult procedure. It requires expanding the basic elements of the paragraph, either saying more about a small subject or choosing a bigger subject. The basic structure remains the same, as you can see in the diagram on page 23.

Expanding the Topic Sentence to the Introduction

A good topic sentence, you remember, is vital for any paragraph, whether it stands alone or is part of a longer essay. A good topic sentence must be complete, clear, and specific, and it must have a narrowed subject and a specific attitude.

86

HBJ material copyrighted under notice appearing earlier in this work.

1. (Carla grew up in Greenport) (Greenport is a busy fishing and boating center) (Carla learned a lot about boats and the sea) [Begin with "Growing up in Greenport . . ."]

Carla grew up . . .

2. (Dr. Charlotte Zirin helps patients) (she works at Hillside Medical Center) (the patients are suffering from crippling fears) [Begin with "Working at Hillside Medical Center . . ."]

Helping patients Dr. C. Z., works at Hillside Medical Center.

3. (six Americans climbed the southeast spur of Mt. McKinley) (they did it in twenty-six days) (Mt. McKinley is the tallest mountain in North America) [Begin with "In twenty-six days . . ."]

In twenty-six days, 6 Americans climbed the southeast spur of the tallest mtn. in North America, Mt. McKinley.

4. (the climbers were approaching the peak) (they had to cross a great glacier) (the glacier was filled with dangerous crevasses) [Begin with "Approaching the peak . . ."]

Approaching the peak, the climbers had to cross a great glacier filled with dangerous crevasses.

5. (Rafael cleared the bar with ease) (he set a new meet record) (he is captain of the track team) [Begin with "Clearing the bar . . ."]

6. (Antonia won the chess match) (she planned her strategy very carefully) (she won in ten bold moves)

Carefully planning her chess match, Antonia won the chess match in ten bold moves.

LESSON 42

Subordination Through Phrases and Appositives

Subordinate clauses can be used to improve sentences by clarifying relationships between ideas and by permitting emphasis of one idea over another. Ideas can also be subordinated by placing them in phrases and appositives. Like subordination through clauses, subordination through phrases and appositives can enable you to combine several ideas into one smooth sentence.

Subordination Through Phrases. Observe how the following ideas are combined into one sentence by placing two of the ideas in phrases.

IDEAS	(Rita took a firm grip on the fence top) (she made a superhuman effort)
	(she pulled herself over to the other side)
COMBINED	Taking a firm grip on the fence top (*participial phrase*), Rita, by a superhuman effort (*prepositional phrase*), pulled herself over to the other side.

Subordination Through Appositives. An appositive is a noun or pronoun —often with modifiers—that follows another noun or pronoun to identify or explain it.

| EXAMPLES | Myung-Wha Chung, **a cellist,** will be the soloist at our spring concert. |
| | Karl audaciously enrolled in advanced calculus, **an extremely difficult course** |

An appositive functions like an adjective clause.

| ADJECTIVE CLAUSE | The European Common Market, which is a cooperative enter-prise of several nations, was formed to stimulate economic growth in Europe. |
| APPOSITIVE | The European Common Market, **a cooperative enterprise of several nations,** was formed to stimulate economic growth in Europe. |

EXERCISE. Show that you understand how to use phrases and appositives to subordinate the ideas in each of the following groups. Combine each group of ideas into a single smooth sentence. Do not write any subordinate clauses. Changes in wording and the order of ideas are permitted, provided they do not change the meaning. Suggestions are given for the first five groups. (Add 10 points for each correct sentence.)

EX. (the driver ahead of me signaled for a right turn) (he nearly caused a serious crash) (he turned left) [Begin with ''Signaling for a right turn . . .'']

Signaling for a right turn, the driver ahead of me turned left, nearly causing a serious crash.

FROM PARAGRAPH TO ESSAY

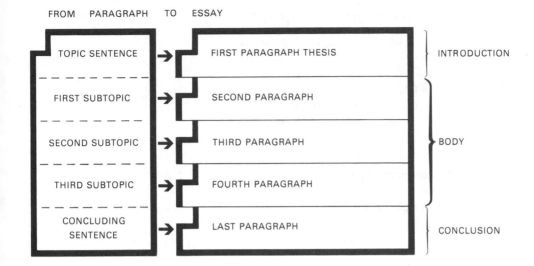

TOPIC SENTENCE →	FIRST PARAGRAPH THESIS	INTRODUCTION
FIRST SUBTOPIC →	SECOND PARAGRAPH	
SECOND SUBTOPIC →	THIRD PARAGRAPH	BODY
THIRD SUBTOPIC →	FOURTH PARAGRAPH	
CONCLUDING SENTENCE →	LAST PARAGRAPH	CONCLUSION

EXAMPLES

FAULTY: Women's lib and how over half of the population of the United States is mistreated. [This is a poor topic sentence because it is not a sentence at all; it is a fragment.]

IMPROVED: The women's liberation movement is fighting against the mistreatment of over one half of the population of the United States.

FAULTY: Fishing is fun but dangerous. [This is a poor topic sentence because "fishing" is not clear and specific. What type of fishing is meant: trolling from a row boat, fly casting from the shore, deep sea fishing from a commercial boat, spear fishing, ice fishing, or net fishing? And how is it "dangerous"? Is the danger from falling out of the boat or stabbing oneself with the hook, or being bitten by fish or snakes or insects, or being bored to death?]

IMPROVED: Ice fishing is fun, but the dangers from the elements are deadly serious.

FAULTY: School teachers are underpaid. [This is a poor topic sentence because the subject "school teachers" is too broad. Some teachers make relatively good salaries.]

IMPROVED: Public school teachers in our area are paid much less than other workers having far less important responsibilities.

FAULTY: The old and deteriorating house sat on the top of the knoll. [This is a poor topic sentence because it expresses no attitude that can be developed.]

IMPROVED: The old and deteriorating house on the top of the knoll both frightened and fascinated the children in the neighborhood.

23

Which of the following would be acceptable topic sentences? Be prepared to tell why they would or would not be.

1. I studied late last night.
2. China is the world's most populous nation.
3. Policemen should not be allowed to go on strike.
4. Blacks and women are treated unfairly in the United States.
5. Shakespeare often uses the "fools" in his plays to speak his wisdom.
6. Basketball is hard on the feet.
7. Decorating an apartment when you have limited funds is difficult, but it's fun, too.
8. Going to college is hard.
9. My favorite sport is riding.
10. That a nation like Iran could hold American diplomats hostage is incredible.

Just as the main idea of a paragraph is expressed in the topic sentence, the main idea in an essay is expressed in a *thesis sentence*, usually the last sentence in a short introductory paragraph. The additional length of the essay allows the writer to use a few sentences to attract the reader's attention by including a relevant incident or anecdote or by presenting factual background for the topic. The introduction can also provide space for a clarification of terms and lead smoothly into the body of the essay. The function of the thesis sentence is the same as that of the topic sentence in that it is also a clearly worded statement presenting the topic to be discussed and a specific attitude toward that subject.

Expanding Subtopic Sentences to Topic Sentences

The body of the essay is made up of paragraphs, so if you can write a paragraph, you can write an essay. Each paragraph in the body has a topic sentence that presents a subject and a controlling idea, which is developed by adequate, relevant, and specific detail. Each topic sentence in the essay supports the thesis statement just as each subtopic sentence in the paragraph supports the topic sentence. In fact, if your paragraph was developed by subtopics, you need only use the subtopics as topic sentences and add relevant detail to each to expand your paragraph to an essay. (However, make sure that the paragraph needs more development. Sometimes a single paragraph is all the development a subject needs.)

Outlining

Before beginning a paragraph or an essay, you may find it useful to write an outline. An outline can do two things: first, it can save a lot of rewriting, and second, it can allow you to check quickly to see whether or not your paragraph or essay is unified.

24

An Example of Expanding

Let's say that you want to expand the following paragraph that you have written on your problems with certain classes in high school.

THE PARAGRAPH

Although generally I liked high school, there were three classes that I really hated because the teachers, all for different reasons, ignored me. My physics teacher ignored me because I couldn't do the math problems associated with the science. He thought I was too stupid to know anything, so he ignored me even when I volunteered some answer not associated with the math.

My gym teacher ignored me because she was terrified that I would get hurt. I was overweight (fat is the word, I believe) and somewhat awkward, and the poor woman trembled when I tried any activity more strenuous than walking. My English teacher ignored me for still a third reason: she thought that I already knew the material she was covering. I was never allowed to recite because she always wanted to see "if any of the others know the reason." I hated these three classes while I was in high school, and I still hate, for whatever reason, to be ignored.

If you examine the above paragraph, you will see that it contains a topic sentence, three subtopic sentences, and a conclusion. It could be outlined thus:

THE OUTLINE: PARAGRAPH

I. Topic sentence: Although generally I liked high school, there were three classes that I really hated because the teachers, all for different reasons, ignored me.
II. Body
    A. Subtopic: My physics teacher ignored me because I couldn't do the math problems associated with the science.
    B. Subtopic: My gym teacher ignored me because she was terrified that I would get hurt.
    C. Subtopic: My English teacher ignored me because she thought I already knew the material she was covering.

III.   Conclusion: I hated these three classes when I was in high school, and I still hate, for whatever reason, to be ignored.

If you wanted to expand this paragraph into an essay, the outline would be much the same.

THE OUTLINE: ESSAY

I.   Introduction, including thesis sentence
II. Body
    A.   Topic sentence: My physics teacher. . . .
    B.   Topic sentence: My gym teacher. . . .
    C.   Topic sentence: My English teacher. . . .
III. Conclusion

Developing the Introduction

Before you start to write, you want to decide what general statement you want to illustrate by your essay. Why do you want to tell the story of the three teachers who ignored you? Is your purpose to show your individuality? To point out weaknesses in the public schools? To show incompetency of teachers? To show differences in students or teachers? To emphasize the different methods of solving problems? The introduction to your essay enables you to focus the reader's attention on the reason for telling your experience: the purpose of your writing, the general truth beyond the actual experience.

The introduction could be developed by any one of the following, each of which could lead into the thesis statement.

If your purpose is to emphasize your individuality, to show that you are not like many other people, you might use this introduction:

Some people try to slip through life unnoticed, feeling that if no one notices them, they won't get blamed for anything. I am not one of those people. If I do poorly at something, I want people to notice and to help. If I do well at something, I want people to notice and to appreciate. I do not want to be ignored. Although generally I liked high school, . . .

If your purpose is to emphasize the different methods teachers use, you might use this introduction:

Some teachers scream at their students, ridicule them, and chastise them. Some teachers always have some encouragement for their charges. Some are pals. And some teach only some students while ignoring the ones that are different. Although generally I liked high school, . . .

If you want to emphasize what teachers teach besides subject matter, you might use this introduction:

I've had a lot of teachers, and all of them have taught me something. Some taught me math, some taught me science, some taught me to spell and punctuate. But some taught me other things: how long fifty minutes can be, how unfair a test can be, how much fun learning can be. And three taught me to hate being ignored. Although generally I liked high school, . . .

If you want to emphasize how different people handle problems, you might use this introduction:

People have different ways of dealing with problems. Clint Eastwood uses a Magnum, Sylvester Stallone uses his fists, Jimmy Carter uses prayer. And some people ignore their problems, probably hoping they'll go away. I met three of the people who use the latter way, but their problems couldn't go away. The problem ignorers were teachers and the problem was me—a captive student in a public school. Although generally I liked high school, . . .

If you want to emphasize what you could not stand in the attitudes of teachers, you might use this introduction.

Teaching is an art, and some teachers are more artful than others. I've been spanked, yelled at, smiled at, fawned upon, berated, encouraged, told off, and put in my place by teachers. I could stand all of these tactics, but I hated being ignored. Although generally I liked high school, . . .

Developing the Body

If you are expanding the essay from a paragraph, you need only use your subtopic sentences as topic sentences.

In an essay you want to give more specific details to support your topic sentences. You think about your three classes and expand upon the ideas in the paragraph. On the first class, physics, you might think about why Mr. Boggs acted as he did. Was he a frustrated math teacher? Did he think you were stupid? You might also think about why his ignoring you bothered you so much. Was it because you really enjoyed the theory and you wanted to talk about it but he wouldn't call on you?

You think about your gym class. Again, you know Mrs. Songerlym acted as she did because she was afraid you would get hurt. Here you think of specific incidents that happened in class and include them in that paragraph.

In this way you develop your body paragraphs by thinking of specific details to support your topic sentences. Include quotations, anecdotes, examples, or comparisons to support or prove the statement made in your topic sentence.

Then you can develop each topic sentence into a paragraph:

My physics teacher ignored me because I couldn't do the math problems associated with the science. Mr. Boggs must have been a frustrated math teacher; he spent all his class time explaining mathematical problems to the four or five boys who understood them. I couldn't do the math, but I loved the theory. I wanted to discuss the things I learned from the book. I raised my hand continually, but Old Bogger never called on me. He always looked pained when he saw my hand up, and he always looked away quickly. He was sure I was severely retarded at best and idiotic at worst. He beamed when one of his boys asked a question about the precious problems and ignored the rest of us. After about four weeks, I stopped raising my hand and started hating Boggs and physics.

My gym teacher, Mrs. Songerlym, was a much nicer person than Mr. Boggs, but she ignored me too, because she was terrified that I would get hurt. Because I was a bit overweight when I was in high school (fat is the word, I believe) and a bit awkward, the poor woman trembled when I tried any activity more strenuous than walking. When it was my turn to vault the horse, Mrs. Songerlym would leap in front of it and move it away. "Now that we've all tried the horse, let's move to the parallel bars, class." If I got to the front of the line for the parallel bars, she would ask me to stand on the base "to steady it." I got three credits for gym but not one hour of exercise.

But neither Bogger nor Mrs. Songerlym was my biggest dislike in high school. I was really good at one subject: English. My English teacher ignored me for still a third reason; she thought I already knew the material she was covering. When I volunteered to diagram a sentence, she would smile and say, "Let's see if someone else knows," and I was ignored. When I rushed into class bursting with indignation over the exploits of Macbeth, I was shushed and nodded to but not called on to discuss his motivation.

I hated these classes and I hated these teachers who ignored me. I wanted to be taught or helped or applauded, but instead I was labeled too dumb or too fat or too smart. Maybe ignorance and ignore have more in common than their opening letters.

Developing the Conclusion

Like the introduction, the conclusion is a necessary part of your essay. You don't just stop—you conclude. Since the conclusion is the last thing you put in your readers' minds, you want it to be a high point. You want it to be strong, interesting, and convincing. You want it to satisfy your readers that you have done what your introduction promised you would do.

The conclusion in the preceding essay would be appropriate if the emphasis was on your individuality. If your purpose were one of the other ones suggested above, the conclusion would be different. If you used the introduction on teachers' methods of handling students, for example, you might use this conclusion:

Teachers use different methods to control their classes and teach their students, and students have their own preferences in the teachers' methods. Most perform better if the teachers encourage them; some do better if they fear ridicule and chastisement; some undoubtedly do better if the teacher is a pal. But no one does better if he is ignored.

In addition to this type of conclusion (the summary), you might conclude with a paragraph of quotation, a little story that dramatizes your thesis, a warning or remedy, or a reminder of the significance of your essay.

Another difference between paragraphs and essays is that essays have titles whereas paragraphs do not. Choose your title carefully. It should do three things:

1. It should gain the reader's interest.
2. It should give some idea of what the essay is about.
3. It should be short and snappy. It need not be a whole sentence. Don't say "Some High School Classes Are Disturbing to Some" but, rather, "Pain in the Class."

Alliteration or the use of two or more words having the same initial sounds helps make a title catchy: "Adolescent Agony."

A title should give you some idea about the author's tone (attitude toward the subject). Often the title is not just a literal label, such as "Ten Sources of Student Complaint." It is also imaginative or allusive as it indicates the author's tone. For instance, E. M. Forster titled one of his essays "Two Cheers for Democracy." In this title Forster indicates his subject—democracy—and because he says "two cheers" rather than the customary "three cheers," he shows that his attitude is not wholly favorable toward it.

What can you intelligently guess about the subject and attitude of the following essays from their titles?

"Confessions of a Female Chauvinist Sow"
"The Ant as a Fraud"
"Co-existence or No Existence: The Choice Is Ours"
"I'd Rather Be Black than Female"
"Custer Died for Your Sins"

EXERCISE Ib: TITLES
Read the following essay and think of a good title.

STUDENT ESSAY
Beginning at noon on October 31, 1978, I suffered from stomach pains, nausea, and a headache. While these symptoms sound like an example of a common virus, they were, in fact, aftereffects of taking an in-class composition test in English Composition I. In comparing these symptoms to the anguish I felt while taking the test, I must admit they seemed mild. Writing my first in-class English composition was a traumatic experience.

Throughout the entire hour allotted for writing my composition, for example, I experienced several physical discomforts. A few of these discomforts interfered dramatically with my manual dexterity. For instance, when I attempted to write, my hands shook violently, causing me difficulty in controlling my pencil. Although I gained control of my shaking hands after a few minutes, my pencil control had not improved. I then had to deal with sweating palms that caused my pencil to slide through my fingers like a loose ski gliding down a steep slope. Just as loss of manual dexterity hampered my writing ability, the fright caused by other physical manifestations caused me debilitating distractions. When I was concerned with physical irregularities, I could not concentrate on writing. An abnormally accelerated heart rate, for instance, was frightening. How could I be expected to think when my heart was making so much noise? Two other physical discomforts that I experienced were a totally dry mouth and a tightly closed throat; swallowing became impossible. As well as being frightening, this inability to swallow was distracting. Trying to force my throat to open and my mouth to produce saliva used all my energy.

In addition to these physical discomforts, I also experienced several distinct emotional effects. Two of these emotional reactions were not only unreasonable, but also distracting. The first was senseless anger. I spent precious writing time deciding where to direct this anger. For instance, I first was angry at everyone, then my instructor, and finally, after seething for half the class period, I decided I was in truth angry with myself for not preparing better. Recognizing that being angry at this point was unproductive, I moved from an emotion of anger to one of unreasoning fear. While I had a legitimate fear of performing poorly in this instance, I also felt a deeper, unreasoning fear. This fear, for example, was similar to the anxiety I felt the last time I sat in my dentist's waiting room. Even though I was only having my teeth cleaned and anticipated no pain, I still panicked and felt hollow inside. I felt this hollow, panicky feeling when I took my first in-class composition test. In both cases, the fear I felt was a reversion to a child's fear of irrational punishment. While waiting in the dentist's waiting room, I irrationally envisioned having my knuckles cracked with a ruler, at the very least, for poor preparation.

All of these physical and emotional problems were further complicated by one final obstruction. This traumatic obstacle was mental collapse. Deciding on a suitable topic became a monumental task. While searching my mind for ideas, I found it was blank. Nothing came to mind but the question: What am I doing here? I only remembered that I was a thirty-year-old competing with recent high school graduates and did not belong in a college classroom. When I finally decided on a topic, I forgot all I had learned about English usage. Writing sentence fragments became my composition style. Proper transitions were forgotten; what were transitions anyhow? I found I could not remember a synonym for *girl,* describe a graphic event, or relate facts I had known prior to that time. Although previously aware of proper English usage, I could not think clearly enough to remember how to use it.

Any event that causes physical discomfort, unreasonable emotions, and mental collapse to occur is traumatic. The only consolation I have is that the severity of all these upsets diminishes by half with each succeeding in-class English composition test I take.   *Janet Gailey*

TECHNIQUES OF CLEAR WRITING

Transitions

In the beginning of this chapter you learned that since an essay is made up of paragraphs, all you have to do to write an essay is to expand upon your paragraph-writing skills. Recalling what you know about writing the paragraph, you remember how important it is to have *coherence,* continuity between your sentences, so your ideas come across smoothly to your reader. Coherence is achieved through *transition.*

The first part of the word, *trans,* meaning "across," suggests movement from one place to the other. Thus, to *trans*port means "to carry across," to *trans*mit means to "send from one place to another," and even the *trans*mission of your car is so named because it is the part of your car that sends power from the engine to the wheels. Transition in a paragraph or essay means to move the reader from clause to clause or from sentence to sentence or from paragraph to paragraph smoothly and easily.

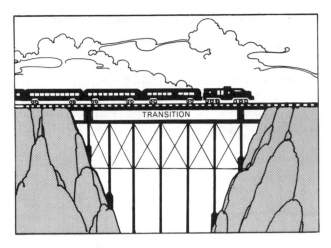

Transition Bridges the Gap

Notice the difference between these two sentences:

I don't like musicals; I loved *Saturday Night Fever.*
Although I don't usually like musicals, I loved *Saturday Night Fever.*

By adding two words, you make the relationship between the thoughts much clearer. Note too how the choice of the transitional word affects the meaning.

I started to study; I liked school.
After I started to study, I liked school.
Before I started to study, I liked school.
Because I started to study, I liked school.
Although I started to study, I liked school.

    OR

I started to study; consequently, I liked school.
I started to study; nevertheless, I liked school.

What are the differences? Notice how careful you must be in choosing transitional words to make sure that you are showing the correct relationship.

Among the more common transitions are the following:

TO SHOW ADDITION: and, too, furthermore, moreover, in addition
TO SHOW COMPARISON OR SIMILARITY: likewise, similarly, in comparison, comparable to, in similar fashion
TO SHOW CONTRAST: in contrast; on the contrary; on the other hand; however; but; not only ... but also ...
TO SHOW CONCESSION: however, yet, still, nevertheless, but, despite, although
TO SHOW SEQUENCE OR TIME: first ... second ... third; to begin with ... later ... finally; then; next; as soon as; just before; immediately after

32

*from
paragraph
to essay*

TO SHOW CONCLUSION OR RESULT: consequently; as a result; thus; therefore; obviously; in short; surely
TO SHOW ALTERNATIVE: if . . . then; either . . . or; neither . . . nor

    In writing both the paragraph and the essay, you can use several other
devices for showing the connecting relationships among the sentences. Basically,
these are divided into two types: the transitional devices and a logical sequence of
organization. The most common transitional devices are these:

1. Enumeration
2. Pronoun reference
3. Repetition of key words and phrases or close synonyms
4. Parallel structure

ENUMERATION

Enumeration—the use of *first, second, third,* and similar connective words—offers a convenient way of indicating a chronological sequence:

First, the trees must be felled . . .
Second, the brush must be burned . . .
Third, the stumps and rocks . . .

**PRONOUN
REFERENCE**

A simple and natural way of providing transition is through the use of pronoun
reference. As long as the antecedent (what the pronoun refers to) is clear, pronouns can be used quite effectively to link ideas smoothly:

The librarian sent a message to the dean of students, **who** suggested. . . .
The children must have immunization shots before entering school. **They** must
be protected. . . .

    A variation of this is the use of *demonstrative adjectives*, which point
toward something previously discussed and tie the new sentence or paragraph to
the previous discussion:

These people . . .
Those incidents . . .
That principle . . .
This notion . . .
As a result of **this** action . . .
The main point of **that** argument is . . .

**REPETITION
OF KEY
WORDS AND
PHRASES**

Note how repeating key words or phrases keeps the central idea before the reader
and keeps the relationship between the parts clear.

Although Thoreau was not a great **naturalist,** what he did supremely well was to
extract meaning from **nature.** He tasted **nature** and extracted from **nature's**
essence a higher meaning.

The **conversational tone** is an essential ingredient in effective business writing. If your reader is to feel that one human being is communicating with another human being, you must cultivate a natural **conversational tone.**

Sometimes groups of words can be repeated to give coherence to your writing. See, for example, how the repetition of *things* and the use of *depression* and *depressing* makes the second set of sentences more informative than the first set below:

Many things contributed to my depression last semester. Biology was very difficult for me.

IMPROVED: Many things contributed to my depression last semester. One of the depressing things was the difficulty I had with Biology.

Repetition of the same word or phrase at the beginning of each of a series of sentences can increase both clarity and emphasis:

It is not a task for the cowardly. . . . It is not the place for the timid. . . . It is not a haven for reckless fools. . . . It is one place where you get just one shot at being a hero or a bum.

**PARALLEL
STRUCTURE**

Parallel structure is a writing technique that increases clarity by putting similar ideas into similar grammatical form. Parallelism makes ideas clear; it also makes reading pleasant and words and ideas easy to remember. Everyone uses it: remember when you were a kid?

One for the money
Two for the show
Three to get ready
And four to go.

and Elvis's:

Love me tender
Love me true . . .

And an oldie:

Tea for two
and two for tea . . .

Much parallel structure comes automatically, especially single-word parallelism:

Bob,
Tom, and
Jim   went to the party. [Parallel subjects]

Sue   hopped,
    skipped, and
      jumped   through the park. [Parallel verbs]
Every day he went out for   breakfast,
    lunch, and
    dinner. [Parallel objects]

Some forms of parallelism, however, are more complex. For instance, the following sentence:

He lied   to his mother,
    to his wife, and
    to his boss.

The words do not have to be the same; just the structure is the same:

She thought   that roses were nice,
    that perfume was romantic, but
    that diamonds were overpowering   for a Christmas gift.

Whole paragraphs can be held together by making most or all of the sentences parallel.

Keito tried to be competitive as the U.S. culture demanded, but when he played basketball, he forgot to keep score. When he took timed tests, he forgot to raise his hand when he was through. When he did something brave, he forgot to tell anyone. But when he was praised for his work, he never forgot to give credit to the others who helped. Keito's god was cooperation, not competition.

Pete wanted to be a scholar without studying; he wanted to be an athlete without practicing; he wanted to be thin without dieting; he wanted to be strong withot exercising. He couldn't understand why he failed consistently.

Application of Old Skills

The important thing for you to remember is that all these devices that work so well to make paragraphs coherent work equally well to make essays coherent. In the essay, however, the transitional word or phrase may be expanded into a transitional sentence to move the reader from paragraph to paragraph. For example, suppose you are writing an essay about the power wielded by various groups in the United States. In the first paragraph of the body you have discussed the power of the industrial leaders. In the second, you have discussed the power of the political leaders. In starting the third paragraph, you might write a transitional sentence like the following to prepare the reader for your last and most important thought:

But the power held by the chiefs of industry and by the politicians combined cannot equal the power of still a third group in the United States....

Organization as Transition

Apart from transitional devices, transition also depends on good organization (again an expansion of the 1-2-3 form, introduction-body-conclusion). For the moment, we will ignore the introduction and the conclusion. **Focus on the development or body section,** which in the essay is usually made up of several paragraphs.

Like all other paragraphs, these body paragraphs have a topic sentence, with a subject and an attitude. But something else must be added: transition. Almost every topic sentence in the body of the essay supplies links to what has gone before, as well as announcing its subject and attitude. Often this kind of sentence begins with a subordinate clause that looks back to the preceding paragraph and continues with an independent clause that announces the topic of the current paragraph. For instance:

While the Germans fought the disastrous Battle of Stalingrad, the British. . . .

Once he has gotten himself elected, he. . . .

Until drastic changes bring the revolution, we. . . .

As soon as we free the hostages, the United States. . . .

As I see it, no simple answer. . . .

If there is no simple answer, the administration. . . .

Although Roger was handsomer than most of his friends, he was too vain to be popular.

In the last sentence the subordinate clause "Although Roger was handsomer . . ." refers to a preceding paragraph in which his good looks were discussed. The independent clause, "he was too vain to be popular," gives the topic of the paragraph now to be written.

Sometimes these transitional links are not so obvious as the subordinate clause, but they are nevertheless precise. In the sentence *All these causes have led to the happiest result,* it is clear that the "causes" have already been discussed and the demonstrative adjective *these* points to those particular causes. Even the occasional use of *but, and, yet, for,* or *so* at the beginning of a topic sentence provides clear and simple transition. However, since these words are connecting words and not introductory words, they should be used very sparingly to begin a sentence.

Note how the writer of the following essay uses topic sentences as transitions:

Original Sin

My mother, the daughter of an Old World clergyman, was a strict Calvinist. To my mother's way of thinking, the devil lay in wait at every corner, ready to ensnare me before I could even reach maturity and the safety of marriage. Thus, while I was growing up, my life was hedged about with all sorts of restrictions and taboos. **Indeed, there was scarcely an activity that was not somehow tinged with sinfulness.**

Among the lesser sins of my early years, for example, was the impulse to whistle. Now boys, of course, could whistle all they wanted to, but for me it was definitely condemned as unladylike. To compound my offense, I developed an uncontrollable urge to whistle during the dullness of Sunday afternoon. Now, in my mother's house on Sunday afternoons, nothing—and I mean nothing—stirred. Dullness clung to the motes of dust in what my mother insisted on calling the "parlor," except when the silence was shattered by my off-key whistling. Promptly banished to my room, I continued to whistle softly to myself while I was supposedly contemplating my sins.

Although I was at the time unaware that whistling was just one indication of my natural sinfulness, it burst forth in my utter disregard for the lustfulness of the world. It would never have occurred to me that my bony shanks could be the focus of lasciviousness, except for the fact that I was constantly told to keep my knees together with the hem of my skirt properly covering my bony kneecaps. Symptomatic of my wantonness, too, was my unconscious desire to straddle things: footstools, chairs, banisters, swing seats, and apple tree limbs. My mother, it seems, saw all my antics as the work of Satan.

The Devil Lay in Wait

The cardinal sin of those years, however, was playing spin-the-bottle in an empty garage two doors down the street. Although at going-on-fourteen I had only the furriest of notions about relations between the sexes, there was something enticingly wanton about kissing one particular neighbor boy. Wilbur was—if such a thing is possible—even more ardently fumbling than I. But whenever chance spun us together, we kissed until my lips were bruised. To this day my mother, of course, remains blissfully unaware of those pubescent interludes. Had she caught me, I'm sure that I would have been condemned, on the spot, to the eternal fire reserved for sinners beyond redemption.

When I look back on those years, what I feel now is not lust or sinfulness but whimsy tinged with pain. Today, my mother grudgingly accepts me as a grown woman, now that I have a daughter of my own; but there is still a certain reserve, a doubt, perhaps, of my having grown up in snow-white purity.

EXERCISE Ic: SENTENCE COMBINING
The following groups of sentences are choppy. Improve their coherence by supplying transitions to join short sentences.

1. Prices at our favorite vacation spot doubled in the past two years. We weren't able to go this year.

2. The wind whispered. The moon shone on the silver sea. John was not there. To me it meant little.

3. The mother was cross with her husband. She was afraid to tell him. She scolded her little boy. He hadn't done anything wrong. He pinched his little sister.

4. The snow started. It fell harder and harder. It was two feet deep. Commuters had a hard time driving.

5. Characters in stories are effective for several basic reasons. They catch the reader's interest and sympathy. He wishes them well or even imagines himself in their places. They are caught up in believable conflicts. The reader is tense until he knows his "friends" have solved their problems. They share some qualities with all mankind. So, most people can be sympathetic. They have some qualities that are all their own. Thus, they seem real. They are consistent with themselves. The reader can tell what they will do in a given situation.

6. We had no reason to believe his excuses. His promises didn't impress us as being acceptable. His errors were not the kind that are easily overlooked.

7. The theme of the novel is people's inability to communicate their loves and desires. These failures are repeated in every incident in the book. This controlling idea is the most important element in the story.

8. His class attendance was good. He was careless in taking lecture notes. He read all his assignments twice. He never made notes on his reading. He was always disappointed in his exam grades.

9. Working with Doris is disagreeable. She thinks her bosses are incompetent. She doesn't have any respect for the intelligence of her co-workers. Her assistants, she believes, are lazy.

10. The movie was exciting. There was a murder. The wrong man was suspected. The police pursued him. The real murderer was about to escape. He made plans to go to South America. The police closed in on the innocent man. There was a chase scene and a shoot-out. New evidence turned up. Justice was done.

EXERCISE Id: UNITY AND COHERENCE
Although the sentences in the following paragraph relate to the controlling idea, the paragraph as a whole appears choppy and disjointed. Using whatever transitional words and phrases may be necessary, rewrite the paragraph to improve unity and coherence without changing the basic ideas.

A new worker usually undergoes two types of testing. The management, directly represented by the supervisor, tries to find out what kind of worker he is. The new worker is frequently given the least desirable tasks. He gets nasty clean-up jobs or monotonous assignments. The testing of the new employee is deliberate. He is being watched by management. His reactions are being observed. The new worker is subjected to an unorganized form of testing by fellow employees. He may be teased, needled, and harassed in various ways. Harassment can become a problem. His fellow workers want to see how he shapes up. He must take care of the problem himself. The employee should not run to the supervisor or the personnel department with every problem. He must establish his own relationship with others on the job. The new employee should anticipate a period of testing and condition himself to making the necessary adjustments.

WORD POWER

Action Verbs

The essential job of you as the writer is to make your material interesting to the reader. There are several ways to do this; one way is to **show** the readers what you are thinking or seeing, not just **tell** them. Readers have to be able to see someone or something doing something. Action verbs enable them to do this. They also add clarity. Note the difference here:

The ketchup **was spilled** all over.

The ketchup bottle **slid** through his fingers, **hit** the floor, and **exploded,** the ketchup shooting in all directions.

The car **went** down the expressway.

The car **hurtled** down the expressway.

The collector **knocked** on the door.

The collector **pounded** on the door.

Verbs such as those in the second sentence of each example give a sense of life, action, forward movement. Readers are carried along with you, when they can "see" the action.

The cow JUMPED over the moon.

Active Versus Passive Voice

In the active voice, the doer of an action, the **actor,** is the subject of the sentence:

```
Jonas    read    the assignment carefully.
  ↓        ↓             ↓
Actor   Action        Object

Betty   spoke   to the militant students.
  ↓       ↓                     ↓
Actor   Action               Object
```

What would be the object or receiver of the action in a sentence in the active voice is the subject of the sentence in passive voice.

The assignment was read carefully by Jonas.

     Object   *Actor*

The militant students were spoken to by Betty.

       Object   *Actor*

Notice that using the passive voice adds words to a sentence without adding meaning. Passive slows the pace of the writing and is generally not so clear and direct as active voice. As a general rule, prefer the active voice.

Note that there are times, however, when the passive voice is more natural and effective than the active. It is the **overuse** of the passive that is to be avoided. The passive voice works effectively in the following cases:

1. When the subject (the doer of the action) is unknown or unimportant:

The bridge was built in 1927. The process was first developed in Egypt. [Who built the bridge or developed the process is unimportant.]

2. When the writer wants to place the emphasis on the receiver of the action:

Old Mrs. Phillips was badly beaten by the mugger.
Detectives were totally baffled by the crime.

Choose the form that best suits your purpose.

Replacing Weak and Colorless Verbs

Weak and colorless verbs, such as *to have, to make, to get, to do,* can often be replaced by more vivid and lively verbs:

After he **had a quarrel** with his boss, Jerry quit.
IMPROVED: After he **quarreled** with his boss, Jerry quit.

A distinction **must be made** between *imply* and *infer.*
IMPROVED: You **must distinguish** between *imply* and *infer.*

The lucky one **gets** a prize.
IMPROVED: The lucky one **wins** a prize.

The combine **does** the harvesting of the grain.
IMPROVED: The combine **harvests** the grain.

Note how another word in the sentence can frequently be converted into an action verb.

Replacing Unnecessary To Be Verbs

The weakest of all verbs is the one we use most often: *to be*. The *to be* verbs—*is, was, were, could have been, should have been*, and so on—provide no sense of action. For example, compare the following sentences:

There **was** a tropical storm off the east coast of Florida.

A tropical storm **lashed** the east coast of Florida.

It **was** the finding of the committee that there **had been** bribes paid by company executives to foreign officials.

The committee **found** that company executives **had bribed** foreign officials.

Most sentences can be strengthened by getting rid of weak verbs. Just change the subject from a nonactor to the doer of the action. For example:

The high scoring record for Alviani High School was broken last night by Ricky "Action" Jackson, who was high man with forty-four points.

Last night, Ricky "Action" Jackson scored forty-four points to break the high scoring record at Alviani High.

Notice that you also become more concise and precise as you eliminate weak verbs.

The Active Voice in Action

Suppose you and another student were competing for a job as a sportswriter for your local newspaper. Both of you have good academic records, and both of you impressed the editor during your job interviews. The editor postpones hiring either one of you until he has evaluated your writing. He assigns you and the other student to cover a crucial Steeler-Oiler football game at Three Rivers Stadium in Pittsburgh, a game that will determine which team goes to the Super Bowl. Suppose you wrote the first article, and the other student wrote the second. Who do you think would get the job?

A Steeler Squeaker I

The game between the Oilers and the Steelers was a nerve-racking one for the Pittsburgh fans. The Steelers **were losing** by two points until the last minutes of the game. Then, about halfway through the final quarter, the Steelers **seemed** to be on their way to victory. Franco Harris **was able** to gain a lot of yardage and soon **had** the Steelers all the way up to the 50-yard line. On the next play, Terry Bradshaw **passed** the ball to Lynn Swann, who **ran** 20 yards before he **was brought** down by the Oilers at the 30-yard line. Things **were looking** good for the Steelers, but their luck **began** to change on the next play. A pass that **was intended** for Swann **was caught** by a Houston linebacker. With only three minutes of playing time left, Pittsburgh had to prevent the Oilers from getting another touchdown. Fortunately for the Steelers, the Oilers **lost** control of the ball on the next play. At this point, the Steeler's strategy **was** to run the ball into good field goal position, but at first this strategy did not **appear** to be successful. Pittsburgh **seemed** to be moving all over the place but not getting anywhere—except at the bottom of a pile of 250-pound Houston players. Then, on the third down,

Rocky Bleier **managed** to take the ball to the 10-yard line. The tension in the crowd **seemed** to mount when Matt Bahr **came** onto the field to kick the ball for Pittsburgh. As seconds **passed,** nine . . . eight . . . seven . . . , the ball **was kicked** right over the goal-post—a perfect field goal. The Pittsburgh fans **were** wild with enthusiasm. Their Steelers **were** victorious. The final score **was** 30 to 29, and the Steelers **were** on their way to the Super Bowl.

A Steeler Squeaker II

It **was** a nerve-racking game for the Pittsburgh fans. The Steelers **trailed** the Oilers by two points until the last quarter, but then, with only minutes left to play, the Steeler offense **leapt** to life. Franco Harris **plowed** through the Oilers' offensive line and **pushed** the Steelers all the way up to the 50-yard line. On the next play, Terry Bradshaw **lobbed** the ball over to Lynn Swann, who **charged** down the field for a 20-yard gain before Houston's defense **sacked** him at the 30-yard line. Now confident of victory, the Steeler fans **let out** a deafening roar that **permeated** every square inch of Three Rivers Stadium, but they celebrated a bit too early. Houston **intercepted** the next pass and **took** possession of the ball at the 30-yard line. With only three minutes left to play, the "Steel Curtain" had to contain Houston's offense. Fortunately for the Steelers, the Oilers **fumbled** the ball on the next play, and the Steelers **recovered** it. Now all they **had** to do **was maneuver** the ball into good field goal position. The first two running attempts **failed;** Pittsburgh's offensive line **scrambled** all over the place, but the ball carriers got nowhere—except to the bottom of a pile of 250-pound Houston bruisers. Then Rocky Bleier **executed** a beautiful 22-yard run for a Steeler first down at the 10-yard line. Tension **mounted** as Steeler kicker Matt Bahr **rushed** onto the field. As seconds **ticked** away, nine . . . eight . . . seven . . . , Bahr **booted** the football straight between the goalposts for a perfect field goal. The Pittsburgh fans **were** ecstatic; nothing **could contain** their enthusiasm. Their Super Steelers had **edged** the Oilers 30 to 29—a real squeaker, but one that would **catapult** them all the way to the Super Bowl.

EXERCISE le: ACTIVE-PASSIVE
Of the following sentences, some clearly must be passive, some would obviously be improved by making them active, and some, depending on what you wish to emphasize, might be either. If they are correct as passives, mark them C. If they ought to be active, rewrite them. If they might be either, say *how* the use of active or passive changes the emphasis.

1. The family was terrified by an explosion in the basement.

   _____

2. The orchestra was applauded by the entire audience.

   _____

3. The freighter *Fitzgerald* was capsized by a ferocious winter storm.

   _____

4. Harvey was chosen by a unanimous vote.

   _____

5. It was announced by Marshall Dillon that the townspeople were threatened by the gang.

   _____

6. Crystal was operated on last Thursday.

    _____

7. The trees were buffeted by the wind; the roofs were bombarded by hailstones.

    _____

8. There was no way the accident could have been avoided.

    _____

9. The strength of the program was known to all.

    _____

10. The Mayhem Corporation's bid was accepted before their competitors knew there was work to be done.

    _____

11. The miser was stifled by his own greed.

    _____

12. The deer were tormented and finally killed by roving bands of wild dogs.

    _____

13. The accelerator was floored by the careless driver.

    _____

14. The silence was shattered by the roar of a motorcycle.

    _____

15. The story was told us by an old sailor and was remembered by us for years.

    _____

CHAPTER II

narrating

ORGANIZATION

> I am the man, I suffered, I was there.
>
> *Walt Whitman*

Often the best source of material to write about is personal experience. It is the one great resource everyone possesses, for each person's experience is unique. No matter how many people may have similar experiences, no two people respond in exactly the same way. Turning this raw material of personal experience into the substance of an essay is the main concern of this chapter.

To use your experience effectively, you must first sift through your memory of people and events and then select the details that suit your purpose.

In the narrative essay you are not just telling a story; you are using a narrative to illustrate, support, or prove a clearly stated thesis. The narrative itself is not an essay but rather a relevant story that can be used as the body of your essay. Thus you have the same three-part organization as in other essays: (1) the introduction leading up to your thesis sentence, (2) the narrative body of the essay using an incident from personal experience to illustrate your thesis, (3) the conclusion, which serves to reemphasize or reinforce the controlling idea of your thesis sentence. When properly shaped to the purpose, your experience may provide powerful testimony. The narrative essay provides a form for using your story to bring home to your reader something that you have learned from experience.

In confronting our own experience, we are often forced to reexamine our feelings and beliefs. You, too, might well begin by examining your own experience and asking yourself some questions:

> What is it that I feel that others don't seem to understand?
> How did I come to feel this way?
> What seems to have been decisive in shaping my attitude?

You might then go on to reexamine a specific event which in some way shaped your life:

> A childhood illness or accident
> A move to new surroundings
> A chance meeting that led to new experiences
> An event that revealed something about yourself

In writing an essay based on personal experience, your best chance for success is to focus upon a single event (or possibly a chain of closely related events) of particular significance to you. Thousands of incidents in your life could be used for this essay: many were funny, some were sad, others were embarrassing, or enlightening, or surprising, or terrifying, or rewarding. Any of these incidents that changed you in any way is worth writing about. Choose an incident that taught you something or made you braver or more cowardly, or made you trust people more or less, or changed you from a loner to a joiner, or helped you decide on a career, or changed your plans. In other words, choose an incident that has had significance in your life. In sifting through your memory of events, the central question you need to ask is, "What did this mean to me?"

Once you have chosen your subject, you must write a clear, concise thesis sentence presenting your subject and its significance. You might start with just the controlling idea: the subject and the attitude.

Subject	Attitude
Going away to college	Drawbacks of independence
Being arrested	Frightening
My trip to Italy	Appreciation of my heritage
Playing basketball in high school	Confidence
My ride down the Grand Canyon	Stifled my adventurousness

Once you have this much, you have only to get this controlling idea into a sentence, making it as interesting to the reader as possible.

I was as eager as any seventeen-year-old to get away from home and parents, but going away to college taught me that there are horrors involved in independence.

Calling a cop a "pig" is one thing, but being arrested is a different matter; it is frightening.

My "overly" emotional and sentimental parents were an embarrassment to me before I learned to appreciate my heritage on an enlightening trip to Italy.

I played ball because I liked it, but playing basketball in high school did more for me than build my muscles; it built my confidence in myself.

Whenever I get the desire to do something daring, I remember my ride down the Grand Canyon—and my adventurousness is stifled.

Having determined your thesis, you need to shape the narrative to suit your purpose. If your essay is to be successful, your reader must see that your story does illustrate the controlling idea. In determining what to include and what to leave out, you must keep your reader in mind. Telling everything "just the way it happened" may provide a poor illustration of your thesis. You must be highly selective. Don't burden your narrative with irrelevant or insignificant details. For example, don't bother telling what you ate for lunch or how much the bus ticket cost unless those details are essential to the story. Don't fuss about whether the event occurred on a Friday or a Tuesday unless that is somehow important to your story. Your purpose is not to bore the reader but to illustrate your point effectively through the story that you tell.

To write an effective narrative essay, you have to remember only one principle of organization: the one-two-three form that governs all standard expository paragraphs and essays. When you apply this three-part form to your essay, remember that one and two and three form a unit. You cannot drop off the introduction or the conclusion. A writer of fiction, on the other hand, need not include all three parts. Indeed, fiction writers usually use only the second, the body, wishing to leave the interpretation up to their readers. Fiction writers often do not explicitly state a controlling idea because they are interested in telling a story for the story's sake. But you, as a writer of exposition, must state your controlling idea clearly in your introduction and again in your conclusion. You are interested in telling a story for the sake of the idea you want to support.

Introductions

If you look again at the diagram at the beginning of Chapter I, you will see that the introductory paragraph is comparable to the topic sentence, except that it is longer. The introduction should attract the reader, should tell the reader what the topic is, should narrow it enough that it can be handled, and should indicate what the author's attitude toward the topic is. Also like the topic sentence, the introductory paragraph commits the essay to that topic and attitude. The essay can do no more or less than the introductory paragraph says it will do.

But how does the writer write interesting introductions? How do you "attract the reader"? There's an old piece of advice to writers that says nothing is interesting—except sex—unless the writer *makes* it interesting. But how is this to be done? Here are some standard approaches:

   Technique 1   One of the most effective methods of introduction is to relate the topic to a contemporary event, especially a controversy. If you had been writing on terrorism in early 1980, you would have attracted readers by relating your subject to the hostages in Iran. Look around you. What is in the news now?

   Technique 2   Another good introductory approach is justification. Sometimes you have to show your reader that you are qualified to write on a particular subject, that your thoughts have merit. It may be that you have studied the matter for years, or that you have had personal experience, or that you have met or are a personal friend of the one you are writing of. For example:

> I have been a lifelong fan of Mark Twain's. I started reading his books at the age of twelve and have continued reading his works for thirty years. I wrote my doctoral dissertation on Twain's later years. Yet, I cannot say I understand all the man believed in, although he did believe in Satan.

   Technique 3   In a method closely related to the preceding one, the introduction gives the background or reason for the topic you are proposing to support. That is, the paragraph is explaining why you are writing. The final sentence, of course, is the statement of the topic.

   In an essay called "The Egalitarian Error," Margaret Mead uses this kind of introduction:

> Almost all Americans want to be democratic but many Americans are confused about what, exactly, democracy means. How do you know when someone is acting in a democratic—or an undemocratic—way? People who do want to be democratic are frequently muddled.

She then goes on to explain what democracy is and why people are muddled about it.

   Technique 4   Another good introductory device is to state your opinion very firmly, especially if it is less popular than opposing opinions. This is sometimes referred to as "the argumentative edge." Its purpose is to provoke the reader into some response. For example, you might wish to start a discussion of the Pittsburgh Steelers with the controlling idea that teams that constantly win are boring.

   Technique 5   A relevant incident or little anecdote that introduces your topic usually gets immediate reader attention (as was mentioned earlier, everyone loves a story). If you were writing on the basketball story mentioned earlier, you might start this way:

> I dribbled down the floor, palms sweating, heart pounding. I felt as though there was a film over my eyes. I looked for Sanchez in the keyhole, Wilson in the corner. I was too nervous to see. Suddenly my opponent reached in and snatched the ball. He threw to his forward breaking down the floor. He was nervous, too, but he could still function.

Then go on with your thesis sentence.

Technique 6   Another method of introducing is to present factual background. You may find that before your reader can understand your essay, he or she must know some details that you do not want to present in the body. Often it is best to give the background at once—in the introduction:

> Thoreau believed that we individuals are the prisoners of our own wants. We want so many things that we must work hard and give up the pleasures of leisure in order to satisfy these wants. He went to Walden, not to study nature, but to "live deliberately, to front only the essential facts of life."

Technique 7   A quotation is often a good way to start an introduction for two reasons: (1) it attracts the reader's attention (and it often makes the reader feel good if he or she recognizes it), and (2) it often states a universal truth. Try to use a less well-known quotation rather than a cliché. A book of quotations or poetry is often a good source.

CAUTION: Make sure the quotation illustrates the significance of your essay. (Don't drag it in just because you like it.)

If writing on prejudice, for example, you might use one of these:

> After all, there is but one race—humanity.   *George Moore*

> I am a citizen, not of Athens or Greece, but of the world.   *Socrates*

> How seldom we weigh our neighbor in the same balance with ourselves.
> *Thomas à Kempis*

Technique 8   The use of startling statistics is also a good way to get a reader's attention if they lead up to the subject you will write on. Suppose you were going to write an essay on the odd value system in the United States. You might start out:

> A schoolteacher in the United States makes about $15,000 annually. An engineer with a good academic background may start out at $20,000. A United States Congressman earns $62,000. A New York prostitute earns an average of $70,000 tax free. And O. J. Simpson earned $733,358 in one year playing football!

Technique 9   A slightly more complicated version of the above is a striking contrast between an idea commonly held and the one you are introducing. If you were writing an essay to support the idea that even famous men had difficulties to overcome on their way to success, you might start with an introduction like this:

> Babe Ruth struck out more times than any other major league player (1,330 times). Humphrey Bogart was thirty-seven years old before he made his first successful film. George Washington lost more battles than he won. Nevertheless, these men became heroes.

Technique 10 Perhaps the most obvious introductory paragraph is one that makes a direct statement of the idea to be supported. Bruce Catton does this in an essay called "Grant and Lee: A Study in Contrasts."

> When Ulysses S. Grant and Robert E. Lee met in the parlor of a modest house at Appomattox Court House, Virginia, on April 9, 1865, to work out the terms for the surrender of Lee's Army of Northern Virginia, a great chapter in American life came to a close, and a great new chapter began.

He then goes on to tell what ended and what began.

These are only a few of the possible introductions you might use. They can be used in many varieties, combinations, and lengths, although generally the introductory paragraph is shorter than the body paragraphs. All you need is an opening that attracts the reader's interest and introduces your thesis and tone. The thesis statement is generally the last sentence of your introduction.

INTRODUC-TIONS TO AVOID

In almost all areas of writing, there are many ways to be correct. Unfortunately, there are many ways to be incorrect too. Here is a list of openings almost sure to turn off your reader:

1. The **complaint or the apology** is a boring way to begin an essay. Avoid such openings as "Segregation is too large a subject to be discussed in a short essay." You're right. It is. So narrow your topic before you begin to write. Or, "I don't really know too much about segregation." If you don't, learn something about it before you begin to write.

2. The **panoramic opening** is poor because it offers so broad a background that it fails to introduce what you are going to talk about. Suppose you are going to write a personal narrative about how your VA benefits have helped your education. A "panoramic opening" might begin by saying, "Warfare has bedeviled man all through history. From the days of Homer men have suffered from war. Any history book records the suffering from warfare. I, however, . . ."

3. Another poor opening is the so-called **mystery introduction** because no one knows what the topic is. Avoid openings like "This book interested me because the leading character reminded me of my Uncle Henry." Or, "It all began when my sister ran into the house screaming." Or, "That experience left me suspicious of dark-haired men with mustaches."

4. **Loading your introduction with definitions** is another poor way to begin your essay. Even though you will find it necessary to clarify the meaning of important terms, squeezing them all into an introduction is a serious mistake. Your readers will become either bored or so confused that they will lose all interest in reading the rest of your paper.

The Body

The body of the narrative consists of several paragraphs, each controlled by a topic sentence. The easiest and most logical order for a narrative is **chronological:** just tell it as it happened—first this, then this, then this, finally this. If you are to demonstrate your thesis by sharing your experience with your reader, you must present the events of your story in the proper time sequence so that you take your reader with you.

MAKE AN OUTLINE

If you were writing the essay mentioned earlier about the ride down the Grand Canyon, you could arrange the details in chronological order. You might jot down the major events as they happened, then divide them into logical divisions such as those shown in the left column. These notes become your outline.

1. The night before: making the decision to go down into the canyon

2. The next morning before we started: bad weather
guide's warnings about what could happen

3. The ride down: who went: members of the train
not too bad at the top
narrow, scary path
what mules did "at rest"

4. The trip up: same dangers
Sheila's idiosyncrasy
the hikers' appearance
Sheila climbs the wall
other mules' actions
my terror

Once you have this list, having removed all the irrelevant detail, you are ready to write topic sentences for each body paragraph.

TOPIC SENTENCE, PARAGRAPH 1
The decision was a tough one to make, but three of us decided the trip was worth the trouble.

TOPIC SENTENCE, PARAGRAPH 2
We realized that the trip down would be rough.

TOPIC SENTENCE, PARAGRAPH 3
The trail was not too bad at the very top, but it got worse quickly.

TOPIC SENTENCE, PARAGRAPH 4
The trip back up the path was a nightmare, punctuated by sheer terror.

PROVIDE TRANSITIONS

As you write the paragraphs, remember that the reader does not have the outline before him and can't see the divisions you have set up (*the night before, the next morning,* etc.). Therefore, you must inform him or her of the changes: Use phrases such as *the night before, the next morning, we started down the trail, later, after three hours, when we reached the bottom,* and the like. Tell your reader of every change in time, place, or direction.

BE SPECIFIC IN DETAIL

In developing your paragraphs, be specific and concrete. If quotations are relevant, use them. Describe the setting so that the reader can see, hear, feel, smell, or taste the situation. Don't say, "It was a frightening situation"; **show** the reader how frightening it was. Don't say, "The man acted crazy"; show the man acting insanely: "He threw his arms around wildly, windmilling them; the veins stood out in his neck like ropes; his eyes bulged, and he lunged at me, but unsteadily, slewing to the left and right."

BE CONSISTENT IN TENSE

Usually, the simple past tense is best for a narrative essay. You must be careful not to switch into present tense as you begin to relive your experience.

BE UNIFIED AND CONCISE

You must make your narrative unified (having no irrelevant details) and concise. You will probably do this best as you revise. As you read over your first draft, check to see that all of your details develop your thesis. Throwing out irrelevant details will serve two purposes: it will unify your essay and it will make it more concise.

The following essay is a good chronological narrative.

It's Easy to Be Brave from a Safe Distance.

Every time I think about my trip to the Grand Canyon, I am reminded of how easy it is to be brave from a distance. Our adventure began when three of my friends and I decided to head west one summer to see the country. When we got to Arizona, I decided that I wanted to see the Grand Canyon—from the bottom. The trip cured me of my adventurousness. Now, whenever I get the urge to do something daring, I remember my ride down the Grand Canyon—and my desire for adventure is promptly stifled.

The decision to go down was not an easy one to make, but three of us decided it was worth the trouble. When we went to the "Mule Trips" office, we found that the trip took eight hours. The cost, we thought, was exorbitant—after all, we didn't want to buy the mules, just rent them for a day. By this time, one friend, Irene, decided that eight hours on a mule was not for her, but I convinced the others to go.

The next morning, when we actually got on the mules, we realized that the trip down would be rough. It had rained the previous night and the day dawned cold and damp and very foggy. Our train leader (the line of mules was called a train) gave us explicit orders and strong warnings:

"Don't lean to either side, or the mule will step out from under you." (Did you ever sit perfectly erect for eight hours?)

"The mules like to walk right on the chasm edge so that they can see it. Don't try to move them in for they might think you are signaling them to turn around and start back. If they do go back, they'll knock every other mule and rider off the trail into the canyon." (I could be a murderer!)

"Don't let your mules eat." (How can you stop them?)

And most frightening: "The trail is only wide enough for one mule. There is no way that I or my assistants can get to you if you get in trouble." (Good grief!)

At this point, I thought Irene was the wisest of us all, but I couldn't quit; it was my idea. We started down the trail, twelve customers, one train leader, two assistant leaders, and one extra mule carrying the lunches. The trail was not too bad at the very top, but it got worse quickly. It became so narrow that my left foot scraped the sheer canyon wall while my right foot hung over the 3,000-foot drop to the canyon floor. The path, knocked out of the canyon wall, was clay, and it was slippery because of the rain. The mules slipped and slid while the neophyte riders gasped and moaned, and it was so foggy I couldn't see across the canyon. The mules had to be rested frequently, so our leader would stop us at some slightly wider area of the trail, and the mules would face

50

the edge of the canyon. My mule, Sheila, would always see some delectable vegetation, seemingly just out of reach, and lean forward to get it while I, horrified, gazed over her shoulders into the sheer drop to the canyon floor. It didn't seem to bother Sheila, though; nothing could have kept her from her repast. After three hours of slipping and sliding, we finally reached the floor of the canyon. Once at the bottom, I heaved a sigh of relief, but my troubles were not over. In fact, the worst part of the journey was yet to come.

The trip back up was a nightmare, punctuated by sheer terror. All of the discomfort and fears of the trip down were still there, but I had an added worry. The train leader had explained to me that Sheila was "head-shy" and that this might be a problem if we met any hikers. I was to keep her head as close as possible to the tail of the donkey just ahead of her. Two thirds of the way up, we met some hikers: a mother and three small children. Since the mules would not pass anyone on the wall side of the canyon, the woman and her children had to stand on the canyon edge, holding on to trees or bushes for support. Our train leader shouted back to me to keep Sheila close to the mule ahead, and the train started moving again. I urged Sheila forward, but as soon as she saw the hikers, she bolted. One leap took her ten or twelve feet up the sheer rocky wall. Her feet raced frantically to take her still higher, but the wall was steep and there were no footholds. She started sliding back down. Mules are smart. The ones ahead galloped ahead, away from where Sheila was performing her anti-gravity stunt, and the mules behind us stopped dead; they wanted no part in this escapade. "Whoa, whoa," I pleaded, but to no avail: Sheila could not stop her slide down the cliff. I figured I was dead and wondered fleetingly if they would bring my body up from the canyon floor. Probably they would—on a mule. Then, as Sheila's hooves hit the path, she miraculously caught herself, her legs straightened, and, now twenty feet past the hikers, she calmed down. Nothing could ever erase those terrifying moments from my memory; I can still see myself sitting in glassy-eyed fear atop a crazed, leaping, scrambling mule as she tried to climb straight up a Grand Canyon wall.

"Whoa, Sheila, whoooa!"

Today, although I am tempted when someone offers me the chance to learn to ski, and I am still fascinated by the birdlike freedom of the skydiver, I always say "no." Every time I am approached by skiers or skydivers or hang gliders or skin divers, I remember my experience with Sheila the Mule and the Grand Canyon, and I decline. I have become a devout coward.

Chronological Order in Writing Other than Narrative

The chronological sequence is important in many types of writing other than the narrative essay. If you are telling someone how to make brownies or color Easter eggs, you need to describe the process in the exact sequence that is to be followed. In various forms of on-the-job writing, too, a precise chronological sequence is crucial; it clarifies descriptions of a process, progress reports, and accident or other reports. After all, your own career or someone else's might depend on the clarity of your report.

The example that follows is from a police report of an accident resulting from a high-speed chase:

On November 6, 1977, at approximately 2:25 A.M., Officer Louis Velasquez was traveling west on Fulmer Street, approaching the intersection of Fulmer and South Barrington Avenue. As he came up to the intersection, he saw a car traveling north on Barrington at a high rate of speed. According to his testimony, Velasquez estimated this car's speed at 85 to 95 mph.

Officer Velasquez testified that he immediately turned on the flasher and siren, swung right into South Barrington Avenue, and began to pursue the violator. Traveling north in pursuit of the offender, Officer Velasquez reached speeds in excess of 115 mph, according to his own testimony.

In the 2100 block of North Barrington Avenue, Velasquez began to overtake the offender. According to his testimony, he was approximately three car lengths behind the offender when he braked suddenly and swung east into Marston Street Extension. Officer Velasquez attempted to follow the car, but he failed to negotiate the turn. The patrol car struck a fire hydrant 20 feet from the intersection of North Barrington and Marston Street Extension. It rolled over and skidded 156 feet, coming to rest on its top on the front lawn of the Carmine residence, 108 Marston Street Extension.

Note the accuracy with which the sequence of events is recorded. Whether you are reporting an auto accident, the results of an experiment, or the behavior of a mental patient, you record your observations in narrative form. Although such reports are expected to be objective and impersonal, they follow the narrative form and adhere to a strict chronological sequence.

The Conclusion

There are several successful techniques for concluding an essay.

THE SUMMARY This method of concluding, though the most common, can be boring and repetitious. Make sure that you summarize only the highlights and that they all emphasize your thesis.

FINAL QUOTATION To conclude with a strong quotation is good because it is brief, has the authority of its author, and pleases the reader's sense of style. Suppose you had written an essay on the age-old question of women's equality with men. An effective close to your thesis might be the quotation from Samuel Johnson when he was asked,

"Which is more intelligent, man or woman?" Dr. Johnson answered, "Which man and which woman?"

THE ANECDOTE

A little story that dramatizes your thesis is an effective conclusion. Suppose, in writing an essay on the popular arts for your sociology class, you want to make a final point that the popular story always ends happily even though such a happy ending is not credible in real life. You might write something like the following:

Ignoring reality, the popular story substitutes sentimentality to provide a happy but unlikely ending. The heroine, Mary Lou, is rescued from her drab life clerking in the fish store to support her worthless brother by Prince Charming, Homer Hoskins. Homer just happens by, happens to see her without her glasses and so recognizes her true beauty, and sweeps her off to romance in his ice-cream truck.

Swept off to an unlikely romance.

THE WARNING OR REMEDY

If you have been writing about something that ought to be changed, you might want to give a warning about what might happen if things don't change or suggest a remedy for making them change. Suppose you had been writing about the student body's failure to elect the best candidates to student government. You might conclude with the following warning:

If the students continue to elect student government officers who are interested only in social events and who ignore academic responsibilities, we will soon have a social committee, not a government. If we have only a social committee, we will have resigned our rights to any control of our academic careers.

If you wanted to conclude on an affirmative note, you might conclude the same essay with this remedy:

53

If we wish our student government really to be a governing body, we must assign social affairs to a social committee and elect to office persons who are concerned with the academic responsibilities and privileges of students. We must have officers who understand that the responsibilities of self-government are at least as important as the privileges. We must elect officers who take themselves and self-government seriously.

THE EMPHASIS ON SIGNIFICANCE

Especially in a narrative essay, in which readers may become so interested in the story you are telling that they almost forget your thesis, you must conclude by reminding them of it. In the essay about the mule trip, you will notice that the writer concluded by restating the significance of his narrative. After all, you've learned something from this experience or you wouldn't be writing about it. Tell what you learned. The rider on the mule learned to be "a devout coward."

CONCLUSIONS TO AVOID

1. A **verbatim repetition** of the thesis sentence, usually preceded by "So you can easily see. . . ."
2. **The colorless summary** which says something like "Students have many problems. They have to worry about their grades. They are frightened about going into a vocation. They are unsure of themselves."
3. **The unsupported claim to interest.** "I have always liked to read about bird watching. This book was an interesting book about bird watching. I couldn't put it down. My mother couldn't put it down. My grandmother couldn't put it down. The dog couldn't put it down." This may show a happy community of interest in your family but tells nothing about the book.
4. **The vague moral.** Moralizing is never very popular and the vague moral is boring as well. "We all should be kind to each other" will not advance your thought or the cause of kindness.
5. **The new idea.** Above all else, make sure your conclusion does conclude and does **not** introduce a new thought: "This reminds me of another thing I should have mentioned. . . ."

Pitfalls to Avoid

1. Don't shrink from using the first-person pronoun *I*. Efforts to avoid *I* often lead to a wordy, impersonal style that deprives your story of its vitality.
2. Don't make the mistake of thinking that you must have an earthshaking story of events in some exotic place. Stick to what you know best. An everyday experience can be transformed into an effective essay by careful observation and thoughtful evaluation. Rather than searching for some bizarre subject, try to present a fresh and vivid personal view that will make even a common experience unique.
3. Avoid any apologetic phrasing throughout the essay as well as in your introduction:

    This may sound dumb, but. . .
    Although I didn't have much time to think about it, . . .
    After all, I was only a third grader, so. . .

Try to present a candid account of your experience, without bragging or apologizing. Even if you acted with less than perfect honesty or wisdom, your reader will more readily accept an honest account than lame apologies or efforts to impress someone.

4. Stick to the simple past tense in telling your story: *We* **went**. . . . *We* **saw**. . . . *We* **heard**. . . . If you need to relate details that took place before the time of your story, use the past perfect:

We **had seen** bear tracks on the day we **arrived** at camp.
We **had heard** about the abandoned mine shaft, so we **went**. . . .

5. Don't use *it*, *this*, or *that* as a vague reference to your title or thesis. For example, in a paper titled "The Day the World Was to End," about your youthful conviction that the world was coming to an end, the following opening sentences start with vague references:

FAULTY: **That** was twelve years ago when I was staying at my grand-parents' farm for the summer.

FAULTY: **It** was not because of anything my grandfather had said.

6. Don't leave a gap between the introduction and the body of your essay. Provide a transition to tie the body of the essay to the introduction and the thesis statement. Look at the following example:

Introduction

My aunt, with whom I lived for several years, was a lady whose dignity few people cared to question. That my mother had married a common millwright who had the indecency to get himself killed seemed, to her, a personal insult. Throughout my stay at my aunt's home, I was constantly reminded of how low in the world my mother had fallen. Since my uncle—poor, harmless fellow—was usually absent on some sort of business, my aunt had an abundance of free time in which to pour into my small ears all the details of my mother's disastrous marriage choice. But the day came when I grew tired of hearing my aunt refer to my father as having been a failure. **In something less than a straightforward way, I determined to take my small revenge.**

First Body Paragraph

Throughout the hot, motionless days of August, I spent much of my time on the banks of the Souris River. I walked along its banks for miles, exploring tiny creeks and ravines. . . .

Note the gap between the introduction and the first body paragraph. A slight revision could supply the transition needed to tie the body of the essay to the introduction.

IMPROVED: During the hot, motionless days of August, a plan of revenge slowly began to take shape in my mind. Wandering the river bank not far from my aunt's home, I developed, bit by bit, a devious scheme to strike a blow at her dignity. . . .

This revised version provides smooth transition and keeps the story's central idea uppermost in the reader's mind.

SUGGESTED TOPICS

Write a narrative essay on one of the following topics.

1. A blind date
2. A traffic accident
3. A childhood prank
4. A courtroom battle
5. A wedding reception
6. A vacation
7. A barroom brawl
8. A hunting trip
9. A surprise party
10. A fraternity party
11. An accident at work
12. An embarrassing incident
13. Your first date
14. Your wedding day
15. Your first child
16. Your first plane ride
17. Your first Christmas away from home
18. Your first day on a new job
19. Your first encounter with death
20. Your first attempt at public speaking
21. Your first attempt at skiing (or hang gliding or other activity)
22. Your high school prom
23. Your first job interview
24. Your first trip to another country
25. Your first experience in unemployment

26. Being arrested
27. Witnessing a crime
28. Getting lost
29. Fighting in Vietnam
30. Winning a championship game
31. Losing your job
32. Learning an important lesson
33. Meeting your future in-laws
34. Getting caught in a lie
35. Making a crucial decision
36. Dealing with an irate customer
37. Being thrown from a horse
38. Running in a marathon
39. Losing a friend
40. Playing a practical joke on someone
41. An experience that taught you:
    a. to think before you act
    b. to respect age
    c. to spend more time with your kids
    d. to change your priorities
    e. to be less critical of others
    f. to appreciate your parents
    g. to appreciate your roots
    h. to have more confidence
    i. to look at both sides of an issue
    j. to appreciate your education

TECHNIQUES OF CLEAR WRITING

The Core Sentence

Often a sentence fails to communicate the writer's idea clearly because the core sentence is faulty. The core sentence consists of the subject, S; the verb, V; and the completer, C. (The completer is anything that completes the sentence; it can be a direct object of an active verb, a complement of a linking verb, or other kinds of words that complete the thought of the sentence.)

Subject	*Verb*	*Completer*
Donnie	passed	French.
S	V	C [*object*]
Mother	felt	sick.
S	V	C [*adjective*]
Stella	is	a good cook.
S	V	C [*predicate nominative, complement of linking verb*]
Ricky	went	to the game.
S	V	C [*prepositional phrase*]
The storm	moved	east.
S	V	C [*adverb*]
David and Lisa	eloped.	
S	V	C [*needs none*]

Whatever the completer might be, it is one of the trio, *SVC*, that must make sense if the sentence is to be clear.

Clarity is sometimes lost because the sentences start off in one direction but stray away in another. Either the subject and verb don't make sense together or the verb and the completer don't go together logically. For instance, in the sentence "Evidence of theft was committed last night," the **subject** is *evidence* and evidence cannot be *committed*. The writer presumably means that theft was committed and evidence was found to prove it. In the sentence *The committee's report replaced John's job,* it is unlikely that a report could take the place of a job. The writer probably meant "The committee reported that John's job was unnecessary."

If words come between the elements of the core sentence, seeing the error is difficult; in order to correct the sentence, you must pick out the **Subject, Verb,** and **Completer** to see if they make sense. For example:

Any one of the members of the Homecoming Queen's Court who didn't show up would mean an unbalanced float.

You may be able to figure out what is meant in such a sentence, but it isn't easy. That's because the *SVC* is faulty:

Anyone	would mean	unbalanced float
S	V	C

Once you see the error, it is not difficult to create a correct sentence:

If anyone in the Homecoming Queen's Court is absent, the float will be unbalanced.

The absence of any of the Homecoming Queen's Court would unbalance the float [*or* destroy the balance of the float].

58

Here is another faulty core sentence:

As you know, the situation in the cafeteria must be resolved.

Situation   must be resolved
   S   *V*

Situations are not resolved; problems and differences are. Situations can improve or worsen, but there is nothing in a situation to resolve.

    As you check your sentences to make sure the Subject-Verb-Completer in each makes sense, don't limit your attention only to the independent clause or clauses. The core within a dependent clause must also be a logical *S-V-C*. For example:

Although the decline in prosperity was turned around, unemployment remained a problem.

    Here the main clause, *unemployment remained a problem*, has a correct *S-V-C*. But in the dependent clause the subject, *decline*, and the verb, *was turned around*, are illogical. A *decline* may level off or bottom out, but it cannot turn around.

EXERCISE IIa: CORE SENTENCE
Pick out the core sentences in the following. If a core sentence is faulty, correct it. Remember that the core sentence must be correct in **all** clauses, not just in the main clause.

1. Motorcycles are a disadvantage over cars.

   _____

2. If the problem gets worse, we will have to employ all our resources and find a response.

   _____

3. One would think the building would supply physical fitness for everyone.

   _____

4. The inclination on the part of some members to put off paying their dues must halt.

   _____

5. The question of the "moral majority" is the basic separation of church and state.

   _____

6. The insolent tone of Mr. Gripper spells out contempt for poets.

   _____

7. Joan decided that her differences with Professor Moriarity were a barrier that she had to submit to.

    _____

8. The new president of the United States is a serious mistake for the people of this country.

    _____

9. An example of the bad food is when I bite into one end of a French fry, grease comes rushing out the other end.

    _____

10. We met many changes when we moved, but one of the worst changes we encountered was our apartment.

    _____

11. This has been a real joy to me to be able to enjoy both my sons and compare their likeness to one another in laughter with them both.

    _____

12. The thing he ought to have done when he was there came to him on the way home.

    _____

13. If you refuse to believe in ghosts, the idea is they will not appear to you no matter what others say they saw.

    _____

14. The piney woods and sandy hills of his home in Carolina believed in country songs and good old time religion.

    _____

15. The school board has made a number of recommendations which are sure to help the discipline problem at Blackwood High School.

    _____

16. This contrast between the readers who love Longfellow and those who ignore him comprehends his mistreatment at the hands of some critics.

    _____

EXERCISE IIb: CORE SENTENCE
In the following, find the core sentences. Correct any faulty cores so that all sentences are logical.

1. O'Grady, since his reach was two inches longer, caused him to lose the fight.

    _____

2. Several people have decided not to vote and became a majority.

   _____

3. The tickets that we sell this year should double by next year.

   _____

4. The plan for the house that Harry designed will take four weeks to build.

   _____

5. The captain of the ship saluted and with all passengers aboard sailed majestically out of the port.

   _____

6. You received a D because your essay had many corrections.

   _____

7. By studying for your test, it will ensure a good grade.

   _____

8. A church is where you go to get religious training.

   _____

9. The problems listed above will make our organization better.

   _____

10. The bridges, which were old and dilapidated, made crossing the river dangerous.

    _____

11. Big trucks pay a mounting toll in lives and road damage.

    _____

12. Teenagers sometimes get the feeling that they were a burden to their parents and wish that they had never been born.

    _____

13. Many of the ornaments were made by past generations of children and hung with pride among the branches.

    _____

14. Oklahoma had not seen a worse winter in forty years, and, like my grandmother, farmers watched their livestock constantly from wolves.

    _____

15. Participation in this session will be on a first come, first served basis.

    _____

16. The possibility of a Sheriff's sale may take place.

    _____

Point of View

One of the ways writers sometimes confuse their readers is by changing point of view. Point of view refers to when, where, how, and by whom the situation is viewed. Errors in point of view can occur in five areas: person, tense, number, voice, and tone.

PERSON Errors in person are the most common errors in point of view. The writer may start off correctly using the third person:

The students were starting to feel uneasy as the smell of smoke grew stronger.

Then he or she lapses into first person:

Someone screamed, and **we** panicked.

Or when starting a narrative, the writer may start with a first-person generalization for the thesis sentence:

Moving to **my** own apartment required some major adjustments.

Then he or she shifts to the second person:

Your parents were very much against **your** moving out.

Shifts in person occur frequently in everyday conversation. In fact, you have probably become so used to **hearing** these errors that you automatically shift from one person to another without even realizing that you have changed your point of view. For example:

INCORRECT: **Those students** thought that **you** could breeze right through Mrs. Griffith's sociology class, but **they** got a rude awakening after the first test. [This sentence shifts from third person (*students*) to second person (**you**), then back to third (*they*).]

CORRECTED: **Those students** thought that **they** could breeze right through Mrs. Griffith's sociology class, but **they** got a rude awakening after the first test.

INCORRECT: I thought that I could breeze right through Mrs. Griffith's sociology class, but **you** get a rude awakening after the first test.

CORRECTED: I thought that I could breeze right through Mrs. Griffith's sociology class, but I got a rude awakening after the first test.

NOTE: Avoid inappropriate use of second person. Keep your reader in mind. For example, it would sound ridiculous to write for a male English instructor, "While washing your nighties in Lux. . . ." It is preferable to use the second person only when you are addressing someone directly. Do not use *you* when you mean *everybody*.

TENSE   Shift in tense is also a common error, especially for inexperienced writers. It is sometimes caused by the writer's getting caught up in the story, especially in a narrative. A student is writing, let's say, about a wreck that changed his choice of careers. He begins correctly using the past tense, but then, excited by his memories, switches to the present tense.

> I started down the narrow twisting road that led to the picnic area. I had the car in second gear because the last thing I wanted from the car was speed. Suddenly, up pops the gear shift. I'm in neutral! The car gathers speed as I brake frantically.

NUMBER   Errors in number, making illogical switches between singular and plural, are usually errors in referring to antecedents: errors in agreement between subject and verb and between subject and pronoun. Essentially errors in grammar, they also confuse the point of view. They are discussed in the Techniques of Clear Writing section in Chapter 4. They include errors such as these:

Each child was told to bring **their** own marbles.

Everybody knows **their** own mind.

VOICE   Changes in voice are changes from active to passive or passive to active. These changes interfere with the flow of thought and force the reader to reread the sentence to understand.

I ordered a ham sandwich, and a hamburger was served to me.

Harry Truman loved bourbon and poker, and an occasional session at the piano was enjoyed by him.

TONE   Basically tone is word choice. Tone can be formal or informal, conversational or pedantic, sardonic or serious. Whatever tone you choose, stick with it; be consistent. When you change tone, you jar the reader.

The ambulance arrived immediately. The white-coated attendants moved quickly and effectively to stem the flow of blood. Cripes, what a mess! The poor sucker looked like he'd been blown away.

Boy, were we having fun. Kids were all over the place, some climbing trees, a few wading in the creek, and a gang playing touch football. A cool breeze permeated the entire area although the sun was a brilliant orb.

The concert was a real bummer. The whole performance was pedestrian.

My brother is a real jerk at school. He mouths off to the teachers, clowns around in class, and neglects his academic preparation. In short, he is a maladjusted, regressive deviant.

You really confuse your reader if you change your point of view.

Revise the following sentences to eliminate needless shifts in point of view.

1. A student like George should try to find a roommate who is conscientious; then you can do some serious studying.

   _____

2. Christopher gives an excellent performance and portrayed the old man flawlessly.

   _____

3. Today he discussed the Paleozoic era; tomorrow the Mesozoic era will be the subject of his discussion.

   _____

4. Visitors should park your cars in the main lot.

   _____

5. For years I have been going to the antique car shows and enjoy every one of them.

   _____

6. Many of the younger horse owners do not join the association because they cannot afford to become a member.

   _____

7. As we came across the bridge, you should see how the cathedral looks.

   _____

8. The instructor called for attention and then announces the examination date.

   _____

9. The men lay in a cold ditch and listen as a dog howls.

   _____

10. If anyone needs dental work, they should first find out exactly what the work will cost.

    _____

EXERCISE IId: POINT OF VIEW
Identify the types of errors in point of view in the following sentences and correct them.

1. Whenever I take the car out for a drive, the engine made a strange noise.

   _____

2. Tennessee is a wonderful state; they grow tobacco and cotton and bluegrass.

   _____

3. I think the ERA should be passed; you'd think a country dedicated to equality would have already passed such a bill.

    _____

4. Trade restrictions on the Soviet Union have been proposed by the President, and he has halted the grain shipments.

    _____

5. Saks Fifth Avenue is a wonderful store; they sell elegant blouses, gracious suits, and groovy shoes.

    _____

6. My pup is really cuddly, a real Teddy bear; she has a fluffy coat, bright button eyes, and a lovely, gracefully curled tail.

    _____

7. The American Film Institute chose *Gone with the Wind* as the best American film ever made, and *Citizen Kane* and *Casablanca* were given second and third place awards by the Institute.

    _____

8. If anyone signs up for Physics II, they're asking for hard work.

    _____

9. If you want to be elected, you had to get out and meet the voters.

    _____

10. Everyone loves literature, even if you don't know you do.

    _____

EXERCISE IIe: POINT OF VIEW

Familiar though you may be with the Declaration of Independence, you will have difficulty at times understanding the version below. It has been rewritten with an inconsistent point of view. Underline the inconsistencies in person, tense, number, voice, and tone. Then revise the inconsistencies so that the excerpt is logically acceptable.

We hold these truths to be self-evident: That all men will be created equal; that his Creator endowed you with certain unalienable rights; that among these will have been life, liberty, and the pursuit of happiness: that, to secure these rights, governments will be instituted among men, deriving its just powers from the consent of the governed: that whenever any form of government becomes destructive of these ends, it was his right to alter or abolish them, and to have a new government instituted by them, laying their foundations on such principles, and organizing its powers in such form, as to you shall seem most likely to effect their safety and to give them whatever they damn well want whenever they damn well want it. Prudence, indeed, will dictate that governments long established should not be changed for itsy-bitsy causes; and accordingly all experience will show that mankind was more disposed to suffer, while evils are sufferable, than to have yourself righted by abolishing the forms to which we are accustomed. But when a long train of unintentional mistakes, pursuing invariably the same object, evinces a design to reduce you under absolute despotism, it is his right, it is duty, to throw the bloody twits out.

WORD POWER

Specific Verbs

In the word section of Chapter I you learned the importance of using action verbs. If you look at the articles written by the two aspiring sportswriters, you will see, however, that the second article is better not just because it contains more action verbs but also because those interesting verbs are more **specific** verbs. In addition to maintaining the readers' interest, the writer of the second article gives the reading audience a clearer picture of what happened at the Steeler-Oiler football game. For example, if you read that "Matt Bahr **came** onto the field," you could picture him walking slowly, jogging casually, or running rapidly onto the field, but if you read Matt Bahr **rushed** onto the field, you can almost feel the excitement as Bahr hurries onto the field to get in field goal position. *Rushed* is more specific than *came*. Thus, the meaning of the entire sentence becomes clearer.

It's not hard to use specific verbs. There are plenty of them in the English language. If, for example, you look under the letter *S* in an unabridged dictionary, you will find over 1,000 verbs, and that's only one letter of the alphabet! So don't say, "I just couldn't think of the right words." That's just an excuse for laziness. All you have to do is take a little extra time to look for them. Thomas Jefferson did. When he wrote the Declaration of Independence in the summer of 1776, there were still quite a few colonists who were not yet convinced that breaking away from England was a good idea. Jefferson wanted to convince these people (and the rest of the world) that the King of England was a tyrant, so he chose his verbs carefully. He was very specific when referring to George III:

He has **plundered** our seas, **ravaged** our coasts, **burned** our towns, and **destroyed** the lives of our people.

If Jefferson had been a lazy writer and used the first verbs that came into his head, the Declaration of Independence would not have been as effective as it is. Suppose, for example, Jefferson had said:

He has **disturbed** our seas and our coasts, and he has **hurt** our towns and our people.

Instead of inspiring colonists to join the rebellion, he might have lost a lot of potential patriots through confusion. "What exactly does he mean?" they might have asked. "Is this supposed to prove that King George is acting like a tyrant?" When you are writing a paper, take time to use specific verbs. You will see your writing improve in a number of ways. You will guard against boredom and confusion, you will automatically reduce wordiness, and you will say exactly what you mean.

EXERCISE IIf: SPECIFIC VERBS

Improve the narrative paragraph below by substituting more specific, interesting verbs for the words in italics.

Agreeing to *stay with* my neighbor's five kids last Friday night was not one of my brighter decisions. For months my next-door neighbors, Rosie and Ralph, had been looking forward to their "escape" weekend at the Marriott Inn. At the last minute, however, their baby-sitter *got in touch with* them and told them that she couldn't come until Saturday morning. Well, God forbid that I should go to my grave knowing that I *interfered with* Ralph and Rosie's only chance to *have* a few days of sanity. I couldn't say no. Well, as soon as I opened my door Friday evening to go over to Rosie's, I knew I had made a big mistake. I could already hear the kids screaming. Ralph and Rosie had their coats on when I *got there,* and they *were* out of the driveway before I could say Jack Frost (correction—before I could say "Help!"). Then the fun began. Ryan and Rebecca, the three-year-old twins, *were running* around the living room on Rosie's plush new light blue carpet trying to *get* Fifi, their neurotic poodle, and eat chocolate ice cream at the same time. Then Randy, the five-year-old neo-Nazi, came *running* down the steps armed with the world's noisiest toy machine gun and *placed* it directly into my left kidney. At this point, Ralphie, Jr., the eight-year-old whiz kid, *proceeded to tell* me precisely how younger brother Randolph should be handled, and then he asked me why I wasn't doing anything to stop the twins from rubbing Mother's makeup into the living room carpet. At that moment we heard a loud crash. One of the twins had *pushed* over a hurricane lamp, which *was* in a million pieces. I immediately *went* in the living room to see if the twins were still alive, and I *saw* one laughing, the other crying, and Fifi bleeding. Obviously, Fifi *had been situated* in the wrong place—right underneath the lamp. (I was beginning to understand why Fifi was neurotic.) Through all of this mayhem, Randy was still blasting away with his machine gun, Ralphie, Jr., was still *bothering* me with his lectures on child psychology, and I didn't know what to do first: *take care of* the broken lamp, *talk to* the frightened twin, *look at* Fifi's wounds, or *get* the blood off the rug. Before I had a chance to make a decision, the baby, who was supposed to be asleep for the night, started *calling* for her mommie. Then the phone started to ring, and someone turned on the TV full blast. If anyone had

Any escape weekends for singles?

walked in at that moment and seen the look on my face, he would have *taken* me straight to the funny farm. I just wanted to scream. I honestly don't know how I *lasted* through the night. I was never so happy to see Saturday morning come. I wished the baby-sitter good luck, *went* home, and immediately *contacted* the Marriott to see if they had any escape weekends for singles.

Specific Nouns and Modifiers

As a child grows, his or her ability to become more specific grows also. The older a child is, the more you expect the child to communicate in specifics rather than generalities. If a three-year-old child pointed to a house and said "house," you would not be surprised. You wouldn't expect him to be any more specific than that. For example, you wouldn't expect him to say, "Look, Mommie, an old Victorian mansion." On the other hand, if you were walking down the street with your twenty-two-year old boyfriend and he said, "There's a house," you probably wouldn't be too impressed with his powers of observation. In the same way, if you use nothing but general words in your papers, your readers won't be too impressed with your powers of observation. No matter what you are writing about, you are not going to get your point across if you are not specific. Your readers might get some idea of what you're trying to say, but the problem is that ten different readers might get ten **different** ideas. If your writing gives them such a choice, you have failed to communicate **your** idea.

When the nouns you use can be interpreted in more than one way, then they are too general. Look at the following example:

Major Cunningham uses **drugs.**

In this sentence, the noun **drugs** is too general. One reader might picture Major Cunningham taking insulin for his diabetes, another might see him smoking marijuana, another might assume that he is popping amphetamines, and still another might conclude that he is shooting heroin every day. The reader doesn't know what kind of drugs the major is taking or how often he is taking them.

Now look at another example:

Mr. Magillacuddy has a **problem.**

This sentence could be interpreted in a number of ways. Maybe Mr. Magillacuddy's problem is only a temporary financial setback—a cut in pay. Maybe he has a serious medical problem, an incurable disease, or maybe his "problem" is that Mrs. Magillacuddy is driving him crazy.

You can clarify the meaning of each of these sentences by

1. Making the noun more specific.
2. Adding specific modifiers:
    a. Adjectives—to modify nouns or pronouns.
    b. Adverbs—to modify verbs, adjectives, or other adverbs.

For example:

Major Cunningham takes **amphetamines daily.** [specific noun and adverb]

Mr. Magillacuddy has had a **devastating financial setback** [specific adjectives and specific noun]; he lost his job.

Notice that in each of these sentences the modifiers as well as the nouns are specific. You can't make a noun specific and then add just any adjective or adverb. For example, if you say that Major Cunningham took amphetamines **regularly,** you are not necessarily saying that he took them every day. You are just saying that he took them at regular intervals—maybe every few hours, maybe every day, maybe every other day. Likewise, if you say that Mr. Magillacuddy has a **bad** problem or a **serious** financial problem, you are not telling the reader that his problem is so bad that it really devastates him.

The illustration below lists general nouns that have been made specific. Notice how you can make nouns more specific by asking yourself a series of questions. Take the word *document,* for example:

What kind   *a legal*
of document?   *document*

                What kind of
                legal document?   *a will*

                                   Whose will?   *Uncle Joe's will*

                                                  What kind of
                                                  will?   *a million
                                                               dollars
                                                               to each
                                                               of us*

GENERAL ————————————————————————————————————> SPECIFIC

document	legal document	a will	my uncle Joe's will	Uncle Joe's surprisingly generous will—a million dollars to each of us
container	glass container	a bottle	a wine bottle	a tapering green Rhine wine bottle
suit	formal suit	a tuxedo	a pastel tuxedo	a mint-green tuxedo, wrinkled and torn
experience	childhood experience	an accident	a bad accident	a fatal automobile accident
executive	business executive	a vice-president	an oil company vice-president	the greedy, unscrupulous vice-president of Mayhem Oil Company

EXERCISE IIg: SPECIFIC NOUNS
Write four increasingly specific words for each of the following nouns.

1. institution _____ _____ _____ _____
2. person _____ _____ _____ _____
3. instrument _____ _____ _____ _____
4. vehicle _____ _____ _____ _____
5. animal _____ _____ _____ _____
6. machine _____ _____ _____ _____
7. store _____ _____ _____ _____
8. place _____ _____ _____ _____
9. furniture _____ _____ _____ _____
10. reward _____ _____ _____ _____

Specific Modifiers

Avoid overused adjectives, such as *nice, pretty, interesting, worthwhile, rewarding, thrilling, wonderful,* and overused adverbs such as *very, actually, really, terribly.* Also avoid stringing a lot of adjectives or adverbs together in one sentence. Don't overdo modifiers.

In almost every instance, vague modifiers can be replaced by more specific ones.

A *nice* house might be **cozy, charming, comfortable, neat,** or **well-constructed.**

A *pretty* girl might be **graceful, elegant, dainty, striking, stunning,** or **provocative.**

An *interesting* scene might be **curious, revealing, absorbing, fascinating,** or **eye-catching.**

A *very dumb* answer might be described as **irrelevant, naive, ignorant,** or **stupid.**

A *very serious* injury might be **grave, critical, dangerous,** or **crippling.**

A *really cold* day might be **icy, frigid, numbing, paralyzing,** or **bone-chilling.**

A *terribly hot* day might be **sweltering, sizzling, scorching, broiling, blistering, blazing,** or **hellish.**

Always try to select the word that conveys the precise meaning you intend.

EXERCISE IIh: SPECIFIC ADJECTIVES
Supply the sentences below with specific adjectives.

1. Jeannie's date was a _____, _____ jock.
2. I found Jack's new home a _____ place to spend an evening.
3. It was a _____, _____ day, fit for neither man nor beast.

69

4. Katie's dog is undoubtedly the most _____, _____ dog I have ever seen.

5. The atmosphere in that restaurant was so _____, I never want to eat there again.

6. Ernie's article provided a _____ look at the proliferation of doctoral degrees in the United States.

7. The _____ killing spree ended in four _____ deaths.

8. My high school offers its students a _____ opportunity to participate in the _____ academic and athletic programs in the state of Arizona.

9. The Y.A.K. television network has bombarded the American public with _____, _____ commercials.

10 Alfred Hitchcock has directed many _____, _____ films.

EXERCISE IIi: SPECIFIC ADVERBS
Vague adverbs weaken the following sentences. Revise each sentence to present the idea suggested by the bracketed vague term in a more specific and interesting way. In some sentences, you may want to revise more completely than by simply replacing vague adverbs with vivid ones.

1. The baby's convulsions stemmed from the [overly large] quantities of alcohol consumed by her mother during pregnancy.

_____

2. The students decided to publish their underground newspaper [periodically].

_____

3. The one-woman post office was so efficient that the postmistress was [soon] thrown out of business by the United States government.

_____

4. Joy's father worries about aging, but he is still a [very] handsome man.

_____

5. The bank president was [somewhat] involved with the embezzlement scheme.

_____

6. The radio announcer [happily] informed me that I had just won the trip to Hawaii.

_____

7. Pete's car was [unusually] situated on the top of a cliff.

_____

70

8. Linda and Rick have a [nicely] decorated home.

_____

9. Al's surprise party was planned [so inadequately] that only half the people who were invited showed up on the right day.

_____

10. Senator Carson introduced a bill that was [smartly] designed to prevent insurance fraud.

_____

CHAPTER III

describing

To describe means "to picture with words." When you describe, you have to get the reader to picture something in his or her mind: a feeling, an impression, an image. If, for example, you are describing a person, you have to convey your central impression of that person (your doctor's *spotless,* almost *antiseptic* appearance, your banker's *rigid, humorless* face). If you are describing a place, you have to convey a mood, an atmosphere (the *cold, impersonal* unemployment office, your grandmother's *warm, cozy* kitchen). The way you interpret what you see will determine your central impression, which in turn becomes the attitude of your thesis statement. For example, one person observing an unemployment office might see only organized chaos, whereas another person observing the same unemployment office might see the quiet desperation on the faces of the unemployed. Your thesis statement, therefore, will not be a factual observation of what you see: it will be an interpretative statement of **how you picture** what you see.

Effective description then makes its point by having the reader see what you see and feel what you feel. You can't do that by just **telling** the reader about something; you must get him to experience, through your words, the sight and sound and feel of what you describe. Good descriptive writing engages the senses: sight, hearing, touch, and sometimes even smell and taste. Your aim in descriptive writing is not just to tell about something but to create in the mind of your reader vivid images that make the scene come alive.

Description as a Help to Other Writing

Although description is one of the four major types of writing (the others are narration, exposition, and persuasion/argumentation), seldom does description stand alone in an entire essay. It is more often written to help convey the meaning of the other types of writing. In narration, for example, description is used to give the setting in which the action takes place. It is also used to make the reader see the characters and understand their actions in the story. Although description seldom stands alone, it is of vital importance in showing both places and people. Through description, you recreate for your reader a sensory experience of a place or of a person which you have already experienced, either in life or in imagination. Your description gives vividness to the story you're telling.

Perhaps you wish to tell about a summer romance at a camp where you worked one summer. You might set the stage with a description like this:

My first morning as a counselor at Camp Tingle began at 6 A.M. with a dip in the lake. Although directly overhead the sky was already bright blue, the high pines that rimmed the lake kept the sun from the round lake's surface. The lake looked almost black and motionless. Only the smallest ripples inched up and fell back on the dark brown sand and rounded pebbles of the beach. It looked primeval, beyond time. Then, suddenly, sixty yelling children rushed from the woodland paths to throw themselves into the lake. The yells changed to screams as the icy, spring-fed water stung their bodies still warm from bed. I followed them more slowly, but they were right. The only bearable way was to jump in. Gasping, but in my best crawl, I crossed the lake and came halfway back again. I rolled over to float a minute before I joined the shouting, splashing children. How beautiful it is, I thought, and with a shiver, how exhilarating.

There you are in a beautiful and exhilarating setting—all ready for a summer love.

In exposition, which is explaining something to your reader, you will also often want to use description to help you. Particularly if you are trying to explain something abstract, it is helpful to show your readers what your abstraction stands for. Simply stated, abstract is the opposite of concrete. If something is abstract, then you can't see it or touch it or smell it or hear it or taste it. In other words, you can't picture it. For example, you can't picture loyalty, but you can picture the old hound trudging after the town drunk. Thus, through description, the abstract becomes concrete. Suppose, for a psychology class, you are writing a paper about the problems of the elderly. You decide to narrow it to the problem of the loneliness of old people. You obviously can't just say, "Old people are often lonely." However, you might describe your neighbor across the street:

"She just hates to let you go."

Mary Carter is a round little dumpling of a woman, who at 79 is far and away the oldest resident of our neighborhood. Her face is as round as her figure, with a network of fine, soft lines around her mouth, lines that cosmetic ads call "smile" lines or "laugh" lines. Mary does smile a lot, but somehow her blue eyes contradict her mouth. They dart glances to every face, looking for warmth, not just tolerance. Since she doesn't have anyone at home to talk to (except for a parakeet who will probably make the *Guinness Book of Records* for the longest silence in bird-dom) and since the neighbors are too busy to talk to her often, when she does get someone to talk to, she talks a lot. If you meet her on the street, she always stops you. If you try to back away from her, she holds onto your wrist or even a button on your coat. She just hates to let you go.

Of course, she really wants to see her son. He's what she talks about most. He does come about once a month. But every day she hopes he's coming. Every day about 5:30 she peeks around her little house to see that everything's neat. Of course it is. Houses with only one old lady in them stay neat. She usually bakes a few cookies or brownies, for he always likes something sweet. But she's a realist, too; she just bakes a few, for somehow, brownies aren't very good when you're alone.

Now if you multiply Mary Carter by thousands, you have your abstraction. Mary Carter dramatizes your subject, the loneliness of old people. Description, the selection of a few vivid details to help the reader see what you see and feel what you feel, is of vital importance in most writing.

ORGANIZATION

Steps in Writing a Description

Learning how to describe is not difficult if you follow this four-step process:

Step 1. Be observant.

Step 2. Form a central impression (this will be the basis of your thesis sentence).

74

Step 3. Select specific, concrete details to support your thesis statement.

Step 4. Determine how your details will be organized.

OBSERVATION Good description begins with close observation. If you are to get your reader to see what you see and feel what you feel, you must first of all be a keen observer. Nothing will aid your description more than a keen eye for detail.

Note the contrast in the following brief descriptive passages:

VAGUE: Jake was an interesting fellow about twenty years old. He seemed to have a lot of interest in his studies. Anyway, he sort of stared at the professor.

SPECIFIC AND CONCRETE: Jake would stand out in any classroom. His sharp eyes peered from under iron rims, sending darts of eagerness and suspicion directly toward his opponent, the professor.

VAGUE: The garage was kind of sloppy and overcrowded. There didn't seem to be any particular place for anything.

SPECIFIC AND CONCRETE: Above the bench at the rear, nuts and bolts and screws and clamps and sockets overflowed from broken drawers and cubbyholes and overturned boxes. Along both walls, snow tires and bald tires, rusted rims and broken springs and shackles, bicycle parts and battered garden tools spilled out onto a floor black with grease.

VAGUE: The landowner, Mr. Larz, sat in his car with the door open and leisurely relit his cigar. Then he told us to go back to work.

SPECIFIC AND CONCRETE: The landowner, Mr. Larz, sat framed in the open door of his green Chrysler, parked in the shade of a live oak. His stubby legs scarcely reached the dirt, and his heavy paunch strained against a brass zipper that bulged into the sunlight. Wiping a drool of tobacco juice from the corner of his mouth with the back of his hand, he scraped the burnt end of the chewed cigar stump against the door frame. Then he leaned backward to fish a battered Zippo lighter from his front pocket and leaned forward again to light the cigar stub. "Aw right, boys," he said, "let's go back to work."

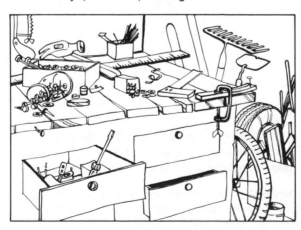

Good description begins with close observation.

75

VAGUE: Mrs. Pelluzzi's garden was neat and orderly. She grew a variety of vegetables and took good care of everything.

SPECIFIC AND CONCRETE: Not one weed was allowed to live in Mrs. Pelluzzi's garden, and every plant was kept in its place. Swiss chard and onions and peppers grew in precisely spaced rows, and flat-headed cabbages, both white and purple, marched across the garden in perfect ranks. Pole beans climbed their neat teepees, the tomatoes pressed against chicken-wire hoops, and even the boisterous zucchini dared to travel just so far and no farther.

As you can see from these examples, it takes more than vague statements to get your reader to visualize what you describe. You've got to make a direct appeal to your reader's senses and emotions, and you do that best through careful observation of specific details.

THE CENTRAL IMPRESSION

Have you ever walked into a room and thought, "How dreary. I don't want to stay here very long"? Or upon entering a room have you immediately thought, "What a happy place this is"? These thoughts are central impressions, the overall atmosphere of a place.

When you meet a person for the first time, you often form an immediate impression:

Boy, is Mark clean-cut; my mother would approve of him.

I think I'll like Pablo; he looks like a regular guy.

Cindy's a real doll, and she's smart, too.

Mimi's a swinger, I'll bet.

These also are central impressions.

You may also remember having seen a quiet farm slumbering in the February cold, and thought, "This is the most peaceful place I've ever seen"— another central impression.

The central impression becomes the attitude of your descriptive essay.

Subject	Attitude
basement den	dreary
mother's kitchen	happy
Mark	clean-cut
Pablo	regular guy
farm	peaceful

Now, having both subject and attitude, you are ready to create your thesis statement. Perhaps you wish to tell your reader why that farm seemed so peaceful to you. You recall the scene in detail and come up with this:

Backed against the protecting hillside and flanked by its sturdy barns, the farmhouse, with its yellow lamplight shining through the dank February twilight, looked like a safe, warm haven.

Your mind constantly gathers details that you perceive through your senses and then generalizes these details into a central impression. Because your mind works so quickly, you often do not consciously know **why** you get the impression you did from the person, place, or thing that you observed. You must think back or reflect on the details that formed that impression or feeling.

SELECTION OF DETAILS

Suppose you want to write an essay about a place that meant a lot to you when you were a child. You remember that when you were twelve your family moved into a big old house you really loved. The very best thing about it was an unused room in the basement which your parents said you could have for your "den."

Filled with twelve-year-old enthusiasm, you pelted down the cellar steps for your first view of **your** den. You still remember the shock of your first impression—that room was so dreary you could have cried. You jot down a list of the details of that dismal room:

dark grey cement floor
bookshelves in bright blue, red, and yellow lining one wall
dirt-streaked windows that let in little light
golden shafts of sunlight piercing the gloom
discarded living room furniture faded into a dull brown
a rickety brown table with legs of unequal length
a dusty glass table lamp with a stained shade that cut out most of the bulb light
a handsome open fireplace clogged with ashes
a crusted, discolored brass floor lamp with a naked bulb
an old threadbare carpet whose pattern could no longer be seen
dust in the corners
well-proportioned window seat with ragged cushions
cobwebs between the ceiling rafters
a dank, musty smell
a smell of mildew or just age coming from the overstuffed couch and chair
stale cigarette smoke
the damp, clammy air
drafts sneaking through the windows
sound of water dripping in the laundry room
creaking in the rafters when someone walked upstairs

Checking over these details, you realize that a few of them don't support the first impression you want to make—that the room was dreary. You go through the list again striking out those details that don't support your central impression of *dreariness*.

dark grey cement floor
~~bookshelves in bright blue, red, and yellow lining one wall~~
dirt-streaked windows that let in little light
~~golden shafts of sunlight piercing the gloom~~
discarded living room furniture faded into a dull brown
a rickety brown table with legs of unequal length
a dusty glass table lamp with a stained shade that cut out most of the bulb light

a handsome open fireplace clogged with ashes
a crusted, discolored brass floor lamp with a naked bulb
an old threadbare carpet whose pattern could no longer be seen
dust in the corners
well-proportioned window seat with ragged cushions
cobwebs between the ceiling rafters
a dank, musty smell
a smell of mildew or just age coming from the overstuffed couch and chair
stale cigarette smoke
the damp, clammy air
drafts sneaking through the windows
sound of water dripping in the laundry room
creaking in the rafters when someone walked upstairs

The description of your first impression might be this:

> Although it soon became the best loved room of my childhood, all I felt when I first saw my basement den was disappointment because it was so dreary. In the little light that struggled through the dirt-streaked windows, the dark grey cement floor seemed to disappear in the dusty corners. The unpainted cement block walls faded away in that dim light. I smelled their clammy dankness rather than saw them. The blackened crossbeams of the ceiling made a grid draped with strings and shreds of cobwebs. The dampness was emphasized by the drip, drip, drip of the faucets in the laundry room. My first thought was that this would make a better den for a bear than a kid.

You might go on to another paragraph beginning:

> But if the room itself was depressing, the furniture was even worse.

You would then go on to support the central impression in that topic sentence. These two paragraphs would act as an introduction to the main section of your essay: the appearance of the loved den *after* you got rid of the dreariness. You would have two descriptions, a "before" and an "after" description.

Writing description is not difficult. Actually your brain has sifted and selected details and formed a central impression without your consciously doing anything. To write a good description, you need only to recall the central impression, then go back to the source of the impression and find the details that inspired it.

For example, suppose you were describing the drill instructor you had in the Marines. You might begin with just a list of physical characteristics, a strictly literal, matter-of-fact description:

> My drill instructor in the Marines was a short, husky man, about five feet, six inches tall, weighing about 200 pounds. He had a big head and a wide neck, and his short legs seemed out of proportion to the rest of his body. He had dark brown eyes and short-cropped hair and a number of wrinkles in his forehead. . . .

So far your reader has no central impression of your drill instructor. He can't form a clear image in his mind. Besides, he is probably so bored that he has lost all interest in reading the rest of your paper. If, on the other hand, you had begun your paper by saying,

"My drill instructor in the Marines always reminded me of a bulldog," then your reader would have a clear picture in his mind. Your descriptive details would mean something. Read the following details and see how they gradually add up to the central impression:

He was a sawed-off, husky-looking guy with an abnormally short pair of legs supporting a five-foot, six-inch, 200-pound frame.

He had an oversized head and a neck so wide that his head seemed to be sitting directly on his shoulders. The only time I noticed his neck was during a fit of rage when his veins bulged out so far, I thought that they were going to burst.

The first time I looked at him, my eyes immediately focused on his vicious-looking face.

The deep, leathery creases in his forehead hung down over his cold, dark eyes in such a way that it would have been physically impossible for him to change his ferocious countenance.

His pudgy, flattened nose seemed perfectly suited to the rest of his bulldog face.

He wore a permanent scowl. His mouth drooped so low that his sagging jowls scraped his collar.

He could absolutely terrorize his men by simply looking them straight in the eye and snarling. All they could see was a savage bulldog on the verge of attack. Even the short bristly hairs on his head stood at attention when he barked out his commands.

Now the physical characteristics of the drill instructor mean something because each of them helps to create the picture of a bulldog. Instead of an unrelated list of physical features, you now have a coherent group of details leading to a specific central impression. Notice that the image of the bulldog was formed not just by what you saw, but also by what you heard and what you felt. For example, you **heard** the drill instructor *snarling* and *barking* out his commands, and you **felt** the *leathery* creases in his forehead along with his *bristly* hair and his *cold,* dark eyes. By observing what you hear, feel, and smell, as well as what you see, you will make your descriptions clearer and more interesting.

Sometimes writers try to improve their descriptions by adding modifiers (mostly adjectives) to their details, but adding modifiers without providing the reader with a clear central impression will not give you a good description. You will still have nothing but a list of meaningless details. For example, suppose your descriptive essay began like this:

My drill instructor was a short, squatty, sawed-off looking guy with a huge, oversized head and a broad, wide neck. He had cold, dark chocolate-brown eyes and a wide, flattened, pudgy, scrunched up nose.

You have more modifiers, but you still don't have a central impression of the drill instructor—not until the details are related to the image of a bulldog.

ORGANIZA-TION OF DETAILS

Once you have determined your central impression, you need to choose some definite principle of organizing your details. Then stick to it. Often, the best principle is that of visual order, the pattern that the eye would naturally follow. In describing a person, you might go from head to foot, or vice versa. In describing a particular scene, you might describe the details from left to right, from right to left, from near to far, or from far to near. You could, of course, start with a central feature or characteristic and then gradually expand the view to include the surrounding details needed to round out the picture.

Quite often you may need to establish a fixed point from which the object or scene is being observed. Let us say, for example, that you are observing a carnival in the town square from a fourth-floor window. Once having established this point of observation, you must be consistent. Don't suddenly shift from the fourth-floor vantage point to a ground-level view. You simply do not shift the point of view without a good reason. In an extended description, of course, you may have good reason to view the same object or scene from different points of view at different times. The important thing is that you take your reader with you by indicating clearly these shifts in point of view.

If, for example, you were describing that "dreary" basement room, you would need to tell the readers where each piece of furniture sits and where the windows are, if they are to get a clear picture of the room. You have your choice as to where to start, but once you do so, you must keep to that direction so that the readers can follow you.

In the following descriptive passage note how the girl is described from a fixed point as she moves toward the observer.

If you see Linda walking toward you, you're apt to think she's taller than she is, for she is fine-boned and beautifully proportioned. As she moves toward you with grace, what strikes you most, perhaps, is her perfect naturalness. Linda doesn't go in for glaring dress or makeup, and no single feature of face or body

Josephine and Linda

strikes you as being extravagant. She wears no fancy hairdo or gaudy jewelry; instead, she radiates sunshine and health. Up close, it's the sparkle in her eyes and the smile from within that captivates you.

Although successful descriptions must be lively, it may at first seem difficult to make them so because there is little or no movement throughout the essay. But you can make your description come alive by using specific and concrete words.

Don't be content to write "Josephine was fat, and as she walked toward me I could see how fat she was." Although the image is quite clear to you as the writer (because you remember Josephine), the reader has only a foggy notion of her appearance. Instead, **describe:** "Josephine was only five feet, two inches, but she weighed over 230 pounds, and as she lumbered toward me, I could see the heavy jowls, the double chin, and the bulges in her dress where rolls of flesh strained against the cloth." Now your reader gets the picture.

Not only must your details be organized and lively, but they must also be unified. Choose only details that point to your central impression. Rule out all irrelevant or contradictory details. Suppose that your thesis sentence says "Willi Hipple is an **utterly grotesque** little man." You would not then go on to describe him as having a strong, straight frame and finely chiseled features. If you say that "Lake Louise is a **jewel in a wilderness setting**," then going on to describe discarded beer cans floating in an oil slick would be totally inconsistent.

Tone is an important element in descriptive writing also. Essentially, tone is the result of the way in which you as a writer view your subject and your reader. In general, your reader is more likely to respond favorably to an honest expression of your feelings and observations. That doesn't mean that your writing should be rough or careless just to keep its naturalness; in fact, you need to give a good deal of thought and care to maintaining the right tone as you revise and polish your work. But the tone should be clearly established in the introduction and maintained throughout the essay. A consistent tone provides a strong unifying element in both narrative and descriptive writing.

Introduction

As for overall pattern of organization, your descriptive essay will have the same beginning, middle, and end as your previous essays. Your introduction should serve to capture your reader's interest and lead up to your **thesis sentence.** Your thesis statement should clearly establish the **central impression**—the controlling idea to which everything else in the essay should relate.

Suppose you have just come back from a trip to Vienna and you want to convey your central impression of those magical two weeks. You might write something like this:

> Franz Joseph's Elevator
> For years I had wanted to go to Vienna. As the song says, Vienna was the city of my dreams. But when I finally got there, I was so excited I stumbled on the train steps and sprained my ankle. So, my sightseeing started on crutches. The first night I went to the opera, where a kindhearted usher, taking pity on me for my third balcony seat, said, "We do have an elevator; it's very special, but I'll take you up in it." I was grateful until I saw the elevator. Then I was ecstatic. That elevator had been the Emperor Franz Joseph's. And I was riding in it. That elevator came to stand for all Vienna to me. It was spacious and well-proportioned, but, above all, I remember the colors: scarlet, and white, and gold—now that I look back, the symbol of Vienna.

Your subject is Vienna. Your controlling idea is that the elevator with its elegant scarlet, white, and gold came to symbolize the beauty of Vienna.

Body

The body of your essay must provide the specific details to support your central impression. Frequently, each paragraph in the body will deal with one specific aspect of your subject. The important thing is that all contribute to the one central impression.

One distinction which you must keep clearly in mind is the difference between **telling about** and **showing.** General statements just tell about; if you are to show, you must use concrete details that create an image in the mind of the reader. The heart and soul of good descriptive writing is showing. The difference between telling and showing, illustrated throughout this chapter, is crucial in developing a good description.

General Statements (Telling About)	*Concrete Details (Showing)*
It was a long twisting road with high trees on each side. At the bottom of a long hill, there was a small river with a cement bridge over it. The square cement sides of the bridge made the road too narrow for two cars to pass.	Winding through tall birches and poplars, the mottled blacktop snaked its way downhill to the river. At the bottom, a straight stretch of tarmac wedged between blunt and ugly cement abutments on either side of a short bridge that arched across the bubbling river.

Note how the general statements that **tell about** are dull and lifeless. To **show** your reader, you must use vivid, active language. For instance, note the contrast in verbs used in the two passages: *was. . .was. . .made* versus *snaked. . .wedged. . . arched.*

Another important element in developing a good description is **selection,** discussed earlier in the chapter. You could never include every minute detail of a given scene; if you tried to, you'd probably end up with a mass of meaningless details. You miss the whole point of good description if you don't strictly follow the process of selection. You must select only those details that support your central impression and ruthlessly weed out details that do not.

Finally, throughout the body of your essay you must provide a sense of movement which takes your reader with you as you show the scene unfolding. The primary movement is visual; let your eyes and the eyes of your reader scan the picture from far to near, from near to far, from left to right, from head to toe, or from the top of the hill to the bottom. Along the way, you need to provide smooth transition from one paragraph to another. Here, too, the most natural way is visual: "Down along the water's edge, . . . Across the narrow bridge, . . . Up the steep side of the ravine, . . . Looking out from the narrow attic window, . . . From his gleaming shoes to the razor crease in his trousers, . . . Around the smooth oval of her face, . . ."

Conclusion

As a counterpart to the introduction, the conclusion serves to sum up all of the details and reinforce your central impression. Together with the introduction, it provides a frame for your picture.

Carefully note how the details in the body of the following essay support the central impression:

The Old Place
In the back of everyone's mind, I suspect, there is a picture of one particular spot that holds a special meaning. As for me, although maybe the lines of the image have softened and what was there gets blurred with what might have been, I know I'll never forget the old farmhouse where I lived until I was sixteen. Yet whenever I try to picture the old place in my mind today, I experience strangely mixed feelings of delight and melancholy.

The narrow farmhouse, wrapped in brownish Insulbrick, seems to lean toward a steep hillside at the bottom end of a lopsided valley. My earliest memories surround the old house and go in and out through the banging screen door, but the images are all fragmented—just bits and pieces of a thousand things. I remember rusty feathers flying in one long squawk and the swirling red fury of the rooster whose fiery beak drove me screaming to the house. I remember the lamp-post stanchions of the brass bed in the attic when my brother and I used to pull the patchwork quilts up over our ears in winter. I remember the mud flying from the fat black lugs of the rear tires as I first drove the "doodlebug," our homemade tractor. I recall the snow scudding up over the hood of the old Dodge pickup as I bucked through to the main road. Best of all, I remember those country meals we ate at the massive butcher-block table in the kitchen: sizzling fried pork and crisp home-fries, glowing fresh ham riveted with cloves, platters of sleek new potatoes sprinkled with parsley, flecked scones and pancakes

I try to picture the old place.

hot from the iron griddle, with raspberry and strawberry and wild plum preserves. I can hear again the family chatter around the loaded table and see my father lean forward with arms akimbo to carve a haunch of beef.

I recall, too, the mournful soughing of the wind in the pines at night, the dead silence that followed a February snowstorm, the long wait for the first signs of spring, and the bleached gravel road that wound over the hills to the world at large. But the world had its own way of intruding: it kept cutting pieces out of the picture. Hard pressed for cash when my sister went to nursing school, my dad sold off a chunk of hardscrabble pasture, which soon became a gravel pit with dump trucks groveling in and out. Little Star Lake, which gleamed through the tops of the hemlocks down behind the house, was bought by a resort developer and quickly sprouted trailers and squat summer cottages. The old farmhouse itself seemed to lean more heavily toward the hillside and shrink a little farther into the ground. Finally, worn down by years of grinding toil, my mother kept urging my dad to sell out and move to the city.

When the screen door had banged for the final time, my dad handed me the keys, and I drove my folks down the white gravel road that my sister and my brothers had traveled, one by one. Sometimes I think, now, about going back to see the old place. I could drive there in two hours. But I won't. Maybe it is just foolish sentiment, but I want to keep in my mind a picture of the old place, not exactly the way it was but the the way I want it to remain.

Note how specific details and visual images help to convey both a picture and a mood. Note, too, how the observer moves into and then away from the scene. And it is not just a static picture: the screen door bangs, the rooster swirls in furious motion, the mud flies, and the pickup bucks through the snow.

Here is a student essay of description, in which the writer carefully chose his details to convey his sense of fear.

Fear

Fear can take many forms. We all have experienced at least one of them at some time in our lives. There is the fear of height and the fear of death, the fear of closed-in places and the fear of the dark, just to name a few. When I think of fear, I remember a little town in South Carolina called Yemassee, where I first experienced lasting fear.

When we left the train that dark, humid night in December, all we could see was the single dim light that hung on the depot platform. A sickly sweet odor filled the air, and the stillness was deafening. The only thing that moved was the fading lights on the rear of the train. The station was in dire need of repair, the windows and doors were boarded shut, and the whole building shook when anyone moved. There was a feeling of apprehension in the air, and the men milling around and talking only seemed to make it worse. The humidity made our clothes stick to our bodies, but the little drops of sweat were ice cold as they ran down our spines. The longer we waited the less talk there was, and everyone began to wonder why we had been abandoned.

Then it happened. Just as the tension reached its peak, a voice shouted at us, "You girls have five seconds to get on that bus!" Out of nowhere appeared the biggest, most sinister looking man I have ever seen. His Smokey Bear hat was pulled down over his face and hid everything but his mouth, which spewed forth some of the vilest profanity ever heard on this earth. His uniform creases looked as though a person could cut his finger on them, and his brass buckles gleamed. He moved with the grace of a leopard with his muscles bunched as though ready to spring. The man, the depot, and the night seemed to work in perfect harmony to create an almost overpowering feeling of fear.

As the bus started to move away, I looked back at the depot. The drill instructor had disappeared. Silence returned. The dim light swayed in the sultry breeze. Nothing moved on the desolate platform, nor would until the next group of young men came on their way to Parris Island and Marine Corps boot camp.   *Mark Custer*

Pitfalls to Avoid

1. Don't clutter your description with strings of repetitious adjectives. "A long, hot, sultry, dragged-out, stifling day" could better be described as "an endless day of oppressive heat" or "a merciless day of stifling heat."

2. Don't use vague or ambiguous wording in your thesis sentence. For example: "The old house was kind of a queer place" does not create a clear central impression. You would have a better thesis sentence if you said, "The old house was filled with curious remnants of the past," or "In the old house, time seemed to have stopped."

3. Don't try to cover the whole waterfront. Limit the area and focus on a specific subject; then try to work in more revealing detail. Don't try to describe all of Florida. Limit yourself to Disney World. Even then, don't try to describe all of Disney World. Limit yourself to the entrance to Fantasy Land.

4. Don't shift from description to a long recital of your personal reaction. For example: "It was a beautiful old mansion. I couldn't help wondering what my mother would think of it. She always did like those old houses with turrets."

5. Don't jump unexpectedly to a new point of observation. For example: "The great stone mansion loomed beyond the iron gates. From the mountaintop it would look like a toy fortress." Instead, open those iron gates and take your reader with you every step of the way.

6. Don't tack on a nebulous conclusion, such as "So that is what the old place was like. It had its good points and its bad points. I guess I kind of miss it, so I like to think of it once in a while." A conclusion such as that does nothing except drain your essay of whatever vitality it had.

SUGGESTED TOPICS

Write a descriptive essay on one of the following topics.

People

1. Your boss
2. Your best friend
3. Your high school sweetheart
4. Your football coach
5. Your insurance salesman
6. Your local funeral director
7. Your husband or wife
8. Your mother or father
9. Your boyfriend or girlfriend
10. Your son or daughter
11. Your grandmother or grandfather
12. Your brother or sister
13. Your doctor
14. Your dentist
15. Your plumber
16. Your TV repairman
17. Your auto mechanic
18. Your high school principal
19. Your neighbor
20. Your teacher
21. Your pastor
22. Your classmate
23. Your accountant
24. Your teammate
25. Your guru

Places

26. An army barracks
27. An old farm
28. An Indian reservation
29. A funeral parlor
30. A steel mill
31. A school cafeteria
32. A fast food restaurant
33. A hospital delivery room
34. An emergency room
35. An unemployment office
36. A doctor's waiting room
37. An empty football stadium
38. A mental institution
39. A fraternity house
40. A day-care center
41. A kindergarten classroom
42. A playground
43. A tenement house
44. A recording studio
45. A discotheque
46. Your workshop
47. Your grandmother's attic
48. Your bedroom
49. Your kitchen
50. Your back yard

TECHNIQUES OF CLEAR WRITING

Coordination and Subordination

Understanding the difference between coordinate clauses and subordinate clauses will make it easier for you to say exactly what you mean. For example, suppose your mother-in-law, who lives with you and your husband, is doing everything she can to make your life miserable. Although you love your husband, you know that you can't be happy as long as your mother-in-law continues to live with you. You therefore decide to talk to your husband and try to make him understand that you are actually thinking about leaving him. If you began your conversation by saying:

I love you, but I can't stand your mother,

you haven't made your point as clearly as you would if you had said:

describing   Although I love you, I can't stand your mother.

Do you see the difference? In the first sentence, you are giving equal importance to both of your feelings: (1) loving your husband, and (2) loathing your mother-in-law. You can tell that each statement has equal weight because each one is an *independent clause*, a sentence. Therefore, the sentence does not indicate your true feelings: that your negative feelings toward your mother-in-law outweigh the positive feelings toward your husband. "**Although** I love you, I can't stand your mother" does show your emphasis. You have lessened the importance of the first part of the sentence by subordinating it, making it a *dependent clause*. A subordinate or dependent clause cannot stand alone. Its meaning depends on the rest of the sentence. The most important thought will be in the strong clause, the independent one.

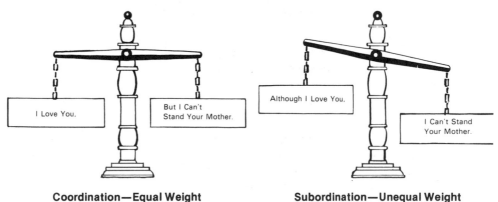

Coordination—Equal Weight   **Subordination—Unequal Weight**

Look at the following sentences:

JANE: Although I hate to cook, I love to give dinner parties.
MARY: Although I love to give dinner parties, I hate to cook.

Who will have dinner parties?

JACK: Even though I love to fish, I have no time for it.
JIM: Even though I have no time for it, I love to fish.

Who will probably go fishing?

BILL: I study a lot because I am a good student.
TONY: I am a good student because I study a lot.

Which makes more sense?

All these examples illustrate the difference between coordination and subordination. When ideas have the same degree of importance, they are *coordinate;* when one idea is less important than the other, then one is *subordinate* to the other. It's easy to remember the difference between **co**ordination and **sub-**

ordination because *co* means equal and *sub* means under or less. Therefore, when you are connecting two clauses of **equal** weight, you connect them with a **co**-ordinate conjunction. When you are connecting a **less important** clause (incomplete thought) to a more important clause (complete thought), then you connect them with a **sub**ordinate conjunction.

Both types of conjunctions are used to show how one part of a sentence relates to another part. Once you know when to use coordinate conjunctions and when to use subordinate conjunctions, you have to make sure that you are using the right ones. Look at each group of conjunctions separately and note the relationship suggested by each individual conjunction:

COORDINATE CONJUNCTIONS

And calls for an additional statement
But calls for a contrast
For calls for a reason
Nor calls for another negative statement
Or calls for an alternative
So calls for an effect
Yet calls for a contrast

SUBORDINATE CONJUNCTIONS

After shows time
Although implies a contrast
As if sets a condition
As long as sets a condition
As soon as shows time
Because gives a reason
Before shows time
Even though implies a contrast
If sets a condition
Since gives a reason
Unless sets a condition
Until shows time
When shows time
Whenever shows time
Wherever shows place
While shows time

Using the right conjunctions is important. If you don't, your sentences won't make much sense. Look at some examples of faulty coordination and faulty subordination.

ILLOGICAL COORDINATION

FAULTY: I love my husband, **and** I can't stand his mother.

IMPROVED: I love my husband, **but** I can't stand his mother.

Although I love my husband, I can't stand his mother.

FAULTY: You hurt my feelings, **yet** I'm going to leave.

IMPROVED: You hurt my feelings, **so** I'm going to leave.

Because you hurt my feelings, I'm going to leave.

ILLOGICAL SUBORDINATION

FAULTY: **While** I spilled coffee on my pants, I cancelled my job interview.

IMPROVED: **After** I spilled coffee on my pants, I cancelled my job interview.

Since I spilled coffee on my pants, I cancelled my job interview.

FAULTY: **Before** you say you love me, I will not marry you.

IMPROVED: **Unless** you say you love me, I will not marry you.

Until you say you love me, I will not marry you.

A NOTE ON PUNCTUATION When two independent clauses are connected with a coordinate conjunction, place a comma **before** the conjunction.

> [*Independent clause*], **but** [*independent clause*].

When you join two independent clauses without a coordinate conjunction, place a semicolon between the clauses.

> [*Independent clause*]; [*independent clause*].

NOTE: The semicolon should be used only when the two ideas are closely related. If they are not, make two sentences.

When a sentence begins with a subordinate clause, place a comma after the clause (as we just did in this sentence).

> [*Dependent clause*], [*independent clause*].

If the subordinate clause comes at the end of the sentence, do **not** insert any punctuation before the clause, as in the example below:

Don't use a comma **if the subordinate clause comes at the end of a sentence.**

EXERCISE IIIa: PUNCTUATION
Correct the punctuation of the following sentences. (Do not add periods or capital letters.)

1. Howard Cosell is hated by many he has made "Monday Night Football" successful.
2. I love driving alone because it gives me time to think.
3. Because the Steelers have won four Super Bowls they have to be considered the "Team of the Seventies."
4. I have many favorite activities among them are seeing plays and playing golf.

5. Although I hate most dogs, I love my neighbor's wolfhound.

6. Television weather forecasters are often wrong, but they never apologize for their mistakes and rarely admit them.

7. Of all the cities I've visited in the United States, I like San Francisco the best.

8. John McEnroe is an emotional tennis player; he lets the whole audience know how he feels.

9. Wishing is good, but working is better.

10. John's father scares me sometimes, so I seldom go to his house.

11. When he called the office, the manager was out; his secretary said she had no idea when he would return.

12. The novel is not highly emotional; it does not move us to tears; it awakens no great sense of awe or pity for the suffering of the human heart.

13. Whereas compounding establishes the equality of ideas, subordination indicates that one idea should receive less emphasis than another; it relegates the secondary idea to a less important position.

14. Since its structure is loose to begin with, if we are to understand *Winesburg* we must first grasp the significance of the prologue.

15. Although he had cheated scores of people, the confidence man was never brought to trial for those he had cheated were too ashamed to admit that they had been victimized through their own greed.

EXERCISE IIIb: FAULTY COORDINATION
The following sentences are examples of faulty coordination. Improve each sentence by inserting a better coordinate conjunction or replacing the coordinate conjunction with a subordinate conjunction to put the less important idea in a subordinate clause.

1. I like the new Coke commercial, ~~and~~ *because* it portrays Mean Joe Green as a nice guy.

2. Marge's husband is a real gutless wonder, ~~but~~ *unfortunately* his son is becoming just like him.

3. I saw the Chief Crazy Horse memorial, ~~and~~ I never realized what a massive monument it was.

4. It takes five hours to digest food completely, ~~but~~ *so* wait at least one hour before you go swimming.

5. *Because* Gregory Peck and Sir Laurence Olivier are two of my favorite actors, ~~and~~ *so* I always watch their movies.

6. Mike said that his hangover was so bad that his hair hurt, ~~and~~ *yet* he kept on drinking.

7. *Although* Larry doesn't like to be interrupted during "60 Minutes," ~~and~~ *so* I called him at 7:15 on Sunday night.

8. *Since* Tom watches Johnny Carson every night, ~~but~~ *and* he has never missed one of his monologues.

9. *When* We heard that our favorite police sergeant was caught smoking marijuana, ~~and~~ we couldn't stop laughing.

10. The average person has 100,000 to 150,000 dreams in a lifetime, ~~and~~ *But* I can't remember any of mine.

90

Relative Pronouns

Relative pronouns offer another way of clarifying your meaning through good subordination. These pronouns (*that, who,* and *which*) used as subjects of dependent clauses enable you to state your main point in the independent clause and less important relationships in dependent constructions.

For instance, suppose you had written this: "Stephen Henderson was a well-known singer. He married my aunt." Your reader would not know which idea you considered more important. But if you wrote, "Stephen Henderson, who was a well-known singer, married my aunt," you would have made it clear the marriage is what you are more interested in. Or, if you reversed it and wrote, "Stephen Henderson, who married my aunt, was a well-known singer," it would be clear that you are emphasizing him as a singer. You want to make sure your reader knows where you are putting your emphasis.

NOTE: It is usually preferable when writing about people to use *who*, rather than *that* or *which*.

EXERCISE IIIc: COMBINING SENTENCES: COORDINATION

In the following sets of sentences, relationships are not made clear. Combine each set, using *who, whom, that,* or *which* to establish a main idea and a dependent one.

1. He bought a new car. It had been custom-built.

   He bought a new car which had been custom built.

2. This book is a best seller. It represents twelve years of research.

   This book is a best seller that represents

3. Americans make up most of the slang in the English language. Americans seem to enjoy the liveliness of slang.

   Americans, who seem to enjoy the liveliness of sla...make

4. The speaker failed to appear. We had asked him to speak at our club dinner.

   The speaker, whom we asked ... failed.

5. Mr. Johnson built the houses to be sold. He was a real estate speculator.

   Mr. Johnson, who was a r.e.s., built the

6. The movie was only partly successful. It was far too long-winded.

   The movie which was fo... was only...

7. The orchestra was playing a waltz. Usually it played rock.

   The orchestra which usually played ... was

8. The statistics had been collected over several months. They were more depressing than we had expected.

   Stats that had ... were

91

9. The Chamber of Commerce tried to support all activities for tourists. They were enthusiastic about the proposed convention hall.

_____

10. This is the dog. He worried the cat. The cat killed the rat. The rat ate the malt. The malt lay in the house that Jack built.

_____

WORD POWER

Eliminating Deadwood and Redundancies

One reason for the lack of liveliness and vitality in the writing of beginners is excess verbiage. Students use too many words to express their ideas. They repeat; they use ten words where two would do. There are various reasons for these types of errors:

1. A fear that the reader will not understand their first explanation.
2. A lack of vocabulary (and an aversion to searching for the exact word).
3. A desire to reach a specified number of words assigned by the instructor.
4. A lack of knowledge of the subject (and an aversion to searching for more information).
5. A lack of careful editing and rewriting.

Actually, the last item is the most important for you to remember. It doesn't really matter how many excess words you have in your first draft; nobody sees that. You should go over your essays carefully, eliminating all unnecessary words and phrases.

You can eliminate unnecessary words many ways. Here are a few:

1. Use a precise word rather than a string of modifiers:

   The large white dog with black spots [7 words]
   The Dalmatian [2 words]

   The second-year physical science course [6 words]
   Physics II [2 words]

2. Reduce a clause to a phrase whenever possible:

   The house which was on the corner [7 words]
   The house on the corner [5 words]

   Or reduce a phrase to a word:

   The corner house [3 words]

Or, if the information is unnecessary for your purpose, leave it out altogether:

   The house [2 words]

3. Avoid phrases that merely add words, not meaning:

Due to the fact that [5 words]
Because [1 word]

In the event that [4 words]
If [1 word]

In view of the fact that [6 words]
Since [1 word]

4. Don't be overly timid. Call a drunk a drunk:

In my opinion, it seems to me that my teacher was behaving in a very odd manner last Thursday, and most people would have assumed, as I did, that he was under the influence of alcohol. [36 words]

Last Thursday my teacher was drunk. [6 words]

5. Don't be repetitious or redundant:

Young juveniles
Youths

7 A.M. in the morning
7 A.M.

He will apply for and try to get a job in accounting.
He will apply for an accounting job.

6. Avoid negatives where possible.

Our cafeteria does not serve good food. [7 words]
Our cafeteria serves poor food. [5 words]

7. Use the active voice.

The test was taken by him. [6 words]
He took the test. [4 words]

EXERCISE IIId: CONCISENESS
Revise each of the following sentences to eliminate excess words.

1. The bed was made by Angela.

   Angela made the bed.

2. She did not have any use for a bicycle.

   She couldn't use a bicycle.

3. The girl who was a blonde won most of the awards in swimming.

   The blonde girl won most of the swim award

4. It seemed to me that the noodles that they served were a bit gummy and stuck together.

   The noodles they served were gummy & stuck together

5. The radio that they had in the car that they used to talk to other drivers with was broken.

   The CB radio in the car was broken

6. The cigarette ash tray was filled and overflowing with butts and ashes.

The ash tray was overflowing with butts & ashes.

7. Due to the fact that I was up all night, I was tired by noon.

I was up all night; I was tired by noon.

8. The lamp which sits on a table in my bedroom is so dim that I can't use it to read with.

The lamp in my room is to dim to read with.

9. The book that I read by Mark Twain called *The Mysterious Stranger* is fascinating.

Mark Twain's, "The Mysterious Stranger" is fasc.

10. My mother was not happy over the fact that I came home late.

My mom wasn't happy that I came home late.

EXERCISE IIIe: CONCISENESS

The following sentences are wordy. Revise them to eliminate redundancies and deadwood.

1. In the event that you decide to change your plans, will you please be so kind as to send me a telegram, to that effect.

_____

2. It was told to me that the president could not always be trusted and did not keep all the promises which he had made. *his*

_____

3. As a rule, in a course that runs in the first semester of any subject you are studying, you usually learn only the basic fundamentals. *a first semester course*

_____

4. It was the consensus of opinion that the government would reduce taxes lower, but instead the taxes have increased steadily upward. *agreed*

_____

5. The life and works of William Faulkner are told about in his biography that was written by John H. Shaver as recently as 1977.

_____

6. Henry Adams is a good writer because he uses words well and chooses the right one for the right place.

_____

7. An automobile driver who drinks while he is driving is really and truly no better than a murderer who runs around all over the place killing people.

_____

8. In considering this aspect of the situation, we must take into consideration that many modern people do not think this way any longer in this day and age.

_____

9. I would like to share with you another piece of information about the possible potential decrease in our earnings.

_____

10. Some of the popular music that is listened to by many people in concerts, on records, and on television seems to revert back to music of the decade of the thirties, I think.

_____

Using Concrete Words

To make your reader see what you see and what you feel, you have to use **concrete** words. Abstract words simply convey information or indicate a general feeling, but concrete words appeal directly to the senses. By engaging the reader's sense of sight, sound, touch, taste, or smell, concrete words enable him or her to picture the scene you describe and relive the experience you relate.

Compare the following pairs of statements:

VAGUE AND ABSTRACT: The foundry was a dirty place to work.

CONCRETE: The black grime of the foundry grated its way into every pore, and six showers couldn't get the grit out of your scalp and eyebrows or the creases of your midriff.

VAGUE AND ABSTRACT: The man in front of the carnival tent had a harsh voice.

CONCRETE: The carnival barker at the girlie show ground out his spiel in a gravel voice.

VAGUE AND ABSTRACT: Tebetha, Josephine's sister, was overweight and inept.

CONCRETE: Truck tires of fat blobbed at every step, and Josephine's sister, Tebetha, seemed to be constantly tripping over her own feet or bashing her head on car doors.

Being concrete is different from being specific. You can be specific in one or two words: Harvard, Chicago, Cleveland Browns, ten feet. However, to be concrete, you must create or recreate an image or a sound or a taste or a feeling or a smell. To do this, you put the situation in time or space, which takes more than a few words.

A tree is general. *A maple tree* is specific. If you want to be concrete, though, you must show the tree in some place or time setting. "I watch the maple tree beneath my window dealing out its yellow leaves to the passing breeze." This sentence clearly indicates place, *beneath my window*, and time, *autumn*. Or "The lone maple tree, its branches covered with ice, glistened in the moonlight." The sentence just as clearly indicates time: *night* and *winter*.

Thus, being concrete appeals to the senses as well as to the intellect. You **show** the reader, not just tell him. If you write, "When I had to give my first speech, I was terrified," you are appealing to the reader's intellect, her memory, perhaps of herself in a similar situation. You are being concrete if you write: "When the emcee introduced me, I felt I couldn't get up; my legs didn't seem to be a part of my body. My mouth and lips were dry, but the palms of my hands were so wet that the note-cards they held were limp and the writing on them smeared. I felt a prickling sensation at the back of my head, and I wondered if my hair were standing on end."

Show the reader how nervous you were.

Here are more examples:

GENERAL	SPECIFIC	CONCRETE
a dog	a beagle puppy	A beagle puppy tripping over his own feet as he runs to greet us
sounds	sounds of food cooking	the sizzling of the bacon, the plop-plop of coffee perking
prison	Alcatraz	the high stone walls atop the barren rock in the middle of the bay
dirt	grit	the grit crackling under our shoes on the old wooden porch
cold air	50° below zero air	the bitter air that froze the spittle on our lips and frosted our eyebrows and stiffened our hair
football player	Lynn Swann	Lynn Swann pirouetting into the air to catch a pass

A writer chooses concrete and specific words to stimulate the reader to visualize. If the writer's choice of words is concrete, most readers will automatically respond with an image. Even commonplace descriptions evoke some sensory experience:

The full moon in a cloudless sky [recreates sight]
The sting of the icy shower [recreates touch]
The squeak of the chalk on the blackboard [recreates sound]
Gingerbread baking [recreates smell]
The first sip of a cold beer [recreates taste]

The sense of motion can be conveyed by a verb: One rabbit *escaped;* another was *seized* in the hound's gaping jaws.

EXERCISE IIIf: CONCRETE WORDS
Revise the following sentences to replace the vague and abstract terms with concrete wording. (Use your dictionary, your thesaurus, and your imagination.)

1. The new immigrants were loyal citizens.

_____

2. The bartender, "Learned Hand" Schlepp, was not an intellectual.

_____

3. The old Rolls-Royce had an opulent interior.

_____

4. Percy Grime was a careless workman.

_____

5. Rita Sandolowsky came from a prosperous family.

_____

6. After the factory closed, Mill River became a depressed area.

_____

7. The new teacher is an asset.

_____

8. Jane McDowell is a nice woman.

_____

9. *One Flew Over the Cuckoo's Nest* is an interesting book.

_____

10. There is no way I can say how I feel.

_____

CHAPTER IV

explaining with examples

Do you realize that you never could have made it through school without the aid of examples? Suppose your fourth-grade teacher had taught you how to divide by simply giving you a definition of division and then expected you to understand it. How would you ever understand if you never saw any examples of division problems? If the only thing you knew was that "division is the operation of determining how many times one quantity is contained in another," how far do you think you would have gotten on your next test when you saw $24 \div 6$? You wouldn't have known what to do. That's why examples are indispensable in learning. It's almost impossible for you to understand general concepts until you are given specific examples. Chapters 1–3 of this book contain over 100 specific examples that were included to help you understand the concepts. General terms such as *central impression* or *consistent point of view* or *subordination* should have become clearer to you after you saw these concepts illustrated with examples.

Examples are used in all fields. For instance, the psychologist and the sociologist use the case study to show the reader such things as the psychotic personality or the environment of the ghetto child. In building the case study of Bob P., the psychologist might include:

The paranoid personality sees enemies everywhere. For example, Bob thinks the clerk at the supermarket is watching him suspiciously. He feels she suspects him of shoplifting.

In explaining the ghetto, the sociologist might include:

The ghetto child lives in a prison. For example, Paco has never been more than five blocks from his home. There are no visible walls, but the invisible ones are there. He said that he feels he is different when he leaves his own "turf."

In the physical sciences the chemist and physicist will cite examples of their own experiments and experiments of others to prove their hypotheses. Sportswriters use examples to illustrate their statements. Notice that examples can serve both of these purposes; they can **illustrate** or **prove.** If the chemist reports the findings of several different scientists in different areas and at different times and they got the same results from a given experiment, he has proved a point. Sportswriters, on the other hand, generally are working with theses that cannot be proved:

Steve Carlson is the best pitcher in baseball.
Joe Louis was the world's greatest heavyweight boxer.
The New York Rangers are the toughest team in hockey.

Nothing could **prove** these statements, but they could be illustrated or supported by examples.

Really, it is hard to think of a subject that examples will not clarify. They can make the difficult easier to understand; they can make the abstract concrete; they can make the academic personal.

Explaining through examples is one of the most effective ways to support your controlling idea. The technique of explaining with examples is closely related to narration. The difference is that narration expands one example into a full story, whereas in explaining with examples you use several brief examples. Like telling a story, giving examples seems to be a natural way of proving your point to someone else because that is usually the way you arrive at your own conclusion. Through certain experiences you have had or events you have witnessed, you form a generalization. The generalization becomes your thesis sentence, the abstract statement that unifies your essay. When you want to prove your generalization to others, show them the examples that led to your conclusion.

Because using examples is one of the most natural and effective ways of proving your point, you use it every day in speaking with your friends.

YOU SAY: Boy, I had a lousy day.
FRIEND: How's that?
YOU: Well, first of all, I got up late and didn't have time for breakfast. I decided to pick up something at McDonald's and eat it in the car on the way to school. I got an Egg McMuffin, and when I took my first bite, the egg

Off to a bad start!

slipped out and slid down my sweater. Now I have egg stains on my new sweater.

FRIEND: That is a bad start.

YOU: That's not all. When I got to my first class—late, of course—I found out the teacher was giving a pop quiz. I flunked it, I'm sure, because for the first time all semester I didn't do the homework.

FRIEND: Wow!

YOU: That's not the worst of it. When I saw my girl, she really snubbed me. I had forgotten that I was supposed to pick her up this morning.

FRIEND: Wow! You did have a bad day.

The three little episodes you related to your friend are examples, and you proved your point by using them.

ORGANIZATION

What Makes Examples Good

To be good, the examples that you choose must be:

1. Specific
2. Relevant
3. Typical

SPECIFIC EXAMPLES   As in all good writing, your details, in this case your examples, must be specific. General statements usually do not prove your point. **For example** (notice how often *for example* comes up), if you were trying to prove that you had "a lousy day," the following examples wouldn't work very well because they are too general to be interesting:

100

I had a lousy breakfast
I flunked a quiz.
I forgot my girl.

Suppose you were writing a paper about men who changed history but whose names are largely forgotten. As examples, you might cite the following individuals:

William Morton, the man who introduced the use of anesthesia in surgery
Edward Muybridge, the father of motion pictures
Howard Aiken, the man who designed the first computer

You could then expand each example in a paragraph and give your reader more details about each man's achievements. However, if you developed your thesis by referring to these examples

A dentist from Massachusetts
An amateur photographer from California
A graduate student from Harvard

you would not be providing your reader with good illustrations. Each one is too general. You have to be more specific if you want your readers to understand you.

**RELEVANT
EXAMPLES**

In addition to being specific, your examples must also be relevant; that is, they must pertain precisely to your controlling idea. If you say "Car buyers need to be alert to the deceptive practices employed by some dealers," then specific examples of those "deceptive practices" would help your reader to understand exactly what you mean. If, however, you proceeded to cite examples of the tricks that people play when they go to trade in their cars, those examples would not provide relevant support.

If, **for example,** in your paper about some of the most important yet least known men in history, you cited Jesus Christ, Albert Einstein, and Adolf Hitler, you would not be giving your reader good examples. They would be specific, but they would not be relevant. These three men certainly changed people's lives, but they are not exactly forgotten names in history. These examples deal with the topic in general (important persons in history), but they do not pertain to your specific comment on that topic—that the names of some of the most influential figures in history are practically unknown.

Here is a paragraph that makes use of relevant examples:

The work of great writers, which we often accept as being natural and spontaneous, is more often, in fact, the result of painstaking rewriting and revision. Ernest Hemingway, for example, is said to have rewritten the final chapter of *Farewell to Arms* more than forty times, and portions of *The Old Man and the Sea* were rewritten at least thirty times. Walt Whitman wrote forty versions of the opening line of "Out of the Cradle Endlessly Rocking," and the poet Dylan Thomas rewrote some of his lines as many as seventy times before his work was published. The list of examples could go on and on; writers by the score have spent years in rewriting and revising their work before it ever got published. Gustave Flaubert, the author of *Madame Bovary,* once wrote to George Sand: "You have no notion what it is to sit out an entire day with your head between your hands beating your unfortunate brain for a word."

**TYPICAL
EXAMPLES**

As well as being specific and relevant, good examples are typical. You cannot use an extraordinary circumstance to **prove** a point. If your examples are to provide effective support, they must be typical.

If you say "I don't like history," you cannot support your point by using an atypical example such as

We had a substitute teacher in history today, and he just droned on and on about the Wars of the Roses, and I didn't understand a thing he said.

This would **not** be an example of the regular history class because usually you don't have a substitute teacher.

Or, if you say "It's easy to make good grades at this school," an example such as this would **not** do:

My oldest brother, who has an I.Q. of 160, made straight *A's* his freshman year here.

Your brother would not be an example of a typical student, even at Harvard.

You are not likely to convince an intelligent reader that most great writers were drug addicts by citing the fact that Edgar Allan Poe took laudanum and that Thomas DeQuincey was an opium eater. And only a naive reader would believe that Iranians are all camel drivers or goat herders, no matter how many examples of primitive tribesmen you present. Intelligent readers would recognize that the examples you offer are simply not typical.

Make sure that all your examples are specific, relevant, and typical.

Introduction

In your introduction, you must arouse the reader's interest and set the tone for the essay. To arouse interest, you might use a relevant incident, startling statistics, or any of the devices mentioned earlier. If your paper is humorous, the tone of your introduction should be light; if your essay is objective and factual, then the introduction should set that kind of tone for the reader.

Suppose that you have been thinking about your own future and looking into job opportunities in various parts of the country. The introductory paragraph of an essay on this topic might explain that your investigation found that the states in the South and Southwest offer excellent job opportunities because of their rapid growth in recent years. You would end your first paragraph with your thesis sentence, which might be something like this: "The Sunbelt continues to offer excellent job opportunities."

Body

You might begin developing your essay with an outline of your main points:

1. In recent years there has been a definite shift in population toward the South and West.
2. The South and Southwest have enjoyed rapid growth and diversification of industry.
3. The job rate has grown rapidly in many Sunbelt cities.

Each of these main points in turn could be made the topic sentence of a body paragraph and could be developed with a series of specific examples. In developing the third point, for instance, you might cite examples of the job growth in such cities as Greenville and Spartanburg, South Carolina; Fort Lauderdale, Tampa, and St. Petersburg, Florida; Austin, Houston, and El Paso, Texas.

To make your essay successful, of course, you would need specific information to support each of your main points. That doesn't mean that you would have to prove that every state and city in the Sunbelt is enjoying phenomenal growth, but you would need enough specific examples in each paragraph to illustrate and support your main point.

Conclusion

An effective essay doesn't just end abruptly with the final example. You don't want to break off as though you had a plane to catch. Although, as Chapter I pointed out, there are a number of ways of effectively concluding an essay, what you usually need is a conclusion that pulls together the main ideas in the body of the essay and points up the significance of the specific examples you have presented.

Here is one possible conclusion for the essay on job opportunities in the Sunbelt:

Not every young man or woman, of course, wants to rush off in search of a job in the Sunbelt, but it might be wise to consider the expanded opportunities that have followed the shift in population toward the South and Southwest. All indications point toward continued growth throughout the Sunbelt area, and that is something you might want to take into consideration in planning your own future.

The Ordering of Examples: Climactic Order

In an essay making use of examples, the details that make up the body are the examples you have selected. Like all selections of details, your chosen examples must be presented in some logical and consistent order. As the author, you decide what that order is. However, just as chronological order is most effective for narrative, and spatial order is most effective for description, climactic order usually works best for examples. In climactic order, you start with the example that is least important and work up to a final example, saving for last the example that you think is the most important.

103

Sometimes two principles of order are at work. In the conversation of the boy who had a bad day, the examples followed both a time order and a climactic order. You recall that he began with dropping his Egg McMuffin, went on to flunk a quiz, and ended up quarreling with his girl. This is a sequence in time, of course, but there is a feeling that his quarrel with his girl looms larger than his earlier problems. Indeed, because climactic order is so conventional, readers assume the thing placed last is meant to be understood as the most important.

In the following student paragraph, notice how the writer has moved in an orderly fashion from the disadvantages that bother her least, through those that are increasingly bothersome, to her ultimate frustration of the good-night kiss:

A short stature is a disadvantage to a teenage girl. She often finds that she has been mistaken for a child; consequently, she receives menus reserved for loyal customers age twelve and under, is refused the right to ride elaborate amusement rides without a parent or guardian, and, to the shocked embarrassment of her date, is admitted to theaters at children's rates. Another disadvantage of being a short teen turns up during clothes shopping. Although the length and fit of a preadolescent style may suit her build, the Junior Petite selection is more appealing to her fashion sense. Thus, the short teen spends endless hours in search of a perfect fit only to settle for a garment in need of hemming and other minor repairs. Another disadvantage bedevils the short teen—the need for short dates. The availability of short males is limited; therefore, the short girl is left to cope with an array of tall, ungainly dates. These dates are often trouble! For example, if the couple want to go to a disco, the girl, to increase her height, usually dons high-heeled shoes. Since many of these styles were never intended for the disco scene, they are soon kicked off, leaving the situation worse than before. Another problem arises when the couple slow dances. The girl finds herself making eye contact with her partner's stomach and trying, in vain, to wrap her arms around his neck. The traditional good-night kiss also poses a problem for the mismatched couple. After contorting his long frame into various uncomfortable positions,

It's tough to be short.

the tall male resorts either to lifting his short date a few inches off the ground or stepping down from the porch to kiss his short date while she stands above him. For a short teenage girl, height's a hindrance! *Jackie Kunzmann*

Examples as a Help to Other Writing

Examples, as you have seen, are an end in themselves. If chosen well, they are an excellent way to explain. In addition, they can be a tremendous help in other, more complex, types of writing. In defining, **for example,** examples are a frequent help. If you look back to the beginning of this chapter, you will see examples used in this way to help in the definition of mathematical division.

Suppose you want to write an essay about odd characters you have known. You narrow your subject to your Uncle Joe. (You remember Uncle Joe. He's the one in Chapter II with the generous will.) Since, among other things, you want to talk about Uncle Joe's collection of limericks, you decide to define a limerick. A limerick, your handbook says, is a "popular type of jingle verse dealing with the peculiarities of people and written in five lines. The first, second, and fifth lines, which have three metrical feet, rhyme. The second and fourth lines, each with two metrical feet, also rhyme."

There's the definition, but you don't find it much help except for that bit about peculiarities, which is Uncle Joe all right. If you're going to get the idea across, you'll have to give an example of a limerick. You find that even the hand-book uses an example by Edward Lear to clarify its definition.

> There was an Old Man of the Dee,
> Who was sadly annoyed by a Flea;
> When he said, "I will scratch it!"
> They gave him a hatchet
> Which grieved that Old Man of the Dee.

With an example, the definition of the limerick is much clearer. However, this example doesn't give the sense of Uncle Joe's rather gamey sense of humor. How, then, will you convey that? You choose another example, this time explaining that it shows the bawdy humor that characterizes most limericks and pleases Uncle Joe. (What limerick would you use?)

Regardless of your subject or the length of the essay, one of the key methods of development is through the use of examples. No matter what the main pattern of development may be, you may need examples to make your ideas clear and show your reader what you mean.

Here is an essay by a student supporting his amusing and unconventional thesis with examples. This is a use of examples for their own sake.

Man's Best Friend?

These days, large amounts of money are spent on dog training. Obedience schools flourish, spreading the notion that a dog can actually be trained. Owners enroll their dogs in these schools expecting a mutt to be transformed into a poised, obedient servant. I have no illusions concerning this matter; I believe the dog trains the owner. My dog has trained me perfectly.

For example, whenever I give my dog a bath, which she totally dislikes, she does everything in her power to make the experience as unpleasant for me as possible. She squirms, shakes, and splashes, anything to get me wet, short of grabbing me and pulling me into the tub. I usually end up with the bath, and she ends up gloating over my injured pride. Consequently, she doesn't get a bath unless it is absolutely necessary.

She is loath to get a bath, but never reluctant to ride in the car; she will go anywhere, anytime. She loves riding in the car so much that she has devised a scheme for taking a ride even though I am not going anywhere. She jumps into the car and sits, oblivious of my attempts at coaxing her out. If I try to grab her and drag her out, she growls and snaps at me. She will get out only after I have taken her for a ride, even if it is just a spin around the block.

Perhaps her favorite pastime of all is being taken for a walk, although I am not sure who is walking whom. She trots merrily down the street, stopping to investigate anything that catches her fancy. I follow at the other end of the leash in the guise of a person in complete control, barking out commands and tugging on the leash, although I fully realize she is not paying any attention to me. I am convinced that she heads for home only after she is satisfied that I have had enough exercise for the day.

I have learned to live with the truth; my dog is the owner of a very obedient human being.

Ron Alberti

Although the next student essay is also lighthearted, it uses examples to support a broader controlling idea than the preceding essay.

Social Rules of a Bygone Society

Through the ages, courtesy and good manners have always been important. However, what is considered good manners has varied throughout the years. Although some of these rules may seem ridiculous to us today, at the time of their inception they were thought to be important. At the turn of the century, a lady or gentleman had many strict rules to abide by.

One of the more important social rules was that of making calls. Ladies were "at home" on certain days to receive callers. Callers, mostly other ladies, would visit, generally staying only about fifteen minutes. If they didn't want to stay at all, they would leave a calling card. The card could mean "Thank you," "I'm returning your call," or "Come see me." Unfortunately, when mixed in with other cards, the meaning could be lost, so a system of bending the corners of cards was devised. The message depended on which corner had been bent. It was very important that the correct corner was bent or chaos and hurt feelings could ensue.

Another problem that confronted the turn-of-the-century lady was that of introductions. It was improper to introduce one lady to another without a previous understanding that it would be agreeable to both. A different set of rules applied when two coaches repeatedly passed each other. Etiquette was strict for such encounters: on first passing, one bowed; on the second, one smiled; and on the third, one looked away.

Some rules are downright ridiculous. One of the more ridiculous stated that a chair which a man had sat on must cool before a lady be seated in the same chair. Words were also subjected to ridiculous rules. Many words were deleted as being vulgar or too harsh for a lady's ear. One did not go to bed; one "retired." A bureau did not have "drawers," nor did a piano have "legs." The delicacy of the ladies was carried so far that, at one point, it was suggested that books written by men and women be kept on separate shelves.

Another consideration of society at the turn of the century was clothing. For instance, when a woman went into mourning, she was swathed in black. Even her gloves and her handkerchief were black. Or her handkerchief had a black edging, the border width determined by who had died. A person in mourning would never attend a

explaining
with examples

dinner dance. However, for those who could, formal attire was required. Both men and women wore white kid gloves, and men were advised to carry an extra pair, in case their first pair became clammy. Married couples avoided dancing with each other at these balls and also avoided speaking with each other for too long. Some couples even went so far as to avoid going to the same parties.

These social rules are only a few of the many that abounded at the turn of the century. And, although they may seem ludicrous to us today, they were taken very seriously then.

Sharon Schavroni

Pitfalls to Avoid

1. Don't forget that you need to provide the transitions which show the relationship between the examples and the main points of your essay. Examples alone are not going to be effective unless your reader clearly sees the connection between the general statements and the examples that illustrate them.
2. Don't stack the cards by giving a series of biased examples. Suppose you want to show that college is worthwhile. If the only examples you cite are those of successful graduates holding high-paying jobs, you are not apt to convince a fair-minded reader.
3. Don't select nontypical examples to support your thesis. Even a large number of exceptional cases will not prove your generalization.
4. Don't just give general examples. Name names, give numbers, provide who, where, when.
5. Don't make the mistake of cramming your essay with nothing but reams of factual details and statistics. Your main job is to interpret the facts and offer examples that clearly show what you mean.

SUGGESTED TOPICS

Select a topic from the following list or choose a subject on which you have some knowledge or experience and write an essay developed by examples. Make sure your topic is narrow enough to be proved.

1.	My father's sense of humor	14.	Ghosts and goblins
2.	Parental punishments	15.	Human characteristics in animals
3.	Embarrassing experiences	16.	Ways people dance
4.	Obnoxious employers	17.	Blind dates
5.	Practical jokes	18.	Misleading ads
6.	Strange neighbors	19.	Lovers' techniques
7.	Strange partners	20.	Controversial heroes
8.	Amusing characters	21.	Contradictions in terms
9.	Funny sayings	22.	Great children's stories
10.	Exercises in futility	23.	Comic strips with a message
11.	Announcers' bloopers	24.	Political dirty tricks
12.	Flying aces	25.	Myths in American history
13.	Famous women in history	26.	Teachers' idiosyncrasies

27.	Children's punishments of parents	39.	Extrasensory perception
28.	Part-time jobs	40.	Animal characteristics in people
29.	Unusual pets	41.	Humor in commercials
30.	Ridiculous clothing fads	42.	Rip-offs
31.	Funny incidents in church	43.	Cults
32.	Odd hobbies	44.	Movie heroes
33.	Annoying commercials	45.	Movie villains
34.	Disappointments	46.	Literary styles
35.	Famous fumbles	47.	Violence in fairy tales
36.	Famous cowards	48.	"Real life" comic strips
37.	Close calls	49.	Unfair test techniques
38.	Famous couples	50.	Having more than one girlfriend

TECHNIQUES OF CLEAR WRITING

Agreement

Two kinds of agreement are necessary to make your sentences clear. The first is *subject-verb agreement;* the second is *pronoun-antecedent agreement.* Although these names may seem a bit bulky, the rules are simple.

SUBJECT-VERB

The basic principle of subject-verb agreement is this:

A subject and a verb must agree in person and number.

Person	Number		Person	Number	
First person	singular	*I*	First person	plural	*we*
Second person	singular	*you*	Second person	plural	*you*
Third person	singular	*he, she, it*	Third person	plural	*they*

I am hungry

You are hungry

He is hungry

We are hungry

You are hungry

They are hungry

I have a new car

You have a new car

He has a new car

We have a new car

You have a new car

They have a new car

(**To be** and **to have** are not only frequently used alone, but they are also used as auxiliary verbs in the compound tenses.)

I sing

You sing

He sing**s**

We sing

You sing

They sing

108

*explaining
with examples*

Except in the irregular verbs **to be** and **to have** and in the third person singular of the **present** tense of other verbs, agreement is consistent. The forms of the verbs do not change. The addition of the *-s* in the third person singular, however, is very important.

It is also important in forming the negative contraction of the third person singular of the verb *to do.*

	Singular	*Contraction*	*Plural*	*Contraction*
First person	I do not	I don't	We do not	We don't
Second person	You do not	You don't	You do not	You don't
Third person	He does not	He doesn't	They do not	They don't

Rules Regarding Subject-Verb Agreement

1. A singular subject has a singular verb.

   The **man bicycles** to work.

2. A plural subject has a plural verb.

   The **men bicycle** to work.
   The **rules are** forgotten.

3. A verb that comes before the subject agrees with the subject.

   There **were** two **dogs** in the yard.
   On the shelf **are** three **textbooks.**

4. Two or more singular subjects joined by *and* have a plural verb

   The **teacher and** the **student are** working together.
   John, Mary, and Beth practice daily.

   unless the combined persons or things are regarded as a unit.

   The **bow and arrow was** the weapon of the Indian.
   Forty-five dollars seems like a high price for that sweater.
   The **Congress is** in session.

5. Compound subjects connected by *or, but,* or *nor* take a singular verb if the subjects are singular.

   The **director or** his **assistant chooses** the cast.

   If the subjects are plural, the verb must be plural.

   Not the **supervisors but** the **workers determine** the work load.

If one subject is singular and one is plural, the verb agrees with the nearer subject.

The **instructor or** the **students collect** the assignments.

The **students or** the **instructor collects** the assignments.

6. The following pronouns take a singular verb:

anybody	anyone
anything	somebody
nobody	someone
each	either
neither	one

All these pronouns have a singular sense; that is, you have a feeling that only a **single** thing is referred to. However, you must remember that even though they sound as if they are plural,

everyone	everybody

also take a singular verb.

7. No matter what comes between subject and verb, only the subject influences the verb.
   a. Modifiers like:

as well as	in addition to
together with	accompanied by

do **not** take the place of *and*. Therefore, they do not form a compound subject.

My **father,** as well as his sisters, **is** a singer. [singular subject, singular verb]

My **dog,** accompanied by all her pups, **was** in the show. [singular subject, singular verb]

My **parents,** in addition to my grandfather, **are** coming for Christmas. [plural subject, plural verb]

   b. Prepositional phrases like

to the skies	by the walls	for the summer months
of the city	with the family	between the hedges

are also only modifiers of the subject and do not influence the verb.

The **cost** to the students **is** fair. [singular subject, singular verb]

A **crate** of oranges **was** delivered from Florida. [singular subject, singular verb]

PRONOUN-ANTECEDENT The basic principle of pronoun-antecedent agreement is this:

A pronoun must agree with its *antecedent*, that is, with the noun to which it refers.

When the **burglar** saw the police car approaching, **he** dropped **his** gun and ran.

When the **burglars** saw the police car approaching, **they** dropped **their** guns and ran.

1. Not *every* pronoun has an antecedent.

    It is very cold today.
    It is a long way from Boston to Phoenix.

    Here, the *it* has no antecedent and needs none.

2. If the antecedent is singular, the pronoun must be singular. Remember that *everyone, someone,* and similar pronouns (listed in item 6 in the subject-verb rules, above) are all singular.

    Everybody is willing to do **her** share.
    Everyone has forgotten to bring **his** notes.
    Each of the girls has **her** own car.

3. When two antecedents are joined by *either . . . or, neither . . . nor, not only . . . but also, both . . . and,* the pronoun must agree with the nearer of the two antecedents.

    Neither the coach nor the **players** have lost **their** enthusiasm.
    Neither the players nor the **coach** has lost **his** enthusiasm.
    Not only the three brothers but the **sister** has had **her** education cut short.
    Either George's sisters or **he** will lose **his** chance to go to college.

    NOTE: A relative pronoun (*who, which, that,* etc.) should also agree with the nearer of two antecedents.

    Sylvia loves everything and **everybody who** is connected with the theater.
    She adores everybody and **everything which** is associated with acting.

4. A collective noun used as an antecedent usually requires a singular pronoun.

    The **team** had made up **its** own schedule for practice.
    The **jury** had arrived at **its** verdict.
    The **company** has changed **its** policy.
    The **group** was free to choose **its** own meeting place.

111

An exception exists: when emphasis is on the individuals who "make up" the body referred to by a collective noun, plural pronouns (and verb forms) are used.

The crowd always express their disapproval in various ways: some shout insults, some cheer, and some toss overripe vegetables.

Here, the members of the crowd were acting individually. Often, you can avoid problems by just saying *members of,* as in the following:

The members of the orchestra were taking **their** seats.
The members of the group were divided in **their** loyalties.

5. The pronouns *who, which,* and *that* may be singular or plural depending on the antecedent. All the following examples are correct:

She is one of those girls who **are** always giggling.
[*Who* is plural because it has a plural antecedent, *girls;* therefore, the verb must be plural.]
The girl who **draws** the winning number will go on the tour. [Since *girl* is singular, *who* is singular.]
Filling out tax forms is one of those tasks which **are** often delayed until the last moment.
He lives on one of those streets that **are** down by the river.
He lives on a street that **is** close to the river.

NOTE: When you have "the only one of . . . ," then the singular verb is used:

She is the only one of the girls who **is** going on the tour.
This is the only one of the books that **was** damaged in the fire.

6. Avoid using the indefinite *they* and *it.*

FAULTY: In Louisiana **they** could produce a lot more sugar cane.
IMPROVED: Louisiana growers could produce a lot more sugar cane.

FAULTY: In the garden book **it** says you should plant the bulbs in October.
IMPROVED: The garden book says you should plant the bulbs in October.

7. With few exceptions, a pronoun should clearly refer to a definite antecedent. If your reader cannot immediately see what the pronoun refers to, then you need to reword the sentence.

FAULTY: Teddy told his dad that **he** had a flat tire.
CLEAR: Teddy told his dad, "You've got a flat tire."

Teddy told his dad, "I've got a flat tire."

Teddy told his dad that the Chevy had a flat tire.

*explaining
with examples*

FAULTY: The two pitchers were from Junction High **who** led the league in shutouts.

CLEAR: The two pitchers who led the league in shutouts were from Junction High.

FAULTY: When the puppy crawled into the cat's box, **it** hissed and scratched sand in his eyes.

CLEAR: When the puppy crawled into the cat's box, the cat hissed and scratched sand in the puppy's eyes.

FAULTY: The lawyer must talk to his client in everyday language since **his** knowledge of the law is limited.

CLEAR: Since his client's knowledge of the law is limited, the lawyer must talk to him in everyday language.

FAULTY: Christopher has deliberately broken almost all his toys, and this is what worries his mother.

CLEAR: Christopher has deliberately broken almost all his toys, and this destructive behavior worries his mother.

EXERCISE IVa: AGREEMENT
Correct any faulty agreement by revising the following sentences.

1. Bud Aiken was the kind of friend who would listen to anyone and try to help them with their problems.

_____

2. Juan's father is an educated man, although he isn't always able to express it clearly in English.

_____

3. William Byrd, whose most important work was his *History of the Dividing Line,* wrote in his notebook while he was surveying it.

_____

4. His CPO told him he would be shipping out on a mine sweeper.

_____

5. To get material for her stories, she often listened to women in beauty parlors, supermarkets, and department stores; these enabled her to write her humorous vignettes.

_____

6. It seems to me that he is a spineless character, and this allows him to bend whichever way the wind blows at the moment.

_____

7. Sara took the bills from the envelopes and tossed them in the trash basket.

_____

8. On the television it said it will rain tomorrow.

_____

9. The benefit the consumers have derived from these new techniques are insignificant.

_____

10. The viscosity of these fluids vary under different atmospheric conditions.

_____

11. Everything that was needed for a grand vacation for all of us were provided.

_____

12. In the new health spa there is a handball court, an olympic-sized pool, and a completely equipped exercise room.

_____

13. He owns one of those cars that is being recalled for faulty brakes.

_____

14. Each of these technicians have a specific job to do, and they must know that job thoroughly.

_____

15. *Ulysses* is one of the books that is missing from the library.

_____

16. Although the average citizen complains about high taxes, they are unwilling to do without government services to which they have been accustomed.

_____

17. Neither absolute truth nor inevitability are assured by such an inquiry.

_____

18. He is the only one of the candidates who are qualified.

_____

19. This is one of those problems which are always on tests.

_____

20. She despaired of ever getting a vacation because it always seemed to be the busy season, and he could never leave his business because of it.

_____

Checking for Errors

All writing is rewriting. If you remember the paragraph in the organization section of this chapter, Ernest Hemingway, Dylan Thomas, Walt Whitman, and Gustave Flaubert rewrote constantly before they were satisfied with their efforts. Marjorie Allingham, a successful mystery writer, says:

> I write every paragraph four times: once to get my meaning down, once to put in everything I left out, once to take out everything that seems unnecessary, and once to make the whole thing sound as if I had only just thought of it.

Editing is an important part of the rewriting process. Make sure that words are spelled correctly, that commas are in the right places, that excess words have been eliminated, and that no words have been left out. You will also want to check to see that subjects and verbs agree and that all the correct words are capitalized. In other words, you check your essay, as the teacher will, for correctness. Once you have made all the corrections, copy your essay. Do not turn in your paper with words scratched out and other words or phrases squeezed in above the blot. Your final copy should be neat and attractive.

Here is a checklist for editing:

1. Do all verbs agree with their subjects and all pronouns with their antecedents?
2. Are all words spelled correctly? Look up in the dictionary any word you're unsure of.
3. Are all sentences complete? Also, are there too many ideas in any one sentence?
4. Are all the proper words capitalized and none of the others?
5. Have any words been omitted? (Your mind works faster than your hand, and often a word or phrase is omitted because your mind has already gone on to the next thought.)
6. Do you have any redundancies or unnecessary words or phrases?
7. Did any clichés slip in?
8. Is the point of view consistent in tense, number, person, voice, and tone?
9. Is all the punctuation correct?
10. Do the words you have chosen say **exactly** what you mean?
11. Did you eliminate all unnecessary *to be* verbs?

Before editing, your first draft might look something like this:

Maybe whenever I become old and gray, my reading tastes will be different. Maybe. I might find myself enjoying Proust and Yeats and maybe even Samuel Butler perhaps. But for right now I liked the stories of action like Huckleberry Finn or The Deerslayer and I enjoyed the novels that teach us about social

115

injustices like to Kill a Mockingbird and The Invisable Man and not just because I'm black either, and stories about teenagers like CATCHER IN THE RYE. And funny stories like Catch 22 and The Education of Hyman Kaplan. Well, that's how it is, that's the bottom line for now. I just don't like what the teacher wants me to read, maybe later I will, but for now I don't like the readings he assigns. But perhaps someday I'll have the Maturity I need to enjoy what he assigns, the maturity he took years to get.

After a careful proofreading, your paragraph might look something like this:

Maybe whenever I become old and gray, my reading tastes will be different. Maybe. I might find myself enjoying Proust and Yeats and maybe even Samuel Butler, perhaps. But for right now, I liked the stories of action like Huckleberry Finn or The Deerslayer and enjoyed the novels that teach us about social injustices like To Kill a Mockingbird and The Invisable Man and not just because I'm black either, and stories about teenagers like CATCHER IN THE RYE, And funny stories like Catch 22 and The Education of Hyman Kaplan. Well, that's how it is, that's the bottom line for now. I just don't like what the teacher wants me to read, maybe later I will, but for now I don't like the readings he assigns. But perhaps someday I'll have the Maturity I need to enjoy what he assigns, the maturity he took years to get.

[handwritten annotations: "no caps", "a", "I feel now.", "the novels that", "no CAP", "it takes"]

Then carefully rewrite, incorporating the changes into a neat copy like this:

Maybe when I become old and gray, my reading tastes will be different. I might find myself enjoying Proust and Yeats and maybe even Samuel Butler. But for now, I like the stories of action like Huckleberry Finn or The Deerslayer, and the novels that teach us about social injustices like To Kill a Mockingbird and The Invisible Man, and stories about teenagers like Catcher in the Rye, and funny stories like Catch 22 and The Education of Hyman Kaplan. Well, that's how I feel now. I just don't like the novels that the teacher wants me to read. Perhaps someday I'll have the maturity I need to enjoy what he assigns, the maturity it takes years to get.

After eliminating all the irrelevant and unnecessary wording in your first draft, you might find that you really don't have enough supporting details in your revised version. You should then reread the draft and make sure that your paragraph or essay is adequately developed. In the revised draft of the paragraph above, for example, the writer does not have enough details to prove his point. His most important examples are crowded together in one sentence. Each of the examples could be explained in greater detail, for an improved paragraph.

Of course, you have to edit the draft each time you revise. When you have done that and copied the results, you should proofread your work to make sure that you have copied the edited version accurately.

EXERCISE IVb: EDITING
Using your editing checklist, correct the errors in the following paragraph.

The United States is the most misunderstood nation in the world. And the most unappreciated. She gives and gives to others and is hated in return. It is a nation that worries constantly about "what the world will think of her actions and published all of her scandles for the world to see. She gives millions in aid for other countries in trouble but she expects and gets nothing in the world when she has problems. They were the most powerful nation in the world in 1945 but they took nothing INSTEAD they gave aid to the countries they had defeated. She holds no grudges, harbors no malice. She made both Japan and Germany modern prosprous nations after it attempted to destroy her. Germany and Japan tried to destroy the United States in World War II. We free the Philippines after the war. We feed the hungry, heel the sick, rebuilt the railroads of others. We give help, we get hate in return.

WORD POWER

Pronouns as Subjects and Objects
There are six pronouns that have forms that differ depending on whether they are used as subject or as object of the sentence:

Subject	Object
I	me
he	him
they	them
we	us
she	her
who, whoever	whom, whomever

If the subject of a sentence is a pronoun, you need to be careful to use the subject form:

Jake and I [*not* me] offered to help Fred.
Mary and I [*not* me] believe in going to church.

In sidewalk English you often hear something like this: "Jeff and me was called into the office." Such sentences contain a compound error: the *me* should be *I* (subject), and the *was* should be *were* because the subject (*Jeff and I*) is plural.

If a pronoun is the object of a verb or preposition, the objective form must be used:

They invited him and **me** [not *I*] to the party.

The gift was intended for Julie and **me** [not *I*].

With **whom** [not *who*] did you discuss your problem?

Those **whom** [not *who*] we invited should be here by seven-thirty.

The history professor made both of us, Jake and **me** [not *I*], write a paper on the French Revolution.

Between you and **me** [not *I*], he is badly mistaken about the cost of owning a car.

Knowing Beth and **me** [not *I*] as well as he does, I'm surprised that he didn't call us.

The Errors of Sidewalk English

In pronoun-noun combinations such as "we husbands" or "us wives," the pronoun form will depend on how the noun is used in the sentence. If the noun is used as a subject, then you must use the subject form of the pronoun:

We husbands are actually benefiting from the women's liberation movement.

If the noun is used as an object, then you must use the object form of the pronoun:

119 The women's liberation movement has opened a lot of doors for **us wives.**

explaining with examples

NOTE: Despite the frequent use of *who* instead of *whom* in informal speech, written English still calls for the use of *whom* or *whomever* in objective constructions:

Whom are you expecting?
From **whom** do you expect to receive this money?
He's a man in **whom** I once had great faith.
Energy costs will continue to rise, no matter **whom** we elect.
Herman Melville was a man **whom** the critics had ignored.
She is a young woman who tells her problems to **whomever** she happens to meet.
We can appoint **whomever** we choose.

Watch out for the form in which the pronoun is the subject of the verb that follows:

The article offers good advice to **whoever** has money to invest. [*Whoever* is the subject of *has.*]
There is little doubt about **who** financed his political campaign. [*Who* is the subject of *financed.*]
Gill asked Ruby **who** she thought should be elected. [*Who* is the subject of *should be elected.*]

In a good many constructions, *that* may be used in place of the more formal *whom* or *whomever.*

He was the sort of man **whom/that** his neighbors scarcely noticed.
The colonists were determined to oppose **whomever/anyone** the governor appointed.

In addition to the subject and object forms of verbs, there are the forms made by adding -*self* or -*selves,* such as *myself, himself, themselves.* These forms have two uses. First, they may show that the subject and the object are the same, as in "He hurt himself." In this case it is called a *reflexive* form. Second, the form may be used for emphasis, as in "My mother herself told me." In this case it is called an *intensive* form. These forms should be used **only** in these two ways.

FAULTY: My wife and myself visited Chautauqua last week.
CORRECT: My wife and I visited Chautauqua last week.
FAULTY: The Ambersons invited Jerry and myself to the party.
CORRECT: The Ambersons invited Jerry and me to the party.

In each of the following sentences, circle the form of the pronoun that completes the sentence correctly.

1. They included my wife and (I/me/myself) in their invitation.
2. Between (we/us) students, there is complete agreement.
3. The instructor and (I/me/myself) compromised.
4. Among John, Mary, and (I/me), no arguments arose.
5. The police officers shouted at both of us, Harry and (me/I), for going through a stop sign.
6. There is opportunity for (whomever/whoever) is willing to work.
7. (Who/Whom) do you wish to speak to?
8. The book offers good advice to students and indeed to all those (who/whom) it reaches.
9. (Who/Whom) is at my window?
10. He, on the telephone, says, "May I speak to Lucille, please?" She answers, "This is (her/she)."
11. Fifi and (her/she) are going swimming.
12. Phil said, "Give it to (him/he) to (who/whom) it belongs."
13. I used to give Richard and (he/him) guitar lessons.
14. (We/Us) girls are going to the movies.
15. The exam asked (who/whom) was the better president.

Tense

Since the verb is the most important part of the sentence, it is important to know how to use verbs properly. The verb not only tells the reader what specific action is taking place, it also tells **when** the action is taking place. Every time you use a verb in a sentence, you are using a specific tense. *Tense* means "time"—the time of the action of the verb. For example:

PRESENT: Jane **screams** at Tarzan every day.
PAST: Jane **screamed** at Tarzan yesterday.
FUTURE: Jane **will scream** at Tarzan tomorrow.

The verb tells WHEN the action takes place.

explaining with examples

The sentences above illustrate the major divisions in time—the simple past, present, and future tenses. Most writers are so familiar with these basic tenses that they use them automatically. In fact, some students think that these are the only tenses in the English language. However, if you listen to yourself carefully the next time you are talking to somebody, you will realize that you can't communicate with anyone very long in just the simple present, past, and future tenses.

PRESENT TENSE AGREEMENT

In spite of their familiarity, present and past tenses present some problems.

In the present tense, the form (the spelling) of the verb changes **only** in the third person singular.

	Singular	*Plural*
First person	I know	We know
Second person	You know	You know
Third person	He knows	They know

To fail to put the -s ending on the third person singular or to put it on any other verb forms is generally considered a serious error in mechanics.

-ED ENDINGS

The simple past tense of regular verbs is formed by adding -ed to the present tense, as in *walked, talked, carried.*

There are two other ways in which -ed is used in forming verbs, the perfect tenses and verb forms in the passive voice.

THE THREE USES OF -ed IN REGULAR VERBS

1. The simple past tense   I **walked** the dog.
2. All perfect tenses   The dog **has walked** here before.
   The dog **had walked** here before he got hurt.
   The dog **will have walked** here for three years by February.
3. Passive voice   The dog **is walked** here every day.
   The dog **was walked** here yesterday.
   The dog **will be walked** here tomorrow.
   The dog **has been** walked here every day for a year.
   The dog **had been walked** here until the highway was built.
   The dog **will have been walked** here for three years by next Thursday.

COMPOUND TENSES

Perfect and progressive tenses show variations of time within the past, present, and future tenses.

Perfect Tenses

The past perfect tense is used for an action completed in the past, before some other action:

The salesman insisted that he **had talked** to my husband.

The present perfect tense is used for an action in the past that is continuing:

I **have talked** to him repeatedly about his drinking problem.

The future perfect tense is used when the action will be completed at some point in the future:

On February 1 we **shall have been married** for fifty years.

Progressive Tenses

The past progressive tense is used for an ongoing action in the past:

The Steelers **were winning** the Superbowl.

The present progressive is used for an ongoing action in the present:

The Steelers **are winning** the Superbowl.

The future progressive is used for an ongoing action in the future:

The Steelers **will be winning** the Superbowl.

BEING CONSISTENT The most important thing to remember about tense is that you must be consistent. You cannot randomly shift from one tense to another. For example, if you were telling a story about what happened to you on your vacation last summer, you would stay in the past tense. If, on the other hand, you were explaining the difference between your German shepherd and your Irish setter, you would stay in the present tense. There will be times, of course, when you have to move to a different tense. If, for example, you were contrasting the driving habits of your old boyfriend with those of your new boyfriend, the part of your paper about your old boyfriend would be written in the past tense and the part about your new boyfriend would be written in the present tense. You should not move to a different tense, however, unless you have a good reason, so proofread your papers carefully and make sure that your writing contains no unnecessary shifts in tense.

EXERCISE IVd: SHIFTS IN TENSE

In the student essay following, some of the verb forms have been changed to make the essay inconsistent in tense. Read the narrative carefully and correct all of the **needless** shifts in tense.

Murphy's Law at Work
One weekend about mid-August last summer, I decided to plan a water-skiing trip to Lake Erie. I knew that my neighbor wanted to go, so we looked for a third person. (The law states that at least three people are needed for water-

skiing.) Knowing that my cousin enjoys water-skiing, I called him and found that he, too, was available. He says that he thought we would have a good time. Well, we all expected to have a good time, but we did not realize how much extra "fun" was to be encountered.

We started to prepare for our little voyage early in the morning since it would take us at least an hour and a half to get to Presque Isle. By seven o'clock we have everything ready to go. The boat trailer was fastened securely to the truck, the trailer lights were connected, the boat and truck had full fuel tanks, and our oversized coolers are packed with all the food we could handle in one day. As we headed north along Route 18, the sun was already glaring upon the hood of the truck. With the boat behind us and the sunny beach ahead of us, we felt like real "beach boys." We will be anxious to launch that boat.

I figured that I knew my way to Lake Erie as well as I knew the way to my grandmother's, but as we traveled east on Interstate 80, I began to wonder if I had missed the Interstate 79 exit. (I am not noted for giving my full attention to road signs once I engage in conversation with my passengers.) The next sign I saw, "Clarion–5 miles," left no doubt in my mind that we had passed the proper exit, so I tell my passengers to watch for police cars because I decided to use the first emergency turnaround available. After making the illegal U-turn, I began frantically racing for that I-79 exit to make up for lost time. Suddenly, we hear a strange noise as we hit a bump in the highway. The three of us casually looked at each other, speechless, until I noticed, by checking through my side mirror, that my trailer had no right fender. (It had one when I left the house.) By this time, we realized that we would need a jet engine and plenty of good luck to make up the time difference. I was tempted to leave the fender behind, but my father owned the whole rig, and I figured that he would not be too happy about buying a new one. Our next move, obviously, was to head back for that fender. This will involve another U-turn. Once accomplishing the U-turn, we were cruising at a comfortable velocity of about sixty miles per hour when I noticed that the boat was rocking on the trailer as if it were in a storm at sea. When I finally realized that it had unhooked from the winch rope, I was forced to slow down and pull into a turnaround. After securing the boat, I make a quick check of the trailer lights and discovered that I had no stop lights; a fuse had blown. As we pulled out onto the highway again, I couldn't help wondering what was going to happen next.

With our first sign of the lake, we felt relieved. Even though it had taken three hours to get there, we made it. After all of the trouble we experienced on the way up, we were hoping for a trouble-free day, and at first it seemed like our luck had changed. We launched the boat with no trouble, and in a matter of minutes we are cruising through the bay. As we crept through the channel, however, we noticed that the water looked slightly rough for water-skiing. In fact, once we started cutting through the waves, we realized that they were not only too rough for skiing; they were also too rough for the boat. Our seventeen-foot, one-half ton boat just could not smooth out those six-foot waves. We decided that there was no point in risking our lives. With no other choice, we will have to head back to the dock, bobbing up and down and getting soaked in the process.

After wasting a lot of time and spending thirty-five dollars for gas, I will think twice before I plan any more little excursions to the lake. Now that I know what can be in store for me, I will definitely make more safety checks, listened to two or three weather forecasts, and call the Coast Guard before I even pull out of the driveway.

Tony Bondi

Use the following verbs in two sentences, putting the verb in a different tense in each sentence.

smoke   1.   Past perfect _____

Present progressive _____

love   2.   Present _____

Future perfect _____

shiver   3.   Past progressive _____

Present perfect _____

be   4.   Present _____

Future perfect _____

alienate   5.   Future perfect _____

Present perfect progressive _____

harass   6.   Past perfect _____

Present perfect progressive _____

stagger   7.   Present perfect _____

Past perfect _____

learn   8.   Present perfect progressive _____

Future perfect _____

pollute   9.   Past _____

Past progressive _____

speak   10.   Past perfect progressive _____

Past perfect _____

Irregular Verbs

Some of the irregularities in the mechanics of English are holdovers from the long history of the language. They are vestiges of language spoken by our ancestors hundreds, even thousands of years ago. Among these remains are the so-called *irregular verbs*.

As you have just seen, the regular verbs have four principal parts:

1.	Present or plain form	I talk, he talks
2.	Present participle	talk*ing*
3.	Past tense	talk*ed*
4.	Past participle	talk*ed*

124

The past participle is the same form as the past tense but is used in combination with various forms of **have**.

I have talk**ed**
She had talk**ed**
We shall have talk**ed**

    Irregular verbs do not conform to this pattern. Although there are only a hundred or so irregular verbs in the language, they are important enough that you should memorize their forms. Fortunately, most of them are so well-known that the forms come to you almost automatically.
    Notice the changing forms in some of the most common irregular verbs. The changes, incidentally, occur only in past tense and in the past participle; the present participle always is made by adding *-ing*.

Present	*Past*	*Past and Past Participle*
begin	began	(have) begun
blow	blew	(have) blown
break	broke	(have) broken
bring	brought	(have) brought
choose	chose	(have) chosen
come	came	(have) come
dig	dug	(have) dug
do	did	(have) done
eat	ate	(have) eaten
fly	flew	(have) flown
go	went	(have) gone
rise	rose	(have) risen
see	saw	(have) seen
sing	sang	(have) sung
write	wrote	(have) written

    If you are ever unsure of the *principal parts* of a verb, your dictionary will give you the forms.
    A few verbs offer you a choice of two acceptable forms:

He dived (dove) off the high board.
They lighted (lit) cigarettes as soon as possible.
The boat sank (sunk) in five feet of water.

    Some few verbs use different forms of the same principal part to show a difference in meaning:

The stockings were *hung* by the chimney with care.

BUT

The murderer was *hanged.*

The sun *shone* brightly.

BUT

The halls were cleaned and *shined.*

To Be

Be is a verb we cannot do without. However, as one scholar pointed out, it is a "badly mixed up verb"; it is the most irregular of all verbs.

Present	*Past*
I am	I was
you are	you were
he, she, it is	he, she, it was
we are	we were
you are	you were
they are	they were

Present Participle	*Past Participle*
being	(have) been

Confusing Forms

Some pairs of verbs have forms similar enough to be confusing.

Lie, lay, lain means that someone or something is somewhere, usually stretched out. (The combined form *lie down* is the same.)

The man *lies* in the hammock.
The dog *lay* in the shade.
We all should have *lain* down.

Lay, laid, laid means that somebody has put something somewhere. You can test the correctness of your form by seeing if *put* can be substituted.

I always *lay* my keys there.
He *laid* his overcoat on the chair.
He had *laid* his tools on the porch.

Sit, sat, sat means that someone is seated. (*Sit down* follows the same pattern.)

He *sits* at his desk.
They *sat* before the fire.
We have *sat* here waiting for hours.

Set, set, set is usually another substitute for *put,* along with *lay.* The few exceptions to this sense include *the sun **sets**, the bird **set**, the cement has **set**.*

Otherwise, *set* is a transitive verb (a verb that takes an object, or completer).

*explaining
with examples*

I *set* the cat down outside the door.
He *set* the luggage on the rack.
They have *set* their burdens down.

Rise, rose, risen means to get up.

I *rise* at seven.
They *rose* quickly.
He has *risen.*

Raise, raised, raised means to lift up.

I *raise* the roof when I'm mad.
I *raised* the flag at school.
I have *raised* my hand every day in class.

EXERCISE IVf: IRREGULAR VERBS
In each of the following groups of sentences, fill in the first blank with the correct form of the **third person singular of the present tense,** the second blank with the **past tense,** and the third with the **past participle** following some form of *have.*

begin 1. The conductor _____ the program. Last night he _____
at 8:30. He has _____ them for several weeks.

blow 2. The wind _____ strongly. It _____ even worse
last week. It has _____ hard during every storm we've had.

break 3. She _____ all the rules. She _____ her promises.
She has _____ her mother's heart.

lie 4. He _____ on the sofa. He _____ there for hours.
They all have _____ down after dinner.

seek 5. He _____ everywhere for an answer. I _____ an
answer yesterday. She has _____ answers since last week.

flee 6. The rabbit _____ the hunter. The hunter _____
the game warden. The whole town has _____ because of rabbit
fever.

light 7. The town _____ its main streets during Christmas. They
_____ even more streets last year. They have _____
these main streets for many years.

bring 8. Winter _____ higher fuel bills. It once _____ only winter sports. Sports now have _____ fun and expenses.

take 9. She _____ gym. The seniors _____ swimming for their gym. We have _____ four different sports this year.

thrive 10. When times are prosperous, business _____. The workers _____ when the times are good. All of us have _____ this year.

write 11. He _____ home every week. He _____ to me last week. They have _____ a new book.

go 12. He _____ his way alone. They _____ east. You have always _____ with us.

lay 13. No man _____ his lunch box in the hot sun. They _____ them in the shade. They usually have _____ them in the coolest spot.

sit 14. She _____ at the window. She _____ there yesterday. She has _____ there every Friday.

rise/set 15. The moon _____ before the sun _____. The moon _____ after the sun _____. In winter, the moon has always _____ after the sun has _____.

wake 16. The rooster _____ early. This morning it _____ and crowed before six. It has _____ that early all year and then has _____ us.

lie 17. He _____ down to read. He _____ down last night to read but he fell asleep. He has always _____ down to study.

break 18. The ocean _____ on the rocks. It _____ with a roar during last night's storm. It has _____ for so long that the rocks are eroded.

do 19. He _____ little all day. He _____ nothing at all today. He has seldom _____ anything worthwhile.

dig 20. He _____ clams for lunch. She _____ some yesterday. They have _____ them daily since they came.

comparing
and
contrasting

In the Alice books, Lewis Carroll has a lot of fun playing with words. One of his jokes is a discussion between Alice and Humpty Dumpty about the meaning of a poem called "Jabberwocky," which is filled with nonsense words:

> 'Twas brillig and the slithy toves
> Did gyre and gimble in the wabe;
> All mimsy were the borogoves,
> And the mome raths outgrabe.

Alice asks, "And what are *toves*?"

Humpty answers, "Well, *toves* are something like badgers—they're something like lizards—and they're something like corkscrews."

He goes on to the *borogove*. "And a *'borogove'* is a thin, shabby looking bird with its feathers sticking out all round—something like a live mop."

Alice: "And what does *'outgrabe'* mean?"

Humpty: "Well, *outgribing* is something between bellowing and whistling, with a kind of a sneeze in the middle."

A Mimsy Borogove

The comparison here, of course, is all in fun. But, nevertheless, comparison is one of the basic techniques for learning something new. You show how the new thing to be learned is like, or **compares** with, something already known. Or, if you are **contrasting,** you show how the new thing is different from something already known.

Comparing and contrasting are nothing new; you do both every day. If you stop at a friend's house, you automatically notice some similarities and differences between his house and your house. If a friend or neighbor buys a car, you quite naturally compare it to the car you have—perhaps turning a little green in the process. How often have you described someone by comparing that person to somebody else? Suppose you were telling your friend about a man you met at your brother's wedding. You might have said something like this: "In a way, he was good-hearted, but he turned me off; he was a typical male chauvinist—kind of a twenty-year-old Archie Bunker." As soon as you compared him to Archie Bunker, your friend probably knew exactly what you meant. On a more complex level, concepts that you have to learn in school are easier to understand when they are compared or contrasted with something more familiar to you. For example, your history teacher might explain indentured servitude by telling you that it is *like* slavery—a form of temporary slavery.

Also, fiction writers often use this device to vivify their characters by confronting one character with a foil, a character who possesses the opposite trait. Thus, the writer points up the stinginess of a Scrooge by showing the generosity of a Tiny Tim, or the romanticism of Tom Sawyer by putting it beside the realism of Huck Finn.

The main difference between your casual, everyday comparisons and the comparisons used in developing an essay is that, in writing the essay, you are comparing or contrasting with a specific purpose in mind. You may want to demonstrate, for example, that one method of studying is more effective than another, that one type of engine is superior to another, or that living in stable Minnesota requires less adaptability than living in booming Arizona. Whatever you are comparing or contrasting, you are doing it for a specific purpose: to prove your point.

On What Basis Are You Comparing or Contrasting?

To have significance, those things you are comparing must be compared on the same basis. For example, you could compare an egg and a seed on the basis that both of them contain the power to reproduce the parent from which they came. You could also compare both egg and seed on the basis of foodstuffs. But you could not logically compare one feature of the egg, the composition of its yolk, for instance, and another feature of the seed, for example, its shape.

Your thesis sentence would be the ideal place in which to point out the basis on which you are comparing the two items or subjects.

Suppose for an English class you decide to contrast two of your favorite short stories. You might have a thesis statement that says, "Although both Mark Twain and Bret Harte are American writers influenced by their experiences in the West, their most important short stories 'The Mysterious Stranger' and 'The Outcasts of Poker Flat' reflect very different outlooks on life." This thesis statement indicates you are going to contrast the two stories. You might point out such differences as Twain's pessimism as opposed to Harte's optimism, and Twain's realistic attitude toward people as contrasted with Harte's sentimental attitude. You could find many more differences, but you give significance to these contrasts on the basis that these men were contemporaries who shared many experiences in their lives which they wrote about. Such a basis of comparison suggests that their work would be similar, not essentially different. Without making such a basis, your thesis statement would say only, "The most important stories of Mark Twain and Bret Harte, "The Mysterious Stranger" and 'The Outcasts of Poker Flat,' are totally different." This would leave your reader at a loss, for why should it be worth comment that two stories are unlike. Without making clear the backgrounds of the two writers, you have not established a basis for making a contrast meaningful.

ORGANIZATION

Once again, your organization will follow the one-two-three development of introduction with thesis statement, body, and conclusion. The comparison-contrast essay, however, requires careful control in the wording of the thesis statement and the development of the body. First of all, you have two subjects rather than the usual one. Furthermore, you must have a clear purpose for the comparison-contrast: you must have a point to make beyond the obvious one of showing likenesses or differences. Providing detailed information on the two subjects is **not** enough. You must make clear to the reader that you are using comparison and contrast **to prove a point.** Telling the reader something that he or she already knows, for example, is pointless. Comparing two items that are obviously alike (baseball and softball) or contrasting two items that are obviously different (a car and an airplane) proves nothing.

Introduction with Thesis Statement

An effective thesis statement for a comparison-contrast essay does three things:

131

1. It names the subjects being compared or contrasted.
2. It establishes the basis for the comparison or contrast.
3. It indicates what you are trying to demonstrate or prove.

Suppose that you decide to compare two different teachers you have known—a very good one and a very poor one. After thinking it over, you decide that a certain math teacher and a former psych teacher would make good subjects. Then, you decide that what you want to show is how a good teacher and a poor teacher differ in their attitudes, methods, and knowledge. Next, you need a carefully worded thesis statement: "When I think about the marvelous math teacher and the terrible psych teacher I had, I see a sharp contrast in their attitudes, methods, and knowledge." With this thesis statement, both your basis of comparison and your purpose are clear.

Body

You seek to organize the details in the body of the essay in the most effective way to support the purpose indicated in your thesis statement.

TWO BASIC METHODS OF ORGANIZA-TION

As you have already learned, in all good writing the details are arranged in some sort of logical order. In comparisons and contrasts there are basically two ways to arrange your material:

1. The block method
2. The point-by-point method

Suppose you were contrasting two actors, Paul Newman and Robert Redford. Using the block method, you would place everything you wanted to say about Paul Newman in one paragraph (one "block") and then in the next paragraph you would explain how Robert Redford is different from Paul Newman. Arranging the same material point by point, you would discuss each actor with respect to one characteristic (one "point"), and then move on to the next characteristic.

You can use either method, as long as you are consistent. Don't begin with the block method and then switch to the point-by-point method. You can see how each method works by skimming through your textbooks. You're bound to find some examples of both. For instance, in the textbook *A Short History of the Movies*, author Gerald Mast devotes one of his chapters to explaining the difference between two masters of comedy: Mack Sennet, the man who created the Keystone Kops, and Charlie Chaplin, the lovable tramp who could make people laugh and cry at the same time. Sometimes the author uses the block method; sometimes he uses the point-by-point method. Sometimes in an essay the author uses both. Notice the effectiveness of each approach:

BLOCK METHOD

Some of the differences between Sennett and Chaplin become most clear when comparing similar devices and motifs they both used. Both Sennett and Chaplin used cops. For Sennett, the cops were purely comic characters, whose good will was balanced by their efforts and frenzy; Sennett's cops can do

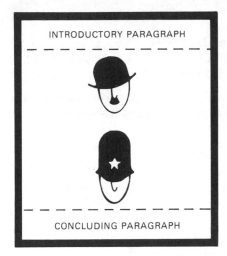

Block Method

nothing right. Their cars crash, their boats sink; they fall all over each other as they swarm to answer a call. They are as earnest and as functional as toy soldiers. Chaplin's cops, though not precisely what contemporary radicals would call pigs, were not very far from it. In *Police,* the cops spend their time leisurely journeying by motor car to answer an emergency call for help; they drink tea and fluff their uniforms and show no concern at all for Edna's distress. The cops in *The Adventurer* are not as satirical, but they do shoot rifles at the escaping Charlie, and their bullets look as though they could kill. . . .

POINT-BY-POINT METHOD

Tempermentally, Chaplin could never see comedy the way Sennett saw it. For Sennett, the comic world was a world of silly surfaces; for Chaplin the comic world was a way of getting at the serious world of men and society. For Sennett, comedy was an end; for Chaplin, it was a means. . . . Both Sennett and Chaplin use the ocean; for Sennett the ocean is a location for watery gags, but for Chaplin the ocean is a place where people can drown. Both Sennett and Chaplin use the chase, but Sennett emphasizes more of the pure motion and frenzy of it whereas Chaplin emphasizes the cleverness and skill of Charlie at avoiding capture. . . .

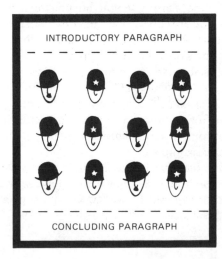

Point-by-Point Method

If you were to develop the essay about the good math teacher and the poor psych teacher, for example, you might begin by grouping the contrasting details under three main headings which establish the basis of comparison:

THESIS STATEMENT: When I think about the marvelous math teacher and the terrible psych teacher I had, I see a sharp contrast in their attitudes, methods, and knowledge.

I.   Attitudes toward students

A. Math teacher	B. Psych teacher
is considerate of feelings, answers questions, seems to care, works with those having trouble	embarrasses students, ignores questions, seems to want students to fail, has no time for slow students

II.   Methods of teaching

is well-organized, gives step-by-step presentation, illustrates	is unorganized, wanders from point to point and back again, gives no examples

III.   Knowledge of subject

has wealth of knowledge, explains "shortcuts," gives items of interest	reads from book, adds nothing, cannot answer peripheral questions

You must decide which of the two methods you will use in the body of the essay. Remember that in the point-by-point method you compare or contrast the two subjects feature for feature, as in the case of the psych and math teachers. If you use the block method, you might still discuss the same details, but the organization of your discussion will be different. In the contrast of the teachers, all of your points about the math teacher will be in one block, then all your points about the psych teacher in the next block. Although you discuss the two subjects in separate blocks, you take up similar points about each. Thus the block method is sometimes referred to as the "parallel-order comparison." If you employ parallel order in your development, you are sure to have a clearer and sharper comparison or contrast.

What aspects you choose are up to you, but you must tell the same things about both. You cannot, if you are contrasting cars, deal with the price of one and the performance of the other. Also, your essay must have balance; you cannot give more information on one side than on the other.

When you have established the principle or basis of comparison and developed your outline, you should have little trouble writing a good comparison or contrast essay. You can use examples to illustrate particular points. In the essay contrasting the math instructor and the psychology instructor, for instance, you could explain each basis of comparison (attitudes, teaching methods, and knowledge of subject) with specific examples.

In a short essay you usually stick to one method of development, either the point-by-point or block method. In a longer essay, however, you may vary the pattern from paragraph to paragraph. However, you must give systematic and balanced treatment to both subjects.

Conclusion

Since you have **two** subjects instead of one, the comparison-contrast essay calls for careful handling to make the purpose of the essay clear. To describe the two subjects in detail is not enough; you must make the point of your comparison or contrast clear, not leave the reader wondering why you wrote the essay. A good conclusion, then, pulls together the various details of your comparison or contrast and reemphasizes your purpose—to show, for example, that A is more practical than B, that A is more economical than B, or that A is inferior in some respects to B.

The conclusion to the essay contrasting the two teachers might read like this:

> In every area that matters to the students, our mathematics teacher is far superior to our psychology teacher. In her whole approach to teaching, she is more positive, more concerned, and more sensitive to student needs. In addition, she knows her subject thoroughly, and, unlike our psychology teacher, she spares no effort in trying to help every student.

Here is a student essay that contrasts two kinds of dates:

Rewards of Being a Late Bloomer

After age thirty, being a single woman and free to date can be very amusing. At first, the average woman in this situation is often disappointed by the type of men who ask her out. As time goes by, however, she begins to think of herself as an individual instead of one part of a pair. It is only when she has reached this stage in her development that she can begin to see the funny side of her social life. One of the first things I noticed was that the men I dated were either "roughnecks" or "sophisticates."

Both types, for a first date, usually suggest dinner and dancing, but each has a style of his own. The roughneck will matter-of-factly assume that you are free, and good-naturedly assume that you will be delighted to go out with him. He generally suggests that you cancel all other plans in order to see him—preferably, tomorrow. If you insist that you are busy, he'll decide that you have spunk. (The roughneck is intrigued by spunk, and he'll become even more determined to take you out.) The sophisticate, on the other hand, will take a little more time and make a greater effort to know you before asking you out. He will ask you if you are busy and if you would like to have dinner with him a week from next Saturday. If you say that you are busy, he will become a little more reserved and say that he'll call next week. If you accept either invitation, you had better decide which category he falls into before getting dressed to go out with him. For a date with a roughneck, you will probably be overdressed if you wear slacks and a sweater. He will be late picking you up, and then he will take you to some smoky bar and grill where the food is good and plentiful and the music is loud and country western. As he drinks more beer, he will think you look fantastic, and he will tell you so—often. If you are able to relax in this atmosphere, you will laugh a lot and have fun. In contrast, the sophisticate will be impressed if you wear a dress and high-heeled shoes and have your hair and nails done. He will pick you up right on time and take you to a lovely restaurant where the food is good and expensive. There will be soft dinner music playing, and the conversation will be a little stilted at first, but as the wine flows, he will become a little less reserved, and he will tell you (just once) how lovely you look.

After dinner, with either date, there will be dancing. The roughneck will dance only the slow dances, and like his cowboy ancestors, will probably hold you a little too close. But because he sometimes displays a little boy charm, you will not protest too much. Emboldened by this, he will (still good-naturedly) suggest that you spend the

135

night together. When you refuse, he will continue to tease, coax, and cajole. The rough-neck doesn't give up easily, and you will probably see the end of this battle on your doorstep when he unwillingly takes you home. The sophisticate, however, handles the same situation differently. He will dance the fast dances as well as the slow dances, although he prefers the slow ones. He will never hold you too tight, and you will gradually be lulled into relaxing your guard and trusting him. The sophisticate moves so slowly that you do not realize, until the last moment, that he is suggesting that you spend the night together. When you refuse, he will look hurt, protest his innocence, and probably swear he never suggested such a thing. He will again pull back, become more reserved, and slowly start to build toward the same tactics for another night.

On a date with either of these types, the dialogue changes from time to time, but the basic script remains the same. If the single woman can maintain her sense of humor, she can have a lot of fun and be well-fed.   *Dorothy Gaydos*

Analogy: A Special Kind of Comparison

You have just read that a comparison or contrast, to be significant, must be made on a common basis. If, for example, you said, "Hitler was a worse tyrant than Mussolini," you would have a straightforward contrast of two men who were both tyrants. Tyranny would be the basis on which you were contrasting them.

However, there is a special type of comparison known as *analogy*. In analogy, the items to be compared come from different classes of things. War and football, for example, obviously fall into separate categories, but in a sense the game of football is similar to the game of war. Both a coach and a general talk in terms of "victory" and "defeat." Both use "blitzes" and "secret weapons" and "front line reinforcements" to plan "offensive" and "defensive" strategies. Both train their men to "defend the flanks" and "crush the opponent."

As a writer, you will find that a vivid analogy can be quite effective in getting your point across, even though the comparison is not literally true. If, for example, you said, "My boss is a snake in the grass," you would be comparing your boss (a man or woman) with a snake (a reptile). When you compare your boss to a snake, however, you mean your boss has only the unpleasant characteristics of a snake; you do not expect the comparison to be carried so far in your readers' minds that they think your boss feeds on mice, sheds skin, and hibernates in the winter. Thus, you would not be making a full comparison. Nevertheless, through your analogy you would be successfully communicating your feelings about your boss —that he or she is a hidden threat, sneaky, and untrustworthy.

Analogy is not literal truth.

In the following paragraph a student makes a cheery analogy between an old woman and a jalopy.

A jalopy reminds me of an old woman. All of the beauty that the new car possessed is now gone. The paint no longer shines; the metal no longer glistens, and the upholstery no longer gleams. The car that once started on the first turn of the ignition now demands much more time before turning over. Instead of giving a smooth, comfortable ride down the road, the jalopy just putters down the road, almost gasping for breath before it reaches its final destination. All of this is the same for an old woman. Her hair no longer shines, her eyes no longer glisten, and her complexion no longer gleams. Instead of waking at the crack of dawn full of vim and vigor, ready to start a full day, the old woman begrudgingly gets out of bed wishing that the day was ending instead of just starting. Her walk is no longer the graceful thing of beauty it once was, but rather a concentrated effort to complete a task. Although neither the jalopy nor the old woman is ready for the used-car lot, both know that they have seen better days.

Cathy Windom

Notice how Ernest Zebrowski in his textbook *Physics for Technicians* simplifies a difficult concept (the radioactive decay process) by making an analogy that is easy for the student to understand:

There is still one thing we have to add to get a complete picture of the radioactive decay process. We might start with a question: If the heavy radioactive nuclei are constantly disintegrating into simpler nuclei, how do we explain the presence of any heavy radioactive substances in nature? Why haven't they all disintegrated?

The answer is that most of them have. Only a relative few can be found in the earth's crust. These naturally occurring radioactive nuclei are unstable, to be sure, but they are not as unstable as the other radioactive nuclei that have long since disappeared from nature. We might envision the process as follows: suppose we have a flat table and a pile of coins containing 100 nickels, 100 dimes, and 100 pennies. We stand all of these coins on their edges, not too close together, and we leave the room. Of course, the coins are in an unstable position, but the dimes are more unstable than the pennies, which in turn are more unstable than the nickels. If we return to the room a few hours later, we might find that a large number of dimes have fallen over. A smaller number of pennies will have toppled, and very few nickels. If left alone for a few days, all the dimes may have fallen while a majority of nickels still stand. The coins on the table are very similar to what happens in a mixture of three different radioactive substances. The most unstable substance decays very quickly, while the others decay at slower rates.

Pitfalls to Avoid

1. Avoid an unbalanced, one-sided comparison. You need to give relatively equal space to the two subjects being compared or contrasted. For instance, if you compare a novel with the movie adaptation, you need to provide equal treatment for both the novel and the movie.

2. Avoid seesaw style. You need to use adequate transition so that you don't just jump back and forth from one subject to another in a series of short, choppy sentences.

3. Just showing the differences or similarities between A and B is not enough. Your comparison–contrast essay must serve a useful purpose:

to show, for example, that A is superior to B or that B is more practical than A.

4. Watch out for false comparison, that is, a few superficial similarities leading to a false conclusion. If you were to compare the Soviet bureaucracy with the American bureaucracy, no doubt you could find a number of similarities; but you would need to be careful not to ignore fundamental differences, for you might easily arrive at a false conclusion.

5. Don't equivocate: have a clear point to make, and state it clearly at the outset. If you start your essay with "There are many similarities and differences between the North and the South," that thesis is useless because you fail to take a stand. You leave your reader asking, "So what? What's the point?"

6. Don't state the obvious. Comparing two obviously similar members of the same class or contrasting two obviously different members of the same class is pointless. Your reader will learn nothing.

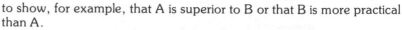

EXERCISE Va: BASES OF COMPARING
Put the following sets of items into a class that will indicate their relationships to each other. Express this relationship in a thesis statement for a possible essay developed by comparison–contrast.

EXAMPLE:
poet, musician
Relationship: Both are artists.
Thesis statement: Through their art, both the poet and the musician attempt to reflect the life around them.

1. **baker, deli owner**
   Relationship _Both run fresh food shops_
   Thesis statement _Because of their professions Bakers & deli owners provide people with fresh meat & bread_

2. **physicians, ministers**
   Relationship _Both are the trained professionals_
   Thesis statement _Ministers & physicians both must relate very well with people._

3. **skiing, water-skiing**
   Relationship _Both are on skiis_
   Thesis statement _Both skiing & w.s. take skill & balance_

4. **sociology, psychology**
   Relationship _Both are work with people_
   Thesis statement _The sociologists job is less difficult than that of a psychologist_

5. **student government, dean of students**
   Relationship _Both are forms of gov't of schools_
   Thesis statement _The dean of students has power over student gov't._

138

EXERCISE Vb: ANALOGIES
Here are some well-known analogies from literature. Read them carefully. Determine what each writer wished to explain, and then point out the way in which the analogy is limited.

1. "A woman's preaching is like a dog's walking on its hind legs. It is not done well, but you are surprised to find it done at all."   *Samuel Johnson*

2. "You were that all to me, love, for which my heart did pine,
   A green isle in the sea, love, a fountain, and a shrine."   *Edgar Allan Poe*

3. "All flesh is grass."   *Bible: Isaiah*

4. "Knowledge is to the mind what light is to the eye."   *Anonymous*

5. "My luve is like a Red, Red Rose. . . ."   *Robert Burns*

6. "Tis with our judgments as our watches, none go just alike, yet each believes his own."   *Alexander Pope*

SUGGESTED TOPICS

Choose a subject from the following list or an approved subject of your own and write an essay developed by comparison or contrast.

1. Two athletes
2. Two teachers
3. Two pets
4. Two actors
5. Two friends
6. Two news broadcasters
7. Two writers
8. Two restaurants
9. Two jobs
10. Two newspapers
11. Two schools
12. Two relatives
13. Two branches of the service
14. Two approaches to coaching
15. Two ways of dealing with terrorists
16. Two ways to discipline children
17. Two cures for hangovers
18. Two methods of childbirth
19. Two types of diets
20. Two types of motorcycles
21. Two styles of politicians
22. Two types of students
23. Two types of salespeople
24. Two types of comedy
25. Two types of architecture
26. Women's rights/then and now
27. Divorce laws/then and now
28. Prison conditions/then and now
29. Workers' rights/then and now
30. Ku Klux Klan/then and now
31. Attitudes toward work/then and now
32. Movie-making/then and now
33. Treatment of insane/then and now
34. Education/then and now
35. Political campaigns/then and now
36. Foreign cars/American cars
37. Solar power/nuclear power
38. Rock/disco
39. Mandatory retirement/voluntary retirement
40. Single life/married life
41. New math/old math
42. Book/movie of the book
43. Open door policy/entrance requirements
44. Practical nurse/registered nurse

139

45. Old movie theaters/modern cinemas
46. Grandmas/then and now
47. Two mothers-in-law
48. Two ways of dealing with failure
49. Two ways of dealing with success
50. Two presidential styles

TECHNIQUES OF CLEAR WRITING

Comparisons Within the Sentence

Since you constantly compare and contrast things, it's important that you know how to do it correctly.

First, you should recognize the three basic degrees of comparison:

Positive: She was a pretty girl.
Comparative: She was prettier than Sally.
Superlative: She was the prettiest girl in the class.

Notice that with most regular adjectives of one syllable you add -er if you are comparing one with one and -est if you are comparing one with more than one:

Positive	Comparative	Superlative
smart	smarter	smartest
big	bigger	biggest
lonely	lonelier	lonliest
rich	richer	richest
busy	busier	busiest
bright	brighter	brightest

If the adjective has two syllables, you have a choice of -er and -est, or more and most (or less and least).

If the adjective has three or more syllables, you form the comparison with more (or less) and the superlative with most (or least).

These rules also apply to the comparison of adverbs.

beautiful	more beautiful	most beautiful
confusing	more confusing	most confusing
disturbed	more disturbed	most disturbed
nervous	more nervous	most nervous
intelligent	more intelligent	most intelligent

Watch out for incomplete, confusing, or illogical comparisons as in the following sections.

INCOMPLETE COMPARISONS   If you remember that a comparison always establishes a relationship between two or more items, you can avoid incomplete comparisons such as the following:

INCOMPLETE: My dog is better. [Better than what?]

CORRECT: My dog is better than your dog.

INCOMPLETE: I was so tired. [So tired that what?]

CORRECT: I was so tired that I couldn't do my homework. (*So* requires a *that* clause, as does *such*.]

INCOMPLETE: He was as **tall** or **taller** than George.

You would not say "He is as tall than George."
The sentence could be corrected in three ways:

He is as tall as or taller than George.
He is as tall as George or taller [than George].
He is as tall as George, if not taller.

CONFUSING COMPARISONS   Some comparisons confuse rather than clarify because they suggest two possible meanings. Always make sure that your reader knows what specific things are being compared. Look at the following examples:

INCORRECT: I like my dog better than my husband.

Words are left out here, and the result is that the reader doesn't know whether you mean:

I like my dog better than my husband does.
I like my dog better than I like my husband.

The wording does make a difference.

I like my dog better than my husband.

ILLOGICAL COMPARISONS   To avoid comparisons that are ridiculous or make no sense at all, you must make sure that the items being compared have a logical basis of comparison. They must belong to the same class of things in order to make the comparison meaningful.

Proofread your papers carefully to correct illogical comparisons like these:

*comparing
and contrasting*

My dog was cheaper than my father.

Surely, the dog was not that cheap! What the writer probably meant was that his dog was "cheaper than his father's dog" or "cheaper than his father's."

The price of steak here is higher than Texas.

You cannot compare *steak* with *Texas.* What was probably meant was

The price of steak here is higher than **it is in** Texas.

Tony Dorsett is better than any football player.

Tony is a football player; how can he be better than himself?

Tony Dorsett is better than any **other** football player.

EXERCISE Vc: CORRECT COMPARISONS
Revise the following sentences to make the comparisons clear and correct.

1. He was so happy.

   _____

2. Maria was as pretty or prettier than the beauty queen.

   _____

3. Elvis was better than any rock singer.

   _____

4. Of all the students who took the test, he was the better.

   _____

5. My house is bigger than any house on our block.

   _____

6. Helga's neck was longer than a giraffe.

   _____

7. Of all the Olympic athletes, I thought Eric Heiden was better
   Of all the Olympic ath, I thought Eric Heiden was better the best

8. The population of Liechtenstein is smaller than Rhode Island.
   The population of L. is smaller that the pop. of R.I.

9. New York is more cosmopolitan than any city.
   New York is more cosmo than any other city.

10. I thought *Jaws II* was as good or better than *Jaws I*.

_____

11. His salary was lower than a garbage collector.

_____

12. The new Zipmobile gives you a better ride and more miles to the gallon.

_____

13. We shouldn't be surprised if our income tax is even higher than last year.

_____

14. Senator Brooks is as rich if not richer than the oil magnate who tried to bribe him.

_____

15. Behr's Bread is better. It has better ingredients, is better baked—it's just plain better.

_____

Parallel Wording

Parallel wording is a technique that makes your writing more coherent, more interesting, and more emphatic. No good writer can do without it. It means that you state similar (parallel) ideas with similar (parallel) wording. (See Chapter 1, page 33.) For example, in the first sentence of this paragraph you were told that parallel wording enhances your writing in three ways: by making it **more coherent, more interesting,** and **more emphatic.** Each idea is similar in the sense that each indicates a quality of good writing, and each idea is equally important. Each then is parallel and thus requires parallel wording. You can state these ideas with words, phrases, or clauses, as long as you make them parallel. For example:

WORDS
Parallel wording is a technique that enhances your writing through **coherence, interest,** and **emphasis.**

PHRASES
Parallel wording is a technique that you can use to **make your writing more coherent, to make it more interesting,** and **to make it more emphatic.**

Notice how this sentence is weakened when the parallel wording is removed:

Parallel wording is a technique that makes your writing more coherent, adding interest, and you can make your writing emphatic with parallelism.

143

As you can see, without parallel wording, you end up with a weak, wordy, confusing sentence. If your reader has a hard time figuring out what you're trying to say, he or she is going to have an even harder time trying to remember what you said. Parallel wording is useful because it makes your writing easier to understand and easier to remember. How far do you think Shakespeare would have gotten without parallel wording? Most of the lines from Shakespeare that people remember are those that contain parallel wording. Look at some of his most famous quotations and see how they lose their effectiveness when they are deprived of their parallel wording.

PARALLEL: **To be** or not **to be:** that is the question. *Hamlet*

NONPARALLEL: To be or not to exist: that is the question.

PARALLEL: I come **to bury** Caesar, not **to praise** him. *Julius Caesar*

NONPARALLEL: I come to bury Caesar, having no intention of praising him.

PARALLEL: **Friends, Romans, Countrymen,** lend me your ears. *Julius Caesar*

NONPARALLEL: Friends, people whose heritage is Roman, men of this great country, lend me your ears.

PARALLEL: I am a Jew. **Hath not a Jew** eyes? **Hath not a Jew** hands, organs, dimensions, senses, affections, passions? . . . **If you prick us, do we not** bleed? **If you tickle us, do we not** laugh? **If you poison us, do we not** die? And **if you wrong us, shall we not** revenge? *The Merchant of Venice*

NONPARALLEL: I am a Jew. Hath not a Jew eyes? Doesn't a member of the Jewish race have hands, organs, dimensions, senses, affections, passions? . . . If you prick us, don't we bleed? We laugh when you tickle us, don't we? Suppose you poison us; do you not think that we would die? And how about wronging us? Wouldn't we try to get revenge?

PARALLEL: **All the** world's a stage,
And **all the men and women** merely players.
They have **their exits** and **their entrances.** *As You Like It*

NONPARALLEL: All the world's a stage,
And men and women are merely players.
They have their exits and entrances are theirs too.

PARALLEL: **A horse! A horse!** My kingdom for **a horse!** *Richard III*

NONPARALLEL: A horse! An equestrian animal! I'd give my kingdom for such a steed!

EXERCISE Vd: PARALLELISM
Revise the following sentences to eliminate faults in parallel structure.

1. Jose not only has been outstanding in basketball but also in his premed studies.

_____

2. The officials in Washington can neither understand the small farmer's problems nor can they solve them by shuffling papers in the Department of Agriculture.

_____

3. The office manager insisted that the girls dress modestly, always being on time, and to limit their phone calls to no more than three minutes.

_____

4. The bumper crop of corn neither helped the farmers nor were the city dwellers benefited.

_____

5. The police not only arrested Jim but his father also.

_____

6. His speech was clear, concise, interesting, and has cleared up many common misconceptions.

_____

7. When the youth has learned the animal's habits, and after many hours practice in tracking, he is ready to take part in the hunt.

_____

8. Discovering a grammar common to all languages would be to discover a bond that unites all people.

_____

9. He was sensitive, intelligent, and knew a good deal about Indian traditions.

_____

10. He should retire for both his own good and because it would be a good thing for the company.

_____

WORD POWER

Good Diction: The Right Word in the Right Place

Diction, according to the **diction**ary, is the choosing of words to create a manner of speaking. It is this choice that, in large part, makes up style. And style in your writing is a reflection of your personality. You develop style through many things, but essential to a pleasing and effective style is the right word in the right place.

To find the right word and put it in the right place sounds easy but involves making a series of choices.

GENERAL - SPECIFIC   One important choice among words is one you have already read about several times in this book: the general and the specific. It is important enough to mention again.

You choose a general word when you wish to convey a broad category, that is, when you want your reader to think of something that is made up of many

145

subdivisions. If you were discussing your selection of a university, for example, you might say, "I want to go where I have a wide choice of *academic disciplines.*" That general phrase covers dozens of specific studies from accounting to zoology. Very often, you need such a general term for your thesis statement or topic sentences.

Having set the broad framework in your thesis statement and topic sentences, you must then narrow your controlling idea as you develop your essay, and so you choose more specific terms. Using the sentence about "academic disciplines" just mentioned, you might have an introductory paragraph like this:

> Our dinner table conversations this winter all seem to end in discussions about what college I should go to next fall. My mother wants me to go to the community college because she would like me to stay near home. My father would like me to go to the very good technical school he went to. Although I can agree with lots of points they make, I yearn for something else. I want to go where I have a wide choice of academic disciplines.

Now as you narrow your thesis, you pick out specific terms naming academic disciplines—astronomy, botany, calculus, and so forth.

**ABSTRACT-
CONCRETE**

The distinction between *abstract* and *concrete* is similar to, but not the same as, the distinction between *general* and *specific.* Here again is a place where you choose your words carefully. Do you want a term that is understood intellectually (abstract) or one that is felt through the senses (concrete)? Usually, the more abstract term is the better choice for thesis statements and topic sentences. The concrete term is better for the supporting paragraphs. Usually, too, you choose the abstract term (or the general) when you are making a judgmental statement, for judgments tend to be generalizations.

JARGON

Doctors, lawyers, psychologists, printers, advertising men, iron workers, oil field roustabouts—people in every trade, profession, or sport have their own kind of jargon, their own specialized vocabularies. Such jargon can be divided into many subclasses: technical jargon, shoptalk, officialese, and the parlance of golfers, yacht owners, and literary critics. The common feature of all jargon is the use of a specialized vocabulary of a particular science, art, trade, profession, or sport. Although it serves a useful purpose for people in a great many walks of life, the big drawback to jargon is that it is clear only to the initiated. For example, imagine yourself a new recruit trying to make sense of the *Handbook of Military Artillery and Offensive and Defensive Strategies:*

> The towed artillery is operationally differentiated from the self-propelled artillery. Both are used in protective reaction strikes involving armoured fighting vehicles and long-range maritime patrol aircraft. The hedgehog is a tactical concept used in defense-in-depth systems in conjunction with the vertical deployment of anti-personnel devices. Close-support, transport, and reconnaissance assistance is provided by the S–3X helicopter which is most

cost effective in a crane configuration. Static artillery and armoured fighting vehicles accompany troop deployment as protection against high-velocity projectiles. . . .

Whenever people use jargon in communicating with others unfamiliar with their trade or profession, there is trouble.

In another sense, which is even more troublesome, jargon means pretentious, obscure language. This language avoids simple words for overblown ones; it overuses abstract nouns, generalizations, nouns modifying other nouns, and passive constructions. The result is wordiness and pomposity, but little meaning.

For example, critic Malcolm Cowley takes to task those sociologists who have become so engrossed in jargon that they can no longer express themselves in clear and simple English. Cowley quotes a sociologist who says:

In effect, it was hypothesized that certain physical data categories including housing types and densities, land use characteristics, and ecological location constitute a scalable content area. This could be called a continuum of residential desirability. Likewise, it was hypothesized that several social data categories, describing the same census tracts, and referring generally to the social stratification system of the city, would also be scalable. This scale could be called a continuum of socioeconomic status. Thirdly, it was hypothesized that there would be a high positive correlation between the scale types on each continuum.

This is boring and says almost nothing. If, as Cowley suggests, you reduce these ninety-three words to standard English, you have the far from startling assumption that rich people live in good neighborhoods.

The scholar Jacques Barzun perceives such jargon as the "unnecessary abstraction (which) is one of the worst faults of modern writing—the string of nouns held together by prepositions and relying on the passive voice to convey the enfeebled sense."

Barzun challenges the reader to make sense out of the following quotation:

The influence exerted by Christianity upon the arts extends to painting and sculpture insofar as their relationship to Christian religious experiences corresponds to that part of this experience which consists of images, and extends to architecture, both with regard to edifices dedicated to worship and to the settlement of religious communities.

In writing for the general reader, there is only one safe rule regarding jargon: **avoid it.**

**GOBBLEDY-
GOOK**

Gobbledygook is a peculiarly American term coined by former Texas Congressman Maury Maverick. The language of Washington bureaucrats reminded the congressman of the sound that a turkey gobbler makes, and the word *gobbledy-*

gook came to stand for a particular type of jargon—the legalistic and evasive wording of government statements. Consider the plight of the veteran who receives the following communication from the Veterans Administration:

The noncompensable evaluation heretofore assigned to you for your service-connected disability is confirmed and continued.

Does the veteran get a pension or not?

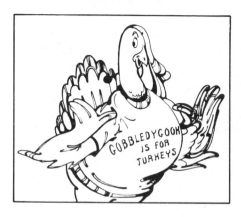

Don't talk like a turkey.

Here is a little game you can play with gobbledygook. First, pick any three-digit number; then select the corresponding word from each of the three columns below:

Column 1	*Column 2*	*Column 3*
0. flexible	ongoing	program
1. innovative	differential	formula
2. comprehensive	clientele	duplication
3. utilitarian	directive	qualification
4. systematized	progression	focus
5. facilitative	flexibility	initiative
6. finalized	program	competencies
7. coordinate	resolution	planning
8. responsive	diffusion	role
9. upgraded	professional	expectation

Suppose, for example, that you select the number 378; that gives you "utilitarian resolution role." If you select 826, that gives you "responsive clientele competencies." Almost any three-digit number will give you a phrase that sounds impressive but says nothing.

EUPHEMISMS   *Euphemisms* are mild, pleasant-sounding words used to hide the blunt truth and perhaps unpleasant facts of life. Poor people are "the underprivileged" or "the lower income brackets." Old people are "golden agers" or "senior citizens." Dead people are referred to as "the deceased" or "the dearly departed"; they never die, they just "pass away."

Not all euphemisms are harmful or deceptive, but they can become a little ridiculous, as when garbage collectors become "sanitary engineers," barbers become "hair stylists" or "tonsorial artists," prison guards become "correctional officers," and rat catchers become "rodent control operators."

A multitude of crimes punishable by law hide behind such euphemisms as "indiscretion," "misconduct," "delinquency," "intimacy," "indecency," "misappropriation," or "negligence." Euphemisms become vicious distortions of language and meaning when brutal aggression becomes "liberation," forced labor becomes "reeducation," and shooting civilians is called "pacification." Since direct and straightforward language best delivers clear, undistorted messages, it makes sense to avoid euphemisms altogether.

DENOTATION

Denotation is the "dictionary meaning" of a word, which means you can look up the word to find out what thing or idea that word points to or denotes. There are several levels of these literal meanings. The first words you ever knew simply denoted things (*teddy bear, cup, cookie*) or actions (*play, fall, cry*) or people (*mother, father, baby*). Since you could actually point to or act out these things, you didn't need other words to explain them.

As you grew older, you learned words that pointed to more complex types of meaning, things that were not really present to be pointed to (last summer's romance, tomorrow's date). As you learned more, you could denote things that never were, like a mermaid or Jack the Giant Killer. You can denote a **class** of things or people, like the tall ships or the faculty. You can denote a generalization, like dreams, or an abstraction, like love. But in all of these word choices, you are still referring to the core meaning, the denotation. Denotative language is objective. It is used when your purpose is to convey factual information, avoiding subjective attitudes and judgments.

CONNOTATION

Whereas denotation points out core meanings giving you information, *connotation* gives you the emotional atmosphere that surrounds these words. Connotation suggests how the writer feels about that information and how he or she wants you to feel about it. Connotative language is subjective. It is used when your purpose is to arouse emotion—fear, hope, enthusiasm.

Connotations arise from the associations that accompany a word. Over years, centuries perhaps, writers have used certain words to express approval or disapproval. These long associations temper feelings about the word. A word that has strong connotations makes the reader feel approval or disapproval, perhaps not even recognizing the reason for such feelings. Suppose, for example, you needed some professional service. Wouldn't you choose someone described as a lawyer rather than a shyster, a surgeon rather than a sawbones, a veterinarian rather than a horse doctor? In each case, the pairs of words might have been applied to the same person, but you probably would not employ a professional whom you thought of as a shyster or sawbones or horse doctor.

LEVELS OF USAGE Still another choice you make in diction is the level of usage you decide upon, based upon the audience you are addressing and how formal or informal you wish to be.

Just as you would not go to the prom in cutoff jeans or wear a dinner jacket on the tennis courts, you would not choose language inappropriate to the occasion or the audience. You would not use exactly the same language to your grandmother as to your best friend, or the same diction to your English instructor as to your baby brother. You would not give a valedictory address in the language you use with your friends at a beer party.

Essentially, there are four levels of usage:

1. **Formal** Used rarely, it is appropriate for important speeches or papers. It avoids contractions and short words; it depends heavily on learned, specialized vocabulary and balanced sentence structure.

2. **Standard** Used constantly as the business and social language of educated people, it strives for preciseness and conciseness in vocabulary, flexible sentence structure, and varying sentence lengths. It is used when people are conscious of their speech and writing.

3. **Colloquial** The spoken language most people use with their families and friends. Since it is spoken, it uses slang freely and sometimes contains cliches. It is used when people are not concentrating on more formal levels of language.

4. **Substandard** The speech of people totally untrained in language, it is characterized by incorrect grammar, imprecise and repetitious vocabulary, and sentence fragments, or at best, simple or compound sentences.

These four levels are broad categories. Within the first three, educated people make narrower choices, generally choosing within the classes of standard and colloquial language. Although some writers of fiction use substandard language in dialogue to characterize people, most users of substandard language are not free to make choices because they lack the knowledge to use the other levels. As Mark Twain once said, "The man who talks corrupt English six days in the week must and will talk it on the seventh; he can't help himself."

Review of Rules Regarding Good Diction

1. Choose the simple word over the long word if the simpler word says what you mean.

2. Choose the precise and concise word to eliminate wordiness.

3. Choose a fresh comparison over a worn-out phrase. If you can't think of an original comparison, choose plain, direct statements rather than clichés.

4. Choose reasonable statements rather than excessive statements of enthusiasm or disapproval. ("Cedar Point Amusement Park is the greatest place in the world for anyone to spend a vacation.")

5. Choose reasonable statements rather than preaching. ("Young people must respect their parents.")

6. Choose a standard word rather than the in-group language of jargon, unless you are writing to an in-group.

7. Choose vigorous action verbs to improve the clarity and force of your writing.

You may have noticed that all the choices discussed in this section have been choices among synonyms, words that mean almost the same thing. The English language is rich in synonyms, so you have ample resources from which to choose words that make distinctions on the basis of connotation, usage, abstraction or concreteness, generalization or specificity.

Notice the distinctions made among the synonyms for the word *sign* in the *American Heritage Dictionary*:

Synonyms: *sign, badge, mark, token, indication, symptom, note.*
These nouns are compared as they denote outward evidence of something. *Sign,* the most general, can mean virtually any [kind of objective evidence]. *Badge* usually refers to something worn that denotes membership in a group, or rank, achievement, or condition: *Her mink coat was a badge of success. Mark* can refer to a personal characteristic or indication of character: *Intolerance is the mark of a bigot.* It can also denote evidence of an experience: *Poverty had left its mark on him. Token* usually refers to a symbol, pledge, or proof of something intangible: *a token of affection. Indication* refers to evidence of a condition. *Symptom* suggests visible evidence of an adverse condition, such as a disease. *Note* applies to a distinguishing characteristic or feature: *the note of mysticism in his novels.*

EXERCISE Ve: JARGON
In the following sentences, turn the jargon into standard English so that something definite and understandable is said.

1. They concluded that they must prioritize their duties to make their lifestyles more viable.

_____

2. We won't know the solution to our problem until we have everyone's input on the bottom line. 'Til then, we only have ballpark figures.

_____

3. In the case of John, who is critical, there are circumstances that indicate his medical situation is serious.

_____

4. The hoopsters of Hoop-la College debut tonight to fire the opening gun of the hardwood circuit.

_____

5. The instructional personnel of our institution of higher learning are frustrated because budgetary limitations make their innovative proposals infeasible.

_____

6. The utilization of computer technology will facilitate the retrieval of information from our data bank.

_____

7. It would seem that nothing more nor less than a value scale of subjective factors renders the range of grades indeterminate.

_____

8. Your son is achieving to expectancy in his skill subjects, but in content areas his development is blocked by a predisposition to underachieve.

_____

9. Due to the fact that the faculty experienced a delay in the distribution of grade cards, it is the decision of the office of student records to extend the period of time permissible for the submission of completed grade reports.

_____

10. Hopefully, all employees are urged to extinguish illumination and other energy-consuming facilities when departing the premises for the night.

_____

EXERCISE Vf: SYNONYMS
Using a good modern desk dictionary, look up the synonyms for the following words. Can the synonyms be used interchangeably? If not, what differences do you see among the synonyms?

1. **mysterious** _____

2. **native** _____

3. **last** _____

4. **recoil** _____

5. **cry** _____

6. **reckless** _____

Franklin P. Adams, a popular writer of humorous verse (what is the distinction between verse and poetry?), wrote a poem addressed to a thesaurus. As you read the poem, observe that scarcely any two of the synonyms could replace each other if the poem were not meant as a joke.

To a Thesaurus

O precious codex, volume, tome,
Book, writing, compilation, work
Attend the while,
A jest, a jape, a quip, a quirk.

For I would pen, engross, indite,
Transcribe, set forth, compose, address,
Record, submit—yea, even write
An ode, an elegy to bless—

To bless, set store by, celebrate,
Approve, esteem, endow with soul,
Commend, acclaim, appreciate,
Immortalize, laud, praise, extol

Without thy help, recruit, support,
Opitulation, furtherance,
Assistance, rescue, aid, resort,
Favour, sustention and advance?

Alas! alack! and well-a-day!
My case would then be dour and sad,
Likewise distressing, dismal, grey,
Pathetic, mournful, dreary, bad.

Though I could keep this up all day,
This lyric, elegiac song,
Meseems hath come the time to say
Farewell! Adieu! Good-bye! So long!

CHAPTER VI

dividing and classifying

"That's not our church! That's the church where the **pedestrians** go," the little girl said. What that little girl was trying to do, although she confused pedestrians with Presbyterians, was to divide and classify churches according to similarities or differences she had noticed. So it is for you and me. From earliest childhood you begin to divide and classify things according to the similarities and differences you observe.

Without the ability to divide and classify information, you would find the world a mass of confusion. You wouldn't be able to make sense out of anything because nothing would be organized; nothing would be categorized, and, as a result, you would find it difficult to accomplish anything. You would never have made it past the fifth grade if you hadn't learned how to break down information (divide) and place it in specific categories (classify). As a matter of fact, one of the first things you learned to do as a child was organize information into categories. For example, when you were learning to recognize sounds, your one-year-old brain might have begun by distinguishing human sounds from mechanical sounds:

Human Sounds	Mechanical Sounds
crying	cars
talking	train whistles
yelling	sweepers
coughing	musical instruments

As you grew older, you learned that each sound could be broken down further. For example, you learned to classify different kinds of musical instruments; you learned to distinguish a drum from a horn and a horn from a piano. As an adult, you divide and classify more complex information, but you are still doing basically the same thing you did as a baby when you were learning to distinguish one sound from another:

1. Dividing information into parts
2. Classifying those parts by placing them in logical categories

Our first attempts at dividing and classifying are crude, and the lines of division may be blurred, as when a child classifies all dogs as big, middle-sized, and puppies. Later, division and classification become more complex; dogs, for example, are seen to be divided in various types and classified according to a variety of characteristics. Finally, you have the specific and exacting kind of classification used by professionals in every branch of science. Geologists, for instance, divide geologic time into various eras, such as Paleozoic, Mesozoic, and Cenozoic. Also the rocks of the earth's crust are divided into various types and classified according to their origin and composition.

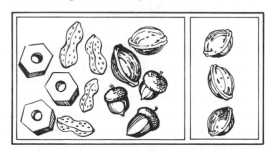

**Four Classifications
—One Subdivision**

Such scientific classification is totally comprehensive. For example, when a biologist classifies animals, he considers **every** creature in the entire animal kingdom. Nonscientific classifications, which are called "literary" or informal, do not try to be all-inclusive. Nevertheless, their aim is the same. They clarify complexity by showing it part by part. They bring order out of chaos.

Poets as well as scientists use classification. For example, almost every creation story tells how the creator made the world by dividing chaos into parts and identifying, through classification, each part. Here is the poet Ovid explaining the Roman version of creation. Notice how he portrays the creator making an understandable and livable world by breaking down chaos, where everything is confusedly mixed together, into its parts:

The Creation

Before the ocean was, or earth, or heaven,
Nature was all alike, a shapelessness,
Chaos, so-called, all rude and lumpy matter
Nothing but bulk, inert, in whose confusion
Discordant atoms warred: there was no sun
To light the universe; there was no moon
With slender silver crescents filling slowly;
No earth hung balanced in surrounding air;
No sea reached far along the fringe of shore.
Land, to be sure, there was, and air, and ocean,
But land on which no man could stand, and water
No man could swim in, air no man could breathe.

Till God, or kindlier Nature,
Settled all argument, and separated
Heaven from earth, water from land, our air
From the high stratosphere.
So things evolved, and out of blind confusion
Found each its place, bound in eternal order.

Whatever god it was, who out of chaos
Brought order to the universe, and gave it
Division, subdivision, he molded earth,
In the beginning, into a great globe,
Even on every side, and bade the waters
To spread and rise, under the rushing winds.

These boundaries given,
Behold, the stars, long hidden under darkness,
Broke through and shone, all over the spangled heaven,
Their home forever, and the gods lived there,
And shining fish were given the waves for dwelling
And beasts the earth, and birds the moving air.

Many ideas that you might want to write about require that you break your subject into smaller units. For instance, if you decide to write your essay on the subject of swearing, you might divide your topic into the four types of swear words: the sacrilegious, the scatological, the anatomical, and the sexual.

Once the subject is broken into parts, it's easy to explain each part in a paragraph; then you add an introduction and a conclusion, and your essay is complete. However, you must be sure that you have used a single principle for your division. If you say, "There are four basic sleeping positions, each of which gives a clue to the sleeper's personality," then it would not be correct, for example, to include in your division of sleeping positions "those who dream," because those who dream could sleep in any of the given positions.

If you were to write an essay on the Olympics, you might begin by dividing the general subject into smaller parts or divisions, such as Individual Sports, Paired Sports, and Team Sports. Then you could develop each part systematically by classifying individual, paired, and team sports according to the skills needed, the method of judging the participants, or whatever classification best suits your purpose.

ORGANIZATION

Division and classification is a **purposeful** grouping of things, activities, or ideas. If the process is to be of any value, you must divide and classify according to some sensible **ruling principle.** For instance, you could classify teachers according to academic degrees, teaching experience, or classroom performance, but to classify them according to hair color would serve no useful purpose. In addition, you need to apply **one** ruling principle at a time to ensure that your purpose remains clear and that your divisions do not overlap.

Thus, to be of any value, the division and classification must be **sensible** and **informative.** Instead of forcing your subject to fit preconceived categories, what you need to do is think about your subject and try to see which divisions or categories fit best. Dividing people into such general categories as rich, poor, and middle income does not in itself reveal anything new. However, if you can define those categories and show a correlation between income and educational level, you may provide new information worth thinking about.

Suppose that you have been reading about hostages seized by terrorists and you decide that hostages might be a good subject to write about. Now there are many possible approaches to that subject, but assume that you decide to concentrate on what happens to the people who are held hostage. After giving the subject a little thought, you might decide to further limit your discussion to those who are held for prolonged periods—not just for an hour or two, but for weeks or months.

After more reading and thinking about hostages held by terrorist groups, you might find that you have a good many notes which could look like this:

1. Helpless and dependent—gun-barrel and butt-stroke obedience.
2. Threat of violence and death hanging over (shot one-by-one or thrown from window, etc.).
3. Physical wearing down—weight loss, etc.
4. Agony of uncertainty—at hands of the desperate and unpredictable.
5. Existing ailments made worse (women and older men probably suffer most).
6. Confinement and restricted movement taking a toll.
7. May develop deep-seated illness (infections, heart and circulation trouble, etc.).
8. Cut off from friends, family, and rest of society—lacking their love and support.
9. Effect on health for rest of life.
10. Suffer from "flashbacks"—agonizing nightmares, etc.

To bring some semblance of order to your random notes, you might first of all divide them into two groups: (1) physical effects, and (2) mental effects of being held captive.

Then you could start sorting out your notes according to these two main divisions:

A. Physical effects of prolonged confinement
  1. Effects of close confinement and restricted physical activity
  2. Physical deterioriation that sets in
  3. Existing ailments made worse by confinement
  4. Deep-seated illnesses that develop from stress
  5. Physical effect continuing after release
B. Psychological effects of prolonged confinement
  1. Continuing fear of violence and death
  2. Agonizing uncertainty of a fate unknown
  3. Utter helplessness, isolation, and dependence
  4. Complete separation from family, friends, and society
  5. Torment of flashbacks following release

Note that each point has been refined and sharpened as you progressed.

What you have done up to this point is to **divide** your subject into two parts according to separate but related bases—physical and mental. Further, you have **classified** these physical and mental effects in a fairly systematic way.

Introduction

Since everything changes as it moves, you may find it necessary to change the order of certain points as you develop your essay. The important thing is that you have a track to run on, a sensible plan for developing your essay. What you need to do now is to define your purpose. What is it that you want to prove or demonstrate with the information you have gathered? Perhaps you would like your reader to understand the various types of physical punishment and mental torture that hostages undergo. If so, you might use an introduction such as this:

Over the past decade, more than forty attacks have been made on diplomatic missions in various parts of the world. To terrorists and guerrillas of whatever stripe, American embassies and diplomatic missions seem inviting targets, for Americans make valuable hostages. Sometimes the hostages, whether embassy personnel or American businessmen seized for ransom, are released after brief periods of negotiations; but some have been held for weeks, months, or years. Those are the ones who suffer most. During their long periods of captivity, hostages are frequently subjected to various types of physical punishment and mental torment.

Body

The body of this essay would be developed by explaining each type of physical and psychological effect of prolonged confinement.

In most essays developed by division and classification, the logical order of arrangement is **climactic.** Having established your main divisions or classifications, you arrange them in the order of increasing importance.

You should never take your reader's interest for granted, and arranging the material in the body of your essay in the order of increasing importance helps to ensure continued interest. Whether you are writing about toadstools or atomic warheads, you create a sense of climax by building from the least dramatic to the most dramatic illustration. If you save the most vivid and dramatic part until last, then the reader will follow you to the climax and may even think, "Gee, that essay really made its point."

Notice how the following essay discusses the various types of problem drinkers in climactic order—from periodic drinker to chronic alcoholic—and then pulls the whole discussion of individual types together in the conclusion.

The Problem Drinker

The stereotyped figure of the skid-row bum sleeping in a doorway with his wine bottle in a brown paper sack is familiar to everyone. Far less easy to recognize are the millions of other problem drinkers in homes, schools, offices, and factories across the nation. They can be found in every occupation and at every level from washroom attendant to top executive. Although they may appear to have little or nothing else in common, they do have one common problem—their inability to handle alcohol. The inability to cope with alcohol comes in many forms and degrees, but problem drinkers can be divided into several recognizable types.

The periodic drinker may be able to hold a job, even a high-level position, because his periodic bouts with alcohol are only occasional deviations from his usually competent performance. Since his sprees may be separated by long periods of diligence and sobriety, the periodic drinker may succeed, for a time at least, in hiding his problem from his co-workers and his superiors. He may, in fact, enlist the aid of a sympathetic doctor who will diagnose his problem as an ulcer or some disorder related to stress. His wife and family, of course, cover for him when he goes on one of his periodic binges. But he has within him a worm that never dies. Unless he quits, and quits permanently, his addiction is almost certain to become more acute, and his periodic bouts with alcohol will become progressively more frequent until his problem becomes obvious to everyone around him.

The convivial drinker who doesn't know when to stop is a familiar figure at the local watering holes and on the cocktail circuit. Even if he works regularly and confines his drinking mainly to weekends and holidays, the quality of his personal life and his on-the-job performance are sure to suffer. His career is frequently checkered with arrests for drunken driving and financial or domestic problems. Sometimes he may go on for years slogging through the hangovers from lost weekends and parties he scarcely remembers, while his friends and acquaintances find him less and less welcome and more and more of a pain. Quite often, such a person may seem to survive one smash-up after another as he goes his not-so-merry way, but he is on a downhill course that may well end in a violent smash-up or total breakdown.

The Jekyll and Hyde drinker is an unpredictable menace to himself and others. Even a few drinks may set off a drastic change in behavior. The courteous and mild-mannered person may suddenly turn foul-mouthed and aggressive, hurling insults at innocent bystanders and heaping abuse on family and friends. His normal caution and restraint may give way suddenly to wild behavior, such as picking a fight with a stranger or driving erratically at a high rate of speed. Later, he may block out the memory of what he did, deny responsibility for his actions, and refuse to believe that he behaved atrociously. The root of his problem goes deep. More than alcohol alone—he may, in fact, consume very little—his trouble is a deep-seated psychological problem, and his drinking behavior may be only a symptom. Yet as long as he continues to drink, his unresolved mental problem is likely to fester until it erupts in some new outbreak of violent and irrational behavior.

The secretive drinker tries to hide his drinking from friends and family. At the same time, he is often trying desperately to hide from himself the reality of his problem. It is not unusual for such a person to hide bottles or wine, whiskey, or vodka in odd corners of the house, even in such places as the dirty clothes hamper or the water closet tank. The secretive drinker steadfastly refuses to admit how much he drinks and constantly searches for ingenious ways to hide the evidence. By maintaining a fairly constant level of consumption, a secret drinker may go for long periods without displaying outward signs of drunkenness. Eventually, of course, the evidence of something amiss becomes as obvious as a cat in a bird cage, but the secretive drinker still refuses to admit the obvious and insists that he has no drinking problem.

The chronic alcoholic is a desperately sick person. Drinking has become a compulsion which rules his life. After years of alcohol abuse, he usually suffers from severe disorders such as cirrhosis, as well as other forms of physical and mental deterioration. The occasional blackouts of an earlier stage have now become routine. Often, he cannot remember where he has been or what he has done, and he may totally forget where he left his car or his overcoat. He may start to confabulate, to make up stories to fill in the frightening blanks in his befuddled mind. In his few moments of relative sobriety he is consumed by one obsession—where to get the next drink. If he tries to stop drinking, he gets the DT's, a terrifying attack of delirium tremens that could prove fatal. Even if he is hospitalized for a drying-out period, he'll be drinking again almost as soon as he hits the street. He can attend the funeral of a friend who died of acute alcoholism and be drinking again before the casket is covered. Unless he can stop drinking completely and permanently—which would be little short of a miracle—his own dance of death has already begun, and whatever life he has left is scarcely worth living.

Chronic alcholism is the state to which most problem drinkers unwittingly aspire, for there is ample evidence to prove that alcoholism is a progressive disease. Taken in time, the disease can be arrested, but the only sure treatment for the problem drinker is to go on the wagon for good. No matter how obvious the solution to the problem may seem to others, few problem drinkers willingly quit drinking.

Conclusion

Your discussion should not end with one division, class, or type. What you need is a brief conclusion which brings out the purpose of your essay of division and classification and leaves its controlling idea clear in the mind of your reader.

In this essay a student presents a humorous complaint about a common problem through the process of division and classification.

The Pennsylvania Pothole

Of all of the things that Pennsylvania produces, the most widely known is the concrete cavity or the common pothole. Potholes are sneaky little devils in that they open overnight and grow to monstrous sizes. The average life of these cement ulcers is about six months, and in that time, they go through three life stages: the teeth grinder, the axle bender, and the killer.

In its infancy, a pothole is a teeth grinder. One knows that he has found teeth grinders when he sees many small holes very close to each other. These holes are usually about one-half inch deep and are usually in narrow strips across the road. Teeth grinders are found in groups of four or five and spaced so that each wheel hits one at different times. To observe a real teeth grinder, all one has to do is go to a nearby road and look because teeth grinders are found everywhere.

As the pothole grows from teeth grinders into its teenage of axle bendership, the hole becomes much more of a pain for the car and its driver. To become an axle bender, many of the teeth grinders get together as a street gang and attack unsuspecting motorists. The typical axle bender is two or three inches deep and about six to eight inches wide (the size of the average tire contact area). Mainly found on moderately traveled roads, axle benders are found alone and spaced about twenty feet apart. It is possible to miss (dodge) an axle bender, but your dodging may result in your being stopped by the police for drunken driving.

When fully grown, the pothole becomes a killer. The killer pothole is one that causes the car to lift one wheel, limp off the road, and whimper. The only way to describe the killer crater is to use the words of one who survived the horrors of a killer attack, "That crater shouldn't be patched, it should be bridged." Though many expeditions have gone down to the floors of killer potholes, the only explanation for them is very rapid growth while in the axle bender stage. (The growth may be caused by the devouring of a few small cars.) The killer pothole is not very common, but it can be found on most moderately to heavily traveled roads, especially ones that big trucks use. A pothole dies after either the killer or axle bender stage. A pothole execution order is issued usually after a Pennsylvania Department of Transportation employee blows a tire or damages his car in a hole. The death has no ceremony, just a shovelful or a truckload of asphalt.

The pothole is a Pennsylvania landmark. People come from many places to hear the bolts of their cars loosen, or to climb down the side of a pothole in search of lost families and treasures. One closing thought: smile when you hit a pothole, and be like the man who was traveling south, hit a pothole, and sent his left rear wheel east; just say, "Raten fraten paten loomer" and you'll feel better.   *Greg Hendry*

Pitfalls to Avoid

1. Avoid simple-minded either-or categories: not all politicians are liberal or conservative; not all restaurants are good or bad. Any such division is faulty because it leaves out some members of the group. Besides, what you end up with is not division and classification but comparison and contrast.

2. Avoid overlapping categories. If you were discussing foods, for example, a classification such as meat, fish, poultry, and veal would be defective. Veal is a type of meat and therefore not a separate category.

3. Be sure to include all members of a group or class. If you are classifying people according to their interest in sports, three categories—great interest, little interest, and no interest—would be inadequate. What about the people who are moderately interested but not great enthusiasts?

4. Avoid trying to cover too many categories for a short essay. You couldn't hope adequately to cover all types of music in one short essay. Often, what you need to do is narrow your focus; you might, for example, discuss the types of dance music that are popular today.

5. Avoid meaningless classification. Just dividing your subject into parts does not necessarily provide a useful classification. Just saying that people can be divided into the young, old, and middle-aged doesn't mean anything unless you have a clear purpose in mind and explain that purpose to your reader.

6. Don't forget to provide the transitions necessary to take your reader with you. Try to provide smooth transition as you move your discussion from one division or category to another.

EXERCISE VIa: CLASSIFYING

Classify the following sets of items in two ways, each on a different basis.

1. Articles in a student's room

	Things for Athletics	School Stuff
accounting text		✓
baseball cap	✓	
chemistry book		✓
half-finished English theme		✓
ski jacket	✓	
employee badge	—	—
pencils		✓
skis and poles	✓	
softball bat	✓	
tennis racket	✓	
socket wrenches	—	—

2. Clothes

	Dress-up Clothes	Seasonal Clothes
yellow bathing trunks		✓
red plaid mackinaw	✓	
black tuxedo	✓	
blue walking shorts		✓
black snow boots		✓
yellow school letter sweater		✓
red woolen stocking cap		✓
blue dinner jacket	✓	
red beach towel		✓
blue cummerbund	✓	
black dress shoes	✓	
black baseball shoes	—	—

162

EXERCISE VIb: CLASSIFYING
Classify in five ways the students in your classroom.

SUGGESTED TOPICS

Write an essay of division and classification using one of the following topics or an approved topic of your own choosing.

1.	Marriages	18.	Jokes	35.	Dreams
2.	Dates	19.	Motives	36.	Ambitions
3.	Pets	20.	Criminals	37.	Symbols
4.	Cars	21.	Textbooks	38.	Vacations
5.	Doctors	22.	Colleges	39.	Engines
6.	Teachers	23.	Parents	40.	Farms
7.	Ministers	24.	Drugs	41.	Athletes
8.	Politicians	25.	Policemen	42.	Tools
9.	Bosses	26.	Occupations	43.	Toys
10.	Girlfriends	27.	Courses	44.	TV programs
11.	Movies	28.	Students	45.	Firearms
12.	Restaurants	29.	Personalities	46.	Prisons
13.	Clothes	30.	Celebrities	47.	Diets
14.	Resorts	31.	Singers	48.	Frustrations
15.	Cities	32.	Dancers	49.	Boyfriends
16.	Alibis	33.	Salespeople	50.	Motorcycles
17.	Fads	34.	Musicians		

TECHNIQUES OF CLEAR WRITING

Clarity Through Emphasis

EMPHASIS THROUGH PLACEMENT WITHIN THE SENTENCE

Explain

If you want your writing to be effective, you have to learn how to emphasize the important points. You must therefore be careful about how you arrange your thoughts. In the following sentences, for example, notice how you can emphasize a point by changing its position in the sentence. Note in particular that it is more effective to place a point that deserves emphasis at the beginning or end of a sentence than to place it in the middle:

Chief Broken Wing heard the distant cannon; **he ordered the attack;** he knew that most of his warriors would not return.

Chief Broken Wing **ordered the attack** even though he could hear the distant cannon and realized that most of his warriors would not return.

163   *2023 ex*

Chief Broken Wing, hearing the distant cannon and realizing that most of his warriors would not return, **ordered the attack.**

All of the sentences above give you the same information; however, they do not give you the same feeling. In the first sentence, the major action, the Chief's order to attack, is buried in the middle of the sentence. In the second sentence, the major action comes first, so it is hard to miss; however, the sentence loses its dramatic effect because the rest of the sentence is anticlimactic. The third sentence is the most dramatic because it makes you wait for the Chief's decision, thus building more tension in your mind as you read. Thus, it is not words alone that make a difference; it is also their position in the sentence. Note the difference in the following sentences:

Archie Bunker, who is a bigot, is the major character in "All in the Family."
Archie Bunker, the major character in "All in the Family," is a bigot.

Note that the first sentence emphasizes Archie's importance in the show. The second sentence emphasizes Archie's bigotry.

In some sentences there is no right or wrong order. It all depends on what the writer wishes to emphasize. For example, look at the following sentences:

Dwight D. Eisenhower, who was the thirty-fourth president of the United States, was a renowned general in World War II.
Dwight D. Eisenhower, who was a renowned general in World War II, was the thirty-fourth president of the United States.

Which Eisenhower do you wish to emphasize?

If you wanted to emphasize Eisenhower's military career, you would use the first sentence; if you wanted to emphasize his presidency, you would use the last sentence.

| EMPHASIS THROUGH POSITION IN CLAUSES | The most important idea in a sentence should be in the main clause; less important ideas should be subordinated. |

INCORRECT: I was walking home from school when I saw the accident occur.

CORRECT: As I was walking home from school, I saw the accident.

INCORRECT: When he learned he had won the Nobel Prize, Ralph Bunche was having dinner with some friends.

CORRECT: While having dinner with his friends, Ralph Bunche learned that he had won the Nobel Prize.

EMPHASIS THROUGH FORCEFUL EXPRESSION

The most obvious way to make your point emphatic is through forceful statement. Emerson advised, "Say what you have to say in words as hard as bullets." Writers find that using strong words to make a blunt, straightforward statement is often the most emphatic way to express profound convictions. Such a statement also gains emphasis through brevity. "War is hell," for example, is more emphatic than "War is a terrible act of violence that creates misery and pain."

Repeating a point, or even a word, also lends emphasis. You make it clear that something is important if you say it more than once: "She was my last hope . . . my last." Also, notice how much more effective it is to repeat a name rather than to say it just once: "John, John . . . my son, my son."

EMPHASIS WITHIN THE ESSAY

Emphasis within the essay works the same way as emphasis within the sentence: the strongest positions are first and last, at the beginning of your essay or the end of your essay. Usually, saving the best for last is the most effective way of developing an essay. Your most convincing argument, your most important detail, your most interesting point, the idea you will leave in the reader's mind—that is what you put last. Then you are using climactic order; your details build to a climax as your discussion progresses from your least important point to your most important point. For example, if you were writing a paper on Pap Finn's treatment of Huck in *The Adventures of Huckleberry Finn,* you might decide to include the following points: (1) he tried to take his money from him, (2) in a bout with the DT's, he tried to kill him, (3) he beat him regularly, and (4) he refused to allow Huck to go to school. However, your paper wouldn't be very effective unless you arranged your points in climactic order:

1. He refused to allow Huck to go to school.
2. He tried to take his money from him.
3. He beat him regularly.
4. In a bout with the DT's, he tried to kill him.

FAULTY EMPHASIS

Seeking emphasis in your writing does require that you emphasize with care. For instance, if you decided that you were going to achieve emphasis by forceful statement, you would have to be careful to choose the most important thing to be forceful about. You would also have to limit your forcefulness to a very few statements. An essay filled with strong, blunt statements would lose its effectiveness and make you sound quarrelsome.

165

Another type of faulty emphasis is the careless use of superlatives. If everything is marvelous, phenomenal, beautiful, fantastic, terrible, awful, or horrifying, then there is no distinction being made between the emphatic and the nonemphatic. Hysterical punctuation also weakens emphasis. Control your use of exclamation points, capital letters, dots, dashes, and underlining. Indeed, control is the key to emphasis. Remember, emphasizing too much will result in emphasizing nothing.

EXERCISE VIc: DECIDING WHAT TO EMPHASIZE

The correct placement of words in a sentence depends upon what you want to emphasize:

a. Stella was trembling with anxiety before she rose to speak.

b. Trembling with anxiety, Stella rose to speak.

c. Rising to speak, Stella trembled with anxiety.

Sentence *a* is weak because "trembling with anxiety" is buried in the middle.

Sentence *b* emphasizes Stella's rising to speak.

Sentence *c* emphasizes Stella's anxiety—the most likely word placement.

Discuss the emphasis in each of the following sentences. Then, choose the one sentence in each set that you feel shows the correct or most effective emphasis. Explain each of your choices.

1. a. John did, nevertheless, try.
   b. Nevertheless, John did try.
   c. John did try, nevertheless.

2. a. The man was told that he would be executed when the sun came up.
   b. The guards told the man that when the sun came up, he would be executed.
   c. The man was told that when the sun came up he would be executed.

3. a. I set the alarm clock before going to bed.
   b. I, before going to bed, set the alarm clock.
   c. Before going to bed, I set the alarm clock.

4. a. Buried under thirty feet of ash and lava was Pompeii.
   b. Pompeii was buried under thirty feet of ash and lava.
   c. Thirty feet of ash and lava covered Pompeii.

5. His kingdom gone, his parents cruelly murdered, his own wretched body torn and bleeding, Prince Krayobv
   a. whimpered.
   b. plotted his revenge.
   c. screamed, "Kill," and lunged forward.

6. a. The war is lost.
   b. Lost is the war.
   c. Lost, lost is the war.

7. a. Of course, General Eisenhower was furious.
   b. General Eisenhower was furious, of course.
   c. General Eisenhower, of course, was furious.

8. a. Max, now a murderer, had been in trouble all his life for stealing cars, mugging old men, and breaking street lights.
   b. Max, who had been in trouble all his life for breaking street lights, stealing cars, and mugging old men, was now a murderer.
   c. Max is a murderer who started out breaking street lights, stealing cars, and then mugging old men.
9. a. He committed a serious error in plagiarizing his term paper.
   b. Plagiarizing his term paper was a serious error.
   c. In plagiarizing his term paper, he committed a serious error.

Revising for Economy and Precision

You have already learned that to write well you must be concise and precise. Good writing depends on strong, active verbs and precise nouns and modifiers. It also demands that you avoid unnecessary *to be* verbs, fuzzy generalizations, jargon, cliches, repetitions, and wordiness. However, knowing the rules and applying them are two different matters. To write concisely and precisely takes careful revision.

In a first draft, a student wrote: "She is a very good person when it comes to making moral decisions based on the Christian aspect of life."

In revising, he first took out *very*. (A statement is usually weakened, not strengthened, by *very*.) *Person* added nothing, so he took it out. Then he realized that *Christian aspects of life* was so vague it had almost no meaning. He then decided that it was repetitious to say that she was good **and** Christian, since Christianity is a highly ethical religion. Also, he wanted to avoid *is* and find a stronger verb. In revising, he recognized that *when it comes to making* was wordy. His first revision read: "She decided moral issues on the basis of Christianity." But he realized that *issues* and *basis of Christianity* were too general. He revised again: "She lives by Christian principles." His final revision cut twenty words to five which **said something.**

When you are revising to make your writing concise and precise, you must consider your sentences as in the example above. You must also consider the paragraph. Are you avoiding repeating yourself? Are you eliminating unnecessary words or phrases? Are you combining elements that go together? Are you reducing clauses to phrases and phrases to single words? (Review the checklist in Chapter IV.)

EXERCISE VId: REVISING FOR ECONOMY AND PRECISION
The following paragraph is a wordy rewriting of a precise and concise paragraph about plagiarism. The thirty-four numbered and italicized items can be made more concise or even eliminated. After you have read the paragraph, rewrite it for conciseness. You will find clues, comments, and suggestions for your rewrite in the list that follows the paragraph.

Plagiarism is [1] *a kind of burglary* [2] *except that it is done in academic work and literary writings.* [3] *It is like* taking things [4] *that really belong to some other person* but [5] *not recognizing their ownership* and [6] *treating their academic findings and their writings* [7] *as if they belonged to the person who is plagiarizing.*

Some [8] *types of* plagiarism [9] *come about as the result of* [10] *pure, straightforward* [11] *failure to be honest;* the student, because he thinks he maybe [12] *has too much work to do,* or maybe he is [13] *the type who doesn't like to work much,* or maybe he [14] *isn't very good at studying and getting his work done,* copies [15] *things printed in books and magazines and newspapers* or even copies [16] *things that other students may have done.* [17] *Of course,* he [18] *really* knows [19] *that what he is doing* is [20] *morally* wrong, but [21] *in spite of this he does it* and he hopes that he will not be found out [22] *by the instructor.* [23] *A student who does this kind of plagiarizing* is [24] *really* a criminal, [25] *though of course not a criminal like a murderer or a bank robber.* Students [26] *like this* [27] *do not deserve to be treated with respect by society,* because society, [28] *by and large,* [29] *does not approve of criminals.* The [30] *greatest number of examples of* plagiarism, however, [31] *does not so much grow out of* [32] *not being honest* as it does from [33] *a failure of being mature* [34] *in an intellectual way.*

1. Useless general phrase since the second clause indicates the specific kind of burglary.
2. Can be reduced to two adjectives modifying *burglary.*
3. It isn't "like" taking things; it *is* taking things.
4. Reduce clause to phrase.
5. Unnecessary because of second following phrase.
6. Combine.
7. Put 4, 5, and 6 into an appositional phrase following *burglary.*
8. Unnecessary.
9. Reduce to verb.
10. Wrong connotation to modify *dishonest;* choose one adjective with correct feeling for *dishonesty.*
11. Reduce to one word.
12. Reduce to one word.
13. Reduce to one word.
14. Reduce to one word.
15. Combine.
16. Reduce to phrase.
17. Unnecessary transition.
18. Unnecessary.
19. Replace with personal pronoun.
20. Unnecessary modifier.
21. Unnecessary.
22. Unnecessary.
23. Use only the personal pronoun.
24. Unnecessary.
25. Replace with one word modifying *criminal,* meaning "an unimportant criminal."
26. Unnecessary and vague. Identify "Students" more precisely.
27. Eliminate negative and condense.
28. Unnecessary.

29. Avoid negative forms; find an antonym.
30. Substitute a one-word modifier of *plagiarism.*
31. Find a more precise verb.
32. Use one noun, a positive, not a negative, form.
33. Find a one-word, positive form.
34. Reduce to a single adjective modifying the form you find for item 33.

After you have revised this paragraph, ask your teacher to show you a copy of the original.

EXERCISE VIe: REVISING FOR ECONOMY AND PRECISION
The following essay is repetitious and wordy. Revise it to turn it into a clear, concise essay.

From all my years of growing up in my school days, there are three times that I will always remember because of the feeling of happiness and accomplishment I felt. The first thing I will remember is being elected to and getting on student council. The second is my first date and the sensational feeling I had inside of myself because it was with a boy I had liked for a long time. The third thing I will always remember is the night I graduated from high school and how proud I felt of the accomplishment I had achieved. The reason I will remember these three events is because each of these feelings were feelings I had never experienced before and that is why I will always cherish them and keep them in my memories forever.

The first thing I will always remember is getting elected to student council because it was a great honor in our school and one that was highly respected. I never really expected to win the election, but my friends and my favorite teacher whom I like more than any of the others urged and coaxed me to become a candidate and run. The reason I never really expected to win was because the opposing candidate I was running against was a boy who was the most popular and best-liked boy in the whole class. Once I was a candidate, however, I wrote up a platform which contained all the principles and plans on which I would base all the aspects of being a student council member. I made a speech which I delivered at an assembly of the whole school the day before election. The next day was election day, and I was surprised to learn when the votes were tallied up and counted that I had won by a sizable margin of seventeen votes. I had won a triumph over the most popular boy in the class.

The second thing I will always remember is my first date and the sensational feeling I had inside of myself and my happiness since it was with that very same boy I had beaten for student council. He came up to me in the library where I was and asked if he could speak to me because he had something to ask me. He sat down and asked if I was busy Friday night because he wanted me to go to a dance the school was sponsoring; with a gleam in my eyes, I accepted. Friday night, he arrived at my house at seven-thirty, and our first date had begun. While at the dance, we danced to all but four dances. As always, time flew by and at eleven the dance was over. After the dance was over, we stopped for hamburgers; then he brought me home. It will be a date I will never forget because of the feeling of joy I felt.

The third thing I will always remember is the night I graduated from high school and how proud I felt of the accomplishment I had made. The night before graduation, my grandparents came from Pittsburgh to see the ceremony of graduation. We left to go on to the high school auditorium where my parents and relatives would go to see graduation. When we arrived, the auditorium was beautifully decorated with Boston ferns and filled with the proud parents of the students who would be graduating. The graduates lined up in a long line and the school band began to play march music. After we reached the stage and listened to several speeches, it was time to receive our diplomas. When the ceremony was over and it was time for the graduates to exit the stage, I suddenly realized how proud I felt of the accomplishment I had made because I had graduated in the top third of my class.

In closing, the things that I will always remember, the things that gave me a feeling of accomplishment and joy are getting elected to the student council, getting my first date, and graduating from high school. The reason I will remember these three events is that each of these feelings were feelings I had never experienced before and that is why I will always cherish them and keep them in my memories forever.

WORD POWER

Idiom

Idiom refers to the characteristic way in which people put together the words of a language. Every language has its natural idioms; people put words together in a certain way to express a particular idea or feeling. These combinations of words may, in the literal sense, be illogical, untranslatable, and even ungrammatical. But idioms grow out of the language and come to have an existence of their own. English has thousands of these peculiar combinations of words. Consider the following examples involving the one word, *heart:*

He's got heart.
She's all heart.
My heart's in the Highlands.
His heart's in the right place.
Her heart was in her mouth.
He didn't have the heart to tell her.
She wore her heart on her sleeve.
We had a real heart-to-heart talk.
I am heartsick at losing my home.
Welcome from the bottom of my heart.
Thomas Paine gave heart to the American Revolution.

They live in the heart of New York City.
Her heart is set on getting a diploma.
We must not lose heart.
He took the rebuke to heart.
She lost her heart to Paris.
He was a scoundrel at heart.
You have a heart of stone.
She loved them with all her heart.
I know that hard-hearted villian's story by heart.
Sit there to your heart's content.
Eat your heart out.

**She wore her heart
on her sleeve.**   **She's all heart.**

For each of hundreds of common verbs such as *do, get, cut, set, hit, put, see, push, pull, take, make,* there are dozens of idiomatic expressions.

If you have ever studied a foreign language, you remember that you had to memorize lists of idioms. Idioms, in any language, must be memorized. You can't just figure out their meanings, because they don't follow any rules. Despite this, idiomatic usage is valuable in that it offers quick, precise communication among most native speakers of a language. Such phrases as *come in handy, make no bones about it,* and *do away with* convey rather complicated ideas quickly and clearly.

For the few times when you do have trouble with idioms, there are two solutions. The long-run solution is to make yourself aware of how idioms are used by educated speakers and writers. The immediate solution is to consult your dictionary. The problem generally concerns what preposition should follow what verb, as in such phrases as *make up, make up for, make after, make much of, make out with.* You will find that most dictionaries will give you directions about this under the entry for the verb, in this case *make.*

Clichés and Trite Expressions

You don't always have time to think before you speak. As a result, you sometimes say the first thing that comes into your head. Once you start to do that, you sometimes load your conversation with trite, overworked expressions. Suppose, for example, that you were listening to the following conversation:

Talking but Saying Nothing

MARTHA: So ... what are you into, George?
GEORGE: Oh, I'm just doin' my own thing.
MARTHA: Yeah? That's beautiful!
GEORGE: Ya' know, Martha, you ought to start doin' your own thing, somewhere down the road.
MARTHA: Yeah ... I know where you're comin' from, George.
GEORGE: Well, hang in there, Martha.

Once you see George and Martha's words written down in black and white, you can see how meaningless their conversation becomes. For example, what did George mean when he said, "I'm just doin' my own thing"? He could have been playing war games with Tom Jefferson or harvesting marijuana from the banks of the Potomac. The truth is that you don't know what he means. Unfortunately, students who depend on such trite, overworked expressions when they talk are just reinforcing a bad habit—**lazy thinking.** If they don't take the time to say exactly what they mean, then they probably won't take the time to **write** exactly what they mean. In other words, meaningless talk turns into meaningless writing. Look at another example—a typical conversation between two students:

DICK: What happened?

JANE: Well, there was this really weird guy, O.K.? And he was tailgating me, ya' know, like all the way to the turnpike, O.K.? So, when I got on to the turnpike, O.K.? Like he's still following me, ya' know? So then, like I really started to panic. I was shaking like a leaf. So at the first rest stop I saw, O.K.? I pulled off, O.K.? And I like pretend that I'm going to stop, O.K.? I was trying to like act as cool as possible, ya' know, but inside I was like really scared stiff, ya' know? So anyway, I slowed the car down to like ten miles per hour, O.K.? And kept looking for anything that resembled a police car, ya' know? Finally, I spotted one, O.K.? And as soon as the guy saw me heading toward the police car, O.K.? He took off, like a bat out of hell. Boy, I was like really relieved, ya' know? I couldn't believe my eyes. I mean like I could have kissed that policeman, ya' know?

If you ever find yourself talking like Jane, watch out. In this reply to Dick's question, Jane used a meaningless word or phrase twenty-five times. Boring and meaningless as this is in speech, such meaningless words and ready-made phrases are even more objectionable in writing. These phrases are often referred to as clichés. A *cliché* is any stale, worn-out expression that has been used so often that it clarifies nothing for the reader and tends to put the reader to sleep.

Some clichés not only are ambiguous and boring, but are sometimes misleading. For example, have you ever told a friend, "You eat like a bird"? If you have, your friend has every right to feel insulted because many birds eat almost their own weight in food every day! Clichés contribute to your writing only evidence of a lack of original thinking. Take care to avoid the clichés listed following, as well as the other tired phrases and trite expressions that fail to communicate real ideas.

LIST OF CLICHÉS AND TRITE EXPRESSIONS

Ugly as sin	Happy as a lark
Pretty as a picture	Soft as silk
Fresh as a daisy	Hard as a rock
Drunk as a skunk	Warm as toast
Old as the hills	Cold as ice
Sober as a judge	Skinny as a rail
Mad as a hornet	Big as a bear

Sly as a fox
Dumb as a doorknob
Quiet as a mouse
Noisy as a zoo
Smart as a whip
Crazy as a loon
Quick as a wink
Slow as a turtle
Stiff as a board
Loose as a goose
Phony as a three-dollar bill
Honest as the day is long
As much fun as a barrel of monkeys
Funny as a crutch
Pure as the driven snow
Snow white
True blue
Pitch black
Sky high
Sparkling clean
Crystal clear
Dirt cheap

Filthy rich
Like pulling teeth
Like a fish out of water
Like a bump on a log
Like finding a needle in a haystack
Like a hot potato
When hell freezes over
When push comes to shove
Between a rock and a hard place
The bottom line
Working one's fingers to the bone
Day in and day out
One in a million
Blowing one's own horn
Come up smelling like a rose
Variety is the spice of life
Stand up and be counted
Giving the best years of one's life
Not wrapped too tight
Raining cats and dogs
Costing an arm and a leg
Have a nice day

EXERCISE VIf: CLICHÉS
Replace the italicized chichés and trite expressions in the following sentences with more original and exact wording.

1. No wonder he's *as sick as a dog;* he *drinks like a fish.*

   _____

2. Mrs. Maloney just said, *"That's the way the cookie crumbles"* when she lost her purse.

   _____

3. *Wild horses couldn't drag* me to Dick's party. His wife *turns me off.*

   _____

4. The production company for *Evita* obviously *pulled out all the stops.*

   _____

5. Terry's face got *as red as a beet* when Lolita walked in.

   _____

6. Laura *took the bull by the horns* and asked her boss for a raise.

   _____

7. I can't buy a new car right now. I'm *waiting for my ship to come in.*

_____

8. The vandals haven't been caught yet, but the police claim to be *hot on the trail.*

_____

9. Molly's new baby is *as cute as a button.*

_____

10. *It is interesting to note* that those twins are *as different as night and day.*

_____

11. That woman bothers me; she always has *an ax to grind.*

_____

12. *Each and every one* of us must *stick by* our friends *through thick and thin.*

_____

13. Joan's boyfriend is *so tight, he squeaks.*

_____

14. I can't figure her out; one minute she's *cool as a cucumber* and the next minute she's *shaking like a leaf.*

_____

15. *Deep in my heart,* I know he'll *cut the apron strings* and ask me to *tie the knot.*

_____

16. Her hair was *as black as coal,* and her *rosy red cheeks* complemented her *sparkling blue eyes.*

_____

17. He was *out like a light,* so I didn't bother him.

_____

18. Ron likes to buy big expensive cars, but I *can't get into that.*

_____

19. Michael is *as sharp as a tack,* but Jim is *as dumb as an ox.*

_____

CHAPTER VII

defining

Combining Methods of Development

In all the essays previously discussed, you have been asked to use one method of development. In writing the essays that follow, however, you may develop your thesis through narration, description, comparison, classification, the use of examples, or any combination of these and other methods. In fact, you are encouraged to use whatever combination of methods best serves your purpose.

If, for example, you are writing an essay on Italy today, you might begin with description:

In Italy the sun still rises early over the shimmering Adriatic and glistens over the red tile roofs and yellow walls of the clustered buildings. The roads that twist and turn suddenly feel hot through the soles of your shoes. Olive trees two thousand years old, their roots a labyrinth of twisted legs, still bear fruit. Medieval walled towns throw shadows down the sides of the cliffs they rest upon.

defining   go on to examples:

Italy today is not Rome of yesterday, but the evidence of ancient Rome is everywhere. Remains of the ancient aqueducts that brought water to the city still stand. Buses that take tourists to and from the airport ride on the original Appian Way and enter the city through gates two thousand years old.

use comparison–contrast:

The old and the new coexist in Italy. A modern eight-lane highway veers left to skirt the ancient ruins of the 110-foot-high Coliseum. New Mercedes scenic-cruiser buses edge through the ancient gates and over roads built for chariots and ox-carts. The walls of the giant Circus Maximus hold back the chic condominiums and modern department stores of the growing city. The Tiber still winds through the city as it did centuries ago, but now it's so polluted with industrial waste that a mouthful of its water can be fatal.

or use a short narrative or anecdote:

The Italian temper is volatile but not physical. Once I saw a driver, held up momentarily by another driver stopping to pick up a passenger, leap from his car and rush up to the offending vehicle. Screaming and waving his arms, he challenged the driver of the first car. This driver also got out of his car, and the two screamed at each other, arms waving threateningly. I thought I was about to witness a murder—or mayhem at least. However, the passenger arrived and got into the first car. When this happened, the two drivers returned to their own vehicles and left. They were whistling as they drove off.

For the assignments throughout the rest of this book, choose whatever combination of methods you feel will best develop your thesis.

The Need for Definition

Defining words is necessary if we are to understand one another, to take the correct action, to do the right job. Yet words have many different meanings; people have different interpretations of words; and people mean different things when they use the same words.

If you ask twenty people to define the word *gentleman,* you'll probably be surprised at the answers you get. Although most people will mention courteousness or good manners, they will disagree on such issues as whether a gentleman must be clean, have money, enjoy the arts, come from a "good" family, or be intelligent. Sometimes it's a wonder we can understand each other at all.

Knowing how to define terms clearly is more important than you might think. If, for example, the world had agreed on the meaning of the word *appeasement,* Hitler might have found it far more difficult to overrun half of Europe. To some, *appeasement* meant peace; to others, it meant dishonor; and to still others, it meant total submission. The political rhetoric of World War II is filled with attempts to define *appeasement.*

In everyday situations we see the confusion created by the failure to define terms. For instance, the dictionary defines *liberal* as "broad-minded," "ample," and "unconfined," among other meanings. But the implications of these meanings are so wide that to communicate clearly, you must define (limit) the word to your meaning. If not, you have Uncle Fritz, who thinks Genghis Khan and Attila the Hun were "liberals" and Aunt Petulia, who thinks that any man who lets his wife wear slacks is a "liberal." Some Republicans are too "liberal" for their own party, and some Democrats are too conservative to gain "liberal" support. Is it any wonder, then, that some people can argue endlessly about politics and get nowhere?

In many such arguments about politics and morality people fail to define the terms. A candidate or platform that is liberal to one voter may be conservative to another; behavior that is moral to one person may be immoral in the eyes of another. Before such people can even begin to understand one another, they must first limit and explain what they mean by such terms as *moral* and *immoral*, *liberal* and *conservative*.

THE LIMITED DEFINITION

Whatever the subject of your essay or the method of development, you may need to provide at least a limited definition of key terms. A limited definition enables you to clarify your ideas by setting clear limits to the area of discussion. You say, in effect, "By such and such a term I mean so and so." For example, the term *free enterprise* is often used in a careless way; you might limit its definition by specifying that you are using the term to apply "only to those businesses that remain free to respond to the laws of supply and demand and the profit motive." In similar fashion, the word *frugality* has various connotations, but you could specify that, for the purpose of your discussion, your definition is limited to "the careful use of resources." In this way you set clear boundaries to the discussion and avoid confusion and misunderstanding.

THE EXTENDED DEFINITION

Some words need a paragraph or even an essay to define them adequately. Words such as *civil disobedience*, *loyalty*, *peace*, *freedom*, *liberty*, *wealth*, *education*, and *art* are examples of words that require extended definitions.

An extended definition offers the opportunity to explore the full meaning of a term. It gives you a chance to go beyond a general definition and explore the implications and possibilities of meaning. If you start with a basic definition, you can expand it in a variety of ways. You may develop your extended definition through one method; however, you will usually find that a combination of methods works best.

Synonym

Extended example

Courage is resistance to fear, mastery of fear—not absence of fear. Except a creature be part coward it is not a compliment to say it is brave; it is merely a loose misapplication of the word. Consider the flea!—incomparably the bravest of all the creatures of God, if ignorance of fear were courage. Whether you are asleep or awake he will attack you, caring nothing for the fact that in bulk and strength you are to him as are the massed armies of the earth to a suckling child; he lives both day and night and all days and nights in the very lap of peril and the immediate presence of death, and yet is no more afraid than is the man

Comparison	who walks the streets of a city that was threatened by an earthquake ten centuries before. When we speak of Clive, Nelson, and Putnam as men who "didn't
Examples	know what fear was," we ought always to add the flea—and put him at the head of the procession. *Mark Twain*

CONCRETE AND ABSTRACT TERMS

The distinction between concrete and abstract terms is a key element in definition, as earlier chapters indicated. Concrete terms refer to and give a name to some physical thing; they refer to something that can be seen, touched, measured, or weighed. Abstract terms, however, give a name to or put a label on certain intellectual and emotional concepts. Thus, the task of defining abstract terms is more complex. Terms such as *integrity, truth, justice,* and *patriotism* have nothing concrete to refer to. Thus, no two people have exactly the same concept of such words.

It is these abstract terms that cause a great deal of difficulty in communication. One individual's idea of patriotism, for example, may be comprised of many intangibles such as religious beliefs, family attitudes, the course of recent events, and the individual's outlook. When you must use abstract terms, you can make them clear by providing relevent, concrete examples.

Methods of Definition

USING FORMAL DEFINITION

A formal definition follows a fixed form that usually provides the clearest short definition. This form always includes three parts:

Term to Be Defined	General Classification	Differentiating Detail
bikini	bathing suit	woman's two piece, very skimpy
theocracy	a form of government	in which power is in the hands of priests or church officials
espalier	an ornamental shrub or fruit tree	trained to grow flat against a wall, often in a symmetrical pattern
obsession	a compulsive preoccupation	with a fixed idea or unwanted feelings or emotions, often accompanied by symptoms of anxiety
manatee	a plant-eating aquatic mammal	found in shallow tropical waters of the coasts of North and South America and West Africa, having flippers and a broad, flat, rounded tail

Formal definition provides a guide and check to your thinking. Here are some guidelines:

1. In placing a term in a class, choose the smallest relevant class to which the term can be conveniently assigned. A manatee could be placed in the class of animal, but then much differentiating detail would be needed because the class is not sufficiently limited. When you place manatee in the class of "plant-eating aquatic mammal," you have narrowed the class and taken a useful step toward definition.
2. Your definition must take into account everything that logically belongs to the term defined. If you define a drill as "a tool for boring holes in wood," you have failed to allow for drills used for boring holes in rock, masonry, and metal.
3. Your definition must exclude everything that does not logically belong to the term being defined. If you define manatee as "a gentle creature of the sea" or "a member of an endangered species," you have failed to exclude other gentle sea creatures or members of endangered species.
4. By following the pattern of formal definition, you avoid creating a circular definition, the kind of definition that just repeats the term to be defined in slightly different words: "An earache is a pain in the ear." So are circular definitions.

DEFINING BY SYNONYMS

One of the easiest and fastest ways to explain the meaning of a word is to define with synonyms, words that mean something similar to the word you are defining. This technique is particularly useful when you are defining a term that may be unfamiliar to your reader. For example, suppose that you have written to a computer-dating firm in an attempt to find a perfect mate. To your dismay, however, the computer comes up with three possibilities who are described respectively as *querulous, obstreperous,* and *propitious.* You have seen these words in print somewhere, but you have no idea what they mean. Without some clarification of the meanings of these terms, you would just have to take pot luck. However, if the computer had supplied you with some synonyms, you could have made an intelligent decision: *querulous,* "whining, complaining, finicky"; *obstreperous,* "noisy, unruly, boisterous"; *propitious,* "gracious, helpful, agreeable."

When you define with synonyms, you must bear two things in mind. First, the word supplied as a synonym must be a simpler word than the term to be defined. Second, the grammatical form of both words must be the same. Notice that the synonyms for *querulous, obstreperous,* and *propitious* are all simpler words of the same grammatical form (adjective) as the words defined. For example:

to osculate (a difficult term) means *"to kiss"* (a simpler term)

> **NOT**
to kiss means "to osculate"

And, making sure to use the same part of speech,

defining

to osculate means "to kiss"

NOT

to osculate means "kissing"

Osculate means "to kiss."
It does!

**DEFINING
BY WORD
ORIGIN**

One of the most obvious, yet often overlooked, methods of clarifying the meaning of a term is to examine the origin of the term. For example, the word *sabotage* means "the intentional destruction of materials, machines, or some productive process." The meaning of the term becomes quite clear when you learn that *sabotage* comes from the French word *sabot,* meaning "shoe," and that it was coined during the French Revolution when the workers "sabotaged" French factories by throwing their shoes into the machinery. Once you learn how and when the word *sabotage* became part of the English language, you not only have a clearer understanding of the word, but you are also less likely to forget the meaning of the word because the picture of French peasants throwing their shoes into factory machinery will always flash into your mind every time you see the word.

Looking up the origin of a word also reminds you that language is constantly changing, with old words gaining new meanings and new words being born. The word *chauvinist,* for example, was never used before 1815. It was coined as a result of the fanatic loyalty of a French soldier, Nicholas Chauvin, to Napoleon. Thus, *chauvinism* has come to mean blind attachment to something, such as one's beliefs or, as it is commonly used today, one's sex. The word *boycott* is another word that has a relatively recent origin, and it also originated from a per-

Put the boots to it.

son's name. In the 1880's, during the struggle between British landlords and Irish tenant farmers, a man by the name of Captain Charles Boycott was hired to collect the rent from the farmers on a large estate in County Mayo. The impoverished Irish peasants, however, got together and decided to ostracize Captain Boycott by ignoring him and refusing to pay.

You cannot depend exclusively on word origin for a sound definition because the meanings of words do change with time. Today, for example, the word *sabotage* does not always refer to the destruction of material objects. It often refers to a more subtle means of obstruction such as interfering with a presidential candidate's campaign strategy. The meaning of the word *boycott* has also undergone some change. Although it still means "refusal to deal with someone," *boycott* today is usually used to refer to a ban on particular goods, such as the grape and lettuce boycotts of the migrant farmworkers or the boycott of the Olympics in 1980. Use word origin in your definition essay only if the word's origin or history helps the reader to understand the meaning that you wish to convey.

DEFINING BY EXAMPLES

One of the most effective ways to clarify the meaning of a term is to provide the reader with specific examples. As you learned in Chapter IV, examples can always aid understanding. Perhaps you could best show what a liberal is by citing examples of prominent figures who are regarded as great liberals. Or, perhaps you want to learn more about vitamins, and as part of your research you decide to read Linus Pauling's book on *Vitamin C and the Common Cold.* In one of the early chapters, however, you come across a term that you have never seen or heard: "orthomolecular medicine." You read Pauling's definition:

Orthomolecular medicine is the preservation of good health and the treatment of disease by varying the concentrations in the human body of substances that are normally present and are required for health.

You still don't understand the term well enough to be able to explain it to somebody else. But after Pauling gives you some specific examples of orthomolecular medicine, such as preventing a cold or treating rheumatoid arthritis with vitamin C (ascorbic acid) or controlling diabetes with injections of insulin (a hormone produced by the pancreas), you have a much clearer understanding of orthomolecular medicine. You now know what he means by "substances that are normally present" in the human body.

DEFINING BY COMPARISON AND CONTRAST

You may define one term by comparing or contrasting its meaning with that of another term. You might define a liberal by showing how his or her views differ from those of a conservative. Comparison and contrast is especially useful in defining closely related terms. For instance, *tragedy* and *misfortune* are closely related terms, yet not every misfortune is a tragedy. By means of comparison and contrast you could show the frequently ignored distinction between these two terms. Specifically, although news reports often refer to events of the day—a fire, an auto accident, an explosion—as being tragic, tragedy, at least in its traditional meaning, always involves a tragic flaw or moral weakness on the part of a central character.

DEFINING BY DIVISION AND CLAS-SIFICATION
A useful method of defining a complex term is to divide and classify the various aspects of its meaning. If you wanted to discuss the economic classes in the United States, you might divide people into various groups, such as the very rich, the affluent professionals, the middle-income workers, the working poor, and the indigent. You might then proceed to classify the members of a particular group. For example, the indigent might be classified to include the disabled workers, the physically handicapped, the mentally unfit, the emotionally disturbed, and the socially maladjusted.

DEFINING BY NEGATION
Sometimes you can help your reader understand what something is by clarifying what is not, as the love-struck cowboy in "Oklahoma" did when he got mad at the peddler who stole his girl: "You're too low to be a man and too big to be a mouse. I reckon you're a rat." When you explain what something is by clarifying what it is **not,** you are using the process of *negation*.

You might start to explain what a liberal is by saying: "A liberal is not one who believes in anarchy. He does not believe that everyone has the right to do just as he pleases. He does not believe in revolution or the violent overthrow of a duly elected government."

Negation alone does not provide a definition, but it does help you to narrow the area of definition. Once having shown what something is not, you can more easily proceed to show what it is: "A liberal, then, is one who believes in orderly change brought about through people's ability to think about issues, discuss them freely, and arrive at solutions democratically. A liberal believes in the free marketplace of ideas and puts faith in the good sense of an informed public to make intelligent judgments and determine for themselves the right course of action."

EXERCISE VIIa: FORMAL DEFINITION
Using an up-to-date desk dictionary, construct a formal definition of each of the following terms.

ohm	1. _____
paddock	2. _____
commissar	3. _____
caravel	4. _____
hollyhock	5. _____
Nazism	6. _____
humanist	7. _____
epaulet	8. _____
clarinet	9. _____
cubism	10. _____
prairie dog	11. _____
Volstead Act	12. _____

182

183

defining

Notice how the following essay makes use of several methods of definition:

The Character of Character

In ordinary speech, we often hear such things as "What a character he is!" or "She's a real character." What the speaker usually means is that he or she is somewhat peculiar or eccentric. The term *character* as used in fiction or drama, however, has quite a different meaning; in fact, it has a dual meaning: it means a person within the story or drama and also a composite of that person's qualities and traits. Thus the meaning of the term *character* changes, depending on the context in which it is used.

As I vividly recall, I once had a neighbor who was generally regarded as "quite a character." The first thing that set him apart from the crowd was a wide-brimmed white fedora from the Al Capone era, which he habitually wore at a rakish angle. An attorney who specialized in criminal law, he seemed to move in mysterious ways, and he had acquired a motley crew of cronies and clients. A strange female client took to sleeping on his front porch until his wife, with malice aforethought, forcefully ejected her. Once, following a night of revelry, he was fished from a snowbank not thirty feet from his own front door, his hat at a little sharper angle than usual. Perhaps my old neighbor should have been a character in fiction; but no—he just was.

Following a night of revelry. . .

In any discussion of fiction or drama, you frequently encounter such terms as "a minor character," "a leading character," or "the protagonist." What these terms refer to is a fictional person who plays a particular role in the story. Character, in this sense, is closely identified with an assigned role in the story or drama. In much of escape fiction and television drama, little is demanded of a character except that he act in a fairly predictable way and fulfill his assigned role.

Character in yet another sense refers to the sum total of beliefs, values, attitudes, and emotions which make a person what he is. In this sense, the characters in escape fiction and television drama can be said to have very little depth. They are mainly one-dimensional stereotypes with whom the reader or viewer can easily identify: the slick detective-hero of the television series making his weekly dash through the underworld, dodging with equal ease the bullets of hired killers and the clutches of sleazy women; the young heroine—originally from somewhere in the boondocks—sashaying with easy virtue through the snares of Hollywood or New York, carrying untarnished a heart of solid gold. The escapades of such characters provide the easy entertainment of manufactured daydreams.

In more serious drama and what is called "interpretive literature," the characters are far more subtle and complex. The leading character in a novel by Dostoevsky or William Faulkner, for example, may be driven by conflicting emotions and propelled into irrational action by the force of inner tensions. Thus, the focus in such novels is on character itself, fully developed multidimensional character. It is this fully rounded quality which makes the fictional people of the story come alive; in fact, we may come to feel that these fictional characters are more real to us than any actual person we have ever known.

In situation comedy, for instance, we expect to find characters who are largely one-dimensional. There, we are entertained by the antics of such stereotyped figures as the bungling father, the sharp-tongued housekeeper, the dumb blonde, or the love-struck teenager. In serious fiction or drama, however, the action springs from character and is determined by character. And the character of the characters is as subtle and varied as the full range of human experience and imagination.

ORGANIZATION

As in all the other essays you are writing, the basic organization remains the three-fold structure: introduction-body-conclusion.

Introduction

The main purpose of the introduction is to bring sharply into focus the term you intend to define. Your thesis sentence differs from a general definition in one significant respect: a thesis sentence presents a specific attitude toward the term. Is the term commonly misunderstood? In what way? What do you consider to be the most important aspect of its meaning? Why do you attach a certain meaning to this term? Do your ideas and associations differ from the generally accepted meaning of the term?

These questions show why the thesis sentence for your definition essay must be carefully worded and why your attitude must be carefully narrowed and made very specific. A thesis sentence such as: "Wealth has many meanings" is too obvious and too general to spark the reader's interest. A better thesis sentence might be: "At every stage in life, we know what wealth is, but it is never the same in any two stages."

Body

Any combination of methods may be used in developing the body of your definition. In defining *prejudice*, for example, you might classify different types of prejudice according to their origin: prejudice resulting from ignorance, prejudice resulting from environment, and prejudice resulting from deprivation. Having explained these different types of prejudice, you might then use examples from various sources or anecdotes from personal experience to show how people's actions reveal their prejudices. Further, you might use statistics to show how prejudice affects income, promotion, and entry into certain professions. In defining *poverty*, you might use figures to show how the official poverty level has changed over the past ten years. You might also compare a rich man's definition of poverty as "an all-encompassing hardship" with a poor man's statement that "it's like being in hell with your back broke."

defining   Or if you are going to define *psychopaths,* you can't just say that "psychopaths are people who are different from ordinary, normal people." This is vague and dull. A better introduction might begin with a quotation from Robert Lindner's *Must You Conform:* "There walk among us men and women who are in but not of our world." Such a sentence might attract the attention of your reader and lead to a more specific thesis sentence: "These men and women are the conscienceless, explosive, unreasoning, and often unrecognized psychopaths who menace society."

After you have introduced your essay with a sentence or two to get the interest of the reader, write your thesis sentence, making sure that it is clear and specific. For example, consider the following introduction to an essay on obsession:

> According to the general definition of the word, obsession strongly suggests an abnormal preoccupation with a fixed idea. It carries with it a notion of abnormal and neurotic behavior as a result of thinking that is definitely lopsided and usually somewhat sick. What is often ignored, however, is that obsession can be a marvelous thing—the focal point around which all of the individual's talents and energies are marshaled. Obsession can produce magnificent results when it serves one great purpose in life, whether that purpose be to write beautiful poetry, carve great monuments, or just build a better mousetrap.

Obsession can produce magnificent results.

This essay could be effectively developed with telling examples of people whose obsessions drove them to achieve their aims in life.

Conclusion

An effective method of concluding an extended definition is to summarize briefly your discussion and then restate the essential meaning of the term. Try to pull together the various aspects of meaning you have discussed, and then conclude with a clear statement that points up the essence of the term's meaning as you interpret it. An apt quotation might serve your purpose, but more often you conclude by restating your thesis sentence. For example, the essay on obsession might be brought to a conclusion with a restatement of the thesis: "Obsession can drive men to great heights and leave everything else—the baseness, the folly, the anguish—forgotten in the presence of their achievement."

Here is one student's definition of marriage:

A Lesson Well Learned

"For better, for worse, for richer, for poorer, in sickness and in health. Till death do us part and I do." As the minister pronounced us husband and wife, I smiled knowingly to myself. I was seventeen years old and my image of marriage was a fairy tale in which I would be queen in my own little castle, a dream in which all was bliss and excitement and independence. At seventeen, I knew it all, especially what the word *marriage* meant—or so I thought. After four years of marriage and two years of divorce, I now know what the word *marriage* means. Marriage is a commitment between two people that involves love, sharing, compromise, and acceptance of one another.

The word *marriage,* to me, cannot be defined in a dictionary. The dictionary definition of marriage is (1) the legal union of a man with a woman for life, and (2) the formal declaration or contract by which act a man and a woman join in wedlock. Those definitions are very cold and broad. A dictionary definition just does not include the implication of emotional involvement—a serious mistake, as I've found out.

The emotional involvement of marriage happens gradually. The first step in this process is the change in self-image which usually occurs during the honeymoon. The introduction of the mate as "Mrs. So and So" or "my wife" brings the realization to the newly married couple that they are no longer two separate people, but united and committed to each other. Responsibilities, as well as obligations, are realized as part of the marriage. The couple begin to know each other, accept one another, and share each other's happiness as well as disappointments. Only through living with one another, through seeing each other's faults and accepting that no one is perfect, and compromising when necessary can a couple achieve the emotional commitment necessary for a marriage to succeed.

For a marriage to succeed, it must not include certain qualities. Jealousy, for one, cannot exist. For example, when I was married, both my husband and I were extremely jealous. Anything more than a fleeting glance in another person's direction would plummet the other into a jealous rage. Jealousy cannot see and would invariably lead into a long, drawn-out verbal battle. Coupled with the plight of jealousy comes the curse of mistrust. For example, one day my father became very ill. Upon learning this from my distressed Mom, I hurriedly dressed and left without leaving a note or calling my husband at work. As it turned out, my Dad was admitted to the hospital in serious condition. As upset as I was, I totally forgot to call my husband to explain the situation. When I returned home very late that night, he was seeing red—he was sure I was cheating. We exchanged angry, hurtful words which only increased my distress. After spending the night on the couch, he awoke with a clearer head. He apologized to me, but it was too late—the damage had been done. These qualities can certainly be detrimental to a marriage.

Now that I'm an old lady of twenty-four, my conception of marriage has changed considerably. I realize fully the commitment involved in the process of learning to accept, share, and love another person. I've learned that to be married is hard work, but that it is something definitely worth working for. And last, had I known at seventeen what I know now, I would have realized that neither of us were ready for the commitment of marriage.

Bonnie Shamrock

Pitfalls to Avoid

1. Avoid such evasions as "Love means different things to different people." Such statements do not help to define; in fact, they usually indicate to the reader that you have given little thought to your subject.

2. Don't try to list every meaning of the term. You are writing an essay, not making a catalog. What you need is a specific attitude concerning the significance of the term; that is what you need to develop.

3. Don't let your discussion drift so that you end up discussing something unrelated to the term you are supposed to be defining. Repeating the term (or recognizable synonyms) at frequent intervals will help you stay on the track and help to keep the thesis before your reader.

4. Avoid starting with such threadbare phrases as "According to my dictionaries. . . ." Consult the most complete and up-to-date dictionaries you can get your hands on, but don't just quote these dictionaries. Try to get a firm grasp of the meaning and then express it in your own words.

5. Avoid vague and sloppy definition. Use specific examples and concrete details to make your meaning clear and vivid.

6. Remember that you may need to use several methods to make your extended definition clear and complete. Negation, for example, is useful in eliminating areas of meaning that do not apply, but negation alone will not provide a complete definition.

EXERCISE VIIb: INADEQUATE DEFINITION
Read the following definitions and explain why they are inadequate. Then write a correct definition of the italicized term.

1. An *armrest* is a thing in your car that you rest your arm on.

_____

2. A *perfectionist* wants everything to be perfect.

_____

3. A *slum* is a place one finds in most big cities.

_____

4. *Liberty* means a lot of things to a lot of people.

_____

5. *Greed* is when a person wants more than he has.

_____

6. A *carburetor* is part of an engine.

_____

7. A *teacher* is a person who is involved in education.

_____

187

8. *Pride* is a vice.

    _____

9. *Hate* is a strong emotion that some people have for others.

    _____

10. A *wagon* is a rectangular-shaped object, usually made of metal or wood, with four wheels on the bottom and a long handle in the front.

    _____

EXERCISE VIIc: METHODS OF DEFINITION
Identify the method or methods of definition used in each of the following:

_____ 1. *Munificent:* Liberal in giving, very generous.

_____ 2. *Rifle:* A firearm with a rifled bore designed to be fired from the shoulder.

_____ 3. *Blunderbuss:* A short musket of wide bore and flaring muzzle, formerly used to scatter shot at close range. The word comes from the Dutch *donderbus—donder* meaning "thunder."

_____ 4. A *romantic* poet is someone like Wordsworth, Coleridge, Keats, Byron, and Shelley who freely express emotions and passions.

_____ 5. A *desman* is an aquatic insect-eating animal similar to a mole or a muskrat.

_____ 6. *Dysentery* is not a pain in the stomach; it is not nausea. It is an infection of the lower digestive track producing pain, fever, and severe diarrhea.

_____ 7. *Glad* means happy, cheerful, lighthearted. But *glad* often means the strong feeling that results from the gratification of a wish or satisfaction with immediate circumstances. *Happy,* however, describes almost any condition of good spirits. *Cheerful* suggests good spirits made obvious by an outgoing personality.

_____ 8. *Sacroscanct* means sacred or inviolable.

_____ 9. *Slogan:* The catchword or motto used by a political party, fraternity, school, or other group. Originally it was a battle cry of the Scottish clans. It comes from the Scottish *slaugh* meaning "host" and *gairm* meaning "shout, cry, or call."

_____ 10. A *wristlock* is a wrestling hold in which an opponent's wrist is gripped and twisted to immobilize him.

SUGGESTED TOPICS

Write an extended definition on one of the following topics.

1. A bigot	8. A humanitarian	15. A muckraker
2. An egghead	9. An alcoholic	16. A lie
3. A chauvinist	10. A workaholic	17. A con artist
4. An optimist	11. An egomaniac	18. An educator
5. A pessimist	12. A gentleman	19. A mercenary
6. A perfectionist	13. A lady	20. A friend
7. A parasite	14. A nonconformist	21. A mother

188

22.	A father	32.	Hell	42.	Common sense
23.	A student	33.	Courage	43.	Learning
24.	A war crime	34.	Wealth	44.	Freedom
25.	A fair price	35.	Happiness	45.	Guilt
26.	Academic freedom	36.	Greed	46.	Victory
27.	Power	37.	Honesty	47.	Failure
28.	Propaganda	38.	Success	48.	Morality
29.	Marriage	39.	Trust	49.	Immorality
30.	Charisma	40.	Ambition	50.	Romantic love
31.	Heaven	41.	Slander		

TECHNIQUES OF CLEAR WRITING

Achieving Economy

VERBAL PHRASES

Dependent clauses and even separate sentences can often be reduced to verbal phrases for clarity and economy. A *verbal* is a verb form used as a noun, adjective, or adverb, not as the main verb of a sentence. A verbal may be preceded by *to,* forming an **infinitive**; or it may end in -*ing* or -*ed,* forming a **gerund** or a **participle.** In the sentence, "*To run* is good exercise," the verbal *to run* is used as a noun. In the phrase "*stationed* at the crossroads," *stationed* is a verbal used as an adjective.

Note the following examples of clauses and sentences reduced to verbal phrases:

ORIGINAL: Julie peered into the rain and the darkness. She could scarcely see the guardrails along the edge of the ravine.

REDUCED: Peering into the rain and the darkness, Julie could scarcely see the guardrails along the edge of the ravine.

ORIGINAL: Charlie Finch felt fine. He strutted down the street in his new camel-hair coat.

REDUCED: Feeling fine, Charlie Finch strutted down the street in his new camel-hair coat.

ORIGINAL: She was wearing her favorite summer dress. She tripped on the steps and fell into the barberry bushes.

REDUCED: Wearing her favorite summer dress, she tripped on the steps and fell into the barberry bushes.

ORIGINAL: Mrs. Carmine wanted to be sure the girls would be safe. She drove to the hall to meet them after the junior prom.

REDUCED: To be sure the girls would be safe, Mrs. Carmine drove to the hall to meet them after the junior prom.

189

Who and which clauses can frequently be reduced to phrases.

defining

ORIGINAL: The old house, which was almost hidden by the overgrown shrubbery, had grown dilapidated over the years.

REDUCED: The old house, almost hidden by the overgrown shrubbery, had grown dilapidated over the years.

ORIGINAL: Old Mr. Zajacs, who had been living alone in the big house since his wife's death, suddenly decided to sell the house and move to Arizona.

REDUCED: Old Mr. Zajacs, living alone in the big house since his wife's death, suddenly decided to sell the house and move to Arizona.

Often the *who* or *which* and the accompanying verb can be cut from such constructions without any loss.

Mrs. Hernandez, who was a woman of considerable determination, managed to rebuild the business.

Mrs. Hernandez, a woman of considerable determination, managed to rebuild the business.

The country store, which was at the intersection of two well-traveled roads, was the only store for miles around.

The country store, at the intersection of two well-traveled roads, was the only store for miles around.

The plantation, which had once been the scene of a Civil War movie, had been established in the 1850's.

The plantation, once the scene of a Civil War movie, had been established in the 1850's.

Mr. Faragutt, who is the present owner, insists on keeping the furnishings authentic in every detail.

Mr. Faragutt, the present owner, insists on keeping the furnishings authentic in every detail.

ABSOLUTE CONSTRUC-TIONS

The ultimate in economy is achieved through **absolute constructions.** In these constructions *every* word not *essential* to the meaning is removed.

ORIGINAL: When their tanks had been refueled, Patton's forces smashed through the last of the German defenses.

ABSOLUTE: Their tanks refueled, Patton's forces smashed through the last of the German defenses.

ORIGINAL: Since her hopes of marrying a wealthy oil man had been shattered, she left Midplains forever.

ABSOLUTE: Her hopes of marrying a wealthy oil man shattered, she left Midplains forever.

ORIGINAL: After the strike had finally been settled, the workers were happy to return to work.

ABSOLUTE: The strike finally settled, the workers were happy to return to work.

NOTE: Such constructions must be used with caution to avoid dangling modifiers. A dangling modifier is called *dangling* because the noun that it modifies is not the subject of the main clause.

DANGLING: Dressed in her new spring finery, a passing taxi splashed her with mud from head to foot.

CORRECT: Dressed in her new spring finery, she was splashed with mud from head to foot by a passing taxi.

DANGLING: Fully armed and completely ruthless, the huddled refugees were defenseless against the pirates.

CORRECT: The huddled refugees were defenseless against the pirates, who were fully armed and completely ruthless.

EXERCISE VIId: REDUCING DEPENDENT CLAUSE TO PHRASE
In each of the following sentences, reduce the subordinate (dependent) clause to a phrase.

1. Harrison Dillard, who was the owner of the building, lived in Columbia, South Carolina.

    _____

2. The army, which was made up largely of young recruits, had never faced an enemy.

    _____

3. The multi-state construction program, which had been started under the Johnson Administration, rapidly doubled and tripled in cost.

    _____

4. As he was sitting by the open window, he was struck by a stray bullet from a hunter's rifle.

    _____

5. While they were playing hopscotch on the sidewalk, the girls saw the car race down the street.

    _____

6. As he was ready to open the door, he stopped for a moment to wonder what she would say.

    _____

7. The famous author, after he had left Nebraska to find fame and fortune in New York, discovered that everything he wrote sprang from his youth on the prairies.

   _____

8. When he was lost in the woods at night, he remembered his Boy Scout training and plotted his course by the stars.

   _____

9. When they had received new supplies, the rebels renewed their attack on the outpost.

   _____

10. The cavalry, which had been waiting all winter for an opportunity to take the offensive, spearheaded the attack that was launched in April.

   _____

EXERCISE VIIe: REDUCING TO A VERBAL PHRASE
In each of the following pairs of sentences, reduce one sentence to a verbal phrase and insert the phrase into the other sentence.

1. He knew nothing about women. He was ready to marry the first girl who said a kind word to him.

   _____

2. Her guests had departed. Edith sat staring at the wreckage of her living room and shaking her head in disbelief.

   _____

3. He had hacked his way through miles of jungle. He was completely exhausted.

   _____

4. She couldn't say that she had any regrets. She knew that she would do it all over again if necessary.

   _____

5. The suspect finally began to talk. He blurted out an unbelievable story about being kidnapped by mysterious bearded men who looked like the Smith brothers.

   _____

6. The boys wanted to be ready for the soapbox derby. They worked all winter on designing the car.

   _____

7. The detective wanted to confirm the truth of her story. He drove her back to the scene of the crime and asked her to retrace her steps.

   _____

8. He had decided to learn more about the stock market. He visited the library and borrowed every book he could find on stocks and bonds.

_____

9. She refused to seek employment. She had become dejected by months of fruit-less job hunting.

_____

10. Levi was becoming homesick. He decided to return to his old neighborhood in Brooklyn.

_____

Sentence Variety

One of the most difficult of all things to define precisely is a sentence. The traditional definition says that a sentence is "A group of words containing a subject and a verb and expressing at least one complete thought." But the sentence is only fully defined when you consider the various kinds of sentences there are. To define sentence variety, you must, as with so many other definitions, turn to classification.

You learned early in your study of English that one classification of sentences is by their function: they make **statements,** ask **questions,** issue **commands,** and make **exclamations.**

In addition, there are two other classifications of sentences:

CLASSIFICATION A: ON THE BASIS OF GRAMMAR
1. Simple
2. Compound
3. Complex
4. Compound-complex

CLASSIFICATION B: ON THE BASIS OF RHETORIC
1. Loose
2. Periodic
3. Balanced
4. Antithetical

Each of these types of sentences has a specific job in communicating, and one of your tasks as a writer is constantly to choose the type that is best for your purpose. If you do so, you will almost automatically have a pleasing variety of sentences. Most of these types of sentences are already familiar to you, so the following is largely review to help you decide which type of sentence is useful in given situations.

CLASSIFICA-TION ON THE BASIS OF GRAMMAR　A *simple sentence* discusses only one topic expressed in one subject–predicate combination or independent clause. (The predicate is the verb or the verb phrase plus the object.) The simple sentence is one independent clause.

Notice that two subject words may be put together to form a compound subject—***Speed and strength*** *are needed for skating contests* — but the sentence remains simple. Similarly, two verbs may be put together to form a compound verb in a simple sentence: *The cannon **volleyed and thundered.*** Two objects may form a compound, but the sentence remains simple: *Literature enriches **our experience and our understanding.***

The simple sentence is used effectively to express a simple thought. You never want a sentence to be more elaborate than the thought it conveys. The simple sentence is also effective to express strong emotion, for its simplicity lends it strength. A strong statement should not be weakened by qualifiers. You would scarcely say, "Because you have a fast car, a big allowance, curly hair, a darling smile, and a good sense of humor, I love you." When you want to indicate that you're in love, the simple "I love you" is more effective.

The *compound sentence* is made of two or more independent clauses linked together with a coordinating conjunction (*and, but, or, nor, for, so,* or *yet*). These sentences are effective when you wish to present several ideas that are equal in importance: *He loved his parents, he respected his teachers, and he responded to his friends.*

The *complex sentence* is the one most often used in mature writing, for it can express a wide variety of relationships other than equality. (See the discussion of subordination in Chapter III.)

The complex sentence is made up of one independent clause and one or more dependent clauses. Since one idea usually is more important than the others, the important idea should be put in the independent clause. The less important ideas should be subordinated. For example:

Stanley stopped to light a cigarette, and a car hit him. (compound sentence)

Obviously, the first clause is less important than the second and should be expressed in single words, phrases, or dependent clauses; in other words, the first clause should be subordinated.

When Stanley stopped to light a cigarette, a car hit him.

Sometimes the important idea is obvious.

COMPOUND: Rose was planting flowers, and the convict approached through the woods.

COMPLEX: As Rose was planting flowers, the convict approached through the woods.

Sometimes the importance is not so obvious:

I like to be well informed; I read a newspaper every day.

In this sentence the reader cannot tell which idea is the more important one, but if you are the writer, you know which is the more important, and you tell the reader by subordinating the less important one.

I like to feel well informed after I read a newspaper every day.

OR

Since I like to feel well informed, I read a newspaper every day.

Decide what you want to emphasize and put that in the independent clause. Don't make the mistake of subordinating the wrong idea:

Stanley stopped to light a cigarette when the car hit him.
Rose was planting flowers while the convict approached through the woods.

You probably should use some form of the complex sentence about 70 percent of the time.
The subordinating conjunction you use is important because it shows the relationship of the subordinate clause to the main clause. The subordinating conjunction can show various relationships and delicate distinctions in meaning. Notice the difference made in the following sentences by changing the subordinating conjunction:

Although he loved his wife, he decided to divorce her.
Because he loved his wife, he decided to divorce her.
Before he loved his wife, he decided to divorce her.

The *compound-complex* sentence, as its name says, is a combination of two types of sentences.

COMPOUND: I called my dog, and she came running.
COMPLEX: When I called my dog, she came running.
COMPOUND–COMPLEX: When I called my dog, she came running, and she refused to leave me.

The compound-complex sentence is effective when you want to show relationships among several ideas that are so closely related that you wish to combine all of them in one sentence.

CLASSIFICA- TION ON THE BASIS OF RHETORIC   The *loose* sentence is the most common type of sentence. You usually put the main idea in the beginning of the loose sentence, and you add on other elements as they occur to you, remembering only to "bury" the weakest words in the middle of the sentence. For example, "Derek sailed to the Fiji Islands, a trip he had always wanted to take, after having sold his business, rented his house, put his furniture in storage, and said good-bye to his friends." The most important idea here is that Derek sailed to the Fijis. As this sentence is set up, the least important idea is that he had always wanted to go there. What he had to do in order to go is rhetorically the second most important thing.

Since the loose sentence is the type that seems most natural in English, you should choose it for most of the more commonplace things you write. Sometimes you will choose to put a subordinate idea both before and after the main clause. You might say, "Having sold his business, rented his house, put his furniture in storage, and said good-bye to his friends, Derek sailed to the Fiji Islands, a trip he had always wanted to take." The most important idea is in the weakest position, but it remains the strongest idea because it is in the independent clause. The loose sentence, as its name suggests, is not rigid in its form.

On the other hand, the *periodic sentence* is fixed in form. It does not complete its meaning until the very end of the sentence. All subordinate ideas come first. Since the strongest position in any writing—whether it be a sentence or longer—is the end, when you wish to be forceful, you choose the periodic sentence. The concluding clause of the periodic sentence has the double importance of being last and being independent: *Having sold his house, rented his business, put his furniture in storage, and said goodbye to his friends,* **Derek at last set sail for the Fiji Islands.**" An effective periodic sentence builds to a climax and so creates a dramatic suspense.

The *balanced sentence* you are already familiar with as parallel structure. In both the sentences about Derek, everything that he did before sailing was presented in parallel form. The parallelism of the balanced sentence is a good choice when you wish to emphasize that your points are of equal value. For example, *The voyage out was smooth and placid; the voyage back was calm and serene.*

The *antithetical sentence* is another familiar type. It is the balanced sentence, but with an additional characteristic: the parts of the parallelism are alike in structure but opposed in meaning.

With malice toward none, with charity toward all

I struggled daily to restore her sanity; I succeeded only in destroying my tranquillity.

Like the balanced sentence, the antithetical should be chosen to make strong points.

The good essay uses a variety of sentence patterns. Such variety, however, should not be strained for. If there are no dramatic points in your essay, do not include any periodic sentences. It would be ludicrous to postpone the ending of such a sentence as this one: *When the blizzards rage outside, when the wind howls through the trees ripping off branches, and when the temperatures reach fifty below zero, I usually stay inside.*

If you work conscientiously on getting the right kind of sentence for each idea, the variety will come of itself.

EXERCISE VIIf: SENTENCE COMBINING, SIMPLE SENTENCE
From your observation of your classroom, make five simple sentences.

EXAMPLE

The classroom smells of chalk dust.

1. _____
2. _____
3. _____
4. _____
5. _____

Now rewrite the sentences so that they have a compound subject.

EXAMPLE

The classroom and hall smell of chalk dust.

1. _____
2. _____
3. _____
4. _____
5. _____

Now rewrite the sentences so that they have a compound predicate.

EXAMPLE

The classroom smelled of chalk dust and looked dingy.

1. _____
2. _____
3. _____
4. _____
5. _____

EXERCISE VIIg: SENTENCE COMBINING, COMPLEX AND COMPOUND-COMPLEX
Following are lists of simple sentences. The sentences in each group can be combined in various ways to make complex or compound-complex sentences. For each group, combine all the sentences in two different forms.

EXAMPLES

GROUP A: The bull pawed the ground.
The bull was in the meadow.
The bull snorted.
The bull was angry.

197

COMBINED: In the meadow, the angry bull snorted and pawed the ground.

The bull, angry and snorting, pawed the ground in the meadow.

GROUP B: The farmer was alarmed.
He told the hired man to help him.
He needed to tether the bull.

COMBINED: The alarmed farmer told the hired man he needed help to tether the bull.

Alarmed, the farmer told the hired man to help him tether the bull.

GROUP C: The bull was dangerous.
He was untied.
He had a ring in his nose.

COMBINED: The dangerous bull had a ring in his nose although he was untied.

Although he had a ring in his nose, the dangerous bull was untied.

GROUP D: A chain could be attached to the ring.
The chain could be attached to a heavy stake.
The bull could be tied.
He wouldn't be a threat anymore.

COMBINED: To keep him from being a threat, the bull could be tied with a chain attached to the ring and to a heavy stake in the ground.

A chain could be attached to the ring in the bull's nose and to a heavy stake in the ground to keep him from being a threat.

Now you try it with the following groups. Remember to combine each group of sentences in two ways.

1.   **GROUP A**   The girl was pretty.
She had red hair.
She had a dusting of freckles.
She was slim and willowy.

GROUP B   The boy looked at her.
He was attracted.
He was sentimental.

GROUP C   She knew he was watching.
She was tickled.
She liked to be admired.

GROUP D   She smiled at him.
She was aware he was shy.
She liked his thoughtful face.

2.   **GROUP A**   The new veterinarian is a woman.
She graduated at the top of her class.
She went to a fine veterinary college.

GROUP B She has invented a new surgical procedure.
It prevents some crippling of dogs by arthritis.
She was honored by her school for this.

GROUP C She is an intelligent woman.
She is a kindhearted woman.
We are lucky to have her in our town.

3. **GROUP A** It is the first warm day of spring.
The sun shines brightly.
The sky is a clear, bright blue.
The classroom seems cramped and hot.

GROUP B There are many types of animals.
They come from all over the world.
Some animals are dangerous.
Some animals are harmless.
Almost all wild animals need great care.

GROUP C Keeping the animals healthy takes a lot of knowledge.
The food has to be properly chosen.
The surroundings must fit the animals' natural needs.
Temperature makes a lot of difference to animals.

4. **GROUP A** Traveling is a lot of fun.
I go to other places to see where famous events took place.
I don't care much about the people who live there now.
They are pretty much like me.
I want to see where great people lived.

GROUP B People of the past seem more alive than people actually living today.
People of the past seem braver and more exciting.
Today everybody seems to dress like everyone else.
They seem to talk like everyone else.
They all seem to think alike.

GROUP C I like to think what it was like "back then."
Let's suppose I go to visit Gettysburg.
I try to imagine Pickett charging across the empty meadows.
I try to figure out why Meade was so slow to bring up his troops.

EXERCISE VIIh: SENTENCE COMBINING, LOOSE SENTENCES
From each of the following groups of sentences, choose the idea you wish to make most important. Write a sentence expressing that idea in an independent clause and putting it first in the sentence, subordinating the other ideas to it.

EXAMPLE
a. The candidate has seven years' experience.
b. The candidate has proved himself competent.
c. The candidate should be reelected. (most important)
d. He had proved himself trustworthy.

defining

COMBINATION A: INDEPENDENT CLAUSE AT BEGINNING OF SENTENCE

The candidate should be reelected because in his seven years' experience he has proved himself competent and trustworthy.

> Now, using the same four sentences, put one subordinate element before and another after the independent clause.

COMBINATION B: INDEPENDENT CLAUSE IN MIDDLE OF SENTENCE

Having proved himself through seven years' experience, the candidate should be reelected for his competence and trustworthiness.

> Combine the following groups of sentences in the ways suggested above.

1. a. Fairy tales are more than stories for children.
   b. Fairy tales express the desires of simple but adult people.
   c. Fairy tales emphasize the values of common sense, courage, and kindness.

2. a. Winds of hurricane force smashed houses, destroyed crops, and uprooted hundreds of trees.
   b. The storm devastated an entire river valley.
   c. All the damage was done in less than half an hour.

3. a. The owners of the baseball team threatened to move it to another city.
   b. The owners didn't like their stadium.
   c. The fans were upset.

4. a. Almost all the students went to the Christmas Dance.
   b. The Christmas Dance was the most important party of the school year.
   c. Many alumni came back for the Christmas Dance.
   d. The Christmas Dance really created school spirit.

5. a. Block Island is only a few miles off the coast of Rhode Island.
   b. Block Island is tiny.
   c. Block Island is a fine place to own a summer home.
   d. Block Island is uncrowded and rather old-fashioned.

> **EXERCISE VIIi: SENTENCE COMBINING, PERIODIC SENTENCES**
> Using the groups of sentences in Exercise VIIh, again decide upon the most important idea and place it at the end of the combined sentence, with all the other sentences subordinated to and preceding it.
>
> **EXERCISE VIIj: SENTENCE COMBINING, BALANCED SENTENCES**
> Combine the following groups of sentences by making them, or some elements of them, parallel.
>
> **EXAMPLE**

Jack Sprat wasn't permitted to eat fat.
Lean meat wasn't enjoyed by Mrs. Sprat either.

Jack Sprat could eat no fat;
his wife could eat no lean.

1. a. The dog loved to ride in the car.
   b. The dog romped happily with its owner.
   c. The dog also liked to hike with its owner.

2.
   a. Doves were murmuring in the trees.
   b. Cicadas shrilled.
   c. The summer evening was filled with country sounds.
   d. I could hear crickets chirping.

3.
   a. The house roof sagged and some of its windows were cracked.
   b. The house looked desolate.
   c. The surrounding grounds were tangled and unkempt.
   d. The whole place had the quality of a nightmare.

4.
   a. John always stuck by his principles.
   b. When he reached a decision, he stayed with it.
   c. John was a man of strong character.
   d. John never permitted anyone to persuade him against his better judgment.

5.
   a. The poetry of Robert Frost is based on natural images.
   b. Frost's themes in his poetry are universal.
   c. The language of Frost's poems is simple.

EXERCISE VIIk: SENTENCE COMBINING ANTITHETICAL IDEAS IN VARIED SENTENCE FORMS

The following groups of sentences contain opposing ideas. Decide what the two ideas are, and, through subordination of some sentences, combine them into one sentence in which the relationship of opposition is clear.

EXAMPLE
   a. The crowd was eager to see the rock stars.
   b. The wait for the doors to open seemed endless.
   c. Most of the crowd had been fans of this group for years.
   d. Rain and a chilling wind made the wait uncomfortable.

COMBINED: The crowd, fans of the rock stars for years, were eager to see them, but the wait in the rain and chilling wind for the doors to open seemed endless.

Although it seemed endless waiting in the rain and chilling wind for the doors to open, the crowd, fans for years, were eager to see the rock stars.

1.
   a. The concert was enjoyable.
   b. The concert was made up of new music.
   c. Some of the audience walked out on it.
   d. Some concert goers only want to hear well-known works.

2.
   a. The crowds downtown some Sunday afternoons are huge.
   b. You scarcely see a passing car.
   c. Some Sunday afternoons downtown are dead.
   d. When the symphony lets out and the ball game is over, there are traffic jams.

3.
   a. Choosing the precise word makes your writing clear and concise.
   b. Wordiness is a fault in writing.
   c. Wordiness tends to make your writing boring.
   d. Wordiness can even obscure your meaning.

4.
   a. Clarity is largely based on good diction and correctness in mechanics.
   b. The first requirement of a good sentence is that it be clear.
   c. A poor sentence is vague.
   d. Vagueness usually comes from poor diction, incorrect mechanics.

201

WORD POWER

The Dictionary

The first people to speak any form of English were known as the Anglo-Saxons and they lived in England almost 1,500 years ago. The language they spoke, now called Old English, was a strong, flexible language with a large vocabulary. The Anglo-Saxons, conscious and proud of their vocabulary, called it their "word horde," which implies that they considered their vocabulary the treasure it is, for the words speakers know are the tools with which they think. Everyone's thinking is limited by the words he or she has to think with.

As protection for the treasure of words, languages today depend upon the dictionary. The dictionary, the best known of reference works, lists the words of a language, supplies much information about each word, and provides its users with standards for usage.

HOW THE DICTIONARY CAN BE MOST HELPFUL

In Defining

You probably use your dictionary most often to find what a word means. When you look up the definition, however, don't just settle for the first meaning the dictionary gives you. Having spent the time to look the word up, read the whole entry because the more you learn, the less you will forget.

In most dictionaries the first meaning given is the oldest and thus the primary meaning. For instance, if you look up the word *red,* you find that its first definition pertains to the specific color, but if you read on, you find that its extended meaning indicates *revolutionary* and, more specifically, *communistic* because of the red color of many revolutionary banners. Since language grows and enriches itself through extended meanings, it is important to read all of them. Take, for example, even so common an adjective as *tame.* Its first or primary meaning is "changed from wildness to domesticity." But its extended meanings go far beyond that to indicate "naturally gentle and unafraid; submissive; fawning; docile; insipid; flat; sluggish; languid." As you consider how *tame* can mean all of these things, you increase your awareness, not just of one word but of several, and so you build your vocabulary.

Just reading the dictionary can be interesting as well as informative. If, for instance, your eye wanders across the page from *tame,* you might spot the word *taleteller* and notice that it has two diverse meanings. Its earlier sense means an oral narrator, but its secondary sense has a connotation of disapproval, for it means a gossip. The closely similar word *talebearer,* however, has only the connotatively disapproving sense of a gossip. Looking up words to find their various meanings is one of the very best ways to increase your language awareness, which is imperative for good writing.

Good dictionaries will usually give you synonyms (and sometimes antonyms) of words being defined. Since there are no exact synonyms, when a word has a number of synonyms, the dictionary frequently distinguishes among them so you can use them precisely. For example, the *American Heritage Dictionary* defines *passion* as "any powerful emotion or appetite, such as love, joy, hatred, anger, or greed." After a full discussion it concludes:

synonyms: passion, fervor, enthusiasm, zeal, ardor.
These all denote strong feeling, either sustained or passing, for or about something or somebody. *Passion* is a deep, overwhelming feeling or emotion. When directed toward a person, it usually connotes love as well as sexual desire, although it can also refer to hostile emotions such as anger and hatred. Used lightly, it suggests an avid interest, as in a hobby: *a passion for gardening. Fervor* is a highly intense, sustained emotional state, frequently (like *passion*) with a potential loss of control implied: *he fought with fervor.* Quite different is *enthusiasm,* which reflects excitement and responsiveness to more specific or concrete things. *Zeal,* sometimes reflecting strong, forceful devotion to a specific cause, expresses a driving attraction to something which grows out of motivation or attitude: *zeal for the project. Ardor* can be for a cause but commonly connotes a warm, rapturous feeling directed toward persons.

In Pronunciation and Spelling

The same care that you give to meanings should also be given to the forms of words. First, what is meant by "forms of words"? Essentially, the form of a word is its spelling, possible variants in spelling (for example, *dialog* and *dialogue*), variations between British spellings and American spellings (*theatre* and *theater*), variations in number (*mouse, mice*), and variations in gender (*goose, gander*). Forms can refer to the various parts of speech a word may take: noun forms, adjective forms, adverb forms, verb forms. Form also shows the principal parts of verbs when they are irregular. When you are attentive to the forms of words, you improve both your pronunciation and spelling, for these two skills help each other. If you are sure of the sound of a word, you probably can spell it correctly and vice versa. However, if you still need help, most dictionaries have not only a guide to pronunciation at the bottom of each page but also sections which give rules for pronunciation and for spelling.

In Usage

Usage refers to the habitual or customary way in which the speakers and writers of a language employ it. Good modern dictionaries will identify for you the accepted usage of a word: standard, colloquial, slang, or subliterate; currently being used, old-fashioned, or no longer used at all.

In Western culture the first important dictionary was that of the eighteenth-century French Academy, which, as well as giving meanings for words, laid down rules for grammar and usage. It was what is now known as a "prescriptive" dictionary, a rule giver. It is widely admired because it was early and comprehensive; it is widely ignored because rules change and no longer apply. All languages that are still spoken and written are "living" languages, and all living things change. Wise dictionary makers today avoid writing a rule-making dictionary; instead, they write dictionaries that are "descriptive," that is, that describe what people do as they use language.

The dictionary that is usually considered the first important one in English is Dr. Samuel Johnson's, published in 1755. Dr. Johnson had announced that he hoped his dictionary would "refine and purify" the English language. However, long before the end of the seven years it took him to make his dictionary, he found that a living language could not be pinned down with rules. The best a lexicographer could do was to describe the language as used by the best writers and speakers.

The "descriptive" approach to dictionary making has been the most influential since Dr. Johnson. In spite of this, however, during the nineteenth century, especially in America, the dictionary was considered a rule giver, and, as such, almost sacred. People would intone "The dictionary says, . . ." and give a rule. You probably have heard someone say smugly, "*Ain't* isn't in the dictionary." Perhaps it isn't in every dictionary, but it is in modern dictionaries because it is in the language. The *American Heritage Dictionary* has this to say about it:

> **ain't.** Nonstandard. Contraction of am not. Also extended in use to mean are not, is not, has not, and have not. . . . Unacceptable in writing . . . according to ninety-nine percent of the Usage Panel [a group of one hundred respected professional writers who advised the lexicographers on usage] and unacceptable in speech to eighty-four percent. . . .

This partial quotation is typical of the advice on usage given in good contemporary dictionaries. They describe how and by whom the word is used. When you know this about a word, you have a basis for choosing exactly the right word for your purpose.

In Miscellaneous Aids

The larger dictionaries usually contain a table of contents telling what other information is available beyond that given for each entry. *Webster's New International*, for instance, includes sections on new words and their sources and a comprehensive history of the English language. The appendices include abbreviations, census figures, forms of address (how to speak or write to a bishop or a U.S. senator, for example), an alphabetized list of short biographies, an alphabetized list of towns, cities, rivers, mountains, and other geographic information. There are also pages of pictures of such things as coins, flags, airplanes, bridges, famous buildings, dogs, wildflowers, and military insignia. Like the pages of other unabridged dictionaries, this dictionary's more than three thousand pages is a hoard of knowledge.

TYPES OF DICTIONARIES

Unabridged Dictionaries

The principle source for complete information on words is an *unabridged* dictionary. For example, *Webster's Third New International Dictionary of the English Language,* found in many college libraries, has 450,000 entries (pocket dictionaries usually have no more than 50,000). In addition, the *Third International* offers complete definitions and ample illustrations of the various uses of words. If you want an even more exhaustive history of a word, your best source would be *The Oxford English Dictionary* (O.E.D.). This scholarly, multivolume dictionary provides the most comprehensive historical study of English words and illustrates in great detail the changes in meaning many words have undergone since they first appeared in the language. Other unabridged dictionaries, such as *The Random House Dictionary of the English Language* (260,000 entries), are more limited in scope but more permissive than the O.E.D., especially with respect to current American usage. Although unabridged dictionaries may not be practical for everyday use, you should become familiar with them so that you know where to turn when you encounter a word not included in an abridged dictionary and when you want detailed information about a word.

Pocket Dictionaries

Pocket dictionaries are generally inadequate for college use. Frequently, you may find that the word you need is not listed or the definition that is offered is insufficient. Furthermore, the pocket dictionaries generally do not provide the advice on usage or the examples you may need to understand the full range of a word's use and meaning.

Desk Dictionaries

A good, up-to-date desk dictionary is your best bet for everyday use. Look for one that has 100,000 or more entries, and be sure to check for a recent copyright date. Many abridged dictionaries are available; any selection from the following list of popular editions would serve you well:

Webster's New World Dictionary of the American Language, 2nd college edition. Cleveland: William Collins and World, 1979.

The American Heritage Dictionary of the English Language, New College Edition. Boston: Houghton Mifflin, 1978.

The Random House Dictionary of the English Language, College edition. New York: Random House, 1975.

Webster's New Collegiate Dictionary, 8th edition. Springfield, MA: G. & C. Merriam, 1976.

Funk and Wagnalls Standard College Dictionary, New York: Funk and Wagnalls, 1975.

TIPS ON INCREASING YOUR VOCABULARY

Although there are more than a million words in the English language, the average person goes through life with a scanty vocabulary of fewer than 25,000. Here are a few suggestions that can help you build a better than average vocabulary:

1. Look at the context in which an unfamiliar word appears; then try to guess its meaning from the way it is used in the sentence. Suppose you encounter the word *excoriate* in a sentence such as this: "The Secretary of Defense *excoriated* those critics who demand that he resign." You might easily guess from the context that *excoriated* meant something like "lashed out at."

2. Look the word up. In this instance, your guess would have been fairly accurate, for the dictionary defines *excoriate* as to "tear or wear off the skin . . . censure strongly; denounce severely; upbraid."

3. Take note of the origin of the word. *Excoriate* comes from Latin *excoriare,* "to strip of skin." Noting the origin of the word will help you to remember it and to recognize other words of similar origin.

4. As soon as you learn a new word, start using it. Check the dictionary guide to pronunciation (ĕk•skôr′•ē•āt) and say the word several times; then write the word in several sentences. You'll be surprised at how often a word you thought was rare will pop up again in writing or conversation.

REMEMBERING WORDS AND THEIR MEANINGS

Mental pictures, no matter how outlandish or silly, can help you remember words and their meanings. For example, take two simple words, *flora* and *fauna*. Do you remember what they mean? Do you remember which is which?

The dictionary definition of *flora* is "the plants of a specified region or time . . . a descriptive, systematic list of such plants." The definition of *fauna* is "the animals of a specified region . . . a descriptive list of such animals."

You can keep the meaning of these words clear in your mind if you make a mental picture, perhaps of tall flowering plants (flora) with a funny long-tailed animal (fauna) scurrying at the roots.

Now take some more unusual words: *monometalism* is "the use of only one metal, usually gold or silver, as the monetary standard." You might remember that word and its meaning by picturing an ingot with a huge numeral one stamped on its face.

An *iconoclast* is "anyone opposed to the religious use of images or advocating the destruction of such images . . . a person who attacks or ridicules traditional or venerated institutions or ideas. . . ." You might remember that word and its meaning by picturing a brawny arm holding a heavy hammer shaped like a capital *I* that is smashing the head from a statue.

The word *serendipity* means "an apparent aptitude for making fortunate discoveries accidentally." You might remember that word and its meaning by picturing the dip of a roller coaster with an open treasure chest at the bottom.

The word *embouchure* is defined as "the mouth of a river . . . the mouthpiece of a wind instrument . . . the method of applying the lips and tongue to the mouthpiece of a wind instrument." You might remember that word and its meaning by picturing, let us say, a lake blowing a river through a trumpet.

The key to this simple technique for remembering a word and its meaning is that as soon as you discover a new word you should create a mental picture somehow associated with that word. Oddly enough, the more ridiculous the picture, the more apt you are to remember the word.

EXERCISE VIII: DICTIONARY DEFINITIONS

The following words frequently appear on vocabulary tests and lists of words that college freshmen should know. For each, complete the following process:

1. Carefully check each word on the list.
2. Unless you are certain that you know the meaning, circle the word.
3. Look up the meaning of each circled word in a modern desk dictionary.
4. After reading the complete dictionary entry, close the dictionary and write your own brief definition.

1. morose	8. temerity	15. declaim	22. eschew
2. sidle	9. simile	16. adroit	23. prerogative
3. arable	10. purport	17. strident	24. lucid
4. desultory	11. tacit	18. extirpate	25. heinous
5. ubiquitous	12. disburse	19. strew	26. innate
6. sedate	13. wry	20. configuration	27. venal
7. congenital	14. dither	21. entourage	28. myriad

29. congenial	**37.** sham	**45.** intrinsic	**53.** consternation
30. docile	**38.** officious	**46.** perverse	**54.** pernicious
31. expunge	**39.** veracity	**47.** flaccid	**55.** maxim
32. volition	**40.** qualm	**48.** marital	**56.** nurture
33. scurrilous	**41.** secular	**49.** regale	**57.** upbraid
34. wheedle	**42.** reticence	**50.** vestige	**58.** rancor
35. surfeit	**43.** litigation	**51.** trundle	**59.** portend
36. verdant	**44.** travesty	**52.** acrimony	**60.** cogent

EXERCISE VIIm: ROOTS

In a good desk dictionary, look up the following words to see how each is related to the Latin word *dictio,* a saying.

1. abdicate	**6.** indicate	**11.** ditto
2. condition	**7.** jurisdiction	**12.** index
3. dedicate	**8.** addict	**13.** interdict
4. diction	**9.** contradict	**14.** paradigm
5. edict	**10.** dictate	**15.** digit

Denotation and Connotation

A mortician never handles a *corpse,* he prepares a *body* or *patient.* This business is carried on in a preparation-room or operating-room, and when it is achieved the patient is put into a casket and stored in the resposing-room or slumber-room of a funeral-home. On the day of the funeral he is moved to the chapel therein for the last exorcism, and then hauled to the cemetery in a funeral-car or casket-coach. The old-time *shroud* is now a *negligee* or *slumber-shirt* or *slumber-robe,* the mortician's *worktruck* is an *ambulance,* and the *cemetery* is fast becoming a *memorial park.*   *H. L. Mencken*

By studying the italicized words in the passage above, you will see that some words have similar meanings but evoke very different responses. Take the words *body* and *corpse,* for example. Although one can be used as a synonym for the other, *corpse* creates a much more negative feeling than *body* because you associate *corpse* with death. These two words illustrate the difference between *denotation*—the literal meaning of a word—and *connotation*—the feelings or impressions that a word calls up. Knowing the dictionary definition of a word (the denotative meaning) is not enough; you must also be aware of what the word **connotes.** Otherwise, you may use wrong words and mislead the reader.

New York Times columnist William Safire gives both the connotative and denotative meanings of words to clarify his interpretations of "Washington talk":

media: a slightly sinister or clinical word for the "the press," often intended to carry a manipulative or mechanical connotation

moratorium: stems from the Latin for "delay" but has a more majestic connotation

In the following terms from *Safire's Political Dictionary*, notice how the meaning of the whole term is affected by the connotations of the italicized words:

Limousine liberal	*Lunatic* fringe
Machine politics	*White* hats
Party *elders*	Official *family*
Spoils system	Merchants of *death*
Truth squad	Saturday night *massacre*

Notice the difference in the connotations of the following words:

Positive	*Neutral*	*Negative*
flexible	indecisive	wishy-washy
public servant	congressman	politician
reserved	shy	backward
student leader	activist	radical
entrepreneur	business person	fat cat

EXERCISE VIIn: SUPPLYING NEUTRAL CONNOTATION
Supply a word with a more neutral connotation than those listed below.

	Positive	*Neutral*	*Negative*
1.	advocate	_____	propagandist
2.	electronic surveillance	_____	bugging
3.	hard-working	_____	opportunistic
4.	negotiated	_____	made a deal with
5.	lady	_____	dame
6.	informed	_____	brainwashed
7.	freethinker	_____	kook
8.	discuss	_____	argue
9.	statesman	_____	demagogue
10.	strong-willed	_____	mulish

EXERCISE VIIo: SUPPLYING FAVORABLE CONNOTATION
Place the words in order in each of the following sets, beginning with the word with the least favorable connotation and ending with the word with the most favorable connotation.

1. drunk, bombed, intoxicated, wasted, blitzed

_____

2. insane, crazy, mentally ill, deranged, feebleminded

_____

3. policeman, fuzz, law-enforcement officer, flatfoot, racist pig

_____

4. a lie, a falsehood, an exaggeration, a fib, a deception

_____

5. getting married, getting hitched, tying the knot, taking the fatal plunge, joining in holy matrimony

_____

6. politician, public servant, statesman, hack, congressman

_____

7. infidel, freethinker, heathen, pagan, unbeliever

_____

8. bacterial infection, Hansen's disease, skin irritation, leprosy

_____

9. inform, brainwash, convince, persuade, indoctrinate

_____

10. cheap, thrifty, frugal, tight, stingy

_____

EXERCISE VIIp: SUPPLYING THE BEST CONNOTATION

Although the denotative meaning of these words is similar, the connotative meaning is different. Of the choices in parentheses, circle the word you should use on each occasion. Then, explain why each word you choose has the best connotation.

1. You tell your boss that his remark was (funny / ridiculous / humorous / witty / ludicrous).

_____

2. You also tell him that you were disappointed with your paycheck because you had (assumed / presumed / banked on / expected / hoped for) a raise.

_____

3. You tell your mother that the birthday meal she cooked for you was (tasty / palatable / edible / epicurean / ambrosial).

_____

4. You prefer to be described as (compliant / malleable / disciplined / meek / pliable).

_____

5. You tell your friend that the cousin you want him to go on a blind date with is (skinny / slim / emaciated / slender / lean / lanky).

_____

6. You tell your teacher that his lecture was (loquacious / long / prolonged / interminable / complete).

    _____

7. You tell your friend that he is (parsimonious / thrifty / stingy / miserly / penny-pinching).

    _____

8. You refer to the gift you bought your father as (inexpensive / cheap / a bargain / economical / worth little).

    _____

9. You call the officer whom you are trying to talk out of giving you a ticket (*buddy / cop / patrolman / officer / protector*).

    _____

10. You tell your employer that during the office party he was (tipsy / drunk / loaded / relaxed / bombed).

    _____

11. You describe yourself to a prospective employer as (pushy / aggressive / motivated / strong-willed / ambitious).

    _____

CHAPTER VIII

cause and effect

From the time we become verbal, we as thinking people seek causes and effects. We want to know why something is the way it is, and what will happen if some action is taken.

The three-year-old who wants to go out to play plagues his father with such questions as "Why can't I go out to play?" and "Why does it rain, Daddy?" Fifteen years later he may be asking his father why he can't have a car, asking his teacher why she gave him a D, and asking his girlfriend why she's mad at him. As a mature adult he might ask the mayor why unemployment is so high, ask the grocer why lettuce is so expensive, and ask his doctor why he feels so sick.

In all these cases, he is seeking the cause of some situation; he assumes that something is responsible, that there is a causal relationship between something in the past and the situation now.

The popular saying that "things don't just happen" assumes that every event must have a cause. Even though it is impossible to prove that **every** event has a cause, the number of times you use the word *because* suggests how often you look for a cause-and-effect relationship in everyday events. The process of seeking the causes for something, of answering the "why" of something, is called *causal* *analysis.* Understanding the causes of some event or situation is one of our most important abilities, for it enables us to prevent future bad situations and encourage future good ones or at least to predict and prepare for what is to come.

Cause really includes all the factors that make some event occur. However, if all these factors were given in answer to "why," the questioner probably would not stay to listen. Usually, therefore, one or more factors are singled out as being "the cause." However, when you identify something as "the cause," you must be sure that it is both a **necessary** and a **sufficient** cause. When you say that *A* is a *necessary cause* of *B*, you are saying that *B* must always occur when *A* does. If *A* does not occur, *B* will not occur. And, to be a *sufficient cause* of *B*, *A* must be significant enough to cause *B* to occur. By applying the basic definition that *cause* is the **necessary and sufficient condition** producing an event, you can avoid many errors in reasoning about events and their causes.

Sufficient Cause

Sometimes an error in cause and effect comes about through mistaking a *contributing* cause for *sufficient* cause. A *contributing* cause helps to bring about a specific event, but it is not enough in itself to be the sole cause of the effect. For example, to say that Germany lost World War II because the nation ran out of gasoline does give a contributing cause, but it is minor compared with more significant reasons, such as the decimation of the German armies by the Russian winter, the stubborn resistance of the RAF, the successful bombing raids on German industrial centers, the German waste of their resources on the "final solution of the Jewish problem."

Causal analysis works in two directions. You may start with the situation as it is and go back in time to discover why. Or you may start at the cause and go forward in time to see what effect some action will have. In other words, you may reason from cause to effect or from effect to cause. If you had a carton of eggs teetering atop a bag of groceries, you might reason that if the eggs drop, they will break (cause to effect). If you found a chocolate cake smashed on the kitchen floor, and you recalled having placed the cake on top of the refrigerator, you would conclude that the cake had fallen from the top of the refrigerator (effect to cause).

When you move from such obvious examples to more remote events, however, you quickly see that accurate cause-and-effect reasoning can become a complex problem. Why did Lee Harvey Oswald kill President Kennedy? Was there any one cause for his action? Does anyone know for certain all of the possible causes and effects?

As you try to analyze the causes or effects of complex situations, you need to guard against seizing upon the first explanation that comes to mind and supposing that you have solved the problem. Much faulty reasoning about cause and effect results from the tendency to oversimplify. Most events involving human beings have multiple causes. Suppose you read in the paper, "ICY ROAD CAUSES FATAL CRASH." That headline implies a simple cause-and-effect relationship, but the reality may be far more complex. The driver may have been driving too fast for the weather conditions; he may have overslept and been rushing to work; he may have been driving on bald tires; the possibilities go on and on. The point is that the icy road by itself is not **sufficient** to explain the fatal crash. Did every car that traveled that road crash? Were other motorists killed at the same spot?

Enough Information

Careful reasoning demands sufficient information to establish a clear connection between cause and effect, yet all too often people rush to conclusions without adequate information. Could the explosion of a hydrogen bomb at Bikini Atoll cause a drought in Nebraska or floods in Arkansas? A surprising number of people blamed local weather conditions on the testing of atomic weapons, and some still do. Is the price of pork chops the result of having a Democrat or a Republican in the White House? Surprisingly, some people will blame the president if prices go up—unless it was their favorite who was elected. If you are to write a good paper, you must have—or find—enough information to provide necessary and sufficient cause or to project probable effects.

Narrowed Topic

To discuss the causes and effects of major events intelligently, you need to narrow the range of your analysis and set careful limits to your discussion. If you tried to explain why Germany was defeated in World War II, for instance, you could spend half a lifetime investigating various causes. If, however, you carefully limited the discussion to the major reasons why the German air force, the Luftwaffe, failed to win the Battle of Britain, you would have a far better chance of presenting a persuasive argument based upon cause and effect. Keep in mind, too, that in cause-and-effect reasoning you are dealing in probabilities. You can seldom be certain that your explanation is the only possible one, so you need to reason carefully from well-established facts to a conclusion that will appeal to intelligent readers.

Analyzing Causes

Causal analysis is one of the great tools of logical thinking; an essay using this method should be logically organized and thoroughly developed. Inadequate preparation can lead to an erroneous conclusion. Let's take a quick look at the two methods of causal analysis: (1) **find the cause,** and (2) **project the effects.**

FINDING THE CAUSE
Why did Henry fail the test?
He was sick the night before.
Before you can assume that this was the cause of the failure, you must investigate further.
Did he fail any other tests?
Yes, he failed two other tests. Was he sick the night before each one? Perhaps the quick answer was not the right one. Unless he failed only those three tests and his health was bad before each one, and you can eliminate all other possible causes for his failure, you probably have not established a cause-and-effect relationship.

Upon further investigation, you may discover more information: (1) Henry attends class irregularly; (2) he spends less than two hours per week studying for the class; (3) he missed three lab sessions; (4) his homework is seldom done, and when it is done, it is often late and incomplete; and (5) he takes few notes and is inattentive during class.

As your investigation proceeds, you see that being sick is not the whole answer to Henry's failing the test. Your investigation has also led you to more fundamental reasons for the failure. There are often larger, more basic reasons for a situation than you see at first:

Henry doesn't really care about school.
Henry has a lackadaisical attitude about all work.
His study habits are poor.
He really doesn't want to be in college; he wants to be a mechanic.

Projecting the effect will not be difficult once you have discovered this information:

PROJECTING THE EFFECT
Henry will probably flunk out of school.

In **projecting the effect** of any situation, make sure that your prediction is logical. Show step by step, without omission, what effect will logically come from what cause or causes. In projecting Henry's fate, you have little difficulty in showing the underlying causes. To be convincing, however, you must **show** them, not just leap over them to the projected effect.

In projecting the effects of more complicated conditions, you have to be even more careful. What are the probable effects of certain chemical pollutants in drinking water? If a pregnant woman smokes heavily, what effect does that have on her unborn child? The process here is still one of reasoning from the known to the unknown, but predicting future effects on the basis of known causes is hazardous at best. You can be fairly safe, of course, when the predicted effect is based upon some natural law or established scientific principle. For example, we know that water will boil at 212°, and we know the effects of mercury poisoning. But predicting what effect the mother's smoking may have on her unborn child is far less certain. There are too many unknowns, too many possible causes and effects, to make any prediction with a high degree of probability. When the evidence will support nothing more than a reasonable guess, say so.

In causal analysis that moves from cause to effects, the cause need not always be in the present and the effects in the future. You might want to identify causes of present or even past effects. The interpretation of history, for example, depends on an analysis of cause and effects that are all in the past.

The Chain of Cause and Effect

When you follow the logical process to establish a sound cause-and-effect relationship, you frequently encounter a cause-and-effect series or chain of events. What you need to do then is to take the chain apart and examine the relationship between each link. Sometimes you reason from cause to effect and other times you must reason from effect to cause. Furthermore, what may be the effect in one link may become the cause in the next link. For example, if severe malnutrition impairs a child's mental development, then the result, deficient intelligence, could become the cause of later effects, such as the inability to find gainful employment. Thus it is often necessary to reason through an extensive chain of causes and effects step by step.

More often than not, your search for causes begins only after something has gone wrong and you are faced with a problem. If you are to solve the problem and perhaps prevent similar occurrences in the future, you must analyze the evidence carefully and take into consideration all of the possible causes. When the FAA sends out a team to investigate an airplane crash, the investigators examine every shred of evidence in an effort to determine the cause of the crash, and, if possible, to prevent similar accidents in the future. Working from the **known,** the physical evidence, they try to find the **unknown,** the probable cause. If they can definitely determine the cause to be a fault in the aircraft design, for example, then design changes can be made in order to reduce the chance of a similar accident in the future. Investigating plane crashes, of course, is a job for experts, but when you are presented with a complex problem, you need to examine the evidence with the same kind of thoroughness and persistence.

ORGANIZATION

Introduction

The introduction should draw attention to and focus upon the controlling idea of your essay. An apt quotation, a striking example, or a brief anecdote may serve to capture your reader's interest and focus it on the point you want to make. Then your thesis sentence should clearly state the controlling idea of your essay, one based upon cause-and-effect reasoning.

Frequently, your thesis sentence will state that A is the cause of B, imply that B is the result of A, or indicate some continuation of causes and effects.

Note the following introduction:

"Men shed their sickness in books," said D. H. Lawrence. Perhaps that idea may seem a little ridiculous to you at first, but literature presents ample evidence to support the idea that great writers often suffered psychic wounds which impelled them to write. *For many, writing was both an obsession and a form of therapy: they had to write because that was the only way they could exorcise the demons within them and maintain their own sanity.*

215

Body

The body of the essay may combine several methods and make use of various types of support, such as examples or brief case histories, comparison or analogy, statistical evidence or authoritative quotations. The only genuine restriction is that the materials presented in the body must provide clear and relevant support for your thesis sentence. To support the thesis about great writers, for example, you could develop the body of the essay by showing the cause-and-effect relationship between the work of great writers and the traumatic experiences they suffered. The following outline suggests the main points in the development of such an essay:

1. Charles Dickens' finest work came directly out of the miseries of his childhood.
2. James Joyce's *Ulysses* seems to reflect every slight and every wound he suffered in his childhood and youth.
3. Alexander Solzhenitzyn's work bears the stamp of one who survived the frozen hell of Soviet labor camps.
4. Some, like Virginia Woolf and Sylvia Plath, were never able to exorcise their demons and eventually committed suicide.

Notice that these four points are examples; each author's experience develops the point made in the thesis statement that writing was both obsession and therapy. Each example involves tracing an effect back to its cause identified in the thesis statement.

Conclusion

The conclusion that will serve you best is one that briefly pulls together the main points of your essay and reinforces your controlling idea. For the essay outlined here, the following might provide a fitting conclusion:

For many great writers, sensitivity and talent were not enough; only the meeting of talent and interior wounds could have driven them to write as they did. For them, writing was a sheer driving necessity, a means of self-salvation. They had to write, even when there was no one who would publish their work. They were compelled to write by an obsession to bring under control the chaos and the torment of their interior lives.

The essay below has a clear three-part organization. Notice how the author leads up to her main idea and then states her thesis clearly in the last sentence of her introduction. Note, also, that the introduction and the conclusion are relatively short compared with the body of the essay, where the main idea is developed. In this essay, the thesis statement is supported mainly with specific examples.

The Decline of Quality

INTRODUCTION   A question that puzzles me is why inexpensive things must be made ugly. . . . I have heard it suggested that raucous colors and hideous decoration are meant to distract the purchaser's eye from shoddy workmanship, but since that only results in a remedy worse than the disease, it cannot be the whole explanation. . . . I do not see why the presumption cannot be made the other way: that the consumer would respond to good design rather than junk. The answer will doubtless be that when this experiment has been tried, the mass of consumers failed to respond. **For this failure, I believe, two institutions of our culture are largely to blame: education and advertising.**

We have some superb schools, public and private, in this country but the dominant tendency, once again, is non-Q. **Education for the majority has slipped to a level undemanding of effort,** satisfied with the least, lacking respect for its own values, and actually teaching very little. We read in the press that, despite the anxious concern and experiments of educators, college entrance scores are sinking and the national rate of schoolchildren reading at below-grade levels hovers at 50 percent. The common tendency is to blame television, and while I suppose that the two-minute attention span it fosters, and the passive involvement of the viewer, must negatively affect the learning process, I suspect something more basic is at fault.

That something, I believe, lies in the new *attitudes* toward both teaching and learning. Schoolchildren are not taught to work. Homework is frivolous or absent. The idea has grown that learning must be fun; students must study what they like; therefore courses have largely become elective. Work is left to the highly motivated, and failure for the others does not matter because, owing to certain socially concerned but ill-conceived rules, students in many school systems cannot be flunked.

Further, one becomes aware through occasional glimpses into *curriculums,* that subject matter makes increasing concessions to junk. Where are the summer reading lists and book reports of former years? A high school student of my acquaintance in affluent suburbia was recently assigned by his English teacher, no less, to watch television for a week and keep a record on 3-by-5 index cards of what he had seen. . . . How will the young become acquainted with quality if they are not exposed to it? . . .

***Advertising* augments the condition.** From infancy to adulthood, advertising is the air Americans breathe, the information we absorb, almost without knowing it. It floods our mind with pictures of perfection and goals of happiness easy to attain. Face cream will banish age, decaffeinated coffee will banish nerves, floor wax will bring in the neighbors for a cheery bridge game or gossip, grandchildren will love you if your disposition improves with the right laxative, storekeepers and pharmacists overflow with sound avuncular advice, the right beer endows you with hearty masculine identity, and almost anything from deodorants to cigarettes, toothpaste, hair shampoo and lately even antacids will bring on love affairs, usually on horseback or on a beach. Moreover, all the people engaged in these delights are beautiful. Dare I suggest that this is not the true world? We are feeding on foolery, of which a steady diet, for those who feed on little else, cannot help but leave a certain fuzziness of perceptions. . . .

I cannot believe we shall founder under the rising tide of incompetence and trash. . . . Although I know we have already grown accustomed to less beauty, less elegance, less excellence, . . . yet perversely I have confidence in the competence and excellence of the best among us. . . . If incompetence does not kill us first, quality will continue the combat against numbers. It will not win, but it will provide a refuge for the trash-beleaguered. It will supply scattered beauty, pride in accomplishment, the charm of fine things. . . . As long as people exist, some will always strive for the best; some will attain it.   *Barbara Tuchman*

Tracing a Complex Cause-and-Effect Relationship

The argument George Orwell presents in "Politics and the English Language" is developed mainly through cause-and-effect reasoning. Although a number of extended examples have been deleted, the following excerpt shows the main trend of his argument and the complex cause-and-effect relationship between language and politics.

Now, it is clear that the decline of a language must ultimately have political and economic causes: it is not due simply to the bad influence of this or that individual writer. But an effect can become a cause, reinforcing the original cause and producing the same effect in an intensified form, and so on indefinitely. A man may take to drink because he feels himself to be a failure, and then fail all the more completely because he drinks. It is rather the same thing that is happening to the English language. It becomes ugly and inaccurate because our thoughts are foolish, but the slovenliness of our language makes it easier for us to have foolish thoughts. The point is that the process is reversible. Modern English, especially written English, is full of bad habits which spread by imitation and which can be avoided if one is willing to take the necessary trouble. If one gets rid of these habits one can think more clearly, and to think clearly is a necessary first step toward political regeneration: so that the fight against bad English is not frivolous and is not the exclusive concern of professional writers.

As I have tried to show, modern writing at its worst does not consist in picking out words for the sake of their meaning and inventing images in order to make the meaning clearer. It consists in gumming together long strips of words which have already been set in order by someone else, and making the results presentable by sheer humbug. The attraction of this way of writing is that it is easy. It is easier—even quicker, once you have the habit—to say *In my opinion it is not an unjustifiable assumption that* than to say *I think.* If you use ready-made phrases, you not only don't have to hunt about for words; you also don't have to bother with the rhythms of your sentences, since these phrases are generally so arranged as to be more or less euphonious. When you are composing in a hurry—when you are dictating to a stenographer, for instance, or making a public speech—it is natural to fall into a pretentious, Latinized style. Tags like *a consideration which we should do well to bear in mind* or *a conclusion to which all of us would readily assent* will save many a sentence from coming down with a bump. By using stale metaphors, similes, and idioms, you save much mental effort, at the cost of leaving your meaning vague, not only for your reader but for yourself. This is the significance of mixed metaphors. The sole aim of a metaphor is to call up a visual image. When these images clash—as in *The Fascist octopus has sung its swan song, the jackboot is thrown into the melting pot*—it can be taken as certain that the writer is not seeing a mental image of the objects he is naming; in other words he is not really thinking.

In our time, political speech and writing are largely the defense of the indefensible. Things like the continuance of British rule in India, the Russian purges and deportations, the dropping of the atom bombs on Japan, can indeed be defended, but only by arguments which are too brutal for most people to face, and which do not square with the professed aims of political parties. Thus political language has to consist largely of euphemism, question-begging and sheer cloudy vagueness. Defenseless villages are bombarded from the air, the inhabitants driven out into the countryside, the cattle machine-gunned, the huts set on fire with incendiary bullets: this is called *pacification.* Millions of peasants are robbed of their farms and sent trudging along the roads with no more than they can carry: this is called *transfer of population* or *rectification of frontiers.* People are imprisoned for years without trial, or shot in the back of the neck or sent to die of scurvy in Arctic lumber camps: this is called *elimination of unreliable elements.* Such phraseology is needed if one wants to name things without calling up mental pictures of them. Consider for instance some comfortable English professor defending Russian totalitarianism. He cannot say outright, "I believe in killing off your opponents when you can get good results by doing so." Probably, therefore, he will say something like this:

*cause
and effect*

"While freely conceding that the Soviet regime exhibits certain features which the humanitarian may be inclined to deplore, we must, I think, agree that a certain curtailment of the right to political opposition is an unavoidable concomitant of transitional periods, and that the rigors which the Russian people have been called upon to undergo have been amply justified in the sphere of concrete achievement."

The inflated style is itself a kind of euphemism. A mass of Latin words falls upon the facts like soft snow, blurring the outlines and covering up all the details. The great enemy of clear language is insincerity. When there is a gap between one's real and one's declared aims, one turns as it were instinctively to long words and exhausted idioms, like a cuttlefish squirting out ink. In our age there is no such thing as "keeping out of politics." All issues are political issues, and politics itself is a mass of lies, evasions, folly, hatred, and schizophrenia. When the general atmosphere is bad, language must suffer. I should expect to find—this is a guess which I have not sufficient knowledge to verify—that the German, Russian, and Italian languages have all deteriorated in the last ten or fifteen years, as a result of dictatorship.

But if thought corrupts language, language can also corrupt thought. A bad usage can spread by tradition and imitation, even among people who should and do know better. The debased language that I have been discussing is in some ways very convenient. Phrases like *a not unjustifiable assumption, leaves much to be desired, would serve no good purpose, a consideration which we should do well to bear in mind,* are a continuous temptation, a packet of aspirins always at one's elbow. . . . This invasion of one's mind by ready-made phrases (*lay the foundations, achieve a radical transformation*) can only be prevented if one is constantly on guard against them, and every such phrase anaesthetizes a portion of one's brain.

. . . one ought to recognize that the present political chaos is connected with the decay of language, and that one can probably bring about some improvement by starting at the verbal end. If you simplify your English, you are freed from the worst follies of orthodoxy. You cannot speak any of the necessary dialects, and when you make a stupid remark its stupidity will be obvious, even to yourself. Political language—and with variations this is true of all political parties, from Conservatives to Anarchists—is designed to make lies sound truthful and murder respectable, and to give an appearance of solidity to pure wind. One cannot change this all in a moment, but one can at least change one's own habits, and from time to time one can even, if one jeers loudly enough, send some worn-out and useless phrase—some *jackboot, Achilles' heel, hot-bed, melting pot, acid test, veritable inferno,* or other lump of verbal refuse—into the dustbin where it belongs.

**QUESTIONS
FOR
DISCUSSION**

1. What purpose is served by Orwell's analogy—the man who takes to drink?
2. Where does Orwell state the main point of his essay?
3. Point out where Orwell moves backward and then forward in cause-and-effect reasoning.
4. What are the abuses of language to which Orwell calls our attention?
5. What remedy for these abuses does Orwell suggest?
6. Orwell's essay was written in the 1940's. Can you give more recent examples of the political abuse of language?

EXERCISE VIIIa: SUFFICIENT CAUSE/CONTRIBUTING CAUSE

Each of the sentences below contains a cause-and-effect relationship. Study each sentence carefully, and see if it contains a sufficient cause or a contributing cause. Mark *S* (sufficient) or *C* (contributing). Be prepared to defend your decisions.

__S__ 1. My dog died because his heart stopped beating.

__C__ 2. Senator Claghorn lost his bid for re-election because some of the younger voters thought that he was too conservative.

__C__ 3. The Steelers won four Super Bowls in a row because Chuck Noll is a good coach.

__C__ 4. The Steelers won four Super Bowls in a row because Terry Bradshaw is a great quarterback.

__C__ 5. The Steelers won four Super Bowls in a row because they have a powerful group of offensive linemen.

__S__ 6. Joe dropped a can of frozen orange juice on his foot and broke his big toe.

__C__ 7. Jack makes good grades because he attends class regularly.

__C__ 8. The I.Q. of American children has decreased because they watch too much television.

__S__ 9. The water boiled because it reached a temperature of 212 degrees Fahrenheit.

__S__ 10. The rapid rise in hospital fees is caused by the cost of malpractice insurance.

__S__ 11. I failed my psychology test because the test questions confused me.

__S__ 12. My husband lost his job because the steel plant where he works had to shut down.

__C__ 13. Americans like small cars because they are easy to park.

__C__ 14. Teenage marriages often end in divorce because young couples can't handle their financial problems.

__S__ 15. Smoking causes cancer.

__C__ 16. Union demands for higher wages have wrecked the American economy.

__S__ 17. Religious cults in America are increasing because young people are getting fed up with organized religion.

__C__ 18. High school students cheat on tests because they like to antagonize their teachers.

__S__ 19. The scores on American College Entrance Exams are dropping because young people in this country aren't learning anything in high school.

__C__ 29. Molly Maguire probably married Barney O'Hara because he was Irish.

Analogy

You remember in the chapter on comparison and contrast you learned about analogy as a special method of comparing two things that really had no conventional basis for comparison—a girl with a red rose, a boss with a snake in the grass. Likewise, when Shakespeare wrote a sonnet beginning "Shall I compare thee to a summer's day," he only meant to **suggest** that his beloved was warm, beautiful, satisfying. He did not expect his reader to extend the comparison to include sweat, sunburn, and bugs. Such comparisons are known as *figurative analogies*. Although vivid figurative analogy can enlarge your readers' understanding of your point without being complete or literally true, you **cannot** substitute figurative analogy for sound cause-and-effect reasoning.

However, analogy can be used to support a cause-and-effect argument when it is limited to a careful comparison of relationships. If you know that your grades went down **when** you cut a lot of classes last semester, that might suggest to you that if you cut a lot this semester that might cause your grades to be low this semester. If all of your friends who miss many classes also have poor grades, that might suggest to you that cutting classes may cause poor grades. Although this is a very simple example of a rather complex idea, it does show what analogy can and cannot do. It cannot ever **prove** anything, but it can suggest ideas to you. If many examples are considered, it makes your argument more probable.

If you wish to use analogy as a support of your cause-and-effect thesis statement, you must choose your analogy upon the following logical grounds:

1. To support a conclusion, an analogy must have a number of important likenesses that are relevant to the comparison you wish to make.
2. To support a conclusion, an analogy must have no important differences that are relevant to the comparison you wish to make.

For example, much medical research is based on the physiological likeness between human beings and laboratory animals such as rats. In the laboratory the researcher experiments upon numbers of rats until he thinks he can make a sound generalization about the reaction of rats. Then, by analogy, he says that men and rats are essentially the same in the area being tested and have no essential differences in that area; thus, the reaction found in rats will probably be found in human beings. For instance, in determining whether or not the caffeine in the coffee drunk by pregnant women can harm unborn children, experimenters are giving doses of caffeine to pregnant rats to test the ultimate possibility of its having harmful effects on human beings.

Reasoning by analogy is one of the most common ways of thinking. Everyone attempts to understand new problems by comparing them to problems already solved. It seems to be almost a natural way of thinking. You notice a pattern of similarities between one thing and another, and, from that observation, you assume that the pattern can be extended. When you reason by analogy, you observe that two things have a number of characteristics in common and no essential characteristics that differ. Analogy **suggests** to you that these two things are probably alike in still more characteristics.

The key word here is *probably*. Since the noted similarities are a generalization, you have to be aware of a possible exception. You also have to determine whether the likenesses you noticed are important or trivial. Once you have seen a pattern of similarities and have checked to see that there are no important differences or exceptions, you still need to observe further to determine whether your analogy will furnish a sound conclusion. Continued observation and thought are necessary.

For example, a legal case may be decided by *precedent*, which is an earlier decision in a similar case. But even here, the effort of the court is directed toward finding an analogy that is close enough to base a decision on. Whenever analogy is used to support a conclusion, it must be tested for the closeness of its similarities and for its lack of differences. Even then, it must be scrutinized carefully.

George Bernard Shaw, arguing for the need for prison reform in his day, attempts to support his conclusion by analogy. The Prison Commissioners, Shaw said, aimed at **punishment and reform** for criminals. Such a double aim was a contradiction, because, says Shaw:

Now, if you are to punish a man retributively, you must injure him. If you are to reform him, you must improve him. And men are not improved by injuries. To propose to punish and reform people by the same operation is exactly as if you were to take a man suffering from pneumonia, and attempt to combine punitive and curative treatment. Arguing that a man with pneumonia is a danger to the community, and that he need not catch it if he takes proper care of his health, you resolve that he shall have a severe lesson, both to punish him for his negligence and pulmonary weakness and to deter others from following his example. You therefore strip him naked, and in that condition stand him all night in the snow. But as you admit the duty of restoring him to health if possible, and discharging him with sound lungs, you engage a doctor to superintend the punishment and administer cough lozenges, made as unpleasant to the taste as possible so as not to pamper the culprit. A Board of Commissioners ordering such treatment would prove thereby that either they were imbeciles or else they were hotly in earnest about punishing the patient and not in the least in earnest about curing him.

When our Prison Commissioners pretend to combine punishment with moral reformation they are in the same dilemma.

Note that, because what Shaw has to say about the man with pneumonia is so convincing, you are liable to accept his analogy that a prisoner is like the pneumonia patient. Bearing in mind the standards that must be applied to an analogy to make it a support for a conclusion, determine whether Shaw has only a persuasive figurative analogy or one that is a sound support for a conclusion. (An analogy, remember, must have many important likenesses and no important differences within the areas being compared.)

Pitfalls to Avoid

1. Don't oversimplify. Remember that many events have multiple causes, so don't settle for the first explanation that comes to mind.
2. Avoid the post-hoc fallacy. Make sure that you are not attributing a cause-effect relationship to a mere coincidence. Remember, just because A happened before B does not mean that A *caused* B.
3. Don't confuse a contributing cause with a sufficient cause. If the cause is not enough in itself to bring about a specific event, then it is only a contributing cause.
4. If you are using an analogy to support a cause-effect thesis, make sure that the two things being compared have a number of *important* characteristics in common and *no* essential characteristics that differ. Also, remember that you can't use an analogy to *prove* a cause-effect thesis—only to *support* a cause-effect thesis.
5. Above all, don't form any conclusion without adequate information.

Make sure that you have enough information to establish a clear connection between cause and effect.

SUGGESTED TOPICS

Choose one of the following topics and write a cause-and-effect essay.

1. Sex and salary
2. Handguns and homicide
3. Cold weather and common colds
4. Drinking and traffic deaths
5. Drug addiction and crime
6. Mouth cancer and tobacco chewing
7. Fertilizer and crop yield
8. Diet and heart disease
9. Exercise and weight loss or gain
10. Unemployment and armed robbery
11. Artificial sweeteners and disease
12. Catalytic converters and exhaust pollution
13. Phases of the moon and crimes of violence
14. Television violence and youthful crime
15. Computer technology and unemployment
16. Broken homes and juvenile delinquency
17. Financial problems and teenager divorces
18. Childhood experiences and adult phobias
19. Supply and demand
20. Pride in workmanship and quality of product
21. Economic needs and career choice
22. Political oppression and revolution
23. Writing ability and earning power
24. Idle time and depression
25. Physical appearance and personality
26. Vitamins and health
27. Skin color and income
28. Physical health and mental health
29. Car size and safety
30. Pot smoking and academic performance
31. Radiation and genetic damage
32. Pornography and sex crimes
33. Quality and price
34. Formal education and earning power
35. Height and managerial success
36. Coal smoke and acid rain
37. Age and value systems
38. Peer pressure and cheating
39. Peer pressure and use of drugs
40. City living and aggressive behavior
41. Personality and style of dress
42. Laughter and mental health
43. American foreign policy and treatment of American tourists
44. Diet and cancer
45. Malpractice insurance and doctors' fees
46. Advertising and consumer buying habits
47. Freedom of expression and creativity
48. Reading level and grades
49. Dress codes and classroom behavior
50. Prenatal nutrition and child development

TECHNIQUES OF CLEAR WRITING

Eliminating Incomplete, Ambiguous, and Confusing Sentences

If you want your reader to understand immediately what you mean, you must eliminate errors that interfere with clarity. Among the most common errors are *fragments*, *comma splices*, and *fused sentences*.

FRAGMENTS

If a group of words that does not contain a complete subject and predicate is set off by a period, then you have a fragment. Most fragments are detached elements which should be joined either to the preceding sentence or to the following sentence.

INCORRECT: Filled with old newspapers, rags, and trash from basement to attic. The old ladies' home was a firetrap.

CORRECT: Filled with old newspapers, rags, and trash from basement to attic, the old ladies' home was a firetrap.

The old ladies' home, filled with old newspapers, rags, and trash from basement to attic, was a firetrap.

INCORRECT: The principal could get nothing done. Especially with the telephone ringing constantly and disgruntled parents barging into his office.

CORRECT: The principal could get nothing done, especially with the telephone ringing constantly and disgruntled parents barging into his office.

(NOTE: Some incomplete sentences are permissible ["What did they gain? Nothing!"], but you should avoid their use except in dialogue or for special effects.)

COMMA SPLICES

If you join two independent clauses with only a comma between them, you have a *comma splice*.

INCORRECT: The stone wall was fourteen feet high, he couldn't possibly climb over it.

CORRECT: The stone wall was fourteen feet high; he couldn't possibly climb over it.

The stone wall was fourteen feet high. He couldn't possibly climb over it.

Since the stone wall was fourteen feet high, he couldn't possibly climb over it.

The stone wall was fourteen feet high; consequently, he couldn't possibly climb over it.

FUSED SENTENCES

If you omit all punctuation between two independent clauses, you have a *fused sentence*.

224

INCORRECT: The Soviets don't worry much about public opinion there is no unified opposition to Kremlin policies.

CORRECT: The Soviets don't worry much about public opinion. There is no unified opposition to Kremlin policies.

Since there is no unified opposition to Kremlin policies, the Soviets don't worry much about public opinion.

The Soviets don't worry much about public opinion because there is no unified opposition to Kremlin policies.

MIXED AND ILLOGICAL CONSTRUC-TIONS

The term *mixed construction* may be applied to a variety of errors in sentence structure. Often, a hasty or careless writer starts off in one direction and ends up going in another. The resulting sentence may be confusing or illogical. Such mixed constructions usually can be corrected by revising the core sentence (see Chapter II, section on Techniques of Clear Writing) and by making sure that the sentence parts are properly placed.

CONFUSED: When you get to the creek is where you will find the fence takes a bend to the left.

CLEAR: You will find that the fence takes a bend to the left at the creek.

CONFUSED: Being that most of the classes I needed were offered at night and I work at night was the reason I didn't go to school this semester.

CLEAR: Since most of the classes I needed were offered at night and I work nights, I didn't go to school this semester.

Since I work nights, I couldn't go to school this semester. All the courses I need are offered only at night.

EXERCISE VIIIb: PUNCTUATING SENTENCES

By adding whatever additional punctuation or wording is needed, revise all incorrect sentences to eliminate fragments, comma splices, and fused sentences. If the sentence is already correct, write *C* beside the number.

1. A nutritionist having received a grant for his study of pistachio nuts.

   _____

2. This is the latest style in men's trousers. Fashioned after the style that was popular in the late 1930's.

   _____

3. The people in the lowest income bracket are hard hit by inflation their income goes mainly for necessities.

   _____

4. A doctor who had practiced medicine in a small Western town for forty-six years and had won the respect of everyone, including the Navajo Indians.

   _____

5. The award-winning documentary was filmed in Thailand, portraying in stark detail the life of Cambodians in a refugee camp.

_____

6. Clem delighted in taking his in-laws to restaurants he had discovered no one else would consider them worth searching for. Places with names like "Tomane Tommy's."

_____

7. Especially when the temperature went down to five below at night.

_____

8. Just to pass the time of day on the long bus ride from Minneapolis to Salt Lake City.

_____

9. To work in a chemical plant that manufactures pesticides and not to wear a respirator.

_____

10. The Morgan trial, the most sensational in the history of Florida, lasted for five months.

_____

11. Dashing in red jackets, gesticulating wildly, and shouting mysterious figures at the top of their voices.

_____

12. My brother witnessed a terrible airplane crash last summer, now he refuses to fly.

_____

13. Gene and Alma sitting on their front porch and surveying their estate.

_____

14. Ice cream is full of air and chemical additives, so I've switched to frozen yogurt.

_____

15. "The Yanks With Their Tanks Will Break the German Ranks" is the title of an old World War I song that my uncle used to sing.

_____

16. A lot of people think that Thomas Edison invented the movie projector they don't realize that the credit should go to a man who worked for Edison—William B. Dickson.

_____

17. Listening to Grace talk about the famous Dionne quintuplets whose birth made history in 1934.

_____

18. Sarah canned fifty jars of apple butter, and Bob ate forty-nine of them.

_____

19. George Gershwin is one of my favorite composers, he wrote "Rhapsody in Blue" when he was only twenty-six years old.

_____

20. Though they visited country homes and strolled the gardens for which Devonshire is famous.

_____

21. I'm afraid that Kelly's Bar has fallen victim to that old Irish curse: "May your beer always be flat."

_____

22. Millard Fillmore wasn't the most famous American president, but he should be remembered for at least one historical first he was the first president to install a bathtub in the White House.

_____

23. Getting sidetracked on Mark Twain's business ventures and forgetting about his literary genius and handing his paper in late.

_____

24. Mr. Eckenrode was trained to coach football, he shouldn't be teaching history.

_____

25. Television advertising is very expensive, costing at least $1,000 per second.

_____

EXERCISE VIIIc: MIXED AND ILLOGICAL CONSTRUCTIONS

_a//_

Revise the following sentences to make the wording clear and sensible.

1. He asked would we take him to the races at Windgate Park?

_____

2. It is good for you like my little brother eats cereal and milk every morning.

_____

3. Her first reaction to riding in Ronny's Corvette was breathtaking speed.

_____

227

4. The results of his ten years' labor had truly brought forth a monstrous machine.

_____

5. Even his most ardent followers realized that being completely obedient to the guru how little fun they were having.

_____

6. His philosophy came to believe why we got here was less important than our responsibility to our fellow humans.

_____

7. Television leads us to where we forget to question morality ahead of ratings.

_____

8. It is a bad painting because I feel the innate beauty should be made more evident to the viewer.

_____

9. His incomplete training, which he was sadly aware of, led to hopes of a professional career.

_____

10. The test was too difficult for what had been taught in the course.

_____

Dangling Modifiers

A *modifier* is a word, phrase, or clause that describes, clarifies, or narrows another word. For example:

> a **tall** building
> a **74-story** building
> a building **made of Italian marble**

These modifiers belong next to the word they modify. If a modifier is placed somewhere else, confusion results and clarity is lost. Sometimes the result becomes ludicrous.

While reading the paper, my dog pestered me to go for a walk. [The dog read the paper?]

If you start the sentence with a participial phrase, the first noun or pronoun after the phrase must be the person or thing the phrase modifies. This is **one way** to correct the dangling modifier.

While reading the paper, I was disturbed by my dog, who was pestering me to go for a walk.

228

While reading the paper, my dog. . .

Another way that such dangling participles can be corrected is by including a subject and changing the participial phrase to a dependent clause:

While I was reading the paper, my dog was pestering me to go for a walk.

A dangling modifier can be found anywhere in a sentence, but the error is most common when the modifier appears at the beginning of the sentence.

EXERCISE VIIId: DANGLING MODIFIERS
Correct the dangling modifiers in the following sentences:

EXAMPLES
INCORRECT: Having won a stuffed bear, the carnival operators wheedled twelve more dollars from Jake.

CORRECT: Having won a stuffed bear, Jake was wheedled into spending twelve more dollars by the carnival operators.

INCORRECT: Being dead tired to start with, the day seemed to stretch into eternity.

CORRECT: Because I was dead tired to start with, the day seemed to stretch into eternity.

 My studying suffers while watching "Barney Miller."

_____

 Feeling compassionate, my letter to the editor lacked the fire I had meant to put into it.

_____

229

3. Having listened to Professor Carter, solar energy fascinated Alfredo.

_____

4. Driven by a fierce desire, the oil well was dug.

_____

5. Drifting across the balmy sky, I watched the clouds.

_____

6. Having written the letter, her stomach began to growl.

_____

7. Studying hard for the test, the exam was easy.

_____

8. Playing a rough game of football, my mother's voice was not heard.

_____

9. My car would not stay on the road having drunk six cans of beer.

_____

10. Watching the Browns play, the cheering was deafening.

_____

EXERCISE VIIIe: DANGLING MODIFIERS
Rewrite the following sentences to avoid dangling modifiers:

1. Loaded down with bank notes and laughing merrily, the police chief watched the bank robbers speed away.

_____

2. Having worked on smoothing the field, the bases were put in place.

_____

3. Ill and friendless, the nursing home was the only place for Mr. Carbonade.

_____

4. Unable to stand the pressures of the office, the move to another job was necessary.

_____

5. The batter missed the ball swinging desperately.

_____

6. Enjoying the play, the theater rocked with applause.

_____

230

7. Having passed the final exam, graduation was assured.

_____

8. Getting permission to go on vacation, my mother warned me about careless friendships.

_____

9. I watched the bus pull away sadly, having forgotten my wallet.

_____

10. Sneezing and choking, smoke filled the room.

_____

WORD POWER

It Ain't Necessarily So!

A very popular American musical has a sprightly character named Sportin' Life who sings a song called "It Ain't Necessarily So." This title shows a healthy attitude toward carelessly accepting a cause-and-effect relationship. Some of the reasons why things carelessly accepted are not "necessarily so" come from language. For instance, one verse of Sportin' Life's song runs:

> Old Methuselah lived 900 years
> Old Methuselah lived 900 years
> But who calls that livin'
> When no gal will give in
> To no man what's 900 years.

They call this livin'?

This verse always brought down the house because of its irreverent gaity about the incredible Methuselah. Part of the fun came from a double meaning. The lyrics use the word "livin'" in a sense other than that meant by Methuselah existing to extreme old age. According to Sportin' Life, "livin'" means having a good time—an impossibility, he thought, without girls.

Ambiguity and vagueness create difficulties for someone trying to arrive at good cause-and-effect conclusions. Vague and ambiguous words permit many shifts in meaning. For example, if you say, "The garage *fixed* my car, and the politician *fixed* my ticket," you are equivocating through the multiple meanings of the verb *to fix*. (Such shifts are numerous—for instance, "I need a fix.") And what is your meaning if you say of someone, "I'm going to give him the business"? Such shifts are fine if your intent, like Sportin' Life's, is to amuse. But if your intent is to support a conclusion, you must choose language that is precise and stable.

EXERCISE VIIIf: AMBIGUOUS SENTENCES
The following sentences can be understood in more than one way. Rewrite them to convey a single clear meaning.

1. Mary Jo has a face like an open fireplace.

   _____

2. Jane's new Honda is really something else.

   Jane's new Honda is an incredible

3. The instructor told the student that he couldn't go.

   The instructor told the student that he couldn't go to the party

4. The club is throwing a party, which is good.

   The club is throwing a radical party

5. Although my school has developmental classes, it didn't do me any good.

   _____

6. My aunt is in the hospital and is critical.

   My aunt is in critical cond. in the hospital

7. "Question 18: Will you give aid and comfort to the enemies of the United States government or the government of the State of Alabama?"

   _____

8. He has a heart condition.

   _____

9. You cannot be happy because you are rich.

   _____

10. The poison center put out a list of poisons children may drink at home.

    The poison center listed poisons children may drink at home

False Implications

A proverb is usually accepted as wisdom. For example, "A stitch in time saves nine" makes sense by itself and in its implication that it is better to do a job when it needs to be done than to put it off. However, a number of proverbs are implied analogies that aren't necessarily so; usually the point of such analogies is to blacken someone's reputation. Consider the proverb "Where there's smoke, there's fire." This is pithy and often quoted, so it seems to have authority. Nevertheless, when you consider it, there is no reasonable basis for the comparison of a fire with a reputation. It may well be that smoke does indicate a fire, but that does not support the implication that someone who is gossiped about is at fault. To accept the implied statement because of the correctness of the direct statement is to depend on slogans and repetition instead of clear ideas sensibly discussed.

EXERCISE VIIIg: IMPLICATIONS
The following sayings all carry implications. Decide what the implications are and if they are "necessarily so." If you are not sure of the meanings of any words, look them up in your dictionary.

1. Like father, like son.
2. If nature intended a ferret, it didn't make it look like a mastiff.
3. A camel is a horse designed by a committee.
4. Birds of a feather flock together.
5. The man who pays the piper calls the tune.
6. "You tell me where a man gets his corn pone, en I'll tell you what his 'pinions is."—Mark Twain
7. Haste makes waste.
8. Fools rush in where angels fear to tread.
9. He who laughs last laughs best.
10. A rolling stone gathers no moss.

Confusing Words

Following are pairs of words that are spelled or pronounced in a similar manner. Check each pair; if you are not sure of the difference in meaning, consult your dictionary.

accede/exceed	coarse/course	eminent/imminent
accelerate/exhilarate	complement/compliment	envelop/envelope
accept/except	comprehensible/comprehensive	explicit/implicit
access/excess	conscience/conscious	formally/formerly
all ready/already	continual/continuous	forth/fourth
attendance/attendants	defective/deficient	ingenious/ingenuous
berth/birth	depreciate/deprecate	it's/its
capital/capitol	desirable/desirous	know/no
censor/censure	device/devise	lay/lie
cereal/serial	discreet/discrete	lead/led
cite/site	dual/duel	leased/least

233

lend/loan	personal/personnel	respectfully/respectively
liable/libel	preceding/proceeding	right/rite
loose/lose	prescribe/proscribe	secret/secrete
pain/pane	principal/principle	to/too
passed/past	quiet/quite	wait/weight

Words and Phrases Frequently Misused

Affect/Effect   *Affect,* a verb, means "to influence the behavior or outcome." *Effect* is usually a noun, meaning "result"; *effect* can also be a verb meaning "to bring about" or "to produce."

CORRECT: The choice may *affect* your whole career.

CORRECT: The *effect* of continued inflation could be disastrous.

Foreign intermediaries helped *effect* the release of the hostages.

Aggravate   To *aggravate* means "to worsen or intensify an existing condition"; it should never be used in the sense of "to irritate" or "to annoy."

CORRECT: Pot smoking *aggravates* heart disease by overstimulating the heart.

CORRECT: She *irritates* people with her constant complaints.

Alot   The only acceptable form is two words, *a lot.*

FAULTY: He had *alot* of money; he paid cash for a house and *alot* on Cherry Street.

CORRECT: He had *a lot* of money; he paid cash for a house and *a lot* on Cherry Street.

All of   *All* is usually sufficient.

FAULTY: All of the faculty members were present.

CORRECT: All the faculty members were present.

Allude/Elude   *Allude* means "to refer to"; *elude* means "to escape."

CORRECT: Democrats frequently *allude* to the Watergate scandal of the Nixon administration.

CORRECT: The escaped prisoner was unable to *elude* the pursuing hounds.

Allusion/Illusion   An *allusion* is a reference to something; an *illusion* is a false or deceptive appearance.

CORRECT: The *allusions* in his sermon were to the parable of the Good Samaritan.

CORRECT: They create the *illusion* of being confident and successful, but they are terrified of failure.

Bad/Badly   *Bad* is an adjective that describes the subject; *badly* is an adverb.

CORRECT: I feel *bad* about leaving Centerville.

234

235

*cause
and effect*

CORRECT: Jeff was *badly* injured in the accident.

Being as/Being that   Never use these. They are not substitutes for *since* or *because.*

CORRECT: *Since* she knew the road, she could get there within an hour. [not *Being as*]

CORRECT: *Because* there was an extra set of keys, he could have taken the car. [not *Being that*]

Between/Among   *Between* is used with two people or items; *among* is used when there are more than two.

CORRECT: There is little difference *between* a Pontiac and an Oldsmobile.

CORRECT: Grading systems vary *among* the Ivy League colleges.

Bunch   Use *bunch* when you refer to things that come in clusters; don't use it in place of *group.*

CORRECT: She selected a huge *bunch* of purple grapes.

CORRECT: A *group* of young people gathered in front of the hall. [not *bunch*]

Bust/Busted/Bursted   There is only one correct form for the principal parts of *burst: burst, burst, burst.*

CORRECT: Because all the water pipes *burst* last winter—except for the ones that had *burst* the winter before—I installed plastic pipes, which won't *burst* as easily.

Calculate   *Calculate* usually refers to a mathematical process, for example, computing costs. It should not be used as a substitute for *guess, think,* or *plan.*

CORRECT: I *guess* that it will be a close election. [not *calculate*]

CORRECT: I will *calculate* the exact fuel cost for the six months.

Case   Expressions like *in the case of* are usually unnecessary.

CORRECT: That is not true *of* doctors and dentists. [not *in the case of*]

Complected   *Complected* should not be used as a substitute for *complexioned.*

CORRECT: He was redheaded and fair-*complexioned.*

Contact   Avoid the use of *contact* both as a noun and a verb; it is vague and overused.

FAULTY: He has several business *contacts* in New York.

IMPROVED: He has several business *acquaintances* in New York.

FAULTY: We will *contact* you in spring.

IMPROVED: We will *call* [*telephone, write to, ask about*] you in spring.

Could of/May of/Must of/Would of/Should of   The correct forms are *could have, may have, must have, would have, should have.*

CORRECT: I *could have* taken the bus. [not *could of*]

Enthused   Avoid using *enthused* for *enthusiastic.*

CORRECT: They were *enthusiastic* over the test results. [not *enthused*]

Farther/Further   Use *farther* when distance is involved; use *further* to express the idea of "to a great extent or degree."

CORRECT: A diesel Volkwagen will take you *farther* for less money than most other cars will.

CORRECT: *Further* research is needed before these drugs are marketed.

Good/Well   *Good* is an adjective; never use it in place of *well,* an adverb.

CORRECT: The pumpkin pie looks *good.*

CORRECT: Martha's new blender works *well.*

CORRECT: Jose did *well* on the test.

Imply/Infer   *Imply* means to suggest; *infer* means to conclude from some evidence or suggestion.

CORRECT: The speaker seemed to *imply* that we were ignorant of the law.

CORRECT: We might *infer* that he had a low opinion of our intelligence.

Irregardless   The standard form is *regardless.* The negative prefix *ir-* is unnecessary.

CORRECT: *Regardless* of the cost, synthetic fuels must be developed.

Kind of/Sort of   Use *somewhat* or *rather.*

FAULTY: The judge's decision in this case seemed *kind of* arbitrary.

CORRECT: The judge's decision in this case seemed *somewhat* arbitrary.

FAULTY: He seemed *sort of* upset by George's question.

CORRECT: He seemed *rather* upset by George's question.

Leave   Leave is not a substitute for *let* or *allow.*

CORRECT: Don't *let* them go before noon [not *leave*]

CORRECT: *Leave* your keys at the service desk.

Liable/Likely   *Liable* means legally responsible or exposed to; *likely* means probable.

CORRECT: They are *likely* to arrive at any time.

CORRECT: You are *liable* to get a parking fine if you park here.

Like   *Like* is a preposition; it should not be used as a substitute for *as if* or *as though*, which are conjunctions.

CORRECT: Victorians treated children *as if* they were little adults. [not *like*]

Literally   *Literally* means "in the strict sense" or "to the letter"; it should never be used figuratively.

FAULTY: She *literally* died from the heat last August. [Is she dead?]

IMPROVED: She thought she would die from the heat last August. [Literally speaking, she had nothing more than a sunburn.]

Lots of   Do not use *lots of* as a substitute for *many.*

CORRECT: There were *many* opportunities for advancement. [not *lots of*]

Maybe/May be   *Maybe* is an adverb meaning "perhaps"; *may be* is a form of the verb *to be.*

CORRECT: *Maybe* they missed the Mayberry exit.

CORRECT: Detective Shocker *may be* arresting the wrong man.

Myself   Avoid the use of *myself* as a substitute for *I* or *me.*

CORRECT: Miss Salisbury and *I* were put in charge of the lunch counter. [not *myself*]

CORRECT: The Steerbusters invited my wife and *me* to the barbecue. [not *myself*]

NOTE: Careful writers limit the use of *myself* to the reflexive and intensive forms.

REFLEXIVE: I hurt *myself* by refusing a promotion.

INTENSIVE: I *myself* saw the vicious dogs attack him.

Number/Amount   Use *number* for countable things; use *amount* for things that are measured by volume.

CORRECT: A large *number* of people had gathered.

CORRECT: A large *amount* of grain will be shipped to China.

Off of   *Off* is sufficient; the *of* is redundant.

CORRECT: He fell *off* the diving board. [not *off of*]

CORRECT: Take my name *off* the list [not *off of*]

Outside of   The *of* is redundant.

CORRECT: Plant the seedlings *outside* the house in May. [not *outside of*]

Real/Really   These words are overused and frequently misused; they should be deleted or replaced wherever possible. Often, action verbs make strong substitutes for these words in weak adverb constructions.

FAULTY: It was a *real* pleasant party.

IMPROVED: It was a *pleasant* party. [or *festive, friendly,* etc.]

FAULTY: Jack Largemouth did *real* well in the debates.

IMPROVED: Jack Largemouth spoke convincingly in the debates.

FAULTY: The debates were *really* difficult for Suzy Smallmouth.

IMPROVED: Susy Smallmouth suffered from stage fright during the debates.

Reason is because   *That,* not *because,* is required in this construction.

CORRECT: The reason he moved is *that* he couldn't get a job in Circleville.

Refer back   *Refer* is sufficient; *back* is redundant.

CORRECT: *Refer* to the earlier chapters. [not *refer back*]

There/Their/They're   *There* means "in that place." *Their* is a possessive. *They're* is a contraction for *they are.*

CORRECT: They arrived *there* just before dark.

CORRECT: They unloaded *their* camping equipment.

CORRECT: *They're* the kind of people who like to sleep with the grizzly bears.

Try and/Go and   Avoid such forms in writing.

CORRECT: We will *try to* get a good seat. [not *try and*]

CORRECT: We will *go to* see the second show. [not *go and*]

Unique   If something is *unique,* it is the only one of its kind. *Unique* should not be used as a substitute for *unusual* or *extraordinary,* and it should never be modified by *very, more,* or *most.* For example, The dress you make for yourself is *unique,* one of a kind; but the dress you buy is *unusual,* not the only one ever made.

FAULTY: It was a *most unique* opportunity for advancement.

IMPROVED: It was an *unusual* opportunity for advancement.

Whether or not   *Whether* is sufficient; the *or not* is redundant.

CORRECT: She wondered *whether* she should go to the party.

Who/Whom   *Who* and *whoever* are used as subjects of verbs; *whom* and *whomever* are used as objects of verbs and of prepositions.

CORRECT: They kept asking us *who* we thought would win. [*Who* is the subject of *would win.*]

CORRECT: The article offers good advice to *whoever* has enough money to invest in real estate.

CORRECT: That is the young man *whom* I met at the auction.

CORRECT: That money may be given to *whomever* they choose.

cause and effect

EXERCISE VIIIh: USAGE
Circle the correct word in each of the following sentences.

1. The Senate (censored/~~censured~~) the members who misused their campaign contributions.
2. When taps were played, the audience became (quiet/quite).
3. Margaret was worried about math, but she (passed/past) it.
4. Carlos had (know/no) time to practice his guitar.
5. Her parents' orders were (explicit/implicit); she was to be home before midnight.
6. The teacher (complemented/complimented) her on the style of her dress; she said the style (complemented/complimented) her figure.
7. The students were (all ready/already) to go at six, but the professor thought that it was (all ready/already) too late.
8. The (eminent/imminent) weather forecaster said that the storm was (eminent/imminent).
9. Each student (accepted/excepted) the (principal's/principle's) award (respectfully/respectively).
10. We have to (device/devise) a method to fix this (device/devise).

EXERCISE VIIIi: MISUSED WORDS AND PHRASES
Draw a line through each misused word or phrase and write the correct form above it.

1. The reason he goes there is because they always treat him ~~royally~~.
2. I will have to refer ~~back~~ to my notes.
3. I was surprised by the amount of people who came to the dance; if I had known there would be that many, I would of gone.
4. Stella looks like the best bet ~~between~~ the five candidates.
5. His allusion to the Bible helped to make his point clear.
6. The unique answer she gave had been heard only rarely before.
7. Being as she lived on a farm, she knew how to take care of horses and cows.
8. It is liable to rain before the end of the week.
9. Jonathan will go further than most students because he goes further into his subject than most of us do.
10. Lori says she will try and discover who called her last night.
11. The mother fought to get off of welfare.
12. I'm sure she will do real well in the finals.
13. The doctor and myself were enthused about the results of the test.
14. In his speech to the delegates, he inferred that they were not doing enough to recruit new members.
15. She is the young lady who we met last night at the dance.

CHAPTER IX

persuading

The essence of persuasion is change. In persuasive writing your purpose is not just to inform your reader but to change your reader's attitude, belief, or behavior. The two basic elements of persuasion are **appeals to reason** and **appeals to emotion.** Even though some people regard emotional appeals as being less legitimate than logical appeals, effective persuasion usually combines both kinds. Therefore, even though the two are presented separately here, keep in mind that successful persuasion usually consists of a combination of an appeal to logic and an appeal to emotion.

Logical Appeals

If you are to convince your reader of your reasonableness and good sense, the first thing you must learn is to distinguish a good argument from a poor one. Unless you can distinguish good evidence from poor evidence, you'll have little chance of persuading anyone. If you hope to present an argument that will appeal to intelligent readers, you must first of all examine the quality of your own reasoning. Being alert to the common fallacies or errors in reasoning will help you to avoid gross errors which would lead your reader to distrust your whole argument.

Hasty Generalization

Jumping to conclusions is one of the most dangerous errors made in reasoning. It has ruined friendships, promoted bigotry, destroyed marriages, and even started wars. (It has also wreaked havoc on countless numbers of writing assignments and essay tests.) The formal name for this type of mistake is *hasty generalization*. For example, suppose you heard the following conversation between two of your neighbors:

HARRY: Don't buy a foreign-made car. You'll be sorry. My son-in-law had one, and he had one problem after another. The carburetor went bad, his brake fluid leaked, and he had to put $300 into transmission repairs. When it wasn't stuck in reverse, it was stalling out. Besides that, the pile of junk rusted out in two years.

CHUCK: Well, my brother brought a foreign-made car, and it runs like a dream. He hasn't had to put one penny into repairs since he bought it. I'm definitely going to buy myself a foreign car.

Neither one of your neighbors has a convincing argument because each of them is jumping to conclusions. Just because **one** foreign-made car is bad doesn't mean that **all** foreign-made cars are bad; likewise, just because **one** foreign-made car is good does not mean that **all** foreign-made cars are good. Each of them is making a hasty generalization about a whole group of cars based on only one example.

Stereotypes

People often rush to unwarranted conclusions when they are forming opinions about other people. Their attitudes toward an entire race or religion is based solely on their attitudes toward one or two members of that race or religion. Thus, *stereotypes* are often formed through ignorance of the first rule of sound reasoning: you can't make a valid general statement about anything based on one or two examples. You, as a reader, should not be so gullible that you can be persuaded by so little evidence, nor should you, as a writer, expect intelligent readers to be persuaded by an argument that fails to examine the evidence adequately before arriving at a conclusion.

The Either-Or Fallacy

In an attempt to deal with complex issues they do not fully understand, people often resort to polarized thinking, in which there are only two sides to every issue—good and bad, black and white, right and wrong. Such constant *oversimplification,* known as the *Either-Or Fallacy,* lowers the reader's opinion of you as a writer. Watch out for thinking that becomes so polarized that there seem to be only two sides to every issue, that it must be either this way or that way with no alternatives:

Either we defeat this bill to control handguns or the government will confiscate our hunting rifles.

Either we let the oil companies make their windfall profits or we freeze to death.

Either-Or Fallacy

Post Hoc Fallacy

Even worse than reaching a conclusion with just a little evidence is the fallacy of reaching a conclusion without any evidence at all. Sometimes people mistake a mere coincidence for a cause-and-effect relationship. They see that A happened before B, so they mistakenly assume that A caused B. This is an error known in logic as *post hoc fallacy* ("after this, therefore because of this"). For example, suppose you see a man in a black jacket hurry into a bank. You notice that he is nervously clutching his briefcase, and a few moments later you hear a siren. You therefore leap to the conclusion that the man in the sinister black jacket has robbed the bank. You have absolutely no evidence to work with—only a suspicion based on coincidence. This is a *post hoc* fallacy.

Circular Reasoning

Another way that people mistakenly reach conclusions without evidence is by engaging in circular reasoning. You have probably met at least one person in your lifetime whom you couldn't understand because he talked in circles. In other words, he kept repeating himself, periodically inserting a *therefore* or a *so you see* to make you think that he was concluding his argument when actually he was just saying the same thing again in different words. His argument might have sounded like this:

Nuclear power is the answer to America's fuel shortage. *Therefore,* nuclear power will solve our energy crisis.

Here, you are given no **reason** to believe that nuclear power is the best answer to America's fuel crisis. In place of evidence, the arguer has presented only a slight rewording of the same idea. Although cause and effect is claimed, no cause is given—only a repetition.

The reasoning in such short examples is so obviously circular that few writers would slip into the error; in more fully developed examples, however, the fallacy is not so easy to spot. Particularly when you are arguing on a subject in which you are emotionally involved or even prejudiced, you may fail to notice that you are guilty of circular reasoning. Notice the circular reasoning in the following example:

Anyone who has real gumption can certainly succeed in America. If a man has good sense, he's going to see to it that his talent is not hidden under a bushel and that other people will recognize his ability. Sooner or later, he is going to make his mark, and other people will beat a path to his door. Anybody who has any gumption can get ahead in the good old U.S.A.

Misuse of Authority

The misuse of authority is another common method of distortion. The use of biased or incompetent authorities has become an increasingly popular sales tactic. You need only switch the channel selector on your television a few times to find an example. For instance, how many times have you seen celebrities on a commercial telling you that you should buy a certain automobile? The automobile company has attracted your attention with the sight of a famous personality, but unless he is also a skilled mechanic or engineer, there is no good reason why the listener should buy the car being advertised. The authority cited is incompetent.

Even when the authority cited has some special knowledge of the subject being discussed, he may be biased on the subject or have a vested interest to protect. If, for example, you cited a statement from the leading members of the American Medical Association to prove that doctors are overworked and underpaid, your evidence would be biased.

False Analogy

Another error in reasoning that misleads the reader is the false analogy. As you learned in Chapter V, an analogy is a specific form of comparison: finding similarities between two things that are normally classified under different categories. For example, "A football coach is like a general" is a valid analogy because you can draw many parallels between them—strategies, goals, vocabulary, and so on. However, the fallacy occurs when a writer finds just one or two vague similarities between two things and then concludes that the two are alike. Look at the following statement:

I'm sixteen years old. I'm old enough to drive a car, so I should be old enough to get married without anyone's permission. Therefore, the marriage age should be lowered to sixteen.

This is a false analogy because the responsibilities required of a good driver are different from the responsibilities required of a good husband or wife. You might say that both require maturity, but that is extremely vague. A person can be an excellent driver and still be a totally self-centered, callous, and unreliable person. The analogy might sound good at first, especially to a sixteen-year-old in love, but upon closer examination, you can see that driving a car and marrying are two entirely different matters.

Card Stacking

Card stacking is both a fallacy and a technique of propagandists. By selecting only the evidence supporting an argument, they stack the deck in their favor. This error is particularly dangerous because it is often subtle. The evidence presented could consist of relevant and accurate facts, but those facts may represent only part of the picture, that part supporting the writer's point of view. For example:

The stock market today is in good shape. Some of the oil company stocks are up 30 percent. Some chemical companies have the highest profits ever.

Some oil company stocks may indeed be up 30 percent, but oil and chemical stocks don't make up the entire stock market. Selecting these stocks and omitting others that are not faring well stacks the deck. It would hardly be accurate to say that the stock market is in "good shape."

The Hidden Assumption

Another error you should watch out for is the hidden assumption. Before you accept any conclusion, you should always make sure that you are aware of the premises on which the argument is based. What is the writer asking you to assume? Look at the following statement:

Jeannie said that Tuesday is going to be a boring day for her because that's the day she has to talk to the patients in the geriatrics ward.

If you are going to accept Jeannie's conclusion, you must first accept her hidden premise, the assumption on which her argument is based:

HIDDEN PREMISE: Talking to old people is boring
STATED PREMISE: I have to talk to old people.
CONCLUSION: I am going to be bored.

The hidden premise, of course, is false. Assuming that old people have nothing interesting to say is ridiculous. Thus, Jeannie's conclusion is also invalid because it is based on a hidden assumption that is false.

Misleading Statistics

Even an intelligent reader can often be misled by statistical evidence. Sometimes people are so impressed with numbers that they don't stop to analyze them. Suppose, for example, that the president of your flying fraternity tells you that girls will never make good pilots because 50 percent of the girls in his class failed the final flight exam. Suppose, however, that he conveniently forgot to tell you that there were only *two* girls in his piloting class: one of them failed the test and the other got the highest grade in the class. True, 50 percent did fail because 50 percent of two is one, but the truth is that the figure actually proves nothing. "Fifty percent" simply sounds more impressive than "one." Don't be fooled by arguments like this.

Whenever you come across an argument supported with percentages, make sure that you know **exactly** what those percentages refer to: 34 percent of what? 50 percent of how many?

Figures dealing with averages, even when the figures are accurate, can often be misleading. Suppose, for example, you read an article stating that five prominent American athletes earned an average of $20,000 on the banquet circuit last year. You would naturally assume that **all** these athletes spent a large part of the off season speaking for pay. However, upon closer examination, you might find that the actual figures lead to a substantially different conclusion:

Bruno Baxter	$3,000
Terrible Tyler	$2,500
Pete Perfection	$86,000
Nancy Nicely	$3,000
Rocky Ricketts	$5,500

It's true that the average of these five figures is $20,000, but the $86,000 figure is so much higher than the rest that it distorts the average. Many people assume that average means typical, but as you can see, the mathematical average of a series of numbers is sometimes misleading. When you have a very high or low number that distorts the average, a more meaningful figure to give your reader is the median (the number that falls midway between the first and last number) or the mode (the number that appears most often). In this case, both the median and the mode are the same—$3,000. So be careful with statistics. Remember, you can drown in a river whose "average" depth is two inches.

PROPAGANDA TECHNIQUES

In addition to avoiding the common fallacies, you need to be alert to the techniques of the propagandist and avoid using them in your own writing. A variety of unethical persuasive tactics are often used by the propagandist in an effort to get others to accept his or her argument without examining the evidence. Among the more frequently used techniques of propaganda are the following.

The Smear Technique

The most common smear technique is one which attacks the person who is proposing an idea rather than attacking the idea itself. The smear technique is often used during the heat of political campaigns. In the 1950 campaign for the U.S. Senate seat in California, for example, the Nixon forces referred to the Democratic candidate, Helen Gahagan Douglas, as the "Pink Lady," thus implying that she was a communist sympathizer (*pink* indicating a light shade of red, a color symbolizing communism). Nixon won that election, perhaps because of the effectiveness of associating Mrs. Douglas's liberalism with communism. Today, however, smear tactics often lose more votes than they gain; voters often lose respect for candidates who resort to such tactics. In the same way, you will destroy your credibility with intelligent readers if they discover that you have resorted to smear tactics.

Bandwagon Technique

Some people feel more comfortable going along with the majority (jumping on the bandwagon) rather than standing alone. This pressure to conform, often coupled with the desire to go with a winner, makes some readers susceptible to the band-wagon approach. In some of television's soft drink ads, for example, you are told, in effect, that you should get with it and join the young generation and drink Brand X. The implication is that everybody else is doing it, so you should too. In similar fashion, insurance salespeople and funeral directors sometimes employ the band-wagon approach to persuade you to buy a more expensive insurance policy or a more elaborate casket:

Almost all our clients are switching to our new Group *B* plan.

We don't sell very many of these models. Most people buy a casket from our deluxe "Rest in Peace" display."

Don't jump on the bandwagon.

Transfer Technique

Through the transfer technique, the propagandist tries to associate himself and his arguments with people or ideas that already have our respect or admiration, thereby getting us to accept blindly his position. The transfer device frequently makes use of labels and symbols. Some of the worst scoundrels have paraded under the flag of patriotism, and some of the most flagrant violations of human rights have been perpetrated under the guise of national security.

Evading the Issue

A skillful propagandist may find many ways of evading the issue whenever the evidence goes against her argument. For instance, she may use spurious or irrele-vant evidence to mislead the reader. Pointing out how good Secretary so-and-so was to his grandmother provides no evidence of his ability to manage the social security system. Spurious arguments frequently focus attention on facts that have little or nothing to do with the central issue. Thus someone may argue that a man or woman who does not play a good game of golf is not fit to be an executive in a prestigious financial institution.

Red Herring Tactic

The red herring tactic is a deliberate attempt to divert attention from the real issue by dragging in a false one. When the unethical persuader knows that his case is weak, he drags in an emotional issue that is designed to mislead the reader. A politician accused of accepting kickbacks from government contracts may try to divert attention by claiming that the investigative agency has persecuted him and his defenseless family. The real issue is whether or not he accepted kickbacks, and the perceptive reader or listener will refuse to be misled by the politician's claim that he is being persecuted.

QUESTIONS TO ASK YOURSELF

Check your final argument by asking yourself these questions:
Did I jump to conclusions?
Did I fail to stick to the issues?
Did I neglect to look at **all** sides of the issue?
Did I make too much of a mere coincidence?
Did I ask the reader to assume something that isn't true?
Did I use any misleading statistics?
Did I make any invalid comparisons?
Did I use any biased or unreliable authorities?
Did I back up my generalizations with specific, relevant examples?
Did I leave out any steps in my argument?
Did I attribute a single cause to a complex series of events?
Did I deliberately ignore evidence that didn't support my thesis?

EXERCISE IXa: VALIDITY OF ARGUMENTS

Examine the validity of the following arguments. If any argument is illogical, identify the specific error or errors in reasoning. If the argument contains no fallacies, mark "valid" in the space provided. Watch out for such errors as the following:

Hasty Generalization	Hidden Assumption
Stereotypes	Misleading Statistics
Either-Or Fallacy	Smear Technique
Post Hoc Fallacy	Bandwagon Technique
Circular Reasoning	Transfer Technique
Misuse of Authority	Evading the Issue
False Analogy	Red Herring Tactic
Card Stacking	

1. Mr. Dempsey is mad at me because I skipped class on Friday. That's why he gave me an F on my midterm.

2. The president of the United States gave a piece of expensive glassware to every foreign head of state that he visited while in office. Therefore, the leader of my church has a right to use our contributions to buy expensive gifts for his foreign friends.

    _____

3. Don't vote for Janice Jolly for mayor. She fell in love with her campaign manager and got a divorce after twenty years of marriage.

    _____

4. You just lost your job, your hospital bill isn't paid off yet, and you still owe over $1,000 on your charge accounts. This is no time to be thinking about buying a new car.

    _____

5. Mrs. Disraeli said that air traffic control majors don't need any math courses, and she should know something about education. After all, she's a member of the school board.

    _____

6. All of the people in your neighborhood must have good jobs if the average home sells for $90,000.

    _____

7. You can't expect him to support a bill outlawing the sale of liquor in super-markets. His brother owns a chain of supermarkets that profit highly from liquor sales.

    _____

8. The Irish and the Polish and the Italians made their way in this society without any help from Uncle Sam, so there's no reason why the blacks can't do the same.

    _____

9. Public employees have no right to strike. Therefore, you should support House Bill 315 because it will make public employee strikes illegal.

    _____

10. Plagiarizing is like stealing: a plagiarist steals literary goods; a burglar steals material goods.

    _____

11. Doctors are all the same. The only thing they care about is making money.

    _____

12. Why should I take any course outside of my major? I'm not going to be a writer or a historian, so why should I know anything about literature or American history?

    _____

13. You should marry me because I can give you financial security and show you the world.

_____

14. Most of my friends at work tell me that Joe is a good mechanic because he charges less than any other mechanic in town.

_____

15. My argument contains a valid analogy, several specific, relevant examples, and the most recent statistical data on the subject. Therefore, I have a logical argument, and there is no reason why you shouldn't accept it.

_____

16. I saw the look on your face when I suggested that _you_ wash the dishes for a change. You just don't love me.

_____

17. If the great Chief Sitting Bull were around today, he would tell his tribe that no one can own the land because people die but the land lives on forever. Therefore, you Indians should give up this legal fight to reclaim 50,000 acres of land and let the oil companies use it for exploration.

_____

18. The police found a gun with Professor Fenton's fingerprints on it right beside his body, and the ballistics experts said that it had been fired within the last hour. A psychiatrist has been treating the professor for depression for over a year now, and his wife found a suicide note on his dresser. I guess the students finally got to poor old Mr. Fenton. He just couldn't take the frustrations of teaching any more.

_____

19. My boyfriend saw "Motorcycle Mania," and he said that it should get an Academy Award, so it must be a good movie.

_____

20. People who have been victims of child abuse seem to have a lot of problems raising their own children. They either beat their kids or they refuse to discipline them at all.

_____

Emotional Appeals

Since people tend to alter their behavior in accordance with their own needs and desires, the key to persuasion is often found in an understanding of human nature. One approach to understanding what motivates people is to consider their basic human needs. These needs may be classified in a great many ways, but the general classification established by psychologists such as A. H. Maslow may prove especially useful to you.

249

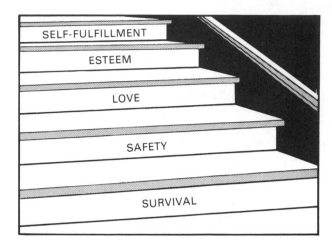

Hierarchy of Needs

Maslow's hierarchy of needs starts with the need for survival and progresses upward: survival, safety, love, esteem, and self-fulfillment. Consideration of basic needs may enable you to see some useful connection between your readers' motives and the persuasiveness of your appeals.

How is this hierarchy of needs related to persuasion? The answer is not always simple, but there is often a fairly direct connection between an individual's needs and what he or she can be persuaded to accept. Certainly, a salesperson who makes a living selling fire alarms plays heavily on the need for survival. People may be persuaded to join unions to secure protection from arbitrary layoffs and gain greater job security. Today's computer dating services extract substantial fees from people with a need to find love. In deciding what clothes to wear or what car to buy, people are motivated as much by the need for esteem as by the desire to get value for their money. Starched collars and tightly laced corsets remained in vogue for years, even though they defied both comfort and health. The need for self-fulfillment motivates people of all ages to take up new courses of study, to explore the far corners of the world, and to push their talents to the limit. Climbing a mountain, building a house with one's own hands, and joining a religious cult all testify to the individual's need for self-fulfillment.

Look around you and you will quickly see that people are not motivated by logic alone. They are impelled by passions and emotions, submerged desires and romantic illusions. Besides, not everything in life adds up like a column of figures; there is still a place for instinctive feeling and intuition. So remember that the most successful persuasive appeals take into consideration **both** the reader's better judgment **and** his or her basic needs.

Both logical and emotional appeals can, of course, be misused. Misleading statistics, card stacking, misuse of authority, smear techniques, and the bandwagon approach are common forms of false and unethical appeals. Unscrupulous persuaders often play upon people's desires and fears for unethical purposes: to encourage prejudice and stereotyped thinking, to stir jealousy and hatred, to instigate irrational action, and to gain blind adherence to fanatical causes.

Your only true defense against deceptive practices is a healthy sense of skepticism. Whenever someone tries to persuade you, you need to ask yourself some sensible questions:

1. Who is trying to prove what? Why?
2. What are the persuader's qualifications? (Does he or she have the necessary training, experience, or relevant expertise?)
3. Are the facts and statistics presented fairly?
4. Does the evidence warrant the conclusion you are to accept?
5. Who stands to gain or lose?

A combination of factual details and emotional appeals can provide a powerful argument. Suppose, for example, that you were a victim of the disastrous 1977 flood in Johnstown, Pennsylvania, a city that was proclaimed "flood-free" in 1943. You are a journalist, and you want to convey the full extent of the horrors of the flood to residents outside the Johnstown area and persuade them to petition the federal authorities for help. You could present them with a factual report of the damages:

The raging waters traveled through seven counties causing $117 million worth of damage, killing 73 people, and leaving 50,000 others homeless. The total damages were estimated at over $200 million....

These facts alone, however, would not necessarily stir your readers' emotions. They are bombarded with statistical information every day. You would have a far better chance of moving them to action if you appealed to their emotions as well. Imagine how much more impact you would have if you reinforced your factual report with an article like Larry Hudson's in Johnstown's *Tribune-Democrat:*

There are some things the history books never told us. They just told us it would never happen again. They never told us about the twisted limbs of the victims and the sudden quickening your heart takes when the rubble falls away, and through the mud a body takes form. They never told us that the image of a dead child can penetrate a sleeping mind and shoot you bolt upright in bed.

We never learned from history books about the rubble, the lifted streets and sidewalks turned and tilted into grotesque heaps.... And they never told us about the mud. Mud piled higher than your head. Mud that's impossible to walk in.... Mud that sticks to your feet, your hands, walls, homes, tires. Mud that can't be swept away with a broom, but has to be boxed and cajoled into tiny floods until it slops over the doorstep and out into the muddy street to join a river of mud going God knows where.

The history books never told us about the smell. Sewer gas so raw that it burns your eyes and throat. The musty, warm odor of brown water.... The smell of death ... the rotten food, wet paper and wet dogs ... the smell of yourself. They never told us that boiled water turns dark and tastes much like we all feel.

They never told us how much it would hurt, or about the unwashed bodies, or the psychological thirst that comes when you know water is limited: the vacant stares from the eyes all around you, everywhere.

And the books contained nothing about the way the sun comes up, pouring incongruous warmth upon devastation. Nothing about the birds singing as the dead lay heaped.

ORGANIZATION

Although there are a great many ways of presenting a persuasive argument, the basic three-part organization will frequently serve you best: (1) You start by taking a clear stand on some issue. (2) You provide specific and detailed support to back up your position. (3) You offer a brief conclusion to wrap up your discussion and reinforce your controlling idea.

Introduction

The introduction to an essay of persuasion usually presents an issue which the writer wishes the reader to consider. An effective introduction may make use of definition, description, narration, an anecdote, or a pertinent quotation, provided it leads to the central issue. What is important is that you set forth the problem clearly and perhaps indicate a solution.

For instance, Paul R. Ehrlich and John P. Holdren, biologists at Stanford University, want their readers to consider the need to limit population. The introduction to their essay "Who Makes the Babies?" identifies the group of Americans that has the highest birth rate:

> Many middle- and upper-class Americans hold the convenient belief that the growth of the population of the United States is due mainly to excessive reproduction among the poor and ethnic minorities. In reality, fewer than one-third of the babies born in the U.S. each year belong to the poor, and fewer than 20 percent to the nonwhite. Evidently, then, the backbone of our population growth is supplied by the parents of "Middle America," many of whom assure themselves that having a third or fourth child is reasonable because they can "afford" it.

This definition of the problem leads to their controlling idea, which is stated in the last two sentences of their introductory paragraph:

> Unfortunately, the heaviest costs of excess births do not show up in the family checkbook. Rather, they are measured in terms of stress on nonrenewable resources, on the life-support systems of the biosphere, and on the overburdened institutions of our society.

In writing your persuasive essay, you will look for some attractive or provocative introduction to capture your reader's attention and to lead them up to your thesis statement. This should be a clear and carefully worded sentence or two in which you take a definite stand that you are prepared to support.

Body

In the body you present both the facts and the logical and emotional appeals to back up your position. You may use comparison, contrast, analogy, statistical evidence, examples, anecdotes, personal experience and observation, or any combination of methods and materials to support your thesis. You need to provide valid evidence to support your stand.

In "Who Makes the Babies?" for instance, the authors develop the body of their essay by several methods. They gather statistical evidence and analyze it to show cause and effect. They say, "Statistically, not only are large families more likely to **be** poor, they are also more likely to **remain** poor." They also use statistics as the basis for a contrast of the average citizen of the United States with the average citizen of India. They say, "—the average American consumes fifty times as much steel—and 300 times as much plastic as the average citizen of India. The ratio of per capita energy consumption . . . for the same two countries is 56 to 1." They also contrast well-to-do and poor Americans. They compare well-to-do black Americans with well-to-do white Americans, saying "Affluent black couples have slightly fewer children than affluent white couples." The authors also use definition as a method to develop concepts like "population control." The body of their essay is a selection of facts and several methods of presenting those facts chosen to make their thesis as persuasive as possible.

KNOWING YOUR AUDIENCE

Before you can be successful in persuading your readers, you must know exactly who those readers are. You must, therefore, know their educational background and their needs and desires. With this knowledge, you can then decide what kind of argument to develop. Different audiences respond to different persuasive techniques. If, for example, you were trying to persuade a group of God-fearing Christian fundamentalists that they should contribute part of their income to the American Poverty Fund, you might appeal to their desire to gain salvation by doing what is right. You might then base a large part of your argument on the Bible:

The righteous considereth the cause of the poor: but the wicked regardeth not to know it.
He that giveth unto the poor shall not lack: but he that hideth his eyes shall have many a curse."

If, however, you were proposing the same idea to your neighbor, a wealthy businessman and an outspoken atheist, you are not likely to persuade him to contribute to the American Poverty Fund by suggesting that he might burn in hell if he doesn't. Instead of dealing with your proposal strictly from a moral standpoint, you could appeal to his material needs and desires. If, for example, you remind him that a sizable contribution could amount to a significant tax write-off or that a large donation would be a great public relations boost to his construction firm, you would have a much better chance of success. He could then view the contribution as a smart business move, something that would appeal to his need for self-esteem and his desire for wealth.

PRESENTING THE EVIDENCE

If you hope to persuade intelligent readers that your argument is sound, you must demonstrate thorough and accurate knowledge of your subject. There is no substitute for a careful study of the subject and a thorough investigation of all the pertinent facts before you begin to write. Careful presentation of accurate factual support is essential to your credibility. Careless statements or exaggerated claims may lead your reader to distrust your argument from the outset. You can't afford to be careless with the facts and just hope that your reader won't know the difference. A single misstatement regarding a significant fact may destroy your credibility. If, for example, you were to claim that handguns are responsible for 75,000 homicides in the United States each year, any knowledgeable reader would see that your claim is grossly exaggerated and would have reason to doubt whether **any** of your statements can be relied upon.

ACKNOWL-EDGING YOUR SOURCES

In presenting a persuasive argument, you must frequently rely on printed sources for facts, statistics, and the testimony of experts to support your opinion. Whenever you use quoted material or statements of fact and opinion other than your own, you must clearly identify your source, either within the text of your paper or in footnotes. Usually, if the references are few and brief, they can be inserted, within parentheses, in the text itself; however, if more extensive documentation is needed and footnotes are required, then consult a reliable guide, such as the *MLA Style Sheet,* for proper footnote form.

STRATEGIES FOR PRESENTING A PERSUASIVE ARGUMENT

Strategy I

INTRODUCTION
1. State the problem so that the issue is clear.
2. Define your terms if necessary.
3. State your thesis in one clear sentence.

BODY
1. Present first main point and supporting evidence.
2. Present second main point and supporting evidence.
3. Present third main point and supporting evidence.
4. Present fourth main point, and so on, as needed.

CONCLUSION
Wrap up your discussion and reemphasize your thesis.

Strategy II
When there is strong opposition to your thesis, an effective strategy is to state the evidence first and conclude with your thesis sentence. In this way, you can pile up the evidence to break down the opposition, then state your thesis after you have had ample opportunity to convince your reader. This type of persuasive argument is flexible in structure, and it offers you a better opportunity to combine logical and emotional appeals. Such an argument might follow these three basic steps:

1. Bring the issue to your reader's attention with a striking example.
2. Pile up more and more details, all pointing toward one conclusion.
3. State your thesis. (In this instance, your thesis and conclusion are the same.)

When your thesis clearly follows from the evidence you have presented, you will have earned an acceptance of your conclusion even from an apathetic or hostile audience. Suppose, for example, that you wanted to convince your readers of the horrors that youthful offenders sometimes face inside our jails and prisons. Some careful research could provide you with telling case histories, and your most effective argument might be one which simply presented case after case of well-documented abuses. By carefully presenting the evidence and avoiding any suggestion of argument, you could lead even the most skeptical reader to accept your thesis.

Conclusion

Offer a conclusion that pulls together the main supporting points of your discussion and reinforces the controlling idea of your thesis sentence. Avoid overstating your case; your conclusion should be warranted by the evidence you have presented. An effective concluding paragraph may provide a careful statement of the implications of the evidence, a striking example or quotation to drive home your main point, a forecast based solidly on the evidence you have presented, or a call for action to remedy the problem you have brought to the reader's attention. An effective conclusion is never just some words tacked on at the end of your essay; it should bring your discussion to a definite close. Having presented your best evidence, you rest your case with the reader.

Many methods may be used in developing a persuasive argument. In some instances, it may be necessary to dispose of an opposing argument before you can present your own argument effectively. When you have two sharply opposing views on a particular issue, you may need to set forth both the pro and con positions. Then, when you have examined these clashing views, you can lead your reader to a more balanced view, a carefully reasoned compromise between the two extremes. Whatever pattern of development you employ, however, you must present your reader with a sensible progression from evidence to reasoned conclusion. In the following essay, notice how the student considers opposing arguments before presenting evidence supporting a different view:

Probing Pot

Marijuana's supporters are almost as varied in their advocacy of the beneficial qualities of the drug as are its opponents in their allegations of its dangers. The advocates are generally eager to neutralize the arguments asserting the drug's harm; there is almost complete uniformity on their side regarding the absence of damaging effects of *cannabis*. They usually consider "pot" far less dangerous than alcohol. In terms of psychological harm, most users of *cannabis* refute the possibility of any significant psychological dependency upon the drug. Likewise, pot smokers vigorously establish clear-cut distinctions concerning the dangers of various drugs, such as amphetamines (speed), alcohol, and LSD. The pro-marijuana people usually base their arguments for legalization on pure hedonism; they want the legal right to use pot because it gives them pleasure. Since I have indulged in the moderate use of pot, I can attest to many pleasurable effects that the drug provides. Nevertheless, my very experiences have convinced me that there are, indeed, more negative aspects of marijuana. Also, I cannot ignore the empirically verified results of pharmaceutical and medical research that indicates several dangers in smoking pot. Although many Americans eagerly support the issue of legalizing marijuana, I am convinced that the legalization of *cannabis* would prove to be a regrettable decision.

First, I consider the legalization of marijuana imprudent because of its intoxicating effect upon drivers. Current research attests that marijuana invariably impairs the smoker's dexterity and discernment when he is operating an automobile. Driving under the influence of a marijuana high is similar to operating a car under the influence of alcohol. The driver feels confident that he can control his vehicle, but, in reality, his abilities are severely impaired. There is marked increase in time required to apply brakes, to recover from glare, and to judge the actual rate of speed. In addition to these impairments, the steering ability of a high driver becomes limited. With the possible increase in the highway death toll, the thought of legalizing the drug and inflicting marijuana-intoxicated drivers on the public seems devastating.

Second, I regard the legalization of marijuana to be unwise because of the greater availability of the dangerous drug to our nation's youth, a significant percent of our population. Several distinct biological dangers are associated with *cannabis.* In particular, long-term pot smoking can cause a breakdown in intellectual activity, and worse, produce a state of pathological drowsiness. Furthermore, evidence concerning the effects of pot on the respiratory system is also frightening. Emphysema, a respiratory disease that usually occurs in later years, has been found to occur often in youthful pot smokers. With such evidence, it seems absurd to make pot legally available. One can only imagine the increase in the drain of potential talent, the leveling off of academic productivity, and the increase in respiratory disorders in our younger generation.

The third basis for my convictions about the marijuana issue concerns the probability that once controls are lifted from the drug, there would be a market for more powerful, dangerous forms of the drug. Experience has shown that when a drug is introduced, stronger forms of it are soon used and abused. For example, cocoa leaves were processed into cocaine, and opium was processed into heroin. In fact, the stronger forms of *cannabis* (such as hashish) that currently are available through illegal channels is evidence of such experience. Most physicians oppose the use of marijuana on the grounds that it leads to the use of more powerful, truly dangerous, and addicting drugs. For many, the less potent drug acts as a kind of introduction to the more potent forms; that is, once the user discovers few or no ill effects from the use of pot, he is more likely than not to consider experimenting with stronger forms of the drug, then possibly using addictive drugs.

In conclusion, since the negative aspects of pot undeniably surpass its euphoric effects, I am thoroughly convinced that legalization of the drug would prove to be a tragic verdict. That marijuana poses the threat of physical impairment, that it predicts an increase in our highway death toll, and that more potent forms of pot could lead to even more serious medical and social consequences—these facts argue for the retention of legal sanctions on marijuana.   *Vicki Schmidt*

Formal Argument

Although the success of your persuasive effort depends on more than just the structure of your argument, some knowledge of the formal structure of arguments can help you to present your case more effectively. The term *formal argument* refers to the structure of an argument. Is the argument logically constructed? Is the logic inductive or deductive? The term *persuasion,* refers to the use of an argument for a specific purpose. When you are persuading, you have to be concerned with how your arguments will affect your audience, so you have to consider more than just the logic of your argument: you have to consider its emotional appeal and the appeal of your "image" as a writer. Do you come across as sincere, authoritative, worth listening to? You need not show every single step in your argument; in fact, you can show your reader valid cause-and-effect relationships without stating all the assumptions and the minor premise of your argument. For example, consider the following statement from a persuasive essay that explores the need for remedial classes:

Many of the high school graduates in ABC County can't read above the fifth-grade level, so ABC County Community College should offer some classes in reading improvement.

This statement shows a clear cause-and-effect relationship even though the minor premise of the argument is not stated. If this statement were presented as a formal argument, it would look like this:

MAJOR PREMISE: Many of the high school graduates in ABC County can't read above the fifth-grade level.
MINOR PREMISE: College students who can't read their textbooks are likely to fail their courses.
CONCLUSION: ABC County Community College should offer some classes in reading improvement.

The statement also makes several assumptions, but they are so obvious that they don't need to be stated. For example:

ASSUMPTION 1: Many of the students who attend ABC County Community College went to high school in ABC County.
ASSUMPTION 2: College textbooks are written at a reading level above the fifth grade.
ASSUMPTION 3: Classes in reading improvement should help students learn to read at a higher grade level.

So don't automatically equate the terms *argument* and *persuasion*. Think of the word *argument* as a process of reasoning. (Certainly don't think of it as a quarrel, as in "She had an argument with her boyfriend.") Argument is a formal structure of reasoning which has two basic patterns: *induction*, which means "to lead to" and *deduction*, which means "to lead away from."

INDUCTIVE REASONING

The process of reasoning from particular facts or observations to a generalization is called *induction*.

In simplified form, the process could be described as

$$S \longrightarrow G$$

Specific examples   to   Generalization

By carefully observing a great many particular examples—of animal behavior, plant growth, people's spending habits, or whatever—you are able to arrive at a reliable generalization or conclusion. For instance, through a great many observations over an extended period, ornithologists (scientists who study birds) have been able to arrive at reliable conclusions about whooping cranes—their flyways, their nesting grounds, and their breeding habits. In a similar process, a poll taker may interview a thousand shoppers concerning their spending habits; then, if his poll is carefully conducted, he may arrive at a reliable generalization, such as "the majority of American shoppers are comparing prices carefully before making major purchases."

Even though it may be on a smaller scale, you make use of inductive reasoning on a day-to-day basis; that is, you look at certain evidence and arrive at a conclusion on the basis of that evidence. If you see that, for the third day in a row, your left rear tire is low, you conclude that it must have a slow leak.

You must keep in mind, however, that any conclusion based upon induction is a **probability.** Generally, the more instances or examples and the more careful the observation, the more reliable the conclusion; however, the conclusion does **not** necessarily follow from evidence, no matter how strong that evidence may be. Sloppy reasoning or hasty examination of the evidence can lead you to a false conclusion. If you see that a neighbor drives a new car every year, you might easily conclude that he must be able to afford to trade in his car every year. However, that conclusion may be unwarranted; he may be leasing the car, not buying it, or his employer may provide him with a new car each year.

A generalization arrived at through induction should never be considered an absolute certainty. However, there are some sensible guidelines that can help to ensure the reliability of your conclusion:

1. Do you have enough examples to support the generalization? If you're not careful, you may be jumping to a conclusion on the basis of too little evidence.
2. Is the generalization carefully limited to what the evidence will support? You need to be especially careful in making generalizations about **all** members of a group. You can seldom justify a generalization that contains such words as *all, always, no one,* or *everyone.*
3. Are the examples typical? You cannot make a fair and accurate generalization based upon bizarre examples or exceptional cases.
4. Is the evidence drawn from up-to-date and reliable sources? If your evidence is out-of-date, or if you rely on biased sources, you're not apt to arrive at a reliable conclusion.
5. Is the evidence relevant to the generalization being drawn from it? Even dozens of examples of poverty-stricken youngsters who became famous athletes earning huge salaries do not support the conclusion that athletics provides a way out for the youth of the ghetto.

DEDUCTIVE REASONING

The process of reasoning from a generalization to a special application of that general principle is called *deduction.* In a schematic form invented by Aristotle, the process is described as a *syllogism.* The syllogism argues from general statements, called *premises,* which follow a fixed form. The argument always goes like this: If A is true, and if B is true, then C must be true. Most books of elementary logic give this as an example of syllogistic form:

MAJOR PREMISE: All men are mortal beings.
MINOR PREMISE: Socrates is a man.
CONCLUSION: Therefore, Socrates is a mortal being.

The broad statement at the beginning is the *major premise*. The more particular statement in the middle is the *minor premise*. The final statement is the *conclusion* which follows from the major and minor premises. If you examine these three statements, you see that they are related on the basis of a common element or *middle term* which appears in both the major and minor premise.

All syllogisms are built on these three terms, which you can identify by grammatical analysis:

The **major term** (*mortal being*) is the predicate of the conclusion.
The **minor term** (*Socrates*) is the subject of the conclusion.
The **middle term** (*men- man*) appears in both premises but does **not** appear in the conclusion.

The *form* of the syllogism does not often appear in real life; you are much more likely to say, "Since Socrates is a man, he must die." However, syllogistic form underlies all argument that moves from the general to the specific. What's more, it serves as an excellent test of the logic of statements you write and read.

For example, if you wanted to convince someone that your local council president should be reelected, you might point out that she has done a lot for the people of the community. Here you are using a generally accepted premise that "Officials who do a lot for the people should be reelected" to support a specific case, the reelection of the council president.

Stated as a syllogism, this would read:

MAJOR PREMISE: Officials who do a lot for the people should be reelected.
MINOR PREMISE: Our local council president has done a lot for the people.
CONCLUSION: Therefore, our local council president should be reelected.

If the person you are trying to convince agrees with your major and minor premises, he or she must agree with your conclusion.

THE CHAIN OF REASONING

In everyday situations, induction and deduction go hand in hand. Through induction you arrive at a generalization; then you apply that generalization to a particular situation and draw a conclusion, which is deduction.

Although both of these patterns of logical arguments are necessary, there is one important difference between them. Inductive reasoning, no matter how painstaking, can never lead to any conclusion stronger than probable, even though it may be very persuasive. Deductive reasoning has greater force because if the syllogism is both valid and true, the conclusion cannot be denied by any reasonable person. Deductive reasoning leads to certainty.

Distributed Middle Term

Logicians say that a valid syllogism must have a *distributed middle term*. This middle term puts the major term and the minor term in the same classification; it provides an overlapping of meaning so that the conclusion follows logically from the premises. For instance, in our example about Socrates the middle term in the major premise is *men* and the middle term in the minor premise is *man*; since *men* and *man* are clearly the singular and plural of the same term, the two belong in the same category and are therefore **distributed,** one in each premise. If the middle term is not distributed, that is, if it does not appear in both major and minor premises, the conclusion is not valid. In the following syllogism, you can instantly spot the fallacy of the undistributed middle by noting that the middle term, *B,* is the **predicate** of both premises and thus is not distributed in subject and predicate. The conclusion is therefore not valid.

All *A* is *B.*
All *C* is *B.*
Therefore, all *C* is *A.*

If the syllogism is to yield a valid conclusion, the middle term not only must be distributed but must remain clear and stable; it must have the same meaning each time it appears.

Now look at the following syllogism:

All nuts are high in nutrients.
My Uncle Fritz is a real nut.
My Uncle Fritz is high in nutrients.

Here, the conclusion is obviously ridiculous because the meaning of the middle term has shifted.

Validity and Truth

When you ask if a syllogism is valid, you are interested in its **form.** When you ask if it is true, you are concerned with its **content.** If you question the truth of a syllogism, you are asking if the premises are statements you consider true. For example, is "All men are mortal beings" a true statement? Common human experience confirms it to be true; there are no exceptions to disprove it. Therefore, the syllogism about Socrates is both valid and true. Some syllogisms, however, are valid but not true. For instance:

All cats speak French.
Some chickens are cats.
Therefore, some chickens speak French.

This is an example of a valid but untrue syllogism.

If you disagree with the conclusion, you must first determine whether you find it invalid or untrue. If you find it invalid, you can immediately offset the argument. If you find it untrue, you may find it harder to disprove the premise—although not in the case of the cats.

EXERCISE IXb: SYLLOGISMS

The syllogism about the French-speaking cats was written by Lewis Carroll, who is best remembered as the author of the *Alice* books but who was also an important logician. Here are some sets of premises he wrote for students. Make up conclusions for these, trying to make them valid and/or true (even if many of them are just jokes). If you cannot make valid and/or true conclusions, tell what prevented you from so doing.

1. Some oysters are silent.
   No silent creatures are amusing.

   Therefore, _____

2. No riddles interest me that can be solved.
   All these riddles are insoluble.

   Therefore, _____

3. All wasps are unfriendly.
   All puppies are friendly.

   Therefore, _____

4. All ducks waddle.
   Nothing that waddles is graceful.

   Therefore, _____

5. Bores are terrible.
   You are a bore.

   Therefore, _____

6. No fossils can be crossed in love.
   An oyster may be crossed in love.

   Therefore, _____

7. A prudent man shuns hyenas.
   No banker is imprudent.

   Therefore, _____

8. Some pillows are soft.
   No pokers are soft.

   Therefore, _____

9. No country that has been explored is infested by dragons.
   Unexplored countries are fascinating.

   Therefore, _____

10. "I saw it in the newspaper."
    "All newspapers tell lies."

    Therefore, _____

11. No emperors are dentists.
    All dentists are dreaded by children.

    Therefore, _____

12. No military men write poetry.
No generals are civilians.

Therefore, _____

13. All owls are satisfactory.
Some excuses are unsatisfactory.

Therefore, _____

14. No unexpected pleasure annoys me.
Your visit is an unexpected pleasure.

Therefore, _____

Pitfalls to Avoid

1. Don't confuse opinion with fact. A fact is subject to verification. The truth or falsity of a statement such as "Hitler was born in 1889" can be verified because there are documents which establish this fact. An opinion, however, is a judgment based upon some sort of evidence: for example, "Hitler was a maniac." Whether this opinion is valid or not is open to question. Someone else might present evidence to show that Hitler was not insane.

2. Don't sound too shrill. No matter how strongly you feel about an issue, a carefully reasoned approach will have a far better chance of persuading intelligent readers than would overblown, hysterical language.

3. Avoid a long-winded introduction. Get to the point. Get down to the question in one brief introductory paragraph.

4. Avoid making statements that are simply unsupportable, such as, "Americans all want smaller, more fuel-efficient cars." Then why are some people still buying the big luxury cars? Watch out for statements that imply "all" or "every"; a single exception can refute any such assertion.

5. Avoid relying on one source for all of your evidence. Unless you can be sure that the source is reliable and unbiased, you could be badly misled, especially on a subject about which you have little or no knowledge.

6. Don't assume that because something appears in print it must be true. Every publication, even the most reliable, contains inaccuracies from time to time. If the printed facts don't square with common sense, check other sources to verify the information.

SUGGESTED TOPICS

Take a stand on one of the topics below and write a carefully worded persuasive essay directed toward an audience of college students. Consider both logical and emotional appeals.

1. Mandatory retirement
2. Gun control
3. Gasoline rationing
4. Paddling in elementary schools
5. Drafting of women
6. Nuclear power

7.	Expelling students for cheating	30.	Busing
8.	Taxing big cars	31.	Right to die naturally
9.	Dress codes in high school	32.	Immigration quotas
10.	Censorship on television	33.	No-fault insurance
11.	Smoking in public places	34.	Generic food products
12.	Alimony	35.	Chemical preservatives in food
13.	Freedom of information	36.	Yearly auto inspections
14.	Four-day work week	37.	Socialized medicine
15.	Test-tube babies	38.	Hunting
16.	Equal rights amendment	39.	Pollution control
17.	Abortion	40.	Foreign language requirements
18.	Capital punishment	41.	Supporting a certain charity
19.	Mandatory class attendance	42.	Investing money in [a specific investment]
20.	Six-year term for U.S. President		
21.	Electoral college	43.	Mandatory union membership
22.	Pass/fail grading	44.	Women in the priesthood
23.	Federal regulations	45.	Volunteer army
24.	Plea bargaining	46.	Aid to parochial schools
25.	Public employee strikes	47.	Pay television
26.	Banning foreign steel imports	48.	Vitamin supplements
27.	Joint bank accounts	49.	Voting
28.	Becoming a vegetarian	50.	Marriage
29.	Third party movement		

TECHNIQUES OF CLEAR WRITING

Parallel Wording

Parallel wording can give clarity and emphasis to your ideas. (see Chapters I and V.) Expressing your ideas in parallel form can help you understand and remember key ideas. Suppose, for example, that you are advocating tax reform. You could begin by lining up your main points and putting them in parallel form:

1. Our tax laws confuse even the experts.
2. Our tax laws leave gaping loopholes.
3. Our tax laws penalize ordinary workers.
4. Our tax laws discourage savings and investment.
5. Our tax laws encourage cheating.

Parallel wording can also be used effectively to drive home your key ideas in a summary statement:

What we must do is **stop calling** on the federal government to meet every local need, **stop using** the federal treasury to bail out private industry, and **stop wasting** taxpayers' money on pork-barrel projects.

Repetition and Restatement

Purposeful repetition can be especially useful in a persuasive effort. Look how advertisers spend thousands of dollars per minute to repeat the same commerical message over and over again. They recognize the value of repetition. You should not hesitate to repeat a key point when you want to emphasize its significance and make sure that your reader hasn't overlooked it. Thoughtless repetition should, of course, be avoided, but when it is used purposefully, repetition can strengthen and clarify your persuasive message.

In restatement, you express the same thought in altered wording, and help your reader understand the point more clearly. One particularly effective method of restatement is that of rephrasing the thought in more common language. Thus, "Not realizing what turn events would take, our expectations of profit were too high-flown" might be later restated as "We all expected to become rich, but our bubble burst."

Notice the effective use of both parallel wording and the repetition of ideas in Martin Luther King, Jr.'s "I Have a Dream" speech, delivered at the nation's capital in 1963. King was trying to persuade white America to recognize the inequalities suffered by blacks in this country.

Five score years ago, a great American, in whose symbolic shadow we stand today, signed the Emancipation Proclamation. This momentous decree came as a beacon of light and hope to millions of Negro slaves who had been seared in the flames of withering injustice.

But **one hundred years later,** the Negro is still not free. **One hundred years later,** the life of the Negro is still sadly crippled by the manacles of segregation and the chains of discrimination. **One hundred years later,** the Negro lives on a lonely island of poverty in the midst of a vast ocean of material prosperity. **One hundred years later,** the Negro is still languishing in the corners of American society and finds himself an exile in his own land. So we have come here today to dramatize a shameful condition. . . .

We can never be satisfied as long as the Negro is the victim of unspeakable horrors of police brutality. **We can never be satisfied** as long as our bodies, heavy with the fatigue of travel, cannot gain lodging. . . . **We can never be satisfied** as long as the Negro's basic mobility is from a smaller ghetto to a larger one. . . . **We cannot be satisfied** as long as a Negro in Mississippi cannot vote and a Negro in New York believes he has nothing for which to vote. No, **we are not satisfied,** and **we will not be satisfied** until justice rolls down like waters and righteousness like a mighty stream. . . .

EXERCISE IXc: PARALLEL FORM IN OUTLINING
Put all the headings in the following outline in parallel sentence form.

Thesis Sentence: If you are to be successful as a job applicant, you must have a carefully prepared plan of action.

I. Plan your job search carefully.
    A. Taking an honest and searching self-inventory
    B. A careful study of the job market
    C. You need to develop a carefully prepared résumé
II. Being prepared in advance for the interview
    A. Find out everything you can about the company

B. Being prepared for typical interview questions
C. Having some intelligent questions you are prepared to ask the interviewer
III. Your best self is what you want to present during the interview
A. Dress and grooming should be given careful attention
B. How to greet the interviewer properly is important
C. To speak clearly and confidently
D. Leaving a good impression at the conclusion of the interview

EXERCISE IXd: PARALLEL WORDING
Rewrite the following sentences, using parallel wording to improve clarity and emphasis.

1. The applicant was pleasant, attractive, and spoke in a soft voice.

   _____

2. It was Eric's job to check all the registers, seeing that the doors were locked, and to take the cash to the night depository.

   _____

3. Either you can read about the investigation in *Time,* or *Newsweek* also carries an account of the investigation.

   _____

4. He met Daphne, was captivated by her charms, and so he went with her to Wilmington to visit her family.

   _____

5. He believed that declining productivity was due to laziness, most workers were overpaid, and to industry, so he thought, the unions were a curse.

   _____

6. She always preached to her daughter that whenever she married to marry a rich man, and thus she would be secure for life.

   _____

7. Julie was dismayed when she discovered that one tire was flat and her spare and jack must have been stolen by someone.

   _____

8. After eight long months of preparation, and when he had acquired skill in the use of the instruments, he was hired by a surveying company.

   _____

9. The computer can teach chemistry formulas, how to balance a checkbook, and calculating compound interest, but can it teach you about getting along with people, how to cook a good meal, or the management of a household?

   _____

10. When you have learned firearms safety, and after a good deal of target practice, then you are capable of the proper handling of a gun.

EXERCISE IXe: REPETITION AND PARALLEL STRUCTURE
Rewrite the following passages, using repetition and parallel structure to make the ideas clearer and more emphatic.

EXAMPLE
ORIGINAL: Television and the press are very powerful in their image-making role. The vicious criminal may be made to look as if he is the victim. Often the victim becomes invisible, or he is made to seem like the criminal. Through television and the press, people can come to hate the victims of oppression while honoring the oppressors.

REVISION: Television and the press are so powerful in their image-making role that they can make the vicious criminal look like a victim and make the invisible victim seem like a criminal. Television and the press are so powerful that they can lead people to honor the oppressors and to hate the victims of oppression.

1. Black people ask why it is that white people should be running all the banks in the community. They notice, too, that the stores are being run by white people. They can see for themselves and wonder why it is that the economy of the community is in the hands of white citizens.

2. The well-prepared job applicant is applying for a specific job. He also knows what the going rate for that job is, and he will act determined to get the job which he is applying for.

3. Most American cars have been built according to a false assumption about what a car ought to do. The occupants are isolated as much as possible from how the road feels and natural shocks and vibrations. The purpose of the design has been to cradle the occupants within a cocoon of inner space, not like a machine on the road.

4. In France, the American tourist does not get to see the French people as they are just by visiting the Left Bank cafes of Paris. The tourist who visits the Leaning Tower of Pisa isn't to gain much insight into the way Italian people live. And to visit Times Square in New York is of little help to a foreign visitor in understanding the average American's way of life.

5. Opportunities to satisfy the desires of a growing population were offered by the Western lands. From that highly favorable condition for expansion came a long era of progress and prosperity. There began to exist a new optimism, and the feeling of sudden availability of wealth spread from the frontier feverishly.

WORD POWER

Wording Your Argument

As a writer, the vocabulary you use will be determined, to a large extent, by the educational level of your audience. You don't want to talk over the heads of your audience, nor do you want to insult them by oversimplifying ideas. You have to communicate with readers on their own level. If, for example, you were a graduate student in marine biology writing a doctoral dissertation on water pollution, you would probably use some highly scientific terminology. Terms such as *chlorinated hydrocarbons* and *phosphoric acids* would be appropriate. But if you were writing an editorial about water pollution for your local newspaper, you would use terms like *insecticides* and *pollutants,* and you would call small gnats *small gnats,* not *Chaoborus asticopus.* Such specialized terms require caution. Also beware of dependence on abstract terms. A highly educated audience can usually deal with abstract terms, but other audiences frequently respond better to more concrete language.

You also have to take your readers' value system into account when you are deciding how to word your argument. If you were trying to convince the National Athletic Association to support an investigation of drug abuse among professional athletes, you wouldn't refer to the athletes as *jocks.* Your use of the term *jocks* would convey a condescending attitude toward sports. You would be likely to lose your goal from the start. The thoughtless use of even one offensive word in an otherwise intelligent essay can destroy all hopes of establishing any common ground between you and your readers. Calling a congressman a "dupe" of organized labor would thwart any hope of your persuading him to work with you. Remember, the language you use will shape your readers' response, so **choose your words carefully.**

Labeling

"Sticks and stones will break my bones, but names will never hurt me." Unfortunately, however, names can and *do* hurt people very much. Phyllis McGinley, a popular poet, rewrote that old saying in a more realistic way:

Sticks and stones are hard on bones
When thrown with hateful art,
And words can sting like anything
But silence breaks the heart.

One of the most common ways that words can sting is in **labeling** people. Identifying people through labels happens constantly in our society: "She's a typical dumb blonde," "He's just a paper shuffler," "They're all a bunch of radicals." A person is thus no longer seen as an individual but only as part of a group. This is what makes labels so dangerous.

... what we call an object or person or situation is going to influence the way we see it and evaluate it, and as a result, affect the way we respond to it ... in our encounters with the world, we are responding more often than we realize not just to something as it exists "out there" ... but rather to something "out there" **as modified by the label we've applied to it.** ... To the extent that our behavior is affected by labels ... we are not entirely sane.

William Dresser and S. I. Hayakawa

As the authors point out, stereotyped thinking that often goes with certain labels can lead us into false perceptions of the world around us. Here is an example that you should immediately recognize: some people associate the word *Mexican* with a stereotyped image of someone leaning against a giant cactus, fast asleep under his broad sombrero. However, the label, when it provokes that kind of non-thinking response, does **not** correspond with reality. Among other things, cactuses (or cacti) are not designed for leaning against; besides—and more to the point—wide-awake young Mexicans would have every right to resent that gringo image of themselves. In fact, millions of people in our own country have suffered because of labels that unfairly characterize an entire group as being dirty, lazy, dumb, or unpatriotic.

So don't use labels thoughtlessly. What you need to do is look behind the label. What are the facts? If a man or woman is labeled as a "troublemaker" or a "pathological liar," make sure that you examine the facts. What did he or she do? What did he or she say? Who has applied this label, and what are his or her prejudices?

Look behind the label.

EXERCISE IXf: LABELS
Examine the list of words below. What do you think of when you hear these labels? Beside each word, write down your understanding of the term. Next ask someone whose views or background differs from yours to define the terms. Then compare his or her definitions with yours. Notice the variety of emotional responses associated with each label.

1. Bleeding heart _____

2. Women's libber _____

3. Jock _____

4. Reactionary _____

5. Paper shuffler _____

6. Acid head _____

7. Macho man _____

8. Jesus freak _____

9. Redneck _____

10. Chauvinist _____

11. Grease monkey _____

12. Hillbilly _____

13. Radical _____

14. Bookworm _____

15. A real politician _____

16. Conservative _____

17. Fat cat _____

18. Wheeler dealer _____

19. Swinger _____

20. Liberal _____

EXERCISE IXg: PERSUASIVE STRATEGIES

For each of the five proposals listed below, briefly explain the persuasive strategies you would use in situation *A* and in situation *B* to convince the audience to accept your position.

1. Terminally ill patients deserve the right to die naturally instead of being kept alive through artificial means.
   A. Editorial in a newspaper distributed to residents of a retirement home
   B. An appeal to a group of young clergymen

2. The United States should stop building nuclear power plants.
   A. A pamphlet distributed to the Harvard Graduate School
   B. A newspaper article in a town where one-third of the residents work at a nuclear power plant

3. Smoking should be prohibited in public places.
   A. An article in a medical journal
   B. An appeal to the president of the American Tobacco Institute

4. The sale of handguns through mail-order catalogs should be outlawed.
   A. A speech written for your boss, who is addressing a convention of the National Rifle Association
   B. An essay in a sociology journal

5. The government should not be permitted to erect high-voltage power lines across private farmlands.
   A. An editorial in a rural newspaper
   B. An editorial in a metropolitan newspaper

269

CHAPTER X

writing about literature

It's a great pleasure to read a good book, but sometimes it's almost as much fun to talk about it with someone else who has read it. Have you ever said to anyone, "Here, read this book; it's terrific!"? Then, every day you ask, "How far have you gotten in the book?" because you want to discuss the parts you really liked or disliked or wondered about. Literature of any type—books, plays, poems, short stories, essays, even movies and TV programs—often present new ideas or new ways of looking at life. After you have thought about these "new" things, you often want to talk about them, to test them, perhaps to adjust your own life to them; therefore you want to hear how others reacted. Did the other person get the same ideas you did? Did he or she agree or disagree with what the author wrote? As you discuss the work, your understanding of it increases, and what you learned from it becomes a part of you. Thus, communicating your ideas about literature is both important and enjoyable.

Reading Literature and Prewriting

In most of the writing you have been doing throughout this book, you have been responding to direct experience, something you have either lived through or

270

observed around you. In writing about literature, you are responding to another writer's interpretation of people's experience or observation.

Why should you be concerned with someone else's interpretation when you could be making your own? There are a number of answers to this question, but perhaps the most obvious is this: any individual's life is limited. Literature, of course, is not life, but it is vicarious living, living through imagination. No matter how fortunate an individual may be, his or her experiences in comparison with all the possibilities of human life are extremely limited. Obviously, you can't experience life as a man and a woman, as an American and a Japanese, as a twentieth-century citizen and a thirteenth-century feudal baron. Good writers can make all experiences come alive for you through imagination. Good writers can vastly extend your experiences.

There is also another answer. Good writers can create experiences similar to, perhaps identical with, your experiences, and as you watch the characters in literature coping with such experiences, you often are better able to interpret what you yourself have lived through. Literature thus can expand your life and make it more understandable.

In trying to reach the understanding that comes through imaginative literature, you might apply what are called "the four critical questions."

1. What is the author attempting to communicate?
2. How does he or she go about communicating it?
3. Is it worth communicating?
4. What does it mean to you, the reader?

Although these four questions seem simple, good answers to them depend on your ability to read sensitively and intelligently. Such reading depends, in turn, upon a careful consideration of the "elements" of literature, which vary from one genre to another; that is, the elements of poetry differ from those of drama and those of drama from those of fiction.

Elements of Fiction

Since fiction—short stories and novels—is the most widely read genre (type) of literature, you'll find its elements make a good starting point for improving your critical reading.

PLOT

Plot involves action, the sequence of events which takes place in a story. Plot also involves motivation, the reason for each action in the sequence. As the plot unfolds, one action impels another until the conclusion. (When you say "That was an exciting story," you are generally referring to the plot.)

The opening action, sometimes called exposition, shows the reader the situation (gives the setting, introduces the characters, and starts the action). *The rising action*, sometimes called complication, shows the main character (protagonist) in conflict with some antagonist (nature, other people, or some conflict within himself or herself). The *climax*, sometimes called crisis, is the point at which some decision is made or some action is taken that determines the outcome of the story. You have probably heard the term *crisis* used medically. If the doctor says, "He has passed the crisis," he means that the patient will survive. In the fictional crisis the coward may run into the burning building to save the child, or he may run away. If he goes in, the story will end one way; if he runs away, the story must end another way. In the biblical story of Abraham and Isaac, you remember, God tells Abraham that he must sacrifice his beloved son, Isaac. Reluctantly but obediently, Abraham leads the boy to the sacrificial altar, but at the crucial moment, just as Abraham lifts his knife, an angel tells him to spare Isaac and substitute a ram. This crucial moment is the crisis or climax. Once the climactic decision has been made, the following action, sometimes called the denouement, leads to the logical ending of the story.

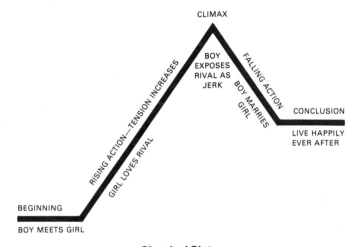

Classical Plot

Notice in the diagram that the falling action is much shorter than the rising action because, once the climax is reached, that particular story is practically over. Plots, like your essays, must have unity. Even though human experience tells you that a falling action as simple as "And so they were married and lived happily ever afterward" is unlikely, what happens after they are married is another story.

These actions are all based on conflict. If there is no conflict or struggle, there is no story. If you have a story about a pilot whose tiny plane crashes in a vast wilderness, the essential conflict is going to be that of man against nature. If you have a woman who defies the rules of the society to which she belongs—for good reasons or bad—then a central element will be the conflict between woman and society. If you have a story about a man who has gained wealth and power but comes to hate himself for the way he has succeeded, then you have man against himself.

These types of conflict are not imposed upon fiction by critics but are the structures by which the authors build their plots and which careful readers can easily observe. For example, conflict between man and nature is seen in Jack London's "To Build a Fire," in which man is pitted against the killing cold of an Alaskan winter; such a conflict appears again in Stephen Crane's "The Open Boat," which is man against the ocean.

The conflict of man or woman against society takes place in two forms. In one, the conflict is between two individuals. An example of this is *Les Misérables*, a great novel of Victor Hugo's in which a detective makes it his life work to hunt down the protagonist, who once committed the "crime" of stealing bread. The second form of the conflict of a person against society is the individual against a group or social institution—for example, the kind of detective fiction in which an entire police department seeks to capture the villain.

Perhaps the most subtle of conflicts is that between an individual and him or herself, where a person is torn between love and friendship, or love and duty. Such a conflict is that of the hero in James Joyce's *Portrait of the Artist;* he wrestles with his conflicting desires to follow the wishes of his dying mother but also to follow his own opposing wishes.

Very often, however, the conflict is not so simple as these examples seem to indicate. There are frequent overlapping conflicts. Even in a story as relatively simple as "To Build a Fire," the protagonist not only is involved in the man-nature conflict, but has secondary conflicts with the group he lives with and with his own personality. Yet, whether they are one or many, conflict is the essence of plot.

After you have read a work and wish to evaluate the element of plot, ask yourself:

1. Did the action carry me along? Was I interested in what happened? (If the answer to this is no, you probably won't go any further for you probably have not finished the work.)
2. In the circumstances that the author created, were the actions believable? Do people behave like this?
3. Given the characters and circumstances that the author created, was the conclusion logical or was common sense defied to force a happy ending?

CHARACTER   Characters are the people who act out the plot. The protagonist is the leading actor who struggles against his antagonist, whether that antagonist is another person or nature or a social force. If you love the protagonist and hate the antagonist, the writer has won your interest so that you will follow the plot avidly in the hope that all will go well for the protagonist.

Basic classifications of characters are round characters, whom you can see from all sides, just as you can walk around a statue to see it from all angles, and flat characters. With well-rounded characters, you learn much more than the physical description. You learn about their natures through what they say about themselves and what others say about them. You discover so much about them that you understand what they do (or don't do). Even if you are surprised at first at their actions, you know them well enough to understand why they took that action. Not all characters in a work must be round, but the protagonist must be, and if the antagonist is a person, he or she usually should be round. Flat characters are those of secondary interest, whose function in the story is to present just one or two

Round Character—Flat Character

traits—for example, a lovable but interfering neighbor. Stereotyped characters are also flat, but in addition they lack originality and individuality. They just fit an overly used role—for example, a mean stepmother.

Another way of considering characters is on the basis of universality and individuality. Good character creations have both these qualities: they are universal in that you recognize in them the common humanity they share with everyone; they are individual in that you find in them distinctive and unusual touches that make them interestingly unlike everybody else. Some characters fall between these two extremes; they represent a segment or class of society that is typical, like a conservative businessman.

Still a third way to analyze characters is to determine if they are dynamic or static. Those who are dynamic grow, develop, change, learn to know themselves in the course of the plot. By the end of the story they are not what they were in the beginning. Static characters are at the end just as they were in the beginning. The protagonist, and sometimes other important characters, are usually dynamic; minor characters usually are static.

Sometimes, however, a minor character does change. When the story is narrated by a character who takes no important part in the action but simply observes and reports, he is often the one who is changed by the experience. He compassionately watches the main characters hurrying on to their happy or tragic ends. The characters themselves are unaware of the meaning of their experience, but the narrator perceives the significance, so his understanding deepens, as does the reader's.

THEME

Theme is the most important element in serious fiction. It is the author's controlling idea, the truth about life that he or she wishes to convey to the reader. Theme is often implied rather than directly stated. Some stories (frequently called "escape fiction") do not even have a theme; they are written just to scare you or make you laugh or test your wits against those of the detective. Serious writers, though, reveal some aspect of life as they see it; what they reveal is the theme.

Theme is not to be confused with a moral, which is a characteristic of the fable, a piece of literature designed primarily to teach. In fact, the writer of the fable

274

is so eager to get his moral across that he often repeats the moral point at the end of his story and labels it Moral.

Theme is often revealed to the reader through the increased awareness of a character, usually either the protagonist or the narrator, the person from whose point of view the story is seen. Because of what happens to the characters in the story, one character learns something which deepens his or her understanding. Since the character has learned this, the author hopes that the reader has also learned it.

SETTING

Setting is the time and place of the action. Sometimes it simply provides a background for the characters and their action. After all, they can't exist in a vacuum. Setting can also add flavor of its own to a work. It makes a difference in the reader's appreciation if the setting is Algiers before World War II or New York City today. But setting is most important when it functions as environment that determines the types of characters and influences the events of the plot.

Sometimes the setting almost becomes an actor. For example, in Stephen Crane's "The Blue Hotel," setting is as important as characters. A man, identified only as "the Swede," is murdered because the setting, from the large background of the desolate plains to the interior of the hotel saloon where even the stove "was humming with god-like violence," leads to brutality and viciousness.

TONE

Tone is the author's attitude toward the material. Authors may be sympathetic or hostile toward characters. They may pity or make fun of them. They may be straightforward or ironic. But whatever the author's attitude, he or she must be consistent in it.

Here is a bit of verse and a short poem, both on the subject of the immediate sense of liking or disliking someone.

> I do not like you, Dr. Fell,
> The reason why I cannot tell.
> But this I know, and know full well,
> I do not like you, Dr. Fell.
>
> *Thomas Brown*

> The soul selects her own society,
> Then shuts the door:
> On her divine majority
> Obtrude no more.
>
> Unmoved, she notes the chariot's pausing
> At her low gate;
> Unmoved, an emperor is kneeling
> Upon her mat.
>
> I've known her from an ample nation
> Choose one;
> Then close the valve of her attention
> Like stone.
>
> *Emily Dickinson*

Although the subjects of these are similar, the tone is widely different. Which one do you think is flip? Which one is serious? What words or phrases make you think this?

Point of view is the vantage point from which the author looks at the story. Imagine yourself caught up in a mob of excited fans who are trying to get close to their idol. What would you see and hear and feel? How would you see the same situation if you were looking out of a fifth-story window across the street from the mob scene? How would you describe the scene ten years later? Do you see that the descriptions of the same event would be vastly different? What you see depends upon your perspective: your point of view. An author chooses to see the characters and their actions through one of several visions. The point of view chosen determines the reader's understanding of the story. Think what a difference it would make if the story of Little Red Ridinghood were told from the point of view of the wolf, or if Star Wars were told by Darth Vader.

Point of view can change the story.

In a novel called *What Maisie Knew*, Henry James tells the story from the point of view of a twelve-year-old girl whose parents are divorcing. What Maisie knows is limited by her twelve-year-old mentality and experiences. It would be an entirely different story if the same events were related by Maisie's mother and still another if those events were told by her father.

Although there are many ways to analyze the point of view, you need be concerned only with the basic types.

1. In the omniscient point of view, the author knows all. He or she goes into the minds of all the characters and tells what each is thinking or feeling. When an author uses this point of view, the reader has no doubt as to what the character is: good or evil, bright or slow, confident or unsure.

276

2. In the limited point of view, the author goes into the mind of only one character. This character may be central to the story or may be on the outskirts. The author may use *I* or *he*. The important thing is that the story is told as it is seen and understood by this character. This point of view appeals to readers, for it parallels the way they see the world every day: through one pair of eyes—their own. It also appeals to authors, for it allows them to reveal the truth as it might be seen by someone other than themselves.

3. The objective point of view is the most demanding on both author and reader. Here, the author goes into no one's mind, makes no speculations or explanations. He records what happens, what is said and done, and the reader must determine the meaning and significance of the actions. The writer must get the point across by showing, not telling.

Here is a short story by the contemporary writer Ray Bradbury. Read it carefully and then see if you agree with the discussion following it.

I See You Never

The soft knock came at the kitchen door, and when Mrs. O'Brian opened it, there on the back porch were her best tenant, Mr. Ramirez, and two police officers, one on each side of him. Mr. Ramirez just stood there, walled in and small.

"Why, Mr. Ramirez!" said Mrs. O'Brian.

Mr. Ramirez was overcome. He did not seem to have words to explain.

He had arrived at Mrs. O'Brian's rooming house more than two years earlier and had lived there ever since. He had come by bus from Mexico City to San Diego and had then gone up to Los Angeles. There he had found the clean little room, with glossy blue linoleum, and the pictures and calendars on the flowered walls, and Mrs. O'Brian as the strict but kindly landlady. During the war he had worked at the airplane factory and made parts for planes that flew off somewhere, and even now, after the war, he still held his job. From the first he had made big money. He saved some of it, and he got drunk only once a week—a privilege that, to Mrs. O'Brian's way of thinking, every good workingman deserved, unquestioned and unreprimanded.

Inside Mrs. O'Brian's kitchen, pies were baking in the oven. Soon the pies would come out with complexions like Mr. Ramirez'—brown and shiny and crisp, with slits in them for the air almost like the slits of Mr. Ramirez' dark eyes. The kitchen smelled good. The policemen leaned forward, lured by the odor. Mr. Ramirez gazed at his feet, as if they had carried him into all this trouble.

"What happened, Mr. Ramirez?" asked Mrs. O'Brian.

Behind Mrs. O'Brian, as he lifted his eyes, Mr. Ramirez saw the long table laid with clean white linen and set with a platter, cool, shining glasses, a water pitcher with ice cubes floating inside it, a bowl of fresh potato salad and one of bananas and oranges, cubed and sugared. At this table sat Mrs. O'Brian's children—her three grown sons, eating and conversing, and her two younger daughters, who were staring at the policemen as they ate.

"I have been here thirty months," said Mr. Ramirez quietly, looking at Mrs. O'Brian's plump hands.

"That's six months too long," said one policeman. "He only had a temporary visa. We've just got around to looking for him."

Soon after Mr. Ramirez had arrived he bought a radio for his little room; evenings, he turned it up very loud and enjoyed it. And he bought a wrist watch and enjoyed that too. And on many nights he had walked silent streets and seen the bright clothes in the windows and bought some of them, and he had seen the jewels and bought some of them for his few lady friends. And he had gone to picture shows five nights a week for a while. Then, also, he had ridden the streetcars—all night some nights—smelling the electricity, his dark eyes moving over the advertisements, feeling the wheels rumble under him, watching the little sleeping houses and big hotels slip by. Besides that, he had gone to large restaurants, where he had eaten many-course dinners, and to the opera and the theater. And he had bought a car, which later, when he forgot to pay for it, the dealer had driven off angrily from in front of the rooming house.

"So here I am," said Mr. Ramirez now, "to tell you I must give up my room, Mrs. O'Brian. I come to get my baggage and clothes and go with these men."

"Back to Mexico?"

"Yes. To Lagos. That is a little town north of Mexico City."

"I'm sorry, Mr. Ramirez."

I'm packed," said Mr. Ramirez hoarsely, blinking his dark eyes rapidly and moving his hands helplessly before him. The policemen did not touch him. There was no necessity for that.

"Here is the key, Mrs. O'Brian," Mr. Ramirez said, "I have my bag already."

Mrs. O'Brian, for the first time, noticed a suitcase standing behind him on the porch.

Mr. Ramirez looked in again at the huge kitchen, at the bright silver cutlery and the young people eating and the shining waxed floor. He turned and looked for a long moment at the apartment house next door, rising up three stories, high and beautiful. He looked at the balconies and fire escapes and back-porch stairs, at the lines of laundry snapping in the wind.

"You've been a good tenant," said Mrs. O'Brian.

"Thank you, thank you, Mrs. O'Brian," he said softly. He closed his eyes.

Mrs. O'Brian stood holding the door half open. One of her sons, behind her, said that her dinner was getting cold, but she shook her head at him and turned back to Mr. Ramirez. She remembered a visit she had once made to some Mexican border towns—the hot days, the endless crickets leaping and falling or lying dead and brittle like the small cigars in the shopwindows, and the canals taking river water out to the farms, the dirt roads, the scorched landscape. She remembered the silent towns, the warm beer, the hot, thick foods each day. She remembered the slow, dragging horses and the parched jack rabbits on the road. She remembered the iron mountains and the dusty valleys and the ocean beaches that spread hundreds of miles with no sound but the waves—no cars, no buildings, nothing.

"I'm sure sorry, Mr. Ramirez," she said.

"I don't want to go back, Mrs. O'Brian," he said weakly. "I like it here. I want to stay here. I've worked, I've got money. I look all right, don't I? And I don't want to go back!"

"I'm sorry, Mr. Ramirez," she said. "I wish there was something I could do."

"Mrs. O'Brian!" he cried suddenly, tears rolling out from under his eyelids. He reached out his hands and took her hand fervently, shaking it, wringing it, holding to it. "Mrs. O'Brian, I see you never, I see you never!"

The policemen smiled at this, but Mr. Ramirez did not notice it, and they stopped smiling very soon.

"Good-by, Mrs. O'Brian. You have been good to me. Oh, good-by, Mrs. O'Brian. I see you never!"

The policemen waited for Mr. Ramirez to turn, pick up his suitcase, and walk away. Then they followed him, tipping their caps to Mrs. O'Brian. She watched them go down the porch steps. Then she shut the door quietly and went slowly back to her chair at the table. She pulled the chair out and sat down. She picked up the shining knife and fork and started once more upon her steak.

"Hurry up, Mom," said one of the sons. "It'll be cold."

Mrs. O'Brian took one bite and chewed on it for a long, slow time; then she stared at the closed door. She laid down her knife and fork.

"What's wrong, Ma?" asked her son.

"I just realized," said Mrs. O'Brian—she put her hand to her face—"I'll never see Mr. Ramirez again."

Analysis of "I See You Never"

If, in preparing to write a critical analysis of "I See You Never," you apply the first critical question to this story (What is the author attempting to communicate?), you are dealing with the element of theme. Your interpretation of theme is subjective; that is, it is your interpretation so long as it does not violate what the story obviously says. To support your interpretation, you look constantly at the story. Here is one possible statement of the theme:

In "I See You Never," Ray Bradbury is conveying his concept that social forces frequently wound—or even destroy—the "little man" because he does not understand them or understand how to cope with them. The law of the country, attempting to protect the majority of the citizens, regulates aliens. Mr. Ramirez has, unknowingly, violated the law which determines the length of time he can work in the United States. The law is not wrong; moreover, its representatives, the two policemen, are kind, courteous, and human. (Bradbury comments on their humanity when he has them lean toward Mrs. O'Brian's door to smell her pies.) The conflict between the law and Mr. Ramirez would be solved if he knew enough to go through the proper channels to have his visa extended and to apply for naturalization. But he doesn't know this; nor does he even know enough to get a lawyer. Mrs. O'Brian, despite her kindness and compassion, doesn't know either. Ignorance is the villain. And social forces destroy Mr. Ramirez.

The second critical question (How does he or she go about communicating it?) deals, first, with identifying the genre. This would be quickly done, perhaps in a subordinate clause or a modifying phrase: "In Ray Bradbury's short-short story 'I See You Never,'..."

The second critical question, however, usually is the largest part of your critical essay because, in answering it, you discuss elements of fiction other than theme. You need not discuss them all, of course, but you would indicate in your thesis statement just what you were going to discuss. For instance, if you were going to discuss plot, you might say this:

Plot, in Ray Bradbury's "I See You Never," is of slight importance. It really is only an incident—a Mexican boarder says good-bye to his American landlady. He explains why he must say good-bye: his visa has expired. And, in flashback, his experiences in the United States are sketched, but they are ordinary. Indeed, the very lack of plot, of action, contributes to the significance of the theme.

To satisfy the second critical question, you probably would need to discuss setting:

Setting in this story is important, perhaps more important than any other element except theme. There are really two settings contrasted with each other to show why Mr. Ramirez wants to stay in the United States. The Mexican setting is lonely , uncomfortable, almost lifeless; the American setting is peopled, comfortable, intensely alive.

The lower-middle class environment is of vital importance. Bradbury establishes that with a few understated touches—linoleum instead of carpeting, calendars instead of pictures. But the story depends on this environment. Neither Mrs. O'Brian nor Mr. Ramirez has the practical knowledge that would be natural in more sophisticated settings. Although their setting is sound and sweet (the house is clean, the food is wholesome and appetizing), it is limited by ignorance. Mr. Ramirez forgot that he had to keep up his car payments; he made parts, during the war, "for airplanes that flew off somewhere."

Setting would then lead into a discussion of character. In such a setting people like Mrs. O'Brian and Mr. Ramirez would be fated to lose. You then might want to identify what kinds of persons these two characters are. They are typical characters, a fact Bradbury underscores by giving them only last names. They have, however, endearing traits that individualize them. Such traits are Mrs. O'Brian's conviction that a good workman ought to be allowed to get drunk once a week and Mr. Ramirez's joy in living, even riding streetcars all night.

Tone also would be considered in the second critical question. Bradbury's tone is compassionate, which he reveals both directly as the omniscient author and by showing compassion developing in Mrs. O'Brian. As the omniscient author, he takes us into the minds of both his characters, and almost always, when we see people through their own eyes, we learn the author's compassion. He does not idealize his characters—indeed, his tone has some overtones of humor—but he consistently shows the pathos of the little man who cannot control his destiny.

Even with so short a story, there are many more points that could be made. These observations are just to give you an idea of approaching a work critically.

For the third question (Is it worth communicating?), the answer is usually yes if the author is artistically serious. Even if the work fails, an honest failure can be enlightening.

The fourth question (What does it mean to me?) will probably be your conclusion, the summing up of your response to the work. Here you must be sure to keep your emphasis on the work, not on the response. You want to avoid conclusions like "I was interested in this book. I couldn't put it down." Focus on the work: "This is a simple, poignant story of good little people who are crushed by social forces which are not evil in themselves."

Writing about literature serves the same purpose as talking about it, but the process is different. It is solitary: you are communicating your thoughts to someone not present, someone who cannot question or react or discuss or present his or her ideas immediately. Therefore, writing about literature is more concentrated and more specific, and the ideas are more carefully supported than they are in talking about it.

ORGANIZATION

Choosing Your Topic

After reading the piece of literature and rereading it if necessary to make sure that you understand it, you must choose some aspect of the work to write about. Here, as with all other essays, you must narrow your topic; you cannot discuss everything.

When you are asked to write about fiction, whether a novel or short story, one of the first things you need to do is to decide upon a manageable topic. A complex novel, for example, may present almost limitless possibilities, yet you must narrow your focus to some specific topic before you can begin to put together a unified essay. Following are six practical approaches to finding a manageable topic.

HISTORICAL APPROACH
Does the work have some historical significance? What does it tell us, for example, about life in czarist Russia or in Paris in the 1920's? What does the work show us about a specific time and place?

BIOGRAPH-ICAL APPROACH
What is the relationship between the author's life experience and the work of fiction he or she has created? Is the work based upon the author's direct experience? What light is shed upon the work by the author's life, letters, and public statements? (Here you need to be wary of oversimplification. Even though a character in a novel, for instance, may seem to represent the author in thought and experience, he is not the author. He is still a fictional character within the work.)

COMPARISON-CONTRAST
Does comparing the work of one author with that of a different author who is writing about the same subject reveal something worthwhile? What specific points of comparison do you see between two characters in different works by the same author? Or between two characters in works by different authors? Or between two characters in the same work?

ANALYSIS OF A SINGLE CHARACTER
How does the author reveal a particular character? What does the author say about the character? What do other characters say about him? How do they react to him? What does the character think and say? What do the character's actions reveal?

ANALYSIS OF THEME
What main idea or set of ideas does the author bring home to the reader? Does the author state the theme? If not, what do you see as the main idea that emerges from the work? What does the story tell us about love, death, honor, duty, ambition, depravity, or human dignity?

DETAILED ANALYSIS OF A SINGLE FEATURE
Is irony, satire, or symbolism important in the work? Does the effectiveness of the story or novel depend upon a certain point of view? Does conflict provide a focal point of interest? Is the author's style—whether simple and straightforward or complex and tortuous—an important element in the story?

281

There are many possible topics to discuss in any worthwhile piece of literature. The possibilities are by no means limited to these six approaches, but each does provide a sensible starting point. The more carefully you read, the more you will find topics suggesting themselves to you.

Introduction

Once you have decided on your topic, you should decide exactly what you want to say about it. Make sure that early in your introduction you give the full title of the work to be discussed and the author's full name. Then write a carefully worded thesis sentence that tells the reader exactly what you are going to write about.

> *INCORRECT:* Satan, in Mark Twain's "The Mysterious Stranger," is unbelievable. [not specific]

> *CORRECT:* Seldom in fiction has Satan been so fully characterized as in Mark Twain's "The Mysterious Stranger," where the monarch is shown as beautiful, compelling, accommodating, and completely without conscience or empathy.

Once you have clearly established your subject and attitude, you should write an introduction that captures the reader's interest and leads into the thesis statement. A quotation from the work itself, a striking comment or anecdote about the work or the author, or a brief definition are among the good introductory gambits.

If, for example, you were writing about *One Day in the Life of Ivan Denisovich,* you might quote Ivan's highly significant line that "A man who is warm cannot understand a man who is cold." This quotation is striking in itself, is applicable to many situations, and is pertinent to the theme of the novel.

If you were writing about *Uncle Tom's Cabin,* you might want to repeat the anecdote about Abraham Lincoln's remark to the author, Harriet Beecher Stowe, when he first met her. Lincoln said, "So you are the little woman who started this great war." This would be a good opening for a discussion of books that changed our lives.

If you were going to write about the comedy in Woody Allen's movies, it might be well to start with a definition of comedy in general. Perhaps something like:

> Comedy is literature that aims to amuse, to provoke laughter, to arouse thought. It ends happily. But until it reaches that happy ending, it skirts disaster and sorrow. Its aim is essentially serious. Someone, year ago, trying to define comedy, said "Comedy is no laughing matter." A Woody Allen movie certainly gets plenty of laughs, but its theme is no laughing matter.

**INTERPRETA-
TION IN
THE THESIS
SENTENCE**

No matter how you introduce your essay, it is imperative that your thesis statement be an interpretation rather than a mere statement of fact. Although it is **your** interpretation, remember that it must come from ideas you have gathered from the work read, not just any that popped into your head. That is, it must be relevant and supportable.

Your job is to provide interpretation and explanation of the work; just retelling what happened in the story or just repeating what the author says is totally inadequate.

Since your essay should be the result of your own thinking, the thesis statement and the topic sentences of the body paragraphs should be in your own words, not words borrowed from some other writer. Although sometimes you may want to use professional criticism to support your points, you are using it **only as support** for your own thoughts expressed in your thesis statement and your topic sentences. To interpret is the purpose of critical writing.

A review, on the other hand, has a different purpose. In a review, the writer assumes that the readers want to know what happens, what a work is about, so that they can decide if they want to read the book or go to the movie or buy the record. In critical writing, the writer assumes that the readers already know what the work is about but want to know more and know more deeply.

Body

In the body of your essay you must support your thesis sentence, just as in the other essays. When writing about literature, however, you have your support right at your fingertips—the work itself. You will use quotations and paraphrases from the literature to prove the statements in the body.

There are two possible directions that you might take once you have your thesis statement: (1) outlining first and then looking for support for your subtopics, and (2) searching for items that support your thesis first and then dividing these bits of evidence into classifications that become your subtopic sentences. Both methods work; it is a matter of personal preference.

GETTING THE SUBTOPICS FIRST

In support of the thesis statement on Mark Twain's "The Mysterious Stranger," you might use the following topic sentences:

TOPIC SENTENCE 1
Satan is beautiful; he is "handsome and had a winning face and a pleasant voice, and was easy and graceful and unembarrassed."

TOPIC SENTENCE 2
Satan is compelling; whether they want it or not, the boys are drawn to him, held by him, bound to obey his wishes.

TOPIC SENTENCE 3
Satan is accommodating; he does what the boys wish, though the result of his actions often turn out to be not exactly what the boys want.

TOPIC SENTENCE 4
Satan seems to have neither conscience nor empathy; when two of the little workmen quarrel, "Satan reached out his hand and crushed the life out of them with his fingers" and ignores the grief of the wives who mourn them.

**"Satan reached out his hand
and crushed the life out of them. . ."**

Once you have decided on a thesis sentence, you become a kind of detective. Much as the detective looks for clues, you look for evidence to support your thesis.

For example, in supporting topic sentence 3, you would read through the story, finding and jotting down on notecards all material to prove that Satan is accommodating but that the results are not always what the boys wish:

CARD 1
Feeling sorry for the grief-stricken mother of a friend of theirs, the boys ask Satan to examine her possible futures. He reports that "the longest . . . gave her forty-two years and her shortest twenty-nine, and that both were charged with grief and hunger and cold and pain." The boys beg Satan to change her future. Satan does. "In three days time, she will go to the stake," he promises.

CARD 2
By this same act, Satan changes the future of Fischer, who will now betray the mother. Instead of dying the following year as was originally his fate, Fischer would "live to be ninety and have a pretty prosperous and comfortable life of it. . . ." The boys are delighted to have done Fischer such a service until Satan adds that his fate after death has also been altered. Had he died in the following year as originally scheduled, he would have gone to heaven. With his new future he is doomed to hell.

CARD 3
Another example of Satan's "accommodation" is his agreeing, at the boys' request, to release Father Peter from prison and ensure him a happy life. Satan does as he is asked, but only later do the boys discover that Father Peter will also be insane.

Then go on searching through the story for more clues, more evidence to prove each of your points.

284

If you use the second method, you would start the same way—reading the story, thinking about it, and coming up with some general impression you would turn into a tentative thesis statement.

Suppose the assignment is a critical paper on Nathaniel Hawthorne's "Young Goodman Brown." After reading the story, perhaps you are a little baffled. The story seems simple enough, but what does it mean? A young man leaves his bride, goes into the forest for a night, meets someone who may or may not be the devil, learns from him that his father and grandfather may not have been the good men he thought they were. He sees and hears—or thinks he does—all the fine, respected people he knows bound on an evil journey, just as he is. They all arrive—or he imagines that they do—at a great witch meeting dedicated to evil. He even thinks he hears his parents and his wife. Hearing them, he faints. When he comes to, the forest is only the forest, silent and solitary. He never knows whether or not he only dreamed this vivid and awesome scene, but all the rest of his life is sad and "distrustful."

From this plot summary you can see that at every step of the way through his journey and through his story, Goodman Brown either does or does not experience something evil. In the Word Power section at the end of this chapter you will see that this either-or situation is called *ambiguity*. So you are ready to try a tentative thesis statement:

Through his repeated use of ambiguity, Hawthorne arrives at his theme that a sense of evil, regardless of whether it is real or imagined, spoils life because it destroys faith in the goodness of man.

Now you collect evidence that can later be classified into subtopics to support your thesis statement. The first thing you notice is the title, "Young Goodman Brown." *Goodman* isn't a name, you find, but a form of address to the ordinary men of early New England colonies. And *Brown* is a common name among the English and their American descendants. Thus, from the title alone, you have learned that the chief character is an ordinary young man, not individualized even by a full name. Thus, you can infer that young Goodman Brown is meant to represent man in general.

The title, also, as mentioned, indicates the setting of early New England. In the early paragraphs, calling Salem a village also indicates time past as well as a specific place. And the terms *tarry, prithee,* and *afeard* all help to set the scene in early days.

You notice that the wife's name is Faith, which of course is a feminine name but is also the name of a quality. This, you recognize, is the first of the ambiguities in the story (unless, of course, there is some doubt about the *good* in Goodman). You see it played upon when Brown tardily meets the man in the forest and says, "Faith kept me back a while."

Within a few lines you have three possible subtopics: first, the universality of the characters; second, the setting; third, the ambiguity of the characters. Careful reading will reveal to you many items under these headings and many other possible headings. Once you classify these bits of information, you will probably have more subtopic ideas than you need, so you will choose the best to form your subtopics and use the others to support them. Some, of course, you will discard. Those selected for subtopics will provide the organizational framework for the body of your essay.

Conclusion

The conclusion of your essay about literature follows the same pattern as the conclusion to any other essay. You may summarize your main points and restate your thesis. Here, also, an apt quotation or a pertinent anecdote often works well.

In writing a possible conclusion for the suggested interpretation of "I See You Never," you might say:

> Almost plotless and with characters so little familiar that we don't even know their first names, this simple story nevertheless conveys a great theme: man's enemy is ignorance. The social forces that exile Mr. Ramirez are destructive only to those who don't know enough to work within those forces. His cry of human loneliness, "I see you never," pertains to more than just Mrs. O'Brian. He cannot "see" his world at all. Mr. Ramirez is one of the good little people who, through ignorance, are crushed by social forces which are not evil in themselves.

Pitfalls to Avoid

1. Don't forget to mention the full title and full name of the author early in your essay. Do not start out with "This story. . ." or "I really love this book."
2. Do not retell the story; you are writing a critical paper, not a book report. In writing a critical essay, you need to show not just what happens, but the significance of what happens.
3. Narrow your topic carefully. Do not try to write on too broad a subject or on too many aspects of a work.
4. Do not use the works of critics without giving credit. This is plagiarism, which is a crime.
5. Do not pretend to more knowledge than you have. Write simply and honestly.
6. Do not state the obvious. "Mark Twain was a great American humorist."
7. Don't just patch together long quotations from various critical works. You need to do your own thinking and provide your own interpretation of the work. But make sure you understand the story before you trust your own interpretation.
8. Don't fail to cite specific evidence from the story that will make your interpretations clear and convincing.

The following passage from Lionel Trilling's "Of This Time, Of That Place" illustrates a situation in which the student clearly does not understand the work he has written about:

> There was a silence between them. Both dropped their eyes to the blue-book on the desk. On its cover Howe had pencilled: "F. This is very poor work."

287

writing
about literature

Howe picked up the blue-book. There was always the possibility of injustice. The teacher may be bored by the mass of papers and not wholly attentive. A phrase, even the student's handwriting, may irritate him unreasonably. "Well," said Howe, "let's go through it."

He opened the first page. "Now here: you write, 'In "The Ancient Mariner," Coleridge lives in and transports us to a honey-sweet world where all is rich and strange, a world of charm to which we can escape from the humdrum existence of our daily lives, the world of romance. Here, in this warm and honey-sweet land of charming dreams we can relax and enjoy ourselves.'"

Howe lowered the paper and waited with a neutral look for Blackburn to speak. Blackburn returned the look boldly, did not speak, sat stolid and lofty. At last Howe said, speaking gently, "Did you mean that, or were you just at a loss for something to say?"

"You imply that I was just 'bluffing'?" The quotation marks hung palpable in the air about the word.

"I'd like to know. I'd prefer believing that you were bluffing to believing that you really thought this."

Blackburn's eyebrows went up. From the height of a great and firm-based idea he looked at his teacher. He clasped the crags for a moment and then pounced, craftily, suavely. "Do you mean, Dr. Howe, that there aren't two opinions possible?"

It was superbly done in its air of putting all of Howe's intellectual life into the balance. Howe remained patient and simple. "Yes, many opinions are possible, but not this one. Whatever anyone believes of 'The Ancient Mariner,' no one can in reason believe that it represents a—a honey-sweet world in which we can relax."

"But that is what I **feel**, sir."

This was well done too. Howe said, "Look, Mr. Blackburn. Do you really relax with hunger and thirst, the heat and the sea-serpents, the dead men with staring eyes, Life in Death and the skeletons? Come now, Mr. Blackburn."

TECHNIQUES OF CLEAR WRITING

The Historical Present Tense

Writing about literature will involve you in using the historical present tense. You use the historical present now whenever you narrate events that happened in the past as though they were happening in the present. For instance, you might write:

Mr. Pumpernickle **jerks** open the door and **shouts,** "Down with Democrats!"

Correct use of the historical present lends a sense of immediacy and action to such writing. Using the historical present for narratives is a stylistic choice available to you, but be sure to stay in the tense if you do choose it. Don't shift inconsistently from the historical present to the past. Avoid mistakes like this:

Mr. Pumpernickle **jerks** open the door and **shouted,** "Down with Democrats!"

Two special circumstances require the historical present. First, it is the right form for expressing universal truths:

Aging is a reality that no one escapes.

Second, when you write about literature, using the historical present permits you to convey the idea that although the work you are discussing was written in the past, the effect and meaning of the words—what they say—exists in the present.

In writing about literature, using both past and historical present tenses lets you make a distinction between what an author has done and what his or her words convey. In other words, the events of the writer's life are in the past, but the words he or she produced still exist and speak. For instance, you might say:

Shakespeare **wrote** many of his sonnets before 1598 and **published** at least part of them by 1609. They **are** among the world's greatest love poems. In them, he **expresses** his belief that literature **exists** far beyond the lifetime of the writer. One sonnet **ends** with the lines:
So long as man can breathe or eyes can see,
So long lives this [poem] . . .

Figurative Language

As you have gone through this book, you have learned that writing that communicates clearly is frequently the result of choices. You choose a topic; then you choose an attitude toward it; then you choose what method will best develop it. When you are writing sentences, you choose among different structures to make sure that the relationships among your ideas are clear. But when you come to selecting individual words and phrases, you have a vast range of choices.

Ford Madox Ford tells how he and Joseph Conrad practiced choosing the right word. Both were novelists who are considered among the great craftsmen of literature. Friends, they spent much time together testing their skills in choosing words. Driving along a country road, for instance, they would challenge each other to choose words to best describe a meadow they were passing. Or, stopping in a country inn, they would test themselves on words that would best convey the atmosphere of the place or the appearance and personality of the landlord. So, you see, even for professional writers, the choice of words takes discrimination— you must choose those words that express exactly what you mean.

The sum total of your choices becomes your style and your style reveals you. Goethe, the great German writer, said, "We should try to use words that correspond as closely as possible with what we feel, see, think, imagine, experience, and reason."

You have already studied word choice under several headings: the specific word and the general word; the concrete word and the abstract word; the denotative word and the connotative word. Still another consideration in effective choice of words is that between literal language and figurative language.

Literal language points to very definite objects or actions or ideas, like a football, or kicking a football, or football strategy. It is concerned chiefly with facts which are stated as plainly and precisely as possible. At its most precise, literal language becomes scientific language. For example, the literal statement that

"Man is an animal who reasons" could be expanded to a biological definition such as: "Man is a biped mammal characterized by his erect posture, his plantigrade foot which permits such posture, a perfectly opposable thumb, scarcity of hair, and, above all, a large cranial cavity which permits the development of a large brain, and, so, of large intellectual capacity."

Figurative language is the opposite of literal; it is imaginative. It is closely allied to connotative language because, like connotation, it has emotional overtones. Figurative language usually depends on the extended rather than the primary meaning. All words have a primary meaning; many words go beyond that first meaning to meanings suggested by it. For example, the primary meaning of green denotes a specific range of color, but its extended meanings refer to things that are green, like a golf course, or money, which, in slang, is sometimes called the "long green." But extended meanings go even beyond that. At a horse show you might hear about a "green horse." Or your grandfather might say about your brother (never about you), "That boy certainly is green." Obviously, neither the horse nor your brother is literally green. What is meant is that both the horse and the boy are inexperienced. How did a color come to express a condition like "inexperienced"?

Language expands through associations. Green is the color associated with spring. After the drab browns and blacks of winter, or the white of its snows, the first sign of spring is the world turning green again. Spring is associated with youth because spring is a new beginning. Youth, of course, does not have the experience of age. Language skips over some of the steps of the associative process and dubs the inexperienced horse and boy "green." (Even that last sentence, though attempting literal definition, uses figurative speech in saying that language "skips" and "dubs.")

You can see language working figuratively throughout literature. In Shakespeare's *Antony and Cleopatra,* the lovers tease each other, sometimes so

Cleopatra's Salad Days

much that one or the other grows bad-tempered. Antony, cross with Cleopatra, twits her about Julius Caesar, who had earlier been her lover. Cleopatra, to reassure Antony, replies, "Those were my salad days, when I was green in judgment." Had she been speaking literally, she would have said something like "Those days with Caesar happened when I was too inexperienced to have the good judgment to wait for you." The term *salad days* has come to mean the times of early maturity, springtime, when the lettuce and other salad greens come up. Later the term picked up another implication. Since youth, when it is looked back to, suggests a carefree happiness, *salad days* implies the good old days.

Language can be almost endlessly extended by association. A poem of Robert Frost's begins "Nature's first green is gold." Again, we associate green with spring and more precisely with the first greening of the trees. But in no literal sense is green gold. The literal statement would be something like this: "The first color that shows on the trees in spring is a yellowish green." That literal statement is not only longer, but it leaves out the suggestion that the turning of the color is both universal and good.

FIGURES OF SPEECH

In addition to having emotional overtones, extended meanings, and suggested associations, figurative language is characterized by its dependence on *figures of speech*. Figures of speech are expressions made up of words used not in their literal sense but to make a forceful and dramatic image. Scholars say that in classical and medieval times students had to learn as many as 250 figures of speech. Modern students need to be familiar with only a handful of the most common.

Antithesis

Antithesis is a figure of speech in which two ideas are contrasted through parallelism. To emphasize the contrast, one idea is balanced against its opposite, with each term in similar grammatical form. For example, "You're wrong, I'm right." or "Man proposes, God disposes." A thesis (the same concept as a thesis statement) is stated and an anti- or opposing thesis is made against it.

Hyperbole

Hyperbole is a figure of speech based on exaggeration. You use it frequently in ordinary conversation: "I'm starved" or "He's a real nut" or "I'll die if he doesn't give me an A on this paper." Such statements are not made to deceive but to emphasize. This is also true of literary hyperbole. In order to emphasize his faithfulness to the girl like the red, red rose, Robert Burns exaggerated:

> And I will luve thee still, my dear,
> Till a' the seas gang dry.
> Till a' the seas gang dry, my dear,
> And the rocks melt wi' the sun.

Samuel Hoffenstein, a comic poet, uses both hyperbole and antithesis in this little verse:

> When I took you for my own,
> You stood 'mong women all alone.

When I let the magic go,
You stood with women in a row.

In literal language, he is saying that when he loved her, she was to him the most important of women; when he no longer loved her, she was just like all other women. Both are exaggerations. In addition, the last two lines are an antithesis to the first two.

How you've changed.

Personification

Personification is a figure of speech which gives human characteristics to non-human things. This, too, you use in everyday speech. You might say of your car on a winter morning: "She's cranky today. She's always hard to get along with on cold days." On a more literary level, John Donne personified death when he wrote, "Death, be not proud." (This line also includes the figure of speech known as *apostrophe*, in which the nonhuman entity or an absent person is spoken to directly.)

Here is a verse by John Hay in which good and bad luck are personified as women. After identifying good and bad luck as women, Hay discusses them totally as if they **were** women.

Identification of good luck as a "gay girl"

Characteristics of the gay girl

Good luck is the gayest of all gay girls.
Long in one place she will not stay,
Back from your brow she strokes the curls,
Kisses you quick and flies away.

Identification of bad luck as a sober-sided matron

Her characteristics

But Madame Bad Luck soberly comes
And stays—no fancy has she for flitting—
Snatches of true-love songs she hums,
And sits by your bed, and brings her knitting.

John Hay

Metonymy

Metonymy is a figure of speech in which a part of the thing meant or something closely related to it stands for the thing itself. Metonymy is frequently used in everyday speech. You might refer to a king as "the crown" and to the king's power as the "scepter." King Richard I often called himself "England" because he so closely associated himself with his country. But he is called by history "the Lionhearted" in a metonymy for the courage of a lion, for normal courage is sometimes called "heart" ("He has no heart for a fight") and extraordinary courage is "lionhearted."

The part chosen to represent the whole must be an important part. You might refer to your car as your wheels, but if you wished to be understood, you would scarcely refer to it as your gas cap. Likewise, because of all the marching they must do, infantry are referred to as "foot" soldiers. It is a metonymy of an important part when the captain of a ship commands, "All hands on deck." He expects the entire sailor to show up, but he calls him a hand because of the amount of manual labor the sailor must do. The same principle is applied in "field hands." By focusing attention on an important part or function, the writer gains emphasis and vividness.

Metaphor

Metaphor is the most important of the figures of speech. Indeed, most of the others are really just subdivisions of metaphor. Metaphor is based on comparison, not literal but imaginative. The word itself means "transfer," the transfer of one kind of meaning to another through comparison. To say that language is metaphoric is almost identical with saying that it is imaginative. The comparisons made by metaphor are essential to any satisfactory handling of language. (Notice that the phrase *handling of language* is a metaphor.) Without metaphor, the users of language could denote only those things that were present with them in time and space. All abstraction rests on metaphor. In fact, every word has a metaphorical root. (Notice that *root* in that sentence is a metaphor.)

Metaphor uses nonliteral comparison to describe and identify one thing in the terms of another. Such describing and identifying is basic to the growth of language, but, even more important, it is basic to understanding. You use metaphor because you can't escape it, but also because, when you use it sucessfully, it is a swift and vivid way to convey understanding.

Sometimes metaphor is broken down into *simile* and *metaphor* for the sake of analysis. Simile uses *like, as,* and *than* to make explicit comparisons. Simile says that *A* is like *B,* as in the following quotation:

> As the flight of a river
> That flows to the sea,
> My soul rushes ever
> In tumult to thee.

Use of Others' Writings

Before you make use of the writings of other people, you must learn the accepted ways of summarizing, paraphrasing, and quoting. These techniques allow you to include the writings of others in your essays without committing the crime of plagiarism. In all of these, you give credit to the original writer by footnote, parentheses, or reference.

Before beginning to write any of these, however, you must first make sure that you understand exactly what the author means. Read the passage as many times as is necessary to feel confident that you know the author's purpose and tone as well as his or her meaning. Once you have a clear idea of the meaning, you must decide which of the devices you wish to use: the summary, the paraphrase, or the quotation.

THE SUMMARY

The use of the summary is not new to you. You used it in high school when you wrote a book review; you used it when you told your friend the plot of a book you read or a movie or a TV program you watched. You probably have used the summary to answer essay questions. The summary is a brief recounting given in your own words. It is usually less than one half as long as the original work, and it follows the same order as the original and includes its major points, major supporting detail, any key facts, and examples.

THE PARAPHRASE

A paraphrase is a restatement, in your own words, of what someone else has written. The paraphrase may be shorter than the original, or it may be as long as or longer than the original, for the purpose here is not so much to condense, as is the case with the summary, but to retell the work in your own words and your own style. Paraphrase allows the writer to concentrate on only one part of the original work or to shift the point of emphasis in the original. However, paraphrase only what the author says, not what you think he or she is implying.

You may, if you wish, quote key words or phrases if they seem better than anything you can come up with. However, the quotations should be clearly marked as such and should be blended into your writing so that the sentences are not choppy. Again, you must have a clear understanding of what the original author is saying, and you must completely reword what he or she writes. Changing the order of the words, changing direct quotation to indirect quotation, or moving a few phrases around is not paraphrasing—it's plagiarizing.

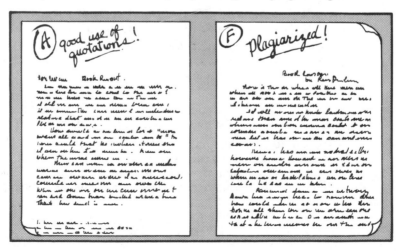

THE QUOTATION

A direct quotation is the use of another's writing exactly as it was written, word for word. You may use a phrase, a clause, a sentence, or even a group of sentences and put it in your paper verbatim. The quotation should be used primarily if the material is written brilliantly, or if the material is controversial or unknown. Otherwise, the paraphrase is usually better, as it is in your style and the writing remains smoother. However, the careful use of quotations can enhance your writing and provide excellent support for your thesis. Generally, phrases, sentences, and short passages are preferable to long passages. **All quotations must be introduced.** Long quotations from various authors strung together with little of your own introductions and comments make for choppy and generally unclear writing. Quotation is not a substitute for your thought and your words. Some instructors restrict the use of quotations to no more than 20 percent of your paper.

Techniques of Quoting

The quotations that you use (a few words or part of a sentence) must fit with the rest of the sentence; that is, the sentence must make sense. A sentence such as

Knowledge, at that time, was not considered essential "could make them discontented with the lot which God had appointed for them."

is unclear and will confuse the reader. To make the meaning clear, the sentence should be changed to

During the Middle Ages, the lower classes were not encouraged to learn because it "could make them discontented with the lot which God had appointed for them."

The Long Quotation

Any quotation of three lines or more is indented five spaces and single-spaced. No quotation marks are necessary; the indentation and single-spacing show that it is a direct quotation.

With all quotations, and especially long ones, you must make clear to the reader the relationship between the quotation and the point you are making. This is usually done in your introduction to the quotation. If, for example, you are attempting to prove that the work you were discussing was, contrary to popular opinion, a tragedy, you might write:

This work is a tragedy because it has the classical properties of a tragedy. John Dryden defined the qualities of tragedy in a 1679 essay:

It ought to be great, and to consist of great persons, to distinguish it from comedy, where the action is trivial and the persons of inferior rank ... it ought to be probable, as well as admirable and great ... the end or scope of tragedy ... is, to rectify or purge our passions, fear and pity.[1]

Then you would show that the work has all of these qualities.

Notice that in the text of the paper the writer has given credit to the author.

Mentioning the author immediately before using his or her ideas or words is useful in showing where your idea (or someone else's ideas) ends and this author's begins.

DOCUMEN-
TATION
You may document (give credit to your sources) either formally or informally. If you are writing formally (a research paper, a thesis or dissertation), or if you are using many sources, you should use formal documentation. In a theme based on a single work, you may use informal documentation. Your instructor will usually tell you what type of documentation is required.

Formal Documentation

Formal documentation requires footnotes. A superscript number in your text following the ideas or words of the writer you are using lets the reader know that the material comes from a source other than your brain. The reader can then look at the footnote to see where the material came from originally.

The first footnote for any work should include the following information (if appropriate) in this order:

> The footnote number that corresponds with the superscript number in your text.
> Author's first and last name, followed by a comma.
> The title of the story, poem, or article enclosed in quotation marks if it is a separate part of but not the whole work.
> The name of the book, magazine, or newspaper (the whole work) under-lined.
> The edition if given.
> The place of publication (the city) followed by a colon.
> The name of the publisher followed by a comma.
> The date of publication. The above three, place of publication, publisher, and date of publication, are enclosed in parentheses and followed by a comma.
> The name or names of the editor followed by ed. or eds.
> The page number or numbers; use a p. for a single page and pp. for two or more pages.
> When quoting poetry, you include line numbers.

For example, if you were using material from this book, the first footnote would read:

[1]Robert B. Donald et al., *Writing Clear Essays* (Englewood Cliffs, N.J.: Prentice-Hall, Inc., 1982) p. 106.

Or the first footnote for "Young Goodman Brown" could read:

[2]Nathaniel Hawthorne, "Young Goodman Brown," *Story and Structure,* 2nd ed., Laurence Perrine, ed. (New York: Harcourt, Brace & World, Inc., 1966), pp. 498–99

295

In your footnote include only information not given in the text of your essay. If you identify the author within your essay, then start your footnote with the name of the work. If you name both the author and the work within the text, your footnote needs to contain only the information not already given.

In Hawthorne's short story "Young Goodman Brown," the hero hears "a scream drowned immediately in a louder murmur of voices fading into far-off laughter...."[3]

[3]*Story and Structure,* 2nd ed., Laurence Perrine ed. (New York: Harcourt, Brace & World, Inc., 1966) p. 503.

Only the first footnote for each work must be so detailed. Subsequent footnotes need only identify the work. For example, the second footnote for the above works could be shortened to

[4]*Writing Clear Essays,* p. 109.
[5]Hawthorne, p. 495.

For more specialized footnotes, see any English handbook, the *MLA Style Sheet,* or your instructor.

Footnotes are numbered consecutively throughout the paper and are usually placed at the bottom of the page where the material is used. They may also be placed at the end of the paper. Footnotes may also be put in the text in parentheses immediately following the material used. Your instructor will tell you which placement to use.

Informal Documentation

Informal documentation is used when you are writing about only one literary work and using only one source. You identify your source in a single footnote, and thereafter you include the necessary information (usually just the page number) in parentheses in the text of your essay.

For example:

The change in Goodman Brown's attitude toward the townspeople was evident. "He shrank from the venerable saint, as if to avoid an anathema...." (507) He "looked sternly and sadly into [his wife's] face, and passed on without a greeting." (508)

DISCUSSION ACTIVITY: PARAPHRASING

Suppose two students are paraphrasing on notecards the following passage. Discuss the errors in and merits of each paraphrase.

PASSAGE TO BE PARAPHRASED

A literary symbol means itself plus more. It stands for what it is and other things that it brings to mind. The flag is a symbol; it stands for a flag plus all the feelings of patriotism, honor, bravery, freedom, and love of country that the flag may bring to mind. Other symbols such as the cross, the swastika, the

Statue of Liberty, and the skull and crossbones evoke their own connotations. In any given story, however, the symbol could take on a different meaning. Certain literary symbols have been used so often that they are almost standardized:

journey = life
spring, summer, fall = youth, adulthood, old age
    morning, afternoon, night = youth, adulthood, old age
crossing a bridge = changing your life
water = purification, life-giving force
light = good, hope, civilization
dark = evil, despair, primitiveness
star = hope

Other symbols have unique meanings; they have a special meaning only in the story in which they appear. The raft, for example, in *Adventures of Huckleberry Finn* represents a kind of Eden, a Paradise, but the raft is not a universal symbol. In other stories, it might represent danger or impermanence, or something else, or nothing else.

PARAPHRASE A

If something means itself plus something else, it is a literary symbol. It stands for what it is and other things that it brings to mind. A military uniform, for example, means a uniform plus all the feelings a uniform brings forth—feelings of patriotism, and bravery, and honor. The same is true of many things, like a skull and crossbones, which makes you think of poison or pirates. Light usually means good things, and dark means bad things, but symbols don't always mean the same things. Sometimes a raft might mean good, but sometimes it might mean evil.

PARAPHRASE B

"A literary symbol means itself plus more."[1] There are two types of literary symbols; one type of symbol has a traditional meaning because it has been used so often: light, for example, has come to symbolize hope or civilization or goodness, while dark represents the opposite. Seasons and times of day have come to be recognized as also representing ages of man. Feelings of patriotism are often evoked by the flag, and other symbols evoke other emotions. Sometimes "symbols are unique; they have a meaning only in the story in which they appear;"[2] in the *Adventures of Huckleberry Finn,* for example, Twain uses a raft as a symbol of Paradise, or it may mean the opposite. Or it may mean just a raft, having no symbolic meaning at all.

EXERCISE Xa: PARAPHRASING
Paraphrase the following paragraphs.

There are no easy rules for literary judgment. Such judgment depends ultimately on our perceptivity, intelligence, and experience; it is a product of how much and how alertly we have lived and how much and how well we have read. Yet at least two basic principles may be set up. First, every story is to be initially judged by how fully it achieves its central purpose. Each element in the story is to be judged by the effectiveness of its contribution to the central purpose. In a good story every element works with every other element for the accomplishment of this central purpose. It follows that no element in the story may be judged in isolation.

Once a story has been judged successful in achieving its central purpose, we may apply a second principle of judgment. A story, if successful, may be judged by the significance of its purpose. . . . If a story's only aim is to entertain, whether by mystifying, surprising, thrilling, provoking to laughter or tears, or furnishing a substitute dream life, we may judge it of less value than a story whose aim is to **reveal.** When a story does provide some revelation—does make some serious statement about life—we may measure it by the breadth and depth of the revelation.

Some stories, then, provide good fun and innocent merriment. Others afford the good reader a deeper enjoyment through the insights they give into life. A third type, like many of the soap operas of television and radio, offer a cheaper and less innocent pleasure by providing escape under the guise of interpretation. Such stories, while professing to present real-life situations and everyday people and happenings, actually, by their shallowness of characterization, their falsifications of plot, their use of stock themes and stock emotions, present us with dangerous oversimplifications and distortions. They seriously misrepresent life and are harmful to the extent that they keep us from a more sensitive, more discriminating response to experience.

Laurence Perrine, Story and Structure

WORD POWER

There are various terms you need to know when discussing literature.

ALLEGORY

Allegory is a form of fiction in which the characters and actions represent abstractions, like Knowledge, Good Deeds, Beauty, Power. The characters and their actions are less important than the political, religious, and moral ideas they stand for. The surface story is just a way to discuss the ideas underlying it.

In an allegory, the characters and incidents are clearly related to the underlying but more important story in a clear-cut and definite relationship. Often the character of Everyman stands for all men. In the most famous of allegories, John Bunyan's *Pilgrim's Progress*, characters such as Christian, Faithful, the Giant Despair, and Mr. Worldly Wiseman represent religious ideas.

ALLUSION

An allusion is a reference to some person or event in history or literature with which the reader is presumed to be familiar. When employed by a skillful writer, an allusion—whether to Hiroshima, Adolph Hitler, or Jesus of Nazareth—can bring into play a whole set of ideas and emotional responses without the author's having made a direct statement about people or events of the past. Much of the work of such modern authors as James Joyce and T. S. Eliot is impossible to understand without some knowledge of the classical allusions.

The title of William Faulkner's novel *The Sound and the Fury,* in which the first section is told by an idiot, is an allusion to these lines from Macbeth:

It is a tale told by an idiot, full of sound and fury, signifying nothing.

AMBIGUITY   Ambiguity refers to the possibility that an object, action, or situation may be subject to more than one interpretation. It is an artistic device used deliberately to enrich the work by suggesting that multiple meanings can be drawn from a single detail. For example, a character may be impelled by contrary impulses, such as ruthless pursuit of power and genuine love for his friends; thus his every move up the ladder is open to contrary interpretations.

In expository writing, where your aim is clear communication, ambiguity is a fault; it simply means vagueness. In literature, however, ambiguity, because it permits more than one interpretation, reflects the richness of human experience. It also reflects the difficulty of perceiving the significance of experience.

ATMOSPHERE   Atmosphere is a general term used to describe the combined effects of setting, tone, and mood. It is the feeling created by the work as a whole. In Edgar Allan Poe's "The Fall of the House of Usher," for instance, the atmosphere is established in the very first sentence:

During the whole of a dull, dark, and soundless day in the autumn of the year, when the clouds hung oppressively low in the heavens, I had been passing, alone, on horseback, through a singularly dreary country, and at length found myself, as the shades of the evening drew on, within view of the melancholy House of Usher.

The author's tone, his attitude toward his subject, also contributes to the atmosphere. Whether he is distant and contemptuous or close and sympathetic, his attitude affects our feeling about his work. Then, too, a skillful writer may establish a mood of wild frenzy, quiet resignation, or romantic moonglow; the sound of the words themselves can powerfully influence the atmosphere.

CATHARSIS   Catharsis is a term associated with tragedy and its effect upon the audience. Through emotional participation in the pity and fear of tragedy, the reader or viewer experiences a purifying or cleansing of the emotions—if not a spiritual renewal, at least relief from anxiety and tension.

COMEDY   One curious feature of comedy is that every attempt to define it turns out to be singularly unfunny. Socrates is said to have put the comic poet Aristophanes to sleep with a lecture on the comic spirit, and modern scholars have written volumes in an attempt to explain what comedy is, so any brief definition is almost certain to prove inadequate. In the traditional sense, comedy implies a situation in which people's fortunes turn from bad to good; they get either what they deserve or better than they deserve. However, in a broader sense, there is no universally accepted set of characteristics which mark the boundaries of comedy, except that it ends well for the protagonist. For example, the New Testament is a comedy. If it ended with the crucifixion, it would, of course, be a tragedy. Much of modern comedy, however, deals with the futility and absurdity of life; thus it could be said that it springs from tragic roots. The distinction between comedy and tragedy which will serve well in most instances is that comedy deals with the light rather than the dark, that it offers an optimistic outlook in the face of folly, absurdity, and death.

299

DEUS EX MACHINA   As originally applied to Greek drama, *deus ex machina* meant the timely intervention of a god who was suddenly lowered onto the stage to resolve the insolvable problems of the human characters. Today, the term is applied to any trick or improbable coincidence used by an author to untangle the difficulties of the novel or story and provide a neat conclusion. In a second-rate romantic novel, for example, you might have the pirate hero snatched from the gallows by the king's pardon or a sudden declaration of war.

FABLE   A fable is a brief tale which carries some sort of moral or cautionary point. The most common form is the beast fable, in which animals talk and act like people, as in Aesop's Fables or the Uncle Remus stories of Joel Chandler Harris. James Thurber uses animal fables for his satires on religion, politics, and human relationships in *Fables for Our Time.*

FARCE   Farce is a type of low comedy marked by improbable characters and actions. The typical farce is a short, loosely structured play designed to amuse with nonsensical antics of one-dimensional characters.

GENRE   In its most commonly accepted meaning, genre refers to the particular form or category to which a literary composition belongs, such as novel, short story, epic, elegy, sonnet, ode, and so on.

IMAGERY   Imagery is the creation in words of some sensory experience. It is usually visual, but it can be an experience of any of the other senses; sometimes it is more than one. For example, the line "the little dog laughed" creates a picture and also a sound.

　　　　The purpose of imagery is to describe and illustrate, but usually the description implies some meaning, suggests some emotion. When you wrote your descriptive essay, you aimed at creating images—helping your readers see what you saw—but you also wanted them to feel what you felt, your implied meaning.

　　　　In the following poem Samuel Allen describes the great baseball pitcher, "Satch" Paige. Paige played for over twenty years on black teams before he went into the big leagues, and there he played until he was almost fifty years old. It seemed as if he would go on forever.

> To Satch
> Sometimes I feel like I will never stop
> Just go on forever
> Til one fine mornin'
> I'm gonna reach up and grab me a handfulla stars
> Throw out my long lean leg
> And whip three hot strikes burnin' down the heavens
> And look over at God and say
> How about that!

This little verse creates, first, an image of a pitcher winding up and then a second image of Satch's almost gloating satisfaction as he delivers three strikes in heaven.

300

Read the following poem to note how the poet moves back and forth from straightforward language to imagery in order to emphasize his theme that, even in small things, there are great meanings.

The Death of a Toad
A toad the power mower caught,
Chewed and clipped of a leg, with a hobbling hop has got
To the garden verge, and sanctuaried him
Under the cineraria leaves, in the shade
Of the ashen heartshaped leaves, in a dim,
Low, and a final glade.

The rare original heartsblood goes,
Spends on the earthen hide, in the folds and wizenings, flows
In the gutters of the banked and staring eyes. He lies
As still as if he would return to stone,
And soundlessly attending, dies
Toward some deep monotone,

Toward misted and ebullient seas
And cooling shores, toward lost Amphibia's emperies.
Day dwindles, drowning, and at length is gone
In the wide and antique eyes, which still appear
To watch, across the castrate lawn,
The haggard daylight steer.

Richard Wilbur

Read the following essay to see how the student writer narrows her discussion to the poet's use of imagery in support of his theme.

Imagery in "The Death of a Toad"

Complete title and full name of author given. Evidence cited from poem to contrast denotative language about the machine with connotative images about the toad's death.

"The Death of a Toad" by Richard Wilbur relies heavily for its effectiveness upon its imagery. The poem begins with blunt, specific, unconnotative language; the power mower "chewed and clipped" the toad's leg. The despair and helplessness of the toad is heightened by his retreat in a "hobbling hop" to the only place he knows protection—his "sanctuary" of "ashen, heartshaped" leaves, where actually he is afforded no protection at all, not even from death. The choice of "ashen" and "heartshaped" are again specific terms of description, but these have connotative overtones of death and compassion. The image of a "dim and final glade" begins a continuing image of the failing of light and sight as a metaphor for the failing life. Blood flows into his eyes, the seas are "misted," "day dwindles and is gone," the daylight grows "haggard."

Further citing of source to support student's interpretation.

Wilbur refers to the "earthen hide" on which the "rare, original heartsblood goes" to show the baseness and importance of this creature. The toad is one of the few creatures existing in its unaltered genetic form today, and it still performs its rudimentary functions of a toad of a million years ago. Wilbur reinforces this view of the primitiveness of the toad by stating that "he lies as still as if he would return to stone," suggesting that the toad cannot regress further into evolution without becoming nonexistent.

Student's analysis of poet's tone by quoting pertinent images.

Wilbur's lament for the loss of the toad is obvious in the last stanza. He refers to the toad's domain as "Amphibia's emperies," suggesting the greatness and power this primitive animal has over his territory, the now "castrate" lawn—"castrate" because it has lost one of the basic elements for its survival, the toad.

Erin Duffy

IRONY

In essence, irony is saying one thing and meaning something else. Suppose that you stay out late and have to get up early, but in the morning, feeling half dead, you say, "Oh, I feel great." Then you are using simple irony. Irony can also be shown through a discrepancy or gap between what one says and what one does, between what a character is and what he or she professes to be, or between what a character expects and the true outcome of events. In Shakespeare's Macbeth the central irony is that Macbeth thinks that by killing Duncan, the king, he will gain power, prestige, and a life of ease; but he gains only sleepless nights of torment until he finally goes to meet his death. In a soap opera, on the other hand, you might have a slick con artist who snares a wealthy widow, only to find out afterward that the widow is bankrupt but believes that he is rich.

MELODRAMA

The term *melodrama* is applied to a dramatic presentation heavily marked by the use of sentiment and sensationalism. Its heroes and villains lack complexity, and the conflict between good and evil is oversimplified; you have only the "good guys" and the "bad guys." The evil characters always get their comeuppance, and a happy ending is predictable. You have a melodramatic situation when, for instance, the mean cattle baron drives the noble Indians from the land of their fore-fathers. If he ends up with an arrow through his middle, so much the better—especially if it is the chief's rebellious but beautiful daughter who lets fly.

Whenever you have the sun suddenly breaking through the dark clouds as the lovers kiss, see the hero being snatched from certain death at the final moment, or find the heroine miraculously escaping the clutches of some fiend, you can be sure that you are in the midst of melodrama.

MOTIF

In literature, *motif* is the term applied to a recurring idea or situation. Just as a few bars may recur from time to time throughout a musical composition, a certain idea or situation may keep recurring in different ways throughout a literary work. The motif may take such forms as a recurring lament for the past, repeated expressions of the joy of life, a wistful longing for a different world, or a merry-go-round of futile activity, but it usually bears some relationship to the dominant theme of the work.

MYTH

A myth is a traditional story of unknown authorship, originally passed on by word of mouth. Typically, myths deal with the heroes, gods, and rituals of a preliterate society. Although once accepted as fact, such stories are now regarded as the fictions of earlier societies. The Greeks and the Norse have provided us with an especially rich collection of myths peopled with monsters, giants, supernatural beings, and ancestral heroes. In a more general sense, but not in the literary sense, the word *myth* is applied to any of the fictions or half-truths that make up the common beliefs of a society: the myth of Hitler's invincibility perished in the Battle of Stalingrad.

REALISM

Realism concerns both the subject of a piece of writing, usually fiction, and the author's attitude toward the subject. The subject of *realism* is **real,** or actual, life as it is lived by ordinary people in an observable world. The realist, being a believer in

302

the value of the common man, focuses on average and everyday events in the lives of ordinary people. These people are not idealized or sentimentalized but are credible human beings attempting to cope with workaday conflicts and emotions.

ROMANTICISM   On the other hand, romanticism tends to place its stories in the faraway and long ago. The romantic writer tends to look at the world through glasses tinted rose by sentimental feelings. His characters yearn upward toward ideal. In the novel, the romantic writer is usually more interested in the hero's adventures than in his character. For the reader romanticism frequently means an escape from life rather than an interpretation of it.

SARCASM   The word *sarcasm* comes from the Green *sarkazein,* meaning "to tear flesh." As its origin suggests, sarcasm consists of biting language or cutting remarks. Thomas Dewey may have lost his bid for the U.S. presidency in 1948 partly because Dorothy Parker said that he looked like the groom on a wedding cake.

SATIRE   Although satire frequently makes use of irony, sarcasm, and caricature, it has a serious underlying purpose: reform. By holding up to ridicule or poking fun at the folly and vice of people and their institutions, satire makes its attack indirectly. For example, instead of telling us that some congressmen are less than honest, a satirist might show us a Bible-quoting congressman swilling liquor on a luxurious yacht provided through the generosity of defense contractors. Satire comes in many shades, from gentle humor to scathing ridicule and contempt.

STREAM OF CONSCIOUS-NESS   The term *stream of consciousness* refers to a technique of fiction in which the writer attempts to capture thoughts as they flow through the mind of a character. In attempting to set forth the thoughts of the character, the writer tries to get closer to the inner reality of ideas and sensations which pass through the mind in a stream of bits and pieces. Conventional sentence structure and punctuation are abandoned in an effort to convey immediate sensations and impressions. The best-known example of the technique is found in James Joyce's *Ulysses.*

TRAGEDY   According to the definition laid down by Aristotle in his *Poetics* (c. 350 B.C.), tragedy involves much more than mere coincidence or a change of fortune from good to bad. Tragedy, Aristotle insists, must inspire pity and fear: "pity . . . aroused by unmerited misfortune, fear by the misfortune of a man like ourselves." The misfortune must be "that of a man who is not eminently good and just, yet whose misfortune is brought about not by vice or depravity, but by some error or frailty." Classical tragedy typically involves a representative person who but acts out of ignorance, only to recognize afterward the tragic error he or she has committed. Neither indifferent nor vicious, the person commits a tragic error out of some weakness or frailty of character, known as "the tragic flaw." Thus, Oedipus, spared by fate from death in infancy, grows to manhood ignorant of his true parentage. He kills his father in a rash quarrel and then marries his own mother. Not until years later does he discover the horror of what he has done.

303

Aristotle's definition of tragedy has been altered quite drastically over the centuries so that today tragedy is often more loosely defined as a human struggle which ends disastrously. However, there can be no tragedy without some exercise of free will and some sort of recognition or tragic knowledge. In Arthur Miller's play *Death of a Salesman*, Willie Loman, the salesman, kills himself after he finally comes to recognize the lies and contradictions of his life.

NOTE: The term *tragicomedy* is used to describe dramas in which the action seems to be moving toward a tragic end but which manages to switch direction and does end happily.

CHAPTER XI

the essay test

The essay test is probably the most misunderstood examination in education. It asks only to be treated with the same respect given to other tests, but instead it is subjected to unmerciful abuse from terrified students who look upon an essay exam as a fate worse than death: "Oh God, I'll just die if he gives essay tests. I'll flunk this course for sure." Unfortunately, statements like this generate immediate anxiety. Pretty soon, the student is accompanied by a chorus of moans and groans from panic-stricken classmates. If these students would only stop to think, they would realize that there is absolutely no need to panic.

When you are answering an essay question, you are simply repeating a process that you are already familiar with. There is no major difference between an essay and essay test. The principles you learn in one apply to the other—with one added advantage: In an essay test, you don't have to think of a topic; your instructor has already done that for you. Actually, many students who once dreaded essay tests find that their attitudes change completely after they have taken one. They begin to like essay tests because they find it much easier to answer questions in their own words than to adapt their thinking to someone else's vocabulary.

You don't scare me any more.

When you are studying lecture notes, for example, you will sometimes find that concepts are easier to understand once you put them in your own words. So remember, if you can write a paragraph, you can take an essay test—assuming, of course, that you studied.

How to Prepare for an Essay Test

TAKE GOOD NOTES

Learn to distinguish between hearing and listening in class. Hearing is an automatic process, but listening requires a concentrated mental effort on your part. You can't evaluate what your instructor is saying if you are just hearing words. You have to **listen** carefully in order to pick out important points and major supporting details.

You must use judgment in deciding what your instructor is emphasizing. He may emphasize by repetition, repeating a point in several different ways; he may give several examples to illustrate a key point; he may explain its causes and effects; he may point out parallels between two ideas or events; he may underscore a point by tone of voice or gesture.

Those points which are not emphasized are not to be ignored, of course, but must be subordinated to major points. Get the important things on paper first, and then, as you have time, expand them with the instructor's relevant lesser supports. NOTE: Don't take notes only when you see your instructor write something on the board. Few instructors will put **all** of their important notes on the board.

READ ALL ASSIGNED MATERIAL MORE THAN ONCE

Some students believe that they can breeze through their reading assignments a night or two before a test and still get a decent grade on their exam. No one, including your instructors, can remember every important point in a chapter, detail by detail, after reading it one time. The human memory doesn't usually work that way. In fact, psychological studies have shown that when you learn something new, you are likely to forget over 60 percent of it. That's why cramming is so dangerous. You will retain more information from ten separate half-hour study periods than you will from one all-night cramming session.

LEARN TO USE YOUR TEXTBOOKS

Don't be afraid to write in your textbooks. They're your books, so use them. Highlight important points, underline definitions, insert additional examples, rewrite difficult concepts in your own words, and jot down any questions that occur to you as you are reading. Make up your own essay questions and see how well you can answer them from memory. Then compare your answers with the information contained in your notes and in your text. If you find that you are particularly weak in a certain area, you will still have time to correct the problem before the test.

STUDY!   *Study! Study! Study!*

How to Take an Essay Test

**BUDGET
YOUR TIME
CAREFULLY**

Before you begin to answer an essay test, find out approximately how much time you can devote to each question. If you have two questions to answer in a fifty-minute period, then don't spend forty-five minutes on one question. If you don't have a watch, then ask your instructor to post the time on the board periodically. Remember, although quality is more important than quantity, your instructor will expect the length of your essay to correspond with the amount of time you have to write it. The more time you have, the more details you should include.

Budget your time.

You can reduce your anxiety and make the best use of your time by answering the easiest question first.

**LOOK
CLOSELY AT
THE VERB
IN EACH
QUESTION**

Students often misinterpret essay questions by overlooking verbs. Make sure that you understand exactly what the question is asking you to do. Does it ask you to . . .

explain	to give reasons for something
evaluate	to decide on the value or significance of something
analyze	to explain something by breaking it down into parts and showing how each part relates to the whole and furthers an understanding of the whole
illustrate	to give examples of something
define	to explain the meaning of something
discuss	to tell all you know about a subject
compare	to point out similarities
contrast	to point out differences
compare and contrast	to point out **both** similarities and differences

When you read an essay question, learn to look for verbal signals—wording that indicates what particular method of development the question is calling for. For example:

EXPLAIN: If you see words such as *reasons, how, why, expound,* or *clarify,* then you'll know that your instructor wants you to explain.

EVALUATE: If you see *judge, weigh, appraise, give the significance of, write a critical analysis* or a *critical commentary,* then you'll know that your instructor wants you to evaluate.

ANALYZE: If you see *kinds, types, classes,* or *categories,* then you'll know that your instructor wants you to show interrelationships among these elements—to analyze.

ILLUSTRATE: If you see *examples, instances, cases, samples, specimens,* or *incidents,* then you'll know that your instructor wants you to illustrate.

DEFINE: If you see the *meaning of,* your *understanding of,* the *distinctive properties of,* or the *nature* of, then you'll know that your instructor wants you to define.

DISCUSS: If you see *examine, consider,* or *comment on,* then you'll know that your instructor wants you to discuss.

COMPARE: If you see *likenesses, similarities, parallels,* traits shared *in common with,* or how *A is like B,* then you'll know that your instructor wants you to compare.

CONTRAST: If you see *differences, dissimilarities, in opposition to,* or how *A is unlike B,* then you'll know that your instructor wants you to contrast.

MAKE A ROUGH OUTLINE BEFORE YOU BEGIN TO WRITE

Read the directions and see how many questions you are supposed to answer, but before you begin to write, jot down any points that you can think of that will help you answer the question. If you don't write them down right away, you might forget them. You'll just end up wasting time and making yourself nervous trying to think of them later. Putting these points into some sort of rough outline can help you a great deal. It's much easier to write a good answer within a limited time if you are following an outline.

GET TO THE POINT

Avoid long-winded introductions. Normally, ten or fifteen minutes is not enough time to spend on an introduction to an essay, but spending that much time on an introduction during an essay test can be fatal, especially if you have less than a half hour to answer the question. The evidence that you present in the body of your essay is more important to your instructor than how you introduce that information. So don't waste time. Get to the point.

A simple but effective way to get to the point quickly is to turn the question into a declarative sentence and treat that sentence both as your thesis statement and as a one-sentence introduction. When you do this, you don't have to spend much time on wording; your instructor has already carefully worded it. More important, since your thesis statement controls what you write, by using a rephrasing of the question, you guarantee that your answer is to the point. Suppose in an English Composition exam your instructor directs, "Discuss the techniques of achieving coherence in an essay." You can turn it around to "Achieving coherence in an essay depends upon two techniques: the first is to establish a sound overall organization; the second is to link the smaller elements within the large plan." Then you would go on to talk about Introduction-Thesis Statement-Development-Conclusion, and the ordering of details within that structure. You would then go on to deal with the subtopics—the smaller elements; there you would discuss enumeration, pronoun reference, transitional phrases, repetition of key terms, and parallelism.

Or suppose your history instructor asks, "Explain by the use of examples the philosophy known as Nineteenth-Century Liberalism as the term refers to government, economics, and the movement called "romantic nationalism."" You might turn it around to answer, "Nineteenth-Century Liberalism can be well explained through examples taken from government, from economics, and from 'romantic nationalism.'"

PROOFREAD YOUR ANSWERS

Too often, when students are taking an essay test, they are so happy to finish that they dash out of the classroom without ever looking at what they have written. This is foolish. When you are writing under the pressure of time, you might make mistakes that you don't normally make—not just in grammar, but in content. You might have left out an important point, or you might have said the exact opposite of what you intended to say. So take a few minutes to reread your answer. It could make a big difference in your grade.

Five Wrong Ways to Answer an Essay Question

1. List a series of facts without relating them to the question.
2. Use a lot of general statements with no specific examples.
3. Pad your answers with irrelevant details.
4. Present your information haphazardly.
5. Express your points in incomplete sentences.

LISTING A SERIES OF FACTS WITHOUT RELATING THEM TO THE QUESTION

When you are answering an essay question, you cannot simply list details. You have to use those details to prove a point. A list of facts will not prove to your instructor that you understand the material you're being tested on; it might only prove that you memorized those facts. After all, an essay is the development of an idea, and you can't develop an idea by listing facts. Look at the following answer to an essay question on the art of American film-making:

QUESTION: Discuss the impact of "Citizen Kane" on the art of film-making.

ANSWER: *Citizen Kane* was directed by Orson Welles when he was 25 years old. He signed a contract which gave him 25 percent of the profits in addition to the authority to write and direct the film. He was also the chief actor in the movie. Most of the actors had a background in theater, but Welles's background was in radio.

Citizen Kane was filmed with a wide-angle lens and high-speed film. Welles used sets with ceilings on them. Welles's basic editing technique consisted of lap dissolves, and he used broad arc lamps for lighting. The sound track blended background music with natural sounds.

The story of Charles Foster Kane, a big newspaper tycoon, was told mostly in flashbacks—through interviews of people who knew Kane. Many people believed that the film was really the life story of William Randolph Hearst, the controversial newspaper publisher of the late nineteenth century. Basically, the story of Charles Foster Kane was the story of a man who could buy everything—except love.

After reading this answer, you still would not know **why** *Citizen Kane* was an important film because the factual details listed are not connected to ideas. In the first paragraph, for example, the student should not have just listed the details of Welles's contract; he should have explained that the contract was the first of its kind. Before *Citizen Kane,* an actor was expected to confine himself to acting, but Welles managed to get a contract that gave him the authority to supervise the production of a film that he was going to star in. The details about the backgrounds of the actors also mean nothing until one understands that the actors used in *Citizen Kane* represented a different approach to film-making. They proved that the transition from stage to screen could work. In fact, many critics believe that the excellent performances of Joseph Cotten and Agnes Moorehead stemmed partly from the fact that they had never acted in front of a camera before. Presumably, they took direction well because neither had yet developed a specific screen style.

The second paragraph also contains many facts, but they don't mean anything unless the student explains that most of the details refer to specific technological innovations in film-making. The creation of the wide-angle lens shot, for example, was a relatively new concept in cinematography. Welles wanted his audience to see things on the screen just as they saw them in real life. When you look at a room, for instance, you can clearly see the furniture in the foreground, the middleground, and the background, which is exactly what the wide-angle lens made possible on the screen. Before *Citizen Kane,* movie audiences had to see things through the eye of the camera, whose focus was limited to one area at a time. The use of ceilinged sets was also a novel idea that achieved a new realism in the art of film-making. It led to more natural lighting effects and more interesting camera angles. For example, filming Charlie Kane from floor level magnified his importance. The audience was looking up at a figure who seemed to be towering over them. Before *Citizen Kane,* actors couldn't be filmed from low angles without showing that "rooms" in films had no ceilings.

In the last paragraph the student should have explained that the complex narrative structure of the film represented a refreshing change from the traditional method of using simple chronological order to tell a story, and the final details about the similarities between Kane and Hearst should have been discussed in terms of the social impact of the film. The controversy became so heated at one point that the Hearst factions actually tried to have the film burned.

USING A LOT OF GENERAL STATEMENTS WITH NO SPECIFIC EXAMPLES

You will never convince your instructor that you understand the material you're being tested on if you can only discuss it in general terms. Vague definitions and general explanations are a clear indication that you don't really understand what you're talking about. Even if all of your general statements are correct, your answer will still be incomplete. Accurate generalizations are simply not enough. An instructor doesn't prepare six lectures on a subject and assign a hundred pages of reading just so her students can get a **general** idea of what she has been explaining in painstaking detail for several weeks. The following answer, for example, would get a very poor grade. It is filled with unsupported generalizations, a clear indication that the student was unprepared to take the test.

QUESTION: Discuss the causes and effects of the Homestead Steel Strike in 1892.

ANSWER: Working conditions in the late nineteenth century were terrible. The economy was bad too, but the head of the Homestead plant didn't like the union. He wanted the workers to take a cut in pay. Henry Clay Frick was running the plant because his boss, Andrew Carnegie, was off in Scotland, so Frick could run the place the way he wanted—and that's exactly what he did. The workers eventually went on srike. They battled it out with the Pinkerton detectives that Frick hired, but, in the end, Frick won and the workers lost. In general, the Homestead Steel Strike had some very damaging effects on the labor movement in this country.

If the student had twenty or thirty minutes to answer this question, the instructor would certainly expect an answer more than a paragraph long. She would expect specific details: What kind of "terrible" working conditions existed in the late nineteenth century? How bad was the economy? How much of a pay cut did Frick impose on the workers? What union did they belong to? What happened when they went on strike? How did the Homestead strike affect American steelworkers? How did it affect the labor movement in general?

PADDING YOUR ANSWERS WITH IRRELEVANT DETAILS

Students often jokingly refer to padding as "the snow job," but they usually stop laughing when they get their tests back: D's and F's are not very funny. Sometimes, in an attempt to tell the instructor everything they know, students make the honest mistake of getting sidetracked on an unimportant detail, but careful outlining can help to eliminate this error. Remember, every irrelevant detail wastes precious time, so make sure that all of your details pertain to the question being asked. Notice the irrelevant details in the following answer from an essay test in Black History:

Turning in the Snow Job

QUESTION: Contrast the progress of the anti-slavery movement during the Revolutionary period with the strength of the anti-slavery movement during the Constitutional period.

ANSWER: During the Revolutionary era, anti-slavery sentiment in this country was rather strong. The signing of the Declaration of Independence bolstered the spirit of freedom and independence in general, so many people thought that the abolition of slavery was only a matter of time. Slaves began to petition for their freedom, and Northern states began to pass their own laws ending slavery in their states. Perhaps if more people today would think about what the Declaration of Independence really says, there would be fewer racial problems in our schools and in our cities. Over 200 years after the signing of this great document, there are still people in this country who don't believe that "all men are created equal." I guess they think that the Declaration of Independence was written just for white people. Some even act like it was just written for men—not women. Other examples of the strong anti-slavery sentiment during the Revolutionary era were the formation of the first anti-slavery society in America and the public recognition of the accomplishments of free blacks. The fact that blacks fought in the Revolutionary War also emphasized the hypocrisy of fighting for independence and, at the same time, owning slaves.

Within a decade, however, the fate of the black man in America took a turn for the worse. The Constitution was written in 1787, and it wiped out much of the progress made by anti-slavery forces during the Revolutionary period. Our founding fathers evidently considered the right to own property (slaves) more important than the right to be free. The power of the slave states at the Constitutional Convention ended any hopes of victory for the anti-slavery forces. Three clauses in the Constitution clearly recognized the existence of slavery. One was particularly dehumanizing—the three-fifths compromise. It provided that every slave would count as three-fifths of a person for purposes of both taxation and representation (5 slaves = 3 whites). The other two clauses were directed toward the slave trade and runaway slaves. Many runaway slaves were aided by the Underground Railroad. It helped thousands of slaves escape to the North and to Canada. The most famous leader of the Underground Railroad was Harriet Tubman. She was a very brave and clever woman. So the Constitution actually legitimized slavery. It would be another forty or fifty years before anti-slavery sentiment would be as strong as it was during the Revolutionary War.

Although this answer contains a lot of specific information, much of it is irrelevant. In the first paragraph, for example, the student got carried away with the discussion of the Declaration of Independence. His comments on twentieth-century political hypocrites and male chauvinists are completely unrelated to the question. In the time it took to formulate those thoughts and write them down, the student could have been presenting details on the significance of the first anti-slavery society—an important point which he glossed over—or discussing the anti-slavery pronouncements of prominent Revolutionary figures. In the last paragraph the student made a similar mistake. Instead of explaining the provisions of the clauses in the Constitution dealing with the slave trade and runaway slaves, he got off on a tangent about the Underground Railroad.

PRESENTING YOUR INFORMATION HAPHAZARDLY

Sometimes students don't understand the importance of presenting their information in some sort of logical order. They think that as long as they cover the most important points, it doesn't matter **how** they present their material. The instructor who is faced with this jumble of disorganized thoughts often has to plod through the answer several times before he can even begin to make sense out of it. Driving your instructor to the brink of insanity is not exactly the brightest way to answer an essay question, but more important, if you can't put your thoughts down in any kind of organized format, then you're really telling your instructor that you don't fully understand the material. If you did, you would see the relationship between one point and another. For example, if A caused B, then you would logically discuss A before B. If you are analyzing reasons for citing examples, you should begin with the least important and end with the most important. The following answer to a test in Child Psychology is very confusing because the details are not placed in any kind of logical order:

> *QUESTION:* Analyze the general trends in a child's physical development.
>
> *ANSWER:* By the age of 6, a child's growth process starts to slow down. An average American child at this age usually weighs around 50 pounds and is close to 4 feet tall. During the first year of life a child experiences extensive growth. His body length increases over one-third, and his weight almost triples. By the age of 3, bone begins to replace cartilage in the child's skeletal system. By the age of 2, the average child is about 2 and a half feet tall and weights around 30 pounds. Myelinization also occurs during this period. During the first few years of life a child's brain increases in weight, becoming three-fourths of its total weight by the age of 2. Immature nerve fibers also develop protective tissues around them. This is a process known as myelinization. During the early adolescent years, from 11 to 15, the child's heart grows faster, but there is no significant increase in brain size. There is also a marked increase in height and weight. Between the ages of 6 and 12, a child's bones become harder, his blood pressure increases, and his pulse rate decreases.

As you can see, the details in this answer are arranged so haphazardly that they make little sense. The confusion could have been eliminated through the use of simple chronological order: first year, second year, preschool years, middle childhood, and adolescence. Also, a term such as *myelinization* should have been defined before it was discussed.

EXPRESSING YOUR POINTS IN INCOMPLETE SENTENCES

When you are answering an essay test, you have to remember that your instructor expects coherent paragraphs containing complete sentences. When you are taking notes in class, you have to use fragments because you are copying information as fast as you can, but on an essay test you can't just jot down bits and pieces of information. If your instructor had wanted two- or three-word answers, she would

313

not have given you an essay test. So don't write any answers like the following from a class in Sociology through Literature:

QUESTION: Describe the various states in the evolution of Malcolm X from a Nebraska preacher's son to the creator of a new political religious movement.

ANSWER: Malcolm X—born a preacher's son
                    —father killed and mother went insane
                    —sent to reform school
                    —lived with white family
                    —moved to big city and lived with half-sister
                    —got a white girlfriend in the city
                    —wanted to look white and act white
                    —got his hair straightened
                    —got a job as a shoe-shine boy, then peddled
                       dope—got caught and went to jail
                    —became a Black Muslim (influence of family)
          Muslim religion—all white men devils, black race superior
                    —became a preacher for Black Muslims
                    —heaven and hell equals your life on earth
          went to Africa—changed—saw both black and white Muslims
                    —white men no longer devils
                    —good and bad in both blacks and whites

The following is an example of a well-written, well-organized, well-documented answer to an essay question in Black History. It is coherent, accurate, and specific. It was also the student's very first essay test:

QUESTION: Trace the development of the Atlantic slave trade from the 1400's to the 1800's.

ANSWER: The Atlantic slave trade took place over a period of 450 years. It occurred along the African coast from Senegal to Angola, a total of 3,000 miles.
          The first contact was made in 1441. Portugal was under the rule of King Phillip, and a Portuguese vessel captained by a man named Gonzales brought home a few slaves along with his material commodities. One of these slaves was the descendent of a chief. He begged for his return to Africa and promised more slaves in exchange for his freedom. In 1452 he was taken back, and his family gave ten other slaves in return for his safety.
          Throughout the 1500's, Portugal and Spain dominated the slave trade. Although a trading system had already developed in gold, iron, and copper, the trade in human cargo developed more gradually. During this early period, slaves were taken mainly from the Upper Guinea Coast. From Senegal and Guinea, Mandingoes and Susus were traded. The trade was relatively small at that time—for example, in 1506, 3,500 slaves were taken from the Upper Guinea Coast. By the 1680's, however, 20,000 a year were taken from the slave coast.

In the 1600's, the Dutch took control of the slave trade, conquering Spanish and Portuguese posts along the coast. By 1640, the demand for slaves had increased so tremendously that the Lower Guinea Coast was tapped for slave supply. From Benin, Nigeria, and Whydah came Ashanti and Fanti tribes, among others. A major reason for the drastic increase in the slave trade at this time was the discovery of the New World and the subsequent need for cheap labor. Africa's needs also played an important part. She needed horses, textiles, and most importantly, guns and gunpowder.

Although France condemned slavery in 1571, the 1700's found France and England dominating the slave trade. Throughout the slave period, the African chiefs cooperated with the traders. Although the first captures were done by piracy, the chiefs soon became the major suppliers of slaves. They captured prisoners of war, and kidnapped and deported criminals and rebels. The slaves did not all go readily into bondage. In 1753, for example, slaves revolted in midocean on the Narborough and killed all of the crew except those necessary to take them home.

The slave trade was declared illegal in 1808. However, illicit slave trade continued until 1862, with most of these slaves being sent to Brazil for work on sugar plantations. An estimated 8 million to 50 million human beings were victims of the slave trade. The second figure includes those who never even made it to slavery, unable to survive one of the many terrible steps to its completion. Basically, slavery flourished because people held their own self-interests above those of humanity.

Pat Tonkovich

The question above called for a chronological understanding of events over a long period of time ("**Trace** the **development** of. . . . "). The student, therefore, organized her information century by century and supported her major points with specific data, mostly facts and statistics.

Many essay questions, like the one above, will call for a specific method of development (comparing, defining, analyzing, and so on) but others will be worded in more general terms. Then it's up to you to decide how to develop your answer. If, for example, an essay question tells you to "discuss" something, you might need to use a combination of methods to develop a good answer. The essay question below was given in a Psychology class on Marriage and the Family. It asks the student to "discuss" the problems encountered in an interracial marriage. Notice how the student uses both classification and illustration to develop his answer. He identifies different **types** of problems and then explains each type with **examples.**

QUESTION: Discuss some of the major problems encountered by a couple who enters into an interracial marriage.

ANSWER: In every society there are certain practices which are seriously frowned upon. In our society, one of the most controversial of these practices is interracial marriage. Sidney Poitier made this a classic topic when the matter was both humorously and dramatically portrayed in the movie *Guess Who's Coming to Dinner.* A large segment of American society looks down on this practice because it is not "standard" behavior—behavior which people are accustomed to living with. Upon entering into an interracial marriage, then, a couple is bound to encounter some problems.

Perhaps the most distressing of these problems is **family disapproval.** The family of an interracial couple often feels that its acceptance in the community has been placed on shaky ground. The real problem usually lies with the parents. Some even go as far as disowning their son or daughter. With others, the disapproval is only temporary, and the couple is eventually welcomed back into the family circle. Most interracial couples, however, have to cope with some form of peer disapproval off and on throughout their married life. Despite protestations of "Your marriage has nothing to do with it," the interracial couple sometimes finds old friends disappearing.

Another obstacle that the interracial couple has to contend with is **societal disapproval.** Although society's rejection of the marriage will not affect the couple as intimately, the total effect will still be damaging because there is no way that the couple can hide from society. They cannot walk down the street without dozens of eyes gawking at them. Even going to church can be a terrible ordeal. Many couples quit going to church altogether rather than suffer the stares of their fellow "Christians." Another discouraging experience often occurs when the interracial couple tries to participate in various social organizations. Even if they should decide to join an organization with no arbitrary membership requirements, their stay is often a short one because, despite an official policy of open membership, they are made to feel unwelcome.

Another potential obstacle in an interracial marriage is the problem that the **children** often encounter. The most abusive treatment frequently comes from other children. Children can sometimes be very cruel because they have not yet learned the rules of tact and diplomacy. They say exactly what's on their minds. It doesn't take long for children to realize that their playmate's skin is not the same color as theirs. The next step is often name calling—"oreo" for example. When the child enters school, he not only has to cope with the common fear of school which he shares with the rest of his class, but he also has to cope with the fear of being different. Outside of school, children of interracial marriages frequently have to contend with societal prejudices, and this problem is often compounded by the rejection of the child by his or her own race. Whatever the case, these children soon learn the need for a thick outer skin.

Interracial marriage, then, poses problems not only for the couple involved, but also for the children of such a marriage. Some day, a more tolerant, unbiased society may judge interracial marriages as acceptable, but until then, those who choose to deviate from society's norms will, in most cases, be forced to suffer the consequences. In most American communities, people still fear that which is different.

Tim Kasunic

The next essay question, given in a Philosophy class, calls for an extended definition of the mind. Notice how the student combines the strategies of formal definition, negation, examples, and classification to answer the question.

QUESTION: What is the mind, and how is it known?

ANSWER: The existence of the mind is best understood through what is usually referred to as "cogito ergo sum," a Latin phrase which means "I think; therefore I am." In other words, to think is to exist. The existence of the mind is one of the basic assertions upon which Descartes bases a good portion of his philosophy. According to Descartes, the very fact that we doubt the validity of something (the sciences, for example) is proof in itself that the mind exists. For if we doubt something, then there must be some part of our essence which doubts, and this doubting entity is the mind. The mind is the only thing that we can ascertain to exist. We have absolutely no definite knowledge of anything else.

Once the existence of the mind has been established, it is next necessary to define it. Descartes begins to define the mind by equating it with a "thinking thing." He does not say that a thinking thing is a body or that it consists of any type of mass, but simply that the mind is some "thing." It is a functional, rational entity—not merely a pocket of knowledge. It has been argued that nothing can be conceived of the mind without the use of the senses. For instance, the mental conception of a triangle consists of picturing these lines joined together. Hence, his critics contend that there is no difference between this mental conception and a simple visual image. Descartes, however, skillfully defends himself by pointing out that a one-thousand sided polygon could not be visually fabricated, but it could be perceived mentally. This supports his theory that the mind functions separate and distinct from the body.

To fully understand the mind, one must understand how it functions. Descartes describes the mind as a thing "which doubts, which understands, which affirms, which denies, which wills, which rejects, which imagines also, and which perceives." These are all conscious processes. That is, they all fall into the category of actions or ideas exhibiting awareness of the environment. The mind also functions in its conception of ideas. These ideas can be divided into three categories: (1) innate ideas, (2) accidental ideas, and (3) self-created ideas. The most far-reaching of these is the category of innate or instinctual ideas. These are ideas with which the mind comes equipped—ideas of self. Accidental ideas are those which have some sort of external cause—a bear, another person. The third group of ideas consists of the fictional or self-created ideas. These are ideas which are conceived of entirely in the mind. For instance, a five-headed horse does not exist, but neither is this image inborn in the mind, nor is it patterned from some external object.

It is these two functions, conscious acts and mental ideas, which compose the mind and what is inside it. The mind, then, is a thinking thing which exists entirely distinct from the body and which performs only those functions which can be grouped under the title of conscious processes.

Tim Kasunic

index

A

Agreement
  exercise, 113-14
  pronoun-antecedent, 111
  pronoun-antecedent, rules for, 111-13
  subject-verb, 108
  subject-verb, rules for, 109-10
Active-passive (*see* Verbs)
Analogy
  definition, 136
  exercise, 139
Attitude in thesis statement, 14, 15
Attitude toward subject, 1, 44
Audience
  knowledge of in persuading, 253
  relating to, 21

B

Body
  cause and effect, 216
  climactic order, 103

definition, 1
development of, 27
methods of organizing, 132
example, 18
outline, 49
structure, 48
subtopics, 283
transitions, 49

C

Cause and effect
  analogy, 220-22
  analyzing causes, 213-14
  chain of, 215
  finding, 214
  narrowed topic, 213
  necessary and sufficient, 212
  pitfalls to avoid, 222
  projecting effect, 214
  questions for discussion, 219

319

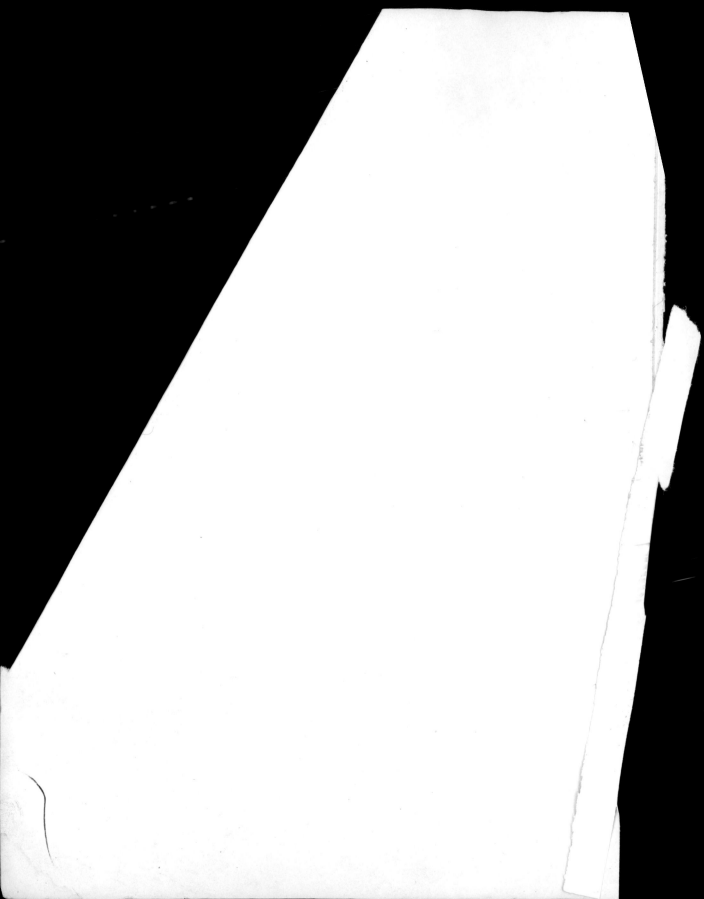